In historical events great men — so called — are but the labels that serve to give a name to an event, and like labels, they have the least possible connection with the event itself. Every action of theirs, that seems to them an act of their own free will, is in an historical sense not free at all, but in bondage to the whole course of previous history, and predestined from all eternity.

Leo Tolstoi

Greenwood County: A History

by

Ann Herd Bowen

1992

Library of Congress Catalog Card Number 92-62150

ISBN 0-9634787-0-2

Grateful acknowledgment is made to William H. Lander for permission to quote from his mother's unpublished letter dating from the 1940s.

Manufactured in the United States of America

Printed by Arcata Graphics Co., Kingsport TN

CONTENTS

PREFACE

WRITING county histories is practically a cottage industry in South Carolina. All sorts of people – from college professors with impeccable credentials all the way to little old ladies in tennis shoes – try their hand at it, with widely varying results. It never occurred to me that one day I might join their ranks as a chronicler of local lore. Although I was never exactly preoccupied with my state's long history of cowboys and Indians, sieges and redcoats, Rebels and Yankees, race problems and politics, I have spent some little time as an adult trying to reconcile our prides and our prejudices, as well as our violent streak, with that certain air of gentility we South Carolinians strive to project. We are, at the very least, a paradoxical people. Only an innocent, or someone utterly terrified at the prospect of retirement, would have been eager to try to trace the evolution of a political subdivision of the State of South Carolina over nearly a hundred years. The fact that I did so – indeed, that I rushed in almost as though I were qualified for the task – really amounts to a leap into the unknown. I have no idea whether I have landed on my feet.

But a book about Greenwood would not be a book about me, county native though I am. Exactly what it would be about is a question that has nagged me for years, not just from the beginning of the project, but from the beginning of my own thoughts about precisely what makes Greenwood the way it is. Oddly enough, I can pinpoint the time when such questions began to occupy my mind; it had something to do with reaching adulthood, a state that in my case arrived rather late. Growing up for me was all tied up with Lander College at the time it was a small and struggling county-supported institution. I went to work there in 1958, and the love affair with the institution that began when I enrolled as a freshman eight years earlier simply resumed as though nothing had intervened. In reality, a great deal had happened to me in the interim, including marriage, children, and five years in New Jersey. I was also well along in the process of disillusionment about life in general when it gradually began to dawn on me how lucky I was to be there. A college environment offers nothing if not the continuous opening of doors and opportunities to contemplate questions to which there are no answers, only more and bigger questions. The place where these magical concepts first entered my consciousness was a college that happened to be owned and operated by Greenwood County; therefore, by extension, the county and I shared an idea so large it had the potential to change the world simply by changing people's lives in somewhat the way mine had been changed.

Greenwood County was different, for me, simply because it owned Lander College from 1948 to 1973. For most of that 25-year period I was part of the connection, not only because of my own awakening interest in its implications but also because I took advantage of opportunities to learn all I could about how the business side of a college operated. That knowledge served me very well indeed. In later years when the college was under state control, my work as budget director and my deep involvement with The Lander Foundation provided opportunities for contacts with many of Greenwood's most prominent businessmen. I like to think we grew in understanding and respect for each other as we pursued a common goal. The solid growth of the Foundation, the many good things that happened for Lander College as a result of that growth, and the way Greenwood people cooperated to make things happen are among my fondest memories of the last fifteen years of my Lander career.

Not long after my retirement in the summer of 1989, Thornwell Dunlap and Boykin Curry, both of whom I knew well from Lander Foundation work, invited me to lunch one day. Over fruit salad at the country club, they popped the question: would I be willing to put together a history of Greenwood County? The county would reach its 100th birthday in 1997, and nothing had been done since Louis Wright published his little memoir *Barefoot in Arcadia* in 1974. Margaret Watson's *Greenwood County Sketches* had appeared in 1970, but the author provided a disclaimer in the introduction. "All of it is local history," she wrote, "but the collection is not the history of Greenwood County in the sense of a chronological exposition of social, economic, and political development." I asked myself if that could be what they wanted; if so, we had a problem. Who on earth was I to come up with a chronological exposition of anything? I had spent most of my life living either in the past or the future; the mere thought of chronological exposition was intensely distasteful to me. But the truth is that I was more than a little intrigued at the prospect of finally understanding Greenwood. My Lander colleagues and I had marveled for years at the reluctance of new graduates, natives and non-natives alike, to leave the area.

I do not remember what I replied to the first query, but, whatever my careful words at the time, they were not meant to be discouraging. In truth, I could think of nothing I'd rather do with the first couple of years of retirement than paw through old records and other people's scrapbooks, but caution was indicated. I didn't know much, chronologically or otherwise, but I did know that barrelling ahead without a plan meant sure disaster sooner or later. My previous experience in book preparation consisted of several small volumes on Cokesbury and a larger work on the South Carolina upcountry written over a three-year period in the late 1970s in collaboration with my late husband Don Herd. Don was the researcher and I the writer/editor of those volumes, but I had simply followed where he led. Curry and Dunlap made it clear that the project would be largely mine from the outset; their interest was in the end product, and their responsibility would be to provide sponsorship and backing.

The next time we met, the lunch group was larger by one member, issues were clarified, and a proposal began to come together. In an amazingly short time the committee reached its final configuration, a sponsor materialized, and the finished proposal cleared all obstacles. The Greenwood County history project was on its way. Officially it was under the aegis of The Museum; its steering committee consisted of R. B. Curry, Jr., R. Thornwell Dunlap, Jr., Emmett I. Davis, W. A. Barnette, Jr., and William John Park; and funding came from a Self Foundation grant matched by five local sources. The County Bank Foundation, the Mary Barratt Park Foundation, Davis & Floyd, Inc., W. A. Barnette, Jr., and R. B. Curry, Jr., all shared in the match. Frank J. Wideman, Jr., Executive Vice President of The Self Foundation, joined the steering committee.

Ready or not, there it was. Commitment in my case looked a great deal like a Macintosh Plus computer, complete with printer and software, that appeared one day in the little room next to my kitchen. A two-hour crash course at the computer store was a jumble of words and concepts that only gradually made sense over the next few months as I groped my way through poorly written instruction manuals and tried to remember what my instructor had said. Three large cardboard boxes, a copy of *Liberty Dethroned*, and a bound copy of *The Index-Journal* for September 14, 1957, (the special edition marking Greenwood's centennial celebration) appeared next, courtesy of Boykin Curry. The boxes held Greenwood memorabilia from the collection of the late May Bailey Smith, granddaughter of one of Greenwood's earliest businessmen. Mrs. Smith's scrapbooks were practically the social history of Greenwood's upper class of another era: there were visiting cards, "at home" cards, letters, menus, and even an invitation to the White House during Woodrow Wilson's administration.

I began to look at existing county histories for guidance in deciding on a format. Many seemed to be written by committees; I tried not to think of camels as I skimmed the long lists of contributors. Somewhere I read that *The History of Georgetown County, South Carolina*, by George C. Rogers, Jr., was the best of the genre. I checked it out. There were 22 chapters averaging nearly 86 footnotes each, four appendices, and an explanation of the alphabetizing used in the index. It was also beautifully written. I had no trouble deciding that my efforts would be much more modest; I would strive for readability and flow but steer away from footnotes and avoid chronological exposition like the plague.

Gradually a format evolved. I knew I wanted to emphasize beginnings and connections, the former for obvious reasons and the latter to link Greenwood with a wider world. Although the county was formed late in South Carolina history, obviously everything about it had a beginning, and connections would reveal themselves in the normal course of events. I settled on a few large topics as headings for fairly long chapters, a format that would provide several opportunities to return to beginnings and pick up connections along the way. In spite of all my protestations, it appeared that "chronological exposition" was my goal after all. A few conditions also seemed important from the first: the book would not be genealogy, living people would not be the subjects of biographical detail, and I would make no attempt to write histories of Greenwood's churches. The steering committee agreed to these stipulations. Finally there were the questions of emphasis and a stopping place. In nearly every case my concern was with the very earliest people, institutions, and events. It seemed to me far more important, for example, to set forth the beginnings of Lander College, trace its founding family, and establish its relationship to the county than to chronicle the ongoing story of a thriving regional state college in the mainstream of American higher education today. Similarly, I was convinced that the first Greenwood County Hospital with its governing board of Greenwood women needed to be remembered for its own sake every bit as much as for its connection to the modern health care facility known as Self Memorial Hospital.

I was acutely aware of the question of perspective throughout the preparation of the book. In the case of anything as sensitive as local history, perspective is everything. Besides, as Theodore H. White and others have written, it is not the way things really are that counts, but the way they seem to be. Put another way, what happened in a given situation is not nearly so important as what people *think* happened, and no amount of argument is likely to change minds long made up. In a couple of instances in this book, my interpretation might well be rather far removed from the popular perspective of the events described.

I am still not sure whether I understand Greenwood exactly, but I found enough material to convince me that the key to the county's development lies in its people. A certain quality of stubborn resolve appears again and again in the Greenwood story, as does that indefinable ingredient loosely called "leadership," or "charisma," or "star quality" in some of its people. Early on I queried several individuals about their feelings for the town. One answer from a native currently living in California gave me something to think about. She said that friendships with Greenwood people hold for her a spiritual quality, and she insisted she did not speak from something as simple as homesickness. She is convinced her memories of growing up in Greenwood are fundamentally different from those of people who grew up elsewhere, and that her conception of "home" holds ramifications shared only by other Greenwood people of her generation. Another young woman said that the town needs to make only a small leap to catch up to what she called the "talent" of its people.

Several acknowledgments are necessary. Members of the steering committee deserve credit for the idea and for their unflagging support during the life of the project; my own debt to six busy businessmen is enormous. The support of two Greenwood institutions – The Museum and The Self Foundation – was necessary for the project to get off the ground. Librarians at Lander College, the Greenwood County Library, and the South Caroliniana Library were courteous, knowledgeable, and helpful. And the enthusiasm of many others, who helped from the first days of research, convinced me that the book was indeed an idea whose time had come. People to whom special thanks are due include Dick Abney, Angelle Adams, Perrin Anderson, Louise Arnold, Harris Bailey, Mary Baker, Helen Taylor Barnette, Charlie and Alice Beaudrot, John Blythe, Gertrude Brabham, Gay Scurry Charles, Virginia Davies, Edgar Davis, Thomas I. Dowling, W. R. Dunn, Helen Harrison, Louise Hodges Hartzog, Bonner Harvley, Mary Beaudrot Herndon, Jessie Julien, Arthur Murray, W. H. Nicholson, Jr., Joe Patrick, Gee Taylor Poe, Betty Emerson Riddle, Clara and Bart Robeson, Furman Smith, Margaret Tinsley, Jimmy Wade, Rose Marie Williams, Rauch Wise, and Ted Wolf. I must also thank my husband, county native John Bowen, for a rather remarkable degree of forbearance as well as an amiable willingness to drive me whenever I had the urge to see some remote corner of the county for myself.

Dixie Highsmith, who is my daughter as well as a teacher of writing, agreed to read several chapters in their early stages for grammar, style, and syntax. She managed to convince me that things have changed considerably since I first wrote a research paper, and it was she who finally persuaded me to buy a style book; we settled on the MLA (Modern Language Association of America) Handbook. Lander English professor Dr. Margaret Marks often allowed me to run stray paragraphs by her fine ear; her criticism was usually funny and always helpful. Dr. Marvin Cann, professor of history, tried his best to curb my excesses; in some cases he succeeded. Whatever is left must be laid at my own door; responsibility for both errors and shortcomings is mine alone.

Ann Herd Bowen

1

ORIGINS AND OVERVIEW

The world and the books are so accustomed to use, and over-use, the word "new" in connection with our country, that we early get and permanently retain the impression that there is nothing old about it.

Mark Twain

SOUTH Carolina has been called "a contentious commonwealth, just south of Eden." This reputation is supported by even the briefest exposure to the state's history, and nowhere is the famous contentiousness more glaring than in accounts of relations between upcountry and lowcountry South Carolina. Culturally the two are distinct and separate regions because of topography and the types of people who settled each. Lowcountry, particularly Charleston, civilization is among the oldest in the United States, while the upcountry still contained elements of frontier conditions until well into the twentieth century. Any discussion of the state's proximity to Eden is more problematic and has no place in these pages.

The area that ultimately became Greenwood County was settled in the second half century of South Carolina's history, from 1720 to the eve of the Revolution. Settlement of the back country – by people of German, French, Scotch-Irish, and English extraction – resulted in enclaves of independent citizens who, because of the lack of any kind of authority, became virtually a law unto themselves before the governmental apparatus at Charleston managed to penetrate the interior of the colony. The back country, with its broad undulating hills, numerous valleys, and hundreds of waterways, was attractive to settlers. Great forests provided ample timber for construction as well as foodstuffs of native nuts and berries. Another abundant source of food was wild game of great variety, and the streams and rivers teemed with fish.

The area was also attractive to its aboriginal inhabitants to whom living was a relatively simple matter. "Fish and game could be caught easily," wrote Louis Wright. "As a consequence, the Southern aborigines, unlike Indians in the frozen North, suffered few if any 'starving times.' The weather was rarely so unfavorable that the capture of game was difficult." Nobody knows exactly when the original inhabitants arrived in the South Carolina upcountry. The subject is one for infinite speculation by ethnologists, and new theories of the origins of man in the region are advanced from time to time. It is known that the Indians had become a mix of several nations by the time the first white men encountered them in the sixteenth century; historians estimate that between 25 and 30 different tribal groups could be found in South Carolina. Many are remembered only by names of streams – Edisto, Congaree, Santee, Saluda, and so on – but the tribal names do not connote any sort of permanency of Indian settlements; these were "wandering folk, constantly at war, pressed by their enemies to seek safer hunting grounds elsewhere." Three principal Indian groups have been identified by linguistic stock: the Iroquoian, represented by the Cherokees; the Siouan, headed by the Catawbas; and the Muskhogean, made up of a number of small groups and tribes. The Cherokees and Catawbas played the most important roles with the white settlers in the colonial period. The area that became Greenwood County was not actually inhabited by Indians but was definitely part of their hunting ground.

An important center of back country settlement had developed at the cross road at Ninety Six by the middle of the eighteenth century. Most historians prefer to settle the origin of the name Ninety Six rather quickly. Marvin Cann, for example, disposed of the issue neatly in one sentence: "Ninety Six . . . received its unusual name from the estimate by English traders that it lay ninety six miles from Keowee, a principal town of the Cherokee Nation located in the foothills of the present Oconee County." Everyone points to the fact that the notation "96" first appeared on George Hunter's map of the Cherokee Nation made in 1730; men whose journals and research corroborate this version of the origin of the name include Methodist Bishop Francis Asbury, diarist Edward Hooker, mapmaker/statistician/architect Robert Mills, local historian John Henry Logan, and state historian Alexander S. Salley. Certainly there is ammunition enough to refute the often-repeated legend that the place was named by an Indian maiden called Cateechee who rode 96 miles to warn her English lover of an impending raid by the Cherokees. Indeed the weight of the evidence almost constitutes overkill . . . or does it? To the amusement of many people, a Laurens businessman and local historian questioned the distance theory in an article published in the *South Carolina Historical Magazine* of April 1991. David P. George, Jr., wrote that the discrepancy between the name and the actual mileage to Keowee is simply too great to lend credence to the accepted theory. Without a more plausible explanation of its name the town should be known as "Seventy Eight," in George's opinion, since the distance to Keowee is actually 78 miles. Indian traders were known for their accuracy in estimating mileage, and George believes they would not have made a mistake of nearly twenty miles. A far more reasonable explanation is the theory that the name came from water courses or streams in the area. A 1738 plat, for example, showed a small stream labeled "one of the creeks commonly called 96." Other evidence and surmise came from a close study of waterways shown on a number of maps. George suggested that Indian traders on the path from Charles Town first crossed nine streams that flowed in one direction and then six that flowed in the opposite direction. "It seems logical to conclude that the term 'Ninety Six' is a reference to the grouping of the unique streams in the area," he wrote, "the digits being considered separately as indicators of the quantity in each group." No proof exists, of course, but *The State's* Cultural Affairs Editor William W. Starr found David George's entry in the game of how Ninety Six got its name "an entertaining and intriguing piece of detective work."

The place that became Ninety Six was at first merely a "convenient campground along the Cherokee Path" on the most direct route from the Indian towns to Charleston. Before permanent settlers made their way to the area, Indian traders had developed a brisk commercial trade with the Cherokees. The first actual residents in the back country near Ninety Six were hunters who arrived about 1730 and threw up "open logg cabins," or crude three-walled shelters, for hunting camps. Another group of adventurers in the very earliest days were cattle drovers whose cow-pens "became a vital economic institution" in the back country. There was a cow-pen, presumably owned by Dr. John Murray of Charleston, near Ninety Six by 1756. Ninety Six grew in importance because of the Indian trade and the increasing demand for fertile land. The first land grant was recorded in 1736. Marvin Cann described an influx of settlers a few years later:

> In January, 1746, John and Thomas Turk appeared in Charleston representing a number of British subjects in the "backparts of Pensylvania (sic) and Virginia." They asked permission to settle near Ninety Six and promised that, if tax concessions were granted, several hundred families would move from the northern colonies. They chose the region near Ninety Six because they could "find no other Body of Land so healthy in its situation (or) so Good in its Kind. . . ." Although it is not clear how many settlers were attracted by the tax concessions and good land at Ninety Six, certainly the development of the back country was profoundly influenced by the waves of Scotch-Irish immigrants who poured down the valleys from Pennsylvania. Patrick Calhoun, the father of John C. Calhoun, first settled near Lancaster and then moved to the prairie country on Long Cane Creek. John Turk returned from Virginia and secured a grant near Ninety Six. James Maxwell and Daniel Burnett became his neighbors. In 1748, James Francis sold his property at Saludy Old Town and secured a tract about ten miles above Ninety Six on the Cherokee Path; Francis became one of the leading citizens in the area and served as captain of the militia and Justice of the Peace. Other prominent

settlers around Ninety Six were Daniel Migler, a blacksmith; Andrew Williamson, who rose from humble beginnings as a cattle drover to become master of White Hall; John Lewis Gervais and John Savage. By mid-century, "Ninety Six had passed the hunting stage and was developing into a fairly prosperous region" of small farms and rudimentary industry.

Robert Goudy is generally regarded as the first permanent settler in Ninety Six and easily the most prominent. An experienced trader with the Cherokees in the Indian Nation, Goudy gave up the business in 1751 and purchased a 250-acre tract on the Cherokee Path at Ninety Six. He built a trading post which soon rivaled some Charleston merchants in its volume of business. Goudy diversified his holdings as his wealth increased and became a sort of frontier banker, loaning money and holding land mortgages. He also acquired 1,500 acres of land in several tracts near Ninety Six where he produced wheat, tobacco, corn, hemp, and indigo, as well as "an excellent Orchard of Peaches." Goudy's store had become the commercial center for a large area by the time of the proprietor's death in 1775.

Upcountry settlers such as Francis and Goudy were exceptional men, a cut above the average of their day. After a visit to Ninety Six in 1753, Governor James Glen reported that the people there "lived like savages." They were probably no better or worse than the vast majority of early settlers who were generally regarded as "ignorant, lazy, poor, and . . . hardly able to exist in a harsh and sometimes hostile land." An Anglican priest who ministered to early settlers near Camden found his parishioners "loose, dissolute, Idle People — Without either Religion or Goodness" and believed much the same was true of the whole body of settlers at the time. The cabins at Ninety Six nearly always contained ten or twelve children, wrote Governor Glen, whose parents could not be bothered to "bestow the least Education on them, they take so much Care in raising a litter of Pigs, [and] their Children are equally naked and full as Nasty." Regardless of the governor's disdain, it is clear that the settlers "who pushed the Carolina frontier westward to Ninety Six" were a hardy breed and brave in the face of constant danger. They clung tenaciously to wilderness outposts where they "battled the elements, wrestled a living from the land, and sometimes fought hostile Indians."

The hostility that developed between settlers and Indians arose from more than one source. The English blamed the trouble on the French, but the official policy for dealing with the Indians was practically a blueprint for conflict in itself. "The Cherokees feared the unrelenting advance of the frontier which destroyed their hunting grounds," wrote Marvin Cann, "and they resented their own growing dependence upon English trade goods. Hunting rifles and steel axes had become essential tools, while red girdles and cheap looking glasses were luxuries desired by every Cherokee squaw. The Indians were perpetually indebted to the traders, some of whom overcharged for shoddy merchandise and cheated their red customers at every turn."

Trade with the Indians influenced the development of South Carolina for generations. Colonial authorities had hoped South Carolina would become a source of silk, olive oil, sugar, wine, oranges, lemons, and other exotic products because of its situation in a latitude believed favorable to tropical products; but experimentation along these lines proved largely futile, and the colony's chief exports turned out to be rice, indigo, and deerskins. The Indians were eager to trade deerskins in return for "cheap hunting rifles, calico, brass pots, and glass beads." They learned quickly to yearn for the white man's goods and for his vices as well. "The introduction of rum, to which Indians became immediately addicted, caused the destruction of some groups," and providing them with guns and ammunition, ostensibly to increase the production of deerskins, was also a calamity. Louis Wright charged that Carolinians dabbled in slave trading in spite of the fact that such trade was forbidden by the Lords Proprietors. Indian slaves were a profitable commodity in the West Indies where they could replace Africans on the sugar plantations, and "a considerable market for Carolina Indian slaves also existed in New England." While the Indian slave trade was a profitable sideline in the earliest days of the colony, cured deerskins were the staple commodity and a valuable export; shipments averaged more than 100,000 skins annually between 1700 and 1745. The Indian trade centered in Charleston determined in large part whether peace or war would prevail between tribes and nations of the aborigines, as well as between the English and their foreign competitors.

Indian uprisings and raids began to occur sporadically as early as 1751. The colonial government built a fort near Keowee, ostensibly to protect the Cherokees from their old enemies the Creeks, but also to strengthen British claims to the back country and block French penetration. Fort Prince George was erected in 1753; Ninety Six supplied about fifty construction workers and became a rest stop and supply station for troops after the fort was completed. An uneasy peace reigned after the fort was completed, but only for a short time. A 90-foot square stockade was built around Robert Goudy's barn in 1759 to provide some protection for the settlers in case of an Indian raid. The stockade was attacked in February and March 1760. The settlers managed to prevail, although Goudy's house was burned to the ground during the first attack and other houses burned and cattle slaughtered after the second. The Cherokee War lasted until the British were able to pacify the Cherokees and restore a shaky peace. The fort at Ninety Six was strengthened with troops and artillery as an assembly point and supply depot for the British army.

Settlement of the back country intensified between the Cherokee War and the Revolution. The area was promising for farmers who expected little beyond subsistence, but markets were too distant to attract planters hoping to get rich from the labor of slaves. Many settlers came with only a pitiful store of worldly goods: "a horse and a cow if they were lucky, the clothes on their backs, the simplest of cooking utensils (one or two pots, two or three pewter spoons, and a knife or two), one or more quilts apiece, and often little else." Most newcomers contrived to procure some sort of firearm, and every man owned an axe. Some, of course, arrived with better tools, abundant household goods, and more livestock. Simple two-room dwellings began to take the place of log cabins on the more prosperous farms.

As time passed and civilization progressed, a few rough wagon roads combined with water transportation allowed the backwoods farmer to market his wheat, peas, corn, cured meats, butter, cheese, and skins and furs obtained from winter hunting and trapping. These products he exchanged for sugar, tea, coffee, powder and shot, cutlery, and utensils he could not make for himself. Most of the cloth for apparel was made at home by spinning and weaving both wool and flax. Wright noted that leisure was not a problem for our upcountry ancestors as they "struggled against the forces of nature for subsistence and a modicum of prosperity." There was neither time nor opportunity to indulge in cultural pursuits even if the inclination were present. Some settlers of religious persuasion brought along Bibles and perhaps a spelling book or reader for the instruction of their children; it was well that they did, for nothing else was available. Schools were totally nonexistent at first, and few teachers could be found in the back country.

In addition to the danger from Indian attacks, the South Carolina upcountry was plagued for many years by an almost complete absence of law and order. Local government was fragmentary, and neither courts nor law officers existed nearer than Charleston. The upcountry had no representation in the Commons House of Assembly and almost no influence over colonial affairs in general. Since criminal cases had to be handled in Charleston, it is not surprising that prosecution of outlaws was a haphazard business. Criminals often openly defied the few constables sent to arrest them. At length the frontiersmen took matters into their own hands and organized groups of vigilantes called Regulators to enforce the law and punish criminals. Even as Regulators and criminals practiced their calling with a great deal of enthusiasm – civil rights on both sides were rampantly violated – the demand for an effective system of courts for the back country and some voice in the government was finally heard in the Assembly. A statute passed in 1769 created seven judicial districts, among them the Ninety Six District, and set up commissions to build courthouses and jails. Governor Glen had urged a similar statute more than fifteen years earlier, but Charleston had blocked the bill to prevent dispersal of the legal business of the colony. A petition demanding redress was signed by 4,000 backcountrymen in 1767; signers talked of marching on Charleston in a body to present the petition. The Regulator Movement hindered as much as it helped in maintaining order since its leaders refused to recognize or obey orders from legal authorities in Charleston. The upcountry was ripe for rebellion, but against a tyranny much nearer than England. "The ill will aroused by Charleston's long disdain of the people on the frontiers," wrote Louis Wright, "helps to account for the unwillingness of backcountrymen to throw up their hats and cheer for the 'Patriots' when the War of Independence broke out." The memory of the long and bitter struggle over the court act created a dilemma: many South Carolinians felt more affinity for the sovereign who had given them their land than for the Charleston politicians who had opposed their efforts toward full participation in government.

The Revolution in the upcountry was more a long series of bloody skirmishes between Whigs and Tories than encounters between opposing armies. Nevertheless, this guerrilla warfare was important to the outcome of the war; the British were never able to "roll up" the South and crush General George Washington between opposing armies moving from both directions. Although the fall of Charleston in 1780 supposedly meant the state was conquered territory, patriot victories at Cowpens and Kings Mountain in the upcountry and hit-and-run raids by Francis Marion, Thomas Sumter, Andrew Pickens, and others "disrupted British plans and encouraged neutrals to join the patriot cause." Only months before the surrender at Yorktown, the patriots attempted to capture the fort at Ninety Six, one of the few strategically important outposts still in British hands. The story of the siege of Star Fort has been told many times. Edward Hooker caught the spirit when he wrote in his diary in 1806:

> The siege of Ninety Six is a favorite topic with the people of this vicinity. It is a pleasure to witness the animation that sparkles in their countenances when, in compliance with my request, they narrate the minute incidents of those trying times. Some of the striking particulars are these – the blockading of the British troops in the fort – the extension of a mine under the British works . . . the marching up of a pick'd company of valiants to haul down with hooks the bags of sand which lay on the top of the entrenchment, while muskets were incessantly blazing from behind them – the act of a courageous Tory who notwithstanding the surrounding crowd of besiegers, galloped through and gained admission at the gate with advices of an approaching reinforcement.

Although the siege was unsuccessful in that the fort was never captured, the nearly month-long struggle convinced the British that its continued defense was impractical. They evacuated the fort and fell back to Charleston, and the surrender at Yorktown soon followed. Now a full-fledged national park, Star Fort at Ninety Six is doubly important as the only Revolutionary outpost still visible in South Carolina.

While South Carolina did not wholeheartedly embrace the idea of war with England, it nevertheless made major contributions to the achievement of independence. Historians generally agree that activity in South Carolina "so hampered Cornwallis's strategy that Yorktown and its aftermath were inevitable." When Charleston was finally evacuated and the troops, along with nearly 9,000 Tories and slaves, sailed away in a fleet of British ships in 1782, South Carolina was at last truly an independent state. In the upcountry the war's aftermath brought a period of vengeance for atrocities committed during the hostilities. Among the most notorious Tories in Ninety Six District was William ("Bloody Bill") Cunningham who was charged with scores of murders, including women and children. Although Cunningham appears to have escaped to Florida, one of his henchmen, Matthew Love, was summarily hanged by kinsmen of men he had murdered. The hanging took place after the case against Love had been dismissed on a technicality. For the most part, however, the upcountry soon settled down after the war. Louis Wright's simple and graceful prose describes the way it was:

> Yet, despite sporadic outbreaks of lynch law and a few riots, the country fairly soon settled into ways of peace. Men and women, sick of fighting and bloodshed, wanted to get on with their farming, cattle raising, and other vocations. Even though the back country had suffered most from civil strife, the farmers and traders quickly recovered. They had little to begin with, and they were resilient. Their plight was less serious than that of many rice planters whose black slaves had been captured and taken away by the British: the planters were left without workers and lacked capital with which to renew their labor force.

The State of South Carolina had its hands full after the war trying to stabilize a government still largely fragmented by tradition and geography. The formation of counties began in 1785, Columbia became the state capital in 1786, and a new constitution was adopted in 1790. Ninety Six had entered the conflict as "the commercial center for an expanding arc of settlement on the frontier and the judicial seat for a huge area of the South Carolina back country." Its first public buildings – a courthouse and a jail – were erected about a mile from Goudy's trading post a short distance southwest of the present site of Star Fort, and a small village grew up around the "hall of justice." No description of the buildings exists beyond a reference in a Revolutionary account to a "brick gaol." After the Revolution the courthouse was described as a "two-story brick structure," but no one knows whether the building was the original or a replacement. A young British officer described Ninety Six in 1780: "It is a village or country-town – contains about twelve dwelling houses, a court-house and a jail . . . Ninety Six is situated on an eminence, the land cleared for a mile around it, in a flourishing part of the country."

The big story after the Revolutionary War was the rise of cotton as *the* staple of an agricultural South. The type of cotton best suited to the upcountry of South Carolina was a hardy short-staple variety "with green seeds to which the lint stuck tenaciously"; it could not be produced profitably until an efficient method of ginning could be devised. Eli Whitney's cotton gin proved to be the answer, but an answer that contained far-reaching consequences of its own: the gin not only revolutionized agriculture but also brought about profound changes in the social structure of the entire South. Cotton production rose to an almost unbelievable 35 million pounds by 1800. Farmers abandoned growing almost everything else. "Cotton was indeed king, and the gin was his throne," wrote David D. Wallace. But the price paid for the virtual enslavement of the South to a single standard based on a cotton economy was enormous. Louis Wright called King Cotton the "road to ruin" for South Carolina.

> [It] imposed the tyranny of a one-crop system on most of the land, extended the plantation system into the Up Country, vastly increased the demand for black slaves, spread slave-holding to regions hitherto free of the curse, and ultimately divided the nation, as slave states and free states battled over the question of slavery in new states entering the Union. In all of this, South Carolina took the lead as the loudest advocate of slavery and states' rights.
>
> From the end of the Revolution to the beginning of the Civil War, South Carolina made significant cultural and social advances and produced a galaxy of brilliant men. Yet, from the perspective of the twentieth century, these were the most dismal and tragic years of the state's history. Not even the actual war years or the miserable decades of Reconstruction and its aftermath were so tragic. In these later years, South Carolina met disaster with courage and nobility. But during the pre-Civil War period, the state exemplified the ultimate in social and political perversity, the wastage of brilliant minds fighting for futile (and often iniquitous) causes, and the enthronement of that worst of the Seven Deadly Sins, Pride. Even more terrible, South Carolina led the whole of the South to ruin.

Before cotton production transformed the upcountry in the late eighteenth century, the population consisted primarily of small farmers practicing a subsistence-to-mildly-prosperous type of agriculture. Few owned slaves. The 1790 census, in fact, reported only 615 blacks in the whole of Greenville County. Seventy years later, in 1860, Greenville's population was nearly 50% black. This dramatic change resulted from the great demand for labor as cotton production grew throughout the state. Cotton brought slavery to the upcountry, "human greed . . . prevailed over humanitarian instincts," and the state found itself forced to defend an institution that many of its citizens had earlier believed wicked. "Few controversies in American history," wrote Louis Wright, "are so lacking in mutual understanding, reasonableness, and charity as the debate over slavery." He found it "discouraging and humiliating to contemplate the verbal excesses" of either "self-righteous abolitionists from the North" or men such as Robert Barnwell Rhett and John C. Calhoun of South Carolina. For many years "emotionalism crowded out intelligence, and extremists on both sides drowned with their clamor the voices of reason and moderation." No peaceful solution was likely to be found amid such uproar. None was found, and the inexorable march to war was the result.

The village of Greenwood had its beginnings almost exactly halfway between the end of one great war and the beginning of another. It can be traced directly to Ninety Six during the period it called itself Cambridge. The name change had come about in honor of the College of Cambridge established in the village in 1785. Ninety Six petitioned for the name of Cambridge two years later, and the first post office in Greenwood County was chartered under that name in 1793. The first postmaster, James Wilson, received his appointment from President George Washington. Cambridge declined as a place name about 1860 as the new town of Ninety six developed along the railroad. The connection between Greenwood and Cambridge was a young lawyer, John McGehee, Jr., who built a log house in 1823 on a 600-acre plantation on the Cambridge-Abbeville road to serve as a summer home for him and his bride, the former Charlotte Dozier. This area, on present-day East Cambridge Street between Elm Court and Brewer School, was considered a "more healthy" location than the farm. According to tradition, Charlotte McGehee named the place Green Wood; any further explanation of the name she chose would no doubt be ludicrous. A settlement eventually grew up around the first house, and the pleasant-sounding name was combined and extended to the little community as well. It is interesting to note that the first post office established in 1837 was called Woodville. No one seems to know exactly why this was so, since the village it served had always been known as Greenwood, and the name was changed officially in 1850. C. M. Calhoun wrote that the town had no prescribed limits until its incorporation in 1857 when the old chapel of the Presbyterian school, an all-purpose building erected by the citizens, was made the center and one mile each way set as town limits. The exact location of the old chapel was between the Seaboard railroad crossing and Cokesbury Road; thus it is possible to pinpoint the very heart of the original village. The first railroad in 1852 was responsible for relocating the center of the village, since stores and other businesses soon moved to cluster themselves around the depot. Although the west side remained undeveloped for another forty years, the beginnings of the Square, an area that still means Uptown to Greenwood residents, were soon in place.

Another means of "placing" the village of Greenwood is its proximity to important early roads. The rough triangle formed by the intersection of three of those roads, in fact, includes the business district and most of the older residential sections of the town. The first important road was the Cambridge-Abbeville Road, now East and West Cambridge Avenues; another was Mathis Road, the remaining segments of which include Spring Street, the Wild Horse Road, and Mathews Road; and, finally, the Barksdale Ferry-New Market Road, which remains as Kirksey Drive and New Market Street. The first of these thoroughfares, the part of the Cambridge-to-Abbeville Road to the eastern edge of Greenwood, was authorized in 1778 but not actually laid out until after the Revolution, in 1785. When the road was extended westward to Abbeville sometime before 1800, the route chosen was identical to the present East and West Cambridge Avenues and Highway 72. Early road-building techniques were a masterpiece of simplicity. Greenwood historian John Henry Logan wrote that road commissioners were ordered to alert citizens to meet at a specified time and place "in order to work two days with axes and hoes, and all their male Negroes."

A road from Greenwood to the village at Cokesbury was opened about 1855. That thoroughfare, the present Cokesbury Road, intersected the Cambridge-Abbeville road at the site of the original village. (Highway 254 is often called Cokesbury Road today, and the street from East Cambridge to East Laurel is generally known as Cokesbury Street.) The names of Greenwood's earliest roads and streets have been changed several times. Cokesbury Road, for example, was once called King Street, and the Cambridge-Abbeville road was first known as Broadway, then Church after all three of the first churches located there, for a time as Main Street, and finally as Cambridge.

The Barksdale Ferry Road several miles south of the village of Greenwood, authorized in 1784, was important because it linked the Savannah and Saluda Rivers. Branches of the road eventually led to both Cambridge and Greenwood; its terminus on the Saluda River was Puckett's Ferry. This road essentially defines the eastern and southern edges of the town of Greenwood along the present New Market and Creswell Streets; early homes include the James Creswell/Abney/Hartzog house on New Market and "Sunnyside" on Dargan Avenue nearby. A lane westward from the Creswell house, first to the railroad and eventually to Spring Street, became East and West Creswell Avenues, still important residential streets.

A street from the Cambridge-Abbeville Road (then called Main Street) to the depot area was opened when the railroad came in 1852 and first called Depot Street. Later it was named Logan and is now known as North Main. When business began to develop around the railroad station, the original village site became almost exclusively a residential section called, appropriately enough, "Old Greenwood." The street that developed southward from the depot area was known as Railroad Avenue until about 1900 when it was changed to South Main Street.

The Mathis, or Mathews, Road, a north-south route along Greenwood's western edge is reflected in the path followed by Highway 178 from below South Greenwood to well above Hodges. This road originally ran "from Oconee to Charleston." Mathis crossed the Abbeville Road (intersection of Highways 178 and 72) and continued across Maxwell Avenue to Spring Street, behind Panola Mill and through Mathews Mill Village as Mathews Road. The stretch below the hospital became known as Wild Horse Road because people supposedly used it in preference to the newer road along the railroad tracks in order not to frighten their horses. The Spring Street area was the home of two of Greenwood's earliest residents: Andrew Logan, who located there before 1800, and William Newton Blake whose home was among the oldest in the town.

Even as Greenwood developed in the midst of several of the state's important early road systems, the sectional disputes between the North and South – over tariffs, extension of slavery, and nullification – continued to grow in the 1840s and 1850s. C. M. Calhoun wrote that Greenwood was a "hot States Right town" from his earliest recollection. He claimed, in fact, that John Henry Logan proposed the resolution that led to Abbeville's secession meeting in 1860. "The war in its embryo state first originated in Greenwood," he wrote. This sort of rhetoric was not unusual; indeed it was typical of the times. One deranged South Carolinian actually concluded a secessionist pamphlet in 1850 with the words "Give us slavery or give us death." The inevitable vote for secession came in December 1860 in an ordinance that represented, in the words of one of its signers, "the wild passions of that mad hour." James Louis Petigru, a Unionist to the last, is supposed to have said, "South Carolina is too small for a Republic and too large for an insane asylum." According to early records, Greenwood sent at least 55 young men into service in the Confederate Army; Calhoun named 57, a number that amounted to 19% of the population of the village at the time.

The area that became Greenwood County escaped most of the direct ravages of the Civil War; no battles were fought within its borders, and no out-of-control armies plundered its towns and villages. Greenwood, in fact, did a wholesale business in dry goods during the second year of the war, according to Calhoun, selling and shipping calico to Charleston. He was proud of Greenwood's enterprise in this regard and noted that shortages were such that ten yards of calico brought, to his own knowledge, the amount of $500. "While all other towns were apparently at a standstill during the war," he wrote, "Greenwood, even after all her male population had gone to the front . . . saw the need of and did carry to execution the only factory of its kind in the State" for the manufacture of "cotton cards" in what is now downtown Greenwood. Except for the "card factory," there was little or no business activity; Calhoun wrote that the village assumed "a rather graveyard appearance" for four long years. Greenwood figured briefly in a dramatic episode at the very end of the war when Confederate President Jefferson Davis, who had fled Richmond some weeks earlier, spent the night of May 1, 1865, at the Cokesbury home of General Martin Witherspoon Gary. The party moved on to Abbeville the next day, and Davis's capture at Irwinville, Georgia, followed a week later.

The formation of Greenwood County dates from 1897, rather late in the state's history; only six of South Carolina's 46 counties are newer than Greenwood. Recovery after the devastation of the Civil War was a long and difficult process, but a period of dynamic growth and development for Greenwood came during the last decade of the nineteenth century. Some of the events of that decade undoubtedly convinced the General Assembly that county status was a reasonable and timely proposal. Important developments of the 1890s, some of which probably influenced the formation of the county, include the following:

- The population more than tripled, from 1,326 in the 1890 census to 4,828 ten years later.
- The first textile plant, Greenwood Cotton Mill, opened in 1891.
- Greenwood was chosen as the site of a state Baptist orphanage in 1890, and the first children were received at Connie Maxwell Orphanage in 1892.
- The first public grade school was opened in 1891 (there had been schools before, but all were private).
- Greenwood's third railroad was completed in 1892.
- Telephone service began in 1896 with 42 subscribers.
- Grendel Mill, Greenwood's second cotton mill, opened in 1897.
- Two newspapers, *The Greenwood Journal* (1894) and *The Greenwood Index* (1897) were launched, following several earlier and unsuccessful efforts at establishing a newspaper. These two merged in 1919 as *The Index-Journal*, the only daily newspaper in Greenwood County.
- The Oregon Hotel, which provided a stopover for traveling salesmen, convention delegates, and other visitors, opened in 1898.
- The first business development on the west side of the square began in 1898 when a group of businessmen bought property and built a block of stores.
- Greenwood began operation of its own power plant for water and electric lights in 1899 with the aid of a $40,000 bond issue voted by the town.

A number of these developments are discussed in more detail in the following pages, along with people and events that help to define the county and county seat. One prominent citizen ticked off three items as examples of the type of enterprising and innovative moves that go a long way toward defining the peculiar, if not unique, quality of Greenwood County: the stories of Lander College, Self Memorial Hospital, and the Buzzard Roost Power Plant. It is perfectly logical to conclude that none of these institutions would have come about without the germ of an idea coupled with a sort of dogged determination typical of Greenwood's leaders in the first half of the century. The county and the twentieth century are virtually the same age. The story of one small county's first hundred years is surely insignificant when compared to the great sweep of global events of the same period; on the other hand, a study of one tends to illuminate the other until one fact becomes clear: Greenwood matters. How much it matters, to whom, and in precisely what ways, are questions for individual contemplation.

2

THE COUNTY SEAT

The trees in the streets are old trees
used to living with people,
Family trees that remember your
grandfather's name.
Stephen Vincent Benet

WHEN the first railroad came to Greenwood in 1852, the business district on what is now lower East Cambridge Street gradually moved nearer the tracks, and Uptown Greenwood as it appears today was born. There can be no question that the railroad led directly to incorporation for the town in 1857. Other lines followed in 1882 and 1890, so that Greenwood was a three-railroad town by the time the county was formed. In the early days of the railroad the town had been known primarily as a "fifty-cent meal stop" on the Greenville and Columbia line, a place that practically disappeared when a schedule change shifted the dinner break to Ninety Six. A journalist of the period wrote that Greenwood nearly ceased to exist after the schedule change "and never was heard of except as the location of a good female school." Warming to his topic, however, he concluded that Greenwood in the 1850s was not yet ready "to show the latent energy within her bounds and to make plain how a few sound-minded, enterprising men could build up a community and set in motion wheels of progress whose velocity increases with time. Greenwood has no history. It is making its record in the present, and a record, too, of which it can be proud." Although Greenwood had no "natural advantages," the writer nevertheless believed it was "fast becoming one of the busiest marts in South Carolina" and was surely "destined to be one of the best distributing points in the upper section of the State." He called the town "pre-eminently an example of what can be accomplished by unremitting energy and boundless self-reliance," a genuine tribute to Greenwood's people.

An article in a Charleston newspaper in 1889 described the circumstances under which the first two railroads were built. The first "was diverted from its natural and most direct route on its way from the Capital of the State to the Mountain City (Greenville) and made to circle round to Greenwood by the enterprising efforts of the townspeople," while the second was "built solely by the people of Greenwood and a few of those living along the line." The Augusta & Knoxville road was completed despite "fearful odds" and with "little encouragement from outsiders," but few railroads ever passed from the hands of original stockholders "with as little loss as did the old Greenwood and Augusta Road." As for the third railroad then under construction the journalist recorded that the Georgia, Carolina, and Northern would be "one of the best roads in the South, running as it does through a section of country ripe for development." The article called Greenwood a "railroad centre" and speculated that where outlets for traffic existed, very soon traffic would spring up to be let out. Greenwood's progress in other areas was also underway: "as a cotton market the town has grown till now it far exceeds in wealth and prosperity any town in the State of its own age and has few peers among those of twice or thrice its age."

After several paragraphs of super-enthusiastic tone, the article described Greenwood's form of government – an intendent and board of wardens – as well as nearly every business house in existence at the time. Greenwood's reputation as a "dry town" was cited as explanation for the lack of any sort of police force; there was only one "night watchman" to keep the peace. Both the Bank of Greenwood, a little more than a year old at the time, and the proposed Greenwood Cotton Mill were described. According to the article, the bank had declared an 8% dividend after only a year of operation, and the mill was to be built "on the co-operative plan," meaning that "no money is allowed to lie idle but is called for just as it is needed." The article also anticipated "cottages of the operatives" to be built on twenty acres of land "about the mill site."

In describing the various enterprises underway in 1889 the Charleston article called Greenwood businessmen "a company of capitalists" and was careful to include the names of officers and directors of every fledgling industry. Greenwood's schools and churches were not neglected, nor were the professions. A reference to lawyers was particularly interesting and indicative of things to come: "for the size of Greenwood there are very few lawyers, due no doubt to its not being a county seat." The article named only three attorneys – W. K. Blake, E. S. F. Giles, and F. H. McMaster – but listed seven physicians and one dentist. Riley's Hotel was accorded a paragraph, and T. F. Riley called "the genial proprietor" who "has done as much as any other man in Greenwood to make the town what it is." Other than Riley's, Greenwood could boast no establishment for "layovers" except "a large number of boarding houses . . . where the accommodations are good and the rates very cheap."

The article concentrated on Greenwood merchants and their places of business as they appeared in 1889. The Durst brothers – John K. and William L. – and S. P. Mathews were called "three as fine business men as one often meets"; the firm of J. K. Durst & Company had done business of more than $142,000 for the fiscal year 1889. Bailey, Barksdale & Company, "one of the oldest and most substantial" in the town, was also described as "a wholesale and retail business in groceries and general merchandise." Abraham Rosenberg was a young man at the time; his store was "continually filled with customers," and Rosenberg, who had "made much money," was "happy that his lot fell in Greenwood." Jervey & Company, dealer in farmers' supplies, cotton, and rice, was "doing a thriving business in supplies" and was the wholesale dealer in rice, besides "handling much cotton every season." The Jerveys were well-known merchants from Charleston.

A. St. Clair Lee and W. R. Bailey were cited as dealers in drugs, paints, oils, and wholesale and retail ice. Theirs was "one of the few granite-front buildings in this part of the State." J. T. Simmons's "carriage emporium" was called "the finest . . . outside of Charleston," with "a stock of vehicles that fills both floors of his repository and a large ware house besides." Other businessmen mentioned in the article include Blyth & Wells, furniture dealers and undertakers; J. W. Sproles, stoves, tinware, and roofing; Calhoun Brothers, groceries; Lee & Hodges, insurance and fertilizers; W. C. Strawhorne, general merchandise; Hartzog and Hays, livestock, horses and mules; and A. McD. Singleton, fancy groceries.

The article's penultimate paragraph stated that Greenwood also had in 1889 "two building and loan associations, through whose workings a number of homes in the town have been built. They are still in successful operation." This reference is a bit of a mystery; most sources indicate that building and loan operations were a phenomenon of the early 1920s. A business brochure from 1910, however, contains a short paragraph entitled "Building and Loan Companies":

> Persons wishing to own a home and not having sufficient money to build will find plenty of aid in their worthy project here. The banks are most liberal in such loans and in addition there are two Building and Loan Companies, the Greenwood Loan and Guarantee Association and The Home Building and Loan Association. Both offer exceedingly liberal terms to those who wish to borrow money for homes to be paid back on the plan of monthly installments.

Possibly these were the same organizations that caught the reporter's eye in 1889.

The long article concluded that Greenwood "bids fair to be a city at no very distant day." Its fair soil, unexcelled climate, railroad facilities, and other enterprises offered "many advantages to young men and capitalists," in the opinion of the reporter, who ended his paean of praise on the high note that Greenwood's "hospitable and progressive" people extended their welcome to "all who may come to" their town.

Surely no chamber of commerce could have done a better job of boosting Greenwood! It is hard not to wonder why a Charleston newspaper chose to spotlight a small upcountry town in such flamboyant style. Editor John Hammond Moore wrote in the introduction to *South*

Carolina in the 1880s: A Gazetteer that more than fifty communities, many of them quite small and not all in South Carolina, were the subjects of these "extensive accounts," which ran in the *News and Courier* between July 1887 and January 1891. He speculated that the newspaper might simply have wished to attract more readers or increase advertising revenue. On the other hand, Moore considered the possibility that the Columbia bureau of the newspaper just might have been "establishing contacts for the yet unborn *State* while ostensibly working in behalf of the *News and Courier.*" Whatever the reason for the series of articles, it is certainly true as Moore suggested that the result is "an unusual windfall" for residents of those towns a century later. In the case of Greenwood, the article serves as a sort of kickoff to the decade of the 1890s, which Louise Watson called "a great upsurge" for the town. That "upsurge" brought about extensive changes in Greenwood's business district and culminated in the formation of the county in 1897.

Only the east side of the square had been developed as the 1880s drew to a close. E. C. McCants wrote in 1935 that the business district he knew when he first came in 1887 lay almost entirely east of the railroad tracks. The west side consisted of either private homes or vacant lots, and the courthouse site was a "strawfield surrounded by a dilapidated fence." The first change came when Joel S. Bailey used his home site on the corner of Main and Maxwell for the construction of a hotel. The site was part of a 34-acre tract of land Bailey's father James had purchased from Dr. E. R. Calhoun in 1848, a tract that included all of the present north side of Maxwell Avenue to beyond the Seaboard Railroad site and part of what is now the mill village. The value of the property in 1848 was the astounding sum of $800. Bailey built his store and a two-story house on the property nearest the square. A newspaper article dated March 1, 1936, stated that the store building was used as a depot for the Augusta and Knoxville Railroad when it was completed in 1882. The house was destined to be moved twice before it was finally torn down in 1935. Joel Smith Bailey owned the home place when he got the idea for a hotel.

Two years later Bailey's sister Alice Boozer consented to sell her cottage located where Thayer's now stands. The blockbusting that began when Joel Bailey decided to build the Oregon Hotel culminated in the purchase of the entire block by a group of local businessmen organized as "The Syndicate." One might expect a group with so intriguing a name to consist of shadowy underworld figures, but this was Greenwood in the 1890s, and the syndicate consisted of perfectly straightforward businessmen H. G. Hartzog, W. G. Gambrell, G. A. Byrd, E. R. Goodwin, and Singleton & Cobb, most of whom opened their own stores in the block. (Note: an earlier newspaper story added J. Spiegel and J. W. McCullough to the list and omitted Byrd.) The architect for the project was D. J. Anderson, who also hailed from Anderson; superintendent of construction was W. V. Blyth. Other houses in the block (some sources indicate it was called Logan Street at that time, but at least one states it was the first location of Waller Street) were those of Samuel B. Hodges and Captain C. A. C. Waller. The Bailey house was moved up the street to the spot now occupied by the federal building. It would be moved yet again when the post office was built a few years later. Presumably the Hodges and Boozer houses were torn down, but Waller's remained standing at the south end of the business block for many years. The Syndicate announced plans to erect five new buildings (some sources say six, or even seven) fronting on the street. All were to be two stories high and contain a "modern opera house" on the second level, as well as some flats, or apartments, for rent to private citizens. Two early tenants, H. G. Hartzog and D. Parker Jordan, were reported to live in "princely style" in these "handsomely appointed" flats. Henry Thayer says that Mr. and Mrs. H. V. R. Schrader, who came to town in 1901, also lived there for a time. The opera house just down the street was used for various road shows, minstrels, and vaudeville performances, as well as what the newspaper called "home talent entertainments," for about ten years, but it vanished when moving pictures came into vogue. Interestingly enough, early reports on the most recent remodeling of Uptown Greenwood contained plans for much the same type of residental units on the second level as were built about 1900. Difficulty with fire codes was cited as the primary reason this plan failed to materialize.

A most interesting illustrated and annotated map of downtown Greenwood as it appeared around 1908 was prepared in 1973 by the Merchants Association and the Index Publishing Company. The authors of this limited edition map were Boykin Curry, Kendall Few, and Margaret Watson. According to the map, the Oregon Hotel building occupied essentially the entire block between Oregon Street and Maxwell Avenue. Several other businesses were located in the building, including the Oregon Pharmacy, LaTour's Barber Shop, a pool room, Western Union offices, and a wholesale grocery business. The Syndicate Block of stores included the Farmers and Merchants Bank, Gambrell Hardware, Greenwood Drug Company, J. P. Jennings Company, G. A. Byrd Company, Greenwood Candy Kitchen (with the Index Publishing Company on the second floor), Wharton & Rush Clothing, M. F. Sanders Dry Goods Company, and the Singer Sewing Machine Company. Wharton & Rush Dry Goods evidently also occupied a separate store building near the Waller residence at the far end of the block.

Businesses on the east side of the square in 1908 included Hodges Drug Store and A. Rosenberg's, both of which are described more fully later in this chapter, as well as the Riley Hotel, the Bank of Greenwood, and J. T. Simmons Furniture Repository, which stood on the present site of The County Bank. The building now occupied by J. C. Bradford and Company was at that time Stalnaker Brothers Grocery on the ground floor and W. V. Blyth's funeral parlor upstairs. The National Loan and Exchange Bank which would later move across the street was just north of the Masonic Temple in what was then known as the "Chipley Block" and now as The Exchange. The voluntary fire department and city jail were just back of the Chipley Block; the town hall lot they would later occupy at the opposite end of the street was purchased in 1908. The three stores in the Barksdale Block at the north end of the square were Sheridan & Hart Book Store (forerunner of McCaslan's), R. L. White Jeweler & Optician, and Singleton Grocery, presumably the successor of Bailey, Barksdale & Company.

The map noted that the population of Greenwood in 1908 was slightly more than 7,500, and the downtown business district comprised some eighty store buildings around the public square. Street paving was underway but would not be completed for another three years or so. Although Greenwood boasted two automobile garages – a Maxwell dealership and the John I. Chipley Auto Exchange which sold Fords – four livery stables did a thriving business as well. Greenwood had electric lights, telephones, two newspapers, three banks, and three hotels.

A newspaper article in the centennial edition of *The Index-Journal* stated that the street-level space at the corner of the Syndicate Block (present site of Thayer's) first served as the post office. A new bank, the Farmers and Merchants Bank organized in 1900, occupied the space until the bank went under in 1930. The third occupant was the Oregon Pharmacy and Jewelry Company, a business that was destined to stay. The corner building was extensively remodeled in 1953, and the business was re-named Thayer's at the same time. The first renovation retained the building's most distinctive feature, a corner turret long considered a Greenwood landmark, but the turret could not withstand progress and vanished in a later remodeling. Henry Thayer still regrets the loss of the turret, which was removed when engineers judged it to be probably structurally unsound. He said it turned out to be securely grounded on granite slabs and would have lasted indefinitely.

Thayer's has an interesting history, primarily because its 80-year life has been spent on one or the other corner of Main Street and Maxwell Avenue, but also because its ownership passed from father to son and out of the family some 65 years after the first Thayer came to Greenwood. The original Henry K. "Kibbie" Thayer came to town in 1911 to enter business with E. L. Norris in his drug store located in the Oregon Hotel building. After the fire in 1912 Norris and Thayer moved their business, the Oregon Pharmacy, across the street temporarily until the hotel was rebuilt. The gift department was Thayer's idea when the only jewelry store in town closed in 1918, and the company expanded to include the Oregon Jewelry Company which opened on the mezzanine floor of the drug store in the hotel building. Norris left Greenwood in 1926, and Thayer became sole owner of the business.

The company moved back across the street for the last time in 1933 and expanded to the building next door and also down Maxwell Avenue.

Thayer opened a second drug store across the square from the Oregon Pharmacy during the war years. That store was called Thayer's Drug Store; its last location was the building at the corner of Main and Magnolia (now the home of J. C. Bradford & Company). The business was bought in 1944 by another long-time Greenwood pharmacist, J. Cecil Dominick, who operated Dominick's Pharmacy in the location for nearly forty years. The building itself was owned by the Blyth family during the entire period, according to Mrs. Dominick. Henry K. Thayer, both father and son, took active roles in the business, civic, and social life of Greenwood, and the staff at Thayer's have always been arbiters of good taste in the town. For some time, at least during the 1940s and 1950s, the store presented every Greenwood High School girl graduate with a sterling silver teaspoon. That spoon often determined the pattern of her wedding silver. Henry Thayer, Sr., a transplanted New Englander, is reported to have said, "Southern people appreciate fine china and silver, and there is always demand for better products." Thayer's also has a long-standing tradition of awarding a medal to the Lander College graduate with the highest grade point ratio. The Thayer Medal dates from the senior Thayer's time and continues to the present day. The current owner of Thayer's, William W. Wilson who bought the business in 1976, sees himself as continuing a Greenwood tradition.

The first important commercial building on the west side of the square was the Oregon Hotel, described in a newspaper article as "the institution that made Greenwood famous." The hotel was the brain child of one of Greenwood's most important early businessmen, Joel Smith Bailey (1854-1900). Bailey was a son of James Bailey who came to Stony Point from Laurens as a young man to work in Joel Smith's store. The conjecture that James Bailey named his son to honor his friend in Stony Point is inescapable. Bailey moved to Greenwood to establish his own store some time around 1855, according to Margaret Watson. The date of 1855 might be only supposition. Bailey purchased property in Greenwood in 1848; it seems odd that he would wait another seven years to move, particularly since he went into business with E. R. Calhoun, the man who sold him the property.

Joel Bailey's business partnership with his brother-in-law George A. Barksdale was Bailey, Barksdale & Company established in 1875. If the date is correct, young Bailey was only 21 years old when the business was formed; of course it is possible that he merely stepped into an established business. An article in the centennial edition of the newspaper, based on an old reference book of the Mercantile Association of the Carolinas for July 1890, stated that the "Bailey" in the firm was William H. Bailey. This reference muddies the waters on Joel Bailey's business interests. His granddaughters Clara Robeson and Margaret Tinsley agree that William H. Bailey was a prominent Greenwood businessman, but they do not associate him with their grandfather's firm. They say that George Barksdale and Joel Bailey were contemporaries who entered business together in the 1870s.

The first store in the Barksdale block that forms the northern boundary of the square was a wooden structure built by James F. Watson of the Mount Moriah section some time during the construction of the first railroad (late 1840s or early 1850s). Watson died before the road reached Greenwood in 1852. James Bailey arrived from Stony Point during the same period and went into business with E. R. Calhoun at another site. A few years later, James Bailey's cousin, another Bailey from Laurens whose name was James A., came to Greenwood and formed a partnership with G. M. Connor of Cokesbury. The firm of Bailey and Connor, located in the store Watson built, was advertised in the Abbeville newspaper in 1858. Yet another Bailey — James A.'s younger brother William H. — came to Greenwood in 1865 to go into business with his brother (Connor had died in the interim), and the firm of J. A. and W. H. Bailey was formed. None of this information, interesting as it is, connects W. H. Bailey's business with that of Joel Smith Bailey; nevertheless, the latter was definitely associated in business with George A. Barksdale, their firm was called Bailey, Barksdale & Company, and it stood on the original Watson site. Joel S. Bailey's name appeared regularly in Greenwood's business news during the decade of progress; he was intendant in 1889, as well as an officer in the brand new cotton mill company.

The idea for the new hotel was apparently Bailey's; an undated newspaper article reported: "Mr. Joel Bailey of the firm of Bailey, Barksdale & Co. will in a few days commence the erection of a three-story brick building on the corner of Main and Maxwell streets fronting the Southern and C.&W.C. Railways. The Bailey residence will be moved further up the street to make room for the new building." The architect for the first Oregon Hotel was G. L. Norman of Atlanta, according to *The Greenwood Index* of February 3, 1898. The general contractor's name was Carson, and W. H. Mays was the brick contractor. Plans included a building with exterior dimensions of 100'x100' with space for stores on the ground floor. Anyone who has seen a picture of the first Oregon Hotel will be pleased to credit Norman, Carson, and Mays with a fine piece of work. Joel Bailey evidently had no plans to run the hotel himself; he leased it before it was completed to H. J. Brinson, proprietor of the Commercial Hotel in Athens, Georgia. Brinson is credited with the naming of the hotel, as well as with its successful operation during his 26-year tenure in Greenwood.

The new hotel had naturally been the subject of much discussion in the little town. The newspaper reported that several names were suggested, but none seemed quite right. The Spanish-American War, which Secretary of State John Hay characterized as "a splendid little war," came along at just the right moment. The war created several instant heroes, among them Commodore (later Admiral) George Dewey, who commanded the battleship "Oregon" in the first important naval engagement, the Battle of Manila Bay. The progress of the ship from Japan to Hong Kong to the Philippines was all over the newspapers of the day, and the battle itself turned out to be a decisive American victory. Headwaiter Charlie Williams, who had worked his way up from water boy in Brinson's Athens hotel and would later accompany him to Greenwood, supposedly called his boss's attention one day to the ship's name screamed from big headlines in the *Atlanta Constitution*, whereupon Brinson supposedly said, with somewhat the emphasis of Archimedes' *Eureka*!, "That's what we will name our hotel at Greenwood!" The name was perfect. Not only did it reflect the nationalist, if not downright chauvinist, spirit of the times, it also allowed for an absolutely stunning souvenir menu booklet for the opening dinner on September 15, 1898. One of those booklets is preserved in May Bailey Smith's scrapbook. The cover is simply a photograph of the ship with a caption reading "U. S. Battle Ship Oregon," and the booklet is tied with three small ribbons – one red, one white, and one blue. The menu page inside offers queen olives, celery, and salted almonds as appetizers; the soup was creme de Volaille a la Reine; and the fish course was fillet of redsnapper a la Maitre D'Hotel. Other courses included croquetts de Dindon petit pois verts, Boston cream puffs souffle D'Orange, Tenderloin de Boeuf aux champignons with snowflake potatoes and a sorbet a la Oregon. There was also broiled chicken on toast au cresson and cold asparagus vinaigrette. Desserts were tutti frutti cream and assorted cakes followed by American cheese, water crackers, and black coffee.

Formal invitations printed in blue ink, mostly in script, were extended: "You are cordially invited to attend the opening dinner of the Oregon Hotel Thursday Evening, Sept. 15, 1898, at 7:30 o'clock. H. J. Brinson, Proprietor; J. S. Bailey, Owner – R.S.V.P." A story in *The Index-Journal* of September 15, 1945, recalled the event and offered additional information on the "brilliant occasion" of the opening reception and dinner exactly 47 years earlier. The reporter interviewed headwaiter Charlie Williams who worked at the Oregon Hotel for 39 years. Williams must have possessed a truly remarkable memory: he could "recall the names of practically all of the diners and guests he ever served during his career there." Williams remembered that some 250 guests attended the festivities on opening night, among them visitors from Columbia, Baltimore, Atlanta, and Nashville. Home town guests included E. C. Rice, J. C. Self, Mrs. Joe Spiegel, Major H. G. Hartzog, Mr. and Mrs. J. J. Caldwell, Mr. and Mrs. S. U. Brunson, Mr. and Mrs. C. W. Garrett, Mr. and Mrs. R. M. Hays, Alfred Hayes, W. H. Bailey, C. A. C. Waller, Major Joseph J. Ligon, Mr. and Mrs. S. P. Wright, J. B. Park, Capt. F. S. Evans, and Parker Jordan.

The headwaiter's description of the hotel floor plan recalled the main office, dining room, kitchen, private dining room, sun parlor, and gentlemen's reception room on the ground floor. The dining room featured a large Maltese cross hung with red, white, and blue lights. The hotel china and other crockery were decorated with a picture of the battleship "Oregon," and the sun parlor sported an electric piano, an aquarium with goldfish, ferns, and other greenery. The hotel also contained a ladies' parlor on the second floor. One singular feature of each guest room was a glass tray with pictures of Admiral Dewey, Theodore Roosevelt, and someone named "Mrs. Slighton." The tray held needles and thread, along with a collar button and a bachelor's button. Charlie Williams was definitely a waiter of the old school. He had no patience with the modern way of dining: an entire meal on a single plate consumed by people in a hurry to get on to something else. Williams much preferred course-by-course service of a meal that might last an hour or two, with time for leisurely conversation around a well-appointed table.

On holidays the hotel offered traditional fare; one souvenir menu described "Ye Thanksgiving Feaste for the Yeare of MDCCCC." Another particularly charming clipping concerned the party at the hotel to celebrate the Baileys' sixteenth wedding anniversary which fell a month or so after the hotel opened. The article was signed only with the initials LMB: "While we sat at the table admiring the jets of electric light around the elegant dining hall, casting a soft glow over the tastefully appointed table, with its 'rich, rare and racy viands,' we could easily fancy ourselves at the St. Nicholas, or the Hoffman House in New York City." It is amusing to think of guests at this dinner nearly a hundred years ago reminiscing about Greenwood fifty years earlier, but the author of the anniversary article did just that. "Verily," LMB wrote, "if some of the spirits who reigned in Greenwood fifty years ago could awake from their long sleep and revisit the spot . . . would they not imagine that some enchanter's wand or Aladdin's lamp had worked some magic around old Greenwood, so wondrous is the progress from ye olden time?" The article commended proprietor Joel Bailey: "All honor to the enterprising builder of this ornament to our growing city!"

Although the claim made for the hotel three years after it opened — that "its fame has spread to the uttermost confines of the country" — might have been something of an exaggeration, the next line, "the laudable efforts of the manager make it a bright oasis in the life of the traveling man," was probably quite true. Because Greenwood was a railroad center with 27 trains coming through every day, a first-class hotel right by the tracks simply had to be a great attraction. The hotel moved rapidly from a favorite stopover for traveling salesmen to a convention center and social gathering place for Greenwood gentry as well. A three-story annex along Maxwell Avenue with space for several more stores was constructed about 1910; Greenwood architect Thomas Cothran designed the annex. No business in Greenwood was more central to the life of the town than the original Oregon Hotel, and no one enjoyed its success more than founder Joel Bailey. Unfortunately, Bailey did not live to see his hotel reach its full potential. He died in 1900 at the age of only 46; his granddaughter Clara Robeson says he developed a mastoid infection for which no treatment was available at the time. A particularly poignant tribute was announced in the March 7, 1901, edition of the newspaper: two memorial windows were to be placed in the hotel – one in the office and another in the lobby; one was to be given by personal friends and Greenwood citizens in general, and the other would be funded by voluntary subscriptions from traveling men who used the hotel. Possibly the plans were altered somewhat; the *Greenwood Index* reported in its May 30 edition that a memorial window in honor of the late Mr. Bailey had been installed in the hotel the preceding week.

And then came the fire on March 3, 1912, that razed the entire block. Fortunately there was no loss of life, but many guests lost their personal effects and fled the flames in their night clothes. Two or three theories of the origin of the fire were advanced, but no one was able to pinpoint the cause exactly. The fire chief blamed a flaw in the wiring in the pool room; others believed the furnace was somehow defective; and still others, including Brinson, thought spontaneous combustion originating in a storeroom was the culprit. At any rate, the loss was set at approximately $140,000, only about half of which was covered by insurance. The hotel building was valued at the time of the fire at $95,000. Other businesses burned out were the Oregon Pharmacy, McKellar-Graham Furniture Company, Holland Brothers (dealer in musical instruments), A. LaTour barber shop, Coleman & Riley's pool room, and Lion Tailors. Another loser was Thomas S. Chipley who had several automobiles stored in a vacant store building.

As evidence of Brinson's determination to continue the enterprise, the newspaper reported that he leased the Moreland Apartments on North Main Street only three days after the fire. There was some talk about taking over the Riley Hotel on the other side of the square, but that option was not pursued. Brinson might have been more eager than the Bailey family; Joel S. Bailey, Jr., saw the rebuilding as too much to undertake alone or as a family project. Times had changed; it was decided the new Oregon Hotel would be a joint venture, or stock company, with several other businessmen taking part. The newspaper reported in March 1912 that plans called for a building of at least five stories, providing for a hotel of from 90-100 rooms with space for business houses on the ground floor, at a cost of not less than $100,000. The undertaking moved very quickly; only three months later, the newspaper reported a stockholders' meeting and election of a board of directors. Officers, in addition to Bailey who was president and treasurer, were Kenneth Baker, vice president, and W. T. Bailey, secretary. Stockholders were listed as the three officers plus G. W. Rush, H. L. Watson, J. C. Self, N. A. Craig, A. Rosenberg, and S. H. McGhee. Brinson was retained as manager of the new hotel which opened for business in November 1914.

The second incarnation of the Oregon Hotel opened in a slightly different location with one entrance farther down Maxwell Avenue. Another entrance faced a courtyard/garden in the area between Oregon Street and Maxwell Avenue. Both entrances were retained when the building was remodeled. The corner lot in the meantime was being developed as the first business venture of the brand new Citizens Trust Company chartered in May 1913. The first floor of the building was leased to the National Loan and Exchange Bank. It was difficult to escape speculation that the two buildings, which seem to have gone up simultaneously, were somehow related in other ways. Although there was no common wall between them and the floor elevations differed slightly, both were five stories high and built of the same materials. Boykin Curry cleared up the question easily enough with the information that the Bailey family was heavily involved in both the bank and the hotel; indeed, Citizens Trust Company was formed as a subsidiary of the bank, and both Joel Bailey and his brother William were officers and directors. That close relationship explains the construction of two such similar buildings on Main Street and Maxwell Avenue. Both were designed by the same architect, A. Ten Eyck Brown of Atlanta, and an Athens builder, Smith Construction Company, secured the $93,000 contract for the two-building complex. Together they made an impressive pair that occupied essentially an entire block, and the two buildings were a most convenient parcel for Greenwood Mills when that company decided to move its administrative offices uptown in 1964. Both were remodeled extensively and became the Greenwood Building in 1966.

The new Oregon Hotel seemed to take up in 1914 where it had left off two years before. Brinson returned as manager and owner of the furnishings, and the real property was now owned by the Oregon Hotel Company, a corporation whose president was Joel S. Bailey, Jr. The first Joel Bailey's widow, who seems to have been addressed ever after as Mrs. C. T. (Clara Tarrant) Bailey, became majority stockholder in the hotel after her husband's death. A fine picture of the hotel appeared in the newspaper article of March 27, 1924, announcing its sale. The new owner was Ira T. Stone of Columbia, a hotel man of long experience. Speculation at the time was that the hotel, with furnishings, brought nearly $250,000. The Oregon was described in the 1924 article as "the best small town hotel in the entire country." The building and surroundings were noted "for their beauty in spring and summer and coziness in winter." Clara Robeson and Louise Hartzog remember the garden on the grounds where they liked to play as children.

A 1937 article called the Oregon Hotel "one of the best advertising mediums for Greenwood" and noted that Stone was "keeping abreast of the times" with a thorough renovation of the interior. One new feature was an electric fan in each guest room; the rooms were also equipped with Wilton and Axminster carpets and "Simmons modernistic beds." (Note: Axminster and Wilton, or Jacquard, are terms that refer to certain types of weaving in carpet manufacture. The invention of the broadloom had made large carpets possible, and wall-to-wall carpeting had just come into vogue. Stone was indeed up-to-date.) On the downside, however, was the fact that the Oregon's famous dining room gave way in 1936 to the coffee shop concept of a smaller restaurant just off the lobby. The dining room was used thereafter only for banquets and service club dinners.

Stone leased the hotel in 1946 to Herman A. Moore and associates of the Auto Finance Company. The hotel thus became a subsidiary of Auto Finance and did business as the Oregon Hotel Company, Inc., with W. D. Tinsley as president. The company exercised its option to buy the property at the expiration of the lease in 1956 and promptly sold the hotel to Stiles-Wallace Hotels, Inc. At some point, presumably during the period 1946-1956, the banquet room, which could seat about 300 people, had been named the Herman Moore Room. A newspaper article at the time of the sale to Stiles-Wallace quoted Tinsley:

> The officials of the company feel that the original purpose of Herman Moore and associates to provide better hotel services for Greenwood have been fully carried out. The hotel facilities in Greenwood compare favorably with those of most cities of similar size. . . . We feel that the record of the Stiles family in operating hotels successfully throughout the South assures Greenwood of even better hotel facilities in the future. That assurance was one of the principal factors in the decision to sell to this group.

The article concluded with a sketch of Moore's successful business career which had begun in Greenwood and noted Moore's view that the remodeling of the Oregon Hotel was a gesture of "appreciation to the people who gave me a start." Boykin Curry supports the idea that Moore was in effect making a gift to Greenwood with the expense of refurbishing, an expense he did not recover.

Although business interests took Herman A. Moore away from Greenwood at the height of his career, the company he founded in 1934, Auto Finance Company, was called "a Greenwood and South Carolina institution" in a 1957 newspaper article, and Moore himself described as "one of the South's great industrialists." He entered the used car business in about 1925 with capital of only $5,000 but also with a plan for weekly or monthly car payments that immediately caught on. So successful was the plan, in fact, that Moore realized he needed a specialized organization to handle his portfolio of receivables; Auto Finance Company was the result. That company's assets in 1957 were nearly $68 million. Its investments, in addition to the Oregon Hotel, included the Augusta Chronicle Company, Southeastern Fire Insurance Company, and Citadel Life Insurance Company. Auto Finance also acquired American Discount Company, a Georgia finance institution.

Although Moore died before 1957, he is well remembered as one of the stars of the business community of Greenwood.

The Stiles group continued to own the hotel until it finally closed in 1963. The new manager was J. M. (Jack) Byrd of Greenwood, who was also one of the owners. Although the Stiles group redecorated and added air conditioning throughout the hotel, business continued to lag. Times had changed yet again. Because of new interstate highways with their network of travelers' stopovers called motels, the country was moving away from downtown hotels with a style of service considered too slow and old fashioned for an America on the move. The demise of the Oregon Hotel brought to an end a 65-year tradition in Greenwood. After it closed the town was without a downtown hostelry for more than twenty years, until the Inn on the Square opened in 1985. Greenwood got the first of its "chain" motels when the Holiday Inn opened in 1966.

As evidence of the impact of the Oregon Hotel on the town of Greenwood, one has only to look at the number of businesses at one time with the word *Oregon* in their names. The Oregon Pharmacy and Oregon Jewelry Company have already been mentioned; references to Oregon Service Stations #1 and #2 have been found; Oregon Street must certainly have derived its name directly from the hotel, although the date of the naming is undetermined; and the Oregon Barber Shop once operated in the basement of the corner building. The Oregon Beauty Shop, which ceased to exist in 1988, was the last of the downtown businesses with that famous name. Its owners were Mrs. George M. (Josie) Bailey and her sister Mrs. F. Q. (Vernetta) Adams; they inherited the shop from an aunt, Mrs. Henry H. Scott, whose husband had owned the Oregon Barber Shop. Bailey still works as a manicurist at Mane Attractions, a salon in Hampton Place shopping center. She recalled in an interview that when the Oregon Beauty Shop finally closed its books, the County Bank wrote that the shop had maintained accounts there for 55 years. Evidently it was among the bank's first depositors in 1933.

At this writing, the only *Oregon* listing in the telephone book is Oregon Farms, an L. B. and Angelle Adams enterprise near Ninety Six. Did a connection exist there? Did the names arise simultaneously, or was this a completely different *Oregon*? A telephone interview with Angelle Adams provided the perfect answer. Of course the *Oregons* are the same. L. B. Adams purchased the property on Kirksey Drive, between New Market Street and the Ninety Six highway, that had been the country place of the Brinson family. Adams remembers that the farm had been lovingly developed and beautified when her husband bought it in the early 1930s. The Brinsons had often taken hotel guests there, and the farm also provided produce for Oregon Hotel dinners. When Adams sold the tract to Greenwood Mills, he simply transferred the name *Oregon Farms* to property he already held near Ninety Six. During the time the Adamses owned the original farm, they began the Oregon Dairy; they also kept horses there and often rode through the countryside.

If any other evidence of the hotel's importance to the town is needed, the fact that it was the first home of newlyweds James C. and Lura Mathews Self in 1916 should take care of that problem.

Although no business in early Greenwood can touch the Oregon Hotel for a certain type of elegance and social cachet, there were others just as closely associated with life in the town and the "interlocking directorate" of the first families of Greenwood. One of those businesses was Hodges Drug Store, with the eminent Dr. Samuel C. Hodges as proprietor. Hodges served a term as county senator in 1928, but that was only a small part of a truly remarkable career.

Samuel Connor Hodges was a descendant of John Hodges who settled in South Carolina before the Revolution and who was a true progenitor of Greenwood County. To broaden the issue still further, Sam Hodges's grandmother was Mary A. D. Connor, daughter of Francis Connor of Cokesbury, and his mother was Harriet Louise Bailey of yet another "first family." Hodges's only child, the redoubtable Louise Hartzog, has just celebrated her 90th birthday at this writing.

Hodges began working in his uncle St. Clair Lee's drug store as a boy, sweeping the store for 25¢ a week. He entered Wofford College in 1892 and graduated with a degree in chemistry three years later. He studied alone, using books borrowed from a pharmacist friend, for the state board examination for a pharmaceutical license. He passed that examination in 1898 and became a partner with his uncle the next year. Eventually he bought out Lee's interest, as well as a drug store owned by another relative, Walter R. Bailey, and launched his own business as Hodges Drug Store. His father and two brothers, both licensed pharmacists, joined Hodges in the business which was eventually incorporated. The store became an institution in uptown Greenwood, and the Hodges name synonymous with the drug store business for more than fifty years. Edgar Davis dubbed it the Presbyterian Club, a reference to the long connection of the Hodges and Bailey families with the First Presbyterian Church. Although the drug store was Hodges's primary business, he also dealt in downtown real estate. The National Loan and Exchange Bank building became known as the Hodges Building when he purchased it in 1936. Samuel Hodges was awarded an honorary degree of doctor of pharmacy from the Medical College of South Carolina in 1951. The citation recognized him for outstanding services and labors for the benefit of humanity. His alma mater honored him with its award of merit at Wofford's Centennial celebration in 1954. That award credited his long public service as elder and Sunday School Superintendent at the First Presbyterian Church and as trustee of Greenwood public schools, the South Carolina Medical College, John de la Howe School, and Columbia Theological Seminary. Hodges also served five terms on the Greenwood City Council, as well as a term as senator.

Hodges's daughter Louise, who carries Greenwood's history in her head, has also accumulated a fine collection of memorabilia in the unlikely event she might forget something. Among these mementos are three publications which ran articles on her father at various times. The first, from the *Southeastern Drug Journal* for February 1930, is particularly interesting because its author was Margaret Wright, sister of Greenwood historian Louis Wright. Wright's opening sentence is a nice summation of her subject: "He started his business career at the age of ten by sweeping out his uncle's drug store for 25 cents a week. Today, at the age of 56, he owns the store and finds time to be a state senator besides." Wright ranked Hodges among the state's leading druggists and added, "a more versatile one could scarcely be found in all the South." Hodges's almost unbelievable list of public service was included in the article; one of those activities surely constitutes a unique connection for Greenwood. It seems that Samuel C. Hodges was elected in 1920 to the convention for the revision of the Pharmacopoeia, the standard work in the fields of drugs, chemicals, and medicinal preparations.

Margaret Wright was as adept as her famous brother in vivid writing; it would be a shame to paraphrase her descriptions of Sam Hodges. After faithfully recording the facts of his busy life, she humanized him delightfully:

> All of which sounds like statistics for a college annual and doesn't give the faintest insight into the delightful and magnetic personality of Greenwood's Sunday-School-superintendent-senator-druggist. When you meet Dr. Hodges on the street, whether it is a cloudy morning in January or a rare day in June, you feel moved to sing out, "Hail to thee, blithe Spirit!" for in all probability he has just swept off his hat in a glorious flourish, given as graceful and courtly a bow as is possible in a modern age of rapidly passing and closely crowding automobiles, and has let loose a flow of debonair eloquence in greeting that would put a poet to shame — and that probably involves an apt quotation of anything from Will Rogers to Socrates.
>
> His spirit is as effervescent as a Seidlitz powder; he bubbles over with quick wit and humor and his tongue is tipped with Irish blarney. "It's just natural with Sam," a former college mate said of him; "he's been that way all his life. He had much rather say the pleasant thing than the critical."
>
> Not that he hasn't his serious side. He is a hard-working and earnest laborer in all phases of church and civic work, in addition to being one of Greenwood's most successful business men, and the message that he passed on to all druggists is: "Take time for outside interests aside from your drugs. Don't let your business cramp and confine you until your mind is warped and your spirit and vision are dwarfed and narrowed."
>
> "The average man," Dr. Hodges said, "uses only a fraction of his mental powers; he rarely plumbs the depth of what he is really capable of." Dr. Hodges hobbies are reading — he has a splendid

> library; walking – he did 1,000 miles in one year; music – he plays the flute and sings; and the study of birds and astronomy. In college he took part in football, baseball and tennis. He still uses his Indian clubs and dumbbells to help him keep in physical trim.
>
> It is characteristic of the excellent balance of the practical with the aesthetic in his nature that he has the vegetable garden on his estate laid off in geometrical patterns with rows of prosaic cabbages and beds of carrots gaily bordered with larkspur and hollyhocks or neatly edged with sweet alyssum.
>
> He is Greenwood's most brilliant and entertaining after-dinner speaker and the training in eloquence and graceful delivery he received in his practice in speaking as a Sunday School superintendent.
>
> In view of his many-sided character and his diversity of interests he was asked if he did not find it a terrible wrench, for instance, to lay down his silver flute, cease reading Shakespeare, or to come back from the interesting life of the political arena to mix up pills and concoct tonics for the ailing.
>
> "A wrench!" he exclaimed. "Why, no! I find no difficulty in transferring my interest from one phase of activity to another. Nor is it boresome and irksome to me to come back to mixing up pills after having been deeply engrossed in politics, athletics, a detective story or a study of the stars. The thing that would be tiresome and monotonous to me would be to have to follow only one line of endeavor or train of thought. It is a diversity of work and hobbies that keeps life perennially interesting and full of zest and piquancy."

The next encomium appeared more than twenty years later in the *South Carolina Magazine.* Hodges was older then, and author Kirby Able wrote about a man who was at the time "the second oldest living man in Greenwood," whatever that means. Able reported that Hodges was losing his eyesight and had been forced to turn gardening chores over to his wife. Although every spring still brought "an urge to go out and stir the earth," Hodges was careful to buy a hoe that was not too heavy for the lady of the house and garden. Able could not resist quoting a line from Hodges to his wife at the time of their 50th anniversary in 1949: "I love you. I love you very much. If there were an exchange for wives, I would not go there." At the time of Able's article, Hodges had been ordered by his doctor to retire, an order he steadfastly disobeyed. He did, however, learn how to take it easy, a procedure he noted as "conducive to longevity." Abel described this procedure:

> On this taking it easy business Doctor Hodges has used a typical scientific approach. If things get too busy, he beats a retreat to the Hodges Building across the square. Busy-ness there forces him to retreat to his farm. Fighting too much hustle and bustle there, he

> will retreat to his home, and from there he will beat a hasty retreat to bed, where he digs in for a long fight.

A final tribute was paid to Hodges in a publication of the Medical University of South Carolina after his death in 1957. That article quoted from the citation accompanying his honorary degree from the institution in 1951:

> For an institution like the Medical College to in any degree pay its debts to the many persons who from time to time serve it, is rarely possible. This year comes one of those rare opportunities. The Board of Trustees has awarded to Dr. Samuel Connor Hodges, of Greenwood, the honorary degree of Doctor of Pharmacy – not merely in acknowledgment of his years of service as a member of the Board, from which he retired this year, but because he has given a full lifetime of devotion to many public services. Gratuitously and happily he has given of himself.

An undated newspaper article (c. 1942) spotlighting Hodges's wife as personality of the week makes clear that May Lily Blake Hodges was every bit as interesting as her husband. A Spartanburg native and alumna of Converse, she adjusted easily to her new home in Greenwood and liked it very much. Her description of the community says it all: "the best town and the best people in all the world." Hodges evidently excelled at everything she did, whether in her home, her church, or a wide variety of public service. May Lily Hodges was a liberated woman long before the phrase was coined, and she was something of a tomboy even as a girl. One line about her college days proves it: "I was never 'Queen of the May,' but I could beat most of the boys running." She also skated, rode horseback, and, of all things in the late 1800s, a bicycle. The latter skill bothered Dr. Sam's grandmother at the time of the Hodgeses' marriage almost as much as her new granddaughter-in-law's Methodism. That lady is supposed to have said: "Poor Sam. He has gone and married a woman who is a Methodist and rides a bicycle." She needn't have worried. Hodges made the transition to the local Presbyterian congregation easily; her record as Sunday school teacher spanned more than forty years. Whether she shocked Greenwood society by tooling around town on a bicycle after her marriage is not recorded. Samuel C. Hodges died in 1957; his wife lived until 1968.

It might be only conventional wisdom that early towns in the American South seemed to number a Jewish merchant or two among their businessmen and boast at least one Greek family who ran a restaurant. While that statement probably could not withstand historical scrutiny, it is true that just that modicum of ethnic diversity existed in early Greenwood. Two businesses dear to the hearts of Greenwood people, and the families associated with those businesses, are considered here. A Polish emigre named Abraham Rosenberg played a unique role in early Greenwood's political and business spheres, and his son not only perpetuated and enlarged that tradition but added also a proud record of military service. The Rosenberg name was a fixture in Greenwood when two Greek brothers named Sterghos came to town in 1909.

Rosenberg's was the oldest retail store in town at the time of Greenwood's centennial in 1957. Abraham Rosenberg established the business in September 1884 when he was only 25 years old. He had emigrated to the United States from Poland at the age of fourteen and lived for a time with an older brother in Abbeville. Phil Rosenberg of the Abbeville branch of the family seems to place Abraham's age at ten when he came to the United States, according to an article in *The Index-Journal* of November 21, 1979. Whatever young Rosenberg's age at the time he emigrated, he found work with merchants in both Camden and Chester before casting his lot with Greenwood, a town he was convinced was destined to grow and prosper. The first store was a small frame structure on North Main Street, but four years later the business moved to the brick building on the east side of the square that would be associated with the name Rosenberg for more than a century. The building, heavily damaged by fire in early 1957, was rebuilt and remodeled so thoroughly that the newspaper story called it an "almost completely new building" when Rosenberg's moved back after a few months in temporary quarters on Maxwell Avenue. The original proprietor was always an innovative merchant, and he did business at a time when the idea of "ready made" clothes was quite new. He dealt in both men's and women's apparel at first and would routinely bring milliners to town to make up a season's supply of women's hats to order. He was also the first to employ women as clerks and bookkeepers and among the first to replace bargaining, or "haggling," with a standard pricing system.

Rosenberg's name was strongly associated with the business and civic life of Greenwood, and his wife was as actively involved as he. Rosenberg served on the committee that brought Lander College to the town, and Mrs. Rosenberg was among the charter members of the Ladies Hospital Association. The store was incorporated in 1910 and known thereafter as Rosenberg's. The name replaced the former *A. Rosenberg*, or "The Old Reliable," as it was familiarly called. The women's department was also dropped that year. Evidently Rosenberg's was a great training ground for merchants; at one point, six downtown stores were managed by men who had worked for Rosenberg.

The business passed to his son Ernest at Abraham Rosenberg's death in 1920. Ernest R. Rosenberg was born in Greenwood in 1892. He attended the College of Charleston and worked in that city for about ten years before returning to Greenwood. He saw service against Pancho Villa on the Mexican border during World War I; later he served in World War II and left military service with the rank of colonel. Rosenberg and

Colonel S. A. Porter had organized a battery of coast artillery just before the second world war, and he was mustered into service with that regiment. After he was discharged, Rosenberg organized a company in the Officers Reserve Corps and commanded the group for the next 27 years. Ernest Rosenberg was as civic-minded as his father; he held offices in the chamber of commerce, the American Legion, the Red Cross, and the Kiwanis Club, in addition to service as a school trustee and even as acting postmaster for a time. After Ernest Rosenberg's death, his nephew Phil Rosenberg supervised another round of remodeling the store "as a gesture of faith in downtown Greenwood." Local firms handled all the improvements, and the owners obviously hoped Rosenberg's would be able to survive the change in business climate brought about by new shopping malls. A grandson, Ernie Gross, managed the business for a time at a new location in Greenwood Plaza, but Rosenberg's finally closed its doors in the late 1980s. A young attorney named Steve Welch opened an office in the Rosenberg building downtown in early 1990. A stipulation of the building's sale was that the name of Rosenberg would be retained; Welch was only too happy to oblige. Ernest Rosenberg was named to the Greenwood County Hall of Fame in 1984.

Mention the term "brain trust," and most people will associate it with President Franklin D. Roosevelt's academic consultants during the New Deal. In Greenwood, however, a very few oldtimers will remember that the businessmen and politicians who gathered daily for coffee and conversation at the Star Cafe were also dubbed with that title. Although he may not have coined the term himself, Lander President Boyce M. Grier was only half joking when he used it to justify his own presence around one of the cafe's tables. He believed one of his duties as the local college president was to keep a finger on the pulse of the community, and there was no better way to do that than face to face with people who made things happen. The Star Cafe was the place those people could be found twice a day, mid-mornings and mid-afternoons.

A newspaper editorial at the time the Star Cafe closed in 1974 compared its importance in Greenwood to that of taverns in Colonial America and local pubs in England. It was just a special kind of place, and its proprietors, the Sterghos family, became a special ingredient in the life of Greenwood. Son-in-law John Kiappes obviously spoke for the whole family when he remarked, "The people of Greenwood have been good to us. We love Greenwood. There is no place in the world like it. The people here are the friendliest anywhere."

The story of the Star Cafe begins with two brothers, Ignatius and Nicholas Sterghos, natives of the Greek island of Mytilene who emigrated, separately, to America in search of economic opportunity. Family members are beneficiaries of a memoir written in 1975 by Nicholas Emmanuel Sterghos. A nephew, Emmanuel "Pot" Sterghos, kindly provided a copy as source material for this sketch. Entitled simply but meaningfully *Land of Opportunity: A Memoir*, the 22-page recollection describes in detail, not only Sterghos's earliest memories of his homeland and his family, but also the devastation of his country in a whole series of wars, especially the political upheaval in 1922. Along the way he provided a unique accounting of his own torturous emigration in 1906, by way of Kemeri to Smyrna to Chios to Piraeus, under an Ottoman passport. At the Greek port of Piraeus Sterghos found passage to America and set off on a 23-day voyage, quite an undertaking for a young man alone and with about $75 in his pocket, particularly since the passage cost $40, and processing at Ellis Island required some $25-30 capital for new immigrants to stay in the United States. Running like a thread through the whole of this remarkable narrative is an accounting of the way Greeks helped each other to establish themselves in a new country. A loan of $2 here and $5 there often made all the difference; Nick Sterghos was part of this network for years until the help he was able to provide his compatriots amounted to much larger sums of money or, even better, a job and a place to stay.

The circumstances that placed the Sterghos brothers in Greenwood in early 1909 add up to mere happenstance. It seems that Nick was working in a New York hotel in 1908, but his brother had moved to the South "through a friend who had a cousin who had a job in Abbeville." The Abbeville job was in a small fruit and candy store and seemed to offer no future at all; indeed, Ignatius had already written his brother to expect him in New York. Before he left the South, however, he traveled to Greenwood to say goodbye to some Greeks he had met, among whom was one Charillaos Tziapas (He was known in Greenwood as the Americanized "Harry Chapas") who, along with his brother, operated a small cafe named the Star. There was a carnival in town the day Ignatius visited, and the cafe was extremely busy. Ignatius agreed to delay his leavetaking and provide some much-needed help for a few days. When things calmed down a bit, the owner revealed that he had decided to move to Savannah and suggested that Ignatius buy his half interest in the business. A couple of weeks later the other Tziapas brother offered his half, and Ignatius persuaded his brother Nick to join him in a new business venture in the little town. Nicholas was dubious at first since he "knew absolutely nothing about cooking," but relented when his brother assured him that the foods people ate in the South were few and simple and their preparation could be mastered in two weeks. Besides, the brothers thought it was a good idea to be together, and they could always go back to New York if the venture did not pan out.

Nicholas Sterghos arrived in Greenwood via the Seaboard Railway, after steamboat passage from New York to Norfolk, on April 1, 1909. He found a town of 5,000-6,000 inhabitants with a railroad station on the edge of town. Sterghos had no trouble locating the restaurant; it bore a "small sign that read 'Star Cafe.'" (Note: a minor point, perhaps, but it should be noted that the restaurant was never called the Star Lunch Room, as has been stated in various Greenwood sources.) How grand not to have to speculate on the beginnings of the love affair between a small southern town and two young Greeks who were still learning to speak English. Nicholas Sterghos summed it up in 1975:

> And from that time to this writing . . . Greenwood has been the Sterghos base. The food we served was extremely simple and, for the most part, prepared to order. And the people generally were simple and unsophisticated. Most of our customers were pretty much simple, unpolished country people. Some – fortunately only a few – had little love for foreigners. With the passage of time, however, we succeeded in convincing them through the way that we conducted ourselves and our affairs, that we were not uncivilized and they came to respect us.

According to a newspaper article, the business was successful from the start, and the brothers had paid their debts and had money in the bank within a year. Nicholas Sterghos wrote instead of the death of his brother Eustratius, who had come to Greenwood to help out, and his fears for his own and Ignatius's health during the early period. Tuberculosis had struck Eustratius; before they sent him home to Greece at his request, the brothers had placed him in a hospital in Augusta for a month or so and had looked after his needs in Greenwood afterward. Both also visited doctors in New York and received a clean bill of health. The business back in Greenwood was "progressing" during this period, in Nicholas's words, and it became clear that more space to accommodate the volume was needed. The 1908 map of Greenwood placed the cafe just behind the Farmers and Merchants Bank building facing Maxwell Avenue, a spot now part of Thayer's. Nicholas wrote that he became close friends with J. P. "Jack" Abney, at that time cashier of the bank and owner of the building next door that housed a hardware store. When the store moved at the beginning of 1913, Sterghos was able to lease the building and greatly enlarge the restaurant. Best of all, the L-shaped space now boasted two entrances, one on Main Street and one on Maxwell Avenue, as well as a kitchen door that opened onto the long alley behind the Syndicate Block. The renovation cost about $7,000 and was done by a restaurant layout specialist from Atlanta.

The fledgling business had already faced the threat of competition. A few years before the restaurant opened an entrance on Main Street, another Greek, a restaurateur from Anderson named Kostas Antonakos, made plans to open a business in Greenwood just across the alley in half the Hagood Brothers livery stable building on Maxwell Avenue. Sterghos promptly bought the other half of the building and promised to open his own restaurant right next door if Antonakos persisted in his plan. It worked, and the competitor backed off.

The World War I years were bad for business until the United States entered the war in 1916. Sterghos wrote that his sales fell about 60%, and he was unable to pay the rent for nearly a year. "Jack Abney stood by me," he wrote, and "kept encouraging me to await better times." Abney also encouraged Sterghos to develop the livery stable property for use as a movie theater; the bank financed the necessary renovation. That property – used as a movie theatre until 1945 and, after another renovation, as two store buildings – produced income for Sterghos until the city decided to turn the entire block into a parking lot. Sterghos was unwilling to accept the $18,000 offered under condemnation proceedings and, with the help of G. P. Callison, sued and received the more equitable settlement of $32,000.

Both brothers returned to Greece to marry, Ignatius in 1915 and Nick in 1920, but both came back to raise families in the town they had made their home. The restaurant moved for the last time toward the end of 1916, this time to a building the business would own for a time at 310 Main Street. Sterghos wrote a full account of his own trip to Greece to find a wife. At that point he was 35 years old; the bride he found was only 17. Still, the young Athena Karatassos agreed to the match, and the wedding took place in Mytilene on July 26, 1920.

Sterghos wrote that he was bitten by the "get rich quick" bug at one point in 1925 and decided to move and open a restaurant in Clearwater, Florida. It was there he learned about the seasonable nature of tourist-dependent business. When visitors left after the season ended, business dropped abruptly to almost nothing. Sterghos decided that Greenwood was better – its ups might not be spectacular, but its downs were at least manageable – so he and his partners sold out at auction and the eight-month experiment ended. Although he lost money, Sterghos was philosophical about the experience: "It was a good lesson for me to learn not to try to get rich quick, especially if it involved picking up the family and moving them to a strange place." Greenwood reporter E. P. Wideman recalled in 1937 his friend's ill-fated Florida venture: Sterghos wrote to cancel his newspaper subscription, "Please stop sending me the paper here. I am coming back to Greenwood to live. I will tell the world that Florida can go to hell forever." Then he added a postscript: "Please do not put this in the paper."

Sterghos's detailed accounting of the fortunes of the Star Cafe ended with the Great Depression era, although he did describe the "fundamental change" of the last remodeling in 1939 which added booths and other modern touches. He found the business reverses of 1929-30 so traumatic that they still bothered him nearly fifty years later. In order to make ends meet for the two families, a drastic cutback in personnel was necessary. The restaurant operated for a time with only four people; one brother would be chief waiter out front while the other acted as chief cook in the kitchen. In a brief editor's note at the end of the narrative, someone wrote that Nicholas Sterghos's primary goal had been to set down events that pre-dated his children's memories, and for that reason he never got around to finishing the memoir. Nicholas Sterghos died in 1981 at the age of 96; his brother Ignagius died in 1956.

While the food at the cafe was an obvious attraction – indeed, one might reason that if it hadn't served a decent meal it would not have lasted to become a legend – its real importance lay elsewhere. Any number of theories could be advanced; i.e., it was in the right place at the right time . . . it managed to attract one or two "leading men," and everyone else played follow-the-leader . . . one or the other Sterghos brother knew just the right politician . . . no other downtown restaurant featured Greek food . . . and so on, but none suffices alone and even in combination they fail to explain the mystique of the Star Cafe. Possibly the institution became simply a meeting place where Greenwood could analyze and criticize and celebrate itself.

All rationales for its longevity aside, the Star Cafe's closing in 1974, which came about for several reasons, was a sad day for Greenwood. Everyone quoted in the newspaper article describing the event was saying in his own way that the closing marked the end of an era for the town. An editorial probably put it best:

> Greenwood has moved off the Square. There is now no focus of commercial activity. And to that extent the close community spirit which was fostered and in turn promoted the Star Cafe is gone. Greenwood has lost something in the process, but that is inevitable when a town spreads out into shopping centers and small buildings serve professional people rather than having them centered in the office buildings around or just off the Square.
>
> That is only part of the story of the closing of the Star Cafe, of course. Those who have operated it for so long have earned a respite from the long hours involved in providing such a center to serve so many people at such varied hours.
>
> But its closing comes as something personal to so many people of Greenwood. Those who have moved into our community only recently probably cannot grasp what it has meant. Each person has his own memories of pleasant incidents connected with it.

A few personal observations illustrate the sentiment described in the editorial. Howard Mabry, who took his coffee breaks at the Star for thirty years, said it had been a Greenwood institution all his life, a gathering place where one "could hear everything discussed from politics to football and finance. I had the feeling that the cafe would always be here." Another man who said he had eaten at least one meal a day at the Star Cafe since 1930 had no idea what he was going to do when the restaurant closed. A waitress with a 36-year tenure said, "This has been home to me. It is the only home I have." Clerk of Court T. R. Pinson recalled "soup and conversation" after midnight at the Star Cafe when he was a young man. C. J. Brabham said, "You could learn more at the Star

Cafe than . . . by reading the *Index*." He also pointed out that one Greenwood mayor, Bob McCaslan, "used to have his office" at a booth in the front corner. One editorial actually called the Star Cafe "the seat of Greenwood government."

There was obviously more at work here than mere food and hot coffee. The indispensable extra ingredient had to be the Sterghos family. The last proprietor was John L. Kiappes, a son-in-law of co-founder Ignatius Sterghos, whose own tenure was more than thirty years. His wife Dora admitted to mixed feelings about the restaurant's closing: "I was born into it. I have been in it all my life. I used to cry when I thought about having to quit some day, but now, I feel somewhat relieved. John has been opening, closing, cooking and shopping for so long and he needs to rest." John and Dora Kiappes live in Greenwood in happy retirement at this writing, having recently celebrated their golden wedding anniversary. No restaurant could ever take the place of the Star Cafe in the affections of Greenwood people, but several other Greek family restaurants have also found a receptive clientele, among them the Grill Cafe, run for many years by the Stathakis family; the Ranch House, owned by partners George Andrews and Ted Kerhoulas for 27 years; the Dixie Drive In; the Caravan; Mig's Pizza Castle, owned by brothers Thomas and Konstantinos Migdalas; and Angelos, recently sold by Angelos Chatos. There was also Gus and Grace Martin's Roseland Drive-In on Montague Avenue. After the restaurant closed, the Martins ran a sort of deli which probably made the very first pizzas Greenwood had ever seen. As for 310 Main Street, home of the Star Cafe for 57 years, a breakfast and lunch business called *Elaine's* now occupies the space. Its owner, Elaine Lewis, is credited in an article in *Nation's Restaurant News* for December 10, 1990, with the line, "This is not an easy business. If I didn't work hard, I'd fail." The Sterghoses and the Kiappeses would surely know what she means.

Two banks, the Farmers and Merchants Bank and the National Loan and Exchange Bank, have been mentioned in connection with the development of the business district of Greenwood. Since neither bank exists today, readers might wish to pause and take a look at banks that came and went (mostly went) as Greenwood grew and developed along with the twentieth century. One important resource in this regard is a brand new book entitled, appropriately enough, *Making Change: South Carolina Banking in the Twentieth Century*, by two history professors, John G. Sproat and Larry Schweikart. But the primary source of information for this section was an interview with the only man in Greenwood who could provide firsthand information, G. Bonner Harvley, Chairman of the Board of The County Bank. Harvley probably holds the record for working in banks that failed, but that is only part of a wonderful personal success story and has to do with the times more than the man. In addition to the story of his own unique experience in Greenwood banking, Harvley provided the names of several other banks that did business in Greenwood at one time or another.

One of the earliest references to local banks appeared in a short sketch of Greenwood written by Joel S. Bailey, Jr., when he was ten years old and a fourth grader in the Graded School. The date was 1893. The sketch mentioned two banks in Greenwood at the time – the Bank of Greenwood and the City Bank. Although the former is one of Greenwood's most interesting success stories, neither Boykin Curry nor Bonner Harvley could recall ever hearing of a bank called the City Bank. Its president, according to young Joel's sketch, was D. A. P. Jordan, whom Curry immediately associated with Grendel Mill and Jordan Street but who was unknown to him as a banker.

The Bank of Greenwood, the town's first, dates from 1888. The Farmers and Merchants Bank followed twelve years later; it opened in 1900 in the building now occupied by Thayer's. Harvley associated the name of M. C. Taggart with this bank. Dr. Moses Clarence Taggart, named in *Greenwood County Sketches* as an early physician and business associate of Dr. Samuel S. Marshall, came to Greenwood in the 1870s; Taggart Street was named in his honor. The tenure of the Farmers and Merchants Bank was only about thirty years. Other officers at another time (c. 1910) were W. R. Cothran, president; John P. Abney, cashier; and A. W. Henderson.

Harvley's banking career had an inauspicious beginning. Born in the Callison section in 1902, he was only two years old when the family moved to Greenwood. In 1918 he was a very young clerk/cashier at Rush Brothers dry goods store on the west, or new, side of the square. World War I was underway, but Bonner Harvley was too young to serve. Other Greenwood men were not too young, and the Commercial Bank, whose president was Goldsby P. Sloan, had lost a number of employees to military service. After about a year at the Rush emporium, Harvley went to work at the Commercial Bank which was located at that time a few doors down the street from the Bank of Greenwood on the east side of the square. The bank moved into new quarters in the Commercial Trust (now Grier) Building when it was finished in 1921, and Harvley worked there until the bank closed in November 1925. He was asked by the receivers to stay on and complete the book work, which he did even after he accepted a short-term job with the state Banking Department as an examiner.

Next in line for Harvley was a job at the National Loan and Exchange Bank, which had moved across the street to its new building completed in 1914. Harvley chuckled at the recollection that his new post in January 1926 was at the very site of a bank he would help form only seven years later. At the time he took the job, however, he was merely replacing a teller who had left Greenwood to go to work for Wachovia in Asheville. Officers of this bank about 1910 were J. T. Medlock, president;

S. H. McGhee, vice president; J. E. Crymes, cashier, and George C. Hodges. The Loan and Exchange Bank, too, was destined to fail; its closing came at noon on January 15, 1930. Harvley happened to run into James C. Self at the post office the same day; he recalled, in fact, that he was mailing a letter to the young woman who was soon to become his wife. Self, who Harvley remembers knew simply everybody in town, expressed sympathy and asked about his plans. Harvley had none just then, and when he admitted he was in the market for a job, Self told him to see John B. Sloan at the Bank of Greenwood. It seems that bank had already taken notice of young Bonner Harvley and had a little something in mind for him. That little something turned out to be opening a branch in Ninety Six, and Harvley spent the rest of the year 1930 accomplishing that chore before coming back to the bank in Greenwood.

When the Bank of Greenwood began having problems during the depression years, most people believed Self would never allow it to close, that he would somehow make sure it survived the panic of the time. But it did close, in January 1933. The reorganization that began immediately had progressed so satisfactorily that the bank was actually ready to reopen on March 6, the date of the famous "Bank Holiday" ordered by President Roosevelt, and was delayed only for that reason. During the reorganization phase, Sloan, in Harvley's words, "severed his relations" with the Bank of Greenwood, but before leaving he told the young man he had something in mind and if it worked out they might get together again. Shortly afterward Sloan contacted Harvley to tell him he had obtained subscriptions of $25,000 ($20,000 capital and $5,000 surplus) to start a new bank and would arrange a loan for him to buy in. In Harvley's words, "It didn't take much thought to go with him instead of what I had, because what I had wasn't all that much." (Harvley had worked during the reorganization and reopening and was at that time a note teller.) The County Bank opened for business on June 5, 1933, with three people: John Benson Sloan, his secretary Jennie Engels, and G. Bonner Harvley. Even Harvley, who is quite matter-of-fact about his long career and who attributes his rise in banking circles to something he calls "luck," views that three-person staff as rather remarkable and something that would be utterly impossible today. He says that changes in the industry over the years have made any such action prohibitive in modern times and points out that Greenwood's newest bank, Greenwood National, started business with a staff of twelve or so. If banking practices were still the same as when he started, however, Harvley believes he could do it all over again. The brave new world of regulations and computerization has made his kind of banking obsolete; the man himself, fortunately, will never go out of style.

In 1983 The County Bank published its 50-year history, a handsome fourteen-page brochure revealing, among other things, that The County Bank is recognized as a Top Performance Bank by the Bank Administration Institute, a distinction accorded to less than 10% of the nation's banks. Conservatism has been the watchword from the beginning, and even the bank's name attests to its original purpose. Emmett I. Davis is credited with the idea for the name, a suggestion that was readily adopted for two reasons: one was to avoid public confusion with the Bank of Greenwood which had recently reopened, and the other was that financing and control were in the hands of Greenwood County residents from the start. The history lists 36 original stockholders, local citizens all, in addition to Sloan and Harvley. Sloan announced the bank's purpose in a statement to the newspaper at the close of the first business day. He said The County Bank "had been opened to serve the people of the city and county of Greenwood," and business would be conducted "along safe and conservative lines." The bank was meant to be "an asset to the community." The author of the bank's history wrote in 1983: "the public believed him (Sloan) when he said, 'If it comes to a choice between losing income for us and taking too great a risk with other people's money . . . there can be only one answer for good banking: we must sacrifice our own income rather than take a chance with other people's money.'" That philosophy has continued to the present day; The County Bank was named one of the hundred safest banks in the country by *Money* magazine in 1989.

The growth of The County Bank was sane and steady, much like the temperament of its founders. The first renovation of the facility came in 1948 when the metal cages, or grilles behind which tellers worked at tall wooden desks, were removed and air conditioning installed. The bank opened branch offices in 1959, 1967, and 1974 and remodeled its main office again in 1966. The bank was forced to move to temporary quarters down the street during that refurbishing. It occupied a building that had once been McCrory's Ten Cent Store, a circumstance that enabled the bank to advertise "Million Dollar Service in 10¢ Store Quarters."

The County Bank moved into its new main office at the south corner of the square in 1979, ending a period of 46 years at the original location in the Hodges Building (now Greenwood Building, where a branch is still maintained). The bank history called the new building "a handsome anchor for the city's business district," and its clock tower a mark of "the bank's desire to create an aesthetic environment in which people can live and work." At this writing, co-founder G. Bonner Harvley serves as chairman of the board. His son-in-law R. Thornwell Dunlap is president, and grandson R. T. Dunlap III is senior vice president of this uniquely Greenwood institution.

Greenwood businessman and civic leader John B. Sloan was a son of Dr. Henry N. Sloan of Ninety Six and a brother of Harvley's first boss at the Commercial Bank. Harvley believes Sloan left the Bank of Greenwood because the bank wanted to make a change in top management, but Sloan's business career was in no sense derailed. In addition to forming a new bank, he served on numerous important boards and commissions and was instrumental in the Buzzard Roost power project in the 1930s. He was also the first president of Mutual Building and Loan Association when it was formed in 1924. Many Greenwood people remember with horror John Sloan's death on October 31, 1957, when his car was struck by a train in Ninety Six. He was nearly eighty years old at the time. Harvley succeeded Sloan as president of The County Bank and served in that capacity until 1970 when he was named board chairman.

Bonner Harvley provided not only a firsthand account of his own more than 70-year career in banking but also the names of several banks that did business, at least for a time, in Greenwood. In addition to those already mentioned, Harvley remembered others: a branch of the Central Union Bank of Rock Hill, the bank that brought F. E. Grier to Greenwood and the one from which he moved to the Bank of Greenwood during its reorganization phase; the Peoples Bank, which began about 1910 with B. F. McKellar, Jr., W. G. Calhoun, O. D. Duckett, and C. E. Klugh; the American Bank under J. D. "Cap" Smith; and the State Bank, connected with a man named Graham who married into the Reynolds family.

Another Greenwoodian with a remarkable memory is Arthur L. Murray, who worked with Harvley in a couple of failing banks in the 1930s. Murray maintains an excellent scrapbook along with other Greenwood memorabilia. He was instrumental in compiling the history of South Main Baptist Church and was presented the first copy of that history when it was published in 1988. Among Murray's most prized artifacts is a sizable booklet published "with more than pardonable pride" by the Greenwood Merchants Association and Board of Trade about 1910. With unpardonable pride or not, Greenwood businesses advertised profusely in the publication, and the text is a litany of praise as well as a gold mine of information for the researcher. The number of wholesale businesses in Greenwood at the time, for example, attests indirectly to the concurrent growth of small towns and communities throughout the county. All had stores that provided the necessities of life for local farm families long before paved roads and automobiles made trips to town feasible. The brochure names ten wholesale firms, all of which did "an enormous business" with "small merchants in other towns." Several were located on Maxwell Avenue. It is possible to date any number of businesses from this publication, and the booklet pictures dozens of store buildings and private homes that no longer exist as well as a priceless few that remain. A description of everything would fill several books; this chapter must, however, continue with sketches of a few more buildings and businesses and a brief description of the beginnings of public utilities.

The construction of Greenwood's three "skyscrapers," or multi-story office buildings, covered a period of about ten years. The first three stories of the Grier-Park building (now the Textile Building) were erected about 1910, and another three floors were added by B. F. McKellar and associates in 1919. The second fireproof office building, erected by Citizens Trust Company in 1914 for the National Loan and Exchange Bank, was described earlier; it became known as the Hodges Building in 1936 and is now part of the Greenwood Building. Third, and last, was the Commercial Trust Building on the site of the old Riley Hotel, which went up during the period 1919-1921. This building was also known as the Professional Building and the Palmetto Building before it was renamed the Grier Building in tribute to Bank of Greenwood and Abney Mills' President F. E. Grier. Many people will remember that the memorable slogan "Greenwood Grows Greater" glowed from the roof of the building for many years.

Other notable early Greenwood businessmen included the brothers W. L. and J. K. Durst who moved from Kirksey where they ran a "bustling country store." J. K. Durst opened another mercantile establishment in Greenwood and became the first president of the Bank of Greenwood. W. L. Durst was chosen as first president of Greenwood Cotton Mill, which began operation in 1891. Both worked actively for county status, and both were connected with various other enterprises as the county developed.

The Chipley family businessmen included John I., first Ford automobile dealer in Greenwood; Thomas S., who ran a store and bicycle shop; and Marvin S. Chipley, a cotton broker in both Greenwood and New Orleans. People like to say that Marvin Chipley made and lost several fortunes during his career; it is clear that he, like many of Greenwood's early businessmen, must be described as a bit of a gambler. The beautiful home he built on North Main Street in 1923 was purchased by Blyth Funeral Home in 1939 and is now headquarters for Citizens Trust Company. John Chipley's fine house on West Cambridge Avenue nearby, one of Thomas Cothran's grand classical designs, was built in 1913. A bit of rivalry with his cousin might have been a motivating force when Marvin Chipley built the vaguely Moorish-style palace around the corner ten years later. The John Chipley house also survives splendidly as the home of Angelle Adams. One of Greenwood's finest, the Chipley-Adams house is an excellent example of Cothran's work when he was at the height of his powers.

Marvin Chipley was the personal choice of Lander College President John O. Willson as trustee after the death of C. A. C. Waller. Willson wrote the Methodist Conference in 1920: "Please give us Marvin Chipley in . . . Waller's place. He will serve and we need just such a man. We have other good men here, but they are already full of duties. Don't fail please – he is the man & I've communicated with him." Another, and later, note reads, "Marvin S. Chipley is the full name of desired trustee. A man of fine spirit, good name, large means and generous to just what we need." One happy result of Marvin Chipley's election to the board of trustees of Lander College was Chipley Hall, built in 1925.

John I. Chipley's name will forever be associated with automobiles in Greenwood, although the very first "horseless carriage" seen in the town showed up in 1900 and advertised Octagon soap. A native of the county, Chipley had spent time as a youth in Macon, Georgia, where he learned the gunsmith trade. He came home in 1890 and opened a bicycle and gun shop on Waller Street. His was the first "safety bicycle" in Greenwood, and he also introduced the motorcycle some time later, according to a 1957 newspaper article. Chipley bought his first car, a second-hand Locomobile Steamer, in Atlanta about 1903. He paid $235 for the machine, which delivered an unimpressive 1.6 miles per gallon of gasoline. Chipley and Jim Self jointly owned the town's second car, an Oldsmobile they purchased from a Greenville man in 1904, or so Chipley remembered years later. That car evidently inspired Chipley's first dealership in Ramblers; a "Rambler parade" from Greenwood to Abbeville one Sunday afternoon was the result. Four Greenwood gentlemen – Chipley, Self, T. J. Crymes, and A. F. McKissick – made the trip, and the trip made the newspapers. It seems they traveled in groups, since no one could be sure his machine would manage the entire distance.

John Chipley switched to Fords in 1906. He built up a large business in both Carolinas, including a thriving agency in Wilmington, North Carolina. He was also busily buying up Waller Street in Greenwood to the extent that it became known as the Chipley Block and is so pictured in the Board of Trade booklet. He built a large garage at the rear of the Masonic Hall about 1911, a building that still stands as part of The Exchange renovation, and completed a four-story addition to his automobile agency in 1928. His business was called the John I. Chipley Auto Exchange, and the famous Ford logo appeared in an ad along with the motto, "High Priced Quality in a Low Priced Car." The text of the publication called Greenwood "a live automobile center." There were two large garages in the town as early as 1910; Chipley's was, in fact, the largest in the state. The other agency was the Greenwood Garage, managed by W. P. Durst, which sold Maxwells. According to the newspaper, Chipley's agency registered 7,000 visitors the first day the Model A Ford went on display in 1929.

The firm of C. L. Beaudrot and Son was called "the oldest continuously operated business in Greenwood" in a 1979 newspaper article. The first C. L. (Charles Louis) Beaudrot worked as a smithy in Charleston during the Civil War; after the war he moved to Ninety Six, and then to Greenwood where he opened a shop in 1879. The shop occupied two buildings in the (now demolished) short block facing the county library before its present location on Reynolds Street was chosen in 1950. Current proprietor and grandson of the founder, Joseph Louis Beaudrot, Jr., calls the survival of the business "just evolution" as it adapted to changing times. He says the need for metalworking is constant, even though the "ancient craft" of smithwork has undergone a number of changes in methodology; welding, for example, began at the shop about 1915 and was greatly stimulated by World War I. The business has been part of the Beaudrot family for 112 years; Louis Beaudrot hopes one of his children or grandchildren will make sure it continues as a family business. As he puts it, "Nobody else would have it"; besides, more than the simple fact of providing a living for three generations of Beaudrots is involved. Louis remembers the depression years when his father would barter his services in return for food and other household necessities. In that era, he says, people fixed broken implements since they couldn't afford to buy new ones; they didn't throw anything away. "The business has been good to the family," he concludes.

A Beaudrot family history compiled in 1982 established both Revolutionary War service – specifically "one hundred twenty-two days militia duty done in General Marion's Brigade" – and a South Carolina land grant in George Towne District for one Joseph Beaudrot in the late 1700s and called him "the first documented Beaudrot in South Carolina." And another Joseph Beaudrot showed up in several Charleston references from the early 1800s. Thus the family is known to have South Carolina roots dating to colonial times, and the same names appeared again and again as its numbers grew over the generations. The Greenwood branch is certainly no exception; sorting the Charleses, the Josephs, the Louises, and the Lelands can be a treacherous exercise. In addition to the welding business that qualifies as Greenwood's oldest, another famous local business can be traced to this solid Greenwood family: Beaudrot's Flowers was the brain child of Mabel Pratt Beaudrot whose husband Thomas Clayton was the fifth of patriarch C. L. Beaudrot's seven children. The couple had lived in several South Carolina towns for the first ten years of their marriage but returned to Greenwood, which was home to both, in 1919. They built a house next door to the family residence on Calhoun Avenue in a stretch that became known over the years as "Beaudrot's Row" or "Beaudrotville," and Thomas Clayton Beaudrot opened a body shop to build wagons, railroad carts, and trucks. He worked also from time to time as a blacksmith and welder. Even as his wife ran the house and raised their four children, she found the time in 1925 to open a flower shop in the basement of her home. That sideline proved to be a lifesaver as the great depression deepened, and her husband joined the business as a partner when normalcy returned. A few years later after military service, the Beaudrots' only son Charles and his wife Alice also joined the family firm. Grandson and namesake of the first Greenwood Beaudrot, Charles Louis was six years old when his mother began her flower business; he quite literally grew up in it. He also exhibited talents in more than one direction: the new building on Calhoun Avenue erected in 1950 was his design, for example, and he proved so adept at growing flowers that the company eventually expanded to three greenhouses. Alice Beaudrot recalls that their excess production was sold to flower shops in nearby towns. The elder Beaudrots retired in 1960, and the flourishing family business became the preoccupation of Charles and Alice Beaudrot who, along with a number of employees, operated the flower shop for the next eleven years, progressing to incorporation along the way. Beaudrot's was simply the place to go in Greenwood when the occasion called for flowers. Eventually the pace grew too hectic for the owners, and the Beaudrots sold out in 1971. Thus a firm which had been in one Greenwood family for 46 years passed quietly to another. The name of the familiar flower shop on Calhoun Avenue, however, remains the same.

The family is honored in the names of two thoroughfares in Greenwood: one is Beaudrot Road on the outskirts of the Harris community, and the other is the short Beaudrot Avenue that runs beside Citizens Trust Company and marks the general vicinity of the first Beaudrot's first business in Greenwood. Any number of Beaudrot descendants still live in the town.

Blyth Funeral Home, also among Greenwood's oldest businesses, can be traced to master craftsman Andrew Alexander Blyth who emigrated from Scotland about 1829 and showed up in the Epworth section of Greenwood County about 1846. A few years later he moved to New Market and added coffins, wagons, and buggies to his cabinetmaking business. His son, the William V. Blyth who figured so prominently in, quite literally, building Greenwood, started his own business in 1884, and that business eventually became Blyth Funeral Home. Blyth built the structure at the corner of Main and Magnolia that housed the company, then called W. V. Blyth, Undertaker, from 1890 until 1939. The name was changed to Blyth Funeral Home when the company bought the Marvin Chipley house and moved there. The Blyth family sold the business to Wayne Gantt and associate Earle Purkerson, Sr., in 1971. Blyth Funeral Home occupied the lovely Chipley house from 1939 until Citizens Trust Company purchased the building in 1977. Blyth Funeral Home is now located at 1425 Montague Avenue.

The name Mauldin is associated in most people's minds with the lumber business – Mauldin Lumber Company is a fixture on Maxwell Avenue – but that company is quite new compared to the first business that bore the family name. William A. Mauldin, who married one of C. L. Beaudrot's daughters in 1908, organized a general contracting company in Greenwood in 1911; sons William and Charles joined their father in business in the late 1930s and continued as partners after his death in 1948, doing business as C. B. and W. F. Mauldin Building Contractors. The lumber company, a completely separate venture, dates from 1952 when the brothers purchased Free's Lumber Company. Both the widows of the Mauldin brothers and several third and fourth generation descendants of the original William Mauldin still live in Greenwood. The business also remains in the family more than eighty years after it was founded.

Carolina Tool Company is another example of a family business of long standing in Greenwood. The company began in one room of E. F. Workman's Cross Hill home in 1923. Workman, described in a newspaper article as a one-man business and a peddler, sold his wares of automotive and textile machinery tools the hard way, traveling from place to place attracting new customers and providing very personalized service to all his patrons. Perhaps because Workman found the life of traveling salesman somewhat wearing, he moved to Greenwood and opened a store on North Main Street in 1927. After a couple of moves the store found a permanent home on South Main Street where it does business today, mostly in wholesale jobbing but also in retail. The founder's son E. F. Workman, Jr., took over the business which has since expanded to well beyond the borders of Greenwood County, in 1946. The nearly 70-year-old Carolina Tool Company is one of the few private businesses in Greenwood still in the hands of the same family.

Citizens Trust Company, the organization chartered in 1913 and responsible for the second fireproof office building in town, has never retreated from that first success, although the bank that spawned it closed in 1930. According to a 1957 newspaper article, the company's principal activity was the general insurance business until 1920, but many people associate Citizens Trust even more with real estate development and property management. In truth, it was involved in all three, with investment banking thrown in for good measure, until that segment was sold in 1979. Citizens Trust is associated in most people's minds with R. B. Curry, who assumed management after he left Bailey Military Institute in 1920. Officers before Curry were J. T. Medlock and J. S. and W. T. Bailey. Clarence A. Smith, Jr., also joined the firm in 1920, and J. E. Young in 1946. R. B. Curry, Jr., who became associated with Citizens Trust in 1937, maintains an office there more than fifty years later. The company has handled the sale of any number of important properties in Greenwood but is perhaps most noted for the residential subdivisions it developed – Forest Hills, Woodfields, Henrietta Heights, and Cherokee Hills, among others.

The building that defines one corner of the area of downtown now called The Exchange is the Chipley Building, once the Masonic Hall of Greenwood. This building was erected in 1908 and provided a home for various bodies of the Masonic Order for about fifty years. Chipley's business occupied the ground floor, the second consisted of offices, and the Masons used the third floor. The building later housed The Vogue for many years and was most recently occupied by a gift shop called Billie's. The old Chipley Block, now owned by Self family interests, was extensively refurbished a few years ago and re-named The Exchange in a project that represents perhaps Greenwood's finest example of retrofitting old buildings for new purposes. The architectural firm of Dorn & Steverson was responsible for the design. Among the first successes was the renovation of a building once used as a garage for new life as a restaurant; Knickers, one of a small chain of restaurants, was the result. The flavor of the entire former Waller and Rush Avenue area was much enhanced, and most of the important buildings escaped drastic changes in their exterior facades. Even the old brick-paved street remained in place. Still another example of successful renovation can be seen at the opposite end of the east side of Main Street where the Inn on the Square defines the southern boundary of uptown Greenwood. The building had been used for any number of businesses, including a funeral home and furniture store, before it was gutted and rebuilt from the inside as a "Charleston-type" inn with 48 guest rooms, plus dining and meeting rooms and a lounge off the lobby.

The Bank of Greenwood, mentioned in the context of Bonner Harvley's story, was one of Greenwood's most important early businesses. In retrospect, its "closing" for a few months in early 1933 might be viewed as merely an unfortunate blip in its long history in Greenwood. As a matter of fact, Harvley pointed out that depositors actually lost very little – only 16-2/3% or about $170,000 in total – during the panic. James C. Self is said to have made that up personally, and depositors' accounts were restored over several years. (Note: this must be true or Harvley would not have said it; nevertheless, "Rooster" Brooks is convinced he never saw more than 13¢ of his original savings account of $13.00.)

The bank was Greenwood's first, having been chartered nearly two years before its actual opening in September 1888. The first location was temporary quarters in J. K. Durst's store until a separate bank building was completed a few months later. The first building was a brick structure a few doors down the street from the current location of NCNB. The bank's quarters changed again when the second building was erected in 1905. That one was a beauty, "a true landmark in Greenwood with its unchanged white marble facade" even after the building's interior was greatly enlarged and completely remodeled in 1953. The bank kept the location but demolished the historic building and erected an entirely new structure in the 1980s. By that time the bank had numerous branches and was among the largest in the state.

The Bank of Greenwood has had as many name changes as presidents in its history. Its first renaming, to State Bank and Trust Company, came in 1955. According to Lynn Boylston of Columbia, other names have been Bankers Trust of South Carolina (1969), Bankers Trust of South Carolina NA (1973, the year "National" was added), Bankers Trust of South Carolina (1974, again), and NCNB-Bankers Trust, NCNB South Carolina, and NCNB National Bank of South Carolina (since the merger in 1986). The bank's most recent incarnation is Nationsbank. John Bowen likes to say he has dealt with seven or eight banks in his fifty years of association with the company and has never moved his account. The bank's presidents before the merger were J. K. Durst, John B. Sloan, F. E. Grier, Dewey H. Johnson, both his sons D. Wellsman and

W. W. "Hootie" Johnson, and Julian B. Turner. Although he never became president, no doubt because he had other things to do, James C. Self got a leg up in business when he left his job as clerk/bookkeeper at Gambrell Hardware for the position of bookkeeper at the Bank of Greenwood in 1899. He was promoted to assistant cashier three years later and to cashier a year after that, a position he held until he resigned for greener pastures in 1916. Perhaps even he did not realize how green they would turn out to be, both for himself and for Greenwood.

McCaslan's Book Store can be traced almost exactly to the beginning of Greenwood County and has connections to the first graded school as well. F. M. Sheridan, who came to Greenwood as school superintendent in 1896, also operated a teachers' agency and organized the "county school book depository" a few years later. Textbooks, along with other school and office supplies, were purchased there. The first location of Sheridan's probably lucrative little business was a second-story shop in the middle of the Syndicate Block. Sheridan resigned his school post in 1901 to devote more time to business interests and joined forces with a brother-in-law, George W. Hart, who moved to Greenwood a year later. Sheridan & Hart lasted for about thirteen years, moving during that time to the marvelous address of "1 Main Street" in the Barksdale Building. Sheridan sold out to Hart in 1915, and Hart's Book Store continued in the location (Sheridan maintained his teachers' agency and a mail-order school supply business; Sheridan School Supply Company continued to operate until some time after the proprietor's death in 1940). When Hart opened a store in Charlotte in 1919 he asked Gus McCaslan to take over the management of the Greenwood operation. By 1921 Hart's North Carolina business was flourishing; he sold the Greenwood store to McCaslan and his brother Foster and moved to Charlotte. The brothers formed a partnership, changed the name of the business, and moved to the present location in 1931. They bought the building and remodeled it extensively, adding the gift and greeting card departments at the same time. The McCaslan brothers credited one saleslady, Ruth Carlay (later Langston) who was hired in 1922, with making the store "one of the nicest book and gift shops in the state."

McCaslan's is a true Greenwood institution. The current proprietor, W. Bartram Robeson, a nephew-in-law of the McCaslan brothers, is associated with Greenwood as surely as though he were a native, although his own tenure in the business covers only 45 years or so at this writing.

A store with a very funny name brought the Burns family to Greenwood: the Red Iron Racket Store came to town in 1902. Perhaps someone understands the meaning of the name, but it seems to be simply an early example of the gimmick, or "come on," so familiar in advertising; it certainly has a vigorous sound. Greenwood's Red Iron Racket was the second of a group that began in Laurens when James C. Burns and his brother Lee opened the original in 1897. After the Greenwood store opened, others appeared in Spartanburg, Greer, Greenville, Anderson, and Charlotte. The brothers anticipated Sam Walton by nearly a hundred years; they stressed "more goods for less money" and had themselves an early group of chain stores. Nothing is more common today, but a 1957 newspaper article called it "one of the state's earliest chain store systems."

The Red Iron Racket Store opened on Maxwell Avenue, the part once called the "Shake Rag" section (??), and remained in business more than thirty years. Burns sold out and retired in 1934. By that time the Burns family had provided Greenwood with three sons – James C., Jr., Howard L., and Byron – who would become deeply involved in the business and social life of the town, and a daughter who married and moved to Columbia.

Talking over the telephone in Greenwood in 1895 meant that one was in J. K. Durst's store, since the line between that business and the store in Kirksey was the only one in town. Both Abbeville and Laurens had telephones at that time, but most people judged Greenwood not quite ready. Evidently only one man disagreed; J. W. Sproles, who sold stoves at the time and who had brought the first coal to town for his wood and coal yard on Maxwell Avenue, didn't know exactly why he was so set on the idea, but set on it he was. He took his plan of organizing a company to other businessmen when he himself had used a phone only once. Most brushed him off, according to a centennial newspaper story, but George A. Barksdale not only listened but also rounded up three others, and five businessmen started Greenwood Telephone Company with capital stock of $2,500 in June 1896. They were Joel S. Bailey, George Barksdale, his brother John Barksdale, D. A. P. Jordan, and J. W. Sproles. The small investment meant expenses had to be minimal; Isaac Giles, a black man who had some experience with a company in Pennsylvania, was hired to install the switchboard and run about five miles of wire. There were 42 subscribers and one operator when the company began, but the system doubled in only eighteen months and has been expanding ever since.

It is not possible to discuss the first telephone company without mentioning three or four families whose interlocking interests – through business, land, marriage, or all three – contributed to the story. Thanks to Norman Dodson's *A History of Ridgewood Circle* (1978), we have sketches of the Barksdale, Sproles, and Reynolds families, a combination of whose properties once made up the area of Greenwood north and slightly east of town. Dodson credited Sproles with bringing Greenwood into the age of the telephone only twenty years after the device had been patented. He also noted that telephones and rural mail delivery started in Greenwood the same year. Although Sproles's first love was the telephone company, of which he was general manager, he continued his involvement in fuels and branched out after the advent of the automobile to service stations and oil companies. "The automobile was good to Mr.

Sproles," Dodson wrote, "although he did not buy one until . . . 1911." The Sproles house, built in 1904, still stands at 723 Grace Street.

Margaret Watson did not trace the Sproles family tree, but Norman Dodson did. He also noted in his small history that Greenwood Telephone Company stock always remained with the original stockholders or with their heirs. Which brings up the Barksdales, two of whom were also founders. John A. Barksdale, originally from Laurens, was described by Dodson as a "landed man." He built a large house outside of town (present site of Grace Street Apartments) in the 1890s and operated a dairy and truck farm on considerable acreage extending as far west as Willson Street and north to Gracemont Drive. When the telephone project came along, John Barksdale was among the first to respond, but he sold his stock after a few years to his brother George and moved on to other business interests. A 1957 newspaper article reported that D. A. P. Jordan also sold out to other stockholders. George A. Barksdale, Joel Bailey's partner in Bailey, Barksdale & Company, was the father of Cecil Bruce Barksdale who personified the telephone company in its latter years before the sale to United. John Barksdale was married twice, to sisters Annie and Kathryn who were daughters of Bennett Reynolds; a number of their descendants still live in Greenwood. Both the Barksdales and the Reynoldses were inveterate street-namers; among the streets definitely traceable to these families are Grace (also Gracemont and Grace Terrace), Barksdale, Reynolds, Henrietta, and Bryte. Sproles Street also fits well here. Dodson wrote in 1978 that the only Barksdale, by name, still in Greenwood was Ruby Hill Devlin (Mrs. C. B.) Barksdale, who lived near Lander College. In 1992, Mrs. Barksdale still lives on Lander Street in a house filled with beautiful objects, none quite as lovely as the lady herself.

The centennial newspaper article noted that stockholders received no dividends for the first thirty years of the telephone company's life, since every dime was needed to keep pace with progress in the industry. That was not the case, however, after about 1926. Owning a utility such as a telephone company is everybody's idea of a dream business; it was a reality to a few early Greenwood families.

The first commissioners of public works in Greenwood were R. M. Hays, J. F. Davis, and A. St. Clair Lee. The commission is nearly as old as the county; it was established in 1897, forty years after the town was incorporated. A special meeting of the town council was called on October 1 to consider a petition from Greenwood citizens requesting a bond issue to build a water and electric power plant. The petition was signed by 199 freeholders (property owners). The minutes of the meeting read in part, "Owing to the absence of the City attorney Mr. Grier whom some of the Council desired to be present to answer certain questions it was agreed to adjourn until Oct. 5th." Council met again four days later; even then, Grier had to be "sent for to explain certain matters relative to the petition. . . ." The minutes of that meeting contain the first mention of the amount of the proposed bond issue; the petitioners evidently thought the project would cost $40,000. Grier explained the basic legal point involved; i.e., petitioners must constitute a majority of those freeholders listed on the tax rolls. A count and cross check revealed a total of 353 names; the petition had indeed been signed by a majority. Satisfied on that point, the council voted unanimously in favor of the proposal and directed the attorney to prepare an ordinance "ordering an Election to submit to the qualified electors of the Town of Greenwood the question of issuing Bonds to meet the cost of building, constructing, equipping, establishing, and operating a system of water works and Electric lights in said Town for the use and benefit of the said Town and its citizens." This was the first bond issue authorized by the town, and the language of the ordinance, particularly the word *operating,* obviously foreshadowed the creation of a board or commission charged with that responsibility. But a question was bound to arise at some point: was the commission a creation of city government and therefore accountable to it, or was it a separate entity accountable directly to the voters who elected its members? The answer is evidently the latter, a determination that has been upheld by state statutes and legal tests.

The groundwork for later and much more adventurous public utilities projects was laid when Greenwood opened the first municipally-owned water and light plant in South Carolina in August 1898. The site was determined by the availability of an adequate water supply at Yoe's Springs (now Grace Street at the By-Pass) when an artesian well nearer the city was found to be inadequate. The disadvantage was that the site was over a mile from town. An article in the *Greenwood Index* of February 24, 1897, reported that the site was selected after several months of patient investigation of other sites nearer the town. An artesian well had been considered preferable but turned out to be impossible; it was "thought that all elements . . . [would] soon adjust themselves to the decisions of the Commissioners." (This quotation, with only minor variations, might be applied to almost the whole of early Greenwood history.) The description of the chosen site noted that several springs produced an aggregate of about sixty gallons of water per minute which would be gathered and poured into a central reservoir – the first standpipe – measuring 18 feet in inside diameter and standing 100 feet high. The contracts to be let were for "the whole work of the two Systems," either together, separately, or in sections. Specifications included two pumps of 750,000-gallon capacity each, the reservoir itself and seven miles of street mains, fifty-two hydrant valves with boxes, "an arc light of fifty-eight capacity," forty arc lamps in place, an incandescent plant of 1,000 light capacity, engine, switchboard, and miscellaneous other items.

The arc lamp, forerunner of modern electric lighting, was rather new, having been exhibited for the first time in Cleveland in 1876. Arc light, produced as the result of an electric discharge between two electrodes, was only a scientific curiosity until efficient methods of generating and distributing electricity were discovered. Carbon arcs, which produced light almost entirely from incandescent carbon rather than an arc stream, followed, and the addition of calcium fluoride to carbon produced the so-called "flame arc" which came about 1898. Greenwood's first electricity must have been of the carbon arc or flame arc variety. Many disadvantages accompanied these early lighting systems, which depended upon automatic feeding devices to maintain the correct arc length; they were more suitable for street lighting than domestic use. One can imagine a great deal of flickering. The development of electric power is beyond the scope of this book, but a certain curiosity about the very earliest days of electricity in Greenwood is surely pertinent, especially since the newspaper article reported that pumping water (which is simple) and generating electricity (which is not) would be carried on simultaneously at the power plant.

About six months after the first story appeared, the newspaper printed a blurb entitled "Let There Be Light." That short article is reprinted in its entirety below, as much for its evocative prose as for the information it contains:

> Last night was the beginning of a new era in the history of Greenwood. Hitherto we have had darkness rather than light, and the midnight straggler was fortunate if he did not strike a corner or stumble over a lamp post, which you had to strike a match to see. Of course we had the moon, but the moon had other duties besides shining in these parts all the time. But last night when all was quiet, an electric button was touched and the whole place was bathed in a soft spray of mellow light. Greenwood has taken a step forward – has discarded her ebony robes and diked herself in an evening dress that bewitches the moon itself.

Less than a month afterward the new Oregon Hotel held its famous opening dinner. The electric lighting in the dining room was among the most novel features of that occasion.

There was no hint of controversy when Benjamin F. Yoe deeded three acres in the middle of a 230-acre tract to the Town of Greenwood for $500 in March 1898. The language of the conveyance waxed almost poetic in fixing the site "where the meadow and woodland join." The deed also included the right "to use and divert all water and watercourses" on the entire tract, but a 4 1/2 page memorandum agreement signed immediately afterward provided two "water cocks" with free water and one "sixteen-candle power incandescent electric light" in Yoe's house as inducements in return for water rights. The controversy arose several years later when the city, eager to expand its holdings at the power plant site, had to deal with a new property owner who was not disposed to sell. Greenwood's struggles with Miss Belle Yoe (B. F.'s daughter) culminated in two lawsuits that reached the South Carolina Supreme Court in 1911. In the process Miss Yoe became a genuine Greenwood "character." Louis Wright called her "an Amazonian woman . . . who hated trespassing boys and was reputed to chase them with sword and gun."

Belle Yoe was a trained nurse who practiced her profession in both Charleston and New York City before settling permanently with her father in Greenwood. Possibly she came home under duress. A 1904 document in the courthouse indicates that B. F. Yoe leased his house and grounds, specifically including the well, to Belle Yoe for a period of five years in return for nursing care. Did his 35-year-old daughter perhaps require that concession before she would come home? Later in the same year he deeded 71 1/4 acres known as the "spring side" of the Yoe property to her. By the time of her troubles with the city, she lived alone in her father's house at the present site of Woodcrest subdivision. Belle Yoe's difficult reputation as described by Louis Wright and others evidently arose from her attitude toward the dispute over the property; Emmaline Tolbert Young remembers her neighbor as a mild and kindly sort who took an interest in her progress in school.

Greenwood sought to buy the land Belle Yoe acquired from her father to extend its holdings at the power plant site. There was just one problem: she refused to sell. The town thereupon considered itself forced to take the property under the laws of eminent domain. Such procedures are provided under state law, and the town was within its rights to proceed with condemnation and assessment of proper compensation. Yoe was compensated for the acreage in the amount of $7,125, and the payment was said to have been placed in escrow since Yoe adamantly refused to cooperate in any way. She appealed to the circuit court on several grounds, only one of which was insufficiency of compensation, but her appeal was dismissed. Another appeal brought Yoe's case to the South Carolina Supreme Court which rendered its verdict on May 11, 1911. In spite of four exceptions, one of which covered sixteen separate grounds, the supreme court found that Yoe's case had no merit, and the circuit court's judgment was upheld. Belle Yoe lost. A couple of months later, however, the same court reversed a ruling of nonsuit by the lower court in another Yoe case. This time she had sued the Savannah River Power Company for trespassing when the company erected power lines under the right-of-way clause in B. F. Yoe's deed for the original three acres. Possibly the suits were simultaneous, since the opinion in the second ruling makes no mention of the condemnation proceedings. At any rate, the order of nonsuit originally resulted from a lack of testimony that the power company had, in fact, trespassed. Although Yoe's appeal won a reversal, hers was a Pyrrhic victory. It is clear that the coming of the railroad had set the precedent in law for all other right-of-way disputes. Progress would always win out; the only thing to be determined, apparently, was the amount of compensation to those who opposed it. In Belle Yoe's case, the amount of $100 per acre would seem to have been fairly generous; she saw it another way entirely. Some people still believe Yoe was jailed at some point during the dispute. Gerald Smart wrote that she "allowed herself to accept a thirty-day jail sentence rather than accede to the demands of the city," but he also claimed the city deposited $20,000 to Yoe's credit in a bank, a payment she refused to acknowledge or use. After all legal appeals were exhausted, she took up residence in a one-room shack "on the apex of a sharp hill across the road from the water and light plant" where she began, in Smart's view, a "new type of life of penury and deprivation." Although Smart's assessment of Belle Yoe's legal troubles was quite unofficial and somewhat suspect, he did provide an eyewitness description of the Yoe cabin in the woods, both inside and out, an account there is no reason to doubt. The "little shack," he wrote, was situated in the midst of "considerable wooded acreage" at the head of a steep incline. Access to Belle Yoe's home was solely by foot, since no vehicle could negotiate the climb. Yoe's landscaping tastes were bizarre indeed if Smart's account is correct:

> She had collected an accumulation of vast proportions of nature's unobserved oddities and objects in the woods. For instance, she had constructed a frieze completely around the outside of the cabin mostly of skeletons. There were rabbit skulls, squirrel, possum, and other wild animals. There were snake, lizard, and skeletons of various small serpents, rodents and such, with which she had become familiar. There were dried bugs, locusts, cicada, crickets, spiders, July flies, and what not. In fact she had gathered a sufficient quantity of animal bones, of birds, of reptiles, of insects, and all life that inhabits the woods and out-of-doors, to completely encircle the entire cabin.

Such a collection of artifacts, no matter how artfully arranged, would not appear to present an overly welcoming aspect to visitors, particularly when one came upon it abruptly not far inside the forbiddingly high fence that surrounded the property. Nevertheless, Smart insisted that Yoe kept a slate, with slate-pencil attached, by the locked gate so that guests could sign in. "She loved visitors," he wrote, "and wanted to know all who came." Some of those who came in response to her "dramatic personality, unrivaled vocabulary, and unexcelled impersonating ability" were Lander students, groups of children, and Gerald H. Smart. It appears that most of Yoe's animosity was directed toward the City of Greenwood.

Belle Yoe was born in Tennessee in 1859; she died in Greenwood nearly 92 years later. In the interim she had graduated from Columbia College and worked for a time as a governess in Winnsboro. Finding that career not to her liking, Yoe enrolled in the first nursing class at Roper Hospital about 1894. Yoe and one of her brothers moved to New York City soon afterward. While she studied and practiced nursing, he paid the tuition and enrolled in a school of embalming. When Yoe's brother developed a case of homesickness and went home, she took his place at the embalming school and added that skill to her repertoire, since she saw no reason to forfeit the tuition he had paid. According to her obituary, Belle Yoe returned to Greenwood about 1895, but other sources indicate the date must have been nearer 1904. The obituary in *The Index-Journal* of April 6, 1951, reveals nothing about the controversy of Yoe vs. Greenwood, unless one reads between the lines:

> Miss Yoe was an unusual woman. She was regarded as a nurse of considerable ability though she had not practiced nursing for years. She had decided convictions and was noted for the courage of her convictions. She had lived alone in her cottage for many years and had no fear of being molested.

Oddly enough, Belle Yoe's legal troubles did not end even with her death in 1951. She left an estate of something over $13,000 and a will bequeathing everything to a niece. One very interesting provision of that will instructs the niece "to plead the statute of limitations to any claim or claims against my estate barred by the statute." This line suggests that Yoe might have anticipated some sort of family problem. If she did, she was absolutely right. A sister-in-law and niece in Alabama, Margaret A. Yoe and Marguerite Yoe Prickett, sued the estate for nearly $20,000 in back rent from 1905 on the grounds that Yoe had promised to leave her estate to her brother, or to his heirs, in return for living on the property rent free for life. The legatee objected, naturally, but the final execution of the estate shows payment of $400 to settle the claim.

Perhaps Belle Yoe can be forgiven for any eccentricities of thought or behavior. No doubt she saw herself as beleaguered, from both inside and outside her family, and protected herself as best she could. Louis Wright's account of youthful shenanigans involving Yoe dates from about the time of her legal troubles with the city. Smart's account was written much later from the perspective of a friend and admirer, but he also described a woman still deeply embittered at the memory of what she considered shabby treatment by the town. Both writers depicted a single woman no longer young. She had given up at least two careers away from Greenwood, and when she came back to live in the family home she faced a number of real problems, none of which was conducive to any hope she might have had of growing old gracefully. Wright called her property "the forbidden premises" which he and other small boys were determined to penetrate through the barbed wire fences and mats of honeysuckle. He wrote that on one occasion she actually charged out of the house, "an apparition in white" waving "a rusty old sword," to chase them away. In spite of everything, Belle Yoe managed to outlive her entire family, except for the sister-in-law who sued the estate. Her final illness at the age of 91 lasted only two months.

Regardless of any difficulty with acquisition, the power house site became a sort of park or picnic area that was used for Sunday outings and other gatherings. The route to the plant was known as the Power House Road for many years. As city limits expanded it became Grace Street. Yoe's Spring furnished Greenwood's water supply until nearby Rocky Creek and, later, Coronaca Creek were utilized. The latter site involved a dam, 20-acre pond, pumping station, and five miles of water lines to the city. Still later, in 1950, Lake Greenwood became the source of Greenwood's water; nevertheless, the original power house site remained dear to the heart of the town. The drama of its acquisition no doubt provided a certain mystique, and the picturesque spot filled the need for a recreational area similar to those associated with natural springs so popular in the nineteenth century. Louise Hartzog, who remembers many outings at the site, has preserved a post card picture of the park as it appeared in the 1930s. Not only was the recreation area at the power plant given a name, it was also set off on the highway side by a high brick wall with the words OAK HILL PARK picked out in granite and built into the wall. But the wall was not merely for decorative purposes; it also served to secure the fairway of the first hole of Greenwood's first municipal golf course. The site must have been just too tempting for Clarence Smith of Citizens Trust Company and Frank Chapman of the Commission of Public Works to resist, especially as it lay idle before the reservoir and the superintendent's house were built, and the two are credited with laying out and building the course. No one remembers exactly when it was built, but many people remember playing golf at the Power House course; William John Park can describe each of the nine holes, and Bill Wilson remembers sneaking off to caddy there when he was a boy. The golf course also explains the name of a popular drive-in restaurant, complete with car hops, that flourished just across the road; everybody met everybody at The Fairway for several years in the 40s and 50s. The building that housed the restaurant still stands; in recent years it was used as a day care center.

The golf course gave way when the power plant expanded, and the brick wall was demolished. Bill Wise recalls that someone on the CPW came up with the idea of saving the granite letters that identified the park. A family named Hill got four, and Park Seed Company was pleased to accept the P, A, R, and K. Wise thinks the last three letters ended up at the city dump; possibly no one named "Oak" could be found. William John Park recalls that one leg of the R was broken when the heavy pieces of granite were unloaded at company headquarters on Spring Street. A repair job, not wholly successful, left the R with a certain rakish tilt. The letters stood beside the Spring Street building for a few years, and when Park moved to its present location the letters went along, this time built into a large brick sign specifically designed to accommodate them. The letters in the official company marker on Highway 254 thus contain a little bit more Greenwood history than meets the eye; in addition, their current "home" is about five miles out the same road that ran beside the power house property when they were first hoisted into their places in the wall.

The relationship between the City of Greenwood and the Commission of Public Works is much more complex today than it was in 1897. The situation is similar to that of the South Carolina Highway Department vis-a-vis the state; indeed, much of South Carolina's state government, with its multitude of quasi-independent boards and commissions, reflects exactly the same pattern of built-in conflict. Mayor John Nave prepared a statement in 1988 in which he reviewed old arguments and posed new questions, recalling almost as an aside the initial provision that the system was to provide "'free' street lights and 'free' front porch lights." Several other sources indicated that a number of Greenwood families found rather ingenious ways to use that front porch light: some ran the long ceiling cord through a window, thereby managing to read the evening paper by electric light, while others suddenly found it convenient to do the family ironing on the front porch. These minor abuses are merely amusing in retrospect; far more serious was Nave's point that the city had been required to provide "seed money" and bail out the commissioners financially for years before the system became the profitable entity it is today. One resolution from 1899 stated that the commissioners required the sum of $3,500 "to meet and defray debts and liabilities in that sum by them incurred in the management and operation" of the system, and unless the amount were forthcoming the town would "be without light and water." What else could the city do but pay up? Nave wrote that the "trend of Council financial support for the utility system continued well into the 1940s." He provided examples of both direct financial assistance and a new bond issue to establish the sewer system before the city found it necessary to levy a five-mill tax to support its utilities in 1915. Still more bond money was required in 1920 to extend the sewer system, which came under the commissioners' control twenty years later. The city also bought the first gas and fuel plant in 1940 and merged all utilities under the Water and Light Commission in 1941. Nave's explanation of the coming of age of the system in the face of annexation and industrial diversification, as well as the concurrent emergence of the CPW as a profitable enterprise, was contained in two paragraphs:

> The Metropolitan Sewer District was formed in 1959 at which time the City Sewer System, consisting of trunk lines and treatment plant, were released to Metro for $1.00 per year. This proved to be a blessing to the Commission of Public Works because they were able to turn over to METRO the responsibility of treating both residential and industrial waste. This strengthened the financial stability of the CPW.
>
> The industrial expansion and the resulting growth has continued to produce increased numbers of paying water and gas cus-

> tomers for the Commission of Public Works. This growth and prosperity expansion has resulted in the CPW becoming very profitable in the expansion of its water and gas, not only to industry, but to more and more residential developments located outside of the City. With this growth, the financial assistance that has been required from the City of Greenwood to make the CPW successful is no longer needed.

Nave's final point – that many customers of CPW pay no city tax, a problem that increases as the community expands outward and forces the city to provide services with ever-declining revenue – must have hit home. In a 1991 telephone interview, he reported a new level of cooperation between the city and the CPW and cited that achievement as a highlight of his administration. Gross sales of the Commission of Public Works amounted to $24.7 million in 1990. Comparison of that figure with sales of about $5,000 in 1900 and $1.2 million in 1957 provides dramatic evidence of the town's growth, as well as the expansion of electricity-dependent trappings of life, over the last ninety years.

Reminiscing about "the way it was," former superintendent of operations Bill Wise provided the information that the first more or less modern power plant, built in 1907 by General Electric, featured a 500-horsepower steam engine fueled by burning cordwood. The engine was started at dark, he said, and turned off at daylight. On the subject of the original $40,000 bond issue to build the power plant, Wise also related the wondrous story that the time for redemption of the bonds, which had a 30-year maturity and paid some 8% interest, fell during the depression when retirement was impossible. The bonds were then renewed at 7% for another twenty years and finally paid off in the 1950s.

The town's first form of government was a town council consisting of the intendant and a board of four wardens. This system was abandoned in 1897 in favor of a mayor and six aldermen, each representing one of six wards. Greenwood added the city manager position in 1939. The town is still served by a mayor, a six-member council, and a city manager appointed by the council. Two or three significant changes in election procedures have been made in fairly recent years. For example, city-wide elections to choose council members were held prior to 1987; in that year, voters approved a referendum favoring single-member districts. Also, city elections are now non-partisan, although party affiliation is still a factor in county elections. City Clerk Mary Edwards recalls that this change came about a number of years ago. When she went to work in the 1960s, candidates' party affiliations were also considered in city elections. Greenwood mayors and council members now serve four-year terms; staggered elections to replace two members at a time are held for city council.

The centennial edition of the newspaper contained a long article on city government, as well as sketches of the fifteen mayors who had served the town from 1897 to 1957. First to hold the title "Intendant" after the town was chartered in 1857 was James Bailey; and Daniel Calhoun DuPre, who was elected in 1897, was the first to be called "Mayor." A. Sidney Hartzog held the record of longest continuous service at that time – four consecutive terms from 1915 to 1923 – but E. DeVore Andrews had actually served longer. Andrews was elected five times, from 1927-1931 and again from 1935-1941; W. A. Barnette was elected mayor for the intervening years from 1931 to 1935. In more recent years, Thomas Wingard served twelve years, and the incumbent, John Nave, will have served for 12 1/2 years by the end of his current term.

There is no such thing as an unimportant mayor, of course, but one three-term mayor in Greenwood's early days as a county seat is sketched here as representative of all the rest. Kenneth Baker, who served from 1907-1913, is remembered as the head of a very progressive city administration and as a man who devoted much of his time and attention to the interests of the city.

Baker's birthplace in 1869 was Kentucky, but he spent his early life in Gaffney, South Carolina. He was educated at Wofford College and the University of South Carolina; his business career is described rather simplistically and loosely as "the cotton business." That business would have been quite enough to bring him to Greenwood in 1901, but surviving information on Baker's public service, church work, and fraternal activities seems to outweigh any emphasis on business pursuits. In that respect he appears to differ from many early Greenwood businessmen who virtually lived their work. A sketch of Baker, written by three Masonic brothers and provided by his daughter Mary Neel Baker, gives a clue to that difference: "He was diligent and industrious in his daily life," the sketch reads, "and accumulated a competency from close attention to every detail of his business." That "competency" might have allowed Baker the time to pursue a variety of other interests.

One of Baker's most avid pursuits was Freemasonry. He attained the highest degrees of all the bodies of both the York and Scottish rites, as well as the offices of Grand Commander of Knights Templar and Grand Patron of the Order of the Eastern Star. Baker was also an active churchman in Immanuel Lutheran Church where he was superintendent of the Sunday School for nearly forty years, as well as an elder, member of the church council, treasurer, and trustee of the church college. There was probably no civic enterprise that did not benefit from Baker's interest, and he was mayor in 1910 when the business brochure described earlier was published.

The house on East Cambridge that Baker purchased soon after he came to Greenwood had once belonged to John Barksdale. Baker's daughter speculates that the house dates originally from the late 1880s. She also remembers that her father greatly enlarged the structure, adding more stories and large columns to the facade, in 1909, the year she entered first grade. The name of the business that now occupies this fine house is R. J. Sprott's, but everybody knows the furniture/interior design company and its beautiful building as "The Baker House." Kenneth Baker died in 1943. Two of his five children made Greenwood their home. Dr. Stanley C. Baker, one of the town's favorite dentists for many years, died in 1980; and Mary Neel Baker, a retired history teacher, long-time Lander College trustee, and source of a great deal of local history, still lives on Blyth Avenue. Grandchildren with some ninety years of Greenwood roots include Dr. Stanley C. Baker, Jr., and Pierrine B. (Mrs. William W. "Hootie") Johnson, of Columbia.

In the days before paved roads and convenient means of transportation, it was common to find private homes built very near, or even in the midst of, business districts of small towns. The west side of Greenwood's square, its southern extremity, and the entire area where the courthouse complex now stands were once residential areas. Naturally, many interesting houses were lost as the town expanded outward in all directions from the railroad tracks and depots that defined its center. Some were moved in an attempt to forestall destruction – the James Bailey house, for example, was moved twice before it succumbed to progress – but most were simply demolished in favor of some business enterprise or other as the town grew. Even so, Greenwood managed to hold on to one spectacular landmark until 1959 when the Barr-Taylor house at the corner of South Main and Marion Streets, along with five others in the block, was sacrificed to allow construction of a new supermarket.

The house became associated with the Taylor family when Andrew E. Taylor purchased it from the C. G. Barr estate in 1918 for the sum of $20,000. A newspaper story at the time of the sale called it "one of the handsomest in town . . . [and] splendidly built." Another grand Thomas Cothran design, the house featured several of the architect's trademarks, such as massive Doric columns supporting a two-story roof, a center balcony over a large fan- and side-lighted front door, and numerous large windows, including dormers above the roof line. Jessie Julien believes that funds to build the house were provided in Barr's will, and his widow carried out her husband's purpose. The house was constructed in 1907 at the beginning of Cothran's most prolific period; it had served several purposes by the time Taylor acquired it. According to a 1918 newspaper article, Mrs. Barr occupied the house only a short time; after her death the Elks Club used it for a few years, and the building was a boarding house run by a "Mrs. Gibbes" at the time Taylor purchased it from the Barr estate.

The house became a real home, evidently for the first time, in 1918, and the new owners were part of a family that had connections to Greenwood from its earliest days. The patriarch, George H. Taylor, moved to the area in 1888 from Newberry County, where he was born in 1847. Thomas C. Anderson wrote that Taylor was among the first three people to make money in the area after the Civil War (the others were Mike Kinard and Andrew Stockman). Evidently these farmers/landowners/entrepreneurs were wise enough to set up what Anderson termed "commissary stores" that provided both fertilizers and mortgages, as early as March each year, against other farmers' cotton crops. He wrote that these merchants would also allow credit for such things as "a sack or two of flour, some sugar, and a little tobacco from time to time," so that by the time the cotton was picked in August and September, farmers usually owed "the return from the whole year's work to settle the account" with the storekeeper. Anderson might have simplified just a bit, but it is easy to understand that the merchant held the upper hand in these annual deals. The George Taylor family lived near the Utopia School community in the early days and attended Mount Lebanon Church before they moved to town. The church history written in 1974 notes that the church lost some of its most valued members – in attendance, service, and financial support – when the George H. Taylors, their three sons, and their families all moved to Greenwood. Mrs. Taylor had presented the first organ and the first pulpit Bible to the church, and her son Andrew had given the oak pews, as well as provided a bequest in his will for youth work. George Taylor died at the age of 71. His obituary cited his "energy and business foresight" as factors in a successful career as "one of the largest planters of the county." He was also credited with helping bring Lander College to Greenwood. He is buried in the cemetery at Mount Lebanon Church.

The three Taylor sons – Ira B., Thomas L., and Andrew E. – all contributed to the business life of Greenwood, and all lived in notable houses, two on South Main Street and one on East Cambridge Avenue at the site of Greenwood Nursing Home. Many people remember these houses; the I. B. Taylor home, for example, was a large Victorian mansion several blocks south of the Barr-Taylor house on the opposite side of South Main Street. Helen Taylor Barnette wrote that her father's family transferred their allegiance to Main Street Methodist Church after the move to Greenwood and also supported the county's schools. Andrew Taylor was, in fact, instrumental in building the new school at Scotch Cross named Utopia, described in a newspaper article as a "handsome building" erected at a cost of $4,000. All four Taylors were among the largest subscribers, along with the Stockman family; someone suggested at the time that the school should be named "Stockman-Taylor" in honor of the two families. Andrew Taylor called the enterprise "a most worthy cause" and thanked the people of Greenwood for their "desire to build Greenwood greater by building up an educated and progressive community."

Andrew E. Taylor built a career in farming and real estate. Like the rest of his family he was active in the church and civic affairs of Greenwood, particularly the Kiwanis Club, of which he was a long-time member. Taylor was educated at the Cokesbury Conference School, Clemson Preparatory School, and Wofford College. When he died at the age of 65 in 1947 his obituary stressed his business acumen and service to church and community, particularly his advocacy of prohibition. His convictions were strong, claimed an editorial, and were upheld with courage and unyielding determination.

Among other legacies Andrew E. Taylor left to Greenwood five beautiful daughters – Evelyn, Louise, Marie, Genevieve ("Gee"), and Helen – four of whom survive at this writing, and three of whom still live in Greenwood. One or more of the sisters continued to live in the Taylor house until it was razed in 1959. Helen Taylor Barnette wrote that her father's influence made Greenwood "a kinder and better place to live." The record of the Taylor family's contributions over the years justifies and confirms Barnette's statement. As for the Taylor home place, Gee Poe says that it was the five sisters' "whole world" when they were children. She remembers that her father had a playhouse constructed in the back yard, and the spacious grounds were scenes of many a girlish adventure. The once-beautiful setting and gracious house on South Main Street gave way to the paved parking lot and Winn-Dixie supermarket building more than thirty years ago, but some people can still close their eyes and visualize the massive magnolia trees and other landscaping features that once defined the magnificent grounds of the Taylor home. Of such, unfortunately, is progress made.

Tracing every single business and building in Greenwood clearly would be impossible. This chapter has tried to hit the highlights and tell a story or two that might not be familiar. Even so, the difficulty has been deciding where and when to stop. It is necessary to write a word or two about trees in downtown Greenwood since their abundance at one time actually gave the town its name. Many people remember primarily the trees and railroad tracks, complete with depots, when they think about Greenwood before 1952. Those large oaks and magnolias are now only memories, although Greenwood's love-hate relationship with trees has meant more than one hewing down and replanting in the downtown area over the years. Several trees in the last large planting died, some say because the earth under the old railroad bed was rock-hard and not friendly to vegetation. There are trees now, to be sure, and a fountain which has not been a notable success, but the look of the town has changed irrevocably from the time large trees defined the median of what would become known as the widest main street in the world. It is true that shading the town watering trough is no longer necessary, but everyone surely agrees that greenery softens the landscape.

Businesses of every kind now abound in Greenwood proper and fan out in every direction from the old square. The town today also has the full complement of by-pass businesses and fast food franchises, most of which are common to nearly every town in the country. Travel writers have commented darkly that American towns now all look the same, at least on their outskirts. Downtown has become, somehow, Uptown Greenwood and is so celebrated on street light banners featuring the awnings that were part of a renovation in the early 1980s. An attempt to draw the area together resulted in either hiding or bifurcating several interesting store fronts, and some old signs can still be seen through new plastic. On the other hand, the copper roofing on the 25-year-old courthouse is oxidizing nicely, and the small dome of the old post office building glistens with a new layer of gold leaf above the repaired slate roof. A most interesting short-and-symmetrical stretch of Montague Avenue, each end of which forms a Y configuration, is currently in process of development. The outer Y features the new building of Greenwood National Bank, with its curved glass brick entrance and high-windowed second-floor boardroom designed by architect Jim Steverson, while the near Y has just lost the Art Deco-inspired Scurry Clinic building erected in 1940 and awaits its replacement. Some Greenwood citizens tried, without success, to save the more than thirty full-grown hardwood trees on the lot. One irreverent preservationist, upset by the loss of the Scurry building, has been heard to say that Greenwood's oldest building will soon be Crosscreek Mall.

Another chapter begins with the sad story behind Greenwood County landowners' general lack of royal land grants. This one ends with one tiny connection of the county seat with royalty, or at least near-royalty. According to Margaret Watson's book, Montague Avenue was named in honor of an ancestor of the Duchess of Windsor who was, on her mother's side, a member of the famous Montague family of Virginia and Maryland. Nobody remembers exactly when, but Wallis Warfield and her mother reportedly visited the grave of her great great grandfather John Montague at Plain Dealing (near Sample Road) at some time before she managed to wreck the career of King Edward VIII of England.

3

THE COUNTY

Knowledge of human nature is the beginning and end of political education.

Practical politics consists in ignoring facts.

Henry Brooke Adams

GREENWOOD had been part of other legal divisions long before either Abbeville or Edgefield county was created in 1785; and Greenwood lost a small part of its own territory when McCormick, the smallest and next to last (only Allendale came later) of the state's counties, was formed in 1916. The earliest subdivision of which Greenwood was a part was Granville, one of four counties created by the Lords Proprietors about 1685. Since the only settlement at that time was along the coast, the original division consisted of four "bands," each with its own coastal boundary, extending inland and westward, presumably to the Pacific Ocean. The four divisions were Craven, Berkeley, Colleton, and Granville, only two of the names of which survived when present-day counties were created much later. These rather loose subdivisions existed primarily for assigning and electing magistrates, organizing militia, and locating land grants in the most general way. The founding of Georgia in 1732 put an end to the "west to the Pacific" idea, since South Carolina territory stopped at the Savannah River.

In 1747 Governor Glen succeeded in buying from the Cherokees all lands south and east of Long Cane Creek in what would eventually become Abbeville county. Subdivisions called "parishes" which were supposed to consist of 100 families came later, but the upcountry was disappointed time and again when no such designation was forthcoming as the provision was met. Settlers were routinely disfranchised, since parishes were the basis for representation in the General Assembly. It is said that John C. Calhoun's father Patrick rode with armed neighbors halfway across the province to vote in Prince William's Parish in 1769. In the same year South Carolina was subdivided into seven circuits, or precincts, or districts as the basis for all later subdivisions. The four original counties ceased to exist, and the districts named were Charles Town, Beaufort, Georgetown, Cheraw, Camden, Orangeburg, and Ninety Six. Court was to be held at least twice a year in each district. The original Ninety Six district embraced all or part of fourteen upcountry counties, and the old village of Ninety Six, later renamed Cambridge, became the courthouse town of the district. Its location was about two miles southwest of the present-day town of Ninety Six.

Greenwood figured in yet another land saga, the origins and final disposition of which are still clouded in mystery and the confusion of claims and counterclaims resulting from the Revolutionary War. According to Don Herd in *The South Carolina Upcountry*, Joseph Salvador, a British citizen descended from a prominent Portuguese Jewish family, purchased 100,000 acres in Ninety Six District of South Carolina from John Hamilton for £2,000 in 1766. Other acreage was acquired until Salvador ultimately held title to some 208,000 acres of what was known as the John Hamilton Grant. Margaret Watson clarified the Hamilton Grant in *Greenwood County Sketches:* the royal government made four grants of about 50,000 acres each to William Livingston and his associates in 1749. One of those associates was John Hamilton, the same Londoner who several years before had tried unsuccessfully to secure land in upper South Carolina for colonization and turpentine production. No one knows why Livingston succeeded where Hamilton failed in acquiring the land that later became most of Greenwood County, but the delay was only temporary, and Hamilton finally gained the territory in a transfer from Livingston. Herd wrote that the Livingston-Hamilton-Salvador transactions – amount of land, methods of acquisition, prices paid, and means of disposition – have long been under a cloud of suspicion and doubt in spite of research and wrangling covering at least fifty years. Quoting from Charleston deed books of the time and adding a line from A. S. Salley that "under the 'more or less' clause they took more," he attempted to sort out the whole matter, to his own satisfaction at least. That sorting can be found in the first volume of Herd's book. The bad news about the Hamilton Grant is that it deprived most county landowners of the greatest status symbol of all – a royal land grant to an ancestor; the good news is that, thanks to the Revolutionary War, county residents need have no inordinate fear of title searches.

An actual survey of this land, known as "The Great Survey," was made in 1751 by George Hunter, and the lines were replotted with the aid of aerial photographs by Carl Julien of Greenwood in 1934. Margaret Watson described the Hamilton grant in *Greenwood County Sketches*:

> Saluda River was the eastern boundary of Hamilton's land. The lower or southern corner was on the west bank of the river just below Ninety Six. From the river the line ran south 45 degrees west for about nine miles to a point marking the end of the first 50,000 acres, then about 10 miles more to the southwestern corner of the second tract, about 64,000 acres. (This southern survey line became the boundary between Abbeville and Edgefield counties when they were created in 1785.) The line made a right angle and went north 45 degrees west for about 18 miles to a

> point a mile or two northeast of the present town of Abbeville. There it made another right angle and ran north 45 degrees east back to Saluda River near the present Ware Shoals.

This acreage amounts to about two-thirds of Greenwood County. From the 1770s to about the 1920s, these lands were often called "Jews Lands," in part because Salvador was Jewish and also because of speculation that the area was originally intended as a haven for persecuted Jews in Europe. About half the land had been sold by 1773; Joseph Salvador's nephew Francis Salvador received nearly 7,000 acres by purchase and mortgage in 1774. The younger Salvador actually moved to the new world and established a plantation which he named Corn Acre. Active in the business and public affairs of the colony and eager to assist in the struggle for independence, Salvador met his death at the hands of the Cherokees in 1776. At Joseph Salvador's death in 1786 the residue of his South Carolina lands was willed to his three daughters, but the intervening war had muddied the waters on any such bequest, for "many English titles to unsettled and undeveloped lands in the backcountry were forfeited . . . [and] the state awarded much of this . . . land to veterans to settle monetary claims." Notwithstanding, legal title to the Salvador lands remained in litigation and dispute for many years; lawyers were still wrangling as late as 1816.

A historical marker stands along Highway 72 near Coronaca Creek a few miles east of Greenwood. Jewish citizens of the area are credited with erecting this marker in 1960 as a tribute to early settler Francis Salvador; he is commemorated in these words: "This young English Jew settled near Coronaca in 1774, represented Ninety Six District in the Provincial congresses of 1775-1776, and died in defense of his adopted home on Aug. 1, 1776. He was the first South Carolinian of his faith to hold an elective public office and the first to die for American independence."

Another law in 1785 began the creation of counties as we know them today, but the district designations were retained to serve for circuit courts. At that time the state consisted of 34 counties; Ninety Six District was divided into Abbeville, Edgefield, Laurens, Newberry, Spartanburg, and Union. The new counties became the basis for representation in the upcountry; the low country retained representation by parish until 1865. The term "district" rather than "county" reappeared in 1799 and continued in use until 1868 when the subdivisions were again called counties. The end of the old county court system came in 1800 when circuit courts were instituted in each of the districts. That meant the end of the judicial importance of the old Ninety Six District, and new counties such as Abbeville and Edgefield grew in importance.

The dream of a new county around the Greenwood area first took root in the town of Ninety Six, which by the 1850s had begun to re-develop at its present site along the Greenville and Columbia railroad. The idea, spearheaded by John R. Tolbert, had gained strong support by the 1870s; H. L. Watson wrote that "it failed by the narrowest sort of squeak" in the General Assembly. Watson wrote a succinct account in 1936 of the county effort sponsored by Ninety Six:

> The citizens of Ninety Six did not have the support of Greenwood in the new county movement because Greenwood had the same ambition. Opponents of the new county idea who lived outside the influence of these two communities soon sized up the situation and followed the time-honored practice in such situations of playing one town against the other, with the inevitable result that neither could get anywhere.
>
> The only way to break down the barrier was for the two communities of Greenwood and Ninety Six to unite. The building of the railroad from Greenwood to Augusta, the failure of the proposal for a railroad through Ninety Six, followed by the building of the present Seaboard through Greenwood, gave Greenwood such an advantage that the good people of Ninety Six not only graciously accepted the result but entered enthusiastically into the move to secure a new county with Greenwood as the county seat.

The formation of Greenwood County might well have happened four years earlier than it did had its proponents been a little less greedy for territory. Although neither *manifest destiny* nor *labensraum* was mentioned, the implications were clear enough in an article written by S. H. McGhee in 1936:

> A very strong effort was made in the session of 1893 of the General Assembly for the formation of Greenwood County. At that time the General Assembly met the last of November and as a rule adjourned a day or two before Christmas. A large delegation from Greenwood went to Columbia and the vote was very close on the formation of the county, but was defeated because our people attempted to take in too much territory, the [proposed] boundaries extending far into Edgefield and to the Anderson county line and far into Laurens County. All these old counties put up a hard fight against us.

Back to the drawing board went the county fathers who by this time had the bit firmly between their teeth with no intention of backing off. Another survey was run in 1894 for a smaller area, but once again the proposed boundary crossed the Saluda River and would have included Cross Hill. Eventually, county proponents agreed among themselves that the natural boundary of the Saluda River should be respected.

One of the leaders in the legislative struggle for the new county was W. H. "Pony" Yeldell, a member of the House from Edgefield who later claimed to have had more to do with the formation of Greenwood County than any other single man. Yeldell managed to prevail in the House, but the Senate demurred because a new constitutional convention was imminent; that convention was expected to support cutting down the required size of new counties. The Senate insisted that Greenwood wait until the convention's work was done. In the meantime, those opposed to the new county effort came up with a proposal they wanted to include in the constitution:

> A constitutional convention having been called in 1895, . . . opponents of the new county idea found a new possibility in the way of blocking the move. These opponents proposed for the new State Constitution a provision which would not allow any new county to have any part of its boundary line come any nearer an old county seat than 10 miles. Abbeville and Greenwood are said to just 12 miles distant in a straight line from each other. If Greenwood could not cut off any area from Abbeville except that which would be included outside a10-mile radius from the older county seat, she could not get the required area for a new county. Greenwood contended for an 8-mile limit. The fight was long and probably bitter . . . [but] the upshot was that Greenwood won and the 8-mile limit was adopted by one vote. W. L. Durst and T. F. Riley were the Greenwood leaders who remained in Columbia during the fight in the Constitutional Convention of 1895. Many others went down from time to time to help.

Although Edgefield in general did not oppose the new county (indeed, its senator, J. M. Gaines, actively supported the proposal in 1894 and was elected Greenwood's second senator in 1900), many Abbeville citizens were indignant at the very notion of countyhood for Greenwood because it would mean "dismemberment" for Abbeville. They spoke freely in the pages of the *Abbeville Medium* of their belief that the plan could easily be defeated in the legislature through what they called "senatorial courtesy."

Mary Hemphill Greene, daughter of *Medium* editor Robert R. Hemphill who was also senator from Abbeville County at the time Greenwood sought county status, contributed a long article to *The Index-Journal* forty years later. "The fight went on for years and every time the subject came up for discussion it made for excitement and vociferous talk in the old town," she wrote. "We were loth (sic) to give up the Greenwood folks. Many thought it a rank piece of heresy for the town to make such a suggestion. . . ." Greene gently reminded Greenwood that it had made much of its fealty to Abbeville when Ninety Six was pushing the move and had sworn nothing could make Greenwood people "leave the county of history and culture." She quoted at length from legislative letters of Senator I. H. McCalla, who defeated Hemphill in the 1894 election largely on the Greenwood County issue. The December 6, 1894, letter made McCalla's position clear: "There is a disposition to postpone all new counties until after the constitutional convention. Now is the time for

Abbeville to move in the matter and preserve the old landmarks. We all think too much of Greenwood to allow her to leave the grand old county of Abbeville. In fact there is no need for a new county with Greenwood as headquarters."

The new county question was debated long and hard during the convention sessions, and some people thought new counties would be created then and there. One – Saluda – actually was, after a lively debate over its name. An interesting aspect of that debate involved the immediate past governor, the notorious Benjamin Ryan ("Pitchfork Ben") Tillman who had defeated General M. C. Butler for the United States Senate in 1894, and his brother George D. Tillman, who supported the name of Butler for the new county as a tribute to the general. Historian D. D. Wallace wrote that the leader of the convention was definitely Ben Tillman – he had it in his pocket, so to speak – and Ben Tillman wanted the county named Saluda. The vote for the name Butler was taken during his absence. When he heard it he was furious, gave the convention a tongue lashing, and demanded another vote to "correct" the name in accordance with his wishes. Mary Hemphill Greene did not cover this issue; she stated merely that the name "Butler" finally prevailed.

No doubt the new county question was quite enough to keep Edgefield and Abbeville delegates enthralled throughout the convention, but D. D. Wallace in his history of South Carolina took another view of the proceedings entirely. He mentioned the new county controversies not at all, and after citing the struggles over suffrage (read, eliminating insofar as possible the Negro vote) and other racial questions that dominated the convention, Wallace wrote:

> The rest of the Constitution merely perpetuates the usual American system of a split-up executive department, with a governor denied adequate power to execute the laws he is sworn to uphold; a legislature encumbered with local legislation and . . . shackled with limitations . . . and a judiciary hamstrung in its functioning against crime and legal delays. . . . Of the enlightened statesmanship which in a number of states has to some extent remedied these chronic evils . . . South Carolina has given slight manifestation. Until something of that lesson is learned another constitutional convention is useless.

Much was made in Mary Greene's article of the high-flown oratory employed by both sides of the great debate. In joking about the number of maps in the hands of Greenwood proponents, who included residents of Honea Path, McCormick, Troy, and Ninety Six, one convention letter commented: "There never before were so many accurate maps of parts of our state which seem to be populated by a set of surveyors and map makers. If cotton proves to be a crop that won't pay our people can strike out through other states and make money by drawing maps. . . ." Another amusing ploy was an attempt to name the county "Mart Gary," both to honor Civil War General Martin Witherspoon Gary, a native of Cokesbury, and to influence Frank Gary, a kinsman and leading opponent of the measure. That attempt was, mercifully, short-lived.

The final fight in the convention came on November 14. The legislative letter of that date stated: "The best fight since the convention assembled was made by our [Abbeville's] delegation against the dismemberment of the old county. George and Ben Tillman . . . were against us . . . [and] were supported by the best organized crowd of lobbyists from Greenwood I ever saw. To these were added friends of new counties . . . Abbeville stood firm and undismayed . . . I have no reproach for the Greenwood lobbyists. I did not hear them abuse anybody."

The movement that began in the 1870s by residents of Ninety Six and gained momentum in the Constitutional Convention of 1895 finally culminated during the last days of the legislative session of 1897 when the Act creating Greenwood County was passed. The efforts of men such as C. A. C. Waller, W. H. Yeldell, J. M. Gaines, W. L. Durst, T. F. Riley, A. Rosenberg, Jack Carr, T. A. Graham, H. J. Kinard, J. B. Holloway, and many others had all been worthwhile. It is significant that two of the most powerful men in the state, Ben Tillman and his older brother George, who agreed on very few things in those days, both supported the move though their motives for doing so probably differed greatly from those of the strictly local delegation. Edgefield was not nearly so vociferously opposed to the move as was Abbeville.

Certain legal moves were necessary long before the actual vote in the General Assembly. The first requirement was a petition to the governor, signed by one-third of the qualified electors in the area proposed for the new county, asking for an election to decide whether a new county should be formed. That election date was set for December 15, 1896, and polling stations were established at Ninety Six, Greenwood, Cokesbury, Hodges, Verdery, and Bradley. *The Greenwood Index* ran in its December 10 edition a resounding call to action headlined "To the Friends of Greenwood": "Take your poll tax receipt and your registration certificate with you to the polls on next Tuesday . . . and tell your friends to do likewise. . . . Many a victory has been lost by indifference to the strength of the enemy." Another article in the same issue reminded citizens to keep their eye on the ball: "If at any future time the people of the proposed New County of Greenwood [wish to] change the name, it can be done very easily and without expense whatever. But it will be hazardous to split on this question now."

An article signed by W. L. Durst, Chairman of the New County Committee, appeared in the December 3 edition of the newspaper:

> We have labored three years to be permitted to choose a more convenient location for a county seat. We were required to await the action of a Constitutional Convention. That convention has

> been held. . . . At last the way is clear for the formation of the New County. If you poll two-thirds of the vote in its favor the legislature cannot refuse to grant you the county. If you fail in this selection you cannot vote on this question again within four years.
>
> Do not underrate the opposition . . . the worst we have to fear is work from enemies outside the lines. They have defeated or delayed the movement for three years. They hope to be able to defeat us again. No more long journeys to a distant county seat to spend day and night away from home; but in this small county each citizen can leave his home in the morning, attend to his business, and return home at night to protect his home and loved ones. . . .

The vote in the special election was 1,019 to 84, far more than the two-thirds majority required; the way was clear for the introduction of the bill itself and its routine journey through the legislative process. When all was accomplished and signed into law by Governor W. H. Ellerbe, which happened on March 2, 1897, Greenwood County became a reality at last. Its boundaries, set in Section 1 of the Act, were adjusted for the first time a year later to include portions of two townships in Abbeville and one in Edgefield which had voted in May 1897 to come into Greenwood, and a part of Cokesbury which had so voted in November of the same year. The lines were changed again when portions were cut off to form McCormick County in 1916.

The complete Act can be found in the 1897 edition of *Statutes at Large of South Carolina;* following is a summary of its sixteen sections:

Section 1 – sets the boundaries.

Section 2 – appoints seven commissioners (Dr. J. C. Maxwell, C. A. C. Waller, W. V. Blyth, T. F. Riley, G. A. Barksdale, S. P. Mathews, and A. B. Ellis) to procure sites and erect buildings for courts, county offices, and jail at a cost not to exceed $25,000.

Section 5 – provides for two members in the House of Representatives [Note: periodic reapportionment over the years has changed this provision in both directions].

Sections 6 and 7 – provide for the election of representatives in the General Assembly, as well as county officers, and set a special election for this purpose on May 4, 1897. A further provision notes that Greenwood County "shall be fully created and established on the 30th day after the date of said special election."

Section 8 – appoints three commissioners (E. W. Watson, Bradley; P. B. Kemp, Kirksey; and R. H. Hughes, Ware Shoals) to set up corners and boundaries and to lay off into school districts and townships.

Sections 9 and 10 – set bonds and salaries of county officers.

Section 11 – places the county in the third congressional district and the seventh judicial circuit (later amended to the eighth judicial circuit) and fixes the times for holding court.

Sections 12 and 13 – provide for transferring all pending cases, liens, and judgements.

Sections 14, 15, and 16 – provide for purchase of books and furniture; make provision for jury lists; and arrange to adjust bonded debt on the two old counties with Greenwood.

No accounting of a county's beginnings should omit the names of its first elected officials. As usual with Greenwood, a certain drama surrounded the first election provided in the Act that created the county. Although the Act provided for two representatives, that representation had to wait since the House membership was at its prescribed maximum of 124, five of whom had been elected from Abbeville to serve through the session of 1898. Accordingly, in the first primary (which at that time, and until much, much later, was "tantamount to election" anywhere in South Carolina), C. A. C. Waller defeated D. H. Magill to become Greenwood County's first senator. Other county officers elected, some in a second, or run-off, primary, were: Tom Turner, clerk of court; Dr. J. A. Marshall, treasurer; Captain W. E. Cothran, judge of probate; Major J. L. White, school commissioner (now county superintendent of education); J. M. Major, supervisor; Captain R. F. McCaslan, sheriff; T. A. Graham, auditor; and A. B. Dean, coroner. The first members of the House of Representatives from the new county were elected in 1898. They were David H. Magill, whom Waller had defeated in the race for the Senate and who had previously represented Abbeville in the House, and R. Hayne Henderson of Coronaca.

* * * *

Greenwood County's first courthouse got off to a rocky start. There were legal problems with the funding; construction was marked by delay and disaster, both natural and man-made; and all sorts of acrimony among the principals reigned for months until the contractor, identified only as N. Partee from Roanoke, Virginia, finally threw in the towel in March 1898. That defection must have seemed an ignominious end to the contract so hopefully awarded less than a year earlier. The *Greenwood Journal* announced in its issue of June 17, 1897, that the Court House Commission had accepted the design of architect Reuben Harrison Hunt of Chattanooga for the courthouse and that of a Mr. Milbourne for the jail. The construction contract for both was awarded to Partee at a cost of $23,000-$25,000.

Although it seems inconceivable, apparently the Commission expected the new courthouse to be ready for occupancy by January 1, 1898, or at the very latest by the second court term scheduled for March. The first term of court in the new county was held in November 1897 in the "Bailey-Barksdale hall" which had been hastily fitted out for use as a courtroom. The first grand jury report given during court week noted that county officials were discharging the duties of their offices with "fidelity and in a businesslike manner" and that the new courthouse which was "rapidly nearing completion" had been inspected. The grand jury, under foreman George W. Lipscomb, reported that "when completed it will be in every sense a modern court house and a fine piece of architecture and entirely suited for the purpose for which it is designed." The grand jury also thanked the town of Greenwood for providing the jail and courthouse without cost to the county. These rosy reports were, as it turned out, premature at best and at worst misleading.

Progress of the construction phase was reported routinely in little newspaper blurbs from time to time, but the first mention of real difficulty came in an article dated January 27, 1898. That article called the enterprise a piece of "masterly inactivity" on the contractor's part. "Plainly and briefly," it continued, "work on the court house is not going on in a business-like or workman-like manner. There is very little material on the ground and scarcely a workman in sight." The writer speculated that January 1899 would be a more likely completion date than the original target of January 1, 1898. At that point the article got really tough:

> Two members of the Commission are outspoken in the belief that the Commission will be forced to take charge of the work and complete it. Not only is the work far behind, but some of it will have to be torn down and made over. Thirty joist[s] are to be changed and some stairways altered. Mr. W. V. Blyth is representing the Commission and, as a practical builder, and a public official, he is not pleased with affairs. It is believed the Commission will sustain his view in the case. This is plain unvarnished statements of facts. It is believed that the time has come for putting a stop to these dilatory proceedings. Indications that the Commissioners will take charge in a vigorous manner and that the people of Greenwood county will sustain the action are very strong. Let foolishness end. The court house can and ought to be finished in time for March Court.

That did it for Partee. Evidently stung beyond endurance he struck back in a long article entitled "Mr. Partee States His Case" published in the *Greenwood Index* of February 24, 1898. But even before his defense appeared, the newspaper reported that a gable of the courthouse had collapsed, "probably on account of the hard wind." No one was hurt "when the several tons of brick fell," the article concluded, "the workmen all being at dinner" at the time.

Partee's side of the story, when he chose to make it public, began as a letter to the editor:

> The article in your issue of Jan. 27th does me gross injustice and while I am averse to newspaper controversies, never having had one, it seems that I should not longer remain silent and be subject to unjust and prejudicial criticism and misconstruction. To this end and that the public may judge rightly, with the facts before them, as to cause of delay in finishing the Court House, and pass on other matters therewith, I submit the following statement:

Partee's submission included copies of the original letter from Mayor D. C. DuPre as well as a couple of contracts between him and the Commission. After thousands of words excoriating everybody, from a disgruntled bricklayer he said he refused to hire all the way to Architect R. H. Hunt, Partee got to his real point: the trouble, he said, had come from the fact that Greenwood wanted too much building for too little money, a charge that may well have been quite true. The contractor pointed out that courthouses in both Anderson and Elberton had cost more than twice the amount Greenwood was willing to spend, and Greenwood's building would be twice as big as either. He even quoted figures, which may or may not be accurate. Anderson's building had cost $27,000 and Elberton's $30,000, according to Partee, whereas he had contracted to build Greenwood's courthouse at a cost of $12,300, plus $5,000 for the jail. (Note: these figures do not include land acquisition costs nor, presumably, architects' fees.)

Poor Mr. Partee. If only a few of his complaints were valid, he had truly made a terrible mistake in pursuing this particular job. There were any number of real problems for the new county in getting the project off the ground; Mayor DuPre's letter made clear his view that the ambiguity of the funding procedure was the stickiest problem of all. The Act creating the county called for an expenditure of $25,000 for the two buildings, with the funds apparently expected to come from a special tax on the citizens of the town. Attorneys decided that city officials had no right to levy such a tax on city residents for the benefit of the whole county. Furthermore, since the Act made no reference to issuing bonds, that option would not be open, according to the attorneys, until the legislature could pass a bill to allow it at the next session the following January. A bond issue seemed to be the answer, and bonds had already been favorably voted in the special election, but the way had not been cleared legally at the time Partee sought the building contract.

The Virginia contractor was nothing if not persistent. He wrote that he submitted a proposal "to buy the ground and erect the buildings [,] provided . . . a note was executed for $5,000 or $10,000, said note to be signed by several solvent citizens, to mature at a date subsequent to the time of the adjournment of the next Legislature and to be placed in bank in escro[w], deliverable only when twice the amount thereof had been expended on the lots and buildings. The balance was to be paid from the proceeds of bonds when an issue was authorized and sold." The Commission accepted this proposal, "provided we could agree on price." Partee said he wanted the Commission to seek bids, the lowest of which he would match, but the group balked at this and asked him to submit his own bid. When he did so, his bid was rejected as too high, and the Commission asked him if he would accept the figure of $12,300. Partee complied, much against his better judgment. "While the price, I felt satisfied, was lower than anyone else would offer," he wrote, "the building was to have a rubble foundation which is never used except for the poorest and cheapest class of buildings, and the local brick to be used were perhaps the poorest made. I naturally presumed the other work would be in keeping – although the specifications, as they always do, called for the best material and workmanship – so I knew with good management there was a small margin for profit."

Partee might have been a frustrated architect. He found "some very serious defects" in Hunt's design and told the Commission the plans would simply have to be changed. Although the members gave him no satisfaction on this point, he said he finally received "an intimation" that they would probably get other plans at some future time and so he forged ahead, even though he was quite concerned that the Commission was ignoring the obligations he had already incurred. He cited his "great inconvenience" over two months, involving half a dozen trips to Greenwood and hundreds of dollars in out-of-pocket expenses. He accused the Commission of stonewalling: "because I had tried to deal frankly with them, in pointing out defects and thus save them complications, it was not right to ignore all obligations to me. One member said all they could do would be to investigate the plans and take a new start at some future time."

Highly indignant but determined to pull his chestnuts out of the fire, Partee wrote that he requested yet another meeting and prepared another written proposal to allow leeway in the plans and specifications. That meeting took place on June 10 with architect Hunt in attendance; the prospect of criticizing the plans in the presence of the man who drew them embarrassed Partee, but he felt he had no choice. The record does not include Hunt's reaction to Partee's charge that other architects were "amused and astounded" at his violation of "every principle of architecture." (Note: Reuben Harrison Hunt buildings can be found all over the Southeast and in several foreign countries. His name is familiar to the United States Department of the Interior and the National Register of Historic Places.) The contractor's desperate move evoked very little response from the commissioners who chose to adhere to Hunt's design with only minor changes. Partee feared that even the few changes the commissioners allowed would incur additional costs, but the Board insisted the changes would offset each other and refused to authorize additional funding. Partee charged next that no one would give him the plans; he wrote that John Barksdale guarded them jealously and refused to give them up until after construction was underway. Problems arose again when the Board decided it was time to borrow the money to pay the contractor; that scheme ran into difficulty when "several solvent citizens" declined to sign the note, and the project virtually ground to a halt. Partee was reduced to pleading by this time, but was finally told he might as well just go away; he was also told that his living expenses would be paid. Commissioner John Maxwell pointed out to the Board that the contractor surely had grounds for a lawsuit; Partee charged that Maxwell also said the town should "get on her knees and beg to be taken back into the old county."

Utterly disgusted by this time, Partee wrote that he decided to give the whole business up as a bad job and regretted he had not done so already, "as enough had transpired to warn me what future treatment to expect, and any submitting to such injustice naturally placed me at a disadvantage, which was only intensified as time advanced." Rather than quit, however, he embarked on the boldest move yet: he proposed to buy the bonds himself in order to insure the completion of the project. He felt no particular qualms about such a course, since the bonds were expected to be legal after January. Commissioner Barksdale, according to Partee, welcomed this as a "happy solution" and told the contractor he "would be doing a second kindness and would be a public benefactor." That contract was signed on June 21. The contractor believed everyone would understand that delays in getting the project underway would mean a delay in completion.

But the absolute worst for Partee was yet to happen. That low point came, he wrote, when W. V. Blyth stopped the work one day about a third of the way into preparing the foundation. Partee hinted darkly that "an old bricklayer" whom he would not hire had carried tales to the Board and brought Blyth into the fray. A builder himself, and one of Greenwood's own, Blyth was hired to second guess the contractor's work for the insulting sum of $1.75 per day. This was simply too much! Nobody could please Blyth, according to Partee, and he felt he could expect no help from the architect whose work he had scorned. While admitting to a grudging respect for Blyth, who "could build a house from a pencil sketch," the contractor accused him of not understanding professional plans and of reading at least one specification backward. Partee's detailed statement dwelt on the controversy between himself and Blyth in the matter of brickwork on the tower. Blyth insisted the brick had to be cut, or beveled, in order to reflect Hunt's design, while Partee feared that the quality of the brick was too poor and the bricks themselves not sufficiently uniform to allow cutting. The beleaguered contractor claimed he ordered the manufacturer to design new molds that would burn brick to suit Blyth. When that procedure proved unworkable in terms of time loss, Partee actually traveled to Chattanooga to consult with Hunt about the brick problem. He wrote that Hunt obligingly showed him the effect he wanted to achieve, using uncut brick laid in an open pattern. It must have cost Partee dearly to go hat-in-hand to a man he had previously maligned, but that visit saved the day insofar as the decorative brickwork in the tower was concerned. Even so, Blyth stubbornly insisted that the contractor cement over the interstices so that the architect's design was thwarted in any case.

Other clashes between Partee and Blyth were not so easily remedied. After laying a foundation of stones considered too small to support the walls, the problem that had alerted Blyth in the first place, Partee next selected very large stones which were cut and shaped to fit and eventually cost, he wrote, more than three times the original estimate for the foundation. The result was a foundation that was almost the equivalent of a cut stone job. Blyth then insisted that the exterior stone trimmings be hand rubbed, even though they were already machine polished to nearly the smoothness of marble; Partee remarked that it would have been better to require roughening the trim to go with the brick which "were perhaps the roughest ever made." Partee reserved his most stinging rebukes for Blyth whose "unreasonable and impossible demands . . . demoralized the labor" until the workers came to him to ask who the boss was. He was especially indignant that Blyth would tell "60 cents a day" laborers that he was going to serve the contractor with written notice "if a most trivial thing was not done."

Although the contractor tried to assure the public that he harbored no ill-feeling against Blyth, he could not quite pull it off:

> While I might fill a book on this it would seem unnecessary as the instances cited are ample to show that *ignorance of work, unreasonable exactions and malice* have been displayed throughout, and although everyday the work was delayed meant $1.75 in his pocket, I do not believe this fact influenced him. I have understood he had some thought of taking the contract himself — but in any case I would be far from doing him an injustice and personally I have no ill-feeling against him. . . . [emphasis added]
>
> I attribute his peculiar course to his extraordinary excentricities (sic), and I have heard even his friends say that he would find fault with his Maker, and if he discovered a knot in a wooden coffin about to be put in the ground he would stop to cut it out.

After Partee had made his point that Greenwood simply wanted too much for too little, he wrote: "No man would build a board house and put a marble floor in it nor would any one buy a common piece of cloth and make it up at the same expense as goods costing five times as much. Further than this we have been put to the delay and expense of trying to make fine work out of common material which any one knows is impracticable." Moreover, the two parties to the contract never could agree on who was entitled to accrued interest on the bonds when they were finally delivered, in installments. Summing up his complaints, Partee whined:

> It seems that almost the entire business of the Board has been conducted by four men (Mr. Blyth being one and making a quorum.) Mr. Blyth is the only one who claims to know much, if anything about building, therefore it is but natural the others should be influenced by him.
>
> Although I appealed to the Board they have systematicaly (sic) refused every request; they have never granted me the least consideration, and on the other hand I regret to say they have been, it seemed to me, conspicuous in their efforts to discommode and mistreat and injure me – some having gone so far as to authorize the publication of a newspaper article which does me a great injustice.
>
> These gentlemen are prominent, representative men, whom, personally, I hold in high esteem, but when I have never given them cause why they should so treat me, is beyond my comprehension. It seems that they regard me a foreign enemy seeking to do them an injury, or a "Wall street shark," whom I hear so loudly abused for swindling the people.

Amazingly, Partee still wanted to finish the job he had started even though he realized that the "general unfriendly spirit" the Board showed at meetings probably meant that would be impossible. "I am anxious to finish the building," he wrote, "but under present circumstances it seems that if I were to empty the national treasury in the effort to please and work till I was as old as Methusaleh (sic) the building would probably never be finished satisfactorily, or controversy averted." Evidently the contractor had been able to overcome his early objections to the building itself. He pronounced the courthouse "a magnificent piece of workmanship, without the slightest crack in it." But he added, "I hardly think the county of Greenwood would desire to accept a gift that was secured . . . at less than its real value, and at the cost of pauperizing the man who worked on it." Partee threw himself on the mercy of the public, concluding his statement to the newspaper with the words, "I do not believe that the people of Greenwood desire to see me so treated that I lose money and at the same time be regarded as a public enemy."

But it was too late. Partee had hanged himself. After rehashing the matter in an article entitled "The Court House Muddle" in the *Greenwood Index* of March 3, 1898, including written rebuttals by both C. A. C. Waller and W. V. Blyth, the newspaper reported two weeks later that N. Partee & Company no longer had a hand in building the courthouse. The contractor, in fact, had been paid up, finished his course in Greenwood, and departed, presumably for Virginia and the less stressful career of building houses. He was paid, according to the March 17 article, a total of $21,000 but required to deposit, "by virtue of the forfeiture clause in the contract," the amount of $3,550 which would be used to finish the work. The Woodward Lumber Company of Atlanta and (surely to no one's surprise) William V. Blyth of Greenwood were charged with completing the project within sixty days for the amount of $3,300. In the understatement of 1898 the reporter noted, "Thus a troublesome matter has been settled." As for a rebuttal of Partee's recital of indignities, the newspaper article concluded in a manner as dignified as possible under the circumstances:

> As to the past conduct of the public building business there is little to be said, as the people generally are in possession of the facts. It is presumed Mr. Partee was in full possession of his mental faculties when he contracted last July to finish the court house and jail by January 1st, 1898, and if he comes out loser he has himself to blame. The Commission has attempted to hold him strictly to the terms of the contract and have succeeded. But the exasperating slowness of the work not only wore out the patience of the Commissioners, but that of the people generally as well. The new Contractors have ordered a sufficiency of material and are in readiness to push the work. All the hands that can be used with the present supply of material are at work – seven or eight of them. By another week work will be well under way.

Perhaps so complete an exposition of this entire matter might be considered overkill. Justification for including so much of Partee's anguished appeal in the newspaper is simply that the general public is seldom allowed to know the extent of squabbling that goes on in nearly every building project of any size. To hear one party's side, biased though it undoubtedly was, must have been pretty heady stuff for Greenwood. No doubt the controversy was the talk of the town for weeks after the contractor's statement appeared. The notice in the newspaper of April 28 that the courthouse had been formally turned over to the county that morning was almost anticlimactic.

While no actual proof exists, it is difficult to escape speculation that the trauma surrounding the county's most important official building somehow seeped into the public consciousness to the point that the structure was never a favorite of the community. What other reason could there possibly be for omitting a picture of the courthouse and some sketch of its history in the centennial edition of the newspaper in 1957? It is true that the building's deterioration was well advanced by that time, but its historical importance remained. Architect Reuben H. Hunt received three important commissions in Greenwood concurrent with and soon after the courthouse project; evidently Partee's opinion of his ability was not shared by building committees of the First Presbyterian Church, Williamston Female (Lander) College, and Magnolia School. Pictures of the first courthouse show a building rather Victorian in feeling and probably reflecting the Gothic Revival style of architecture more than any other, although Hunt's favorite rounded arches, many-featured tower, and stone trim softened the angular feel of the steeply-pitched sections of roof and a number of chimneys. The four-faced clock tower (the clock was a later addition) guaranteed a Greenwood landmark for the 65 or so years of the building's life. Perhaps the modern brick clock tower in front of the County Bank-United Savings Bank complex on Main Street was meant to evoke memories of that feature of the first courthouse.

Considering the financial and contractual constraints of getting the courthouse built in the first place, perhaps the speculation is not too far-fetched that deferred rather than preventive maintenance was the order of the day for the next fifty years. Whatever the reasons for the building's decline, decline it most certainly did, and many people seem to believe it was just a "bad building." Leaks in the roof and squirrels in the attic would seem to imply inadequate attention to maintenance, but carping thirty years after the building's demise is probably both counter-productive and reactionary. The fact that the county had outgrown the building by the time it was replaced in the 1960s is indisputable; counties and other governmental agencies usually outgrow their quarters. The "new" courthouse was designed by local engineer Hearst Coleman (of Coleman & Townes) and built by local contractor C. Y. Thomason and Company. The building cost about $1 million; there is no record of impolite exchanges among the principals during the planning and construction phases.

By way of contrast with information on the courthouse, the centennial edition of the newspaper featured both a picture and an article describing the Confederate Memorial which once stood in front of the courthouse and now stands at the side and toward the rear of the building. The 35-foot monument, erected in 1903 by the Ladies Memorial Associations of Greenwood County, is an impressive fluted column resting on a base of South Carolina and Vermont granite and topped by a life-sized Italian marble figure of a private soldier at parade rest. Two marvelous connections are contained in the monument. One is that the column was originally cut for the State Capitol in Columbia. Somehow broken in preparation and unusable for its intended purpose, the column was donated to the ladies by special act of the legislature. The City of Spartanburg received a similar column. The other connection is that the statue of the soldier was modeled after a photograph of James Leonidas Waller, a Greenwood native and Confederate soldier who fell at Sharpsburg. Senator C. A. C. Waller provided the statue of his brother as his contribution to the project.

The Confederate Memorial owes its existence to the women of Greenwood who organized themselves in 1898 "to keep alive reverence for the

Confederate cause and its defenders," but its first instigator was L. M. Moore who wrote a series of letters to the editor to get the project off the ground. This gentleman must have been Lewis Mathews Moore; Margaret Watson wrote that he served as postmaster for several years. One of Moore's letters reads in part: "I expect I will be classed with the cranks before I am done with this, but if our women . . . will stand by me . . . we will see the monument erected." He called it "the great ambition (earthly) of my life." The ladies' associations raised more than $1,000 toward the monument, the overall value of which Waller placed at about $4,000.

Although everyone would probably agree that C. A. C. Waller was a natural for the office of first senator, it is interesting to note that his first term was cut short because 1900 was a regular election year, and J. M. Gaines won the senate seat in that election. Gaines had been a senator from Edgefield County but had worked actively in favor of the Greenwood petition. Perhaps his election was a sort of reward for that work; it also made him the only man in the state believed to have served as senator from two different counties. Waller was elected again, this time for a full term, in 1908.

No name comes up more often in early Greenwood County history than Waller's; there was apparently no movement in which he was not an active participant, and his influence was felt in every area of Greenwood life. A great-grandson of the Reverend John Waller who moved to the area from Virginia in 1793, Chris Waller spent his entire life in Greenwood except for service in the Civil War. A sketch of his career printed in *The Index-Journal* of May 6, 1920, states that he "served with distinction throughout the whole of the War Between the States." His rank of captain rested on merit, according to the sketch, and he commanded his company during the last seven battles of the war.

The Waller family genealogy contains references to William the Conqueror on the Waller side and George Washington's grandfather Joseph Ball on the Creswell side, with a United States Senator from the late eighteenth century thrown in for good measure. With such a family tree it is not surprising that Waller seemed destined for public service. His father Albert, called "Squire" Waller, moved to Greenwood from his first home a few miles south of the town in 1834 and was appointed first postmaster for Woodville three years later. The squire and his wife, Jane Elizabeth "Betsy" Creswell, had eleven children, eight of whom lived to maturity and three of whom were killed in the Civil War. Most of the Waller sons were christened with most interesting classical names, as detailed in another chapter, but none was more fancifully named than Creswell Archimedes Calhoun, who was born in either 1838 or 1840, depending upon which version of his age at his death in 1920 one believes. His obituary insists that he died only a month shy of his 80th birthday, while his tombstone in Magnolia Cemetery is engraved "Aged

82 Years." A newspaper sketch of Waller's career states that the first brick houses built as schools by the Baptists and Methodists (presumably including both Fuller Institute and Hodges Institute) were part of Albert Waller's estate at his death and, "by consent of the family became at a nominal figure religious and education edifices for a few years." Strangely enough, the sketch notes that Waller "never received a dollar for this part of the building and grounds." (Note: the records consulted for the section on Brewer School state that the Hodges Institute building was sold after the war to satisfy a mortgage held by Albert Waller. Chris Waller was evidently sensitive on the matter and wished it known that he realized no personal gain from this transaction.)

Although Waller's first business venture after the war was the firm of Waller, Gaillard, and Waller, which he formed with his brother Cadmus Garlington and I. V. Gaillard, his profession as merchant always allowed room for public service and great involvement in educational pursuits. His career was described as "restless almost in its activity for the growth of Greenwood." Waller is credited with holding fast to the town square, or plaza, configuration first proposed by Dr. E. R. Calhoun. Some businessmen wanted to build stores and warehouses with their backs to the railroad tracks for the sake of convenience. Waller's steadfast resistance on the grounds that such moves would effectively destroy the square as he and others envisioned it made enemies for a time of those who proposed them, but in the long run Waller was proved right and the square eventually developed as the city fathers hoped it would. Waller was among the first to realize that Greenwood was handicapped by bad public roads which made for difficult access to the trading center. His solution was simple: open up the public roads and open new streets. This preoccupation with roads and streets might be considered the opening wedge to Waller's interest in "the bigger field of railroads."

Waller was elected Intendant (Mayor) of Greenwood in 1872. The term *intendant* was evidently a holdover from colonial times, since it is defined as an administrative post in a monarchy. The office of intendant was created in the 1600s by Cardinal Richelieu to strengthen royal authority in the provinces of France. Intendants were meant to represent the crown in provincial administration: they supervised the collection of taxes, the administration of justice, and the raising of troops. It is interesting indeed that this appellation for the highest elected official in a town was still in use more than a hundred years after America won its independence from the British crown. In Greenwood, the office was first called mayor in 1897.

Captain Waller served several terms as intendant. In addition to his first term, he is known to have been elected also in 1879, 1886, and 1887. There were probably other terms as well; the records are far from complete. Terms of office in the early days were for only one year, and municipal elections were held in January. In Waller's day the town also had four wardens who, along with the intendant, formed the town council. The newspaper described Waller's first term as particularly "troublous," since black council members outnumbered whites three to two. But Waller's famous tact and grit prevailed, and he managed to push through a new charter for the town during his first term.

Waller was also instrumental in the struggle to build direct railroad connections between Greenwood and Augusta, Georgia. Freight rates for the roundabout method of shipping goods to that distribution center were becoming prohibitive in the late 1860s, and Greenwood druggist and physician Dr. E. R. Calhoun, along with Waller and other businessmen, decided to see what could be done about another railroad. The outcome was the opening of the Augusta and Knoxville Railroad in 1882, fourteen years after discussions commenced. Waller gave credit for the route finally chosen to a Dr. Parks of Parksville, but it was Waller's idea for work to begin at the Greenwood end; he feared the money might run out before the line was finished, and Abbeville might be able to step in and "get the fruits of Greenwood's labors."

C. M. Calhoun confirmed the story of the Augusta-Knoxville line in *Liberty Dethroned* and included in his account a few shenanigans recognizable today as effective public relations tactics. It seems that E. R. Calhoun dreamed up the idea of publishing a story describing a great mass meeting in Greenwood on the subject of a railroad line to Augusta. The "mass meeting" had, in fact, been nothing more than a conversation among three men in Calhoun's drug store. Evidently it worked, since real public meetings, including barbecues and picnics with speakers for the railroad, began soon afterward. One ploy was particularly effective: after the overthrow of Radical Rule in 1876, supporters hit on the idea of a railroad meeting after Democrat Party gatherings. Calhoun wrote that the turning point came when the state provided "100 able bodied convicts for their board, clothes and three dollars per month," thus virtually assuring the grading for the road. Work was begun, in Calhoun's colorful phrase, "on a bushel of meal and a side of bacon." For its part in the enterprise, Augusta finally agreed to built twelve miles of road and an iron bridge over the Savannah River. Calhoun called the building of this railroad a "gigantic scheme" which, in spite of continued opposition from Abbeville, was carried through to "successful termination." But there was a dark side to the use of convict labor. One hundred twenty-eight prisoners working under a convict-lease system on the Greenwood-Augusta line died in 1879, mostly from sickness caused by the appalling living conditions in the stockade.

Waller participated in another railroad venture in 1886 with, once again, Abbeville in opposition. This time Waller subjected Abbeville Judge W. C. Benet to public humiliation at a meeting in Columbia. Benet's remarks had left the impression that towns around Greenwood were anxious for the road, but Greenwood's contribution had been nothing but hot air. The charge infuriated Waller. He rose to rebut the speaker and immediately began to call out actual dollar subscriptions from Greenwood backers with a challenge to Abbeville to match the offers. Abbeville delegates had not reached the point of pledges and were in no position to meet such a challenge. Some Abbeville men quietly approached Waller and urged him to let up on Judge Benet who was by this time painfully embarrassed. Waller responded with a parable of sorts: in the old days, he said, a baby crying in church was either spanked or taken out. If he were not taken out, Benet would simply have to be spanked, and he wanted the crowd to know that C. A. C. Waller was equal to the task. That railroad, too, became a reality from Monroe, North Carolina, to Greenwood in 1890 and to Atlanta two years later. Nor was this the last of Waller's interest in Greenwood as a railroad center. During his second term as state senator (1908-1912), Waller was among those who actively promoted the sale of railroad stock to fulfill the pledges Greenwood had made for service by the Piedmont & Northern Railway.

An early venture into politics came in 1888 when Waller was elected to the General Assembly as a representative from Abbeville County. Two years later he was defeated by less than 100 votes in a race for the senate. The newspaper sketch hinted, perhaps as a face saver, that Waller ran only because he was urged to do so and "against his personal wishes." From that time on Waller was untiring in his efforts for the new county. Those efforts constituted a "memorable struggle," primarily on the question of the eight or ten mile limit between county seats and county lines. Mary Hemphill Green provided an amusing Waller anecdote from the early days of the fight in the General Assembly when setbacks came thick and fast. When one bill went down to defeat, it happened so quickly that Waller was unable to follow. He kept asking, "What happened? What happened?" When told the bill had been knocked out on a technicality, his response was, "Technicality! Technicality! Well, damn technicality!"

C. M. Calhoun also related a couple of amusing incidents in the great battle between Abbeville and Greenwood. One concerned a delegation from Abbeville to Governor Tillman's wife beseeching her to intervene on their behalf with her husband. Their argument was that two anti-Tillman counties would be the result of splitting Abbeville, which at that time was considered pro-Tillman territory. Calhoun heaped this effort with self-righteous scorn in the line: "Oh! for shame to use such an argument." Another outrage came "on the very eve of dismemberment" when Abbeville County incurred a debt for eight road scrapers and 32 fine mules to pull them. Greenwood was expected to pay its share and had voted for the expenditure with the expectation that Greenwood would receive part of this important asset at the proper time. As it turned out, Abbeville officials balked at any division and refused to use the scrapers on Greenwood's side of the new county line. The case was fought all the way to the state supreme court, and the matter was eventually resolved by a referee who awarded to Greenwood the appropriate share of scrapers and mules.

Abbeville did not give up easily and tried one maneuver after another to defeat Greenwood's bid. Calhoun charged that one prominent Abbeville delegate tried to get a Greenwood supporter too drunk to cast his vote, only to have his scheme backfire when the Greenwood delegate proved he could outdrink his opponent and still show up for the vote. After the smoke cleared, Calhoun wrote rather smugly but with a certain magnanimity that the separation proved a "great advantage to Greenwood and Abbeville too. It has . . . created a pleasant rivalry between the two towns urging each on to greater deeds of progress." Among the greater deeds of progress for Greenwood was Waller's successful bid to bring a female college to the town. That story is told in the chapter on Lander College.

Chris Waller's private life, alas, was not nearly so successful as his public career. His wife was Mary Elizabeth "Molly" Vance, a daughter of leading citizen Allen Vance who is believed to have built the historic Vance-Maxwell house on East Cambridge Avenue about 1850. Some people said Vance accepted Waller only to please her family; at any rate, the marriage was not a happy union, and at some point this childless couple "of distinguished lineage" parted company. Louis Wright described them in later life as "two of the most conspicuous oddities" in a town that "teemed with picturesque characters known for their idiosyncrasies." Wright observed that they often could be seen walking their separate ways about the town square, each asserting that the other was crazy. One episode involving this interesting couple is included here just as Louis Wright recorded it in *Barefoot in Arcadia*:

> Chris cultivated cats, some thirty or forty, which followed him about the streets. Every butcher shop in town was instructed to save liver and scraps, which Chris collected for his trooping gang of cats. Miss Mollie favored geese, ducks, and scrawny chickens, which roosted in and about her house. She gathered up old boxes and barrels, filled them with straw, and scattered them around her front piazza for the convenience of nesting poultry. Every spring, flocks of goslings and ducklings emerged from Miss Mollie's front yard to dodge wagons and buggies as they headed for a puddle of water under the nearby standpipe, receptacle of the town's water supply.
>
> What to do about obvious violations of health ordinances by Chris's cats and Miss Mollie's poultry, visible and troublesome to the fastidious, was the subject of frequent debate in town council. But both had been honored residents of the town since the Civil War, nobody wanted to cause them embarrassment, and the

> authorities did nothing. Perhaps they were wise, for Miss Mollie got in the habit of sitting on her front steps with a shotgun lest anyone molest a nesting goose or try to cart off any of her precious trash.
>
> For his part, Chris continued to feed his cats in his rooms during rainy spells, but on fine days he scattered liver on the sidewalks and let the cats fight over it. If a few dozen mangy cats growling over bloody scraps disturbed citizens walking that way, Chris took no notice of them.
>
> Finally, the town council concluded that something must be done to clean up the mess made by Chris's cats and Miss Mollie's fowls. So a delegation of diplomats was chosen to try to reason with them. Tactfully, they approached Miss Mollie with offers of help with her "spring-cleaning" or the care of her expanding flocks of poultry. For a time she listened, then a light dawned. "I know what you think. You believe I'm crazy. I tell you what I'll do. Let both Chris and me go to the Asylum [for the insane] in Columbia. Then whoever the doctors decide is the craziest they can keep." When this proposition was broached to Chris, he refused to risk it. The council's efforts came to naught, and only illness and death a few years later solved the problem.

A final scrap of information on this beloved Greenwood character was contained in an undated newspaper clipping in May Bailey Smith's collection. The writer's name is unknown, but the title, "Capt. Waller's Squirt Gun Got a Sousing," probably insured that everyone made a point of reading the anecdote:

> Several incidents of the long ago published in this column recently have reminded one old-timer who was a member of the Voluntary Fire Department back in the 1890's of a sousing given Capt. C. A. C. Waller and his squirt gun at a conflagration. The Department answered a call to the warehouse at the Greenwood Mill and Capt. Waller with his gun and bucket of water was already there. This seemed to confuse the fire fighters and all of a sudden by accident (and on purpose) the hose got unmanageable and the flow of water splashed on Capt. Waller and his gun, completely sousing him while the little stream about the size of a pencil was squirting a flow about 15 feet long.
>
> As soon as he could get himself and his little gun together he picked up his bucket and left. The record does not show what he said as he strode away.

Jimmy Wade believes C. A. C. Waller possessed "foresight, perseverance, stubbornness, and conviction," traits that combined to make him a leading figure in the development of Greenwood County. His home for many years was a large house at 428 Main Street, diagonally across from the C&WC Railroad freight depot on the square. Waller Street is named in his honor.

* * * *

Certainly no county office, particularly an elective or constitutional office, is unimportant. Some, however, are simply more interesting than others, and those dealing with law enforcement might be the most interesting of all. No county office has an older or more romantic history than that of sheriff. The very name conjures up visions of Robin Hood and his merry band of outlaws outwitting the Sheriff of Nottingham, and the office itself dates from Anglo-Saxon times (generally regarded as lasting from sometime in the fifth century to the Norman Conquest in 1066). The word *sheriff* derives from two words: *shire*, an administrative district comprising several smaller districts united for the purpose of more efficient governance and inaugurated in England by Alfred the Great (849-899), and *reeve*, defined as a local administrative agent of an Anglo-Saxon king. The "shire-reeve" was, in fact, the hands-on, or practical, representative of the king, although nominally he was subordinate to the alderman, who was the appointed royal officer over the shire.

Oddly enough, the English sheriff is becoming an endangered species. According to an article in *The Atlanta Constitution* of May 2, 1985, the number of sheriffs in England and Wales dwindled from more than thirty in the 1950s to only sixteen in 1985. A group of sheriffs met that year to form the National Shrievalty Association in an attempt to save their office from extinction. Their superiors, called county high sheriffs, had formed an association of their own ten years earlier. Most people blamed Prime Minister Margaret Thatcher's tight money policies for the decline of the office of sheriff to largely ceremonial status. The most visible duty of English sheriffs – summoning juries and serving writs for the assize courts – ended in 1972 when the assize court system was dismantled, and sheriffs were left without a practical function. Although county high sheriffs still have duties, primarily those of seizing debtors' property and evicting illegal tenants, everybody agrees that sheriffs are a vanishing breed in modern England.

Fortunately such is not the case in South Carolina, and the office of sheriff in Greenwood County is in a flourishing state indeed with its staff of 58, including 38 deputies, and a 78-bed jail currently housing 95 inmates. Greenwood County has had only six sheriffs in its history; framed portraits and biographical sketches of the first five are displayed on the wall of Sheriff Samuel P. Riley's office in the city-county law enforcement center on Edgefield Street. Greenwood County Sheriffs from the beginning are Robert Foster McCaslan, 1897-1907; T. W. McMillian, 1907-1920; Eugene Melvin White, 1920-1941; J. Cal White, 1941-1964;

L. Giles Daniel, 1965-1989; and Samuel P. Riley, 1990 -. McCaslan's sketch covers primarily his Civil War service but also includes the dates of his birth (September 4, 1836) and death (May 5, 1907) and the names of his children, all of whom evidently lived in Greenwood. Two McCaslan sons – Robert Foster, Jr., and Gustavus Walker – became partners in McCaslan's Book Store, and a daughter married one of early businessman Joel Bailey's sons. McCaslan was a member of the South Carolina Constitutional Convention of 1895 and is supposed to have switched his support to Greenwood's bid to become a county when he was promised the office of first sheriff.

The biographical sketch of the second sheriff reveals very little about him but gives a great deal of information on the last three hangings in Greenwood before the electric chair was adopted as the means of execution by the state. All three hangings took place during a period of less than three years, all were for the crime of murder, and all happened during Sheriff McMillian's time in office. The names of the honorees are surely irrelevant after eighty years or so, but, in the same macabre vein, readers might be interested in a blurb included in a column of outstanding news events from 1912-1917 by E. P. Wideman. That item, entitled "Electric Chair is Ready," is dated June 1912:

> Five prisoners in South Carolina are standing within the shadow of the electric chair and these will be the first to pay the death penalty since the substitution of the chair for the gallows. Samuel N. Hyde, Anderson man who killed his wife and her father, asked Judge Prince, who sentenced him last week, to place the time so that he might be the first man to die in the chair in South Carolina. July 5 was the date named for the execution of Hyde. [Note: Hyde may have been a murderer, but no one can question that he had a sense of history. Even his name fits.]

Greenwood's executions took place "in the jail yard on a scaffold erected each time for the purpose." One hopes Sheriff McMillian is remembered for something else by somebody. On the other hand, he undoubtedly did his duty.

Greenwood's third sheriff, Eugene Melvin White, is described as "one of the best known and most highly respected men in this part of South Carolina. . . . He enjoyed a very fine reputation as an exceptionally able, efficient and conscientious public official and was popular with all classes." Sheriff White was remembered also as a farmer and fox hunter.

The next sheriff was the colorful J. Cal White, whose career in law enforcement spanned 44 years. He was the county's first motorcycle officer under Sheriff E. M. White and was elected sheriff upon the retirement of his predecessor. The two Sheriffs White were not related, nor was former Chief Deputy Harold White related to either sheriff. Modern law enforcement techniques began during Sheriff Cal White's 24-year tenure. The official sketch tells it best:

> [I]n 1947, the Sheriff's department consisted of the Sheriff, three deputies and several mill deputies. Mill deputies were assigned to the various mill villages. Half of the deputy's salary was paid by the County, the other half by the textile firms. Uncovering liquor stills and arresting bootleggers was one of the Sheriff department's biggest activities at that time.
>
> During the time White served as Sheriff, there was no South Carolina Criminal Justice Academy, nor were there training schools or seminars for law enforcement officers. It was more or less on the job training. When you went to work they gave you a gun and a badge and told you to go to work. However . . . Sheriff White was a great believer in sending his deputies to the few training courses that were available and was very enthusiastic about scientific methods of criminal investigation. Greenwood County's first murderer to be convicted on ballistic evidence presented by FBI experts was during Sheriff White's tenure. The law enforcement officers' major clue was the bullet recovered from the body. The break in the case came when the man who was eventually convicted of the murder pawned a 22 automatic pistol.

Cal White is also remembered as the father of a rather famous Clemson quarterback, Harvey White.

Sheriff No. 5 was L. Giles Daniel who, like his predecessor, served for 24 years. Seventeen years a deputy under Cal White, Giles Daniel's career as sheriff was very different from that of his mentor. He graduated from the FBI National Academy, for one thing, and he saw service on the USS Hornet aircraft carrier while serving a three-year stint in the navy. For another, while Daniel himself received only on-the-job, practical training, his staff were required to complete a course at the Criminal Justice Academy which was established during his tenure. Daniel was also shot in the line of duty in 1961. As for working conditions in the sheriff's department, Daniel's sketch reads: "In 1965, there were ten deputies. When Sheriff Daniel first came to work there was only one shift, seven days a week, 24 hours a day. During his tenure he established a work schedule with four shifts and a detective division. At the time of his retirement there were fifty deputies and two secretaries on the work force." Giles Daniel was honored many times, including an award for Outstanding Sheriff's Department in South Carolina in 1971, and Governor Carroll Campbell presented him with the state's highest award, the Order of the Palmetto, at his retirement dinner in 1989.

Most Greenwood County sheriffs were well versed in department matters before they were elected, and county native Sam Riley is no exception. He began his career as a deputy in 1966 and has participated firsthand in a great many changes in law enforcement in Greenwood County. The present courthouse, for example, was brand new when Riley went to work, and the chief deputy, Sonny Cooper, lived in the county jail, a rather forbidding white-painted brick structure on Edgefield Street. Riley pointed out that until 1968 the sheriff was compensated (one hopes only in part) on a per-prisoner basis, and at one time the sheriff's wife was expected to provide meals for the prisoners. She received no compensation, official or otherwise, for this service, unless her husband chose to provide a little butter-and-egg money now and then. The same jail served until the new center was built with the aid of a federal grant in 1975. The sheriff does not live there.

In addition to its able-bodied male deputies and other employees, Greenwood County law enforcement boasts a female captain and division head with thirty years of service. Lina Riley Blizzard went to work after graduation from Lander College in 1961. After about ten years of doing "deputy-type" work outside her job description simply because it had to be done, she was deputized as a full member of the department, including qualifying to carry a gun. Blizzard's career has concentrated primarily in the criminal records division which she currently heads, but she has also worked with female prisoners almost from the beginning. She observes that the steady increase of female lawbreakers would have necessitated a female officer at some point. The fact that she was already in place simply meant her job didn't have to be invented somewhere along the way.

Emphasizing the point that sheriffs are in a class by themselves in county government, Greenville County Sheriff Johnny Mack Brown wrote in a publication of the National Sheriffs' Association:

> Clearly, the office of sheriff is not simply another department of county government. Its internal operations are the sole responsibility of the sheriff. County department heads are subordinate to a county administrator or manager because they are truly only a division of county government, and they work for him and for the governing body of the county council (or the board of commissioners). The office of sheriff, on the other hand, is a constitutional office in 35 states having exclusive powers and authority. These powers are not subject to the dictates of a county manager or the whims of a county council. The powers of this office have been exercised for over a millennium.

* * * *

With its county status firmly in place and with growth underway, in the county seat at least, Greenwood probably felt itself ready to face whatever the twentieth century might bring. For many years after Reconstruction, which was more harshly visited on South Carolina as the instigator of war than on other southern states, there was really nowhere to go but up. Though the whole state was rural, South Carolina's economy in no sense represented the noble Jeffersonian ideal of a nation of (presumably self-sufficient) small farms. What would become known as "the farm problem" began as the state tried to put itself together after Radical Rule and culminated with the agricultural depression of the 1920s. An article in *The State's* centennial edition of February 24, 1991, could have been written about Greenwood County: "Not only was the land poor," the article reads, "but so were those who farmed it." The agricultural sector virtually collapsed during the 1920s from overproduction of cotton followed by loss of overseas markets, drought, and the boll weevil. All that was bad enough; even worse was the fact that much of the state's farmland, particularly in the upstate, was poor in comparison to elsewhere in the South, and a great deal was actually worn out from the one-crop economy. The abuse of the land was so severe that by 1934 eight million acres were declared "destroyed." Many farmers, who at best had tilled only 15-25 acres, were forced to a life of tenant farming or migratory labor in order to feed their families. Worst of all, neither tenants nor landowners made money in the 1920s, according to the article. (Note: this is a very broad generalization; almost anyone could cite exceptions.)

Against such a backdrop, it is not surprising that county services in the first decades of the new century left much to be desired in Greenwood. The sad state of the school districts of that era is covered in another chapter. Building an infrastructure of roads and bridges was a slow and torturous process because of the simple fact that there was no money. And the amenities of life that most citizens now take for granted, such as electricity, running water, and indoor plumbing, came to Greenwood county residents about forty years after they were introduced into the town. Telephones took even longer; many homes lacked phones until well into the 1950s. As a matter of fact, the electrification of the county had to wait until the federal government got into the act after the election of Franklin D. Roosevelt in 1932. An article in *The Index-Journal* centennial edition covered the county's entry into this new world succinctly: "In 1938 the Buzzard Roost power project was made certain after five years' effort by Greenwood County, and the county-owned hydro-electric plant went into operation in August 1940."

But that single sentence holds many stories. One is contained in a full page ad sponsored by the Greenwood County Electric Power Commission in the same edition. Copy for that ad states that access to electricity on the nation's farms jumped from 11% to almost 100% as the result of the rural electrification program and that none of the systems was built by the federal government itself. The government loaned money only after local groups designed plans for building economically sound systems and signed up enough consumers to support the system and insure repayment of the loan. What could be simpler or more ordinary? Nothing, it seems in retrospect, except the determination whether it was legal for a public entity such as Greenwood County to instigate such a project with federal funds, thus in effect denying business to private utility companies already in existence. That determination would take five years to finalize, even though the original application by the county for the first loan took only seven months for approval. The Rural Electrification Administration executive order, which came about later, specifically allowed loans to farmers' cooperatives, public power districts, private utilities, and "other agencies," but the funds that built the Buzzard Roost power plant on the Saluda River were granted under the auspices of the Public Works Administration (PWA), an agency of the federal government designed to put the country back to work. Greenwood made its application simply as a county, or political subdivision. A chronology of events was provided in a special edition of the newspaper on April 14, 1938: the county filed with the State PWA Board in November 1933 and gained approval the following month. Duke Power Company, a North Carolina utility, filed its first protest at the time of approval by the PWA in Washington, and the disputed issue then went to the Power Board of Review at which Greenwood was asked to substantiate its estimate of the project's cost. The net result of the review was that Greenwood not only won the skirmish but also had its allotment increased by $90,000. Next, the PWA required the county to bring a test suit in the state supreme court. Duke asked to intervene in that suit but was told it could do so only if no new issues were raised. Since it was marshaling quite a few arguments, the power company took no further action at that point, and the county won in the state court also, in September 1934. The first federal court hearing was held in December of that year; Duke appealed that verdict, and the case went first to the circuit court of appeals and from there to the United States Supreme Court in 1936. The matter was referred again to lower courts, and Greenwood finally won a favorable decision in December 1937. The first Supreme Court hearing, in November 1936, is considered here; the second was merely a review and affirmation of a decree by the circuit court that private power companies had no right to challenge the action of the government in making loans and grants. The question might have been moot at that point in any event, since the REA had been established in 1935.

Duke Power Company's position was that the county would be acting in a proprietary function by operating a utility, and the strictly intrastate character of that utility did not answer any constitutional requirement for using federal funds. Besides, the power company argued, the county would be in direct competition with Duke in the matter of setting rates and would be in an unfairly advantageous position because of its federal subsidy. The county's position was that its power to act came directly from the general welfare clause of the constitution and that projects such as Buzzard Roost served to promote employment throughout the nation, a not insignificant argument at that period of the depression. Furthermore, the county was "in darkness" because of "inadequate facilities" provided by Duke, its counsel argued, and Greenwood had a clear duty to rectify that situation when the means came its way.

As the case meandered its way through the courts, gathering steam and growing more and more complex, it attracted a great deal of attention in the press. When it reached the Supreme Court in late 1936, the Raleigh *News and Observer* wrote that the justices' decision, when it came, might not be the final word. Difficulties over technical procedures in the appeals court still threatened. An opinion by one judge enjoining the government from spending, and Greenwood County from receiving, funds for such a purpose on the grounds of unconstitutionality had been reversed by another judge. But that problem was merely a sidebar when the United States Supreme Court heard the case on November 10, 1936. Since the arguments would be along constitutional lines and would affect a great many similar projects, Greenwood County found itself a litigant in one of the landmark cases dealing with New Deal legislation. The importance of the issue was impossible to overstate even at the time. Not only would the court's decision settle Greenwood's case and about eighty others still pending, it would also determine the validity of the government's entire program of aiding local power plants. The *News and Observer* noted that the "court itself recognized the importance of the case in two ways: by doubling the time usually allotted for argument of a case and by the unusual number of questions asked counsel from the bench."

Counsel participating in the argument included W. S. O'B. Robinson and Newton D. Baker for Duke Power Company, Solicitor General Stanley Reed and Jerome N. Frank for the government, and State Senator W. H. Nicholson and D. W. Robinson, Jr., of Columbia, for Greenwood County. Duke's attorneys tried to assert that Greenwood's acceptance of federal funds violated the entire principle of states' rights and placed the federal government, in effect, in competition with private enterprise. Newspaper accounts judged the participation of Greenwood's attorneys "far from perfunctory," adding, "They pretty well exploded the arguments . . . that the project was really that of the federal government rather than Greenwood County." The *News and Observer* devoted several paragraphs to the performance of the attorneys for Greenwood. Reporter Robert E. Williams's version of that performance is preferable to any paraphrasing:

> Senator Nicholson, whose Southern drawl attracted attention as he repeatedly said "May it please the cote," spoke with as little

> restraint or embarrassment as if he had been addressing a jury in his own county instead of the most august tribunal in the world.
>
> Mr. Nicholson, who was interrupted less than any of the attorneys, denied the contention of Mr. Baker that South Carolina had surrendered its sovereignty by permitting its counties to accept federal funds. He declared that the project did not initiate with PWA, but with the governing board of Greenwood County, because nine-tenths of the electric power used in that vicinity was generated by cotton mills unwilling to pay the rates of the Duke Power Company and because there was virtually no rural electrification available. Both he and Mr. Robinson stressed the relative unimportance of the project compared to the operations of the Duke Power Company, and Mr. Robinson also stressed the fact that under the South Carolina statute the PWA would have no more control than would the bond holders of a private power company.
>
> Today was homespun day in the court, neither of the South Carolina lawyers, the North Carolina Robinson, nor Mr. Frank wearing the formal clothes usually affected by attorneys arguing cases before the court, a convention observed today only by Solicitor General Reed and Mr. Baker.

The New York Times reported the case as "the contest between the Roosevelt Administration and the power corporations over the government's right to make grants and loans for publicly owned hydroelectric plants as part of the relief program." The newspaper viewed the suit as one of the most important involving New Deal issues and one that could determine the fate of the entire $3.3 billion originally set aside for public works relief projects. Greenwood's grant/loan of $2,852,000 to build the power plant at Buzzard Roost was directly at stake. *The Times* devoted about two columns to the four-hour argument and noted especially the presence of Governor Olin D. Johnston in the chamber. The story seemed to dwell on Duke's contention that the whole purpose of the loan to Greenwood County was no more than an unfair attack on Duke's rates. Newton Baker personalized the issue: "With the treasury open to his hand . . . the PWA administrator has made up his mind that the rates of the Duke Company are too high." One terse Nicholson quote made the *Times* article: in response to Baker's assertion that the state was abdicating to the federal government, he drawled, "They say South Carolina sold her birthright, but I daresay that if counsel looked up the record he would find that every state takes all the money it can get." The *Columbia Record* also covered the case minutely, but its story focused more on the probing questions of the justices directed at Duke's attorneys than on Greenwood's arguments. The *Record* also reported Nicholson's assertion that Duke had provided only seven miles of rural electric lines in Greenwood County.

During closing arguments on Greenwood's day in (United States Supreme) court, Solicitor General Reed stated that the authority for the grant and loan had been sustained by the court in the TVA case, and also that the loan was similar to RFC (Reconstruction Finance Corporation) loans and grants to banks and railroads, thus making it clear that no new ground was being broken. That there were motives beyond the obvious behind most New Deal legislation was made clear in his line, "When a national, widespread situation arises, the government has power to spend under the general welfare clause. The law was not intended to build up local utilities but to relieve distress."

The case was finally settled in Greenwood's favor, but not for another year. A great many issues had to be considered during the first two terms of Franklin D. Roosevelt's administration, since it is generally conceded that the New Deal changed forever the scope of government power in the United States. The sentiment contained in a line by American humorist Finley Peter Dunne in *Mr. Dooley's Opinions* might have had something to do with the decision: "No matter whether the constitution follows the flag or not, the supreme court follows the election returns." And so, as *The Index-Journal* reported in banner headlines on January 3, 1938, the Buzzard Roost project was finally approved with not one dissenting vote, and the way was cleared not only for Greenwood's but also for 51 other power projects across the country costing more than $84 million. Both Alabama Power Company and Duke had challenged the projects, but the court held that the government indeed had the power to make the loans and grants and that any competition engendered thereby was "entirely lawful."

Greenwood was jubilant! At another time and place its citizens might have felt some foreboding about the long-term implications of the court's decision, particularly in view of Wendell Wilkie's comments as reported in the newspaper story of January 3:

> It simply means the federal government now has the right to continue its policy of making outright gifts to municipalities with which to build competing distribution systems to those of private utilities now functioning. No utility, of course, can compete successfully against a . . . plant built in whole or in part with free gifts from the federal government and upon which the municipality does not have to make any return. This is particularly true where it gets its wholesale supply of power at less than cost from such federal agencies as the Tennessee Valley Administration.

But the decision also meant a dramatic improvement in the standard of living for county citizens, and if anyone spoke out against the project, his objections did not make the newspapers. Instead, a victory meeting with PWA administrator Harold L. Ickes as speaker and guest of honor was scheduled for January 5 at the high school auditorium. The newspaper called it a celebration of "the biggest story ever to come Greenwood's way." The meeting would be a three-county affair, since Newberry and Laurens counties would also be affected by "the huge plant to be built on the Saluda River at a total cost of $2,850,000." In addition to federal, state, and county officials invited to participate, the planners announced that the 263rd Coast Artillery Band would lead a parade around the public square before the program at the high school. In case readers missed the point, the newspaper also announced that the Roosevelt campaign song, "Happy Days Are Here Again," would be a feature of the program. One of the most important speeches would be delivered by Dan T. Duncan, project engineer and county native, who would outline plans for the construction phase of the project about to begin.

The Index-Journal printed a special edition dedicated to the Buzzard Roost project on April 14, 1938. The front page featured a copy of a letter to Editor H. L. Watson from President Franklin D. Roosevelt congratulating the county on its victory and expressing the hope that the people would administer the plant and distribution system as a testimonial "to cooperation between local and Federal Government." United States Senator Ellison DuRant "Cotton Ed" Smith, a lukewarm New Dealer who would be elected to his sixth term later in the year, sent his best wishes. He regarded the project as "one of the finest pieces of work ever undertaken in South Carolina." Senator Smith saw it as a story in two parts: one part representing the people's work for five long years, and the other a time when the project would work for the people. Always a champion of the farmer, Smith emphasized the benefits of "lighting and power facilities to hundreds of families previously denied the use of electricity." He echoed the "general welfare" argument from the courtroom when he pointed out the benefits of "the expansive body of water behind the dam" that would be available for fishing, boating, and other forms of recreation.

One article covered the county's progress in land acquisition, stating that the finance board had purchased 228 separate tracts in the basin area, as well as approximately 500 rights of way for power lines. The land purchases ranged from less than an acre to 700 acres in three counties and amounted to a total of about 10,000 acres, most of which would be covered by waters of the lake. Other articles covered Chief Engineer Duncan's description of the dam and details of the construction contracts for dam, power house, and spillway which had been awarded in March. E. W. Grannis of Fayetteville and Lee Construction Company of Charlotte submitted the low bid of $509,678.75 in a contract that called for completion within 365 working days. The dam was to be "an earth structure of selected material composed of fine clay for the center and coarse rock and sandy material for the outer portions." The 50' center portion would be "carried to the rock all the way across the river valley," a plan that required removing 40,000 cubic yards of sand, mud, and river bottom material and pumping out all water until the rock was dry enough to "be swept with a broom." The dam would be 525' thick at the highest point, with a maximum height of 89', some 17' higher than the final water level in the lake. The total length of the dam from Buzzard Roost bluff to the hill on the Greenwood side would be 2,279'. The resulting lake would be at least twenty miles long with about 200 miles of shoreline. Engineers anticipated that two months of normal weather conditions would be sufficient time for the lake to be filled completely after the dam was constructed. Power transmission lines would deliver current to Newberry, Laurens, Clinton, Ninety Six, and Greenwood; power was to be furnished wholesale to cities and manufacturing interests. Duncan stated the cost to consumers would be about 40% under current rates of Duke Power Company. First estimates of the labor force required were about 1,500 workers within the first few months and several hundred more before the project was completed.

The project was under the control of the county finance board during the construction phase. The board's secretary, Emmett I. Davis, was heavily involved, as were the county supervisor, auditor, superintendent of education, and treasurer. It is easy to believe that the county came of age in important ways as it worked on the most far-reaching project it had ever undertaken. The plant began operation in August 1940 with the first delivery of energy to Panola and Grendel Mills of the Abney chain. Countywide service was under the auspices of the Greenwood County Rural Electric System which had been formed in 1937 with the aid of REA loans. Responsibility for operating Buzzard Roost rested with the Greenwood County Electric Power Commission created by the legislature in 1940. The Commission also governed the rural electric system and was itself answerable directly to the county. John B. Sloan was chairman, Emmett I. Davis was secretary-treasurer, and O. A. Moore was operating superintendent. The new plant operated with an installed capacity of 21,000 kilowatts – three 5,000 kw hydro-turbine generators and one 6,000 kw steam turbo-generator. An additional 10,000 kw steam generator was installed in 1948 at a cost of $1.4 million. A 1957 newspaper article reported that the system employed 39 people at that time.

No one argues even today that the Buzzard Roost project was anything but a success. It would be hard to imagine life without Lake Greenwood, and the county's legal struggles at the beginning became simply another dramatic episode in the county's rather dramatic history. Greenwood County operated the facility for more than 25 years until, in another dramatic move in 1966, voters approved the sale of the plant to the county's old nemesis, Duke Power Company, for the equivalent of $20 million, payable over a period of years. A book, or at least a large pamphlet, could be written on the moves and countermoves that culminated in the sale. For purposes of this chapter, however, only one rather homespun point will be made: State Senator W. H. Nicholson, the lawyer-legislator who established a unique place for himself in county history when he argued Greenwood's case before the United States Supreme Court, served in the General Assembly during the entire time the project was planned, fought for, and built; his son, Francis B. Nicholson, happened to be in the South Carolina Senate at the time of the negotiations and sale to Duke Power Company. Not surprisingly, Senator Francis Nicholson personally opposed the sale.

* * * *

Greenwood's current status as a major regional medical center evolved very slowly, although the first recorded convention held in the village was a meeting of the South Carolina Medical Association on July 18, 1855. The prominence of Dr. John Perkins Barratt was almost certainly the overriding reason for that meeting; evidently he alone was the "committee of arrangement" that advertised it in Abbeville newspapers. The stated purpose was to "show forth the aims of the association" and invite practitioners of the profession to join. In addition to a speech by Barratt that "enchained the audience for more than an hour," the convention featured papers on dysentery, tumors, and "medical faith." Best of all were the "elegant entertainments" at Dr. E. R. Calhoun's hotel and a visit to Barratt's "delightful residence" and museum at Chinquapin Ridge.

Greenwood was well supplied with medical men from its first days as a village; an article in a Charleston newspaper in 1889 mentioned seven by name and called the profession the only one that could "lay claim to being crowded." The article noted, however, that most had other sources of livelihood besides their profession; obviously there were still traces of the gentleman-physician concept of an earlier era. Medical care was provided in doctors' offices, most likely in their homes, or through house calls. Dr. G. Pressly Neel, for example, practiced with Dr. J. C. Maxwell and observed office hours daily, both mornings and afternoons. There was no clinic or hospital for more than fifty years after the town was chartered and for more than a decade after it became a county seat. And the move for a hospital, when it came, had the usual interesting twist.

The first Greenwood hospital, which opened in 1911 and served the county until Self Memorial was completed in 1951, was not only planned and built by women but was also under their control and management for 34 years of its operation. Certainly that might not be unique, since women's contributions to society in no sense began with the women's liberation movement of modern vintage, but it is a notable achievement in Greenwood County history. Plans to build a hospital were first discussed seriously in 1907 at a meeting called by physicians, but no definite steps were taken for another year. The Greenwood County Hospital Association was formed in May 1908 under the guidance of Dr. R. B. Epting, but officers and directors were all female from the start. This level of responsibility had not been sought by the women themselves; indeed they probably expected to be relegated to their customary auxiliary roles when they attended the organizational meeting at the courthouse. But, if a 1957 newspaper article is correct, a "prominent Greenwood attorney" urged that the project be placed directly in the hands of women on the grounds that they had more time and would work more enthusiastically than men. Time and enthusiasm they undoubtedly had, as well as organizational skill and tenacity; they also had an advisory board made up of town and county men who could be counted on to contribute money and work on committees. No doubt men were also available to give advice and encouragement. Mrs. B. F. Duckett, the first president of the Association, served only one year, but the second, Mrs. E. D. Andrews, presided until the women gave up management 33 years later. Other prominent officers and board members included Mrs. H. J. Brinson, Mrs. G. W. Rush, Mrs. E. H. Williams, Mrs. H. V. R. Schrader, and Mrs. A. Rosenberg. These women and other recruits "struggled valiantly with bazaars, entertainments and suppers to raise money for the hospital" until they were able to purchase the site on West Creswell and Edgefield Avenues in late 1909. At that point the men threw their support wholeheartedly into the effort. County citizens bought stock certificates; individuals contributed $150 each to furnish a room; the doctors themselves gave the operating room equipment; and, of all things, the ladies had the idea of throwing a shower to provide linens, pillows, and other small items. A nursing school with six students opened concurrently with the hospital in 1911; one of the first two graduates was still doing private duty nursing at Self Memorial as late as 1957.

The first Greenwood hospital was built at a cost of $12,000 and could accommodate only 35 patients. Still, it was undoubtedly a hospital, and Greenwood was on its way. A two-story nurses' residence, made possible by a $5,000 gift from William H. Bailey, was added to the complex in 1914; and a second wing, identical to the first, that increased the hospital's capacity to 52 was built in 1924 for $25,000. Still another substantial addition was built in 1937, but the hospital lost its nursing school that year because it was still too small to meet the requirements set by the American College of Surgeons. The school did, however, reopen for a time to aid the war effort during World War II.

Having demonstrated that they were equal to the task of management, the women of the Greenwood County Hospital Association voted a hand-picked board of men in, and themselves out of office, in 1942. The men they chose were first rate, as proven by the letter of acceptance sent by John B. Sloan, R. B. Curry, Douglas Featherstone, H. E. Keifer, Jr., James C. Self, and F. E. Grier at the time of the transfer of authority:

> We are well aware of the untiring efforts of your board over a period of 30-odd years and we consider it one of the most outstanding contributions ever made to Greenwood. No other community, city or county, can boast of a hospital such as Greenwood's due to the work of a small group of civic-minded women. [Perhaps the undertaking was unique after all.]

Only two years after the transition to male control, the hospital suffered severe damage from a devastating tornado that roared through Greenwood and was forced to close for repairs and renovations. During that period James C. Self announced that The Self Foundation would build a new hospital as a gift to the community as soon as materials became available after the war. Possibly Self would have done it anyway, since such thinking was definitely part of his philosophy, but one can speculate that the notion of a reward for the county's own efforts for more than thirty years was somewhere in his mind at the time. Of all the damage wrought by the tornado, somehow that to the hospital was among the most poignant: a place of healing, much of which was suddenly rubble. The roof of the main structure was ripped off, several walls were shattered, and extensive other damage was sustained. Self's announcement must have meant a great deal to a board facing the trauma of rebuilding.

Self Memorial Hospital was originally planned as a concrete and steel structure with a capacity of 100 beds, but that estimate had nearly doubled to a 179-bed facility by the time it was actually built. The first patients were accepted in November 1951; since that time the hospital has seldom been without a major building program – on the drawing board, in progress, just completed, or all three. The hospital is now among the largest employers in the county and encompasses medical specialties and facilities undreamed of only a generation ago. James C. Self believed that no medical service or facility could be too fine for the community he called home. That conception has been sustained in a remarkable way as the hospital grew in service and capacity over the years. From its humble beginnings in the early years of the twentieth century when a few women brought a dream to reality, the hospital has evolved into a state-of-the-art monolith that fills the space between Edgefield and Spring Streets for several blocks and spills over into related complexes nearby. Now the hub of a busy medical center, Self Memorial Hospital has also grown from one man's notion of a gift to his home town all the way to an institution that serves an entire region.

The story of Greenwood County Library began in 1901 when a small room over a store was fitted out by interested merchants and 368 books contributed by individuals were placed in the care of a volunteer librarian. This modest beginning was the result of the formation of the Library Association earlier the same year. Membership dues of association members provided the bulk of financial support for the new "library"; other sources of revenue were occasional benefit suppers and entertainments. The newspaper reported that the room "in the Riley Annex building over Bolton's store" was the result of the largess of C. A. C. Waller; potential patrons were reminded that anyone could visit the library and read there, but only association members were permitted to check books out. The library was moved later "to the upstairs of the new city hall," according to a 1957 article. If this account of the library's first two locations on the east side of the square is correct, a map of Greenwood as it appeared in 1908 must be in error, since it places the library upstairs in the Oregon Hotel building on the west side. Regardless of the various locations of Greenwood's first library, which was in reality little more than a reading room, the association continued to prosper and elected its first advisory board of men in 1905. The first named librarian, presumably a volunteer, was Julia Lee; presidents of the Library Association also donated their services behind the circulation desk from time to time.

The movement to obtain a separate public library was spearheaded by H. L. Watson and Samuel C. Hodges early in 1916. Greenwood received a grant of $12,500 from the Andrew Carnegie Foundation to construct a building, and three ministers presented a petition to the town asking for the donation of an appropriate site. Greenwood complied with a spot on Monument Street in the courthouse block and an annual appropriation of $1,200 for the library's support. Building plans drawn by Greenwood architect James C. Hemphill were approved in June 1917. The library's collection by the time the first building was finished consisted of 4,000 books donated to the new city library by the Library Association; the building was planned for a maximum expansion to 15,000 volumes. The first staff in the Carnegie building was one librarian, Ivy Calhoun. Other early librarians included Mazie Trammell, who resigned just before her marriage to C. A. Mays in 1920, and Mary Ferguson. The latter is credited with building up the rare book collection, called the "locked case" volumes, which consisted chiefly of South Caroliniana. Ferguson became a favorite of Greenwood's book lovers, and the "enthusiasm and charm" she brought to the position helped to popularize the library in the community.

A children's department opened in 1928 under the sponsorship of the Greenwood Kiwanis Club, which provided equipment, books, and salary for a part-time children's librarian. Mrs. George W. Rush served in that capacity until 1940; Netta Engels is also remembered as a long-time children's librarian. The library board incorporated the youth division into the regular library services in 1933, but the Kiwanis Club continued to provide funds for books.

The Greenwood County Council of Farm Women, which worked to bring library services to rural communities, is credited with gaining county tax support for the purpose. Greenwood County provided a one-half mill appropriation in 1937, and the library opened a "county department" to provide the first services to a wider community, particularly rural schools and other locations in the hinterlands. Significant in this regard was the first "bookmobile," a primitive affair made by adding shelves to an ordinary pickup truck chassis. Kathleen Snead McCabe, the first "truck librarian," served in that capacity for seven years, making regular twice-a-month visits to about twenty locations in suburban and rural communities. The converted truck served for eleven years before it gave way to a more modern "steel bookmobile" in 1948. Other state-of-the-art vehicles followed over the years; the first air conditioned model was purchased in 1974.

A branch library for black citizens opened in 1940 with a deposit of fifty books at the Brewer High School Library. That branch, named in honor of Benjamin Mays, a county native who was at the time President of Morehouse College in Atlanta, was moved from Brewer to other locations and finally dissolved, after having "outlived its usefulness," in 1971. Black school children in the county received bookmobile services about once a month beginning in 1951.

The county library building on North Main Street was erected on the site of the original First Baptist Church and occupied in 1958. By that time the library's holdings totaled more than twice the projected maximum collection the Carnegie building could accommodate. The same architect who had designed the Carnegie library – James C. Hemphill – drew the plans, assisted this time by associate Lawrence Cobb. The building was designed to accommodate a collection of 100,000 volumes and a staff that had grown to seven librarians by the time it was built. The facility was expected to take care of the library's needs "for the next four to eight years." The new building seemed to spur growth in all directions at once. The county increased its appropriation to two mills in 1962, and the first branch location, or depository, opened in Ninety six a year later. The idea of creating a regional system in cooperation with the Abbeville Library was implemented in 1966, and the Ware Shoals branch library joined the system in 1969. The first contract establishing the Abbeville-Greenwood Regional Library was renewed in 1971 after a five-year "demonstration period" indicated a mutually advantageous relationship. Bookmobile services were provided by contract to McCormick County for two intervals in the 1960s and 1970s.

The library building ran out of space in the mid-1970s. Sparked by a challenge grant from The Self Foundation and fueled by federal funds from the Library Services and Construction Act, the trustees and friends of the library launched a program of additions and renovations that nearly doubled the size of the building on North Main Street. County Council increased the public library appropriation to three mills in 1979. Ninety Six erected an attractive new library building in the middle of town in the 1980s.

Public library services for Greenwood County seem to have followed an orderly pattern of growth and development. The first "place to read" was provided more than ninety years ago, and both library amenities and library services have reflected the ebb and flow of the county's fortunes over the years. In the words of a brief sketch of its history, the library has "kept pace with the growth of the county" as it added new services and reached out "to a more diverse readership." Many librarians have served Greenwood since Miss Julia Lee "gave certain hours per day" as volunteer librarian in the early days, but only three have served as Head

Librarian (now Regional Library Director) since 1950. They are Elizabeth Porcher, Mary McCord, and Bruce Heimburger.

Greenwood's repository of antiquities and oddities, known simply as The Museum, is much newer than the library, having been "talked about for several years before . . . definitive actions were taken" between 1967 and the grand opening on January 25, 1970, in a room of the old armory on Phoenix Street. Vacated for new quarters by the South Carolina National Guard, the armory was used as a temporary courthouse while the new building was under construction. As county offices one by one moved out of the armory and into the new courthouse, museum supporters moved in to renovate the interior of the old building for its new purpose. The Greenwood Kiwanis Club adopted the museum as a project, and prime mover and first president James W. Durst directed a volunteer crew, including high school students, for nearly a year before The Museum opened to the public. Exhibit cases were either built, purchased used, or donated by businesses; fluorescent lights came from a store undergoing renovation; and paint was contributed, as was cloth from Greenwood Mills. As for exhibit materials, collectors began to bring in items from their personal collections to add to those contributed by The Museum's organizers and trustees. Materials for exhibition actually came in faster than display cases and plans for security could be provided. The Museum's initial funding consisted of a grant of $5,000 from the South Carolina Arts Commission matched by $5,000 in local funds.

Durst was the first curator (at no salary); his staff consisted of volunteers, a part-time employee who managed the office and helped with exhibits, and a Museum Auxiliary formed to give talks to schools and conduct guided tours through the facility. The first traveling exhibit, put together in the fall of 1969, consisted of a rock collection shown on request to fifth grade classrooms in the district. After the official opening The Museum entertained visitors "by request and on special occasions."

Although Greenwood County contributed $4,000 a year toward operation and provided space, utilities, and maintenance free of charge, the years in the armory building were a mixed bag for The Museum:

> Even though the building was located on a side street, had a forbidding exterior and certainly did not suggest a museum, for the next ten years people came in ever increasing numbers. They saw Greenwood memorabilia, rocks, minerals, Indian artifacts, Confederate relics, mounted birds and mammals, shells, fossils and items from Asia, Africa, South America and the Pacific Islands. There were items from private collections such as bottles, keys, locks and dolls. They saw all kinds of things and each one of them of interest to someone. The collectibles continued to grow and more and more items were put on view. In addition to the exhibits the museum's programs included suitcase exhibits (to be used extra-murally) talks and lectures to the various community

> clubs and the use of a meeting room. Visiting hours had expanded. . . .

The trustees of The Museum found themselves in a dilemma. After ten years in what was essentially a most unsatisfactory location and with only a skeleton staff, the institution had managed somehow not only to survive but also to become integrated with the community. They had a decision to make: "could the museum continue as it was . . . primarily exhibiting an assortment of individual collections . . . in haphazard fashion, in one large, open space, dark, difficult to heat and to cool, and almost impossible to keep clean, staffed by two part timers, or . . . move on to a more meaningful program of planned exhibits, and . . . institute correct museum procedures for recording and storing materials." The trustees decided on the latter course, with a building as the first priority.

A commercial building near the center of town was located in 1981. The site had several advantages, among them the fact that it was adjacent to the Greenwood Community Theater, across the street from the county library, and a few blocks from Lander College. A professional curator, Fred Schlein, was hired the same year and charged with a number of responsibilities. Among other duties Schlein was expected to organize exhibit materials, develop an acceptable system of records, work out a comprehensive exhibit plan for the future, and bring The Museum up to established standards. He was also to determine the feasibility of the building for museum operations and plan and supervise the move from the old armory bulding to the new location.

The building at 106 Main Street was purchased with the aid of a $30,000 grant from the State of South Carolina and a Self Foundation challenge grant of $27,500 matched with local funds. A volunteer drew up the interior plans, and other volunteers papered and painted the new model rooms; even so, the cost of $40,000 to remodel the building for museum purposes was considerably more than had been anticipated. Volunteers stepped in again when moving time came: local garden and study clubs pitched in, businesses loaned trucks and trailers, individuals loaded cartons in cars and station wagons, Boy Scouts and Girl Scouts helped unpack, and the staff, plus an intern on loan from the South Carolina State Museum, prepared the exhibits in their new location. The Museum held another Grand Opening with a ribbon-cutting and appropriate ceremony on July 23, 1982. Guests included Greenwood dignitaries and representatives from museums across the state.

The interior layout of The Museum's quarters has proved quite satisfactory. The major theme for the main floor is Greenwood as it appeared about the turn of the century. The "model rooms" – a Victorian parlor and farm kitchen on one side and a drug store, doctor's office, general store and schoolroom on the other – are furnished to suggest the period with artifacts contributed by Greenwood residents.

The main floor also contains natural history exhibits. The second floor houses materials from foreign countries, plus some from nineteenth-century America, and contains a gallery for art exhibitions and craft shows. The lower level is used for collections storage and inventory. Volunteers are currently engaged in accessioning all the objects in all the collections, correlating each artifact with the written record and affixing an accession number before the object goes into the organized storage area. The sophistication of this orderly cataloging process stands in sharp contrast to the early days when the institution was essentially nothing but open space in an old building where everything was on exhibit, records were scanty, and numbering of objects was minimal. At the end of the current phase of development The Museum will have a complete physical inventory of its holdings.

The Museum sponsors field trips in the community, including "bud" walks and tours led by visiting naturalists, and plans wild flower and geology walks for the immediate future. It also collaborates with the Social Science Department of Lander College in an internship program for senior history students. A major interest is to develop and interpret the Greenwood area by means of exhibits spotlighting the natural history of the region and illustrating changes in the uses of the land. Future plans include offering classes in arts, crafts, and basic sciences, as well as strengthening ties to the public schools and supplementing students' classroom experiences. The Museum also plans to expand its gallery exhibits from works of regional artists to shows by artists of national significance.

Operational costs rose significantly after The Museum moved from its first location. The county continued its $4,000 appropriation, but maintenance and utilities, as well as mortgage payments, became part of the operating expenses. Like many other public institutions, The Museum continually fights the battle of the budget, but its tenth anniversary as a fixture on Main Street occurs in 1992, and the building recently underwent change when a modern facade was removed from the front. Although The Museum is young, it is a viable institution with a firm foundation and plans for a strong future in Greenwood. Directors, or curators, from the beginning have been only three: Jim Durst, Fred Schlein, and V. W. Hayes. Despina Panagakos currently serves as Administrator.

* * * *

South Carolina is known as a "legislative state," meaning that power ultimately rests with the General Assembly, and all other governmental agencies are subordinate. A couple of professors at the University of South Carolina – Walter B. Edgar and Blease Graham – wrote a three-part analysis of what they called the "hydra-headed monster of state government" for *The State* in 1990. The articles pointed out that the system worked reasonably well so long as the state was dominated by one-party politics, but that the period of change since World War II had spotlighted the need for more effective state government and more authority for the governor's office. Edgar and Graham wrote that the year 1950 was perhaps "the high-water mark" of dominance by the General Assembly when, among other forms of control, its individual members actually governed the state's 46 counties. Those individual members were the county delegations who controlled "what went on in their respective counties – from which roads got paved to who was hired to teach school." Hence the vital interest in county politics; the senator and representatives *were* county government for more than sixty years of Greenwood's history as a county.

Change began in the 1960s, and the county eventually came around to the county council form of government, the system that exists today. A newspaper headline from *The Index-Journal* of December 31, 1971, called 1971 the "year of politics" in Greenwood County. The transition period really deserves its own separate treatment; for purposes of this chapter, however, only the election of the first county council, a genuine two-party battle, will be considered. One reporter wrote that there were "more hats in the ring than in most men's clothing stores" during the filing period which began on February 9, 1971. The actual election process had begun with the November 1970 general election when voters chose the council form of government almost two to one. Twenty candidates ran in the Democrat primary, Republicans fielded eight, and two more qualified by petition. After the smoke cleared from the primaries – two Democrat and one Republican – the final election on June 8 seated the first five members of Greenwood County Council: Democrats Dr. Stanley C. Baker, A. L. Atkinson, R. Thornwell Dunlap, and Frank Jones, with William H. Harrison the lone Republican. Harrison called himself "the Southern member," a reference to his home in lower Greenwood County, in contrast to "Northern" member Frank Jones, who hailed from Ware Shoals. There can be little question that the council system was responsible for the move toward hiring a single county manager charged with the day-to-day administration of county business. Greenwood is one of only two counties in the state to adopt the county manager system.

The work of Greenwood County Council has most certainly grown since that first election twenty years ago; in fact, Carroll Brooks, who retired as chairman in January 1991, called it "rough," a reference to the shift of responsibility from Congress and Legislature to the local level. Brooks cited the problem of the county's being forced to raise taxes for programs mandated, but not funded, at higher levels of government. "That's frustrating," he said, "especially when you don't believe in some of them." Brooks wound up a long career of public service when he retired twice, first from the South Carolina Tax Commission and ten years later from Council. As noted in another chapter, this descendant of "Cap'n Ham" Brooks, an early supporter of the movement to form Greenwood County who served as both representative and county senator in its earliest days, simply carried out a family tradition. His father, E. Loudon Brooks, Sr., served as Greenwood County supervisor for more than twenty years.

In addition to the move to a new form of county government, Greenwood became part of a mandated regional subdivision when the Upper Savannah Council of Governments was formed in 1967. The state was divided into ten such councils, defined as voluntary associations of governmental units formed to assist in dealing with issues and needs that cross city and county boundaries. The regional councils were funded with a combination of local, state, and federal dollars and designed to provide advisory and other services geared to the needs of a particular area of the state. Greenwood's council, which also includes the counties of Abbeville, Edgefield, Laurens, McCormick, and Saluda, was the first to be established in the state; as another first, Upper Savannah's current executive director, Patricia Edmonds, is the only woman to hold that position.

The state's network of regional councils was a natural outgrowth of the federal government's move to organize and coordinate its grant-making apparatus at the state and local levels. South Carolina lawmakers recognized that a regional approach could facilitate intergovernmental coordination in areas other than federal grants; an act creating a statewide network of regional councils was the result. The most glaring need addressed was for studies and recommendations in the public arena. The Act specifically covers "matters affecting the public health, safety, general welfare, education, recreation, pollution control, utilities, planning, [and] development" as well as "technical assistance and information" to be provided by a professional staff. The Upper Savannah Council has provided any number of demographic studies, reports, manuals, directories, and planning documents since its inception nearly 25 years ago. Among its most visible successes in Greenwood is the civic center, built with the aid of a grant from the Economic Development Administration, a federal agency. In addition to the economic development of its six-county region, the Council is involved in housing programs, drug control, personnel studies, recreational projects, job training, and many other matters of public concern. One program has unfortunately been lost to budgetary constraints in recent years: though historic preservation is no longer on the list of Upper Savannah's priorities, Greenwood is fortunate that many of its historic sites were pinpointed, researched, and in several instances recorded in the National Register of Historic Places as a result of the efforts of the Upper Savannah Council of Governments.

This chapter ends with sketches of two important Greenwood County senators who happened to be father and son and whose terms of office were 25 years apart. There is no temptation to call them typical since the county has sent only distinct individuals – men such as Chris Waller, Ham Brooks, J. K. Durst, D. A. G. Ouzts, William Jennings Bryan Dorn, C. A. Mays, G. P. Callison, J. W. Bradford, John Drummond, and others of their ilk – to the South Carolina Senate over the last century. But the two Nicholsons were undoubtedly among the county's most interesting and influential men, and their careers covered times of far-reaching change for Greenwood County.

William Hughes Nicholson was born near Ridge Spring (now Saluda County) in 1879 but moved as a boy with his mother and eight siblings to her family home, Cedar Grove, which still stands near Edgefield. Young Nicholson always worked on the farm, even while attending South Carolina College (now the University of South Carolina). He moved to Greenwood in 1904 where he read law to qualify for practice. After a time in the firm of Grier, Park and Nicholson, he opened his own office and specialized in criminal cases. Many people considered "Lawyer Nicholson" the only way to go if one were in *real* trouble; indeed, his "ability to extricate defendants from difficult situations" is still legendary. Nicholson himself often boasted that none of his clients was ever executed, although some ended up in the penitentiary. His son calls him "an orator of the old school" who spoke with both vigor and volume. So far as is known, the senior Nicholson was the only Greenwood lawyer ever to argue a case before the United States Supreme Court.

Nicholson served in the South Carolina House of Representatives from 1908 to 1914, co-authoring during that time a bill to provide the first state aid to poor school districts. He also worked on the first marriage license law in the state. His senate terms fell during the Great Depression, 1932-1940, and he sponsored a resolution delaying mortgage foreclosures to allow time for some property owners to save their homes and farms. In addition to a busy law practice and state house service, Nicholson was an avid fox hunter as well as a farmer with a fine herd of Jersey cows. He was also a faithful churchman, noted for teaching a Sunday School class at Main Street Methodist Church with much the same vigor he displayed in the courtroom.

William H. Nicholson died at the age of 86 in 1966, having been at work in his office only the week before. He was fortunate enough to practice law with two of his sons in the firm of Nicholson and Nicholson, and his secretary, Frances Drake, worked for him more than fifty years.

Francis Bates Nicholson was born in 1929 in Greenwood. A victim of a polio epidemic at the age of twelve, young Francis was left disabled, but only in his legs. He kept up with his school work and finished Greenwood High School with his class. His brother recalls that he never sought special favors nor showed the slightest bitterness because of his handicap. A graduate of Wofford College and the University of South Carolina Law School, Nicholson later obtained the master of law degree from George Washington University and taught for two years at Stetson University Law School in Florida. He returned to Greenwood in 1956 and practiced in the family law firm until his election to the South Carolina Senate in 1960.

Francis Nicholson's time in the senate coincided with the beginnings of Piedmont Technical Education Center and the new county courthouse, both of which claimed his attention. Also, he was senator when Greenwood County sold its power facility to Duke after a county-wide referendum determined that citizens favored the sale. Nicholson was elected Judge of the Eighth Judicial Circuit in 1967. A poll of practicing attorneys not long before his death named him one of the three top judges in the state in terms of ability, judicial temperament, and integrity. Like his father, Nicholson was always active in church work and was a charter member of the Church At Greenwood. He was only 55 years old when he died in 1984; at his request, Francis Nicholson was buried on the family farm where he had built his home.

* * * *

What criteria can be used to sum up a county? Nothing in our system is more ordinary than the subdivision of political entities called states, and even states are actually only political subdivisions that together make up the United States of America. The political subdivision notion can be taken to inordinate lengths, yet no concept is more important to the ideal of self government. The people and their government meet and even merge in the environs of a small county, but it is easy to forget the vital importance of such a concept. So commonplace are the comings and goings that hardly anyone realizes that the underlying philosophy of a high school civics course is played out as county citizens enact their private and public roles in the system. But Greenwood has never lacked a sense of its own importance in the scheme of things. Its leaders, in fact, were convinced of the validity of their case for countyhood for several years before it became a reality. The Act creating the county was little more than formal recognition of a foregone conclusion in the minds of many supporters who had worked for years to make Greenwood a courthouse town. It follows therefore that its "leading men" must be numbered among the criteria that matter in assessing the impact of Greenwood County.

Another criterion might be the timing of significant events, which could simply be another way of looking at the leadership qualities of individuals. Superior leaders know that timing is crucial. The development of Greenwood's railroad system is a case in point: more than one of the five railroad lines that once converged on the town owed their routes to the enthusiastic work of individuals blessed with the ability to discern when the time was right to act. And railroads were by no means the only examples of fortuitous timing in Greenwood's past. From erecting schools and other public buildings to spearheading countywide projects such as bringing a four-year college from another town, building a major dam and hydroelectric plant, or securing a modern health facility to rival any in the state, Greenwood County has gained kudos for the timing of its efforts as well as for its determination to see projects through.

Some people point to the issue of transportation as Greenwood's single most glaring weakness as a county. The more than thirty miles from the county seat to the nearest interstate, the lack of air service, and the shortage of four-lane highways to the metropolitan centers of Greenville and Augusta might seem on the face of things formidable obstacles to proper county development. One businessman commented that many deals have foundered on the forty or so two-lane miles of Highway 25 between Greenwood and the Greenville-Spartanburg Airport. Others counter that this apparent shortcoming has allowed for a controlled growth pattern that might not have been possible had Greenwood been more accessible to businesses in search of a location. The transportation question thus remains moot.

Business questions aside, nearly everyone can agree that the peculiar charm of Greenwood County is a question for endless subjective speculation. The county is finally old enough for its citizens to think in terms of generations, and the First Families of Greenwood know very well who they are and where they fit in the county's history. But relative newcomers, too, are able to find a place for themselves in one of the several distinct periods of the county's development as the twentieth century unfolded. Finally, Greenwood's standing vis-a-vis South Carolina's older counties lends itself neatly to a paraphrase of a famous Ralph Waldo Emerson line contrasting England with America: "In Charleston every man you meet is some man's son; in Greenwood, he may be some man's father."

4

SCHOOLS AND EDUCATION

The things taught in colleges and schools are not an education, but the means of education.
Ralph Waldo Emerson

THE editors of *The Encyclopedia of Southern Culture* (1989) begin the section entitled "Education" with the observation that education in the American South is characterized by the incessant search – they call it a "self-conscious quest" – for equality with systems outside the region and claim that most significant changes have occurred in response to non-southern influences. During colonial times southerners accepted the English notion of education as a private responsibility; as a consequence the very notion of public education carried a certain stigma. Further, the sparseness of settlement, particularly in the backcountry, and the lack of effective governmental apparatus also inhibited the growth of schools in the South. Though the "liberation ideal" of the Revolutionary era contributed to a new interest in state systems, common schools, and colleges throughout the new United States, systems in the South tended to reflect the region's social structure and conservative philosophy until long after the Civil War. Wealthy southerners hired private tutors, the moderately well-to-do created private schools and academies, and the working classes got along as best they could with "field schools" and such itinerant teachers as came their way. Public education was a totally foreign concept; higher education was reserved for the elite and reflected a fondness for classicism and the values of an earlier age. There are indications that this system was not without certain merits. For example, literacy rates among southern whites were approximately on a par with those of midwestern states by 1861.

The Civil War disrupted education in the South just as thoroughly as it disrupted the activity of every other social institution. The region was left with a high population of school-age children and a low level of taxable wealth after the war ended, as well as the stark political realities of Radical Reconstruction and the prevailing notion that education was somehow connected with social instability or a disruption of the class system. It is fruitless to speculate on what might have been, but the reality of widespread poverty, white resistance to educating blacks, and political corruption combined to limit educational reforms to the point that southern schools were far behind those of the rest of the nation as the twentieth century approached. In the South as a whole, only about 40% of the children went to school regularly, and only about 10% of those who did completed the fourth grade. Teachers were poorly trained and badly paid, secondary schools were virtually nonexistent, and illiteracy rates greatly exceeded those of the rest of the country. Even after 1900, the agricultural depression of the 1920s followed by the Great Depression of the 30s compounded the problems of the region.

As for South Carolina, Ernest Lander began his chapter on education and religion in *A History of South Carolina, 1865-1960,* with the optimistic subtitle "The Decline in Ignorance." The foundations of the public school system in South Carolina were laid in the Constitution of 1868 which called for free public education without segregation for "all children of school age." In the era of Radical Reconstruction, however, perhaps it is not surprising that no attempt at racial mixing of school children was made, since neither Radical Governor Robert K. Scott nor Radical Superintendent of Education Justus K. Jillson favored such a policy. Other provisions of the constitution, such as the subdivision of counties into school districts, selection of uniform textbooks, and election of county superintendents and commissioners, were carried out so that groundwork of a sort was laid. South Carolina's illiteracy statistics at about the time of this first attempt to reduce ignorance are revealing: when the national average of persons over the age of ten unable to read or write was 17% of the population, South Carolina's average was 55.4% (21.9% of native whites, 78.5% of blacks). The percentages had improved by 1950 but were still more than twice the national average. True expansion and progress in educating its children would come to the South only after World War II.

While the elaborate design mandated by the constitution attracted thousands of both white and black youths to school, the results were still quite unsatisfactory. Jillson reported in 1873 that the legislature was slow to provide its share of financial support even when funds had been appropriated. He also pointed out that many school officials were "eminently disqualified" for their positions, and a large majority of teachers were "wholly unworthy, either morally or intellectually," to instruct their charges. The condition of physical facilities was even worse. Whatever buildings and related equipment were available had been pressed into service for schools, and Jillson's report charged that 1,129 of the 1,908 schoolhouses in use in 1873 were made of logs. Despite James A. Garfield's eloquent line – "Give me a log hut with only a simple bench, Mark Hopkins on one end and I on the other, and you may have all the buildings, apparatus and libraries without him." – it is easy to support Lander's contention that thousands of school children received only a smattering of education. Besides, there have never been enough Mark Hopkinses to go around.

Another serious problem of education during the Reconstruction era was that of indifference in several areas of the state. Other needs, mostly involving adjustment to the new economic realities of the postwar South, seemed paramount. Thomas Dowling noted that "people were very impatient and really did not care whether schools operated." Every hand was needed on the farm if families were to make a living, and, of course, the really big question of the time was that of mixing the races. There was general agreement that establishing mixed schools, regardless of the constitutional mandate, would be the kiss of death for any state system of public education.

The regime of Conservative Democrats which followed hard on the heels of that of Radical Republicans came near to finishing off any tentative moves toward a public system of education such as we know today. Indeed, a number of "leading men" of the state, in response to a poll taken in the 1880s by the Abbeville *Press and Banner*, voted 35 to 7 against the notion of a two-mill tax for educational purposes. The same newspaper editorially called teachers "organized raiders on the public treasury." There can be no question that the race problem and the backlash of Reconstruction were at the root of this strange attitude.

But what were the motives that brought about a change in that attitude, in South Carolina and throughout the South, toward at least a common school education for all its citizens, both black and white? No doubt there are many answers to this question, but one of the most compelling was provided by Wilbur J. Cash in *The Mind of the South* (1941). Cash argued that the concern of the landowner after the Civil War centered on the plight of the poor white and yeoman classes who, owning practically nothing and never having developed any sort of class pride, suddenly found themselves in economic competition with black freedmen. In a burst of Faulkner-like prose, Cash wrote: "the South was hurrying fatally, and indeed already distinctly coming into a time when there wouldn't be room enough on the plantation to take care of both the main body of the blacks and this always multiplying army of white candidates – when these whites would be hurled, not only into competition with these blacks, but into the most naked and brutal competition – into a struggle to the death for the means of subsistence." Even though such an eventuality held a certain temptation for landowners to "beat down the hire of both contestants" to their own advantage, the end result would inevitably be to drive both white and black workers to a far lower standard of living than either race had ever known before. Cash argued that such a prospect was utterly intolerable for the "ruling order," not only from the standpoint of noblesse oblige, but also from those of racial sympathy, racial pride, and love for the South. Fearing social equality between blacks and whites most of all, the ruling order believed firmly that the chaos engendered by a bitter struggle for survival between blacks and desperate poor whites, stripped of their last bastion of an imagined racial superiority, threatened to destroy the entire fabric of the South. As Cash put it, nearly all of the "master class" and in some sense "the whole body of the South" simply had to find another way to extend the arm of the land without the abandonment of cotton-growing.

Wilbur Cash firmly linked industrial development and education as twin solutions proposed for the dilemma of the postwar South. He called it "an idea – a dream . . . a page from the book of Yankeedom . . . in short, . . . Progress." Cotton mills, even in the midst of cotton fields, would be the answer to white unemployment; and mass, but certainly not equal, education would be the answer to the great fear of social equality between the races. There was already concern that northern teachers were making inroads on black illiteracy while poor whites still basked in their prewar state of blissful ignorance. Arguments for providing schools for blacks ranged from the idea "that we ought to do it, if for no other reason, because we have got him here and owe it to him" all the way to "since the Yankee is plainly determined on it . . . it would be better if we beat him to the draw and did it ourselves." Somewhere in between lay the strange reasoning that "the instructed black man can be trusted never to commit rape, and that taught the elementals and perhaps some mechanics (we shall rigidly veto the idea of academic schools for him), he will be distinctly more useful, both to himself and to us."

Cash stressed that the development of an industrial economy concurrent with educational opportunity throughout the South was in no sense the result of any real change in the southern mindset. Indeed, it was quite the opposite: "far from representing a deliberate break with the past, the turn to Progress clearly flowed straight out of that past and constituted in a real sense an emanation from the will to maintain the South in its essential integrity." Cash did not, however, suggest that these developments lacked innovation nor question that they were truly revolutionary.

Meanwhile, the South Carolina Constitution of 1895 set up a State Board of Education to regulate teacher examinations for qualifying certificates, provided "a liberal system of free public schools for all children between the ages of six and twenty-one years," specified the size of school districts ("as compact in form as practicable, having regard for natural boundaries, and not to exceed forty-nine nor be less than nine square miles in area"), and empowered these districts to levy property taxes for school purposes, within limits of not more than 8% of assessed value. Section 7 of Article XI of the Constitution makes the state's position in the matter of race crystal clear: "Separate schools shall be provided for children of the white and colored races, and no child of either race shall ever be permitted to attend a school provided for children of the other race."

Greenwood County's educational efforts fit rather neatly into the time frame of the state's move toward public education. Six years before the county was formed Greenwood adopted the "graded system" then being introduced in some parts of the state, and its own charter included a provision for laying off school districts in the new county. That activity, which ultimately resulted in the creation of 48 separate districts, had to be reversed beginning in 1952 in response to a new state school act providing for a large school building program financed by sales tax monies, as well as drastic consolidation of each county's unwieldy number of school districts with local financing. Today the county comprises only three districts, one in Greenwood proper and one each in the Ninety Six and Ware Shoals areas. Interestingly enough, *The Index-Journal* reported in its edition of March 20, 1990, that tentative moves toward consolidating the three districts financially were under discussion.

This brief introductory sketch covering only a little over a hundred years is in no sense adequate as the story of education in Greenwood County and simply will not do for purposes of this chapter. Practically every county, as opposed to city, Greenwoodian over the age of 40 received a grade school education in one of those small local school districts in which the schoolhouse was the center of community life and the schoolteacher, or teachers, if one were lucky enough to attend a two- or three-teacher school, among the most respected and beloved citizens.

The Index-Journal has printed a number of long articles on the development of Greenwood's public schools since 1891. There is also sketchy information, consisting mostly of personal recollections, of a number of private schools existing before that time. The edition of September 14, 1957, contains a long article entitled "Good Private Schools Educated Greenwood Young until 1891" which provides perhaps the most comprehensive coverage of the years before public education. That article is the basis for the following sketch.

The first school in Greenwood can be traced directly from the demise of the College of Cambridge established by the General Assembly in 1785 in the town of Ninety Six. Despite the high-flown connotations of the name, which was actually to change that of the town for awhile, and the high hopes that undoubtedly surrounded its beginnings, the school was never more than a preparatory school with one teacher, or possibly two for a brief time. One of the teachers in 1806, identified as Edward Hooker in Margaret Watson's *Greenwood County Sketches*, wrote in his diary that the school consisted of one brick building erected as the president's home, but "which is now designed by the Trustees for the Academy building itself." Hooker added that over the years the school had "flourished less, and finally became quite neglected — in which state it has been for several years past." The problem was the usual one of lack of funds; there was "great difficulty in getting the board together; and also in collecting the monies subscribed." The institution "began to decline about 1789 or 90 and . . . [had] fallen into almost total neglect about 1795 or 6. Great sums were subscribed which were never paid." It is clear from this evidence that Cambridge enjoyed something less than ten years of success. One of its board members, Richard C. Griffin, Jr., who at that time lived in Greenwood and who wrote that the school "became extinct" in 1825 "owing to disease and emigration," made up his mind "to collect the funds due the Cambridge institution and establish a school at Greenwood as it was a more healthy and eligible situation."

Griffin wrote his own account in a letter to the Reverend John McLees, an early Presbyterian minister. As a member of the legislature in 1832 he introduced a bill to allow surviving members of the Cambridge Association to collect debts and sell the property of Cambridge College. The bill passed, and Griffin was able to secure the services of Samuel Trowbridge as schoolmaster at a salary of $300 per year. The thirteen scholars who enrolled for the first term were housed in a new building which Griffin had erected as a dwelling for his son Franklin. Unfortunately we know nothing further about Schoolmaster Trowbridge, but we do know that the "schoolhouse" was located on a site "slightly northeast of Brewer High School." Griffin added that the school more than tripled in enrollment after the first term. Trowbridge was forced to leave in 1835 because of ill health, and Charles R. Moseley, described as "a local young man who later became a physician," was hired as his replacement, along with Rebecca Chapman of Columbia, who was employed "to take charge of the female department." Thus the village was able to boast that it had two schools – one for boys and one for girls – in the 1830s. The first trustees in addition to Griffin and nominated by him were Thomas Wier, John T. Coleman, and Dr. John Logan.

The Greenwood Association for the Promotion of Education was formed in 1835 to operate the schools, and a young graduate of the South Carolina College, James Leslie, was hired as teacher of the male school in 1836. This young man, who taught for a time in Greenwood then left for greener pastures only to return in the 1860s, was regarded as an excellent teacher. His reputation was so fine, in fact, that Greenwood's Leslie School was named in his honor.

The old chapel, mentioned in the very earliest records as the town center of Greenwood, arises once again in tracing the growth of schools. This building was erected in 1839 and used as a sort of community center. "School exercises, lectures, music programs, and meetings were held here for years," according to the centennial newspaper article, "and preaching, prayer meetings and communion services were regularly conducted here by the pastor of Rock Presbyterian Church years before that church bought the Education Association's property in 1855. It has sometimes been indicated that the Presbyterians were in control of the first schools in Greenwood, but Griffin's sketch and the Charter of the Education Association do not mention Presbyterian control, and known members of other denominations were long members of the Education Association."

In his short history of Greenwood published as a pamphlet in 1901, C. M. Calhoun wrote that the Presbyterians erected a "two story building on each side of the old Chapel for male and female" schools, and that "Joshua Jones, his wife and Miss Mary Jane Jones, taught the Presbyterian school at the Pelot house during the construction of the large building at the chapel, which when completed was occupied respectively by Dr. Auld, Rumple, Wm. H. Logan and Rev. Donnelly, principals of the male school. Robert Anderson, Rev. Robert Logan, Miss Pelot and Dr. J. H. Logan were principals of the Female school." The Pelot house was located on East Cambridge about where Brewer Hospital was later built, and the Pelot daughters were among the early teachers.

The chapel apparently saw service as a school throughout the war years and for some time afterward. The Education Association, however, had sunk so deeply in debt by 1855 that it turned the school property over to Rock Presbyterian Church whose members had voted to pay the debt and operate the school under the auspices of the South Carolina Presbytery. Other sources state that the Presbyterians purchased the school for $6,000.

Meanwhile, other denominations had entered the education picture. The Methodists at this period were heavily committed to the school at Cokesbury which had entered its "manual labor" phase in 1834. That experiment lasted only a few years, and the school was officially designated the Cokesbury Conference Institute in 1843. Three years later, in 1846, a meeting was held at Mount Moriah Baptist Church a few miles southwest of Greenwood "to devise measures to establish Male and Female Academies in the village of Greenwood under the control of the Baptist denomination." Two Baptist-sponsored schools, both named for prominent ministers of the day, opened in January 1847. The boys' school was Hodges Institute, named for the Reverend Nicholas Ware Hodges; Fuller Institute, named in honor of the Reverend Dr. Richard Fuller, was the school for girls. The first catalog, issued in 1849, described Fuller as "a large, handsome and comfortable building . . . 50 feet in front and 40 feet in depth, containing a school room and two Music rooms. . . . [I]t has a fine entry, a handsome portico and a belfry." As for the boys' school, "the building of the Hodges Institute is found to be too small and inconvenient for its increasing prospects; hence the Board have commenced a large and commodious brick building, with two school rooms, a chapel or exercise room, and Apparatus and Library room, all enclosed in a house 60 by 60 feet, a Cupola in the centre of the roof, and a portico in front." The first principal of Hodges Institute was Allen Dedrick, and the rector of Fuller Institute was Robert H. Nichols. William P. McKellar was a later principal of Hodges.

Although the Fuller Institute building burned in 1849, it must have been rebuilt on the same site – the present 400 block of East Cambridge – since the organizers of the first Methodist Church in the village "bought a brick building which had been the Baptist girls' school" in 1858 and used it as a church until a new building was erected some forty years later on the present site of Main Street Methodist Church. In fact, the Methodist cemetery on East Cambridge was located behind the church. The fate of the Hodges Institute building was quite different. A 1956 *Index-Journal* editorial noted that Hodges survived as a boys' school "until the Confederate War," a period of less than twenty years. After the war the building "was sold at public auction to satisfy a mortgage which had been given to Albert Waller." It was acquired by the American Missionary Association representing the Congregational Churches in the United States and became the home of Brewer Institute, the first school for blacks in Greenwood, which opened in 1872. Though neither of the early Baptist schools managed to weather the Civil War period, the Hodges Institute building, renamed Beadle Hall, did survive for more than eighty years as Brewer's main building. This historic building was razed in 1957 to make room for a modern administration unit at Brewer High School. It was the oldest public building in Greenwood at the time. The 1970 Brewer yearbook, *Bulldog*, contains eight pages of pictures from Brewer's early years, including several photographs of the original building. Sadly, these are all that is left of one of Greenwood's most significant landmarks. The 1956 editorial concluded with the hopeful sentence: "There would seem to be justifiable reasons, on the part of those interested in heritage and tradition, for attempting to preserve this landmark with its notable history and its record of educational service to the entire community." But it was not to be.

The newspaper description of education in post-Civil War Greenwood contained the brave assertion that there were "schools of some sort here both through the war and the lean years immediately following." Notable teachers who struggled during this period were W. K. Blake, Miss Bettie Crews, Miss Beaufort DeVore, James Leslie, W. P. McKellar, Mrs. L. Sheppard, and Miss Florrie Wilson. As A. G. McLees, son of the Reverend John L. McLees, wrote in his autobiography *Opening Doors*, "Anyone could teach, if he wished, provided he could get together groups of pupils." McLees, who was born in 1864, noted that he went to four such schools before the age of fourteen. These were all one-teacher schools with no grades and no promotions involved, and instruction consisted mostly of the three R's. The demise of any sort of school in the old chapel came at this period. The building was sold to private individuals in 1877, and its two school wings were taken down.

Things were a little brighter by the 1880s, specifically because of the three red-haired Misses Bright, two of whom were named Mollie and Maggie, who conducted a private school on what is now Magnolia Street. Samuel C. Hodges recalled in 1957 that this was his first school. In fact, a newspaper advertisement in 1884 announced that the Misses E. R. and M. E. Bright taught the Greenwood High School. It should be noted that a "high school education" meant instruction approximating the ninth grade level, a condition that prevailed until the 10th grade was added in 1905, fourteen years after the first graded school began. The 11th grade followed fairly soon, in 1914, and the 12th came about in the 1940s.

George C. Hodges, who also taught at both Cokesbury and Ninety Six, is listed in a newspaper article as a teacher with a Miss Bright in 1878. This George Hodges, an uncle of the Sam Hodges mentioned above, figured prominently in the Greenwood Male High School which opened in the fall of 1887. In the meantime, the Greenwood Female College under the leadership of the Misses Giles of North Carolina had begun operation in 1885. The three Giles sisters – Theresa, Persis, and Mary – were described as "the first women graduates of Trinity College, now Duke University"; their school was housed in a two-story frame building on the present East Cambridge Avenue at Elm Court. Unfortunately, very little specific information on this school is available, although one newspaper article cited its "high reputation" and called its programs "highlights of community life" in the late 1880s. The Male High School was launched two years later "to give boys as fine a school as the Misses Giles were providing for girls." Its founders were a group of citizens led by R. W. Major, Dr. J. C. Maxwell, C. A. C. Waller, and Professor Simon P. Boozer who was everybody's choice for principal, or headmaster. Boozer had come to Greenwood from Adger College in Walhalla after it closed in 1881. His first Greenwood venture was a boys' school in the middle of town on the east side of the square; Sam Hodges recalled that the schoolboys used the square as a playground. That school moved next to North Main and finally to what is now Grace Street where its history abruptly ended. Boozer's school either died or was incorporated into the new Male High School. George Hodges, former county school commissioner for Abbeville, was employed as co-principal of the new enterprise. A lot of ten acres was acquired, and a two-story brick building containing three classrooms and an assembly hall was erected on what is now Hampton Avenue. That building was still standing and known as the Snead Apartments as late as 1948. Boozer died before the building was completed, which left Hodges in charge, and two additional teachers – Amon Stallworth and E. Crayton McCants – were added to complete the faculty.

Teacher, school administrator, and writer McCants, who later made his home in Anderson, wrote a long recollection of the male high school which was published in *The Index-Journal* of January 6, 1935. He speculated that one reason he was hired, in addition to having been mentored by Professor Hodges earlier at a school in Ninety Six, was to handle the military training which figured prominently in the curriculum. "The Confederate veterans who were the leading men of that day," he wrote, "lacked a great deal of being pacifists." McCants named some of the boys but came no closer to estimating enrollment than the line, "the school opened with a large attendance" representing "nearly the whole of the western section of the State . . . and . . . several from Georgia." His penultimate paragraph deserves quoting in full:

> In looking back over the matter I can clearly perceive that the Greenwood Male High School was a pioneer in its field – the dawn which preceded a new day in public education – and I firmly believe that it contributed no small share toward hastening the coming of that day. The school was never adequately financed with

> the result that the original teachers one by one drifted away to other schools or other occupations. I have always regretted the loss to the youth of the state when Mr. Hodges turned to the insurance business. He was a born teacher. When will South Carolina learn that cheap teachers are apt to prove an expensive luxury and that on the money saved by employing such the next generation pays an exorbitant rate of interest.

Possibly the reader has guessed by this time that the Male High School and Greenwood Female College were destined to merge in 1891 as the first public graded school and usher in a new era for education in Greenwood County. But before that story is told, it is important to go back a few years and pick up the fortunes of Brewer School established in 1872 on the former Hodges Institute property on East Cambridge Street. The name Brewer honored the Reverend Josiah Brewer, a well-known missionary to Africa, and the Greenwood institution was not the first to honor him. The name had in fact been transferred from an orphanage in Wilmington, North Carolina, when its benefactress, identified only as "Mrs. Perry" from Boston, decided to sell the property and shift her allegiance to the new institution in Greenwood. The school was first called Brewer Institute; its stated purpose was "to educate and train the recently emancipated youth in the principles of christian living and good citizenship." The name was changed to Brewer Normal a few years later. The designation of "normal school" is a translation of the French *ecole normale* and refers to the fact that the first school so named was intended to serve as a model. Normal schools were also identifiable as those schools whose primary purpose was to train teachers.

Brewer Normal progressed from a one-teacher school in its earliest days to a boarding school with dormitories for both males and females. By 1897 the school had a principal, seven teachers, and an enrollment of 280 students, 78 of whom lived on the campus. The boys' dormitory became the nurses' residence when Brewer Hospital was built on the site in 1924. Brewer served students from first grade through high school until 1925 when the first six grades were eliminated. There was an effort in the early 1930s to turn Brewer into a junior college, but enrollments in courses beyond the high school level were too small, and the experiment was abandoned. Brewer became part of Greenwood City School District No. 18 in 1925 and of the county system in 1927 as a high school for black students. Financial support from the American Missionary Association ended in 1935, and all property was deeded to the school district with the reservation that it would continue to be used for educational purposes. A new plant was built in 1957, and Brewer High School remained in the system until the school year 1970-71 when it was designated to serve the middle grades and renamed Brewer School.

Brewer's principals and teachers were all white until 1925; its first black principal was W. H. Hillyard. Not surprisingly, most of the early teacher-principals were male ministers from the North, but at least one was a woman: Henrietta Stewart of Des Moines, Iowa, served as principal in 1892.

Most people would probably agree that longtime Brewer principal Benjamin J. Sanders, Jr., ranked as one of Greenwood's leading citizens for many years, both during his career and following his retirement in 1969 after more than forty years at the school. Sanders died in March 1990 at the age of ninety. His leadership qualities were called "quiet, inspiring, low-key" in the front-page obituary in the April 1 edition of the newspaper, and he was credited in large measure with helping Greenwood avoid the bloody racial conflicts that marked other communities in the late 1960s. Sanders, a native of Barnwell County (now Allendale) and the son of a poor farmer, came to Greenwood in 1927 to teach at Brewer, remained as a teacher for eighteen years, and headed the institution for 24 more, from 1945 to 1969. He was honored for a life of service by the Brewer High School alumni at a ceremony on October 20, 1984. Sanders held the B. A. from Pennsylvania State College and the M. S. from South Carolina State. He was awarded the honorary degree of Doctor of Humanities by Lander College in 1979 and elected to the Greenwood County Hall of Fame in 1981. The accompanying citation emphasized his "outstanding contributions in the field of education and . . . to positive relations among all people in the community. Without fanfare, he pursued a better educational system for the youth in the Black community and as a result he helped establish an atmosphere of cooperation and community interaction that contributes greatly to the quality of life in Greenwood." The citation also credited his business acumen, longtime connection with South Carolina Freemasonry, and record of community service. Retired guidance counselor Bernice Duckett probably described Sanders best: "He walked with dignity," she said.

The record of public education in Greenwood County is reasonably well documented in long newspaper articles published from time to time. Superintendent W. E. Black, for example, undertook a bit of historical research for a story spotlighting the new Greenwood High School published in *The Index-Journal* of May 10, 1925, and Thomas I. Dowling wrote a long article entitled "Greenwood Schools – From the Wilderness to 1970" which was published in *The Index-Journal* of November 12, 1970. Dowling served as superintendent of District No. 50 for about seventeen years; more than forty districts were consolidated into one during his tenure. His account summarized Greenwood's earliest foray into public education just four years after it became a county seat: "In 1891 the citizens in the town of Greenwood purchased the property of the girls' school, united it with the boys' school, and organized the present system of public schools." The first graded school building was that of the Misses Giles on East Cambridge Avenue, and the first superintendent was Professor Rufus B. Wilson who had been headmaster of the boys' school. The trustees erected Magnolia Street School with the aid of a bond issue after the first building burned in 1903. Neither Black nor Dowling mentioned the architect who drew the plans for this landmark even though the same man designed four important public buildings in Greenwood during its first few years as a county. No one knows the reason the trustees chose Reuben Harrison Hunt of Chattanooga, beyond the fact that he was well known in his field. One could speculate that Greenwood's civic affairs were the business of the same tightly knit group of leading men, a fact that might have given Hunt four important commissions in the new county seat. Whatever the reason, for many years Greenwood could boast (though it did not) the presence of four typical Hunt designs within a few blocks of each other. The courthouse came first, followed closely by Magnolia School, Lander College, and the First Presbyterian Church. Magnolia was a fine example of Hunt's work, particularly its towers and arches which were virtually his trademarks. Reuben H. Hunt (1862-1937) was one of the most prominent architects of his day, with literally hundreds of public buildings to his credit all over the Southeast and some in foreign countries. So distinctive was his work on churches, in fact, that his name was given to a particular style of church building.

The addition of several more classrooms and an auditorium to the basic building over the next few years allowed Magnolia to "provide for most of the elementary school children and the high school pupils in the County Seat." Dowling wrote in 1970 that the building was "still in a state of good repair and has served as the administrative offices of Greenwood School District No. 50 for some years." It would serve for ten more, until a fire in November 1980 destroyed the building that not only represented Greenwood County's first venture into a graded public school system but also one that was still in active use after 77 years.

An annual report of the South Carolina Superintendent of Education, presumably issued in the first decade of the 1900s, provides a succinct assessment of the state of public education in South Carolina at that time:

> It is a misnomer to say that we have a system of public education. In the actual working of the great majority of the schools of this State, there is no system, no orderly organization. Each county supports its own schools with practically no help from the State as a whole. Each district has as poor schools as its people will tolerate, and in some districts anything will be tolerated. Each teacher works along in her own way, whatever that may be, almost uninfluenced by the existence of any other school or authority. Isolation reigns. This is not inspiring or stimulating.

The use of the feminine pronoun in the superintendent's report brings up a significant point. *The Encyclopedia of Southern Culture* noted a new breed of teacher: young unmarried women who, in addition to possessing the presumed traits of virtue, complacency, and reliability, made ideal employees because they would work for lower wages than men. Teaching became stereotyped, particularly in the South, as "women's work." The South has the highest percentage of female teachers in the nation.

It is important also to look at educational activity in sections of Greenwood outside the county seat. The experiments with academies, or "colleges," in both Ninety Six and Cokesbury are covered elsewhere, but there were others in relatively remote areas which would spring up when a teacher could be found, flourish after a fashion for a few years, and gradually decline. H. T. Cook mentioned a Woodlawn Academy in his book *The Hard Labor Section.* Woodlawn was located "not far from William Bradley's home"; it had flourished for a brief time after the Civil War under the tutelage of the Reverend Edmund L. Patton and his sister Kate, both of whom Cook called "eminent educators, born and reared on Long Cane." Another such school was Woodville Academy in the Phoenix section. Woodville was the predecessor of Phoenix School, later designated District No. 37. Its history was the subject of a paper prepared by H. L. Watson and read at its homecoming on July 14, 1938. The school existed prior to 1845 in a log house near Damascus Church. Watson wrote that the church and school actually swapped locations at one time, a move coincidentally similar to the transfer between the Masonic Female Institute and the Presbyterian Church in Cokesbury in 1875. Through personal interviews with former students Watson managed to determine the names of some of Woodville's early teachers, among them David Richardson, who might well have been the first. Other teachers were Charlie May, John Wilson, and Rosa Ann Wright, who is said to have been a native of Switzerland. How grand it would be to know more about how a Swiss miss managed to find herself teaching in the South Carolina backcountry before the Civil War. Still other teachers Watson identified were W. H. (Hodge) Stallworth and his son Amon, who also taught at the Greenwood Male High School in the late 1880s, and James H. Burnett.

The school was named Woodville about 1858 upon completion of the frame building that replaced the original log structure. Watson speculated that the name was a reference to the first post office in Greenwood (the post office had been established in 1832 as Woodville and its name changed to Greenwood in 1850). He noted the same situation in Phoenix between the name of the post office and the school; that community had been known as New Boston before Watson's own ancestor Jonathan Sale brought the name Phoenix from its first location near Epworth.

Woodville Academy was forced to close at some point during the last two years of the Civil War because many of its students volunteered for service; at least one, Pickens Vaughan, was killed in action. After the war the school reopened with a succession of teachers, including several ministers and a number of women, the most memorable of whom was the strict Miss Beaufort DeVore. Watson wrote that "Miss Beaufort" taught five years in all, then "married the Rev. J. K. Fant, a well known Baptist preacher and taught school no more."

Woodville Academy became Phoenix High School about 1897, concurrent with the formation of the county and the laying off of school districts. It was never a real high school in modern terms and became known simply as Phoenix School in its later years as a grammar school. Watson also mentioned three other schools in the area – Pineville, Moss Hill, and "one at Rehoboth" – which were absorbed into Phoenix. Moss Hill was located in the Breezewood section and is notable as the early school of Margaret Ethridge (Mrs. James L.) Tedards whose teaching career spanned 41 years, most of them in small county schools.

Margaret Ethridge (she disliked the nickname "Maggie") was born in 1889 in Greenwood County. She attended Moss Hill from 1895 to 1904 when she entered Williamston Female College of Greenwood. She was ready for college at the age of fifteen and was a member of the first class of the school that had moved from Williamston and opened in Greenwood the year she enrolled. It would not become officially Lander College until early 1905.

After graduation in November 1907 (this is the date Mrs. Tedards gave; college records indicate 1908. Since graduation could happen at the end of any section of the year, possibly the college simply grouped all graduates of the school year 1907-08), Miss Ethridge began her teaching career at the age of most of today's college freshmen. She stayed a year here and two years there; her longest tenure was at Bold Spring School in Callison where she served as teacher and principal from 1936 to 1950.

There was absolutely no nonsense about Mrs. Tedards. "To my five-year-old eyes," recalled one of her pupils, "she was doubly awesome; not only did she outrank the first grade teacher, Miss Sullivan, who was no mean authority figure herself, but she also knew enough to teach seventh graders. And we never doubted that indeed she knew quite enough. My brother said he didn't need to study until the 10th grade, because Mrs. Tedards had covered all that." Another of her pupils, Bill Logan, whose first opportunity to attend college came more than twenty years after high school, wrote in 1987, "I was curious to see if I could pass a course. In grammar school I had an English teacher who . . . worked so hard it made an impression. In high school I really didn't learn anything new because she had already taught me so much." One hardly needs to add that Bill Logan had no trouble with college courses. He graduated from Lander College, *summa cum laude*, in 1991. Although Louis Wright was probably correct when he wrote, "Boys brought up in the country and in country towns learned more outside of school than in," somehow teachers like Mrs. Tedards managed to cajole or browbeat even the most reluctant scholars to try their best. It was as though their own pride and self-respect were at stake. Perhaps they were.

Margaret Ethridge Tedards wrote the barest possible sketch of her life before she died in early 1968. One line in that spare narrative says it all for those who knew her: "1959, May 28 – Last day I taught, from then on most unhappy."

Watson's description of "the machinery" of Woodville Academy as he knew it – "how the thing got started and how it ran and who ran it" – is general enough to serve as a description of most of the early county schools, although his own tenure dated from before 1897. There were, of course, many changes in later years as districts were formed, trustees named, and local taxes levied, but most of those who attended small county schools can recognize many elements of Watson's school days from their own experiences, even fifty years after the time he depicts:

> If you ask who elected the teacher or teachers I could not tell you for I never knew and I do not think the teacher ever was actually elected as that process is followed today. There were no trustees. In fact there was no semblance of the system of public schools which we accept today as a matter of fact. As well as I can express it from information picked up here and there the matter of securing a teacher was somewhat of a neighborhood affair and was usually arranged before or after church on preaching days or perhaps by a group gathered at our country store for the mail and these were, naturally, parents of children of school age interested in getting them taught. It was a sort of informal conference at which those present would agree to send so many children at so much in the way of tuition, the rate was not uniform but largely what the individual "felt able to pay." It was then left to one member of the group to draw up an agreement to which patrons signed their names with the amount of tuition they were to pay oposite [sic] their names. . . .
>
> The "petition" as it was called by some or paper having been circulated through the neighborhood the amount available for salary or compensation for a teacher was then known and the business of getting the teacher was also left much in the hands of the individual who had been designated to "go ahead" by the informal group in the beginning. If the teacher was attracted by the total of the emoluments, he or she would arrange whatever details were in order with the same individual who started negotiations, and the school was started. The length of the term varied. Usually it started in October or even November and ran until June or July. In some places not so far away the school term began in January and ran to the following November, all through the hot Summer. After school started the teacher was the whole thing, no board of trustees no anything to interfere. There was a little pittance of public money, so called, amounting to about twenty-five dollars each month for about three months only. A teacher had to have a first grade certificate to get this and it necessitated a trip to either Abbeville or Edgefield where the County Commissioner of Education would issue a warrant or scrip which

> would be paid when taxes came in. If the teacher wanted or needed the money before that time, there was usually some well-to-do man in a nearby town who would "discount" the warrant at what today would seem to be an ungodly rate of interest but money was hard to get then and the demand regulated the amount of hire the money could or did command.
>
> This little bit of public money, as it was called, hardly figured in the teacher's salary in the eyes of the patrons. It was more of a bonus which was given the teacher and not a contribution from the community. However, Woodville, about 1893, did step up into an organized district when these were first authorized and a small tax, presumably, made the matter of salary more certain or less as the price of cotton happened to be.

The *Twenty-Second Annual Report of the Public Schools of Greenwood, South Carolina* issued for the year 1913-14 contains some rather bleak statistics, including the information that a total of 32 teachers served 2,055 students, an unweighted student-to-teacher ratio of 64:1. But the whole picture was even more starkly drawn; for example, white teachers actually averaged 48 students each in enrollment, while the black teachers' average was 117. The fact that the report shows enrollment and attendance statistics separately has a significance of its own since it demonstrates the wide variance between what might be termed the county's philosophy and its practice. The student-teacher ratios in attendance were 36:1 for whites and 72:1 for black students. Not surprisingly, white teachers' salaries averaged $58.38 per month, while black teachers made $27.75. In what seems a rather feeble attempt to accentuate the positive, the report also contains the information that the library (presumably located in a white school) contained 900 books, and 88 white pupils had been neither absent nor tardy for the whole year.

Former County Superintendent of Education W. R. Dunn recalls there were more than forty school districts in Greenwood County when he took office in 1943, down somewhat from the all-time high of 48. This was not at all unusual, according to Dunn, since the state was divided into about 1,600 school districts at one time. The 48 in Greenwood County had been gradually reduced to 33 by the time of the state's mandate to consolidate, and in 1952 these districts were compressed into only two – District No. 50 was made up of thirty former districts, and three were represented in Ware Shoals District No. 51. In 1955 part of District 50 became Ninety Six No. 52. Dunn's job at first covered 78 schools, of which 28 had only one teacher. That number had decreased to 26 by 1968 – nineteen elementary, five senior high, and two junior high schools.

A directory of Greenwood County public schools for the year 1948-49, only a few years before consolidation began in earnest, provides perhaps the best information we have on county schools and their separate districts at a critical time. Space does not permit a full discussion of each school, and someone's favorite teacher will not be mentioned; nevertheless, the sheer number of schools listed below gives an idea of the unwieldy state of public education in Greenwood County just after World War II:

Algary District No. 1 – 2 teachers, 3 trustees
Ware Shoals District No. 2 – 37 staff, 3 trustees
Walnut Grove District No. 3 – pupils transported to Ware Shoals, 3 trustees
Hodges District No. 4 – 3 teachers, 3 trustees
Leith District No. 5 – pupils transported to Hodges, 4 trustees
Ellis District No. 6 – pupils transported to Greenwood, 3 trustees
Cokesbury District No. 7 – 2 teachers, 3 trustees
Andrews Chapel District No. 8 – 1 teacher, 3 trustees
Coronaca District No. 9 – 2 teachers, 3 trustees
Saluca District No. 10 – pupils transported to Ninety Six, 3 trustees
Pine Grove District No. 11 – 2 teachers, 3 trustees
Woodlawn District No. 12 – 2 teachers, 3 trustees
Ninety Six District No. 13 – 23 staff, 5 trustees
Iuka District No. 14 – 1 teacher, 2 trustees
Utopia District No. 15 – 5 teachers, 3 trustees
Lebanon District No. 16 – pupils transported to Greenwood, 3 trustees
Quarry District No. 17 – 2 teachers, 3 trustees
Greenwood District No. 18 – 8 schools, 144 staff, 9 trustees
Calhoun District No. 19 – pupils transported to Ninety Six, 3 trustees
Salem District No. 20 – pupils transported to Ninety Six, 3 trustees
Verdery District No. 21 – 1 teacher, 2 trustees
White Hall District No. 22 – pupils transported to Utopia, 3 trustees
Bradley District No. 24 – 2 teachers, 2 trustees
Troy District No. 27 – 2 teachers, 3 trustees
Union District No. 31 – pupils transported to Bradley, 3 trustees
Bold Spring District No. 32 – 3 teachers, 3 trustees
Kirksey District No. 34 – 1 teacher, 3 trustees
Pittsburg District No. 35 – 1 teacher, 3 trustees
Phoenix District No. 37 – 2 teachers, 3 trustees
Fellowship District No. 39 – pupils transported to Greenwood, 3 trustees
Sandridge District No. 40 – 1 teacher, 3 trustees
Oak Grove District No. 41 – 1 teacher, 3 trustees
Fairview District No. 42 – pupils transported to Ninety Six, 3 trustees
Kinards District No. 43 – pupils transported to Ninety Six, 3 trustees
Central District No. 44 – pupils transported to Ninety Six, 3 trustees

There were 35 separate districts at this point, 22 of which were staffed with at least one teacher, and all provided with a board of trustees. Perrin Anderson, writing of this period in *Recollections of My Life* (1989), recalled his appointment to the committee charged with devising a plan for consolidation. Anderson's committee held meetings all over the county to explain the need for consolidation and listen to patrons' responses. "There was considerable opposition in rural areas to giving up the community schools," he wrote, but the committee's recommendation for only one school district with schools in Greenwood, Ninety Six, and Ware Shoals was adopted by the County Board of Education. Both Ware Shoals and Ninety Six were able to establish separate districts within a few years so that the county now has three. "There was much to be said in favor of the more populous farm communities, such as Troy, Callison, Coronaca, and Hodges having separate schools," Anderson concluded, "and the one and two-teacher schools may not have been that bad where there were good teachers. Certainly they did not have some of the problems that beset the large city schools today. A good case can be made for decentralizing the school system."

Public education in the county seat virtually began with Magnolia School, although the graded school concept had been implemented twelve years before a bond issue allowed the construction of Magnolia. The school was first enlarged in 1908; by 1911, Greenwood's schools consisted of Magnolia and one-room branches at both Greenwood Mill and Grendel Mill. Separate schools for black students were operated: one source notes that the first school building for blacks was on New Market Street, a later and larger building was erected on Baptist Street, and West Side School was built in 1906. By that time the city had grown to a population of about 6,600, and a new school was needed. Another bond issue raised $25,000, and Leslie and Grenola Schools were built. Grenola was a two-classroom affair, with a meeting hall on the second floor, located between Panola Mill and Mathews Mill. This frame building burned in 1924 and was replaced by a brick structure in 1925. A six-room addition was built in 1938.

Long-time principal Martha McCabe wrote a short history of Leslie School in 1981, noting that the school was named in honor of James Leslie, an early teacher in Greenwood, at the request of Charles Montague Calhoun from whom the property on the corner of Stanley and Crews Streets was purchased. Leslie was the third teacher hired at Greenwood's first school; his teaching career spanned more than fifty years. Leslie School opened in early 1913 with 285 pupils and seven teachers, one of whom was another famous Greenwood educator, Emma ("Sunbeam") Andrews. Leslie was enlarged in 1929 and extensively modernized in the boom period of the 1950s. Enrollments hovered around 600 students even after Northside Junior High School was opened and Leslie lost two grades in 1956. Other changes came with full integration of public schools in 1970 when Leslie became an elementary school serving grades one through four. Leslie's final chapter was written in 1981 when the school was closed; it was replaced by Oakland Elementary School located on East Durst Avenue Extension. McCabe pointed out the rather remarkable stability of the school during most of its 68-year lifespan. Although there were three principals in the first seven years, only three more served for the remaining 61 years of the school's existence. The Leslie School building is now owned by Lander College, which has plans to demolish this historic structure.

The next important step in building Greenwood's schools was the construction of Blake School on Phoenix Street. Named in honor of Professor John Rennie Blake, a native of Greenwood and an eminent college teacher, it opened in 1916 with eight teachers and 180 pupils. The property had been purchased by the school district as early as 1911 with other parcels added in 1914 and 1916. Blake was dealt a double blow in the 1940s: first, the school was virtually destroyed by a fire in 1943, and the walls, which had remained standing after the fire, were so badly damaged by the great tornado a year later that nothing was salvageable for a new school. The present building was erected in 1946. Blake passed out of the school system in 1981; its property now serves as headquarters for Emerald Center, an organization serving the needs of retarded citizens.

The Connie Maxwell Orphanage School established in 1892 became part of the Greenwood school system in 1931. For nearly forty years the orphanage had demonstrated its self sufficiency by operating its own school. The full story of both school and institution is well told in two histories and a book of drawings of the buildings, all of which can be found in the Greenwood County Library. The books are: *Forty Years of Connie Maxwell History*, by A.T. Jamison, D.D. (1932); *A History of Connie Maxwell Children's Home 1892-1977*, by Alan Keith-Lucas (1982); and *Connie Maxwell, A Pictorial History, 1892-1968*, by Mack Baltzegar (1968). It is interesting to note that Connie Maxwell Orphanage, renamed Connie Maxwell Children's Home in 1945, predates the county's formation by five years. Its location in Greenwood can be traced to the town's early efforts to bring, in C. M. Calhoun's phrase, "everything to its betterment as a growing city." The year 1992 marks the centennial of this uniquely Greenwood institution.

An article by W. E. Black, "Growth of Greenwood Public Schools Amounts to Three Hundred Percent in 20 Years," appeared in *The Index-Journal* of May 10, 1925. Black, superintendent of city schools from 1919 to 1945, traced in three short paragraphs the history of the public school system to 1925 as a lead-in to a discussion of the new Greenwood

High School building then on the drawing board. Even though Greenwood had eight schools – six white and two black – in 1925, overcrowding threatened, and a new school appeared to be the answer. Black's contention that "Greenwood has never stood in the way of progress, no matter what the cost, if within her ability" was not only politic but also quite true; the rebuilding of Blake School, for example, was financed under a "pay as you go" plan worked out by the trustees and the county delegation, a plan which left the district with no bonded indebtedness. But that coup was more than twenty years in the future when Black wrote about the $225,000 bond issue that financed the first Greenwood High School.

In May 1924 an overwhelming majority of county voters approved the bond issue to construct a separate and modern high school for Greenwood County. Several sites were proposed and examined before the trustees, in a move still somewhat suspect in a few people's minds, chose the Southern Cotton Oil Company property consisting of 6 1/2 acres, complete with buildings, on South Main Street. Matters appeared to move very slowly: bond approval came in May, architect selection took until October, and the land acquisition was finalized the following February, a full nine months after the referendum. Nor was this the only delay in the project; construction bids received in June 1925 were all higher than the budget for the entire project, and the trustees were forced to delay construction of the gymnasium for another four years. The main building was opened on September 22, 1926, even though the auditorium was not yet finished and landscaping not begun. Formal dedication of the new school was delayed until January 21, 1927.

Black provided the names of the architects for the high school building. They were Wilson, Berryman and Kennedy of Columbia and James C. Hemphill of Greenwood. He called the building "a handsome addition to the public buildings of the city," which indeed it was, and its size was based on realistic expectations. The auditorium, for example, was planned to seat 1,250 people. In striking contrast, the Lander College auditorium built in 1987 seats fewer than 700; college enrollment at the time it opened was more than 2,500. This contrast says something important about the differences in planning, budgeting, and funding of two public projects about sixty years apart.

In addition to its massive auditorium, the new high school boasted 27 brand new classrooms, plus laboratories, domestic science rooms with the latest equipment, and "all the latest and best features of a thoroughly modern high school." Extant accounts vary as to the order of erection of the three segments of the old high school building. Black's contemporaneous article seems to state that the gymnasium wing would be built first and the auditorium later; a 1957 newspaper article indicates just the opposite; and Thomas Dowling's 1970 account reads, "an auditorium and the gymnasium were added a few years later." A 1965 master's thesis by Edna Elledge states that most of the building was completed in 1925 and the rest in 1926. Its author added that the gymnasium and additional classrooms were built in 1929 and the cafeteria and vocational building in 1947-48. Although a 1965 study concluded that the building was seriously overcrowded, having been built for 600 students when the then-current enrollment numbered more than 1,200, the original building continued to serve until 1969 when a new and much larger Greenwood High School was constructed on Highway 254. The building housed Emerald Junior High School during the 1970s, but it was finally abandoned when the new junior high school on Highway 225 was opened in 1981. Many people feared the old building would be demolished, but it was sold in 1984, converted to a modern apartment building, and re-named, appropriately enough, Greenwood High Apartments.

The Greenwood High School building is listed in the National Register of Historic Places, even though the agreement between the trustees and the purchaser protects the building's exterior architectural character for only twenty years from the date of purchase in 1984. The National Register nomination not only clears up the order of construction of the three-part complex but also provides a great deal of justification for the structure's historic significance to Greenwood County, a justification that includes nods to both art and utility. Some people still believe the decision to save the building was based merely on sentimentality and therefore was not good business. Others believe that tangible artifacts of another era are valuable in themselves, in addition to their function as reminders of certain romantic intangibles that remain constant from generation to generation. That debate will not be settled in these pages; excerpts from the National Register nomination are included not to try to change people's attitudes but merely as facts that might not be generally known, or that might have been forgotten, by Greenwood people:

> The Old Greenwood High School is a complex of three buildings located at 857 South Main Street in the city of Greenwood, South Carolina. Two of the buildings – the auditorium building and the main building – were constructed in 1925-26; the gymnasium building was added in 1929-30. All three buildings were designed in 1925 by Greenwood architect James C. Hemphill and the Columbia, South Carolina, architectural firm of Wilson, Berryman and Kennedy. The school is built in the Georgian revival style, with the buildings arranged in a Palladian configuration. The complex was utilized as a school from 1926 until 1982; few alterations were made to the buildings as a result.

The detailed description of each section of the building is too long to quote here. Fortunately, however, anyone who is interested in the exterior architectural details has only to make a slow tour of the building to satisfy himself that they are still intact. The ornamentation was concentrated in the interior of the auditorium building since the other two sections were designed primarily for function and were therefore more restrained, and the permanent and decorative bulletin boards outside the auditorium entrance were shown on the original plans. The sensitivity of the architects is further noted in the line: "the restrained use of stone for trim and ornamentation and the Palladian arrangement of the buildings demonstrate the great care that was taken to beautify a large, institutional complex."

The Greenwood High School building is important also for the collaboration of several noteworthy architects in its design, although exactly how that collaboration occurred is unclear. While James Hemphill actually drew the plans, the senior architect on the project was Charles Coker Wilson of Columbia. Wilson was well known throughout the Southeast and was perhaps the state's most prominent architect in the 1920s. According to the National Register nomination, Wilson designed many public buildings and was the "final architect for the completion of the South Carolina State House." He died in 1933 only a few years after his work on the Greenwood project.

James C. Hemphill (1889-1970) was an Abbeville native who opened an office in Greenwood in 1916. The National Register nomination establishes a significant connection for Hemphill: he once worked as a draftsman for Thomas A. Edison in East Orange, New Jersey. Hemphill's practice in Greenwood covered two distinct phases – from 1916-1933 and again from 1945 until his death in 1970. During the interim he lived and worked in Columbia and Washington, D. C. where he specialized in depression-era reconstruction and, during World War II, worked on military projects. Though Hemphill is known primarily for his work on private residences in Greenwood and Columbia, he also designed many churches and schools. Some of his projects took him as far away as Alabama and even Mexico, but his name is most closely associated with Greenwood.

The building program begun in the early 1950s in response to the state school act continued almost unabated in Greenwood County for about ten years. Mathews School was erected in 1951; the first junior high school, Northside, was built in 1956; West Hodges Elementary opened in 1957; Southside Junior High and Woodfields Elementary were erected in 1958; and Merrywood Elementary was added in 1961. The story of Harris School is particularly interesting in that Greenwood Mills not only erected and equipped this school as part of the Harris Plant project in 1950 but also paid the bills until Harris was absorbed into the county system in 1964. The Harris School building now serves as the home of Cambridge Academy.

Progress in Districts 51 and 52 was similar. *From Hill to Dale to Hollow,* the history of Ware Shoals published in 1983, traces the development of schools in the northernmost part of Greenwood County and ties that development directly to Riegel Textile Corporation's impact on the town dating from 1906. Anyone who reads the section "The Schools" in that little history will come away convinced that a large corporation and two citizens, one black and one white, dominated the educational arena in Ware Shoals. Emma Mauldin Walker Maddox, whom the book calls "a great woman," came to Ware Shoals as a minister's wife in 1917 to teach in such schools for blacks as existed at that time. Because of her persistence in the cause over many years, a new school to replace Briar Hollow was erected and named Emma Maddox School in her honor. Maddox died in 1942.

The other name synonymous with Ware Shoals and education is Professor Marion Boyd (M. B.) Camak, who came to the town from Anderson County in 1924. Camak is credited with the building of Ware Shoals High School, the "beautiful school building on the hill," which opened in 1926. He encouraged nearby Laurens County schools to send their pupils to Ware Shoals High as a means of increasing enrollment so that a better curriculum would be possible. Camak was ahead of his time also in obtaining federal grants. Indeed, he used the depression era public works programs combined with Riegel funds to build a sports stadium for use by the schools, the plant, and the community as early as 1934. Camak retired as district superintendent in 1955. Camak Middle School is named in his honor.

As for the Ninety Six district which separated from Greenwood in 1955, approximately 1,400 students attend three schools – Ninety Six Elementary (grades 1-5), Edgewood Middle School (grades 6-8), and Ninety Six High School (grades 9-12).

The latest annual report of Greenwood School District No. 50 states that the system today consists of fifteen schools serving more than 8,700 students in grades K-12. The district operates with a staff of nearly 1,000, of whom 537 are teachers. The raw student-to-teacher ratio is 16.3:1. A nine-member board of trustees chaired by William B. Patrick, Jr., governs the district's operation.

Another key ingredient of the county education system is the Greenwood County Board of Education, the "fourth player" in shaping educational policy. The Board serves as a sort of liaison between the three districts on the one hand and Greenwood County Council on the other. The importance of that role is readily apparent in that district budgets must be approved by Council. Board members study proposed budgets and make recommendations. The Board also sets up and oversees trustee elections in each district, approves all building projects or renovations using state funds, appoints members to the County

Library Board, and approves any disposition of property held by a district. Finally, the Board serves in appellant capacity for student/parent grievances. It is interesting to note the comment of administrative secretary Toni Ross that only three such cases have been brought to the Board during her tenure, which dates from 1969.

Although the County Board of Education has power to alter or consolidate school districts at will in accordance with a tested and upheld state law, the seven members of the Greenwood County Board apparently share the philosophy that their appointive status makes it inappropriate for them to exercise such sweeping power. One member, Paul Johnson, says, "We have a county that believes power should lie in each district that has trustees elected directly by the people." Other terms used by board members, such as "checks and balances," "buffer between the County Council and the districts," "last chance for students in trouble," and "sounding board," probably sum up the current board members' attitude toward their job. In addition to Ross, other board employees are the county attendance supervisor and the county food service supervisor.

Greenwood's schools began with private initiative, attracted some denominational interest, and gradually evolved into a vigorous public system of education. In 1968, however, something akin to full circle was reached when a group of citizens met to organize the Greenwood Independent School Association with the intent of establishing an alternative to public education. Many people will argue that the real purpose was to avoid the sweeping plan for integration instituted by federal courts in 1967, but a sketch of the history of Cambridge Academy states that one overreaching goal – "to offer an educational program of excellence" – motivated the organizers. That goal led to a school with a single college preparatory track, the most significant departure from the mission of the public school system. The school's name was chosen both for its association with education in general and for its prominence in the history of Greenwood County. Citizens of Ninety Six had had much the same idea nearly two hundred years earlier when the College of Cambridge was established. In 1972 the new school formally adopted a philosophy that "declares belief in stimulating and challenging students toward sound scholastic achievement by providing a program of academic excellence that will enable its graduates to continue their education in college."

Cambridge Academy opened in 1968 with 72 students in grades one through six. It was housed for the first year in the former Durst School building but moved in 1969 to the newly-purchased Harris School. Enrollment increase was rapid, particularly since another grade was added each year; by its third year the school had grown to 216 students in grades K-9, and a branch was opened in McCormick for the first six grades. A major addition was built and the Upper School added in 1974, but the experiment with the McCormick branch ended that year as well, since McCormick parents were supporting an independent school of their own by that time. Enrollment hovers around 300 at present; the rate of college acceptance is a solid 100%, and most graduates are accepted by their first choice of college. Full accreditation by the Southern Association of Colleges and Schools came in 1984. Cambridge is governed by a 20-member board of trustees. Its support arm is CAPA (Cambridge Academy Parents' Association), a name chosen in 1986 as better reflective of the status of the group than the earlier name, Greenwood Independent School Association. The school is currently headed by Jean Kirkpatrick, Headmistress, whose predecessors were Frank Holroyd (1969-71), Kenneth Hauck (1971-81), Glenn Holliman (1981-82), and Russell B. Glenn (1982-1986).

While Cambridge Academy is the only independent school not associated with any other institution, Greenwood does have several schools operated in connection with churches. The largest of these is East Side Christian School established in 1979 by the East Side Baptist Church. The school began with 34 students in kindergarten-4 through third grade and grew in only seven years to an enrollment of 291 students. The first official graduating class of six seniors "marched down the aisle at the end of the 1988-89 school year." The school's kindergarten program graduated 364 children in the first eleven years of its existence. The principal of East Side is an associate pastor of the church, and the school is operated as a church ministry.

Probably no school in Greenwood's history holds more sentimental sway over the town than Bailey Military Institute (or Academy, as it was named for the last six years of its existence). This school's tenure was longer than most, dating as it did from 1913 to 1936 – just before World War I to just before World War II. Juxtaposing the school with two world wars is no accident; a story in the centennial edition of the newspaper notes that it gave the entire town a "military flavor." Bailey was a boys' preparatory school located where Self Memorial Hospital now stands. The school originated in Williston in 1891 as the South Carolina Co-Educational Institute, moved to Edgefield in 1898, and to Greenwood in 1913 where it was re-named to honor its founder, "Colonel" F. N. K. Bailey. This gentleman was one of the more intriguing individuals connected with Greenwood's earlier days. A formidable figure in education, he was cast in the same mold as Samuel Lander, whose story is told in another chapter, although Bailey's contributions were in the fields of co-education and the military academy. In those fields he more nearly resembles the Cokesbury educators of an earlier period, with one notable exception: Cokesbury was Methodist to the core, while Bailey was a staunch Southern Baptist, the son of a minister, and a lifelong supporter of Baptist institutions. An entire scrapbook devoted to Bailey's life and career has been preserved by his granddaughter, Lillie Fuller Simonson of Greenwood.

Franklin Newton Kierulf Bailey (1867-1955) was born in Alabama to a cultured and literate family. He graduated from Howard College (now Samford University) in Birmingham and entered the teaching profession immediately. The move to South Carolina came in 1891 after Bailey had made a successful beginning as principal and superintendent of schools in Alabama. The young man held rather progressive ideas; evidently he saw the need for a co-educational boarding school, something that did not exist in South Carolina at the time. Some will argue that while that statement might be technically true, it is a little misleading. The Cokesbury Conference School, for example, had become co-ed in 1882; by 1890-91, however, most of the students were local, and those who were not boarded with families in the village. In addition, an 1899-90 catalog of Colonel Bailey's school reads: "In 1890 there was no college or *prominent* Boarding School in our State that was Co-Educational" (emphasis added). No one could argue that Cokesbury remained prominent after the Civil War. Further, its patrons were sharply divided over the question of co-education, and some had become disenchanted with the concept of sectarian education as well. Regardless of the question of its uniqueness, the South Carolina Co-Educational Institute established in Williston (Barnwell County) in 1891 was something quite different in the upcountry. A printed page preserved in the scrapbook pictures the school as a frame building two stories high and states that the building later became the first high school in Williston. Although Bailey moved his school to Edgefield in 1898, the building he left behind continued in service as a school until it was replaced by a new brick structure in 1912. The paragraphs describing Bailey's first venture in South Carolina are revealing. It was said that his boldness "revolutionized" education in the whole area. The school opened in 1891 and began taking boarding pupils the next year. "At first they were boarded in private homes, but later a large dormitory was built." Since it is inconceivable that Bailey could have pioneered co-ed dorms before 1900, smart money would have to be on the single dormitory as male only, although there seems to be no proof. The Edgefield catalog mentions "dormitories," to our great relief. It also assures patrons that "young men and young ladies are never thrown together only at stated times and then under the watch-care of the teachers."

The move to Edgefield came when "flattering inducements in the way of buildings and equipments" were offered by that "beautiful little city." Enrollment for the first year in the new location, 280 pupils of whom 101 were boarding students, was cited as proof of the wisdom of the move. The catalog states, however, that Bailey's school had been a success from the very beginning.

The little catalog of the South Carolina Co-Educational Institute at Edgefield is remarkable for much more than its sixteen pages of information. It contains six full-page photographs, for example, and it is the first of several excellent extant publications put out by Bailey's schools. Detailed descriptions of those priceless photographs are included here with the full realization that they are no substitute for the pictures themselves. The first shows the 14-member faculty in 1898-99; six men and eight women, not one of whom is smiling, gaze steadily at the camera. The second picture shows the main building, a marvelous frame structure with verandas, cupolas, turrets, and shutters. Students are everywhere – gathered on porches and balconies, even leaning out of windows. One group, obviously the white-gloved and uniformed corps of cadets, is lined up on a porch roof! The American flag flies from the tallest part of the building, a sort of tower rising above several chimneys, and a stack of rifles appears alongside a drum just inside the wooden front gate. This is an impressive photograph indeed; the pride and enthusiasm it depicts are almost palpable. Next comes a group of eight "commissioned officers" in two types of military uniform, evidence that Bailey's school had been at least quasi-military from its earliest days. In the section entitled "Discipline," in fact, these revealing lines appear: "From the founding of our school, strict military rules have been observed in every department. At that time there were only two other military schools in the State: The Citadel and Col. Patrick's School. . . . The Military Department is well equipped with guns and all necessary accouterments for first-class training. An experienced military instructor has charge of the cadets." The next picture shows the S. C. C. I. Band, a group of fifteen students, including one female, and a mustached gentleman with high collar and pince-nez who is evidently the director, Professor P. P. Blalock. The band members, except for the woman, are attired in natty uniforms. Music was quite prominent in the curriculum, perhaps because both Bailey's wife and sister were fine musicians. Instruction was offered in piano, voice, mandolin, and wind instruments.

The next picture shows the graduating class of 1899, the first after the school moved to Edgefield. There are two women and six men. The catalog describes both the curriculum and the degrees available through the fifteen "schools," (loosely, academic departments, although one, "Telegraphy," might be somewhat suspect), as well as the kindergarten, primary, and preparatory programs offered. The basic degree was evidently the B. E. (Bachelor of English) which, with the addition of one ancient language, would become the B. S. (Bachelor of Science) or, with one ancient and one modern language, would be the A. B. (Bachelor of Arts). Commercial course graduates received only a "diploma." The last picture shows a group of college girls, 1898-99, eight young women attired in what was evidently the "college cap," a mortarboard with tassel, and some sort of military-type uniform with two rows of buttons and leg-of-mutton sleeves. The catalog refers more than once to the "school uniform" required for both sexes. Not surprisingly, the men's outfit cost more: women paid from $7-10, including the college cap, while the cost to young men was from $12-14. It was necessary to purchase these uniforms immediately upon enrollment.

A rigorous day, from the rising bell at 6:30 to the bugle for lights out at 9:45, is laid out in the catalog, with increments in some cases of only ten minutes. Evidently room inspection was an everyday occurrence. The catalog guaranteed that students could attend a whole year for $125 maximum; moreover, the school promised to secure positions as teachers for those who completed the full collegiate and normal courses. In spite of the military flavor that permeated the school, Bailey identified himself only as "President" in the catalog. But there was a "Colonel" Bailey in the future, and a future that lay in Greenwood.

The school at Edgefield lasted for fifteen years, until its president was once again seduced by an offer too good to be refused. There is no evidence that anyone tried to pick up where Bailey left off in Edgefield; the school simply vanished to appear again in a different guise in Greenwood. But, thanks to Simonson's scrapbook, we find one last hurrah for the South Carolina Co-Educational Institute in Edgefield. In October 1975 the county historical society dedicated two historical markers commemorating Edgefield's early schools. One cited Furman Academy and Theological Institution, established in 1826 and forerunner of both Furman University and the Southern Baptist Theological Seminary at Louisville, Kentucky; the other memorialized the Edgefield Village Academy, organized in 1811, and the South Carolina Co-Educational Institute, both of which once flourished in "Academy Grove." The scrapbook contains a copy of the dedicatory program as well as a history of the latter school and its founder written by Bailey's granddaughter, Evelyn Fuller Rigby.

The relocation of the school seems, not surprisingly, to have been Greenwood's idea. The desire to have the school in Greenwood is somehow reminiscent of the Male High School which had been established as a counterpart to the Misses Giles's Greenwood Female College about 25 years earlier. In the later case the existence of a flourishing Lander College in the same town allowed Bailey to abandon co-education and indulge what had evidently been a dream of long standing – a full-fledged military academy modeled along the lines of West Point but without what he called its "rigid and unsympathetic features." It must have been at this juncture that he appointed himself a full "Colonel" (only one source, a 1944 article from a journal in Florida, credited him with military service of any kind; that credit was evidently only an assumption) and provided appropriate rankings for all his faculty as well. R. B. Curry is shown in the 1919 catalog as both Headmaster and

Lieutenant-Colonel (Greenwood still calls him, erroneously, "Major"), and the other faculty members are mostly majors and captains. The lone lieutenant is one Herbert Putnam Bailey, who taught history and science that year. Major Walter Benson was Post Adjutant and mathematics teacher, as well as a member of two faculty committees. Three years later he was head of the department of mathematics and still adjutant, but by that time a member of four important administrative committees as well. Lieutenant Colonel Curry left in 1920, in spite of his promotion, for greener pastures in the business arena of Greenwood. Major Benson would also leave the school in a few years. Both went on to lasting prominence in the town.

Justification of the school's military format is probably unnecessary for southern readers. Bailey had evidently incorporated the military system, at least for boys, in his schools at the beginning, though there is no proof in the case of the Williston school. His rationale seems to have been primarily for discipline, but sectional chauvinism might well have played a part; it is important to remember that Bailey was born only two years after the Civil War ended. In addition to many other attributes, Bailey was no mean promoter. Two extant school catalogs (1919-20 and 1922-23) are not only beautiful pieces of work but also contain an entire section of testimonials called "Expressions of Appreciation." These sections reprint letters from prominent individuals in all walks of life – from college presidents, missionaries, judges, politicians, religious leaders, and businessmen all the way to a mother or two. All praise Bailey for the mix of discipline and "moral tone" he managed to achieve. There can be no doubt that military discipline, which the catalog describes as "the habit of obedience to constituted authority," was the bedrock of Bailey's philosophy. He argued that moral, mental, and physical fitness was the inevitable result of the military training and spirit that permeated the Bailey campus. By an act of Congress in 1916, schools which offered courses prescribed by the Secretary of War were granted weapons and other military equipment for the training of cadets. Bailey Military Institute qualified fully. The government also provided an active officer of the Regular Army as instructor in military science and tactics. In these respects Bailey probably had the equivalent of a modern R. O. T. C. unit on its campus for many years.

The section of the catalog entitled "The City of Greenwood" described the town in glowing terms. Its climate, for example, was said to be equaled only by that "of Southern France, which is conceded to be the best in the world." Similarly, the educational system was regarded as "unsurpassed by any in the State," and business conditions made Greenwood "logically and literally the industrial center of Western Carolina." The town was "surrounded by a fertile farming section . . . practically in the center of the great cotton manufacturing industry . . . [,] situated between the great water powers of the Savannah and Saluda rivers and . . . in the midst of the great electrical development." Furthermore, Greenwood's population of about 12,000 people was doubling every ten years, according to the catalog; the town had four railroads, five banks, seven miles of streets, five cotton mills handling 30,000 bales of cotton annually, one of the best hotels in the South, a modern city hospital, an orphanage, the best and lowest-priced water and light service in the state, and no vacant buildings. Most important of all, Greenwood was "the best moral town of like size in the South" with many strong churches, the buildings of which always impressed visitors by their "imposing appearance." The last sentence, italicized in the original, reads as follows: *"Greenwood has never permitted the legalized sale of intoxicants, never had licensed drinking clubs, gambling houses, places of ill-fame, nor other such institutions for the corruption of the citizenship. Its laws in reference to such are strictly enforced."*

All available evidence indicates that Bailey Military Institute was a superb example of its type, and there can be no doubt the school loomed large in the life of Greenwood for more than twenty years. Bailey himself, however, sold out in 1922 to three faculty members, Majors J. E. Burnside, Jr., S. B. Marshall, and John Moore. In an announcement made on September 20, he cited health reasons for the sale but also admitted that he wanted to spend all the winter months in Florida and would therefore be unable to remain as active superintendent. The new owners were all Greenwood natives, and at least one – Burnside – was a Bailey alumnus. The newspaper announcement made clear that Bailey was not exactly retiring: he planned to retain an interest in the institution as well as his residence in Greenwood. But the new owners managed the institution only about three years; Colonel J. D. Fulp succeeded Burnside, Marshall, and Moore.

Most of the principal faculty members in the early days in Greenwood had been with Bailey in Edgefield. Those gentlemen included R. B. Cain, R. B. Curry, J. F. Entzminger, and Thomas J. Lyon. A four-page history of Bailey Military Institute (author unknown) states that all moved to Greenwood except Major Lyon. While he does not appear in the 1917 yearbook – Captain S. A. Porter held Lyon's former title of Commandant of Cadets that year – two later catalogs from the Greenwood years list Lyon as Commandant and show his picture. Evidently Lyon rejoined the faculty after 1917. Curry became headmaster after the move to Greenwood, and Walter Benson joined the faculty in 1915.

The local governing board in 1919, called the Board of Visitors, was chaired by H. V. R. Schrader. Its membership consisted of prominent Greenwoodians Kenneth Baker, C. C. Featherstone, S. C. Hodges, A. F. McKissick, C. A. Mays, D. A. G. Ouzts, W. J. Snead, and H. L. Watson. J. B. Park was the only addition shown in the 1922 catalog.

The school had six superintendents, or presidents, during its tenure in Greenwood, one of whom was Walter William Benson who served in 1923-24, the year before he was named principal of Greenwood High School. Its period of peak enrollment was 1917-21, when the student body hovered between 350 and 500. The newspaper noted that Bailey's service flag for World War I held 156 stars. An editorial from August 23, 1936, cited the "earnest service of the high-toned faculty which distinguished it," as well as the "reflected services of the thousands of young men who were recipients of . . . [its] training and development." Other benefits of the school came from "drills and parades of the snappily-dressed cadets" which were features of all its public functions. Everybody loves a parade, but the most important legacy of BMA might have been those faculty members who stayed in Greenwood after the school closed. In addition to Benson, who became principal of Greenwood High School, and Curry, who headed Citizens Trust Company, there were R. B. Cain, G. L. Dickson, S. A. Porter, and J. Lide Wilson.

Evidently Bailey Military Academy died a natural death in the years after its founder withdrew. One source cited the steady growth of the public school system as a contributing factor to its demise; other causes might have been the loss of key faculty members and a certain disenchantment with the military school concept, particularly between the two world wars. In any event the school was not in a flourishing state at the time of a devastating fire that destroyed one whole wing of the barracks in 1936. The fire must have delivered the coup de grace. When it became known that the school would not reopen that fall, Greenwood School District No. 18 purchased the property and subsequently sold it to the Self Foundation as a hospital site. Funds from that sale were used to buy property on Phoenix Street for the high school athletic field. The original barracks building continued in use as apartments, medical offices, and offices for the school district for several years. In a final touch of sentimental irony, the daughter of the school's founder, Thelma Bailey, worked there for some years as secretary to the superintendent of School District No. 50.

As for the founder, Bailey's health improved so remarkably after the move to Florida that he built a whole new career in the citrus industry and re-directed his educational fervor to a seat on the board of Stetson University and as superintendent of schools of Highlands County, a position he held for about twenty years. Naturally, he became president of the Stetson board, and the University awarded him an honorary Doctor of Laws in 1943. Bailey retained his lifelong interest in Baptist institutions; in addition to his service at Stetson, he headed the board of the Florida Baptist Children's Home. He was cited as one of the "Men Who Made Florida" in 1940. Bailey's private life was nearly as varied as his public career; he was married three times. He maintained contact through friends and family with both Edgefield and Greenwood throughout his Florida years. Stories and articles about him appeared in many upstate newspapers; one written by Eugene Blake made the *State Magazine* in 1954. When Bailey died in 1955 at the age of 88, funeral services were held in Sebring, Florida, but his body was brought to Greenwood for burial in Edgewood Cemetery. John Murdoch of Connie Maxwell and James A. Bowers, pastor of the First Baptist Church, spoke at the Greenwood services. Murdoch called Bailey a "practical idealist" and a man of "indomitable courage" who had outlived his own generation but not his usefulness. The House of Representatives of the State of Florida adopted a resolution in Bailey's memory on May 6, 1955.

Another proprietary school with a longer tenure than BMA was Greenwood College of Commerce which opened in 1917 as Peterson Business College. At one time the school occupied the seventh floor of the Textile Building which many people will remember was surrounded on three sides by windows. That floor has since been removed. The late Clyde Stephens of Greenwood recalled that the school's name was changed to Greenwood Business College while he was a student in the year 1926-27. He also remembered that there were four teachers at the time. In 1938 Frank Reed purchased the school and changed the name again, this time to Greenwood College of Commerce.

The school was sold yet again in 1940. The new owner was Edward L. Wolf who had owned a business school in Meadeville, Pennsylvania. Mr. and Mrs. Wolf moved their family to Greenwood and operated the College of Commerce until their deaths in a tragic automobile accident in December 1963. The Wolfs' son Ted took over management of the school and lasted until 1969, at which time he was forced to close its doors because of declining enrollment. Wolf attributed the decision to competition from Piedmont Technical Education Center which had opened three years before. He also noted that eight other business schools around the state had already succumbed for the same reason.

Greenwood College of Commerce, located for most of its life on the second floor of the Textile Building, met a real need in Greenwood for many years. Wolf has preserved an old school register dating from 1943 which lists the names of students who enrolled each session. The first entry is Sara Frances Lowe, 327 Norwood Street, whose course is listed as "Complete Business." The last name is Alfredia Adams who indicated a preference for "Private Secretarial." In between are literally hundreds of names of students from Greenwood and the surrounding area. Wolf estimates that the school has more than 2,000 alumni, many of whom continue to staff Greenwood offices and a number of whom went on to open businesses of their own. Among the latter are Walker Byrd who until his recent retirement owned Charzanne Beauty College, another proprietary school located on Highway 72, and Ruth Ivester Polattie, proprietor of the Hash House, a Greenwood legend on East Cambridge Avenue.

An undated Greenwood College of Commerce catalog lists the school's programs of study: Complete Business, Private Secretarial, Stenographic, Junior Accounting, and Advanced Accounting. The catalog also identifies a number of special courses for those students not enrolled in a complete program. The school's philosophy and purpose were intensely practical. Its motto, "Business Education Doesn't Cost, It Pays," appears on nearly every page of the catalog, and a quote from the title page illustrates the school's position: "general education is desirable; . . . polite education is a luxury; but a practical, everyday business education is a necessity." Since the College of Commerce enrolled more females than males, women will enjoy the irony of another quote from the same author, lawyer and politician Chauncey M. Depew, which also appears on the title page: "I feel the young man who enters business without going to a business school is enormously hampered in his progress in life." Depew, who died in 1928, no doubt had little experience with young women who entered business.

The fact that the College of Commerce filled a real need in Greenwood is evinced by its 52-year history and the events during the time it operated. Opening about the time of World War I, the school provided opportunity during a period of great occupational change in the South. There is no evidence that it closed during the depression years, and it was definitely important at the time of World War II. One graduate noted that a number of students found wartime jobs in Washington as a result of their business and clerical training.

Many alumni remember Etta M. Dorn as their favorite teacher, and a couple of telephone conversations some forty years after she left Greenwood help to explain why she is remembered so fondly. Dorn recounted during one interview that she had recently attended her 65th reunion at Coker College and had a wonderful time reminiscing with the lone classmate who showed up. She also recalled the circumstances of her employment at the College of Commerce: her then-husband, one of Congressman Bryan Dorn's six brothers, was employed there when he was called to active military duty at the beginning of World War II, and Mrs. Dorn simply stepped into his job. She remembers that she taught about nine years and worked for a time later at the Chamber of Commerce. Etta Dorn is now in her mid-80s. She lives in Columbia.

Public vocational and technical education came to Greenwood in two stages. First came *A Study of the Need for an Area Vocational School in Greenwood County, South Carolina* by Clemson University, in cooperation with the Division of Vocational Education and the State Department of Education, in 1966. The preface notes that the study was undertaken at the request of a group of interested citizens of Greenwood County and that it was the first of its kind in South Carolina. Only Greenwood High School had any sort of vocational program, and educators believed there was clearly a need for facilities to serve all high schools in the county. Accordingly, a combination of local and federal funds was secured and a building erected on Airport Road to serve as an area vocational high school. Thomas I. Dowling reported that the facility was opened in 1968 and offered courses such as food and health services, auto mechanics, machine shop, clothing design, cosmetology, small engine repair, and construction trades.

The second phase of vocational/technical education in Greenwood was the Piedmont Technical Education Center, established as the eighth such center in the state in 1966. A statewide system of technical education centers was mandated by the General Assembly in 1961, in large part to insure a well-trained work force for industry attracted by the state's massive push toward industrial diversification. A 1984 Piedmont TEC news release called the system "unique" and "among the finest in the nation." It was conceived as a new venture in post-secondary education with a mandate "to serve the actual, documented needs of the area's business, industry and general populace." Possibly because of the breadth of this stated mission, the technical education network has evolved into virtually a statewide system of two-year community colleges in the years since its inception. Piedmont Technical Education Center became Piedmont Technical College in 1974, according to the news release, "to reflect its post-secondary education mission." Many educators believe the original purpose of the technical education system has become blurred by the change to college status; they point, for example, to needless competition for students and duplication of effort in many towns, including Greenwood, with both a technical college and a four-year college within a few miles of each other.

Even before Piedmont TEC became Piedmont Technical College, Lander College had sought some means of capitalizing on the opportunities the new system provided, both to expand its own curriculum and to contribute its share to a new era of post-secondary education in South Carolina. At that time a county institution with a local governing board, Lander became the first college in the state to accept credits earned at technical centers. But Lander went even further, all the way to initiating a degree program in Vocational/Technical Education. Under this "upside-down" program, students would complete two years in a particular area at a technical school, then enter Lander for academic courses and professional education requirements. It was expected that these graduates would be well prepared to staff technical education centers themselves, as well as vocational high schools, all over the state. Though the program, which had barely begun when the college became a state agency in 1973, was almost immediately abandoned by the new administration, Lander continued to accept credits from Piedmont Tech. Indeed, credits earned in academic divisions of technical colleges are now routinely transferable to four-year colleges and universities.

The value of tracing the development of a public school system within a county, beyond the obvious importance of education itself, probably derives more from the beginnings than the end product at any given moment. In the last decade of the twentieth century nothing is more ordinary than public schools, and nothing is more fraught with controversy. Indeed, nothing is harder to measure qualitatively than the impact of mass public education. The reliability of test scores is always a problem, as is every effort to meet the needs of some group or other, whether ethnic, physically handicapped, learning disabled, economically deprived, or otherwise labeled. For want of a better standard, per-pupil expenditure of public funds has become the means by which states are compared in their commitment to education. South Carolina has never fared well on that criterion and prefers to publicize the percentage of its total budget expended for education, a percentage that has increased consistently over the years. Tracing a single system in a single county in a single state is almost necessarily an exercise of numbers and years and dollars. Evaluation will be the province of sociologists and educational historians years hence. But every town had its pioneers and their dreams, and Greenwood is no exception. A few of those pioneers have already been mentioned, and this journey through the county's battles with ignorance will end with sketches of a few more, among the hundreds who deserve mention.

Three women, only one a Greenwood County native, share "first teacher" honors in the new graded school that opened in 1891 under Superintendent Rufus B. Wilson, himself a North Carolinian. They were Laura Maner, of Allendale; Eva Smart, from Troy; and Nellie Screws, a native of Alabama. It is unclear from surviving records whether this was Screws's first teaching job, nor is her date of birth available, but the fact that Nellie Screws was very important in the life of Greenwood is evident from the number of newspaper articles and editorials run soon after her death. May Bailey Smith's scrapbook, preserved by nieces Clara Robeson and Margaret Tinsley, contains two pages devoted to Screws, including a couple of photographs, and a search of *The Greenwood Index* turned up a good deal more. Screws died while still actively teaching, and most intriguing of all was the discovery that the community tried hard, but unsuccessfully, to have her body interred in Greenwood. That story appeared on the front page of the newspaper of June 9, 1917.

"At half past one o'clock Friday morning," ran the story, "Miss Nellie Screws passed into rest, rest that she would not have any other way, for on this earth she was at her work from day to day regardless of her physical weakness and she knew no rest." It appeared she had "broken down the day the schools closed" and succumbed to pleurisy and pneumonia soon thereafter. Her family in Alabama was duly notified, and a niece arrived about an hour after Screws's death. The next morning, according to the newspaper, "a delegation of citizens went to the home of Mrs. C. T. Bailey where the body was and urged upon Miss Ferrell [the niece] the wishes of the community that Miss Nellie be allowed to be buried here." Not only was Miss Nellie's niece importuned in person by many prominent Greenwood citizens, her mother and brother back in

Alabama received more than one telegram with the same urgent appeal. Trustee chairman H. L. Watson's wire cited the "great feeling" of the entire community in the matter. The Ferrell family was, however, adamant that Screws's body be returned to be "buried . . . where her mother rests," though Greenwood was thanked for its "thoughtful offer."

Notwithstanding its disappointment, Greenwood went ahead with a funeral service at the First Baptist Church. That service was meticulously covered in the newspaper, including the strange revelation that the Reverend B. H. DeMent used the occasion to reminisce about his association with Mrs. DeMent, a former Greenwood school superintendent, and Screws's landlord Dr. J. B. Green, all of whom were graduates of Peabody College. Since there was no hint that Screws herself ever attended Peabody, the reader is left to speculate on the reason for such a departure. After the services three Greenwood representatives accompanied Ferrell on the journey to Seale, Alabama, for Screws's burial. The newspaper noted that the train was three hours late.

But Greenwood's preoccupation with memorializing Miss Nellie had only just begun. An editorial the day after her death called her "the frail and timid body who had become so large a factor in the life of Greenwood," and added, "We feel, in every home almost, as if a member of the family had slipped away from us." Other tributes followed, including a long letter from colleague Nannie G. Major who wrote that Miss Nellie had taught at least 1,500 Greenwood children. Some, whom she called her "grandchildren," were the offspring of earlier students.

The June 12 issue of the newspaper announced the formation of the Nellie Screws Memorial Association to raise funds to erect a permanent memorial. The Association had five officers and an executive committee of fifteen, including the entire board of trustees. The newspaper noted that one Greenwood gentleman had already sent a contribution of $5.00 along with the line that he "would make it more but done [don't] want to rob some one else of a gracious privilege." Fund raising was slow; at one point the newspaper noted that the Red Cross canvass then in progress hampered the local effort on behalf of the Nellie Screws Memorial. The newspaper of June 23 reported $33.75 in hand toward a goal of "not less than $500." Things looked bleak, but no one spoke of abandoning the effort. Persistence was the key for the promoters.

And persist they did, all through World War I apparently; nearly five years after the effort had begun, the Nellie Screws Memorial in the middle of Magnolia Cemetery became a reality. The unveiling took place on January 10, 1922, with appropriate ceremony and an address by A. J. Sproles. The tributes were long and flowery; not surprisingly, considering the teacher pay scale of the day, Miss Nellie was extolled for "self sacrifice" and a "beautiful life, noble deeds, unselfish motives, devotion to duty, and consecrated service." Among Sproles's most telling lines was this: "the position of the elementary teacher is far more important than that of the college professor, although your paycheck does not always indicate that your constituency believe it."

Miss Nellie just might have appealed more to parents during her lifetime than to her students. She is remembered as a stern disciplinarian whom no six-year-old could possibly escape, since she was the only first grade teacher in Greenwood. A little memoir by Lucia McLees Mercer entitled "The Second Layer of My Life – First Grade" (1986) described Miss Nellie's habit of slapping her students. It was said that "no one, literally no one, ever, ever completed the first grade without being slapped." Mercer's own personal slap came one day when Miss Nellie noticed that a corner of her report card was bent. Mercer wrote that her reaction was humiliation which quickly turned to relief that she needn't dread it any more. She also defended Miss Nellie as "a product of her day [when] parents and teachers believed in discipline, and that a child was spoiled by sparing the rod." She added: "It was said that when Miss Nellie 'learned you, you stayed learned.' And that was true."

An undated newspaper article in Smith's scrapbook details another memorial to Miss Nellie, one that evidently failed to materialize. That article states, "A bronze tablet to the memory of Miss Nellie Screws will be placed in the room in which she taught so many years at Magnolia Street School and a Nellie Screws Library will be established as a part of the juvenile department of the Carnegie Library, the room for this library being designated by a suitable tablet." Greenwood's first separate library building dates from 1917, but no source mentions a memorial to Nellie Screws either there or in the building that replaced it; presumably the committee members changed their minds in favor of the Magnolia Cemetery memorial.

Two photographs of Nellie Screws, one a posed photographer's shot and the other captioned by May Smith, "taken in our front yard on Hampton Ave.," show two views of the schoolmarm of that day. In the first, a young woman in white organdy and ruffles, hair up except for a fringe on the forehead, is leaning slightly forward, with the whole body, and certainly the face, caught in an attitude something like expectancy. The eyes are intelligent, the nose rather long and patrician, and the thin lips are curved in a hint of a smile. The later snapshot, with the face in profile, depicts a mature woman, ramrod straight, in a high-necked shirtwaist and long black skirt. Heavy dark hair is swept up, and there is no smile playing about the mouth. Her hands are relaxed by her side, but there is an air of authority in the set of her head and shoulders. This is unmistakably the photograph of a schoolteacher; one can almost smell the chalk dust. It is interesting to speculate whether the teachers of that day really found fulfillment in their profession, but there can be no doubt that their pupils remember them with something akin to awe.

Although there is a great deal more printed information on Nellie Screws than on any other of Greenwood's early teachers, no accounting of the early days of Greenwood's schools would be complete without mention of Nannie Major, a colleague of Miss Nellie's for 23 years, and Maude Pratt. The centennial edition of the newspaper noted that Major began her teaching career in "nearby county schools." Those schools, according to her obituary, were Pertville, Stoney Point, and The Nation, all near Major's home in the Quarry section of the county. Miss Nannie taught at all three before she graduated from Winthrop College in 1894 (Winthrop was established in 1886). Major began her career with the city schools as teacher of the 5th and 6th grades. When Magnolia School opened, she took over the 5th grade. Major was named principal in 1926 and served in that capacity until 1945. Since she would shortly reach the age of 75, no doubt her retirement was mandatory; nevertheless, she continued for one more year in the Magnolia School Library. Nannie Major holds the record for sheer longevity as an educator: she taught for 55 years.

When Miss Nannie finally retired, no doubt with great reluctance even at the age of nearly 76, the Magnolia PTA unveiled a plaque in her honor at its meeting on November 19, 1946. The plaque read: "In recognition of Miss Nannie Major — this tablet is erected by the Board of Trustees of Greenwood City Schools as a tribute to her faithful and inspiring leadership as teacher and principal for 55 years." There is no record that Miss Nannie's plaque survived the fire that destroyed the school in 1980.

As usual, the newspaper recapped Major's career in the account of her death on December 30, 1956, after a long illness. This time, however, there was a little something extra in the way of remembrance. W. H. Nicholson wrote what he termed a "humble tribute" in a letter to the editor which was printed in the edition of January 2, 1957. That letter read in part: "An incident occurred after her retirement as principal of Magnolia and after her personal faculties had weakened: we found her one morning at the door of the school, then not in session, trying to open the door. Some see only pathos in that occurrence, to others it was a crowning touch to a long record of devotion to duty. There was other symbolism in that incident; she was always 'opening doors' for little children, the doors to the wonders of knowledge and the higher planes of conduct." Nicholson also wrote that "it would be difficult for many of us who knew the school over the last thirty years to think of it without thinking of Miss Nannie and Miss Maude Pratt."

Many people in Greenwood speak of Major and Pratt almost in the same breath. Apparently both could be considered genuine "characters" of their day. Miss Maude, for example, is widely remembered for her devotion to her car — one irreverent high school student of the 1940s was overheard one day calling her "T-Model Maude." The story goes that Miss Pratt was continually frustrated in trying to keep her old Ford running during the war years when auto parts were in short supply. Finally she wrote a letter to the Ford Motor Company detailing her plight, the result of which was that the parts she needed were actually flown to Greenwood. How wonderful it would be to be able to reprint that letter!

Pratt's teaching career began in 1902 when she became the first teacher at Grendel School, according to the newspaper, but she "soon went to Magnolia and taught there until 1945." Her obituary in *The Index-Journal* of March 3, 1958, reads somewhat differently. According to that article, Pratt was born in Due West and moved to Greenwood as a child. A graduate of Erskine, she had taught at Bradley for a few years before she came to Greenwood in 1900. After 46 years as an elementary teacher, mostly at Magnolia, Pratt retired at the age of 72. She died in March 1958 after a long illness. Although her obituary lists membership in the UDC and the First Baptist Church, there can be little doubt that Pratt's chief interest, as well as that of other teachers of her day, lay in her work in the classroom. These women appear to have considered their students as their families. While there is no way to be sure, it is pleasant to believe that each child's progress brought a measure of personal gratification to these dedicated teachers.

The private lives of these remarkable women are virtually unknown to us. It is easy to believe from such records as remain that their entire lives were lived either at school or in church. For example, they seem to have spent many summers doing graduate work at Teachers College of Columbia University in New York City, and their obituaries never omit mentioning their devotion to their churches. They really appear to have looked upon their profession as a "calling" not unlike that of the ministry. One thing is clear: they did **not** do what they did for the money, for teachers' salaries were pitifully small, even by prevailing standards of the day. The particular type of selfless dedication these women's lives represent is rather rare today, and there is a certain irony attached in that public school teachers are finally able to earn reasonably decent salaries.

Another beloved educator whose career in Greenwood spanned more than forty years was Major Walter William Benson, a native of Travelers Rest who came to Greenwood in 1915 as a professor at Bailey Military Institute. The rank of major was purely honorary and bestowed because the superintendent believed a military school required at least military-sounding titles for its teachers. Boykin Curry provided this information and stated also that Superintendent "Colonel" F. N. K. Bailey liked to substitute military "promotions" for salary increases. Curry's father, Major R. B. Curry, attained his rank (and his small salary) in the same way. There is one bit of evidence, however, that Benson's military credentials had some basis in fact. He won the Star of the West Medal as a cadet at The Citadel in 1906. That medal is still awarded:

> [It] is presented each year to the cadet who wins the competitive drill in the manual of arms held just before the Awards Parade at the end of the year. The medal was originally presented to The Citadel in 1893 by Dr. B. H. Teague, a veteran of the Civil War. The medal derives its name from a central piece of wood, in the shape of a star, taken from the U. S. Vessel, The Star of The West. The

> competition is for members of the three under classes in order that the winner may wear it while a cadet. The names of the winners are engraved on the original medal which is kept in the office of the president. A replica is given to the winner to wear on his dress uniform.

Local sources indicate that Benson graduated in 1908, but that date is incorrect. He was a member of the class of 1907; a biographical sketch appears in a little book, *History of the Class of 1907, The Citadel,* published in 1965. Classmate James Henry Hammond, grandson and namesake of a South Carolina governor and United States Senator and quite a personage in his own right, is listed as publisher of the book, a copy of which he inscribed to Benson's wife: "[My] only regret is that a real volume could not be written about Benson. Great. Honest in every way. One of those that The Citadel could take pride in." The Citadel book is special for many reasons, among them the fact that it was the first published class history, according to General Mark Clark who at that time had just announced his retirement as president. Hammond was evidently something of a wit as well as a poet, and the book contains examples of both talents. He had roomed with Walter Benson during their junior year and described his roommate in these words: "Benson was the most wonderful person I ever knew, rigidly straight in all things and brilliant." This from a man of Hammond's stature and accomplishments is high praise indeed.

Benson graduated second in his class with a degree in English. The class had dwindled from more than fifty members originally to only nineteen on graduation day, a situation that seems to have been typical of the times. Hammond attributed the attrition to economic conditions, noting that South Carolina was overwhelmingly an agricultural state and the price of cotton stood at five or six cents a pound. Benson was listed as a "beneficiary cadet," which probably means a scholarship student. His Citadel career was quite varied – not surprising was his involvement in the literary society, the oratorical association, and the college yearbook, but he was president of the athletic association and helped plan the senior hop and class picnic as well. His career was always in education. He taught at Staunton Military Academy in Virginia for one year and at the Furman Preparatory School in Greenville for two. At that point he became superintendent of schools, first in Ridge Spring and later in Easley. He was thirty years old when he joined the faculty at Bailey in 1915. One account states that he was superintendent of Bailey for nine years. If that is true, another account which credits him with one year is in error. At any rate, Benson accepted the position of principal of Greenwood High School in 1924 and served in that capacity until his retirement in 1953.

The citation accompanying Benson's induction to the Greenwood Hall of Fame in 1982 states that he "influenced in a remarkable way hundreds of young people who attended Greenwood High School." While that statement is undoubtedly true, it is somewhat less than satisfactory to anyone in search of the real person who exerted that influence or the precise nature of the remarkable way he used it. In the absence of any documentary proof, perhaps it is risky to state the belief that Benson was one of those rare individuals who possessed a fully developed self, one who had formulated a philosophy quite interchangeable with any aspect of his life. His work was therefore essentially himself, and his motto, astounding in its simplicity, yet endures as the measure of a man. That motto – "Do Right Because It Is Right" – was so pervasive, in fact, that it was finally emblazoned over the entrance to the school as a tribute to the man who coined it. A former student remembers that at one point someone tried to add the words "and not because you are afraid to do wrong" to Major Benson's famous line, but that attempt was short-lived.

Trying to describe Benson without using words such as *honor, character, integrity,* and *nobility* is impossible. One tribute called him "a man who accepted others, and yet even in his acceptance . . . demanded a stringent code of ethics and morality, and sought for them a very high standard of achievement." An article in the school newspaper noted that he was vitally interested in every student and always fair. Gertrude Brabham, who was the first secretary at Greenwood High School and who worked for the superintendent as well as the principal, believes that Benson's most remarkable trait in dealing with rowdy students was his patience. He understood the futility of trying to reason with an angry adolescent, and his methods included a waiting period; that is, the student had to sit cooling his heels in the secretary's office while Benson quietly went about other business. After the danger of explosion was past – students sat sometimes for a half hour or even longer, depending on their temper span – the principal did his duty in his characteristically pleasant, but firm, fashion. Very rarely, that duty took the form of a few strokes with a leather strap. In those extreme moments, the student would straddle a straight chair and receive the punishment across his back. Rumor had it in those days that Benson used the tower for this drastic act, but according to Brabham it took place in his office. She thinks he would never have climbed those tower steps, and it was too hot up there anyway. Some students believed the tower area was the scene of other types of teenage experimentation, but Brabham doubts that. A common prank in her day was students' dropping lighted matches in the large trash cans at the end of each corridor. Benson was usually able to wring a confession from the perpetrators.

Brabham worked with Benson for about sixteen years, and her admiration for the man and the way he did his job never faltered. "There will never be another like him," she said. She was also the source for the information that Benson spent his summers for many years as a counselor at Camp Transylvania in North Carolina. Since one would think rest and relaxation for a high school principal would mean the luxury of not having to deal with youngsters, this activity merely confirms the view that Benson genuinely enjoyed working with children both in and out of school.

Helen Watkins Harrison, who also worked with Major Benson, remembers that he was somehow able to make students see unacceptable behavior as the result of a lack of self respect. She believes he truly cared, and he made a point of knowing every student by name, even when enrollment reached 1,000 or more, in part to enable him to deal with the person and not merely the offense he had committed. It must have been humiliating to hear the simple words, "I'm disappointed in you," when one had managed to exasperate a teacher to the point of being sent "to the office." Harrison herself remembers feeling she would rather be caught misbehaving by anyone – her parents, her pastor, anyone – other than Major Benson. "Both as a student and a teacher," she said, "I remember trying to live up to his expectations, and I'm sure others did the same. Our aim was high and our goals ambitious because he made us feel we owed it to ourselves to be the best we could be."

Walter Benson was so universally admired that some people wonder why he never served in a higher administrative capacity than high school principal. His best chance at the office of superintendent would seem to have been in 1945 when William E. Black retired after more than 25 years, and he actually did serve in an acting capacity for a few months in 1951 following Superintendent J. C. Turner's death. But according to Boykin Curry who joined the board of trustees in 1946, Benson sincerely believed he had found his niche and had no ambition for higher office or even higher pay. So strong was his dedication to his work, in fact, and so indifferent was he to personal gain, that retirement time in 1953 found him with practically nothing to live on. At least four sources indicate that J. S. Abney arranged for a job with Abney Mills after Benson's retirement so that he would be eligible for social security benefits and a little more retirement income. Interestingly enough, the Abney Mills job was in the personnel department where his supervisor was Edgar Davis, the same Edgar Davis who, as a junior teacher and band director at Greenwood High School about ten years earlier, had reported to Major Benson. The two men were close friends in both associations, and Davis's recollections parallel those of others who knew Benson well.

Several friends relate that Benson liked to give them gifts of books from his own library. These books nearly always carried an inscription on the flyleaf, and their texts were often underlined or annotated in some way. The inscriptions were usually quotations from other sources; attempts to find something original from Benson's own pen have been unsuccessful. Whether he kept copies of correspondence and other papers is not known. Hammond noted in a letter accompanying copies of The Citadel book that for several years before tackling it himself he had urged Benson, among others, to undertake writing the class history.

Benson's honors during his lifetime, in addition to the Star of the West medal, include an award in 1952 from the Woodmen of the World for service to the community of Greenwood and the Greenwood Rotary Club Man of the Year Award in 1956. The Woodmen citation reads: "An educator true to the highest tradition of his profession – One who teaches by precept and example as well as through efficient presentation of technical knowledge – A friend of youth and always a champion of right."

Walter W. Benson died at his home on Elm Court on June 22, 1959. An editorial in *The Index-Journal* printed the day after his death reads in part:

> His relations with young people were marked by patience and understanding, by occasional righteous indignation and leavened with gentle humor. He had qualities of mind and spirit which commanded respect and a personality which prompted affection. In his lifetime this tall, thin man with the piercing dark eyes and soft voice exerted an influence for good on thousands of students. Through them he leaves an indelible mark on this community.

On November 30, 1982, some 23 years after his death, Major Walter William Benson was elected to the Greenwood County Hall of Fame.

Julius Wistar "Pinky" Babb was a great deal younger than Walter Benson, but for the period from 1943 to Benson's retirement the two men worked closely together as principal and head football coach/athletic director at Greenwood High School. It would be difficult to decide which of the two posts was more important at the time – Greenwood has always been a sports town, and the sport of choice is probably football. A native of Princeton in Laurens County, Babb was a standout on the Furman University football teams of the late 1930s; he came to Greenwood High after short stints at other schools.

Most of his peers called Babb "Pinky," a reference to his red hair and ruddy coloring, but to everybody else, including his family and his players, he was simply "Coach" or "Coach Babb." Benson and Babb, the two supreme authority figures on the high school campus, evidently understood each other from the first. It is significant that the principal and the football coach together set an example for the faculty by going back to school for the master's degree. Babb's widow says that Benson foresaw the need for advanced degrees for high school teachers and administrators and suggested that Babb join him in graduate school at Furman University. And both were involved in an innovation that continues to move in and out of the national news. At Greenwood High School in the 1940s and 1950s, it was possible to earn one's letter in academics as well as in varsity sports. A tiny lamp of knowledge was sewn onto the letter at the spot a football or basketball might be expected to appear, but the academic block G otherwise was identical to the athletic. Furthermore, no one seemed to find anything odd or unusual about very different types of students wearing green or gold sweaters adorned with the letter. In the late 1970s a newspaper story revealed that a high school in Pittsburgh, the only one in town to do so, had inaugurated the same program as a means of stimulating interest in learning; the novelty was such that the Associated Press picked up the story, and newspapers all across the country ran it. And a high school in Summerville implemented the notion for the first time in 1991. No one remembers exactly how the program originated in Greenwood, but most people would probably agree that it was a winning idea and typical of the Benson/Babb team.

As a coach Babb was first of all a winner. Only one high school coach in the country compiled a record better than his in career wins and losses. Babb's record at Greenwood High School was 336-81-23 with only two losing seasons – 1950 and 1969. He compiled a 9-1 record in his first year, losing only the season opener, and the first of several undefeated seasons came in 1947. Babb's coaching honors during his career ranged from the strictly local all the way to national recognition: he was selected for the National High School Coaches Association Hall of Fame in 1976 and was named the South Carolina AAAA Coach of the Year four times. Babb made the South Carolina Athletic Hall of Fame in 1973; two years later, he was named both regional and national Coach of the Year by the National Coaches Association. He was named to the Furman University Athletic Hall of Fame and honored at a Day of Recognition at his alma mater. The Greenwood Rotary Club named Babb its Man of the Year in 1974, the Lions Club followed suit in 1977, and the Chamber of Commerce named him to its County Hall of Fame in 1978.

Babb retired in 1981 to pursue, as he put it, "other game plans" for his life. The National High School Coaches Association honored him that year with its Dwight Keith Award for "outstanding contribution to the advancement of interscholastic athletics and the coaching profession." He became a member of the South Carolina Order of the Palmetto, the state's highest award, in 1982 and in 1983 won the Distinguished Service Award of the National Coaches Athletic Association.

Although every season was a championship to Babb and every player a champion, his admirers drew somewhat finer distinctions. The quality of the quarterbacks Babb always seemed to turn out once prompted Clemson Coach Frank Howard to quip that his own job was in no jeopardy so long as Babb stayed in Greenwood and sent him players such as Harvey White, Lowndes Shingler, and Joe Anderson. A few years earlier when "Doc" Blanchard and Glenn Davis starred as "Mr. Inside" and "Mr. Outside" of a championship Army team, Babb trained his own Blanchard and Davis in two Greenwood players named "Sonny" Horton and "Hootie" Johnson.

The nomination of Greenwood's legendary football coach to the County Hall of Fame ignored the specifics of his career and instead stressed the recognition and honor Babb had brought to Greenwood. His contributions were termed unique and far beyond the expectations of his profession. The penultimate paragraph of the nomination also reveals a tidbit of county history:

> When Pinky Babb came to Greenwood, football games were played on a converted baseball field at Mathews Mill. Through his leadership and much personal labor, the old field located behind the present Emerald Junior High building [original Greenwood High School on South Main Street] was built. Largely through his leadership and the willingness of a grateful community to show what his presence in Greenwood had meant, a stadium valued in excess of $300,000 is owned by School District 50 at no cost to this School District.

Babb's widow has kept her husband's study in the house on Janeway just as it was while he lived, and she has only to glance at the inscriptions and citations that line the walls for reassurance of the regard of his peers. She admits to pride in his achievements, but she treasures even more her husband's investment in the lives of the boys he worked with for 39 years. "My reward," he wrote in his retirement announcement, "has been to watch boys develop into young men, and to make their contributions in the game of life."

Babb died on November 26, 1983. More than a thousand people crowded the First Baptist Church for his memorial service.

Emma (Sunbeam) Andrews is another Greenwood educator whose name at one time was almost synonymous with teaching algebra and whose teaching career spanned nearly fifty years. Miss Sunbeam (nobody ever called her Emma, nor her sister Amelia anything but "Pet"), who lived to be 84 years old, was one of six children born to George Worth and Amelia Reeder Andrews. Her father is identified as a "Confederate soldier" in *Greenwood County Sketches*, and indeed he was sixteen years old when the war began in 1861. Miss Sunbeam was born in what is now McCormick County in 1887 and came to Greenwood as a small child. The record shows that she was a member of the class of 1904 at Greenwood High School. According to an article in the centennial edition of *The Index-Journal*, no class had as many as twenty graduates until 1909, and a high school graduate in Miss Sunbeam's day had received nine years of more or less formal instruction. Miss Sunbeam finished high school about the time Magnolia School was built, and she graduated from Lander College in 1908. Evidently her teaching career began at Magnolia School the same year, and her name appears on the faculty roster when Leslie opened in 1913. We know very little about her years as an elementary teacher, but that she became "almost a legend in her own time in Greenwood" is a statement referring to her status as algebra teacher par excellence at Greenwood High School. She moved from Leslie to Greenwood High at some time prior to 1924 and taught there until retirement in 1955.

It seems in retrospect that Miss Sunbeam taught simply everybody who attended Greenwood High School for about 35 years. If one were lucky (or very unlucky, depending upon one's propensity for math), he or she might draw one of Miss Sunbeam's classes for more than one year; and a few, including this writer, sat at her feet for four whole years – from 8th grade math through algebra and trigonometry (geometry must have been her least favorite course; Ruth Bowles was probably Greenwood's most famous geometry teacher). Miss Sunbeam's class was a world of its own, and one entered with either great trepidation or wild exhilaration, depending upon how the inevitable homework had gone the night before. Miss Sunbeam's teaching methods were a mixture of smiling approval and sometimes scathing criticism. She once said she could tell from the front of the room the exact moment when the "light dawned" on some hapless student who might have been struggling mightily but in vain for weeks. "At that point," she said, "I could begin to teach that student math." One of her favorite themes was the number of store clerks who had difficulty making change. She would regale her classes with stories about some girl at McCrory's whose fumblings with change had exasperated her the day before. No doubt some of her students identified strongly with that poor girl; no one relished the thought of a one-on-one with Miss Sunbeam in any matter involving adding and subtracting. Her eagle eye, tapping foot, and snapping fingers were not calculated to instill confidence while that all-important learning process was going on.

Miss Sunbeam's name and fame were not limited to Greenwood. Clemson and Lander professors recognized her fine hand in the work of students who had come from Greenwood High School. Miss Sunbeam always demanded that her students show their work; that is, it was necessary to write down every step in solving an equation or word problem. Similarly, she required that students draw a box around their answers so they could be more readily found when she corrected papers. Neatness was always less important to her than students' ability to demonstrate total understanding of the mathematical process. That procedure became a habit so ingrained that students simply continued it in college. One scoffing Lander professor began referring to the box around the answer as a "pig pen." The same professor, while demonstrating one day a math problem involving the length of a shadow, commented dryly that the shadow had been cast by a ray of sunshine which was not to be confused with a certain famous "sunbeam." His students, most of whom had graduated from Greenwood High School, were not amused.

A newspaper editorial commemorating Miss Sunbeam contains the usual tributes, including the statement that she was "a remarkable woman," and an unidentified former pupil wrote the following lines which were printed on the editorial page of April 28, 1972:

> Sunbeam Andrews was a great character. She was great because she loved and served people – all sorts of people, but especially young people.
>
> As a teacher, she had the ability to stimulate her pupils and make learning an exciting rather than a dull experience. Her teaching was a fine mixture of firm discipline and sincere affection that reached and warmed thousands of indifferent or discouraged students.
>
> She kept no hours at home or at school and her door was always open to someone who "didn't understand." She rarely forgot that a slice of fruitcake often made math more palatable. . . .
>
> Even in old age and ill health, she kept a large group of devoted friends around her.

The tribute on the dedication page of the 1946 high school yearbook is more succinct: "The staff of 1946 considers it a privilege and a pleasure to dedicate this edition of *The Sapling* to Miss Sunbeam, who through the years has given her time and energy freely and untiringly, who at any time is ready to give her advice and assistance. She is an unforgetable [sic] personality of our high school life." The accompanying photographs show a lovely lady of about sixty with snow white hair in soft waves around her face and pinned up in back. She was always beautifully groomed and quite well-dressed; in fact, she was a very handsome woman. One of her students, a famous football player of the late 1940s, was heard to remark one day that Miss Sunbeam had good looking legs; one wants to believe she would have been pleased on some level with that assessment, which might have been the highest compliment a high school boy could pay in that more innocent time.

Miss Sunbeam Andrews was awarded an honorary Doctor of Science from her alma mater, Lander College, as part of the Founder's Day program in February 1970. She died in Greenwood on April 26, 1972.

The history of Greenwood County is studded with the record of its schools, from private to public and in between. Some, such as the schools at Cokesbury, were so integral to the community that their story must be told in context; for that reason, Cokesbury's schools are sketched in the chapter on towns, sections, and place names in Greenwood County. Others rose and fell or came and went, finally succumbing either to overwhelming forces such as war or to the more whimsical realities of a shifting popular demand. Still others died from simple competition in the marketplace. Most of the uncertainty and upheaval in the story of education in Greenwood County came about well before the county was formed; from the time graded schools were adopted in 1891, Greenwood appears to have made reasonable progress in providing schools for its youngsters. The record of that hundred-year effort is simply part of the continuum we choose to call *education*. As for knowledge itself, an entirely different concept, we are told it doubles every few years. Certainly today's elementary school students are proficient in areas their parents and grandparents never dreamed of, and everyone knows that only a youngster can manipulate the family-room VCR. At the same time, reading and writing skills even of college graduates are often the despair of potential employers, and developmental courses have become routine in most college curriculums. Mass illiteracy on the scale of that prevailing after the Civil War is, thankfully, a thing of the past, but everyone believes there is still a long way to go. And it would be foolish to pretend that Greenwood's long "battle with ignorance" was untainted by prevailing realities of economic hardship, unsettled race relations, inadequate planning, and a certain indifference to the concepts of formalization and standardization which allow better comparison with other regions.

5

BUSINESS AND INDUSTRY

To work! To work! In Heaven's name!
The wolf is at the door!
Charlotte Perkins Gilman

"GREENWOOD has no history. It is making its record in the present . . ." runs a story in an 1889 Charleston newspaper. That line, of course, refers to the development of the business section, and it strikes the right chord in describing the bustling beginnings of a town with a progressive philosophy. In another sense, however, the line is ludicrous. Not only Greenwood, but the whole state of South Carolina and, indeed, the entire South, was almost literally mired in history for many years after the Civil War. Professor Walter Edgar, director of the Institute of Southern Studies at the University of South Carolina, wrote in the centennial edition of *The State* that South Carolina and its people were considered "quaint relics" to many Americans as late as the 1920s and 1930s. Writers have explored the phenomenon of what Eleanor Roosevelt once called "the poor and unhappy South" ad infinitum, and at least one, Wilbur J. Cash, actually attempted to delineate the mind of the South as though it were a single entity in his masterwork of the same title. Some have attributed the mystique of the region to the fact that the South is the only part of the country ever to have experienced the trauma of a conquered nation. That experience is supposed to explain both the South's literature and its philosophy, neither of which is the subject of this book. Most southerners seem finally to have arrived at a sort of equilibrium; we still stop to smell the magnolias, but we have learned to balance our heritage of monuments and memories against the simple need to make a living in a constantly changing world.

The business of making a living in Greenwood County has not always been easy, but many county citizens managed to improve their standard of living from barely a subsistence level on the family farm as the county began its slow march away from an agrarian base. Agriculture dominated the entire South after the Civil War until the agricultural depression, the Great Depression, and World War II forced an economic redefinition of the region. With a great deal of help from politicians, chambers of commerce, and industry search committees, the South was "discovered" by companies becoming hamstrung by demands of powerful labor unions in other sections of the country. Added inducements for industry to move included cheap land, low taxes and other concessions, as well as specialized training programs for employees. Suddenly, the Sun Belt was the place to be. Greenwood County has benefited enormously in the last thirty years from this phenomenon. The county seat has also changed irrevocably from the time it was known, somewhat derisively, as merely a railroad and mill town.

Greenwood was once unquestionably a railroad town. The fact that five lines crisscrossed the county and converged in the town at one time is really rather remarkable, considering that Greenwood was not directly between any larger cities, except perhaps Greenville and Augusta. Jimmy Wade has traced the entire story of railroads in Greenwood County, including every merger and particularly the track removal from the center of town, in a manuscript that awaits publication. Wade kindly provided a synopsis of his forthcoming book for purposes of this chapter.

The City of Greenwood is currently served by only two railroad systems, quite a change from 1929 when the entrance of the Georgia & Florida Railroad brought the number of rail lines to five, more than any other city in the state had at that time. Three railroads served Charleston; Greenville, Columbia, and Spartanburg each boasted four; but Greenwood topped them all with Southern Railway, Charleston & Western Carolina Railway, Seaboard Air Line Railway, Piedmont & Northern Railway, and Georgia & Florida Railroad. The development of railroads opened the entire country and played a particularly vital role in the growth of Greenwood County. Indeed, without the railroads, the area doubtless would have developed quite differently, if at all. The town actually moved its business district to the railway site in the 1850s, and Bradley, Ninety Six, Hodges, Troy, and Verdery owe their existence and initial growth to railroads.

Wade discovered in his research that little information exists for the period from 1857 to 1866. Certainly this lack of documentation comes as no surprise; the political, social, and economic unrest between the North and South, followed by the Civil War, is reason enough for the general lack of information on early railroads. We do know, however, that the Greenville & Columbia Railroad, Greenwood's first, suffered no damage until the war was almost over; even so, operations in the area that became Greenwood County remained unscathed throughout the period. Sherman's troops managed to destroy the line only between Columbia and Alston.

The second railroad, the Augusta & Knoxville line, came about because of Greenwood's business initiative and single-minded attention to obtaining reasonable freight rates to Augusta, which for a long time had been "the distribution center for goods and merchandise for Western South Carolina and the lower Piedmont, including Greenwood." The indirect rail connection – by way of Branchville, a distance of more than 200 miles – made for an almost prohibitive freight cost, Wade wrote, and a local druggist complained "that it was a shame to have to pay such rates when the straight-line distance was less than 60 miles." This remark, uttered about three years after the war, "was the spark that ignited a 14-year struggle" to obtain direct rail connection with Augusta. The opening of the Augusta & Knoxville Railroad on May 1, 1882, was the result.

Wade traced this railroad, which through various mergers and reorganizations eventually became the Charleston & Western Carolina, as a venture that first provided rail service to Spartanburg, the second terminus for Greenwood in the Piedmont (Greenville was the first). This line – the Greenwood, Laurens, and Spartanburg Railroad – merged with the existing Augusta & Knoxville line into the Port Royal & Western Railway in 1886. Another reorganization created the C&WC ten years later.

The next railroad was an east-west line extending from Monroe, North Carolina, via Greenwood and Abbeville to Atlanta. The Georgia, Carolina, & Northern Railway reached Greenwood in 1890 and opened to Atlanta two years later. This line became part of Seaboard Air Line Railway in 1901. The third railroad seemed to usher in an unprecedented period of growth for the area, although the timing might simply have coincided with the push for county status, and each influenced the other during an exciting era of the "Gay Nineties." Wade pointed out that the notorious "Jim Crow" laws requiring racial segregation on trains, in waiting rooms and restrooms, and at ticket windows and water fountains, were passed only a year after Greenwood became a county.

Another tiny railroad came to Greenwood County in 1904. A five-mile connector between the Southern Railway at Shoals Junction and the textile mill at Ware Shoals, while never actually reaching the town of Greenwood, nevertheless became a common carrier in 1908. This line was christened the Ware Shoals Railroad and later connected with the Piedmont & Northern Railway. And a railroad Wade called "James B. Duke's electric line, the Greenville, Spartanburg, & Anderson Railway," (later the Piedmont & Northern, or P&N, also dubbed the "Poor and Needy"), was opened from Greenwood to Greenville in 1912 and to Spartanburg two years later.

Greenwood's last railroad came at a time when railroad expansion nationwide had slowed almost to a standstill; the Georgia & Florida Railroad built a new line from Augusta which terminated at Greenwood. One can imagine the fanfare when it opened on June 19, 1929, not long before the stock market crash which ushered in the Great Depression.

With such emphasis on railroads it is not surprising that Greenwood reveled in its standing as a railroad town. The lines meant not only business but also pleasure, with convenient and even luxurious passenger service available to cities and resorts everywhere. While no such amenities exist today – Greenwood lost its passenger train service in 1969 – Seaboard offered excellent accommodations for many years, including the popular and streamlined "Silver Comet" which many Greenwood people rode to Washington, Philadelphia, and New York. Other railroads provided only local service, but some of their schedules offered connections with through trains at Atlanta, Augusta, Columbia, Greenville, and Spartanburg. A description of an excursion of Greenwood women to a flower show in New York is part of Wade's manuscript.

The Maxwell Yards facility at Greenwood, originally constructed by the C&WC, was greatly enlarged after the merger of its successor, the Atlantic Coast Line, with Seaboard to create the Seaboard Coast Line Railroad (which later also absorbed the P&N). These mergers brought about a substantial increase in freight interchange to the point that all CSX Transportation (successor to Seaboard Coast Line) trains are routed into Maxwell Yards just outside Greenwood. Much of the drama that accompanied the era of the railroad in downtown Greenwood is now concentrated at a maze of tracks visible from an overpass on Highway 225.

Wade wrote a succinct account of downtown Greenwood's long love-hate relationship with railroads:

> The rails of both the Southern Railway (originally the Greenville & Columbia) and the Seaboard Coast Line Railroad (ex-Atlantic Coast Line, ex-C&WC, nee Augusta & Knoxville) were laid through the heart of Greenwood's Square. As trains gradually grew longer, they became more and more of a nuisance to motorists and pedestrians, especially when more than a hundred cars, moving at a restrictive speed limit of 10 miles per hour, blocked uptown street crossings, at times, for as long as 15 minutes. In an effort to solve that problem, a plan was devised by an engineer in 1934 for removal of the downtown railroad tracks. Later, a group of prominent citizens organized a track removal committee and laid the groundwork for the project that subsequent generations completed some 48 years later, using a combination of city, county, federal, and railroad funds. All trains, having been routed over other tracks within the city, are now gone from the Square. No evidence can be seen today of the multitude of tracks and three railroad depots that were once located there.

Wade's synopsis concluded with the information that at least eighteen other railroad companies obtained charters to construct lines in the county, but most never progressed beyond the organizational stage. After more than 140 years of development, reorganization, consolidation, and mergers, none of the original corporate names of Greenwood's railroads has survived. Ironically, the county's first and last lines are both represented in one of the two remaining companies serving Greenwood: the Norfolk Southern Corporation includes the original Greenville & Columbia (1852) and the Georgia & Florida (1929). The other original carriers are represented in CSX Transportation.

It is difficult now to recall the sort of accommodations to trains that had to be made whenever one had business downtown, but one ritual nearly everybody remembers was the positioning of fire trucks on either side of the tracks in case of a fire somewhere during the times the longest trains came through. Teachers at the old Greenwood High School also remember how difficult it was to hold students' attention at the times trains were being maneuvered on and off the giant turntable or taking on water for the steam engines from the water tower across the street.

As for the "mill town" designation, Greenwood pleads guilty with a great deal of pride; indeed, the growth of the textile industry is considered largely responsible for the rather remarkable development of the city and county as a whole. Greenwood Cotton Mill, the county's first, was chartered in 1889 and built the following year with capital stock at first paid in at the rate of 50¢ per share per week. The initial investment was less than $100,000, and only 75 people were employed in an operation that used, according to Margaret Watson, four bales of cotton per day. At that point, James Cuthbert Self, whose name would loom large as a master builder of lasting value in the county, was a teenager, the son of a country doctor and a former schoolteacher in the Kirksey section of what is now Greenwood County. Although Self's time had not yet come, his neighbors the Durst brothers pioneered the textile business in which he would make his own name and fortune some years later. Nor were the Dursts and Jim Self the only county residents who would become notables in the industry. Other natives of the area were Daniel A. Tompkins, who as a contractor helped organize and build any number of mills across the South; John Pope Abney, a pioneer of the Abney Mills chain; and John H. Cheatham, whose name is associated with the industry in Georgia. These men were described later as "the mill-buildingest boys that ever was," a designation every southerner understands.

Textile pioneers evidently took their cue from Atlanta editor Henry Grady's famous "New South" speech delivered to the New England Society at a meeting in New York City in 1886. Grady contrasted the dead South of slavery and secession with the living and breathing South of unity and freedom which, he said, was growing every hour. This new South had come about, "not through protest against the old, but because of new conditions, new adjustments, and . . . new ideas and aspirations." Grady's ideas expressed in that speech were almost the blueprint for Greenwood County, at least so it seems in retrospect. Even as he spoke in New York, Greenwood already had access to a couple of railroads and had become known as a transportation center. It is probably true, as G. O. Robinson pointed out in *The Character of Quality*, that "transportation centers attract men of action," and there is no question that Greenwood had those as well.

Among the men of action in the town were William Lowndes and John Kemp Durst whose reputation as businessmen would have been secure whether or not they nourished ambitions beyond their mercantile establishments. Members of the Durst family (originally spelled Darst or Dorst) were among the German immigrants who landed in Charleston in 1764 and migrated to the Londonborough settlement in Greenwood County. Several generations later, young William Durst found himself a Confederate soldier at the age of 17. Wounded twice, once in the foot and again in the knee, he was said to have kept on display the rest of his life the Yankee bullet taken from his leg. After the war he worked for a time on the family farm at Kirksey before opening a general store with his brother John. Robinson wrote that the brothers "set up" the store, while Margaret Watson indicated it had been established in 1870 by James Marion Dorn and purchased by the Dursts six years later. At any rate, that store became Durst and Mathews when Simon Pierce Mathews, another Kirksey neighbor, acquired an interest in 1888; it remained a Kirksey landmark until a fire destroyed the building in 1953.

In the 1880s both the Dursts were lured to nearby Greenwood which offered a more promising arena for their business ambitions; the brothers soon opened other stores in the bustling little town, as did their partner S. P. Mathews. They must have done well from the beginning; Robinson wrote that before long "they had accepted the challenge of providing the capital and the jobs for an economy still nursing the wounds of the Civil War." Accepting the purely altruistic motivation attributed to the gentlemen in that statement might be a little difficult, but there is no question that jobs were provided and Greenwood's economy improved because of W. L. and J. K. Durst. John Durst decided to take up banking; it was he who organized the Bank of Greenwood and became its first president in 1888. William, on the other hand, "turned to the world of weaving," in the words of the Greenwood Mills historian, thereby constructing the foundation of the textile empire that Greenwood County would eventually become.

Even though South Carolina is generally credited with one of the first textile mills in the country – at James Island in 1789 – a more lasting foundation was laid by William Gregg, who established the first cotton mill at Graniteville in 1845. That company may or may not be in existence today; it was still operating when the first Greenwood Mills book was published in 1964. I. A. Newby called it one of the "larger mills" in *Plain Folk in the New South* (1989), and Jack Temple Kirby described it as "William Gregg's pre-Civil War model mill" in *Rural Worlds Lost* (1987). Gregg was evidently something of a pioneer with a bit of the reformer's zeal thrown in; Robinson called him the "father of Southern cotton manufacturing." At least one early Greenwood County settler, James Callison of the section that bears his name, came to the area to work in the new cotton mill in Graniteville before 1850. David D. Wallace called William Gregg an "industrial statesman" who had the misfortune to be overshadowed by that famous expounder of "metaphysical doctrines of the Constitution," John C. Calhoun. Wallace wrote that Calhoun's philosophy of blindly protecting the slave system held the state "in a bondage that could only grow worse the better he succeeded"; whereas Gregg, who had come to South Carolina from Pennsylvania in 1824, saw the South's economic situation plainly and as a whole, including the plight of the poor white class which had been "created, neglected, and despised by the plantation system."

Gregg himself had amassed a fortune as a master jewelry craftsman in Columbia and Charleston before he entered the textile field. So interested was he in the theoretical and social implications of southern industry that he spent a great deal of time making speeches and writing articles on the subject. He had hoped to establish and organize Graniteville and then depend on hired experts to run it. When that plan turned out to be unworkable, he pitched in himself, providing his own services free for eight years. Gregg and his directors never agreed on certain business policies; one director, for example, made more money as sales agent than Gregg ever received as president. Given the systematic opposition to manufacturing and the small scale of such industry as existed in the state at the time, Wallace considered that Gregg's factory in Graniteville, as well as his writings on the subject, constituted no less than a revolution in both opinion and production. Further, Gregg's contributions to the industry marked him as "an apostle of a new social and industrial era" as well as a "benevolent despot" in the lives of mill operatives who constituted virtually a new class of South Carolinian as the industry expanded. Evidently the state is indebted to Gregg for the paternalistic spirit of early cotton mill owners no less than for other aspects of the industry as a whole. Surely it is reasonable to believe that Greenwood's first mill owners followed the example of William Gregg set more than forty years before cotton manufacturing came to the county.

Perhaps the point should be emphasized here that "cotton factories" were intended primarily as economic opportunity for the state's large population of impoverished white citizens. One notable exception in 1880 was a small factory in Saluda which employed 25 blacks among its 100 operatives. Newby called this phenomenon "a survival, not a portent," since only a few years later the mills reserved essentially all production line work for whites, with blacks restricted to menial work as helpers, sweepers, scrubbers, and yard men. The subtitle of *Plain Folk in the New South* is "Social Change and Cultural Persistence, 1880-1915," and the book deals primarily with the sociological themes of class, race, and patterns of folk life. Among Newby's most important sources were the Coleman L. Blease papers which contain a great deal of actual correspondence from cotton mill workers to the governor during the years 1911-1915. These remarkable letters – a blend of touching naivete and appalling illiteracy – are a striking record in themselves. While the book lists fifty cotton mills in South Carolina – more than in any other state – in its index, none of the Greenwood County mills is included. *Plain Folk in the New South* adds nothing concrete to a study of the textile industry in Greenwood County; it is, however, good collateral reading. One statement from the book sums up the entire question of the race issue vis-a-vis the early days of cotton mills: the author noted that blacks accounted for some 5.5% of the adult work force in 152 selected mills in 1907. "These patterns," he wrote, "conformed to New South racial theory." Since the Greenwood Mills history mentions the subject not at all, it is probably not unfair to conclude that local mills also reflected the tenor of their times.

When William L. Durst began planning Greenwood Cotton Mill, the nearest such plant was in Newberry, according to Robinson's book. Possibly the Saluda factory mentioned above escaped the author's notice or was no longer in operation by 1889. At any rate, nothing comparable existed in adjoining Laurens, Edgefield, or Abbeville Counties, so that Durst was, in effect, "plowing new ground" for Greenwood as he cast about for some means of capitalizing the venture. Cash was short and working capital scarce in 1889, but Durst was both persistent and persuasive. Robinson called him a "financial innovator" for hitting on the idea of an installment plan: he offered a $100 stock certificate payable at nothing down and 50¢ per week. "His unorthodoxy, *plus additional financial arrangements*, brought results (emphasis added)." The "additional financial arrangements" were not described. Margaret Watson's account in the centennial edition of the newspaper was evidently among Robinson's sources. Both wrote that 376 shares were represented at the first stockholders' meeting on March 18, 1889, at the call of chairman J. C. Maxwell. At that meeting Durst was unanimously elected temporary president and Joel S. Bailey temporary secretary-treasurer. (The "temporary" designations are interesting; with capitalization so hard-wrought the whole enterprise might have seemed temporary to the participants.) The first directors were named a month later: W. H. Bailey, G. A. Barksdale, W. L. Durst, J. N. Godsey, Dr. John C. Maxwell, and Dr. W. B. Milwee share that distinction. The charter was issued on October 5, 1889; a photograph of the original is reprinted in the mill history. Robinson wrote that the first plant – a two-story brick structure erected at the "old mill" site just off Maxwell Avenue – was placed in operation in 1890. It contained 2,500 spindles and 84 looms operated by 75 employees and processed five bales of cotton per day. (Note: there is a discrepancy between Watson's and Robinson's accounts: was it four bales, or five? One is inclined somehow to trust the mill's official history on this important point.) China and other Oriental countries were customers from the start for the cotton print cloth, sheetings, and twills produced by Greenwood Cotton Mill.

A story on the first mill appeared in the *Abbeville Press and Banner* sometime in 1893. The second paragraph of the following excerpt is revealing:

> This factory is a well-constructed two-story building 200 by 76 feet. The company owns 30 acres of land upon which 15 comfortable and substantial dwellings for operatives were erected in 1890, and soon 10 more similar buildings will have been completed. The operatives are furnished with clear, cool water from five conveniently-located wells.
>
> President Durst informs us that the factory employs only first class people, and that they freely associate with the best citizens of Greenwood, their children attending the graded school there, joining the Sunday schools and the different churches just the same as other children do. He encourages parents to send their children to school as regularly as circumstances will permit.
>
> In addition to burning coal, the mill annually consumes about one and a half thousand cords of wood which is supplied by farmers living in the surrounding country. Besides the main building, three large rooms – engine room, boiler department and warehouse – are connected with the factory. The engine room contains a 250-horsepower engine for running the mill which is beautifully lighted by electricity produced by a 200-light dynamo, driven by a 25-horsepower engine which is separate from the engine that drives the factory machinery. . . .
>
> Within a few yards of the factory is a reservoir containing about one million gallons of water as clear as crystal. Mr. Durst says the insurance is only one-fourth of regular rates; every arrangement possible has been made to prevent and to extinguish fire in the building. Automatic fire extinguishers are equally distributed throughout the building. Besides this means of extinguishing fire, there is a regularly organized fire company and buckets of water are constantly kept in various parts of the building. . . .

Working conditions at the beginning were certainly primitive by modern standards but probably welcomed by those who had found farming a perilous way of making ends meet. Operatives knew the job meant food and shelter; they were happy to have work, even though the hours from 6 a.m. to 6 p.m. with a half hour lunch break made for a long day (Saturday hours were from 6 a.m. to 4 p.m.). Another sobering revelation was that, at first, lighting was provided by kerosene lamps, with reflectors, hung around the walls, and the humidification apparatus consisted of an ordinary flower sprinkler used to dampen the floors at intervals. The operatives in company houses lived by the whistle; that is, the mill whistle at 4:30 a.m. started their day, a second summoned them to their posts, and the third, known as the "dock whistle," was the signal for work to begin. If workers were not in the right place when the third whistle blew, their pay was docked – hence the name. Wages were computed by the number of looms operated; a full load was six looms which, at 12 1/2¢ each, meant 75¢ per day. Younger employees, some nine to twelve years old, were allowed recesses when machinery was down for repair. (Note: the large question of child labor is not addressed in *The Character of Quality* and will not be considered here for several reasons. Newby wrote that it was a pervasive feature of mill work and one of the most misunderstood subjects in the history of the mill experience.)

The financial picture by May 1891 appeared singularly unpromising. The board issued a statement advising that stockholders had paid in only a little over $32,000, while the company owed more than $57,000 on the building and machinery. There were only fifteen company-owned houses in 1892, but that number had increased significantly by 1900. Growth picked up in all areas, in fact. When the charter was re-recorded in the new county clerk's office in Greenwood in 1898, there were 10,000 spindles and 384 looms, as well as a capital stock increase to $400,000. Greenwood Mill No. 2 came in 1905; spindles and looms increased again, to 20,556 and 485 respectively.

Meanwhile, the Greenwood Cotton Mill had stimulated interest in other textile ventures in the town. Grendel Mill, Greenwood's second, was chartered in 1896 and began operations a year later under its first president D. A. P. (David Augustus Parker) Jordan. Grendel, too, expanded almost immediately; its capital stock more than tripled in three years. Jordan died in 1901 and was succeeded by Anthony Foster McKissick who moved to Greenwood (Watson said from Pelzer, but Robinson wrote that he left a teaching job at Alabama Polytechnic Institute, now Auburn University). W. L. Durst died in 1902; his brother J. K. succeeded him as president of Greenwood Cotton Mill. The year 1902 also marked the beginning of a cotton mill at Ninety Six. Some familiar names appeared on its first board: in addition to Ellison A. Smyth, J. P. Phillips, F. G. Brown and first president E. M. Lipscomb, A. F. McKissick and J. K. Durst were named directors. Both John B. Sloan, who was secretary at the time, and Lipscomb resigned in 1904, and Smyth and McKissick took over as president and secretary-treasurer respectively. Four years later McKissick was named president.

The first generation, so to speak, of the textile business in Greenwood ended and a whole new era began in 1908. J. K. Durst resigned after six years as president of Greenwood Cotton Mill, and James C. Self, at that time the 32-year-old cashier of the Bank of Greenwood, was elected to the position. Robinson wrote that the board's regard for young Self's managerial ability, as well as his financial interest in the mill – he held fourteen shares of stock – prompted his selection. The value of the new president's stock nearly equaled his first year's salary of $1,800, and all the business news was grim when he assumed his post. Greenwood Cotton Mill consisted of two plants with total spindleage of 20,000, but one plant had already closed and the other faced certain doom unless its obsolete machinery could be replaced by new spindles and looms. The automatic loom had been invented in 1889 and further developed by the Draper Corporation in Massachusetts; Draper looms were the standard for the textile industry. Greenwood Cotton Mill's situation was truly desperate. Its operation went forward under debt amounting to $10 per spindle, greater than the mill's total value, and on which the bank had $40,000 of its $60,000 capitalization in a mill mortgage that the bank was forced to call. A contributing factor was the nationwide business recession, or panic, of 1907 which was just beginning to lift when Self surveyed the faltering enterprise that was his new domain. Robinson put it well: "The last, laboring gasps of a local industry were depressingly loud" in 1908.

New spindles and new looms obviously had to be acquired, and suddenly the means of acquiring them was James C. Self's problem. There was nothing to do but go, hat in hand, to the manufacturers in New England. Acquiring new spindles was a simple matter compared to the much larger investment required for the purchase of automatic looms. On Self's first visit to Massachusetts he dealt with a Draper who was not the firm's manager at all but his brother, who happened to be governor of the state at the time. Eben Draper was willing to listen while Self outlined his plans to save the mill and, with it, Greenwood's budding industrial development. The earnest young executive must have made a good case, at least for himself; Governor Draper invited him to dinner and gave him a chance to raise the issue again in after-dinner conversations. Finally Draper made up his mind: "Your collateral is worthless," he is supposed to have said, "but I'll take a chance on your integrity. Give your specifications to our engineers tomorrow." His mission, he thought, accomplished, Self returned to Greenwood to prepare for the arrival of the new machinery. Unfortunately he got a letter instead, from manager George Draper, who wrote that the deal was off. His company would accept nothing but good, hard collateral; taking chances on integrity was evidently not the way this particular Draper did business. Back to the company's headquarters on the next train to Boston went James C. Self, no doubt hearing "those last, laboring gasps" of his mill every mile of the way. Soon he found himself in Draper's office mulling over the discouraging words, "We can't do a thing for you," spoken from the other side of the desk. Self's answer, as recorded by Robinson, was a true classic: "We're not exactly begging," he said, "but Eben, your brother, promised me on my last visit here to help us and . . . in the South, sir, we do what we promise." George Draper must have entertained a thought or two about integrity as he considered the young man's words. At the very least he had to admire the vigor and tone of his visitor's statement so that his answer, when it came this time, was the same as his brother's. The two trips, and Self's own conviction, had carried the day. Robinson called the Draper deal "the first step in an expansion program which was to cover many exciting years of progress." This story, dating from the very beginning of Self's career in textiles, must have been a mainstay of company and family lore. It bears the mark of much repeating, and the mill history was first published about nine years after Self's death and more than fifty after the Draper incident took place.

The year 1876 was pivotal for South Carolina, for it was in that year the state began to emerge from the yoke of radical rule it had borne since the end of the Civil War. Evidently it is quite true that each voter considered it his duty to vote as many times as possible in order to insure the election of Wade Hampton as governor. On July 1, 1876, not long before the election, James Cuthbert Self was born on a farm in the Bowles Mountain section of Edgefield (now Greenwood) County. Mill historian Robinson pointed out that General George Custer made his last stand just seven days later, and Wild Bill Hickok was shot dead from ambush the next month. The juxtaposition of these three events is hilarious, but Robinson was making the serious point that the westward expansion of the United States was not nearly over at that point, and the wild, wild West was still just that. Nor, of course, was Greenwood's expansion even begun. More than twenty years would pass, in fact, before there was a Greenwood County to be known as the birthplace of its most honored citizen.

Self was named *James* for his father and *Cuthbert* in honor of a Baptist minister of the community. The Self family name *Callie* is a diminutive of his mother's name, *Mary California,* given in commemoration of the California Gold Rush the year before she was born. James was the middle of three brothers and was less than ten years old when a skating accident resulted in his father's death at the age of 37. Mrs. Self suddenly found herself with a farm to manage and three sons to raise by herself. She did well; one became a doctor, another a banker, and the third a pioneer industrialist. None of these connections is insignificant: Self honored his mother throughout his life and built a church as a memorial; Self Memorial Hospital was dedicated to the memory of his father and brother, both doctors; and Self's middle name might have had something to do with his lifelong generosity to churches and ministers. In addition, the names of the mills in the Self chain are nearly all tributes to individuals.

Young Jim Self wanted an education more than anything, but hard times dogged that ambition. He had to drop out of Wofford Fitting School in 1891 because of illness, and he worked as a manual laborer for 8¢ an hour as a Clemson student in 1893. Mostly he worked on his mother's farm, but he realized his dream of college was over when four bales of cotton brought less than $100. That transaction also convinced him that cotton was the most vexing thing in the world (he might have thought too that he would prefer to be on the other side of the deal). Self was finally able to go to school; he completed a course at Smithdeal Business College in Richmond, Virginia. He had saved the money himself from his earnings at two country stores near his home – J. M. Gaines's Store in the Phoenix section and Durst and Mathews at Kirksey.

Jim Self returned to Greenwood and another job as store clerk, this time at W. G. Gambrell's Department Store. No longer a $10 per month worker, he was now able to command the munificent sum of $58 monthly. To a young man who in his own words "had nothing in this world but two suits of clothes and fifteen dollars," it must have seemed a lot. Family connections might have had something to do with Self's first job in banking. The president of the Bank of Greenwood in 1899 was J. K. Durst, whose wife was Self's aunt, and the bank needed a bookkeeper. Self advanced to the position of cashier rapidly and would hold on to his base in banking until well after he had established himself in textiles. He resigned his position in 1916, although he later served as vice president for a time and remained as a director until 1933. The reasoning behind Self's resignation from the bank provided the intriguing title of Chapter Two of the mill history, "A Blind Mule and Fifty Dollars." It seems that tobacco tycoon James B. Duke once chided him for continuing to divide his time between mill and bank duties. In a comment that speaks volumes about banking at that period, Duke is supposed to have said, "Jim, you'll never get anywhere lending fifty dollars on a blind mule." Self must have thought about that remark many times; "Blind Mule" is a registered brand name of Greenwood Mills.

The first few years under Self's control made all the difference in firming up the mill operations, but the job was never easy in those days. "I was there before day [and] I figured till long after midnight every night trying to cut a few more corners, trying to figure a way to get hold of a little more money to keep going," he said. "There never was enough money to buy enough cotton to operate with, and it was always nip-and-tuck to meet payrolls. If we had not obtained the new machinery from Draper, we would have been sunk." With that stark life-or-death problem overcome, Self was able to turn his attention to smaller issues, and it might have been at this point that he began acquiring the reputation as a "duty and detail man" that clung to him the rest of his life. Self always emphasized the importance of details, and nothing was too small to escape his notice. Certainly the question of employee housing was a large issue, but the small matter of replacing wells and dippers with piped-in drinking water caught Self's attention as well. It would be foolish to pretend that James C. Self's sole purpose in life was to "save" Greenwood by providing jobs for displaced farmers. It is true, however, that Self and other men of ambition who depend upon the labor of others to produce a product would be dense indeed not to realize that workers perform better if their needs and desires are considered important in the process. This question at its loftiest level is one of human dignity; at the very least, it is simply good business, and James C. Self was always noted for good business sense.

Other mills had begun appearing with some regularity in Greenwood, and the weeding-out process of ownership began in earnest. Panola Mill was chartered in 1910. According to Margaret Watson, *panola* is an Indian word meaning *cotton,* but no verification of this intriguing connection has been found. Although Panola was organized by F. S. Evans, capital ran out before construction could be completed, and local attorney and banker Samuel H. McGhee and his associates stepped in. McGhee, a native of Cokesbury whose mother was a Hodges, joined forces with Greenwood newcomer C. C. Featherstone in the law firm of Featherstone and McGhee at about the same time. He was also president of the National Loan and Exchange Bank, according to *The Index-Journal* of September 14, 1957. (Another article in the same issue named him "president of the newly-formed First National Bank" about 1903; the name of the bank is probably incorrect.) S. H. McGhee was quite important in the business and political life of Greenwood; he served two terms as state senator and was president of Panola Mill from 1912-1921. He had also taught school for a time in Marion County and even owned a Greenwood newspaper, *The Index,* for some years. Boykin Curry recalls that McGhee was "Mr. Greenwood" at one time, and it is easy to see why. Teacher . . . lawyer . . . editor . . . banker . . . mill executive . . . politician . . . the list is rather long, even for Greenwood; in fact, the only surprise is that no comprehensive sketch of Samuel H. McGhee seems to exist. He is mentioned, but only barely, in *Greenwood County Sketches.* Evidently his family experimented a great deal with the spelling of their name; several variations – McGee, McGhee, and even Magee – appeared over the generations. McGhee must have accumulated something of a fortune in his heyday, but Curry hints that he was not only a bit of a gambler in business dealings but also inordinately fond of Scotch whisky. Probably it is best not to speculate how McGhee and others might have managed to indulge that particular vice. A 1910 publication of the Merchants Association and Board of Trade boasted that the county had been "dry" since its organization, which means only that the sale of alcoholic beverages had never been legalized, and the official Greenwood line was that law and order prevailed.

Panola appeared to owe its existence to S. H. McGhee, and he remained as president until John Pope Abney acquired a controlling interest and became president in 1921. Work on Grendel Mill No. 2 also began in 1910 while A. F. McKissick was president. McKissick's interest in the mill at Ninety Six ended when he resigned as president in 1917 and was succeeded by the same John P. Abney, who also acquired McKissick's interest in Grendel Mill. Abney, however, lost out in 1921 when Ninety Six Cotton Mill was acquired by James C. Self. He acquired another important mill ten years later: in a single line with absolutely no explanation, Margaret Watson wrote, "Mr. Self became president and treasurer of Mathews Mill, the new name for Grendel No. Two, on September 15, 1931." There simply have to be dozens of stories buried, perhaps with the people involved, concerning that acquisition, as well as other maneuverings during the 20-year period from 1910 to 1930. A business brochure from 1910 contains a statistical table of the textile mills in Greenwood County. There were seven, counting Ware Shoals, and James C. Self was involved with only two. By 1931 he was firmly in control of four, having weathered hard times again following the first world war. Describing that period, which he called the worst in his experience, he said, "I sometimes thought we would have to close."

John Pope Abney, or Jack as he was known to simply everybody, was a native of Edgefield (now Saluda) County where his family had lived for more than a hundred years before he was born in 1885. The Abneys moved to Greenwood, primarily for better educational opportunities for their children, according to J. R. (Dick) Abney, Jr., and Jack finished high school in 1900. He entered Wofford College where his lifelong love of sports began; although he probably weighed no more than 120 pounds at the time, he played football at Wofford and also developed an interest in baseball that lasted throughout his life. Returning to Greenwood after he left college, Abney took a job as messenger boy at the Bank of Greenwood, then moved in 1905 to the Farmers and Merchants Bank where he progressed from bookkeeper to assistant cashier to cashier to president over the ensuing years. Abney was nearly ten years younger than Self and his mill interests developed about ten years later, but in a striking parallel the two men managed to marry sisters within the space of three years. Jack Abney was married to Miss Susie Mathews of Kirksey on June 24, 1913, and James C. Self married Miss Lura Mathews on October 16, 1916. To complete the circle, the Mathews sisters were daughters of one of Self's first employers, the wealthy and prominent Simon P. Mathews. Dick Abney believes these two women might have controlled more wealth at one time than any other pair in South Carolina.

The story of Abney's very first venture into cotton manufacturing, as related by Boykin Curry, is in a class by itself. Curry believes the following is a true story, since it was told to him by banker John Sloan. He also thinks it provides a remarkable contrast with the way a similar deal would be handled today. Lawyers, CPAs, and IRS agents would spend months in negotiation and produce reams of computer-generated data on such a deal in today's world, but McKissick and Abney got the job done quickly with a couple of conversations, some figures scribbled on waste paper, and a handshake. McKissick, who was president of both Grendel Mill and Ninety Six Cotton Mill in 1917, made up his mind to move to Greenville (one reason, though surely not the only one, was to please his wife who had found Greenwood somewhat lacking in terms of social opportunities). McKissick contacted Abney at the bank, invited him to the mill office on a matter of business, and surprised him with the suggestion that he figure out a way to buy both mills as soon as possible. Abney was flabbergasted. He expressed appreciation for the offer but told McKissick that he lacked the security to find financing and would be unable to accept. McKissick's reply was to think about it over the weekend and come back the following Monday.

Abney returned at the appointed time. He had thought long and hard about it, he said, but his answer had to be the same. There was simply no way he could come up with the money. McKissick had not changed his mind either. "I want you to have these mills," he said. "You are the man to run them, and I will sell both to you for $_____." At that point Abney reached into the wastebasket, took out a used envelope, and asked McKissick to put his offer in writing. The mill president took up his pen and obligingly wrote on the back of the envelope: "I, A. Foster McKissick, hereby agree to sell to J. P. Abney two textile plants, Grendel and Ninety Six, for $_____." Abney thanked him and left, promising to see his friend again in a few days.

That very day Abney left Greenwood by train. He arrived in Boston the next day, but several more passed before he was able to see the president of Saco-Lowell Corporation. He wasted no time when he finally managed to get inside that gentleman's office. "I want to borrow enough money to buy these two plants," he said, pointing to the offer on the envelope. The president almost threw him out, but Abney must have been persuasive; perhaps he had already heard Self's Draper story. At any rate, by the end of the day the two men had reached agreement. John P. Abney came back to Greenwood with a check made payable to A. Foster McKissick for the full amount. Nor was that all: Saco-Lowell also agreed to provide new machinery on credit, taking preferred stock in the mill as collateral. After Abney took over, business picked up to the point that he was able to repay the loans in about two and a half years. Curry believes this story reveals a great deal about Abney's exceptional personality traits, including a brashness and willingness to gamble not every 32-year-old possesses. It also fits well with stories of other mill owners of the period.

A biographical sketch from the November 1951 issue of the Abney Mills magazine *Quills* states that Abney recognized the bright future of the textile industry more than most businessmen of his day, and it was that recognition that led him to purchase several cotton mills which were being operated inefficiently and therefore unsuccessfully by absentee owners. He reached outside Greenwood County to acquire controlling interests in mills in Anderson, Belton, and Newry in the late 1930s and early 1940s. Margaret Watson called this the beginning of an expansion that grew to seventeen plants in South Carolina, as well as control of the Erwin Mills chain of ten mills in North Carolina and Mississippi, by 1957. Abney's death in 1942 came when he was only 57 years old. The biographical sketch notes that Jack Abney figured prominently in the textile world as a man of both courage and ability. The word *courage* in this context is quite interesting, but a little reflection reveals that it is a good choice. All the ability in the world is useless without the courage to take risks.

Dick Abney recalls his uncle as a quiet sort of man but one who had the soul of a gambler. Abney had few hobbies or interests apart from his work. One serious preoccupation was his farm, in part because it provided the country hams he loved, and he was also very fond of animals. Abney's nephew believes the stress of constant speculation in cotton futures – like many men Jack Abney dreamed of cornering the market – might have contributed to an early death. Dick Abney's own father Joel's make-up was much the same, he says, at least where business was concerned, but the brothers were quite different socially. Jack Abney's few leisure hours might be spent mostly on his own front porch. He was a bit of a loner, not as open and gregarious as his brother, and with a smaller circle of friends, whereas Joel Abney liked to hunt, play poker, and golf with groups of cronies.

Abney's successor as President of Abney Mills was the notable F. E. Grier, who guided the company to greater prominence than it had ever known and whose name became known throughout the textile industry. Born in 1899, Grier was a descendant of two formidable families who were instrumental in founding both the Associate Reformed Presbyterian Church and Erskine College. Three of Grier's brothers entered the ministry, and three members of his immediate family – a grandfather, an uncle, and a brother – served as presidents of Erskine. Himself a graduate of the family college, Grier spent most of his working life in banking; he was President of the Bank of Greenwood in 1942 when Jack Abney died. Grier assumed the presidency of the Abney chain, which at the time consisted of five mills, at the request of Abney's family. Other plants, as well as working control of Erwin Mills in North Carolina, were added during Grier's tenure as president. Most people probably agree with Bill Bradford's assessment that Grier was "a genius in corporate management and finance." But Ebe Grier also died young, of a sudden heart attack on October 13, 1959, a month before his 60th birthday. At the time of his death he held the management reins over 27 textile plants employing about 15,000 people in North Carolina, South Carolina, and Mississippi. He had served as president of both the South Carolina Textile Manufacturers Association and the American Cotton Manufacturers Institute in 1956, an achievement unique in the annals of the two organizations. In addition to directorships too numerous to mention, Grier held honorary degrees from Clemson, Erskine, and Lander, and was named to the South Carolina Hall of Fame for the Living in 1953. An editorial at the time of his death called him "a great man by virtue of accomplishments, by strength of character, forceful personality, and ability of the first order." Inman Mills President James A. Chapman said that no man ever contributed more to the American textile industry. Greenwood County named F. E. Grier to its Hall of Fame in 1987.

In view of Grier's succession to the helm of Abney Mills, another Boykin Curry story about the time Abney and Grier locked horns over certain banking practices is particularly amusing. The time must have been about 1933. Grier headed the Bank of Greenwood where Jack Abney did business. The cavalier Abney could not be bothered to check his bank balances before writing checks, a practice the more meticulous banker found extremely frustrating. When Grier's repeated admonishments about overdrafts went unheeded, he simply allowed a couple of Abney's checks to bounce, whereupon that gentleman charged into the bank one day to demand an explanation. When Grier stood firm, Abney retaliated by moving his accounts to the new County Bank across the street, to the great satisfaction of its president John B. Sloan. But such flare-ups had no real effect on the mutual regard of the two men; not only did Grier replace his friend at Abney Mills, he was also named executor of Abney's estate. Anecdotes such as the banking story might be trivial, but if they help us see the men behind the legends they are worth retelling for that reason alone.

Thus Greenwood was the home of not one, but two, titans of the same industry at the same time. In one sense they were competitors, but in others they seem to have been cut from the same mold: from farm boy to lowly bank employee to banking prominence to mill executive. Hard work characterized both, as did vision, incisiveness, and judgment. One particular quality both men seemed to possess and exercise frequently was that of offering a leg up to those who were willing to help themselves and others. The *Quills* article noted that Abney liked to help students who wanted to go to college and asked, not for repayment to him, but that the recipient help someone else do the same thing. The Self Foundation even today likes to provide matching funds as an incentive to organizations and groups willing to view a Self grant as a challenge. That philosophy appears to emanate directly from the personal and business creed of James C. Self.

The sorting-out phase – the determination of just who would end up owning what mills in Greenwood – was probably the greatest test of Jim Self's mettle since the Draper interviews in 1908. The management skills Self brought to the fore in the years between the two world wars might have been the final determination of the viability of the enterprise. Even though times were hard soon after World War I, Self's move toward serious expansion began in the early 1920s. He deliberately kept his company "in a liquid position so that when opportunities arise, we can take advantage of them and not depend on borrowing." A shrewd judge of good men, he already had the first of his lieutenants, John B. Harris, on board when he looked around for another mill to buy after the war ended. Robinson credited him with "a delicate sense of timing" when he bought the Ninety Six mill in 1921 and placed Harris in charge. That timing was also a factor when he pulled off his famous coup in the cotton market, a strategy that many people thought would break him. As cotton prices fell, Self bought, and bought, and bought. He filled up warehouses until they overflowed, then stacked cotton bales under tarpaulins in the open, until he had built up more than a two-year supply. People wondered, and asked, and Self was ready with an answer: "Cotton can't be raised . . . for the price for which it is selling," he said. "If we stay in business, which I think we're going to do, we've got to have cotton, and I'm buying it because I think it is below the cost of production." Nothing could be simpler; Self was merely echoing the age-old admonition of "buy low, . . ." With the addition of Grendel Mill No. 2, which he renamed Mathews in honor of his father-in-law and took over as president in 1931, Jim Self became the foremost textile magnate in Greenwood County. Four years later, in the depths of the depression, he purchased all outstanding stock and became sole owner.

Greenwood Mills did not entirely escape the unrest in the industry in the 1930s when labor unions attempted to organize textile workers, but Self's position made him almost invulnerable, and his attitude must have given the labor organizers some pause. He said, no doubt quite calmly, to one delegation in 1934: "We are not mad at anyone, but if the employees want to work the mills are there. If not, the mills will be closed until such time as the employees desire to return." Was there a lockout, or wasn't there? Perhaps it depends upon one's point of view. A recent book, *Like A Family* (1987) by several University of North Carolina scholars, records the story this way: "Self responded with a ten-week lockout." The mill history states laconically, "Closure was reluctantly decreed. Only his Ninety Six Cotton Mill continued to operate." The general strike was called off at the end of three weeks, but Greenwood remained closed for an additional five weeks, and Mathews held out for ten. There were picket lines, but no violence has been recorded.

Self's wisdom and financial prudence insured that his mills weathered everything the faltering economy could throw in their way in the 1920s and 30s. He even managed to meet weekly payrolls with cash during the bank holiday early in the depression. By that time his employees saw nothing particularly unusual about that; indeed, the surprise was that he could not manage to keep the Bank of Greenwood open during that period. Self's enterprises grew and production increased during a time (1921-1938) when the industry as a whole registered a net deficit of $150 million. The demands of World War II created a boom for Greenwood Mills and set in place greater expansion than the company had ever known. Mathews plant alone wove more than 40 million yards of special wind-resistant, water-repellent poplin used as the outer covering of cold-weather garments for the military, a performance that brought the plant the Army-Navy "E" award four times and a commendation for energy, initiative, and efficiency. The first line of management, or "old guard," of Self's organization included John B.

Harris, L. B. Adams, H. W. Brinson, and James F. Chalmers, four men with an average tenure of 39.5 years. These pioneers retired in 1962 and 1963; Greenwood Mills named plants in honor of Harris, Adams, and Chalmers.

James C. Self's private life appeared to follow the same orderly pattern he brought to the mills' operation. It is easy to speculate that he was married to the mill until the pivotal year 1916 when three important events occurred, none of which changed his direction but instead set him even more firmly on track. In that year the 40-year-old tycoon acquired just over 50% of Greenwood Cotton Mill stock . . . he finally resigned as Cashier of the Bank of Greenwood . . . and, on October 16, he ended a long bachelorhood when he married Miss Lura Mathews. In a move that says quite a lot about the couple's built-in social standing, not to mention its own dash, verve, and elan, Mr. and Mrs. Self set up housekeeping in the Oregon Hotel, a very Greenwood-like thing to do. Of course there would be a house in the near future; and the house, when it came in 1917-1918, was a Greenwood product as well. Designed by local architect Thomas W. Cothran, the James C. Self house gained listing in the National Register of Historic Places in the late 1980s.

The Self house is important to Greenwood, not only because of its beauty and architectural significance, but also because of the historical importance of its connection to notable people and events. At the same time, it is a lovingly preserved private home. Since Mrs. James C. Self, Jr., sought the National Register listing and worked with historic planner John Blythe on the nomination, perhaps she will not mind if information from the nomination is shared in these pages. The two-paragraph section on architecture deserves to be quoted in full, primarily because of the sketch of Thomas Cothran it provides:

> The Self House is one of the best examples of the neoclassical style of architecture in the Greenwood area. Its setting, proportions, and ornamentation have been carefully preserved, making it one of the most imposing residences of its period and style in the Upper Savannah region. Many such residences were built in and around the city of Greenwood ca. 1910-25, but the Self House is among the larger and more elaborate of the houses that remain. It is unusual that construction of the house took place during the United States' participation in the First World War, a period when few private buildings of this scale were being erected.
>
> The architect for the Self House was Thomas White Cothran (1874-1923), a Greenwood County native who was one of the most prolific architects in Greenwood from 1908 to 1923. During this period, he designed residences and commercial buildings for many of Greenwood's most prominent individuals. He also was architect for numerous railroad-related buildings and for the 1911 Willson

TONY POINT — Constructed between
318 and 1829. First owned by William
ıd Joel Smith. Now the home of Donald
ıd Marilyn Hawthorne.

ROSELANDS — Built by Whitfield Brooks. Located on Highway 246 nine miles south of Ninety Six. Restored by current owner Mrs. Allen W. Eddy.

EWPOINT — Built in 1856 by Dr. Lewis
ıderson. Restored by current owner Mrs.
B. Adams.

MOORE-KINARD HOUSE — Built c. 1835 by Wright Nicholson Moore. Sold in 1884 to W. P. B. Kinard and still owned by Kinard family.

LVANIA — Built in 1825 by Dr. John
ırst. Located about one mile off High-
y 221 near Bradley. Home of Frank and
ly Wideman.

GREEN PASTURES — Built c. 1815-20. Purchased in 1932 by H. R. Maxon who restored the property. Purchased in 1942 by David Dows and in 1968 by W. H. Harrison.

CONNOR HOUSE — Built in 1850 by Francis A. Connor of Cokesbury. Moved to site just off Highway 254 and restored by Karen & Jack Jennings.

SUNNYSIDE — Built in 1850 by Robert Gillam. Home of the H. L. Watson family for more than fifty years. Located on Dargan Avenue near Taggart Street.

SMITH-LOMAX HOUSE — Built c. 1820 by James Lomax, Jr. Located about two miles west of Hodges, the house is owned by the estate of Wilbur Smith.

EDEN HALL — Built in 1850 by Dr. John Wardlaw Hearst. Owned by Emmett I. Davis and currently undergoing restoration.

DURST HOME — Built by W. L. Durst at corner of Cambridge and Durst Streets. Site of Greenwood's first post office.

BAILEY HOUSE — Built by James Bailey at corner of Main and Maxwell. First moved to site of Federal Building and later to site of The Museum.

STATE CHAMPS — In 1916 this team established a state record in spreading and connecting fire hose.

TWO NEW ENGINES — Greenwood's Pride, with personnel, in the 1940s.

GREENWOOD'S FIRST FIRE ENGINE — Coal-fired and horse-drawn.

CLARENCE BEAUDROT — Greenwood's first regular fireman who began sleeping with No. 1 in 1909 to keep boiler fired and horses ready. Fire chief from 1913 to 1953.

FIRE DEPARTMENT AND "SPEED COP" — In front of City Hall on Main Street in the early 1920s.

CITY AND COMMISSION OF PUBLIC WORKS EMPLOYEES — In the 1920s

FIRE WAGON — Ready for a State Convention parade. Courthouse and Law Range in rear of picture.

THE SQUARE (in 1896) — Old Barksdale Building before it was destroyed in a fire in 1904. Much cotton was sold here.

THE SQUARE (about 1905) — With the "new" Barksdale Building in background.

ORIGINAL COURTHOUSE – Completed in 1898 after a long struggle, as recounted in Chapter Three.

MAGNOLIA STREET SCHOOL – Built in 1904 when schools were supposed to be pretty. Burned in November 1980.

THE SQUARE (east side) — This photograph taken before brick paving was installed.

THE SQUARE (east side) — Taken in 1920s featuring Commercial Bank Building (now Grier Building), one of Greenwood's three "skyscrapers."

BANK OF GREENWOOD & RILEY HOTEL — Nationsbank now occupies this space at Main & Riley Streets.

SYNDICATE BLOCK — Built in 1898 on the west side of the Square by group of prominent businessmen. Second-floor apartments popular with bachelors and young couples.

INDEX BUILDING – On south side of Maxwell Avenue. Election returns and World Series games coming over the "wire" were announced to large crowds filling Maxwell Avenue.

MISS MAUDE'S MODEL T – And a racy DeSoto from the mid-1950s.

GREENWOOD GARAGE – Located on north side of Maxwell Avenue. As it appeared in the early 1900s

POST OFFICE — Located at corner of Hampton and Oregon Avenues. Now the Federal Building, the structure cost $60,000 when built in 1911.

AMERICAN BANK BUILDING — As it appeared in the 1920s. Later named the Central Union Bank Building and finally The Textile Building.

THE SQUARE (still another view) — As it appeared in 1902 before the Grier & Park Building (now Textile Building) was built at corner of Main & Oak Streets.

FIRST OREGON HOTEL – Built by Joel Smith Bailey and opened in 1898 at corner of Main Street & Maxwell Avenue.

(right) CONFEDERATE MONUMENT – Erected in 1903 by the Ladies Memorial Associations of Greenwood County. Courthouse and lawyers office building in background.

ANOTHER VIEW – The Oregon attracted not only traveling salesmen, or "drummers," but also weekend guests from near and far. Featured exceptional food and hospitality.

THE OREGON BURNS — No lives were lost in this fire of March 3, 1912, but property damage was severe.

THE NEW OREGON — Plans materialized rapidly, and the new hotel opened in 1914

NATIONAL LOAN & EXCHANGE BANK BUILDING — Built by the Bailey family at the same time as the Oregon Hotel #2. Became the Hodges Building in 1936, then the County Bank Building, and now the Greenwood Building.

GREENWOOD BAKERY – Built in 1895 by the Feuthenberger family who came from Germany. Children and grand-children of the Hollingsworth family continued the business.

TRAVELING ADVERTISEMENT – for early Greenwood business.

EADY" – William A. Lomax and Thomas urst.

FLOAT IN COUNTY FAIR PARADE – About 1904, showing Janelle Arnold, Graeme Smith, Dr. Hugh Fellers, Ruby Aiken, Gus Henderson, May Bailey, Clara Neel Bailey, and James Crymes.

ELUXE TOURING CAR – John I. Chipley t the wheel, with Mrs. Chipley and Lanier hipley in the front seat. Marvin S. hipley, along with Cora and Lula Felker, ccupy the rear.

A MERRY OLDSMOBILE – James C. Self driving, with Miss Susan Arnold up front.

THE YOE WELL — After supplying all the water needs for several years, this free-flowing well still contributes to the town's water system.

THE MILL HOUSE AT PARKTON — where Dr. Corbett's health food was produced.

PARKTON — A view of the boat house.

CTURE TAKEN DURING PASTORATE OF MR. GEORGE N. COWAN(1909-1914)FIRST BAPTIST CH

Gerald Smart
D.M.NIXON
Mr.DeShazo
R.B.Norris
J.C,BURNS-Sr.
Mrs.Joel Burnett
Mary Sue Sproles
Genevieve Singleton
Mrs. DeShazo
Mrs.Napier

11=Mrs.Mary Beaudrot
12=Mrs. Wideman
13=Mrs.Susan Hill
14=Mrs.J.R.Leavell
15+Mr.Cowan(Pastor)
16=Elizabeth Cowan
17=Theodosia Sproles
18=Mrs.Duckett
19=Mrs.A.F.Hagan
20=Mrs.Bessie Andrews

21=Mrs.Lizzie Harrison
22=Mrs.J.W.Sproles
23=Joe Beaudrot
24=L.C.Craig
25=J.W.Sproles
26=Press Devore
27=Mr.Graham
28=Mr.Watts
29=Mrs.A.T.Jamison
30=Mrs.J.G.Mattison

31=Mr.A.F.Hagan
32=Mr.Youngblood

IF YOU HAVE OTHER OLD PICTURES, CONSIDER GIVING THEM TO =THE MUSEUM= WHERE MANY PEOPLE CAN SEE AND ENJOY THEM.

FIRST BAPTIST CHURCH MEMBERS — Taken in 1912.

NORTH MAIN STREET — Showing First Baptist Church at far right and First Presbyterian Church in the center.

DURST & MATHEWS STORE — Kirksey.

(Right) BANK OF GREENWOOD OFFICERS — Left to right: H. T. Medlock; J. K. Durst, President; J. C. Self. Organized in 1888.

THE DEPOT — Southern Railroad Station in Greenwood.

Hall wing of the Lander College Old Main Building (listed in the National Register in 1984). Although the majority of Mr. Cothran's projects are in the Greenwood area, he also was associated with buildings in other parts of the state, including the YMCA building at Clemson College (now University). The Self House is one of the best-preserved examples of Cothran's residential work.

According to family tradition, construction required about a year. Considering the number of important details contained in both exterior and interior, that length of time is not at all surprising. The contractor, reportedly Charles L. Rounds of Clinton, deserves full credit for executing architectural details one needs a dictionary to define. At the risk of losing readers who do not deal with such terms every day, the description of the mansion's exterior from the nomination is also included here:

> The James C. Self House is a two-story, brick veneer residence with a green Spanish tile, hip roof. It rests on a brick foundation faced with rock face granite blocks. There is a partial basement and an attic. The exterior walls are composed of textured brick laid in stretcher bond. Most of the windows are double-hung, with six-over-six lights and louvered shutters. The windows have concrete sills and flat arches with keystones. Three interior end brick chimneys and one brick flue, all with corbelled caps, pierce the roof.
>
> The five-bay facade (east elevation) is symmetrical, with central entrances on each story. The first-story entrance has a single door with beveled glass sidelights, recessed within an architrave framed by four fluted pilasters. The second story entrance opens onto a small balcony that is supported by four acanthus leaf consoles and has a square-picketed balustrade with simple pedestals. This entrance has double doors, sidelights, corner lights, and transom, all recessed within an architrave featuring two fluted pilasters.
>
> The facade is dominated by a colossal Ionic portico that projects from the three central bays. The portico has four fluted Ionic columns (and two corresponding pilasters) with Scamozzi capitals and rosette ornamentation. The entablature has a plain architrave and frieze, and a cornice with dentil molding and acanthus leaf brackets. The portico is surmounted by a balustraded parapet, composed of turned posts and panelled pedestals, which engages the front slope of the roof. Centrally located behind the portico is a gabled dormer that has a Palladian window, boxed cornice with returns, and an acroterion.
>
> The porch has a tile floor, which extends to form terraces to the north and south. The terraces have balustrades with turned posts and brick pedestals, and intersect with single-story porches on the north and south elevations. The north porch extends to form

> a porte-cochere; the south porch has been enclosed with glass to form a sun room. Both porches and the porte-cochere feature grouped, fluted, Doric columns; turned balustrades; balustraded parapets; and dentil molding. The portico, terraces, porches, and porte-cochere have granite steps and granite trim.
>
> Two large, two-story wings extend from the rear of the house. Other notable exterior features include a single-story polygonal bay window on the south elevation, a gabled dormer on the south roof slope (similar to the dormer on the facade), and a granite water table. The roof has a wide overhang with dentil molding and acanthus leaf brackets. There have been no additions to the house.

The house's interior is no less impressive; especially noteworthy is the fact that the interior remains largely unchanged from the time of construction, with the exception of alterations made for modern conveniences. Outbuildings contemporary to the main house, including a smokehouse/wellhouse, garage, and boys' playhouse, are also described in the nomination, as is the newer girls' playhouse.

The ultimate paragraph of the National Register nomination provides a thumbnail sketch of James C. Self's career and introduces the subject of his model mill villages:

> James C. Self was one of the most prominent textile industrialists of the first half of the twentieth century. When he became president of the Greenwood Cotton Mill in 1908, the company was deeply in debt and on the verge of collapse. Through continual modernization and expansion, Mr. Self built the small company into a textile giant. A 1939 survey of textile industries in South Carolina showed that Mr. Self was president of five of the ten textile plants in Greenwood County. The five plants had an aggregate of 160,928 spindles and 3,860 looms, well over half of the total number in the county. By 1955, Greenwood Mills was reported to be one of the largest privately-owned textile empires in the world. The mill villages that Mr. Self had built, beginning in the 1920s, were model communities, with wide streets; brick veneer, tile-roofed houses; modern schools; and spacious churches. His position as an industry leader was affirmed by many colleagues and editorialists at the time of his death in 1955. By this time, Greenwood Mills included five large plants that employed approximately 6,000 workers.

The term "mill village," taken out of context, somehow conjures up a whole spectrum of images ranging from a sort of second-class neighborhood at best to a repellent place of pure squalor at worst. Erskine Caldwell's descriptions of life in an Augusta mill village immediately come to mind. Because of the lack of transportation in the earliest days of the textile industry, company-owned housing was a necessity; but it is quite true that mill villages often were simply the means to an end, an end that had much more to do with production than with the everyday lives of the people who produced. Of particular significance is the fact that people generally left the farm and went to mills in families, a move that suited employers very well since it brought in several operatives at one time. Not only was this arrangement practical, it was also desirable and even essential to the mills' functioning as they did. But it did mean company housing, and the quality of housing provided for these farm-to-mill families varied widely. Mill villages in the early years of the industry were so diverse that visitors could find whatever their preconceived notions had led them to expect. Descriptions might be anything from "exposes of poverty and social wretchedness" to "portraits of material well-being, civic advancement, and social harmony." Some writers had their own axes to grind: two reform-minded ladies named Van Horst, for example, wrote in 1903 that mill villages were "pest-ridden, epidemic-filled, filthy settlements where mill hands lived their horrible honeycomb of lives, shocking morals and decency." Another writer, not hostile to mill interests, recorded in 1899 that mill housing in Columbus, Georgia, consisted of "germ-breeding and poverty-engendering 'shacks' whose bare floors and walls, broken windows, and battered doors bespoke the human misery they might otherwise have obscured." Whole families lived there, according to the columnist, "sleeping, eating, cooking in a single room, in health or sickness, with no sanitary guards whatever."

Certainly this is enough said on the extremes that could be found, if one were looking, in company-owned mill housing. Much more common were the utterly drab groups of identical houses, often painted the same dull color and arranged in two, three, or four rows quite near the mills. These plots were generally innocent of any attempt at landscaping and featured only "wells spaced at regular intervals between houses and privies placed at uniform distances behind them on otherwise barren lots."

These examples were chosen by way of contrast with what happened in Greenwood when James C. Self turned his attention to housing for his employees. One of the best anecdotes in Robinson's book concerns this question. It seems that a long-time employee once quit because of some grievance. His foreman was unable to resolve the matter, and there seemed nothing to do but pay the worker off and let him go. The next morning he was back. "I thought you didn't want to work here," the foreman said. "Well," the ex-employee replied, "my wife won't move." One hopes he got his job back. He must have, since the book records that Self told the story often.

Jim Self was definitely not a slumlord; neither was he simply a social reformer, although a case could be made that he was undertaking an experiment of sorts when he planned the communities. Certainly decent villages could have been provided with less costly materials than those he chose. Plain folk (Newby's term for mill workers during the farm-to-factory transition period) were accustomed to housing much inferior to that offered by Self's company. Nor did his interest wane after the communities were constructed; instead, Self made regular visits, taking notes in his little book and stopping to inquire about the smallest thing that might need improvement. If it is true that Self actually listened when housewives complained about the placement of a kitchen cabinet, and there is no reason to doubt it, then it is easy to believe that he genuinely cared about how his workers lived. The move to upgrade housing for Greenwood and Ninety Six cotton mill workers began in 1921, when the latter was acquired, and continued until every village met the standard Self set. Because of their familiarity there is no point in describing the houses and mill communities themselves, and Greenwood residents are surely aware that they represent, in Robinson's words, "an understanding of employee needs and comforts rarely equalled in the modern industrial world." Greenwood people might not know, however, that the communities were the result of Self's personal attention to every detail of design, construction, and maintenance. The company history claims that the millions of dollars spent on construction, landscaping, maintenance, taxes, and insurance far exceeded the rent receipts of $1 per room per week, but Self never seemed to regret the decision to build model communities that reflected his philosophy of challenging Greenwood Mills employees to pride in themselves and their product. The decision to sell some 1,500 company-owned houses came in 1962, and by 1967 every house in the Mathews and Greenwood villages was privately owned. James C. Self would have approved; the importance of home ownership was another of his maxims.

Before his death in 1955 Self had opened his own selling house in New York, formed the present-day corporate structure of Greenwood Mills, and launched a $21 million building and modernization program to be accomplished without outside financial assistance. Two new mills were part of the expansion plan: Harris Plant, named for J. B. Harris and placed in operation in 1950, and Durst Plant, named for W. L. Durst, which followed in 1953. Others in the county would come later under the next generation of management, and the company would move into its first expansion beyond Greenwood in 1965.

The term *philanthropy* is perhaps better defined by example than by the dictionary. The simple words, "goodwill to fellow men," could characterize almost anyone; there is no reason to doubt the goodwill of the average bum. But one who practices philanthropy, or a philanthropist, must not only feel that goodwill but also possess the means to convert attitude to action and the good sense to bring vague idealism into focus. James C. Self's philanthropy sprang not only from his wealth, which was considerable, but also from his brains, his energy, and his faith. The simple truth is that Greenwood would not be the same had Self not been the person he was or made the choices he made. Boykin Curry made a pointed suggestion at the time of Self's death. It might be well, he said, for every citizen to pause and consider the question: what would Greenwood be today if J. C. Self had moved to another city fifty years ago? Which is not to say that the man was some sort of plaster saint. Complaints about some of his business practices are still part of Greenwood lore; Perrin Anderson's memoir *Recollections of My Life* took the balanced view in assessing the way Self did business:

> One case which is worth telling about is the case in which I represented Bethlehem Steel Company vs. Greenwood Mills. One day I received a call from an official of this company wanting to know if I would represent them in collecting an account against Greenwood Mills. "What is the amount of the account?" I asked. He replied, "About $200,000." I agreed very readily. This was something big in my experience. As soon as I got the papers from Bethlehem, I wrote Mr. Jim Self telling him that I had been employed in the case and that before commencing suit I would be glad to discuss the claim with him or his attorneys with a view to settling the matter without suit. He immediately called me on the phone saying "Perrin, I got your letter. I knew that they would hire some Greenwood lawyer and I'm glad you got the case. I hope you get a good fee. My lawyers will contact you." The claim was for the unpaid portion of an account Greenwood Mills owed for the purchase of steel used in building Harris Plant. Mr. Self claimed that Bethlehem was late in shipping the steel and that had held up construction of the plant and caused a loss in profits. So he was claiming damages as an offset against the bill. . . .
>
> I recall a Lions Club meeting at which Mr. Self was to be given an award. Congressman Bryan Dorn was the featured speaker. He praised Mr. Self for his "unselfish service" and other superlative statements. Mr. Self, who was sitting near me, said, "Young man, you should not be so careless with the truth." I don't think Mr. Self ever sought praise or made any false pretenses.

The tactic Self used with Bethlehem was nearly always successful in gaining a "discount" of a few percentage points, since it was generally simpler and less expensive for suppliers to acquiesce than to press for full payment. The Bethlehem claim, for example, was finally settled out of court, but only barely, and for $192,000. Anderson also speculated that Self might have regretted the time he spent pursuing business interests; he wrote that he once heard him advise someone not to become a slave to his work and wondered if he might be thinking of his own life. No one really knows whether Self's great business success brought corresponding personal fulfillment. Perhaps it is true, as Anderson suggested, that Self spent Sundays going through the mills when some of the machinery was idle. But it is also true that if he had wanted to be on the Riviera instead, that option was assuredly his.

When James C. Self died in July 1955, *The Index-Journal* printed nearly a full page of tributes from South Carolina newspapers and individual textile executives from all over the South. Speaking on behalf of the chamber of commerce, Boykin Curry struck the keynote with the observation that everyone shared one overriding memory of Jim Self – the way he felt about his home town. "He loved Greenwood," Curry said, and that was undoubtedly true. Other tributes also noted this particular aspect of Self's business and personal life, but *The Charlotte Observer's* editorial covered the touchy subject of labor relations as well:

> Union men will tell you that Jim Self was one of a vanishing breed of anti-labor barons who resisted organization with all the vigor of a backwoods parson wrestling the devil. The estimate may be reasonably valid, but Jim Self wrestled with humanitarian skill. . . .
>
> Whether Jim Self was motivated by his dislike for organized labor, as the union men claim, or by his deep regard for his fellow man, as his friends maintain, the unions haven't moved in. We prefer, with his friends, to believe that Jim Self's motive was that of a grateful man who looked upon himself as a temporary trustee of the millions his people had helped him acquire.
>
> More than a man died yesterday. A giant is gone.

Any listing of awards Self received in his lifetime – and even since his death as new halls of fame were created – seems quite unnecessary since it would add nothing to the measure of the man already taken by the monuments of functional value he left behind. All are notable, of course, but perhaps the Man of the South award from 1952 should be singled out since he was the first South Carolinian to win it. And a tribute from Louis Wright's *Barefoot in Arcadia* deserves mention here. Wright recorded a number of stories and observations from the time he worked for the newspaper in the early 1920s, but there was one man he was never able to interview:

> There was one story I always wanted to write but never did because the subject was a reticent man and, unlike the common run of humanity, had no love of publicity. The wealthiest man in town was James C. Self, known to everybody as Jim Self, owner of the Greenwood Cotton Mills and one of the greatest textile magnates in the South. . . .
>
> By hard work, shrewd judgment, and fair dealing, he made the Greenwood Cotton Mills and other mills that he developed into a

> vast textile complex recognized everywhere for the quality of its product. He also became a philanthropist: the builder of hospitals and the benefactor of charitable causes. Many of his achievements reached fruition after I had long given over reporting, but already in my time he was a legendary figure of the poor boy making good; Dick Whittington becoming Lord Mayor of London was no more astounding than Jim Self, country clerk from Kirksey, rising to such eminence that Wall Street bankers spoke of him with reverence. Although I wrote many stories about the growth of his enterprises, I never could get a story about the personality behind them. He was a modest man. Not until age had mellowed him would he talk to a reporter about himself. But by that time I was no longer writing news stories.

The story of Greenwood Mills is by no means ended; in fact, recording its history is an ongoing project of the company. *The Character of Quality* is now in the third or fourth revision since its original publication in 1964. Both the second and third generations of Self family management, by James C. Self's only son and two grandsons, are filled with accomplishments recorded in the book, along with descriptions of subsidiary companies and interesting accounts of diversification in recent years. These subsidiary companies include Ninety Six Manufacturing Company, Greenwood Motor Lines, Coleman Oil Company, Greenwood Warehouse, Inc., Greenwood Mills Credit Association, Central Trust Company, and Greenwood Development Corporation. Another subsidiary, although technically not an actual company, is the Forestry/Land Management Department. Most of these companies are familiar to Greenwood County people and will not be described in any depth. Two, however, are particularly interesting for almost opposite reasons and merit further examination in these pages.

Ninety Six Manufacturing is an example of the cottonseed, or "oil," mill so familiar from the early days when cotton production was high. South Carolina boasted 36 cottonseed mills in 1931; today there are only four, according to the mill history. Greenwood County produced 50,000 bales of cotton annually in the early 1900s. Eli Whitney's cotton gin, invented in the late eighteenth century, had been the first practical step toward processing cotton, but its byproduct — the seeds themselves — created another problem. Cottonseeds were essentially waste: they were supposedly poisonous to animals in their natural state, storage created a fire hazard, and their sheer volume contributed to a sort of environmental nightmare. Greenwood Mills' current historian, Ryan C. Amacher, wrote that the county once had 25 tons of cottonseed to dispose of annually. (Amacher's paragraph on cottonseed creates a problem of its own: if the 50,000 bales produced 1,000 pounds of seed each as he indicated, then 25 is only 1/1000 of the tonnage of cottonseed the county accumulated in a year. Twenty-five tons sounds like a lot, but 25,000 tons is almost mind-boggling.) Agricultural researchers discovered in the early 1900s that cottonseed could be turned into valuable products for sale on the market. But, as usual, the story goes back a bit further. Other sources indicate that the Chinese produced oil from cottonseed as early as the sixteenth century, and some cottonseed oil was refined in England a couple of centuries later. It is true that the industry did not assume commercial importance in the United States until after the Civil War, but once established it grew rapidly. By 1900 more than half the cotton crop in the country was fully processed through cottonseed oil mills. Although oil is the most important by-product, it is by no means the only use of cottonseed. Both long- and short-staple cotton fibers are the first usable products to result from processing. These are consumed by the paper industry and also used as mattress filler, weiner casings, and in the manufacture of gunpowder. Next come the cottonseed hulls which are sold as filler for animal food. After the seeds yield their oil, the resulting "meal cake" is mixed with hulls and ground into feed for cattle. Ninety Six Manufacturing Company purchased cottonseed from outside the region when county cotton production dwindled and served the farming community directly as a dealer for a leading South Carolina livestock feed company.

While the cottonseed oil industry is a holdover from the days when cotton was king, another Greenwood Mills subsidiary, Greenwood Development Corporation, represents activity in a field that is not only quite modern but also has strong connections to South Carolina's foremost industry of tourism. Amacher called the formation of the company a natural transition, considering that Greenwood Mills had been involved in property development since the time of the original Jim Self; indeed, the company had built houses outside the mill villages for sale to employees and others as early as the 1930s, and Mathews Heights and Wade Heights were the first residential property developments in South Carolina. Self's grandson James C. Self III was credited with the idea of diversification into areas outside the basic textile industry. He researched several possibilities before the decision to enter the field of recreational/retirement development was made. The company was formed in 1978; the next year it purchased a partially developed 2,000-acre resort on Hilton Head Island. Palmetto Dunes is the major star in Greenwood Development Corporation's firmament, but it is not the only one. The company has also acquired property in North Carolina, Georgia, and Florida; its goal is resort/retirement developments all along the eastern seaboard.

A photograph of the Self family in the 1989 edition of *The Character of Quality* shows a total of 21 individuals, from babies to elder statesman James C. Self, most of whom live in Greenwood. The name of the book has been adopted as the motto of Greenwood Mills to represent its dedication to quality improvement. The original Jim Self would surely be proud.

Most people are familiar with the term *multiplier effect,* meaning the economic impact of payrolls and other business expenditure within a community. The rounds of spending created by the multiplier, or ripple, effect are among the most fascinating features of a free-market economy. Economists have developed methods of measuring the impact of economic activity which have been codified for more or less uniform application, thus the multiplier effect is now a measurable phenomenon. Another notable feature of a free economic system is the rise of support industries of various types in response to some large-scale advance such as railroads, automobile manufacture, textile mills, and so on. One quick example is the proliferation of video rental stores at a time of fundamental change in the home entertainment field. Several examples of textile support activity still exist in Greenwood, but one of the most important, Aldrich Machine Works, passed off the local scene some years ago. Many Greenwood people remember the company well and consider its owners uniquely interesting and important to the story of Greenwood business and industry.

One of Greenwood's star businessmen and a contemporary of James C. Self was Robert Aldrich. He might also have been one of Greenwood's star eccentrics if it is true, as Jimmy Wade suggests, that he sometimes dressed in a cowboy suit to listen to "The Lone Ranger" radio program. But Aldrich Machine Works was a serious business indeed and one of Greenwood's oldest. The company made machinery and parts for textile mills which were sold all over the world. The original A. P. (Alfred Proctor) Aldrich came to Greenwood from Barnwell in 1898. His first job, repairing machinery for Greenwood and Grendel Mills, led directly to opening a small repair shop near his home on Reynolds Street about 1900. At first the shop handled only repairs, but Aldrich began making "ball bearing applications" in a limited way about 1914. Five years later Aldrich's two sons, A. P., Jr., and Robert, bought their father's business, formed a partnership, gave up repair work, and concentrated on the manufacture of ball bearing equipment for textile mills. The brothers also persuaded their father to change the name of the business from A. P. Aldrich Shop to Aldrich Machine Works in 1918, the year before they bought him out. Both sons were graduate engineers – A. P., Jr., from Auburn and Bob from Clemson – and both saw service in World War I. A fire in 1928 forced the Aldrich brothers to move their business to a 26-acre site on Montague Avenue Extension, the spot it continued to occupy until the company passed out of existence many years later.

A centennial newspaper article noted that the plant gradually expanded to the point of manufacturing machinery rather than simply parts and specialized in the picking and opening departments of textile mills. The business was incorporated in 1953. A. P., Jr., moved to New Hampshire to represent the company in New England and Canada, while in Greenwood both the machine works and Bob Aldrich became fixtures in the town's business and civic life.

The Greenwood Chamber of Commerce sponsored a Robert Aldrich Testimonial Dinner at the Oregon Hotel in 1959. Aldrich was presented the Distinguished Service Award that evening, and testimonials were offered by a number of the town's business leaders, each representing a civic organization. Among them were J. B. Harris (Kiwanis Club), William John Park (Greenwood Jaycees, of which Aldrich was the first member, as well as an honorary life member), Dr. James A. Bowers (Tuberculosis Association), W. D. Tinsley (Community Chest), Dr. B. M. Grier (Lander College), and Douglas Featherstone (Northside Junior High School and several other recipients of Aldrich's largesse). One of his favorite charities was Brewer Hospital; Ed Chaffin spoke of his 25 years of service on its board and his many contributions to its needs.

As for Aldrich's eccentricities, quite a few are remembered by those who knew him. Walter Roark, who was hired as manager in 1962 and stayed for more than six years, found Aldrich difficult to work with, probably because he resented his new manager and could accept no way to do things but his own. Roark considered both Aldrich brothers intelligent but called salesman A. P. "the brains of the business." He also said that Aldrich Machine Works was among the first of Greenwood's businesses to provide a profit-sharing plan for its employees. But that enlightened attitude did not carry over into other company policies; for example, sheriff's deputies and telephone operators could expect to receive Christmas gifts from Aldrich Machine Works, but not its own employees. Possibly management was doing its bit to discourage idle expectation and crass materialism among the staff, but a more likely explanation is that Bob Aldrich was paying off debts he incurred during the year to law enforcement agencies. He enjoyed riding around the county with deputies and highway patrolmen. He reportedly carried a state constable's badge in his wallet and was likely to show up at any time and any place a law enforcement vehicle might go. Sometimes that would be the hospital, in company with a trooper investigating an automobile accident.

Dan Hammett, retired purchasing agent for Greenwood Mills, remembers that he sent an associate to see Aldrich one day. Finding the gate locked and no one around to open it, that gentleman simply climbed the fence and walked to the office. After Aldrich determined how his visitor had managed to gain entrance, he ordered him to leave the same way he came. Hammett's representative was forced to reclimb the fence under Aldrich's steady gaze, at which point Aldrich unlocked the gate and cordially invited him inside. One can almost feel the poor man's chagrin; he was probably not able to laugh about the incident for some time afterward.

Gordon Bailes, on the other hand, managed to impress Bob Aldrich during his first business call by returning a chair to its proper place after the two men finished their business at Aldrich's desk. Bailes recalled that Aldrich gave him money to buy a Coke as a reward for his thoughtfulness. Neatness, punctuality, and cleanliness were almost fetishes with Aldrich. He was married twice, but home life and home cooking were not among his favorite things. He much preferred the Oregon Hotel for the morning and evening meal, and he lived between marriages in an apartment on the plant site.

Boykin Curry recalls that Citizens Trust Company once mailed renewal insurance policies to Aldrich with insufficient postage. Bob Aldrich was incensed at the notion of paying the 2¢ postage due and returned the policies with a letter refusing to renew. Several meetings with Clarence Smith, a personal friend and manager of the insurance department, were required before Aldrich could be persuaded to reinstate the insurance.

Louis Wright recorded a story in *Barefoot in Arcadia* about a Mr. Aldrich who because of the time factor must have been Bob Aldrich's father. Wright left himself an out in the first line just in case the story is apocryphal. It has been repeated about other individuals; one hopes in this case it is actually true, but there are no guarantees:

> [S]omeone could always recall the way Mr. Aldrich, operator of a machine shop on the edge of town, put down an officer of a local cotton mill who had complained about the size of a bill. The circumstances, as related, concerned a troublesome engine at the mill, which no mechanic on the work force could repair. In desperation, the mill sent for Mr. Aldrich, famous throughout the region for his skill. In less than half an hour, he had the engine going and sent in a bill for $500, an enormous sum in those days. The management grumbled and asked for an itemized statement. Mr. Aldrich was glad to comply. It read: "One leather washer, $.20. Knowing where to put it, $499.80." The bill was paid.

Wright recalled the elder Aldrich from his boyhood, in part because he was reputed to be an atheist, but also because Aldrich had a long black beard and rode a white Harley-Davidson motorcycle, the first of its kind ever seen in Greenwood: "When he went roaring down the street, bareheaded and his black beard parted by the wind, children ran to stare. If Beelzebub himself had ridden past in a cloud of sulphur, he would not have excited more wonder in us." These brief accounts of A. P. Aldrich, Sr., might explain, at least in part, the almost legendary quality of his children's lives in Greenwood.

Angelle Adams remembers Rose Aldrich, who would become as eccentric as her half-brother, as a lovely and accomplished woman in her youth. A graduate of Lander College who also studied at the University of North Carolina, Miss Aldrich shared her talents in music and dance with Greenwood's young people. She lived in the family home, the interesting brick house built about 1898 in the second block of Reynolds Street, only a few doors from the house where Adams grew up. Rose Aldrich held kindergarten classes and taught music and dance in her home. She was cultured and well-read, Adams remembers, and the children of the neighborhood loved her. Boykin Curry recalls that the sight of Rose Aldrich, clad in a black dancer's leotard and standing up in a convertible, made a distinct impression on him at the fairground one day. In later life, however, Aldrich grew ever more reclusive behind the closed doors of her home, which more than one child of the next generation began to call the "witch's house." Adams believes Aldrich's difficulties were twofold: a heart problem of some sort evidently kept her from embarking on a full-scale career as a dancer even though the talent and interest were there, and other careers might have been ruled out for the same reason. In addition, Aldrich had no money to call her own, and indulging her wide-ranging cultural interests was impossible because of financial constraints. It seems reasonable to speculate also that the "heart problem" might have limited Rose Aldrich's social contacts at a critical point. Though it is possible she had absolutely no desire to marry, somehow one can picture Greenwood's own Miss Havisham brooding over a mouldering wedding cake. Rose Aldrich died in 1980 not long before her 76th birthday. Her brother Robert died of a heart attack in 1964.

The business brochure printed by the merchants' association and board of trade in 1910 contains a section entitled "Manufacturing Enterprises." In addition to the seven cotton mills in the county, Greenwood boasted two lumber companies (W. J. Snead and Greenwood Lumber and Manufacturing), three bottling plants (Coca-Cola, Pepsi Cola, and soda water), two marble yards, a granite quarry, and a handkerchief factory. The latter company not only gave "employment to a number of ladies" but also specialized in making striped suits for convicts. The handkerchief part of the business was discontinued in favor of convict clothing in 1907, but the name of the company was not changed, and the fifteen female employees produced thirty dozen garments per day. Greenwood also had two fertilizer factories in 1910, as well as the "largest cotton ginnery east of the Mississippi" and one of the largest oil mills in the state. Mays Brick Company advertised in the brochure, but for some reason was not listed among Greenwood's manufacturing enterprises.

When Greenwood County was predominantly agricultural, farmers produced not only cotton and small grains but herds of fine livestock as well. A 1910 brochure called the Greenwood County Fair "one of the leading county fairs of the State." The editor of the *Southern Cultivator,* an Atlanta publication, wrote in 1909:

> We have seen one Fair that fulfilled our ideal. It was at Greenwood, S.C. The best county fair we ever saw. We never saw so many good Jerseys, hogs, horses, colts, stallions and Jacks. There were five fine herds of Jerseys present, and one, as good as any south of Mason & Dixon line, owned by Mr. T. P. Henderson, of Phoenix, Greenwood County. We had no idea Greenwood County was such a center of blooded stock.

The county fair is now only fond memories of rides, sideshows, and cotton candy, but remnants of the livestock industry remain. A number of people, most of whom earn their livelihood in other ways, still "fool with cows" as the saying goes, and a related Greenwood company has managed to progress from merely a slaughterhouse to a major meat packing operation doing business throughout the Southeast. Members of the Henderson family mentioned in the Atlanta periodical are still involved in both farming and the packing plant. One descendant, Greg Henderson, manages to grow cotton successfully.

Greenwood Packing Plant dates from 1919 when W. P. Corley and Dr. W. A. Barnette took over the Greenwood Abattoir and made it a city slaughterhouse to distribute dressed hogs and cattle at wholesale. The business started with four employees. Barnette, a veterinarian and one-time mayor of Greenwood, always believed the county had a future in the livestock and meat industry. He was a Clemson graduate with a D. V. M. from Ohio State who settled in Greenwood after the first world war. His wife was Mary Payne Henderson, daughter of T. P. (Thomas Payne) Henderson. Barnette became sole owner of the business in the early 1940s and served as president until his death in 1962. Barnette and his three sons — Bill, Henderson, and Ed — built the company into a leading industry in Greenwood with the most modern plant in the state. Greenwood Packing Plant is still a leading Greenwood industry with many more "firsts" to its credit now than in 1957 when it was already the first in the state to initiate United States Department of Agriculture grading of beef, as well as the first to use vacuum packaging to insure freshness of its famous Carolina Pride line of luncheon meats. The company today, managed by surviving sons W. A., Jr., and P. Henderson Barnette (J. E. Barnette died in 1982), is the largest full process meat packer in the state, producing some two million pounds of meat products per week. Its distribution area is South Carolina, North Carolina, Georgia, Florida, Alabama, and Tennessee.

Brick-making in Greenwood County dates from the very beginning. The industry was cited in a long story on Greenwood in an 1889 Charleston newspaper, and other articles in early newspapers nearly always mentioned the on-site production of brick for new construction in the town. Obviously Greenwood County contains large deposits of sedimentary clay and shale, the most common materials used to manufacture brick, and the reason for on-site production in the early days was, just as obviously, the difficulty of transportation. The evolution of the brick industry in Greenwood County is a story of growth in both quantity and quality of a product, as well as one of almost inordinate dependence on factors external to the end product itself. No one could tell that story better than Joseph H. Patrick, retired president and chairman of the board of Southern Brick Company.

Journeyman brick-makers followed contractors to building sites until as late as 1915. The brick-maker brought along his "forms," four-brick-sized wooden boxes used to mold hand-made brick, and a hoe for mixing clay. After selecting a site where the clay was best, the brick-maker would mix and "throw" the brick, then set the forms on the ground to dry. Many old brick, with animal tracks clearly visible in their sides, remain as evidence of this stage of the industry's evolution. After the brick were sun-dried, they were stacked into a "scove kiln" to be burned. The kiln consisted of the dried brick themselves arranged so that they created spaces, or tunnels, which made a series of "fire boxes" the entire length of the kiln. Fuel was, naturally, wood; a good brick maker could judge when the brick were ready by the amount of shrinkage in the kiln.

The beginnings of the modern era of brick manufacture in Greenwood County were linked to the railroad, since transportation "was, and still is, a major factor" in any successful operation. Opportunities for manufacturing brick on a large scale opened when railroads came to Greenwood, and clay from the bottom land along Ninety Six, Wilson, and Coronaca Creeks took on new importance. The first business contract involving brick-making was made in 1908 between W. G. Sligh of Newberry and George W. Reid of Dyson. The contract, an elaborate arrangement of land, leases, and commissions, was never implemented; Patrick wrote that it "came to naught." Since Sligh's name comes up no more in the Greenwood County brick industry, perhaps he must be considered a "would be" rather than a "has been" brick manufacturer.

The first brick plant set along a railroad in the county opened about 1910 when Reid sold 98 acres bounded by Ninety Six Creek, Wilson Creek, the Old Anderson Road, and Southern Railway to J. L. McMillan and W. E. Owen. This plant, one of three that opened in the years between 1910 and 1920, had a rather straightforward history and a couple of different names. During the McMillan family years (Owen sold his interest to his partner in 1916), the company was known as Dyson Brick and was so deeded to Joe F. Park, Receiver, in 1932. Patrick wrote that the original McMillan had apparently contemplated a partnership with Frank Fetzer under the name Angus Brick Company, but McMillan died suddenly in about 1926, and that name was not used until the company was acquired by Nell and Sterling Graydon in 1932. Graydon operated the company for thirteen years and sold his interest to Southern

Brick Company in 1945. Chartered Angus Brick and Tile Company by the new owners, the business was first improved and then operated with eight bee hive kilns until 1971 when labor problems brought it to its knees. Patrick wrote that the company "never reopened after a labor dispute." But there had been certain problems with the site even before labor difficulties erupted. The area was subject to flooding, so that installation of modern equipment and labor-saving devices would have been impractical in any case. The property was sold in 1982 and is now planted in pine trees. The rest of the story is that current owner L. B. Adams, Jr., was careful to preserve the bee hive kilns on the property, almost certainly for their historical value.

A second brick company of the period provides the link between early brick maker W. H. Mays and the modern era. A. C. Stockman leased forty acres of land along the Seaboard Railroad about five miles from Greenwood to Mays Brick Company in 1914. The location, in today's terms, is directly behind Moore Business Forms and Jarvis Tool Company. The company did business at this site, called Mays Siding, for about 23 years; the plant also explains the name of Old Brickyard Road which runs between Highway 221 and Emerald Road. Mays leased the plant site to J. W. and H. P. Mitchell in 1919; the Mitchells were the operators when foreclosure came in the great depression year 1932. The fact that the National Loan and Exchange Bank sold the property the day after foreclosure to Ben A. Osborne, d.b.a. Greenwood Brick Company, might possibly be significant but has no real relevance here. Osborne sold the plant to Southern Brick Company which operated it as Plant #2 for a time. A new owner, Seaboard Brick Company under President C. W. Kinard, emerged in 1940. After five years Seaboard sold the land to E. W. Milford and Paul Watkins and the business to Greenwood Lumber Company. When that business was sold to C. Y. Thomason, the Greenwood contractor found himself in the brick-making business, a rather normal extension of his involvement in the building industry. The brick company that began with Greenwood's W. H. Mays and ended with Greenwood's C. Y. Thomason was sold in 1956 to Dixie Chemical Company, a branch of Greenwood Packing Plant, and no longer produces brick.

The third, and most successful, brick manufacturing plant in Greenwood County was chartered as Southern Brick Company. The company bought an abandoned brickyard, along with an additional 100-acre tract, on March 15, 1935, and immediately set out to rebuild the facility. The first president was J. W. Holloway, and J. B. Britt was superintendent. The new owners were faced with the formidable task of reconditioning the entire plant which had been idle since foreclosure two years earlier. Patrick wrote that labor was plentiful, even though the going rate was 5¢ per hour before actual brick production started up again. At that point wages increased by a hundred percent; the new rate of 10¢ per hour no doubt meant a great deal to workers, as did the added morale booster of actually making a product. Brick sold at that time for about $10 per thousand.

A reorganization in the first year not only resulted in new officers – Bank of Greenwood President F. E. Grier, Greenwood Mills executive L. B. Adams, and Lois P. Stuart – but also marked the beginning of Joe Patrick's career with the company. He was hired as assistant to Superintendent Britt on September 1, 1935. The company's books were kept in the Bank of Greenwood, where Stuart was employed as Grier's secretary, until the late 1930s when a business office was opened at the site. Ben A. Osborne replaced Britt as superintendent in 1939. By that time three new bee-hive kilns had been built, the plant had been converted from steam power to electricity, and dump trucks had replaced the "Dinky" rail line. The plant was closed during World War II because its priority rating for supplies was too low to operate, but Patrick stayed on "to hold the plant together" during the war. He had, in fact, been made president in 1940 and bought Grier's shares in 1942. The plant reopened on a limited basis when coal became available again after the war, and the company bought the Angus Brick Company from Sterling and Nell Graydon.

The truly modern era of Southern Brick Company began when presumably Precambrian shale of the Carolina slate belt was located in 1945 only four miles from the plant. (The Cambrian period is a geological time span of some 70 million years during which the highest life forms on the planet were invertebrates. Possibly the only way for the layman to visualize this period is to learn, albeit simplistically, that its end was marked by the elevation of land when the seas retreated from the continents. Precambrian must be viewed as the farthest reaches of the geologic time chart.) Clay reserves had already been found to be inadequate, and the company converted to shale in the late 1940s. Patrick wrote that the discovery provided the company with an unlimited supply of "superior raw material." Coal was abandoned in favor of heavy fuel oil in 1948, and natural gas was first utilized in 1954. The progression of kiln modernization was similar. The company installed its first tunnel kiln in 1956, a "Harrop 8-wide" which allows brick to be "pushed through a heated stationary zone on cars with a refractory deck." After more than twenty years the company was finally in a position to grow. Kiln No. 2 was built in 1959, No. 3 followed in 1963, and No. 4 was completed in 1969 to provide a production capacity of 110 million brick per year. Modernization took care of quantity, but quality suffered until the company learned proper methods of processing shale brick. A description of this process appeared in an industry journal, *Brick & Clay Record*, for October 1971. Brick-making starts with a "dark red burning shale, a river bottom plastic clay, and a buff burning clay." The shale, mixed with some of the plastic clay to improve absorption, produces a very deep red brick; the amount of buff clay added determines final shades of lighter red and pink. The mixing, crushing, grinding and blending, as well as the shale mining itself, are all part of the operation. A rather complex description of a new machine for automating the unloading, or "de-hacking," operation appeared in the same journal: Southern Brick acquired a "Platypus" machine to replace the old monorail system for half the plant's production in 1971. The article predicted that a second such machine would make Southern Brick Company "the most automated brick plant in the country." The company's sales, primarily through building supply dealers and lumber yards, have climbed dramatically as quality improved.

Individuals with exceptionally long service at Southern Brick Company include H. G. Bledsoe and G. L. Kennedy. Patrick retired after 52 years of service in 1987. His son, Joe H. Patrick, Jr., succeeded him as president and board chairman; L. B. Adams, Jr., holds the office of vice president, the same position his father filled until his death a few years ago. Perhaps the most interesting innovation undertaken by the company occurred when it converted, once again and in response to the potential deregulation of natural gas, to a new power source for its kilns. That "new" source is, of all things, wood, the very same fuel that powered the journeyman brick-maker's scove kiln a hundred years ago. The wood used is in the form of sawdust, an age-old byproduct of the sawmill industry; Southern Brick uses one ton of sawdust per hour per kiln, a potential use of some 96 tons per day of production. The fuel burns in suspension with no residue. Of course the technology is light years away from that represented by cords of wood stacked somewhere near the kiln, but the fact remains that in one sense the company has come full circle, and Joseph H. Patrick emerges as a modern pioneer in the field of brick-making in Greenwood County. His summation of the company's history and prospects is a blend of the practical and the romantic:

> Southern Brick continues the manufacture of, principally, face brick used for the outside of many buildings of all sizes. The market served is roughly described as all areas east of the Mississippi River. With good, abundant raw materials and using a southern renewable resource, wood, for fuel, the future looks promising for Southern Brick, the sole survivor of the clay industry in Greenwood County. With each sale, a little bit of Greenwood goes out to beautify America.

Southern Brick Company employs about 200 people and generates sales of about $12 million annually. Production capacity is now more than 115 million bricks per year. Joseph H. Patrick was elected to the Greenwood Hall of Fame in 1991, along with P. Henderson Barnette of Greenwood Packing Plant.

A town's newspapers might not qualify as industry exactly, but they are certainly businesses, and their impact on a community is often just as significant in its own way as a new plant in the industrial park. Greenwood's only daily newspaper, *The Index-Journal*, has been a fixture only since 1919, but its story, as well as those of its forebears, is surely worth telling in these pages. Southerners, even those who claim to be non-readers, seem to devour newspapers assiduously; omitting the beginnings of Greenwood's ventures in this important realm would be unforgivable.

While no one really needs a definition of a newspaper, it might be noted that the word was first used in a letter to the editor of the *Oxford Gazette* in 1670 when a reader wrote: "I wanted your news paper Monday last past." *The Chicago Tribune* called the public press "an institution developed by modern civilization to present the news of the day, to foster commerce and industry by widely circulated advertisements, to lead and inform public opinion, and to furnish that check upon government which no constitution has ever been able to provide." Even though radio, television, and other electronic gadgetry have diminished its influence over the last half of the twentieth century, the fourth estate occupies a unique place in American society. Recognized specifically in the first amendment to the Constitution of the United States, newspaper enterprises are not solely businesses, professions, nor public utilities, but actually combine elements of all three. The intriguing phrase "fourth estate," a generic term denoting the entire public press, was first used in 1828 in Thomas Macaulay's description of the British Parliament: "The gallery in which the reporters sit has become a fourth estate of the realm."

Nearly every town's history contains some endeavor in the field of journalism. A half dozen papers were published briefly in Greenwood before the 1890s. Although all were weeklies that lasted only a short time, they did prepare the way for two that would prove sufficiently hardy to merge into the single daily that serves Greenwood today. The first attempt to publish a newspaper, to be edited by teacher and historian Dr. John Henry Logan, never got off the ground. C. M. Calhoun wrote in *Liberty Dethroned*: "The old . . . village with not two dozen residences, as early as 1848, made an effort to get up a paper to be published here, . . . possibly in the interest of the schools as well as to have a home medium in which he [Logan] could give full vent to some of his pent up feelings as to the state of the country's politics then existing. The enterprise fell through almost still born." No one tried again until ten years after the Civil War; lawyer William K. Blake began publishing *The New Era* in 1875. Blake worked at his editorial venture about two years before returning to his law practice. He sold his printing equipment to Miles B. McSweeney, who launched *The Ninety Six Guardian*. That newspaper, a strictly political venture that also lasted two years, and its founders are described elsewhere in this book.

The next newspaper to be published in Greenwood was, oddly enough, *The Saluda Argus,* which appeared in 1881. Its editor was a man named Hogan and its place of business an upstairs room of a building on Waller Avenue. Possibly another editor from Pickens named John P. Carey succeeded Hogan for a time. Whether with one editor or two, *The Argus* managed to survive about four years.

The first issue of *The Greenwood Light,* edited by E. S. F. Giles, appeared on August 1, 1885. This newspaper had school connections; its publisher was H. S. Cunningham, an assistant to Professor Simon Boozer of the Male High School. Though *The Light* lasted hardly a year, another newspaper, *The Greenwood Tribune,* also began as a stock company in 1885; its editors included R. G. McLees, E. C. McCants, and Dr. W. P. Barratt. No one knows exactly what happened, but *The Tribune* quietly died in the summer of 1888. *The Greenwood Times* showed up in 1889 with Fitz Hugh McMaster as editor. *The Times* also published an ARP paper and church literature, but the paper folded when that part of the business was moved to Due West. It had lasted all of six months. The next effort was *The Greenwood Atlas,* which also survived only briefly.

As Greenwood approached county status and began to grow in advertising potential as a consequence, things began looking up for a newspaper that might make it. *The Greenwood Journal* appeared in 1894, and *The Greenwood Index* followed three years later. Their survival as separate entities was fairly typical of the times, as was their merger 25 years after the former was founded. Both had become afternoon dailies by the time of the merger, although each had begun as a weekly. The first attempt at daily publication came in 1902, but that effort was abandoned after about six months, and the paper reverted to its weekly schedule. *The Journal* became *The Daily Journal* in 1911, and *The Index* followed in 1918 as an afternoon daily.

Perhaps it is not surprising that school men and lawyers had a great deal to do with early newspapers in Greenwood. Rufus B. Wilson, head of the new graded school, was editor of *The Greenwood Journal.* After a year the paper passed to F. M. Allen and J. L. Carr. Carr sold his interest to Dr. George W. Gardner, who had come to Greenwood to publish a statewide denominational paper called *The South Carolina Baptist.* A frame building on Oak Street was the home of both papers for a time. Allen sold out to another Baptist preacher, the Reverend A. Pittman, and soon thereafter Gardner and Pittman themselves split up. The Baptist paper remained in the building on Oak Street, and Gardner moved to a second-floor location on the east side of the square.

In the meantime *The Greenwood Index* had been established with William Gregg Chafee as proprietor and editor. *The Index* was published upstairs in a brick building on Waller Avenue. Like several other would-be editors, Chafee was a lawyer who had come to Greenwood to set up a practice. He had two assistants in the newspaper business: A. M. Carpenter and M. Leland Smith were both printers and writers. One long-timer who began work as a small boy and stayed until retirement 55 years later was Claude P. Seymour. When Chafee left for military service in 1898, S. H. McGhee purchased *The Index.* The paper moved into quarters in the newly-constructed Syndicate Block in 1899 and stayed there for about ten years. The next move, to 123 Maxwell Avenue, would be the last for quite a long time. The Maxwell Avenue address remained headquarters for more than fifty years; the company's "new" building on Phoenix Street was occupied in the summer of 1962. Editor Bill Collins remembers moving on a Saturday and putting out the paper as usual the following Monday.

Harry L. Watson acquired an interest in *The Index* in 1900. After the merger of the two papers in 1919 Watson and Joel S. Bailey evolved into a partnership that lasted until Bailey's death in 1935. Watson, a native of the Phoenix section, thus emerged as Greenwood's first newspaperman of both note and longevity, although Bailey's tenure of about thirty years is also impressive. Watson also became Greenwood's foremost resident historian. A collection of his newspaper columns called "Our Old Roads," which appeared in *The Index-Journal* regularly for the years 1940-50, became the basis for a book, *Greenwood County Sketches*, published by his daughter Margaret in 1970. The introduction to that book notes that Watson wrote "countless local history articles" during the more than fifty years of his newspaper career. The citation accompanying his honorary degree from the University of South Carolina in 1938 reads in part: "Collector, preserver and publisher of much South Carolina history that would otherwise have been lost, [he is] an outstanding representative of the editors of the smaller daily and weekly press of this state whose immense service in its upbuilding is too little understood and appreciated." Lander College awarded Watson an honorary degree in 1956, the year he died. Both Margaret Watson, who was primarily a newspaperwoman, and her sister Louise, a librarian, carried on their father's work in local history until their own deaths in recent years.

There have been other papers in the county from time to time. William John Park remembers the *Greenwood Plain Dealer* from his high school days in the late 1930s, and two weeklies, the Ninety Six *Star* and the Ware Shoals *Observer,* currently serve their respected communities.

Watson's heirs sold their controlling interest in The Index-Journal Company to three men – James E. Chaffin, R. Frank Mundy, and William W. Wilson – each of whom had been associated with the newspaper for about twenty years. Another partner, board chairman Major Arthur Lee, retired from active participation before 1957. Chaffin succeeded Watson as editor of *The Index-Journal* upon the latter's death in 1956. A native of Chapin, Chaffin held a degree in journalism from the University of South Carolina. He worked on weekly papers in Denmark and Lexington in his home state, as well as a newspaper in New Orleans, before joining the news staff of *The Index-Journal* in 1937. He left in 1940 to work for a time in Atlanta before military service claimed him during World War II; Chaffin returned to Greenwood as managing editor of the newspaper in 1946. An editorial in a black-bordered box in the edition of February 22, 1977, two days after his death, called Chaffin "a builder," a reference to one of his most significant honors. The Greenwood Kiwanis Club had presented him with a special, one-time award in 1965 with an accompanying plaque inscribed: "To J. E. Chaffin, a community builder on the foundation stone of truth, informed and informing clearly, eloquently, and vigorously through news and editorials." Kiwanis President Jack Lawrence cited him as a builder "in the educational, in the cultural, the social, the political, civic and religious and business areas of the community."

Chaffin's interests and influence were broad indeed. He was the first chairman of the South Carolina Economic Opportunity Board, a member of the statewide Task Force for Correction and Rehabilitation, and he sat on the original committee that established Piedmont Tech. He was a life member of the county historical society, a member of the county library board, and director of the chamber of commerce at various times in his career. He led a group of South Carolina business and professional leaders on a trip to eastern Europe in 1960 and followed up by organizing a statewide seminar to study the theory of communism and its possible effects on American society. Chaffin received an honorary degree from Lander College in 1970.

Both black and white community leaders credited the newspaperman for his cool objectivity during a period of racial tension in the late 1960s. Chaffin's outspoken advocacy of peaceful integration of the public schools marked him as a liberal in many people's minds, but he seemed truly concerned that minorities, whether political parties or a particular group, were treated fairly. Chaffin himself would probably have appreciated most a paragraph from the February 22 editorial: "He was born with a need to know about the world around him and he read and asked questions. His home is filled with evidence of his dedication to getting the information; books can be seen in almost every room." Ed Chaffin's death came suddenly at the end of a golf weekend with Greenwood friends at Charleston and Fripp Island. He was not quite 64 years old.

Index-Journal President and Publisher Frank Mundy survived his partner by only five years. Another activist and "cheerleader for Greenwood," Mundy was a native who began his career as a paper boy. His university degree was in economics, his military service in the U. S. Navy, and his niche at the newspaper in circulation and management. Mundy's civic service was as wide as Chaffin's, and the South Carolina Press Association Foundation, which he served as president, was actually renamed after his death "The R. Frank Mundy Newspaper

Foundation, Inc." An editorial in the January 6, 1982, edition of *The Index-Journal* referred to his love for his home town: "Seldom did he speak with anyone that somewhere, somehow in the conversation he didn't manage to get in a good word about Greenwood. To him, there was no better place to be found and he let the world know it."

The newspaper continues to operate under the management of Mundy's widow Eleanor and his daughter Judi Burns. Bill Collins is editor.

Besides its international reputation, one of the most intriguing aspects of Greenwood's George W. Park Seed Company is the fact that a son of the founder is still active in the business. If that does not seem at all unusual, one has only to consider that the company itself dates from 1868. The founder's son, Chairman of the Board William John Park, is also a direct descendant of the famous Dr. John Perkins Barratt, who lived and worked in what is now Greenwood County long before the Civil War.

George Watt Park began his business in Pennsylvania when he was sixteen years old. A company publication tells the story best:

> When he was just a young child, George's mother noticed his interest in horticulture and encouraged him to raise flowers in a corner of her garden. Later, when George Park was 16, he bought a hand press and printed a list of seeds and sent it around to friends and neighbors. After Park printed his catalog, he bought an advertisement in *The Rural American* for $3.50, which brought him $6.50 in seed orders. With this success, the young entrepreneur learned one of the cardinal rules in business: "It pays to advertise."
>
> Park's first catalog in 1868 was just eight pages and used two illustrations – wood engravings of an aster and a pansy. In 1871 the young seedsman started a monthly paper, *The Floral Gazette,* in which he offered advice on gardening and created a forum where people could share gardening experiences. The magazine gave even the poorest gardener an opportunity to grow many different varieties through its exchange column which enabled readers to trade seeds, bulbs, and plants. Circulation of the magazine grew to 20,000 subscribers in 1877, and to over 800,000 by 1918.

Young George Park was so successful in business that he sent himself to Michigan State University at the age of thirty to fulfill a life-long ambition to earn a college degree. Not surprisingly, that degree was in horticulture. A few years later he moved his business from its original location in Libonia to a spot nearer the railroad line in LaPark, (now Paradise) Pennsylvania. Park was no longer young when he met Mary Barratt of the Breezewood section of Greenwood County. As a matter of fact, he was 66 and his bride only 28 when they married in

1918. William John Park likes to tell the story of their courtship. It seems his mother, while working as a home demonstration agent in Cherokee County, wrote Park for advice on teaching horticulture to homemakers. Her letter must have intrigued him, and a regular correspondence, not always focusing on gardening, began. Park was by this time a frequent business traveler, and on one of his trips to the area he made a point of meeting his pen pal in South Carolina. Each was favorably impressed with the other, and a May-December marriage was the result. Other results were two sons – George Barratt and William John – and a new business for Greenwood about six years later. After his second marriage Park was ready to "retire," at least from Pennsylvania if not from the mail-order seed business, and the couple moved to Dunedin, Florida, where their first son was born in 1920. The Parks found that the heat and humidity of that state were not suitable for the seed business and decided to relocate in Greenwood about 1924.

Park found the perfect spot, an already developed tract of land west of Spring Street which he named "Parkton." He spoke of his choice later in a newspaper interview. "I have a lovely place here," he said. "The mild, healthful climate, the genial, intelligent people, and the beautiful surroundings all combine to make it ideal." The site was still lovely many years later; Angelle Adams remembers that her garden club was named Lotus in honor of the plants that flourished in the Park gardens. A centennial newspaper article added that the site had been a recreation area from the time A. L. Blake capitalized on the natural mineral spring and opened Greenwood's first "bathing pool" there. Two Greenwood streets – Spring and Mineral – owe their names to Blake's version of an early tourist attraction. According to William John Park, the spot was known as "White City Park" by the time his father bought seventeen acres from a man named Mays. Some recreational amenities, such as boating, swimming, and picnicking facilities, were already in place when Park acquired the property. From this promising beginning the seedsman lost no time developing the entire area "into one of the beauty spots of Greenwood," in the center of which he built the combination seed house and print shop where his seed catalog was prepared and mailed to some 20,000 subscribers every spring. Park also installed a genuine water wheel on a small stream near the lake and built "Ye Old Water Mill" around it. The purpose of the mill was to grind a concoction of various grains called Dr. Corbett's Health Food, the recipe for which had been given to Park by its inventor, Dr. L. G. Corbett, and which Park intended to market along with his flower and vegetable seeds. Although the product was sold from grocery store shelves in Greenwood, he apparently never offered the health food through his catalogs. William John Park recalls, however, that it did appear with some regularity on the family breakfast table. It was not a favorite of the Park sons.

George W. Park died in 1935 while his sons were still quite young, and it was during the early period of her widowhood that Mary Barratt Park truly came into her own. She raised the boys, ran the business by herself during their college and military service years, and remained active in the company long after they relieved her of management responsibilities. Many people remember that Mary Park brought new meaning to the terms *frugality* and *employee relations* during the early years. Most of the employees were women whose time on the job belonged in no uncertain terms to Mrs. Park. Some say she employed draconian measures to discourage goldbricking and gossiping on company time, common enough complaints lodged against young female employees of the period. In retrospect, Mary Park must not have been too tough; former employee Emma R. Deal, who retired in 1990 after fifty years on the job, remarked that she wouldn't change a thing about those years, in spite of the fact that she was hired at $7 per week on the condition that she was "fast with her hands." If she were not fast enough, her pay would be cut to $6. Deal spoke with particular nostalgia about the years in the original building, which survived until 1950. She recalled the chicken wire "cage" where the mail was opened every day and the steep staircase with a particularly bad turn at the landing. Other employees with many years of service were Mrs. Walter Rush of Callison and the late Myrtle Stevens.

The business had outgrown its first building well before the new facility on Spring Street was occupied in 1950, but a brochure states that the company "entered the modern era of environmental control for seed quality" during the years at its second location. The basic concept of Park's current facility, occupied in 1961, was also developed at the Spring Street location. The 500-acre tract on Highway 254 is a total business complex considered "unequaled in the horticultural world." Tragedy struck in 1967. George Barratt Park and his wife Margaret were killed when their plane crashed immediately after takeoff from the airport in Greenwood, a disaster that shook the town to its roots. Family and friends rallied around the four Park children as they grew up to take their places in a business which had continued to expand under the leadership of Barratt Park's younger brother William. Acquisition in 1975 of the Wayside Gardens Company, a highly respected mail-order nursery business from Ohio, added another dimension to Park Seed Company. A company paper states that Park "had long sought [to acquire] a company with business philosophies and practices that coincided with" its own. The paper also describes Park as "the last major, family-owned seed company in the United States."

And major it undoubtedly is. Even Greenwood people probably have no conception of the vast scope of Park's research and development activities. Most, however, know that the company's name is familiar all over the world and that 44 varieties of its flower and vegetable seeds spent five days in space aboard the Challenger shuttle a few years ago.

Although the company might be said to be on the cutting edge of technology in the industry, possibly its importance is best summed up by the fact that it has its own separate zip code – two separate zip codes in fact, one for the seed company and another for Wayside Gardens. If even that distinction seems a little too prosaic, then the dazzling show of Park's trial gardens during Festival of Flowers week in Greenwood every year would have to be the clincher.

The site of the original Park complex in Greenwood is now a tract of almost completely cleared land. Nothing remains of the first or second seed house, the lake, the picnic area, or the grain mill complete with water wheel. But the Park home still stands where West Creswell Avenue ends at Spring Street. It has recently been remodeled into several apartments.

The church James C. Self built and named for his mother led directly to a most unusual industry for Greenwood. As Callie Self Memorial Baptist Church in South Greenwood was nearing completion, Self found the perfect instrument for installation in an 87-foot carillon tower to be built just behind the main structure. On a visit to the New York World's Fair in 1939 he was so impressed with the tone and sound quality of a carillon in The Netherlands pavilion that he immediately opened negotiations to purchase the instrument for delivery to Greenwood when the Fair closed. The carillon was a product of the van Bergen Bell Foundry, a family firm that had manufactured church and carillon bells in the town of Heiligerlee for more than 200 years. The expert in charge of the exhibit at the Fair was master bellfounder and company executive H. T. van Bergen. Typically, Self persuaded van Bergen to come to Greenwood to supervise the installation; he also engaged Dr. Kamiel Lefever, carilloneur at Riverside Church in New York and the man who brought carillon music to America, as a special consultant.

The original 25-bell instrument – and H. T. van Bergen – arrived in Greenwood in January 1940, and both quickly became fixtures in the town. The carillon was successfully installed in its brick-and-limestone tower, and van Bergen accepted a position as manager of Greenwood Mills Foundry. In spite of wartime travel restrictions, he was able to bring his wife and son from the old country to a new home and a new life in Greenwood. Later van Bergen opened his own business to continue the family tradition in a very different location.

Carillon bells are different in that they are cast and tuned at the foundry. A true carillon consists of at least 23 bells (an instrument with fewer bells is a chime) to as many as anyone could wish; Riverside Church's carillon is the world's largest at 72 bells. Individual bells also vary greatly in size, ranging from as small as twenty pounds to behemoths of many tons. The largest in the world is supposed to weigh nearly 41,000 pounds; the largest in the Callie Self tower weighs in at only 3,500 pounds.

Bell-making is a most intricate art. The bell contains a whole series of notes which must be aligned both aesthetically and mathematically by a master craftsman. A 1980 newspaper article detailed the process: it begins with a "clay mold for which the tone has been worked out scientifically" in arithmetic figures. The figures are then transferred to a sketch on matured wood that reflects both inside and outside contours of the bell-to-be. Next, the contours are sawed out and a clay mold "built around the rib and the heart of the bell." Even the nomenclature is revealing. At that point wax decorations are applied, and another layer of clay reinforced with hemp and cord is added. When the mold is finished the inner "false bell" is removed, and a molten alloy of 80% pure copper and 20% pure tin is poured into the cavity. But casting is simple compared to the art of the tuning process that follows. Van Bergen wrote that the reason people think cast bells sound out of tune is that most of those they hear are either untuned or tuned improperly. The van Bergen method was quite precise: by means of special tuning forks and sensitive frequency counters, as well as his own trained ear, the master tuner determines whether a bell's tonal quality coincides with the true tone on the chromatic scale. If not, he must patiently shave off minute fractions of the bell's surface until the tone is perfect. Each van Bergen bell contained a minimum of five tones, and its tuning required not only patience but also knowledge and experience. Greenwood's bellfounder was one of only five people in the world who practiced this "unique art" when health reasons forced his retirement in 1980. Most people associate carillons with "the varied effect of bells striking in alternating rhythms" and especially thrill to "the jubilant tumbling sound" of bells celebrating events such as coronations and royal weddings. Since Greenwood's opportunities to celebrate either are virtually nonexistent, its carillon concerts are necessarily a little more prosaic, but even Greenwood is familiar with a peal of bells, defined as "a musical combination of two, three, or more bells in harmony with one another."

Although the first worship service actually took place in December 1939, Callie Self Memorial Baptist Church and Carillon were dedicated on February 2, 1941, at a service led by Dr. George W. Truett, a world famous minister and former president of both the Southern Baptist Convention and the Baptist World Alliance. James C. Self was so pleased with the day that he named a street in Truett's honor, and more than 2,000 people – far more than the church could hold – attended the services. The church history, written in 1977, explained that the erection of a major church building was an exciting event in the years immediately following the depression. "[It] attracted attention and interest from far and near" and resulted in a period of great growth for the church; membership grew from 163 resident members in 1938 to more than 600 only three years later. The tower housing the 35-bell instrument was Greenwood's first. A few lines from the dedicatory program described the impressive structure:

> The carillon tower, to the rear of the church, is eighty seven and a half feet high, made of red brick, with sixteen two and a half by eighteen feet glass brick windows, the sixteen doors of the arcade are lined with limestone, and all the insets have limestone coping. The arcade is entered over four large granite steps, which surround the base, and the floor is of six inch quarry tile. Above the bells there is a three foot limestone belt and the top is finished with a heavy metal rail rising four feet above the coping.

The placement of the bells in the openings of the tower was said to be at Self's suggestion.

Not every small southern town boasts a bell foundry; as a matter of fact, van Bergen Bellfoundries, Inc. of Greenwood was the only tuned bell foundry in the United States when it closed its doors in 1980 as the result of its founder's age and state of health. The foundry in its last years was located just across the bypass on Highway 25 North. The work carried on there included not only casting and tuning bells for installation throughout the United States and Canada and as far away as the Philippines, Japan, Vietnam, Hong Kong, and Indonesia, but also tuning bells in existing untuned and out-of-tune carillons. A three-year project testing van Bergen's expertise resulted in the ranking of Deeds Carillon in Dayton, Ohio, as one of the finest instruments in the country. The last bronze carillon made in Greenwood was shipped to its destination in Brazil only a few months before the business closed. Because of van Bergen, it was said that Greenwood at one time had five carillons, more than any other town of its size in the world. The instrument in the Lander College bell tower, installed in 1976 after a fund-raising drive of only a few months, is a van Bergen product.

Although both the bell foundry in Greenwood and the original Dutch firm have ceased operations, the corporate name still exists, with offices in Atlanta and Charleston, in association with the Paccard Foundry in Annecy, France. H. T. van Bergen's son Harmannus (Harry), who grew up in Greenwood, is president of van Bergen Bellfoundries, Inc.

Greenwood's first and most famous carillon has been upgraded from time to time over the years, always by a van Bergen. The first major change came in 1947 when ten van Bergen-made bells were added to increase the size of the instrument to its present configuration of 35. And the most recent undertaking – extensive refurbishing of the entire playing system, including manual, electric, and automatic operations – was no exception. Since H. T. van Bergen built the very first console installed about 1940 at Callie Self Memorial Baptist Church, it is particularly appropriate that his son Harry wrote the specifications for the 1990 renovation and personally supervised the work. The state-of-the-art equipment now in place "allows maximum expression from the tower." The cost of the two-year renovation project, about $90,000, was borne largely by The Self Foundation.

Although Greenwood is no longer home to the only tuned bell foundry in the United States, it is still a "bell town" as envisioned by James C. Self more than fifty years ago. His remarks at the Callie Self dedication are even more meaningful today. "Let these bells with their lovely voices," he said, "bring some happiness to this sad world."

Historians generally concede that the second world war was probably as great a catalyst for change in South Carolina as the Civil War. The state's manufacturing sector prior to the war was primarily devoted to processing cotton, but the mobilization movement brought in new industries that employed large numbers and opened the state to possibilities of attracting manufacturing enterprises from outside the area. Local communities took the lead, but politicians were not far behind. Governor Strom Thurmond was the first to "put out the welcome mat for corporate executives." So diligently did Thurmond woo out-of-state industry that the Governor's Mansion was used extensively to entertain business prospects during his term of office from 1947 to 1951. The next governor, James F. Byrnes, who had not expected industry-recruiting to be part of his job description, nevertheless pitched in to do his part. Byrnes, who had ranked high in the Roosevelt administration and had come within a hair of the presidency, issued the rather lukewarm statement: "South Carolina's government is basically sound and it is friendly toward industry. Our government, our communities, and our people want industry and want to see that it is prosperous and happy. No state and no people can offer more." Historian Walter Edgar wrote that the wooing of northern manufacturers by local business and civic leaders actually amounted to regional competition for new industry, and the state's leadership was rather suddenly faced with an image problem that had to be overcome. This concern led to educational and social changes in the 1960s that would have been unthinkable only twenty years earlier. The State Development Board was created in 1954 in reaction to a certain unevenness of new industry distribution throughout the state as a result of many strictly local efforts. So diverse were its activities and so dynamic the impact of this prestigious board that some northern legislators began to mutter darkly that South Carolina was practicing "carpetbagging in reverse" at the expense of the industrial strength of their region.

The story of Greenwood's industrial diversification fits rather neatly into this scenario. Perhaps it would not be quite fair to imply that Greenwood and Abney Mills considered the county work force their own private fief, but it is true that Greenwood's search for outside industry seemed to coincide with the willingness of local mill executives to co-operate. Much was made of the presence of Greenwood and Abney Mills executives at the press conference to announce the first new plant, and Greenwood Mills was credited with an attitude of "responsible cooperation." Whatever the reasons for the timing, Greenwood County made its own jump to broader industrialization in 1959. The announcement in June of that year that the Chemstrand Corporation would build a multi-million dollar nylon plant on a 1400-acre tract in the county opened a whole new era for Greenwood. The company had been teetering between two sites in the state. Several sources credited executives of Greenwood and Abney Mills, as well as Charles E. Daniel of Greenville, with tipping the company's choice toward Greenwood. Boykin Curry, who spearheaded the drive for new industry on behalf of the chamber of commerce, credits not only Daniel and local mill executives but also nearly every public agency in the county and numerous individuals for the united front and coordinated "push" necessary to pull off the coup represented by Chemstrand in 1959. He remembers particularly the formation of the Metropolitan Sewer District and other accommodations undertaken specifically to facilitate the relocation of existing industry to Greenwood County. Many people believe, in fact, that Greenwood was saved from economic strangulation, or "dying on the vine," by its emphasis on diversification as the 1950s drew to a close. A committed cadre of leaders was the key; many counties with advantages Greenwood could not boast still lacked the type of enlightened leadership that allowed Greenwood to grow in industrial strength at a critical time. This growth and diversification have served the county well through the ups and downs of any number of business cycles over more than thirty years, with the result that the recession of the early 1990s left Greenwood relatively unscathed. Not truly a metropolis, Greenwood is considered a "small regional hub" for the six-county Upper Savannah area. This means that the county's business is drawn from a wider region, and a broader and stronger industrial and business base supports its economy. Greenwood's per-person retail spending pattern is far above that of the five surrounding counties.

Although no one could argue that economics is an exact science, some of the advantages that have accrued to Greenwood were no doubt rather easily foreseen as its leaders worked with the Chemstrand Corporation in 1959. Negotiations were a closely guarded secret so that nothing would detract from the impact of the announcement on the big day. One Greenwood wife who knew about it had, in her words, "withdrawn from circulation" and become a gardener. "I was so excited I didn't dare get around my friends for fear I'd let something out," she said, "so I stayed in my yard and pulled weeds." The announcement at a press conference held at the Oregon Hotel and its long-term implications for Greenwood were quite enough to excite anyone. The gathering featured a number of dignitaries, most of whom had something to say. State Senator Bill Bradford, for example, promised Chemstrand an "ample supply of skilled labor" and the county an end to its unemployment problems, while for its part the company projected a $14-15 million building project and jobs for some 4,000 workers.

The Chemstrand Corporation, now Monsanto, was the first large-scale industry from outside the region to choose a location in Greenwood. It was followed by many more over the next several years, notably Parke-Davis & Company (later sold to Professional Medical Products), Capsugel (originally part of Parke-Davis), Neptune Meter Company, Moore Business Forms, International Paper Company, McGraw-Edison, Cincinnati-Milacron, Inc., Jarvis Corporation, Westinghouse Electric Corporation, Union Carbide, Velux Corporation, and several others. The year 1979, in fact, was notable for the announcements within one week that five or six industries planned to locate in the county. Greenwood also welcomed a division of Pirelli Cable Corporation and its first Japanese firm, Fuji Photo Film, Inc., in recent years. Just as its first industry brought new families to the area, so has the more recent industrialization changed forever the population and flavor of the county. Greenwood County's established institutions – churches, schools, colleges, libraries, hospital, nursing homes, and recreational facilities – as well as its building and real estate industry, banks, small businesses, and shopping malls, have grown and changed also in response to new configurations among the population. Most people would probably agree that the changes on the whole have been for the better. On the other hand, there is definitely new meaning to the term "rush hour" around town, especially on Thursdays and Fridays, and the phrase "Old Greenwood" probably holds meaning for fewer and fewer residents. There can be little doubt that pay scales are now more competitive, and manufacturing is still the largest of the eight sectors considered in the "gross county product," or the dollar value of all goods and services produced in the county. That product in 1989 amounted to something over $3 billion, according to economist David Dumont of Lander College. The eight sectors are manufacturing; construction; transportation and utilities; wholesale; retail; financial, insurance and real estate; services; and government. Interestingly enough, the agricultural sector, once the economic definition of the entire region, is now too insignificant to be included. A notable comparison in this regard is the gross county product as reported in the centennial newspaper edition in 1957. That figure was something over $123 million in 1956. Possibly the methods of computation were totally different, and inflation is certainly a major factor; but the increase from 1955 had been nearly $3 million in one year alone, and more than thirty years of intense economic activity separate the GCPs of 1956 and 1989.

The article on Greenwood in a Charleston newspaper in the year 1889 predicted a bright future for the town, but that reporter could not have known the county would contain 64 manufacturing plants in 22 different classifications less than seventy years after he gave his optimistic forecast of things to come. Louise Watson wrote in 1957 that "made-in-Greenwood" products included items "from ice to machinery, from shirts to monuments, and food products to neon signs." Many of the businesses and industries she listed no longer exist, but many more have begun operations since she described the "considerable variety" of the county's industrial picture. One of the most significant departures from the corporate scene in recent years was Abney Mills. It must have been difficult, but the company made the decision to divest its holdings in the textile industry and concentrate its investments in other areas. The Abney Foundation, a significant private foundation which provides grants for various charitable, educational, and cultural endeavors, remains as an intangible reminder of a truly important Greenwood-based industry that exists no more. There are tangible reminders as well: Grendel Mill is now listed as a division of Amtex, Inc., with offices on Jordan Street, and the Greenwood Mop Factory occupies the former Panola Mill building in South Greenwood. On the other hand, several firms besides Greenwood Mills are classified as "Textile Manufacturers," including Adobe South, CJN Textiles & Knitting Company in Ware Shoals, Chickasaw Processing Company, and Medical Textiles, Inc. In spite of "mergers, consolidations, closings, and rebuilding throughout the industry," textiles are still a mainstay of the county's economy, and manufacturing is alive and well in Greenwood County.

6

THE PROFESSIONS

A lawyer without history or literature is a mechanic, a mere working mason; if he possesses some knowledge of these, he may venture to call himself an architect.
Sir Walter Scott

DESPITE the proliferation of lawyer jokes, Greenwood takes the legal profession very seriously indeed as befits its standing as a courthouse town. Actually, the legal fraternity has been a conspicuous presence in the county for more than two centuries – since Ninety Six became the seat of a judicial district in 1769. And even as Cambridge (Ninety Six) declined from the height of its influence in legal circles, nearby Greenwood was slowly emerging to take its place. The rise in importance of the legal profession in Greenwood can be traced directly to its becoming a courthouse town in 1897, and although the number of lawyers quite naturally increased when county status was attained, the fact that the town's very first resident was a lawyer was indicative of things to come. Other early attorneys were named in the newspaper commemorating Greenwood's centennial in 1957. Louise Watson wrote that article, drawing on a paper her father had delivered at a Greenwood Bar Association dinner ten years earlier. Greenwood editor and historian H. L. Watson took a lively interest in the profession, having practiced law himself for a brief time in the early 1900s.

Greenwood's first lawyer, John McGehee, moved on to Florida about 1830 and eventually became a circuit judge and a signatory to that state's Ordinance of Secession. McGehee's tenure in the future county seat spanned only seven years; after he left, the village had no lawyer in residence for nearly fifty years. Native son William K. Blake, who received his legal training at the University of Virginia, was the second attorney to hang out a shingle in Greenwood. His partner, W. A. Lee of Abbeville, also edited the *Abbeville Banner,* an activity that might have influenced Blake's own short-lived effort to establish a newspaper in Greenwood in 1875. Edward S. F. Giles, another lawyer-editor, moved to Greenwood in 1882. Giles's sisters followed him from North Carolina and opened a school for young ladies in the early 1880s. W. J. Rook, another University of Virginia law school product, rounded out Greenwood's three-lawyer contingent when the Newberry native moved to the village from his farm ten miles away. R. Hayne Henderson of Coronaca came next; Henderson was, in fact, the first of a long succession of lawyer-legislators on the delegation from the new county of Greenwood. Watson's article included a tantalizing reference to a contretemps between two lawyers who practiced in Greenwood for a short time before the county was created. It seems that Waddy Thompson of Union and his partner, a man named Rowell, exchanged pistol shots on Waller Avenue one day. Obviously a dispute of some sort prompted the exchange, but if members of the Watson family knew more about the shooting they kept it to themselves. While speculation about a particular affair of honor might be futile, the propensity for settling disagreements with a brace of dueling pistols was certainly not unknown in South Carolina.

The creation of the new county brought "quite a group" of lawyers to the town, seemingly all at once, either to open new offices or establish Greenwood locations for firms in other towns. William Gregg Chafee of Aiken; Ben Cunningham and James B. Park of Laurens; David H. Magill, W. P. Greene, and Ellis Graydon of Abbeville; F. Barron Grier of Kingstree; Leland C. Spears of Newberry; Walter F. Stackhouse of Marion; and Erasmus H. Youngblood of Winterseat arrived, but "quick changes" reduced their ranks in short order. Evidently Greenwood's need for legal services was insufficient to occupy the time of the number of lawyers who suddenly appeared on the scene. This early period, however, saw the beginnings of one of Greenwood's most prestigious law firms, one that is still in existence today. After several other business configurations for each, F. B. Grier and James B. Park formed a partnership in 1906 that lasted until their deaths some 25 years later. The law firm these men established – Grier & Park – became, after a number of name changes along the way, the present Burns, McDonald, Bradford, Patrick and Dean.

Still other early Greenwood attorneys were W. J. (Bid) Moore of Cokesbury, who became the first master in equity for the new county; D. A. G. Ouzts of Edgefield, who spent most of his life in Greenwood and served a term as county senator; S. H. McGhee, who was also a banker, state senator, editor, and mill executive; E. L. Richardson, one-time partner with McGhee who moved to Oklahoma and eventually became a judge; and W. H. Nicholson, a native of Edgefield whose singular career is sketched in another chapter. Others were Jones Fuller, a firm named McDowell, Brunson and Blease (could this be the famous Colie Blease, or a relative?), and John W. Spence. In addition, C. C. Featherstone of Laurens was persuaded to move to Greenwood in 1911; he entered partnership with McGhee and became a circuit judge in 1922. Featherstone's son Douglas also practiced law in Greenwood for many years.

Many Greenwood attorneys have also served on the county delegation during their careers. A few who are remembered for dual careers are J. Perrin Anderson, J. William Bradford, G. P. Callison, William Lowndes Daniel, Thomas L. Hughston, William T. Jones, C. A. Mays, W. H. Nicholson (both father and son), Francis B. Nicholson, and James E.

Moore. Current representative Jim Johnson is also an attorney. The town might be considered notable, but in a negative sense, for its current dearth of female attorneys. Only three women – Andrea Loney, LaDonna Johnson, and Linda Whisenhunt – currently practice law in Greenwood; two more, Selma Jones and Mary Daniel, have moved to other towns. The William T. Jones family surely holds the record for the sheer number of attorneys in one family. Four of Jones's five children made the legal profession their career choice, and one, W. Townes Jones IV, succeeded his father as circuit solicitor.

Circuit Judge and Greenwood native James E. Moore was elected to the South Carolina Supreme Court in 1991, the first Greenwood attorney ever to achieve such standing. *The Index-Journal* of June 2 called his election a "good news-bad news" event, a reference to his move to the top of his profession in the state vs. the loss of his services on the circuit court bench. Fortunately, as Louise Watson wrote in 1957, Greenwood lawyers no longer have to supplement their incomes with sideline businesses as was the case in earlier years.

While possibly not as well represented in public affairs as their counterparts in the legal profession, Greenwood physicians nevertheless have been held in the highest esteem since the very earliest days, and many took leading roles in the development of both town and county. One whose name comes up quite often is John Chappell Maxwell, a native of Newberry who came to Greenwood soon after the Civil War. Though Maxwell was on the leading edge of nearly every new venture in the town a hundred years ago, he is perhaps best remembered as the financial founder of Connie Maxwell Children's Home. And Maxwell's home on East Cambridge Avenue, which was also the home of the W. H. Nicholson family somewhat later, survives as a very special Greenwood landmark. The Vance-Maxwell House was added to the National Register of Historic Places a few years ago.

Although the house is believed to have been constructed by Allen Vance about 1850, its true significance lies in an 1870s remodeling in accord with the Second Empire fashion and in its second owner, John C. Maxwell. Among its most important architectural features are the bracketed mansard roof, double-run, open-well staircase with carved newels, and tiled fireplaces. Although few would dispute later owner W. H. Nicholson's claim to fame in Greenwood, Maxwell was considered the most prominent resident of the historic house, at least for purposes of the National Register nomination. A regimental surgeon in the Civil War, Maxwell moved to Greenwood soon after the war ended. He acquired the Vance property in 1871 and enlarged and remodeled the residence soon thereafter. John Maxwell served for nine years in the state senate before Greenwood became a county; he was first elected in 1876, that very special year of "Wade Hampton and the Red Shirts, who broke the Republican Party's control of the South Carolina legislature."

Maxwell's most conspicuous act of philanthropy occurred in 1890 when he donated 470 acres of land, provided a proposed Baptist orphanage were built in Greenwood. The gift was in memory of the Maxwells' only child to survive infancy, a daughter named Constance Pope (Connie) who had died of scarlet fever at the age of eight in 1883. The denomination accepted the offer, and Connie Maxwell Orphanage opened its doors in 1892. Its location is on the edge of town along both sides of Highway 10, a spot that might easily be considered an extension of Maxwell Avenue, an important early street also named in honor of the doctor. Maxwell played an active role in the formation of Greenwood County; it was he who chaired the committee charged with building the courthouse and jail, the first public buildings in the new county. Maxwell's devotion to the medical profession lasted throughout his life, though he was perhaps even more active in the public life of Greenwood than in the dispensary. He died in 1899.

The Vance-Maxwell House reverted to Connie Maxwell Orphanage upon the death of Mrs. Maxwell in 1902 but was sold the next year to Maxwell's medical partner, Dr. George Pressly Neel. W. H. Nicholson bought the property in 1918, and the house remained in that family until 1972. The current owner, Lander Professor Dr. Elizabeth R. Bethel, is engaged in rehabilitation of the historic Vance-Maxwell House.

While John Maxwell was certainly important to early Greenwood, a much earlier medical practitioner might well be regarded as the most distinguished professional of the entire region. John Perkins Barratt, in fact, came near to practicing virtually all the arts and sciences of his day in one remarkable lifetime. Thanks to his own productivity and to the preservation efforts of members of his family and others who recognized his genius, examples of Barratt's work can still be seen nearly 150 years after his death.

Don Herd introduced the chapter on Barratt in *The South Carolina Upcountry* with one of his favorite anecdotes, President John F. Kennedy's remark at a White House dinner honoring American Nobel Laureates in 1962: "I think this is the most extraordinary collection of talent, of human knowledge, that has ever been gathered together at the White House, with the possible exception of when Thomas Jefferson dined alone." Herd believed Kennedy's tribute to Jefferson might just as easily describe the "universal intellect" of John Perkins Barratt. It was his opinion that early nineteenth century men such as Barratt deliberately chose to live in the backcountry because they believed the frontier afforded unusual opportunities for freedom of thought and expression. Nothing was accepted as a given; instead, men of scientific bent were open-minded to all considerations. The older coastal or "tidewater" society, on the other hand, embraced a more constricted view; its pseudo-aristocracy "attempted to reflect modes of life and thought of a European civilization that never really existed in the new world." The intellectual curiosity of men such as Barratt actually helped develop a true American civilization, one that "continually honed its edges against a wilderness that had to be pushed farther west with each generation." Herd called this push an "epic struggle of mind against frontier" and suggested it might help to explain the uniqueness of the American intellectual experiment.

We do not know very much about the first 21 years of Barratt's life, and we are not even sure that he was born in Wakefield in the West Riding of Yorkshire in northern England. One source states that he came from Surrey, which is in the southeast. We know only that he was an Englishman and that he came to the new world in 1816 with the help of an aunt who paid his passage. Although the young man was without funds when he arrived in Charleston, he was certainly not without resources. Barratt's education, which had begun at his mother's knee, continued unabated throughout his life. An early apprenticeship to an apothecary uncle had inspired a keen interest in science and awakened in the boy a desire to study medicine. But that ambition had to wait until Barratt was able to finance the necessary training; in the interim he moved to the backcountry and taught school for about five years in a wilderness area called the "Ridge" in Edgefield District. Saving money at the pay scale of that day was probably very slow going. Although Barratt did not know it at the time, two young men who befriended him at Red Bank Baptist Church were destined to help speed the process. Both Dr. Samuel Perryman and Zebulon Rudulph were members of well-to-do families. Barratt read medicine with Perryman, as was the custom for young men who wanted to enter the profession, and the doctor and his friend were sufficiently impressed with Barratt's ability and promise that they offered to finance further study at a medical school in the North. In a singular twist, these two men later became Barratt's stepsons-in-law; both married daughters of Lavina Brooks Watson, the widow whom Barratt married in 1826.

Barratt enrolled in the American College of Physicians and Surgeons in New York City, one of the finest medical schools in the country in the years before the Civil War. Its president just prior to Barratt's enrollment was Samuel Bard, a noted medical man who had been George Washington's personal physician. Bard was a leader in the drive to establish one of the first public hospitals in New York City in 1791; he also brought together a number of eminent physicians, surgeons, and scientists to enhance the prestige of the medical college. Since the study of medicine at that time still ran to the humoral theory, or the idea that illness was the result of some sort of imbalance among the four humors of the body, medical students could hardly spend all their time on "medical" studies. The school offered lectures in natural history and earth sciences as well. One of Barratt's teachers was Samuel Latham Mitchill, whose expertise included botany, natural history, mineralogy, geology, paleontology, and horticulture, as well as "materia medica." Barratt was an avid student; he managed to obtain in the two years he studied at the school a good general knowledge of the "liberal scientific arts." If that phrase sounds like a contradiction of terms, one has only to reflect that the time was the early 1820s when the sorting out of specialties such as we know them today had not yet begun. Surgery in those days, for example, was considered a last resort. Barratt's lecture notes indicated that medical science could offer little to alleviate suffering beyond periodic bleeding, cold or warm baths, herb tonics and wines, or some form of crude surgery.

Among the avocations Barratt pursued when he was not in the lecture hall or laboratory was painting. One of his oils from the New York period now hangs in the president's office at Lander College, having been moved there from the lobby of Barratt Science Hall. Dated 1821, the painting depicts The Narrows, a tidal strait leading to the Upper Bay and forming part of the New York and New Jersey harbor system; it was presented to the College by members of the Barratt family when the science building was dedicated in 1967. An art preserver who happened to see it in the early 1980s pronounced the painting a genuine American primitive of great value, not because Barratt was a great painter but because the subject is a specific place at a specific time, two qualities that spell value to collectors. College officials agreed that the security-protected environs of the president's office provided a better setting for a valuable Barratt original than the exposed lobby of the science hall.

Barratt brought with him quite a variety of interests and expertise when he returned to South Carolina to begin his medical practice in 1823. He settled in the White Hall community, and it was there he met the young widow with four children who became his wife three years later. Her name was Lavina Brooks Watson, and her dowry consisted of about eight square miles of the former William Watson plantation. Barratt named the main house, which stood on the present site of Abney Hall, "Chinquapin Ridge." Although the house had been built by Richard Watson, Barratt enlarged and improved it to his own exacting standards. Chinquapin Ridge was "a wonder to behold" after Barratt worked his magic on house and grounds. In addition to murals on all four walls of the dining and drawing rooms, the house featured marble-tiled fireplaces with brass appointments and a two-story conservatory with a southern exposure where Barratt experimented with tropical plants and fruit trees. He grew oranges, lemons, and bananas at Chinquapin Ridge, using special soil brought from Beaufort by the wagonload for the purpose. Barratt had decided that lowcountry soil would be just right for citrus cultivation.

Barratt's two-acre formal garden was among the finest in the up-country. He is said to have been the first to grow the Osage orange shrub in this part of the country; the plants were trimmed to form hedges. Barratt collected other rare and unusual plants as well. He had a Cedar of Lebanon tree sent by a friend in Palestine, for example, and he accented his garden with petrified tree trunks. He even harvested enough silk from his own silkworms and mulberry trees to produce a vest. We do not know what happened to his silkworm farm; perhaps, like the Huguenots, he found the manufacture of silk impractical in the long run. Barratt encouraged rice-growing in damp areas of the plantation, and he bought rice, as well as chickens and eggs, from his own slaves. Although the plantation was a working farm of 800 acres, Barratt made it a workshop and laboratory as well. He built a museum to display specimens of birds, animals, reptiles, and insects he had preserved himself. He was an expert taxidermist, so good that the preparation of the Alabama Swamp Hare featured in John Bachman and John J. Audubon's *Quadrupeds of North America* is credited to Barratt. He also furnished stuffed and mounted specimens of the Carolina shrew and white weasel for Audubon's drawings. The star attraction of Barratt's museum was probably the stuffed two-headed calf it contained. It was not unusual for "ten to twenty carriages filled with visitors" to call at the Barratt home nearly every day. Visitors to The Museum in Greenwood can still view a most eccentric piece of Barratt's work: a specimen cabinet encrusted with shells and wood carvings and containing several well-preserved examples of the taxidermist's art. In addition, two unique specimens of Barratt's work are displayed in the home of William John and Jean Park: a colorful stuffed and mounted bird rests under a large glass dome on either side of the fireplace. One is the Carolina Parakeet and the other is a Passenger Pigeon; both species are now extinct.

When not occupied with his primary avocation of medicine, Barratt delved into all sorts of pursuits, many of them at least fifty years ahead of their time. He became interested in cotton manufacturing in the 1830s, for example, and invested in a very early factory in Spartanburg. He anticipated the coming of the railroad, envisioned its traversing his property, and planned his own village to be called "Barrattville." Although the railroad was laid a couple of miles to the east and his most ambitious scheme failed to materialize, it is interesting to note that in this respect Barratt foreshadowed the man his great-granddaughter Mary would marry more than 75 years later; George W. Park dreamed much the same dreams, except that his "LaPark" and "Parkton" became realities. Barratt also built a school for his own children and others of the community and personally chose the teachers.

Always, Barratt indulged his passionate interest in the natural sciences. One boon companion was Michael Tuomey, whose *Geology of South Carolina*, published in 1848, is still a standard work in the field. The two men traveled together to Orangeburg, Barnwell, and Beaufort Districts, supposedly in Barratt's carriage with slaves on horseback as outriders. Although the purpose of the trip was to compile geological data for Tuomey's book, Barratt used it also as an opportunity to keep a daily journal. As he put it, "the onward march of improvement . . . [makes it] necessary, with all great men and not a few of the small ones too, to give to the world a kind of journal of all their doings and seeings." Barratt's journal included entries not only on the flora, fauna, climate, and economy of the regions the two men visited, but also notes on their society and even their inhabitants. Some of his observations were glaringly unscientific: Barratt thought, for example, that the population of the lowcountry could be divided generally into "two distinct grades." The upper grade he found "remarkable for gentlemanly appearance and hospitality to strangers," while the "common classes" appeared somewhat "sallow and sun burnt" and lacking in that "dont-care independent bearing of the poor man of the up country."

Barratt began to develop certain radical ideas and theories about the bearing of natural science on the human race, perhaps as one result of his association and correspondence with eminent scientists of the time. In short, he speculated that since certain species and varieties of flora and fauna appeared to be indigenous to each of the great geographical and climatic divisions of the earth, possibly the human race was similarly diverse. The speech in which he first propounded this theory was delivered at Erskine College in 1846; in the same speech he predicted air and space travel, including trips to the moon. Barratt's ideas were bound to create an uproar at some point. The inevitable happened four years later when he advanced the same theory in an address to the State Medical Association. The Reverend John Bachman immediately took issue with Barratt's notion, insisting that "all mankind is of one single species"; but another friend, the zoologist Louis Agassiz, came to Barratt's defense in an essay entitled "Sketch of the Natural Provinces of the Animal World and their Relation to the Different Types of Man." Michael Tuomey understood the situation very well indeed but feared that Barratt was toying with an old taboo. "The parsons will be down upon you," he wrote in a letter to his friend, "fortunately for you we have no Inquisition." Barratt's only response was to express the hope that his ideas might "awaken a single individual to observation and exploration of the fact of creation and its laws."

Barratt's speech "was like an exploding bombshell to the scientific world" of his day. The controversy coalesced into a heated debate played out in newspapers and periodicals over the next five or six years between Agassiz and Bachman, thereby focusing "the spotlight of the clash over the origins of the human race" on South Carolina (Agassiz, though not a South Carolinian, was a professor at the Medical College in Charleston at the time). Barratt himself took no part in the battle of words that raged between his two friends. He had fulfilled his desire to awaken interest in the subject and deferred to those whom he regarded as "giants of science" to fight it out.

A few years before his death Barratt took up the cause of agriculture, having been elected president of a convention called to discuss problems common to South Carolina farmers. Barratt undertook to canvass the Abbeville District "for the purpose of awakening a deeper interest in the cause of agriculture." A typical meeting was one at Cokesbury in 1855.

Barratt's speech at that meeting urged the necessity of leaving the old and beaten track for a new system of agri- and other culture improved by science and art. Farmers are considered notoriously difficult to influence, even when their own benefit is at stake; the newspaper article describing the meeting did not cover the audience reaction when Barratt begged for kinder feelings for the generous earth, the resources of which he called exhausted and maltreated. Finally the distinguished speaker committed his hopes for the salvation of agriculture to the youth of the country. The question of whether Barratt's words that evening fell on fertile ground is still unanswered.

John Perkins Barratt died of stomach cancer on September 26, 1859. His death was described by the Abbeville *Independent Press* as a "public loss," two small words that carried a world of meaning. Barratt died nearly forty years before Greenwood County was formed; nevertheless, he belongs in no uncertain terms to any history of the county, and he richly merits his own biography as one of the "universal intellects" of the South Carolina upcountry in the nineteenth century.

Early Greenwood physicians with names familiar from other ventures include William P. Barratt (grandson of John Perkins Barratt), R. B. Epting, Joseph Augustus Marshall, William Brewster Milwee, Moses Clarence Taggart, and John Maxwell's partner George Pressly Neel. For some reason Neel's name presented a problem to chroniclers of Greenwood history. Louis Wright got the initials right but spelled the surname *Neale,* while the first county mapmakers preferred *Neal.* (The correct spelling is definitely *Neel,* as proven by a visiting card and letter in his own handwriting preserved in May Bailey Smith's scrapbook.) Wright called Neel "one of the town's heroes . . . whose medical knowledge, skill, and technical audacity were reputed to have brought many souls back from the brink of death." Neel was not only a prominent figure in Greenwood, where he practiced medicine for fifty years, but also a member of a distinguished family from Troy. His father was a doctor, as was a sister born in 1872. Female physicians during that period were rare indeed. In addition, several members of the Neel family were missionaries, in India, Pakistan and Mexico. Although Neel was evidently quite the social lion in Greenwood, he never married. He died in 1939.

Medical men from a "middle period" in Greenwood's history included James Clarence Harper, who died in 1950 after 48 years of practice that included several years of partnership with Neel; Clough Henry Blake, "a beloved family physician and community-minded citizen" from 1917 to his death in 1954; and William Preston Turner, who came to Greenwood in 1910 and practiced with Neel, Blake, and John Lyon long before his association with his son, W. P. Turner, Jr. Two Turner grandsons currently practice urology in Greenwood. The original Dr. Turner, whom Watson characterized as "widely known and much beloved," died in 1957. Still others were John Lyon, Ralsa Marshall Fuller, James Luther Ward, Samuel Watson Page, John L. Marshall, and John Douglass Harrison, whose son followed him in the profession.

The practice of medicine in the early days meant primarily house calls and clinic hours, often in the doctor's office at his home. Greenwood had no hospital until 1911; even so, it is clear that not everything changed with the advent of Greenwood County Hospital or even Self Memorial forty years later. For example, the first three of Troy native John Bowen's six children, all born during the eleven-year period 1950-1961, were delivered in Dr. C. H. Workman's office in McCormick (Workman had practiced earlier in Troy), where the lying-in included an overnight stay and the fee was about $50. The modern era of Greenwood as a medical center clearly began with the hospital, and the practice of medicine in the county gradually changed. The centennial edition of the newspaper noted that the number of doctors increased from about a dozen in 1860 to more than thirty nearly a hundred years later. Today the number is at least three times that figure, and Greenwood physicians represent a wide variety of specialties in both practice and research. The Greenwood Genetic Center, for example, recently announced a breakthrough in identifying and analyzing a gene that causes mental retardation in males, the result of a study of a particular family that was begun by pioneer American geneticists in 1939. That breakthrough led to the center's first major research grant from the National Institutes of Health. Director Dr. Roger Stevenson said in acknowledgement of the $500,000 grant, "The Center's new emphasis on research coincides with a similar commitment by the international scientific community to understand human heredity. The goal is to have basic knowledge of all human genes by the year 2005." It is entirely possible that much of that basic knowledge will be gained in Greenwood.

Whether engaged in sophisticated research involving techniques unheard of only a few years ago or making routine hospital rounds and processing dozens of office patients daily, Greenwood doctors are definitely in the mainstream of American life. The list of medical men in 1957 included a few who still practice today, among them Stanley C. Baker, William S. Brockington, James A. McQuown, Hunter May, and Wiley Price. Others, recently retired or semi-retired, include Elbert Adams, Phil Bates, Richard M. Christian, John Harrison, William Klauber, Vernon Moore, John C. Scurry, and R. Brooks Scurry. Still other noted Greenwood doctors have died since the town celebrated its centennial. Somehow all doctors seem rather special to their communities – surely nearly everybody remembers Charles Crosby, Furman Daniel, Paul Massengill, and Frank Shealy – but two physicians, one the first Chief of Staff of Self Memorial Hospital and the other a unique man-of-all-medical-work, are profiled here as representative of the profession. Carroll Jenkins Scurry and Walter Grady Bishop were contemporaries, it is true, but each was so clearly his own man that the story of one is not the story of the other.

Scurry was born in 1893 in the crossroads community of Chappells near the Saluda River in Newberry county. His was a well-known name in the area; some family members at the time still lived on land their pioneer ancestors had settled more than a century earlier. It seems that Scurry's father was always called "Doc," a nickname derived from the initials "D. R." which stood for Drury Ralph. Scurry's daughter Gay Charles speculates that this nickname, undoubtedly a household word, as well as young Carroll's duty as the oldest son to fetch the doctor when several of his nine brothers and sisters were born, might account for his choice of profession. "He learned early on how important a doctor is to a family and to a community," she wrote. Scurry was definitely a country boy; the activities he enjoyed as a youth – hunting, fishing, boating, swimming – remained important as leisure pursuits throughout his life.

Wofford Finishing School prepared Scurry for medical studies at Emory University. Graduation came in 1916, and a residency at St. John's Hospital in Pittsburgh, Pennsylvania, followed. Scurry met a student nurse, Lila Catherine Malone, while he was a resident and married her shortly before enlisting in the U. S. Medical Corps at the beginning of World War I. His tour consisted of assignment to the British Medical Corps in field hospitals on the front lines. The family settled in Greenwood when the doctor returned from military service. Scurry practiced for a time with G. P. Neel and was associated with several other doctors, including his two sons, over the years that followed. His daughter believes the "pursuit and joy of learning" were keys to Scurry's success as a physician and as a person. He regularly attended medical meetings and seminars to keep his knowledge current, and he promoted learning always in his own family. No doctor was more understanding than Scurry of the "hunger, embarrassment and poverty" that accompanied the Great Depression in the rural South of the 1930s, and none was more compassionate. He would not charge those who were unable to pay, and he accepted many a basket of garden vegetables and other farm products in lieu of cash payment for his services.

Scurry studied for a semester at the University of Vienna in 1937 where he was exposed to the latest medical and surgical techniques in the "progressive atmosphere" that had surrounded Sigmund Freud during his pioneer work in psychiatry. Perhaps the Vienna experience inspired Scurry's dream to build his own clinic to house doctors of varying specialties in one place. The Scurry Clinic, a landmark building erected on the corner of Hampton and Cambridge Avenues about 1940, was the result. Scurry set up his own office there and confidently prepared the way for his two sons to join him when they finished their medical training and military service. In the meantime, other physicians hung out shingles, and Minton's Pharmacy set up shop in the building to complete a sort of one-stop treatment center; one simply had the prescription filled on the way out. The Scurry Clinic building has only recently been demolished, much to the chagrin of preservationists.

James C. Self chose Scurry as his primary local consultant during the planning stage of Self Memorial Hospital, and he was named chief of staff when the new facility opened in 1951. The idea for an annual scientific meeting sponsored by and for the medical staff of the hospital belongs to Scurry, and he was instrumental in securing nationally known physicians and surgeons as speakers.

Dr. Scurry's career spanned a period during which medicine progressed, both literally and figuratively, from a horse and buggy practice to sleekly modern specialties. He was a general practitioner, the grandest kind of family doctor, one who "felt the call to perform medical tasks, whatever they were and wherever they required him to be." That meant day and night house calls, in addition to office hours and hospital rounds; Scurry's schedule included house calls for at least 35 of his working years. He never complained about the demands of his profession, and he counted among his friends people from all walks of life. His daughter attributes his capacity for friendship to his "way of life," which she describes as a philosophy of building rather than demolishing, including as opposed to excluding, and sharing instead of hoarding. She calls his generosity during his lifetime "immeasurable" and believes that helping people was his greatest pleasure. Scurry died, after a lifetime of service, on July 1, 1967.

Walter Grady Bishop was another beloved family doctor cut from much the same mold as Scurry but with certain characteristics unique to himself. A native of Inman, Bishop came to Greenwood in 1927 only a year after graduation from the Medical University of South Carolina. Bishop's practice in Greenwood spanned the next 51 years, except for five years spent in military service during World War II. In addition to a term as chief of staff of the hospital, his career included approximately thirty years as county physician and twenty as campus doctor for Lander College. A doctor who treats both convicts and co-eds, as well as a basketball team, babies, and nearly everybody else at one time or another, must be a remarkable individual, and those who knew Bishop probably would agree that he was just that. Not quite as suave and urbane as his friend and colleague Scurry, but every bit as outwardly gruff and inwardly compassionate, Bishop endeared himself to generations of Greenwood people and left an unforgettable imprint of plain common sense that has seldom been equaled. Bishop died at the age of 85 in 1984. Two of his four sons currently practice medicine, one of them in Greenwood, and his widow, Martha Thurmond Bishop, was named "Mother of the Year" for South Carolina in 1991.

An editorial in *The Index-Journal* of July 18, 1984, cited Walter Bishop for his willingness to go "the extra mile" in his profession and added that "he did that in everything" even as he kept "a low profile" in his personal life. "The world will miss him, as it does all those who offer a helping hand without seeking something in return." Many people remember Walter Bishop with special fondness.

It is amusing to think of a traveling dentist, but it is true that the dental profession was first practiced in this area by itinerants. An article in the centennial edition of the newspaper provided what must be the first mention of the availability of dental service in the village of Greenwood. John Donald McKellar advertised as a "surgeon dentist" in The *Abbeville Banner* in 1857. Louise Watson wrote that McKellar had completed a dental course in Philadelphia a short time earlier.

The art of dentistry developed along with that of medicine; documents from as early as 3700 B.C. describe methods of treating teeth, although the assumption is that no actual dental operations were performed prior to about 500 B.C. The separation of dental procedures from medicine began in the sixteenth century, but the independent and organized development of modern scientific dentistry actually dates from about 200 years later. A Frenchman named Fauchard is credited with establishing a firm scientific base and emphasizing dentistry's importance as a health science profession. While it may be true that barbers were the first dentists and the striped barber pole their symbol, as is popularly believed, there is no record that any Greenwood barber ever pulled a tooth, and even surgeons of the Middle Ages warned that barbers should perform extractions only in the presence of a physician.

Greenwood's first resident dentist was West Allen Williams of Williamston who opened an office in about 1872. Williams had practiced as an itinerant for a time; he first met his wife, in fact, on a visit to Greenwood and decided to hang out his shingle in the village. Williams died in Greenwood in 1877. Other very early Greenwood dentists included J. H. Wilson, Madison Augustus Bailey, Truman J. Crymes, Louis H. Russell, Preston Brooks Connor, Hugh L. Fellers, Robert W. McCord, and William E. McCord.

Ten dentists were in active practice in Greenwood at the time of the town's centennial in 1957, and one other had died shortly before that time. Many people will find their family dentist in a list of practitioners from the late 1950s: Stanley Cyril Baker (son of one-time Greenwood mayor Kenneth Baker and father of physician-surgeon Stanley C. Baker, Jr.), Carl Eugene Bailey, Elisha Brandon, Lewis Monroe Cheek, Charles Calhoun Fuller, Joseph Gwynne Jenkins (father of current dentist J. G. Jenkins, Jr.), John Hudson Kirkland, Jr., James Maxie McLees (father and two sons), and Russell Hanahan Park.

Greenwood dentists have proliferated, both in number and specialties, over the last thirty years as the profession itself has advanced. Greenwood people now have access to resident specialists in both orthodontics and periodontics, as well as the entire spectrum of modern scientific dentistry.

Surely there can be no doubt that Thomas Carson Anderson holds the record for longevity as a professional surveyor (maybe everywhere, but definitely in Greenwood); Perrin Anderson recorded in *Recollections of My Life* that his stepfather actually took on surveying jobs after his 100th birthday even though he had given up driving at the age of 95 or so. Anderson's memoir contains a number of anecdotes about the man he called "Dad"; clearly the two men shared great affection, family loyalty, and deep respect over many years.

The elder Anderson was born in 1868. Although the times meant his early education was probably the "catch as catch can" affair described elsewhere in this book, Anderson was able to attend the University of South Carolina for two years before the money ran out. He regretted the lack of a degree for the rest of his life. While Anderson's father might have been unable to manage the cost of a full college education, he did teach surveying to both his sons when they were still quite young. Tom Anderson tried farming but soon ran into what his son called "the woes of the cotton farmer" of that day. He operated on the "share crop" system with two black families who lived in tenant houses on the farm. Perrin Anderson provided a good description of the system in only three sentences:

> The share-cropper furnished his labor and that of his children, one-half of the fertilizer and one-half of the cost of the seed. Since the share-cropper had no capital, the landowner had to "carry" him; that is, advance him the money for his living until the cotton was picked and sold. When the cotton was sold, the landowner and the share-cropper divided the proceeds, one-half each, after the landowner was paid for his advances.

Tom Anderson was never a successful cotton grower. One reason was the red clay of the Anderson land, but another, the vagarious weather, was actually a blessing in disguise for a man whose skills ran more to surveying than to farming. Excessive rainfall on freshly-plowed cotton land can mean serious erosion, and terracing proved one method of coping with this problem. Anderson became more and more involved in "laying off" terraces for neighboring farmers and gradually moved from cotton farming to surveying as a more dependable source of income. He never got rich as a result because he never quite learned to charge fees commensurate with the prevailing market value of his professional services. The usual rate for a job was about $10 at the time he started surveying, but he couldn't seem to adjust as prices went up. His son wrote that Anderson could never force himself to charge full value because he remembered the times when Greenwood County people had very little money.

The lack of cash in the Anderson household when Perrin Anderson was a youngster spells "poverty level" in today's parlance, but neither he nor others who grew up as he did regard their farm background as a low standard of living. The only thing missing was actual cash; but, as Anderson put it, children seldom went to town anyway, except to go to school, and were therefore not constantly reminded of their deficiency in pocket money. There did come a time, however, when the money situation created a genuine crisis for the family. Perrin Anderson's mother was determined all her children would have the chance for a college education. Both Perrin and his brother Tom got through college before the depression hit, but there seemed no way to send the Anderson daughters at a time of unpaid taxes and delinquent mortgage payments. Mrs. Anderson's quiet assertion, "Well, they *are* going," led to her famous potato chip business, a venture that not only financed the four Anderson daughters' education but also furnished a delicacy considered necessary at nearly every party or other entertainment for miles around. The business went on for years, and every member of the family was pressed into service in some capacity. Anderson wrote, "My wife says that very often in attending some party she would deliver the potato chips to the back door and then go in the front door as a guest." No one knows how many chips Nannie Anderson turned, one by one, while "standing over a hot wood-burning cook stove, winter and summer," but turn them she did until her financial goals were reached and college expenses paid. Even after the Anderson sisters had their degrees, their mother couldn't quite get out of the food business. She took on the job of school lunch supervisor at Grenola School in South Greenwood when she was about seventy years old. Originally, the job was simply to fill in until another supervisor could be found; Anderson "filled in" for eleven years. In her church, in her home, and in a wide community, Nannie Anderson was every bit the good citizen her husband was. A good wife also, she dutifully attended Mount Lebanon Church with her staunchly Methodist husband during the years her children were young, but Anderson never faltered in her own allegiance to the Baptist denomination. A Sunday School class at Ninety Six First Baptist Church still bears her name.

Tom Anderson eventually became everybody's favorite senior citizen and a true legend in his own lifetime in Greenwood. His son wrote that his mind was clear and active to the day of his death. He had a strong sense of humor, a lively but questioning religious faith, a love of poetry and the Bible, and a willingness to try new things all his life. Born only three years after the end of the Civil War, Thomas C. Anderson died not long before his 108th birthday, on August 6, 1976.

An editorial in the March 26, 1970, edition of *The Index-Journal* begins: "Few people have been so closely identified with a community as J. Hearst Coleman was with Greenwood." Coleman had been probably the town's most prominent engineer for more than forty years at the time of his death, at the age of 72, on March 24, 1970. His mother was a Hearst, and Coleman might have been one of the last Greenwood County connections to the remarkable family that moved to the American West and grew in fame, fortune, and notoriety over the ensuing generations.

Coleman studied engineering at The Citadel and Cornell University and served as an officer in the first world war. His Greenwood career, although quite varied, was never far removed from his primary occupation as engineer and builder. For example, he served on the city council for a term in the 1940s, but he was city engineer before that and chief engineer for Abney Mills simultaneously. He also chaired the city zoning commission. Coleman organized his own firm in 1940. According to an editorial, he might have carried a topographic map of Greenwood in his head, so closely did he "become acquainted with all its geographic features." Not only an engineer, Coleman was also a builder whose expertise can still be seen in the courthouse, the municipal building, Piedmont Technical College, and Greenwood High School.

Greenwood connections for Coleman were not limited to the family name. He was born in the historic White Hall community, for example, and he attended Bailey Military Institute for part of his school years. He also taught at BMI and at Columbia Military Academy. Before returning to Greenwood after college and graduate school, Coleman worked for a time as a structural engineer and designer with the Cleveland Union Terminals Company and as a bridge engineer for the Wheeling and Lake Erie Railway in Ohio. Coleman was an active member of the ARP Church and served as a counselor at Erskine College. He was also quite interested in local history, especially in preservation and restoration of historic structures.

Coleman's sole survivor at the time of his death was his wife; their only child had died as a young boy in 1949. A small area along Highway 25 South was designated for many years "The Jimmy Coleman Park," but nothing remains of the modest wood sign that once marked the spot. The Hearst Coleman estate passed to Erskine College upon Esther Hunter Coleman's death a few years ago.

Greenwood has been singularly fortunate in the number of professional engineers who have made the town their own. Pete Marshall's long service with the city comes to mind, as well as the careers of men such as C. Y. Thomason and G. E. Moore. Another engineer, whose fame as a photographer actually outweighs that of a long career with the South Carolina Highway Department, was Carl Julien. A Newberry native and Clemson graduate, Julien came to Greenwood before the first world war. He married Greenwood native Jessie Fouche during the war and settled in at the highway department afterward. But Julien had developed more interests along the way than a single career could possibly satisfy. Although he lost the sight in one eye rather early in life, his photographic output was simply astonishing, and his other avocations, such as cabinet work, local history, and amateur botany, were not curtailed by a lack of full vision. Jessie Julien, who in her mid-90s pursues extensive hobbies of her own, believes her husband's seven books are probably his greatest legacy. Most of the books for which Carl Julien provided the photographs are of the "coffee table" variety – large volumes of historical text and stunning black-and-white photographs of South Carolina scenes. An Associated Press review on the jacket of an early volume, *Beneath so Kind a Sky* (1947), credits the photographer with "a handsome job of merging what meets the eye with what speaks to the heart." *Photographic Trade News* called Julien's photographs "simple and dignified" work that other photographers might "study with profit." *The News and Courier* noted Julien's "wide taste, knowledge of the subject, and rare technical skill." Other books followed, including *Ninety Six*, prepared in collaboration with H. L. Watson; *Pee Dee Panorama*; *Sea Islands to Sand Hills*; and *Look to the Rock*, Julien's last work.

Carl Julien's books are considered rare treasures by the people who own them. Surely no one, South Carolinian or otherwise, who studies the quiet beauty and power of Julien's photographs could fail to be interested in the artist who created them. Although the sites themselves are familiar South Carolina scenes, the emotions Julien's images evoke are part of the mystery of the universe. Julien must have understood what he was doing very well indeed; his widow says her husband was an "inward" sort of person, one with few intimate friends and almost no small talk. She thinks he would laugh at the notion that he was not fully appreciated in his lifetime, since the approbation of others did not interest him in the least. Carl Julien found his greatest fulfillment in the work he did with his own hands and his own brain.

While the interests of the two Juliens did not always coincide, theirs was a symbiotic relationship. For example, he brought home masses of wildflowers because he was interested in their taxonomy; she, on the other hand, had a passion to grow the flowers and try to duplicate their natural habitat. Fortunately, water from photographic processing can be re-used, and the Julien home on Gracemont Drive was chosen, at least in part, so that the basement darkroom runoff would provide water for plant cultivation. Unwilling to leave her natural garden behind when she moved, Julien gave some of the plants to fellow wildflower lover Jean Park. Also, while Carl Julien worked on his projects, his wife began her own accidental career as Greenwood's most famous cookie-maker. She says it all started at Christmas in 1948 with the problem of what to give a neighbor who already had everything. That year the neighbor got a jar of Julien's cookies, as did a couple of other friends in town. Even the jar became a sort of trademark. Some cookies come in boxes, but not Julien's. Her recipe exactly fills a wide-mouthed glass or plastic gallon container, unmistakably a jar. The word spread, and Julien found herself responding to more and more requests for cookies; one day she realized she had been in business for some time without knowing it. That realization came when a request for cookies sounded suspiciously like an order. The ever-practical Julien accepted the inevitable but was sufficiently shrewd to raise the price a bit over the years. Though the selling price of a jar of cookies gradually rose from one to five dollars, escalating prices made absolutely no difference; more and more customers demanded more and more cookies every year. Orders for Christmas had to be on the books by December 1 or cookie-lovers were out of luck. One year she decided to count cookies and found her production totaled 10,000 in Christmas orders alone. This went on for 23 years; Julien fears it might start again if she were to relent even so far as one batch of cookies baked at midnight for a special friend. Nowadays she makes only birthday cakes for Hospice patients. So much for baking; Julien also gardens and sews. Although she still makes clothes, her specialties are fabric-covered boxes in a fanciful shape cut from a very old pattern and delicately-worked linen handkerchiefs. One window in Julien's room at the Bayberry Apartments is filled with African violets, a bird bath surrounded by caladiums she planted is just outside another window, and more plants grow in pots and on trellises beside the porch railing.

Carl Julien took early retirement from the highway department. His widow believes his decline began when he lost interest in the pursuits of a lifetime. He died at the age of 80 in 1977.

One of Greenwood's most impressive engineering firms today is Davis & Floyd, which was established in 1954 by Emmett I. Davis, older son of a Greenwood County engineer primarily associated with the Buzzard Roost project, and Philip R. Floyd. The firm encompasses a number of engineering specialties, including a great deal of work in the environmental sciences, and has branches in Columbia, Charleston, and Boston.

Greenwood is a town of churches, most of which employ professional ministers. Any discussion of ministers would seem to require some mention of their churches, although church histories per se are not a significant part of this narrative. The county is dotted with famous old churches. Among others, there are Greenville Presbyterian in the northwest corner; Horeb, near Troy; Cedar Springs on the Abbeville County line; Mountain Creek and Antioch in the southeast; Siloam, Mount Moriah, Tranquil and Rock Presbyterian nearer the county seat; Mount Lebanon toward Ninety Six; Rehoboth and Damascus, near Breezewood; and Bold Spring in Callison. At least two of these churches, Rock Presbyterian and Cedar Springs, date their origins from the late eighteenth century. These historic old churches, as well as several large city congregations, insure that the county lists among its professionals any number of ministers. Several Greenwood churches have published their own histories and documented the tenure of their pastors. One famous early minister, John McLees, is generally credited as the "father" of First Presbyterian Church. His pastorate at Rock Presbyterian dates from 1847 to his death in 1882. The Greenwood church, which began as a chapel nearly ten years before McLees came to Rock, was formed by members of the mother church and fully organized as a separate entity shortly after McLees's death. A much later and much beloved pastor of First Presbyterian Church was Robert L. Alexander who served the church from 1951 to his retirement only a few years ago.

One might naturally assume that Main Street Methodist Church grew out of the all-Methodist community of Cokesbury, but Louise Watson's sketch of Main Street's history made no such connection. Early records listed seven charter members, all women, of the first Methodist church in town; it was organized in 1858 by a group "who had no ties with any of the long-established rural churches." Watson's article named ministers who had served Main Street Methodist Church practically from its beginning at the site of the cemetery on East Cambridge Avenue. Famous Methodist ministers who filled Main Street's pulpit at one time or another include R. E. Stackhouse, B. Rhett Turnipseed, John M. Shingler, and James F. Lupo.

The meeting-house for most Baptists in early Greenwood was Mount Moriah Church organized in 1810. This church was considered one of the wealthiest in the Edgefield Association by the 1860s. Its wealth was inferred in part from the number of slaves its members owned; more than a hundred were carried as members on the church rolls. The time was considered ripe for a Baptist church in Greenwood by 1870; twenty-three charter members, of whom eighteen moved from Mount Moriah, organized the earliest Baptist church in town on September 25 of that year. The first building was erected a few years later somewhere on East Cambridge (then Church Street), and the second was built on North Main Street where the county library now stands. The entire front page of the first issue of *The Greenwood Index* on November 11, 1897, was devoted to the new First Baptist Church building. One result of the burgeoning membership of First Baptist Church was South Main Street Baptist Church which dates from 1911. Notable pastors at South Main include D. D. May, Walter L. Coker, George H. Moore, and James Buckingham. Callie Self Memorial, which began as Grendel Mill No. 2 Baptist Church in 1912, published its history in 1977. Connie Maxwell Baptist Church also dates from 1912, West Side Baptist from 1914, and several other Baptist churches were organized in later years.

Other protestant denominations are also well represented in Greenwood, and the lone Catholic Church, Our Lady of Lourdes, appeared in 1920. The Episcopal Church of the Resurrection was established as a mission in 1892; its first chapel building dates from 1896. Immanuel Lutheran Church began in 1902 with 23 charter members, among them the Kenneth Bakers and Dr. R. B. Epting. Many people remember that the first Lutheran church building stood at the corner of Oak and Monument Streets. That building was erected in 1910 and sold to the Masonic Order in 1952 when the new building at East Creswell and McLees Streets was finished. Two ministers – Muller R. Wingard and Frank L. Roof – are remembered for long service at Immanuel Lutheran. Greenwood Associate Reformed Presbyterians have had a church in Greenwood since 1914. Due West and Long Cane connections are evident in the names of the seventeen charter members, who included Hearsts, Widemans, Youngs, and Lipscombs. The building at the corner of Calhoun Avenue and Lander Street served the church for about fifty years until a new church complex was erected on Highway 254 near Greenwood High School. Noted and well-remembered ministers to the Greenwood ARP congregation include William L. Pressly and S. P. Tinkler.

Since any decent accounting of Greenwood's churches would fill several volumes, the brief sketches of the few included here are not intended as a comprehensive look at either the churches or their most notable pastors. Clearly many professional ministers have preached the gospel in many different pulpits for many years. The single minister whose life and career are sketched here was chosen simply as representative of the type of man Greenwood had taken to its heart. James Augustus Bowers was an Arkansas native who had served two other churches for a total of seven years before he came to Greenwood as pastor of the First Baptist Church in 1943. He was thirty years old. Bowers's undergraduate degree was from Baylor University, and he earned the Master of Theology from Southern Baptist Theological Seminary in 1936. Furman University awarded Bowers the honorary Doctor of Divinity in 1965. In addition to the usual pastoral duties of a large congregation, Bowers was at the helm of the church during a massive building program that began at about the time he came. In spite of all that, he was always involved with community affairs and even made a name for himself as an actor with community theater in both Greenwood and Abbeville. Any listing of Bowers's civic activities would include the YMCA, Kiwanis Club, the Crippled Children's Society, the County Library, and the National Tuberculosis Association. Along the way he also chaired the County Board of Social Services and served the Lung Associations of both the area and the state. The Rotary Club chose Bowers as its "Man of the Year" in 1957, and the Kiwanis Club honored him with its highest award in 1977.

The range of Bowers's denominational activities was equally wide: during his career he served as state pastor-advisor for the Baptist Student Union, a member of the General Board and its executive committee, moderator of the Abbeville Association, chairman of the board of the Bethea Home for the Aging, and president of the Greenwood Ministerial Association at two different times.

Bowers was pastor of Greenwood's First Baptist Church when it was voted out of the Abbeville Association in 1970 for its policy of accepting members by transfer from other denominations without requiring baptism by immersion. Most people credit Bowers with the policy and regard his stand as evidence of superior leadership during a time of questioning and change. Not only has the church maintained disfellowship from its local association for more than twenty years, it recently formed a new organization, the Covenant Association, with the

First Baptist Church of Clemson which was expelled from its association in 1976.

Bowers retired in 1977 after 34 years of service and was named Pastor Emeritus of First Baptist Church. He died on February 15, 1991, at the age of 78. His funeral service, reportedly of his own choosing, included a number of his favorite musical selections, and one item, "A Call to Celebration," seemed particularly evocative of the Bowers style. Many people remember Jim Bowers as especially effective at the funerals of old friends. No one who heard it could ever forget his opening line at one memorial service: "When I learned that L. B. Adams had died, it was as though a mighty tree had fallen in the forest."

The words *profession* and *professional* are tricky. In one sense, everybody who has a job is a professional, and some people seem to regard not working as a career in itself. One Greenwood man considers himself a "professional heir," an occupation with a number of interesting ramifications. The terms are generally understood, however, to connote training and specialized study. The perfectly legitimate job of bookkeeper has evolved into the classier designation of accountant and all the way to the profession of Certified Public Accountant. Hardly anyone is called "bookkeeper" these days, but it should be remembered that Greenwood's most famous practitioners of that honorable calling include John P. Abney and James C. Self. And hundreds of Greenwood women worked for years simply as secretaries before a national association codified the work into the Certified Professional Secretary licensure. Job titles such as "assistant" or "administrative assistant" have replaced that of secretary in many large companies because they sound more "professional," but Greenwood can remember many legal secretaries, for example, who were so capable they practiced law in all but name. Nurses are definitely professionals, as are schoolteachers and college professors – their diplomas, licenses, and certificates prove it. In general, musicians, writers, athletes, artists, and actors are considered professionals as opposed to amateurs when they are able to command remuneration for what they do. But janitors and maids are often trained in the latest cleaning techniques, bank tellers must undergo hours of specialized instruction, and police officers and firefighters must learn in a structured fashion the standard practices of their craft. Indeed, every trade has its own distinctive tricks that must be learned if its adherents are to practice it successfully.

There is really no end to the circular argument of occupation vs. profession, but clearly most people today seek to be regarded as professionals for rather obvious reasons, only one of which is a larger paycheck. Many early Greenwood notables, on the other hand, just as clearly preferred to see themselves as generalists, and not simply because specialization was a concept of the future. Of course many good reasons for specialization and licensure exist. Perrin Anderson wrote that his father exploded when told he needed a surveyor's license – "I was surveying before those fellers were born!" – but relented when Hearst Coleman explained that the procedure protected the public from persons pretending to an expertise they did not possess. The downside of specialization is contained in the wag's remark: "We learn more and more about less and less; pretty soon we will know everything about nothing."

Once open in its admiration of the Renaissance Man, society no longer knows quite what to do with the generalist. It is revealing to note that the word "generalist" appears in the 1967 edition of *Webster's Seventh New Collegiate Dictionary* as "one who is conversant with several different fields or aptitudes"; whereas *The American Heritage Dictionary*, which has been revised "to reflect the language of the '80's," does not include the word in its 1983 paperback edition. The whole matter in its larger sense might be simply a question of semantics, but doubtless only a professional linguist would be qualified to decide.

7

LANDER COLLEGE

Those who wish graduation without education are respectfully notified that this is not the school they are seeking.

Samuel Lander
(from an 1883 catalogue)

ANY number of Greenwood schools over the years have been called colleges, but Greenwood County can boast of only one institution that conforms to the most commonly accepted definition of the word *college* as "an independent institution of higher learning offering a course of general studies leading to a bachelor's degree." That school is the four-year, coeducational Lander College which has been part of the South Carolina system of public colleges and universities since 1973. It has also been several other things since it was founded in Williamston, South Carolina, in 1872 as Williamston Female College by Samuel Lander, a noted educator and Methodist clergyman. The move to Greenwood as a fully established institution in 1903-1904 was neither accident nor whim of the moment; indeed, no event in the county's history was more calculated and none more significant – with the possible exception of the first railroad in 1852 – in the dreams for Greenwood's future woven in the minds of its early planners. The story would be worth telling for itself alone, but the fact is that Greenwood County and Lander College have grown up together. The story of one is very much the story of the other.

That story begins sometime in 1902 when Greenwood had been a county seat for five years. Its courthouse had been completed and formally turned over to the county in April 1898, and all sorts of other construction – from private homes to churches to businesses – was in full swing throughout the town. Forty-foot-wide streets with sidewalks on either side were being built using the "city chaingang and a few hired hands." J. S. Bailey's Oregon Hotel was still new. Brick-making was a bustling industry; one anonymous article describing Greenwood in 1889 stated that Messrs. Mays & Weeks, contractors, made brick of "superior quality" from local clay and were unable to "supply the demand . . . which has come from all sections." The town square was becoming just that – a square – with the completion of the "Syndicate Block" of stores on the west side. C. M. Calhoun reflected the spirit of the time quite well (except for certain problems with grammar and punctuation) when he wrote in *Liberty Dethroned*:

> This city has always been wide awake, and ever on the alert, reaching out and grasping hold of any good thing afloat, which is beneficial to the welfare of its people, and has never yet failed to acquire anything sought for, which could be acquired by money and hard work. While some other towns have stood dormant waiting for something to turn up. Greenwood has always pushed forward, like the Octopus, stretching out its arms taking in its coils, everything to her beterment [sic] as a growing city, while at [the] same time grander enterprises . . . [have] originated within her gates . . . than can be found in any town or city of much greater size in the State. One thing can be said of the city, while among themselves they are not by any means a unit and homogeneous, in sentiment, on the many details of a private and business nature, but just let the tocsin be sounded for a measure which bids fair to redound to the upbuilding of the city. When just then they became a band of working brothers, all of one mind and inclination.

The push for a college in Greenwood began when the South Carolina Methodist Conference met in the winter of 1901 and passed certain resolutions concerning the removal of Columbia Female College from its original location on the corner of Pickens and Hampton Streets in downtown Columbia. Having been conceived in 1854 and opened in 1859, the school was five years in the building. Hardly begun, Columbia Female College was forced to close its doors in 1864 due both to debt and the conditions of war. While the building was not among those destroyed when Columbia was burned in 1865, its location caused it to sustain great damage from the invading army nevertheless. There seemed no possibility of reopening at the close of the war since the school's debts were still five times greater than its assets; the building was leased for a time as a hotel. According to a sketch in the Methodist publication *Builders*, the school managed to reopen in 1872 after eight years of suspension, with Samuel B. Jones as president. The dates of both closing and reopening as reported in the sketch are off by one year. The Columbia College Alumni Office confirmed 1865 and 1873 as the correct dates.

Sentiment to move the college remained strong, however, because of certain dissatisfactions with the Columbia location, among them the fact that it lacked room to expand and Calhoun's contention that "Columbia had not supported the college as she ought to have done." The conference went so far as to appoint a committee to visit those towns whose citizens had expressed an interest in having the college and had actually pledged a sum of money to that end. A rivalry developed between Laurens and Greenwood, both of which were under consideration. Evidence of the sincerity of Greenwood's effort to secure Columbia College exists in the form of a small pamphlet preserved in the Greenwood County Collection at the public library. Entitled *Greenwood's*

Superior Advantages and Splendid Offer to the Board of Trustees, Columbia Female College, the pamphlet reads in part:

> Greenwood can furnish all kinds of building material at reasonable cost. Within a few miles of the city are fields and quarries of superior granite. In and around the city are fine brickyards supplying brick at very low prices. The soil of Greenwood is well suited to brick making. Wood and coal are comparatively cheap, labor is good and abundant and brick can be made at a very low cost. Saw mills, planing mills, and lumber yards will furnish material at moderate prices. Being a strong competitive point the railroad freight rates on lumber, coal, and all kinds of material are very low.

The visiting committee reported to the 1902 Conference its choice of Greenwood as the new home of Columbia Female College based on the amount of money subscribed (some $49,000), the fine railroad facilities, the distance from other colleges, and Greenwood's "very great progressive spirit." Notwithstanding, the conference voted by a small majority to keep the college in Columbia but to move it to a new site in the northern suburbs. Columbia Female College opened at its new location in 1905.

Concerning this period and his own link with the Columbia Female College situation, Samuel Lander wrote his son-in-law, John O. Willson, in April 1904:

> At the close of our first year – December, 1872 – I went to the Anderson Conference with full authority to offer our school to the Conference as a Church institution. But soon after my arrival, my good friend, Brother J. W. Kelly, then president of the Columbia Female College trustees, persuaded me to postpone my proposition till the next session of the Conference, urging that the acceptance of our college would be a serious hindrance to the success of the Columbia College, just then about to be reopened. So far from being willing to interfere with the Columbia College, I felt an unusually deep interest in its success. Indeed, the occasion for my withdrawal from the Spartanburg Female College in November, 1871, was the fact that I had been conditionally chosen president of Columbia College, provided the trustees found it practicable to reopen the institution in October, 1872. . . .

It should be noted that Samuel B. Jones and Samuel Lander served as co-presidents of Spartanburg Female College for one year only, 1870-71. Lander went on to start his own college, while Jones became President of Columbia Female College a year later. He served for the period 1873-1876 and again from 1890-1894. The several coincidences of the Greenwood/Lander/Columbia College/Methodist network in the very earliest days should not be missed. They will arise again in the late 1940s.

Back to Greenwood in 1902 and the chagrin following the conference vote. Calhoun wrote, "All of our labor seemed to have been in vain, as we had been led to believe this point [relocation] had previously been settled and all we had to do was to raise a certain amount of money for its accomplishment. . . . We felt somewhat agrived [sic], at the action of conference . . . but even felt more determined than ever to have a college."

Every source agrees that the prime mover in the quest to secure a college for Greenwood was the county's first senator, C. A. C. Waller. Of course there were others – Greenwood people have interested themselves in every phase of the college's development – but there can be no doubt that Waller was the earliest champion of the enterprise. The original Lander auditorium, which according to early catalogs could seat 1,200 people, was christened "Waller Hall" in his honor. Waller was by all accounts something of a character, the sort of man who was personally and vociferously involved in every aspect of Greenwood life. H. L. Watson described him well in an address delivered at Founder's Day exercises on February 10, 1955: "Captain Waller was the dominating figure and spokesman for the Greenwood interests. He carried a cane, and in his excitement over the whole project he would wave that stick around his head as if he were still handling the sword of a Confederate captain and was ready to charge . . . anybody who questioned any of his plans or visions."

Nobody knows exactly how the fiery Chris Waller and the gentle Samuel Lander found each other the first time; but, as often happens when mutual interests are at stake, find each other they did, late in 1902. Waller made an offer that Lander could not refuse; indeed it must have seemed a godsend to a man who had become almost a victim of his own success as an educator of young women. When Greenwood made its proposition, Lander was 69 years old and a veteran of many pulpits and classrooms; his own education had begun 65 years earlier, and a long commitment to education for women had found fulfillment in a school that reflected his philosophy from top to bottom. But without adequate backing and room to grow, that school faced almost certain retrenchment and eventual failure. Lander's willingness to undertake so fundamental a change as moving the entire institution reflected a determination to do what he could to secure the school's future. This attitude of supreme self-confidence and a sure sense of direction were typical of Samuel Lander throughout a long and productive life.

Samuel Lander was born in 1833, the seventh child of Samuel and Eliza Miller Lander, in Lincolnton, North Carolina. His father was an Irishman whose family was originally English, and his mother's ancestors were members of the Protestant colony from the Alsace-Lorraine who had emigrated to southern Ireland during the reign of Queen Anne (1702-1714). Both the elder Landers were unusually strong-willed people, according to a family sketch written by a granddaughter, and both were staunch Protestants who were not only tolerant of, but even sympathetic with, the new sect of Methodists. Indeed, they entertained John Wesley himself on several of his visits to Cork. "This interesting Irish couple, whose ancestors had known and suffered religious persecution, came to this country when the Roman Catholic Church made things unhappy for them in Cork." The Landers came to America in 1818; eventually the family settled in Lincolnton where Lander worked successfully at the coach maker's trade even after he became a local Methodist preacher. Eliza Lander was described as "better educated than most women of her day and . . . fond of reading." Her granddaughter noted particularly that she "continued to read fiction even after her husband became a Methodist preacher" as an example of her courage in breaking away from "commonly accepted customs" of the time.

Young Samuel managed to survive infancy, even though he was born a "frail and unpromising" child, and lived the life of a normal boy in a family with seven children. Learning apparently came early and easily. By the time he was sent to school at the age of four to a Mrs. Bevins from Charleston, he knew his letters and had already learned to read. He had also received a taste of Greek and Latin at home before he learned English grammar. The Reverend J. W. Murphy, an uncle described as a "classical scholar and a rigid disciplinarian," took over young Samuel's education after he left Mrs. Bevins's school and prepared him for college. Lander later said that the only rule in Murphy's school was twelve inches long, one inch wide, and applied to the palm of the hand.

Lander was ready for college in 1849 at the age of sixteen and was admitted after examination to the sophomore class at Randolph-Macon. Having deliberately subjected himself to physical discomforts in preparation for hardship, having already adopted a regimen of stern self-discipline in all his pursuits, and having always viewed learning as adventure, Lander's graduation as valedictorian of his class in 1852 was probably a surprise to no one who knew him. After graduation he tried out civil engineering and sampled the study of law for a year or so but found neither to his liking. College teaching, however, appealed to Lander from the first; his introduction to the front of the classroom came at Catawba College in Newton, North Carolina, in 1853, the same year he married Laura MacPherson. Lander returned to Randolph-Macon as a professor of languages in 1855 and found time to earn the master's degree while on the faculty there. Other teaching assignments followed: he taught Latin and mathematics as well as languages at various schools in North Carolina and was licensed to preach in 1861.

During the war years Lander occupied himself with problems of education in his state. His daughter wrote that during the war the need arose for textbooks adapted to the circumstances of the time. The North Carolina State Education Association had determined to use what it called "home publications" in preference to any other; accordingly, a whole series of school books bearing the proud name *Our Own* was prepared and published during this period. Two *Our Own Arithmetics* were written by the Reverend S. Lander. William L. Sherrill stated in a 1909 Founder's Day address: "During the Civil War, when communication with the outside world was cut off and necessity became the mother of invention, books were scarce and his [Lander's] thorough knowledge of mathematics enabled him to prepare *Lander's Common School Arithmetic*, which was the standard in the early days of my school life. . . ." No doubt this was the same series, and Sherrill was merely applying the terminology of the day to indicate the wide acceptance of this textbook.

Lander left active school work in favor of the ministry for only two years soon after the close of the war. His daughter wrote that he was disposed at this time to devote his life entirely to the ministry, but another school called and he answered in 1868. Three years later, after the Columbia College proposal fell through, he asked for an appointment in the Methodist itinerancy and was sent to Williamston, South Carolina.

Church officials at Williamston had requested a preacher who could also teach; they also asked for a single man. Samuel Lander met the former requirement admirably, so admirably, in fact, that a wife and seven children did not jeopardize his appointment. The church could provide only a small salary, and no living quarters were available. The only building in town large enough to accommodate the family and any pupils Lander might attract was an old hotel building. The resourceful Lander knew an opportunity when he saw one; he asked that the church pay the rent on the building in lieu of salary and grant permission for him to open a school for women. The church and the presiding elder, no doubt with great relief, complied, and Williamston Female College was launched. Lander recalled his thinking at the time in a letter dated many years later: his desire was "to elevate the standard of female education which at that time throughout this region of the country was lamentably low," and his faith in the new enterprise was complete. "I felt perfectly sure that, with the resources at my command, it would be . . . worthy of patronage," he wrote. Lander went to Williamston in December 1871; the college opened on February 12, 1872. "It was a gratifying surprise when on that date seventeen boarding students appeared with twenty-one from the town," his daughter wrote later. The total enrollment reached 61 before the spring term ended.

For the first time Lander was able to put into effect his own ideas on education, formulated and refined over the preceding eighteen years. One conviction he had held for some time was that graduation depended upon individual preparation and examination. No one earned a degree during Lander's three-year tenure as president of one school in North Carolina because he said he found none prepared to graduate. At Williamston, however, three young women satisfied the requirements for graduation at the end of the first session.

School sessions were of twenty weeks each, with the vacation period from late November to early February. Lander felt that the cooler summer climate in Williamston would be beneficial to young ladies from the "unhealthful" lowcountry. He was also pleased to be able to offer daily access to the waters of the chalybeate spring for which Williamston was noted, and he took advantage of the opportunity for nature study in early morning pilgrimages, with students in tow, to the spring. But these advantages were secondary to the all-important question of scholarship. Lander found many students deficient in elementary studies and instituted a system of reviews to remedy this condition. Every student was required to review reading, writing, spelling, and arithmetic throughout her college course. His word was *review*; today we call it developmental education.

Lander was much opposed to prizes, nor would he tolerate what he called "public exhibitions," believing they required too much time that would be better expended on scholarly pursuits. Education was meant for culture, he said, and not mere accomplishment. But a practical system of rewards or premiums by which students could earn a reduction in tuition made sense to Samuel Lander. This system not only encouraged students to excel, but also meant that costs could be substantially reduced; best of all, the inducement was open to every student. After 1874 it was possible for a student with a 95 average to attend Williamston for one-half the normal tuition costs. Lower averages could also earn fee reductions; a modest average of 75-80 earned a 10% discount. Samuel Lander would surely find today's concepts of financial aid mind-boggling, but he clearly anticipated the notion of academic scholarships.

Williamston Female College operated the second kindergarten department in the state, offering both practical application and instruction in methods. Early Childhood Education is a sizable major field at Lander College today; it was not unknown to Samuel Lander in 1875.

Perhaps Lander's most unusual innovation was his "one-study" plan introduced in 1877. Lander believed that deeper and more accurate knowledge could be acquired by concentrating on each discipline in turn. Consequently, one subject was emphasized during each five-week section of a session, with secondary subjects given only review or preparatory attention during that time. There was a practical side as well: if a student sustained herself in every study, it was possible to accomplish the entire collegiate course in three years. Was Samuel Lander anticipating the modern concept of majors and minors?

Lander believed that the education of women was a serious and vital business and that broad and accurate scholarship was as necessary for women as for men. He spoke of "possibilities" for educated women rather than relegating females to the merely decorative or utilitarian status then considered their station in life. While he emphasized useful knowledge, he did not neglect cultural pursuits. Music and art were in the curriculum from the first, to be studied for the pleasure they gave and not for ostentatious display in their performance. He disdained formal commencements; rather, when a young woman completed the requirements for a degree, which was possible eight times in any given year, she was handed her choice of a diploma or an engraved gold pin and quietly took her leave. Lander was firmly opposed to the notion of lowering standards in order to attract students. An 1883 bulletin carries the admonition: "Those who wish graduation without education are respectfully notified that this is not the school they are seeking." Emerson could not have said it better.

Trinity College (now Duke University) conferred the honorary degree of Doctor of Divinity on Samuel Lander in 1878. His daughter wrote that the honor seemed to oppress his "modest soul"; he considered himself unworthy on the grounds that he knew only Greek and not the language of the Old Testament. He took up the study of Hebrew at once and made it a rule thereafter to read portions of the Old and New Testaments daily in their original languages. Concerning her father's study of languages, daughter Kathleen Willson commented: "He gratified his love of language by studying, without a teacher, German, French, Spanish, and Italian until he could read these languages, though he never attempted to speak them." Lander began studying Portuguese in 1889 when his son John went to Brazil as a missionary, and he took up the study of the ancient Irish language only three years before his death.

No sketch of Samuel Lander would be complete without a discussion of his educational philosophy. An anonymous chronicler, who signed herself "One of his many loving 'daughters'" and who was probably one of his biological daughters as well, wrote that an adequate conception of his educational ideas depended upon understanding his character as a man. She added that his most pronounced characteristic, next to his quiet modesty, was a fearless love of truth. In a nice turn of phrase, she wrote that no pupil ever had as a teacher a more exhaustive student, that "whenever a subject came up for his consideration he was tireless in his efforts to learn all that human research had discovered, not content till every possible avenue of information had been critically searched, till he had ferretted [sic] out the primal, basal facts in the case." Although his teaching career had spanned nearly twenty years by the time he founded Williamston Female College, it was there Lander found himself for the first time sufficiently untrammeled to carry out many of his original ideas regarding education. The writer believed the Williamston years produced "the ripest and most permanent results of his life."

Every source stressed Lander's emphasis on thoroughness and accuracy in study, preparation, and recitation, and one also noted his conviction that study must be *intensive* before it can be *extensive*. An unvarying rule in Lander's schools was that a student could not advance in any study before she had mastered it. One wonders what he would make of the modern concept of "social promotion." Lander had adopted as his own the motto of his native state, *Esse quam videri* (to be rather than to seem); the motto was displayed conspicuously in the study hall.

Certainly Samuel Lander's reputation was made well before he and Waller began negotiating the move to Greenwood. Williamston Female College had been a fixture in the village of Williamston for more than thirty years. It had undergone a number of changes during that time, including joint stock company ownership of the hotel/school building and some additions to the plant, as well as receiving a charter issued by the county. Lander had tried repeatedly since 1872 to turn the school over to the Methodist Conference in an attempt to secure its future. Offers were made and rejected in 1886, 1889, and 1890; conditional acceptance came in 1898. The only problems were space and money. It had become evident that the village of Williamston, which was never again to enjoy the prominence it held for a brief period before the war as the "Saratoga of the State," simply lacked the resources to provide a new and larger physical plant. There was no financial backing and no room to expand even if resources had been available. Such were the circumstances when the offer came. Willson wrote simply that the "city of Greenwood, South Carolina, offered a site and suitable building if it [the college] would remove to that town. Enlargement at Williamston was impossible; so the offer . . . was accepted gratefully, though with no little reluctance at the prospect of leaving its first home. Dr. Lander felt that the move to Greenwood would put on a permanent foundation the College to which he had given the best of his life."

Greenwood's offer met Lander's needs so admirably that one imagines few snags in the negotiations that followed. In fact, the *Greenwood Index* ran an announcement in its issue of January 8, 1903:

> The Index is in possession of some valuable information. As the immortal Greeley used to say, "its [sic] mighty interesting reading." Everybody knows how a college has been talked about, how the people have been worked up over the effort to get a college here and The Index is greatly pleased to be able to say that the efforts of the committee have not been in vain. The Williamston Female College is to be moved to Greenwood. This decision was reached yesterday. Nine tenths of the trustees of that institution decided to move it here. A vote of the students of the college resulted in over seventy-five per cent agreeing to come to Greenwood. There are at present one hundred and five boarders in the college.
>
> The Williamston Female college is said to possess the most extensive and valuable equipment of any female college in the

> State, Winthrop alone possible [sic] excepted. The college has about five thousand dollars worth of apparatus. All of this, the furniture, pianos, etc, etc, will be moved here. The building will be furnished by Greenwood. Dr. Lander, the well known president of the college will subscribe liberally to the fund. He will have charge of the school. He will also keep the buildings in repair and run the college. If he should leave the college, the property will be tendered to the Methodist conference, and that great body will not allow so splendid a gift to pass. The college is a certainty.

An editorial from the same issue is included here, more for its ebullience than for any new information and as an example of a journalistic style no longer in vogue:

> As told in The Index this morning Greenwood is to have a college. This much is settled. The Williamston Female College is to be moved here. . . . Greenwood has the opportunity of a life time. Let us make it count. Let us show to the world more of the pluck that has made Greenwood famous. We give an instance of it in the successful effort to get a college. We tried to get the Columbia Female College but had to fight against unsurmountable obstacles. Other communities might have lapsed into indifference, but not so with Greenwood. Our fighting blood was up. Our war horses were on their mettle, and their labors were not diminished one whit, but simply turned into another channel. And now they have accomplished their end. They have given us a college. Which same is pleasing to us. Let us show our pleasure and our appreciation by holding up their hands. Stand by Mr. Waller and the committee. Help them in the Greenwood way to show the State that Greenwood NEVER FAILS when she sets out to do a thing.

Several prominent citizens were associated with Waller in the grand design to bring a college to Greenwood. The members of the committee who prepared the nine-page proposal to the trustees of Columbia College in 1902 were: J. L. Andrews, R. P. Blake, R. A. Childs, D. C. DuPre, J. K. Durst, R. B. Epting, S. F. Evans, F. B. Grier, George C. Hodges, J. B. Park, A. Rosenberg, J. T. Simmons, C. A. C. Waller, Chairman, and J. B. Wharton, Secretary. Presumably, though not indisputably, the same group continued the effort after the Columbia proposal fell through; the names of the directors of the fund to build the female college were reported in the April 16, 1903, issue of the *Greenwood Index*. The second group was only half as large, and most were carryovers from the original committee. Perhaps the intention was a smaller group for the more concentrated effort of raising funds – a more lean and mean team, as it were. The final directors were: J. L. Andrews, R. P. Blake, Dr. R. B. Epting, R. M. Hays, Dr. Samuel Lander, J. T. Medlock, Mayor J. B. Park, A. Rosenberg, and C. A. C. Waller. Only Hays, Lander, and Medlock were new names.

The town had promised a site of not less than fifteen acres and a modern building to accommodate at least 100 students at a cost of no less than $25,000. Lander himself was to select the site from among several possibilities. The actual acquisition was 12.3 acres of the H. B. Reynolds property, plus an additional six acres purchased from John A. Barksdale, and the sum of $38,500 had already been subscribed by April 1903. Waller was recognized for his efforts in a resolution worded as follows: "Whereas: Our fellow citizen, the Hon. C. A. C. Waller has been untiring in his efforts to raise a sum of money which guarantees us a female college second to none – Be it resolved: that we accord to him more than all the others the praise, extend him our heartfelt congratulations and thanks without reserve."

The record of property transfers about this time would be incomplete without mention of the purchase by "S. Lander & Son" of a 45.6 acre tract of land adjoining the college property. Lander evidently formed a company with his son William Tertius and bought property in the name of S. Lander & Son from the same John A. Barksdale who sold six acres to the Williamston Female College of Greenwood Corporation. The purchase price was $2,736, and the deed was dated January 4, 1904. This farm appeared again in property transfers after Samuel Lander's death and eventually became part of the college property.

The actual method of fundraising was described in a 1950 master's thesis, *Lander College and Doctor Samuel Lander*, by Faye Tucker Bryant: a corporation was formed and shares sold at par value of $50, "each payable one fourth in cash and the balance by notes of the subscribers in three equal installments without interest until after maturity." The first charter of Williamston Female College of Greenwood, South Carolina, a Corporation, was dated April 23, 1903.

The newspaper faithfully recorded the progress of the enterprise practically month by month as the summer of 1903 wore on. These articles are merely sketched here but should be read in their entirety for a complete picture of the project. The super enthusiastic tone grows somewhat repetitive after awhile, but one purpose of the articles was obviously to remind Greenwood citizens of just what they had undertaken. One line from an August 6 article entitled "Our College" was particularly revealing in this regard: "The magnitude of the undertaking we have imposed upon ourselves is not generally understood. It is proposed to build a female college the equal of any and the work is to be done by Greenwood, town and county. It is a big work, but a great one in a larger sense. Now is the time for concerted action and when applied never let it be withdrawn." Most of the article concerned Waller's appeal for all amounts due on the first subscription to be paid at once, since brick-making at the rate of 50,000 per day had been underway for a month at that point.

The same 1903 article cleared up a point somehow overlooked in researching the history of Old Main Building many years later. In a conversation with the author in June 1989, President Larry Jackson stated that one architect believed the building had a foundation of granite slabs, which probably accounted for the fact that the exterior brick walls had no cracks, even after 85 years. A line in the article reads, "His [Waller's] idea is to have the *rock foundation work* completed by December the first and is pushing everything to that end" (emphasis added). The foundation is indeed rock, and that rock almost undoubtedly granite.

Once again the architect was given short shrift in the articles, but at least Reuben Harrison Hunt's name was mentioned, and he was credited with both the courthouse and the Presbyterian Church. Magnolia School was a Hunt building also, but that commission must have come a few months later since the building Magnolia replaced burned at some point in 1903. The newspaper reported that Hunt was quite experienced in designing school buildings and "knows exactly what is wanted here." Also, an April article describing the college site reported that a landscape artist had been contacted to insure "college grounds that will not be surpassed in the state."

An impressive groundbreaking ceremony took place on August 27, 1903, and was covered in detail in the newspaper a week later. One very special touch was that the "footprint" of the building was marked off by chalk lines, and the main ceremonies took place within these lines. Crowds of people, many of whom had never visited the site, began gathering well before the scheduled hour. The site had been described earlier as a plowed field so far on the edge of town that most residents thought of the new college as "out in the country." On groundbreaking day, however, Greenwood people and others seemed to view the incipient campus in more positive terms. The newspaper noted its "beauty and elegance" and went on to affirm that "the general, in fact universal, opinion is that it would be hard to find a site more admirable in all particulars. It is central, high above the surrounding country and one that with but little cost can be made beautiful in the hands of an expert landscape gardener." That particular landscape "artist" or "gardener" was never employed – Mrs. Lander and her son William Tertius Lander undertook the task – and most people would probably agree that the Lander College grounds grew ever more beautiful over the years with imaginative and unusual plantings of great variety. Professor Shelton E. Stewart, whose tenure dates from the late 1950s, documented the flora of the Lander campus in a small publication entitled *Trees of the Lander College Campus* in 1972.

The groundbreaking ceremony was hardly under way when a messenger boy arrived with a telegram from the citizens of Williamston. The message it contained – "We congratulate you on this great occasion.

Build wisely and well" – was greeted with cheers and applause. The speaker for the occasion was Professor W. P. Hood who had taught for many years at Erskine College. Hood struck exactly the right note when he "showed with emphasis the most convincing argument to be used in soliciting money; showed how it [the college] saved money for those in the town and how the coming to the town of students from other sections would bring other money into circulation." Dr. Lander's concluding remarks were romantic rather than economic: he noted that the cornerstone at Williamston had been laid on the same date exactly thirty years before. In a final touch of sentiment, Lander and the oldest alumna of Williamston Female College, Ella Calhoun Turner of Ninety Six, turned up the first spade of earth in a symbolic gesture of launching the college in its new home.

The first physical description of the building to result from Reuben Harrison Hunt's design appeared in the newspaper story of the groundbreaking. "Located on the highest point on the site . . . [facing] a broad avenue leading down to Calhoun Avenue," the completed building would be 240 feet long and would contain "one of the largest auditoriums in this part of the state," as well as "every modern convenience." It was sure to compare with any in the state. In a paragraph long on faith but somewhat short on prophecy, readers were also assured:

> It is not intended that Greenwood shall manage this college after it is built. All that Greenwood wants to do is have it built, and have that done properly. That done she will be perfectly satisfied to leave the management of the college to that most excellent man, Dr. Samuel Lander, and may his life be spared for many years to preside over their college is the wish of the people of Greenwood.

The actual construction of the building on its rock foundation required about a year. The bricks were made on the college property; the contractor, T. J. Hannon, finished the brick-making on schedule before the end of October. The general contractor, George W. Buchanan, was credited with "shoving things along in great shape" in a June 16, 1904, article entitled "Brick Work Finished." But there had been yet another red letter day about a month earlier when not one, but two, cornerstones were laid in the tower walls with full Masonic ritual. The program for that high noon ceremony listed fifteen separate items, including four hymns and three Masonic odes, to accompany the laying of the new cornerstone. Children from both the Greenwood graded school and Connie Maxwell Orphanage were featured on the program, as well as the entire student body of Williamston Female College, who had arrived, together with the faculty, on a special train from Williamston earlier that morning. The newspaper of May 12, 1904, reported the attendance of Masons representing Abbeville, Laurens, Newberry, Prosperity, Honea Path, Donalds, Williamston, and Ninety Six, as well as a large contingent from Greenwood.

Following the main address by United States Senator A. C. Latimer, Dr. Lander laid the old cornerstone from Williamston which had been placed in 1873 by Grand Master Frank Connor of Cokesbury. An extant photograph captures the moment when a frail-looking gentleman in black suit and hat guided the stone, secured by ropes and pulleys, into its prepared niche. That moment must have been poignant indeed for Lander; the newspaper recorded that he was "visibly affected" as he placed the stone and "stated the facts connected with its being laid in the walls of the old college." The new stone was then laid in accordance with Masonic ritual by Deputy Grand Master F. E. Harrison of Abbeville. The newspaper reported that hundreds of people attended the ceremony.

Even as the walls of his college rose on the site of his own choosing in Greenwood, Lander's health steadily declined. He died at his home in Williamston on July 14, 1904, at the age of 71. There was universal sorrow in Greenwood at the news of the death of this "excellent man" who had personified the college in the minds of many since that day about a year and a half earlier when they learned of the success of the relocation project. Tributes to Lander's life and career were many, from a newspaper headline calling his death a "loss to the state" all the way to personal recollections of family members, friends, and colleagues. A number of these reminiscences found their way into college publications.

An address on Samuel Lander's methods as an educator by Dr. Henry Nelson Snyder, President of Wofford College, was reprinted in the 1906-07 catalog. Snyder's speech is a lovely example of the high-flown oratory of the day, and it contains one priceless paragraph on the education of women. Many women will be highly offended, but they will forgive Snyder's excesses when they remember the address was delivered about fifteen years before women were allowed to vote:

> Many sins have been committed in the name of education as well as of liberty – particularly in the matter of female education. Superficial show, shallow shams, bedizened and bedecked pretence, the cheap tawdriness and glittering tinsel of brassy decoration, have been too often the glaring characteristics of what the so-called female college stands for. A loud-mouth profession of even university standards and methods have [sic] been permitted to cover up flabby and loose, not to say consciously dishonest, work. The dazzling glare of exhibitions of parrot-like music and elocution, lurid splashes of color under the name of art, the beguiling presence of pretty faces and white dresses, ribbons and laces, have had the charm of confusing the unthinking public as to the utter hollowness of it all. Now against this sort of thing in the education of women the spirit of your founder was at perpetual war. Him the showy ornamentation, the thin gilding that wore off at the first touch of real life, never seduced. It seems to me that, if

> his gentle nature hated anything, it was these things – sham and show and the tinkling brass and sounding cymbal of educational pretence. Perhaps this quality of his character, his unmitigated honesty, led him too far in the other direction – led him to make of his institution something too severely simple and private, withholding from the public those occasional presentations of its work we call commencements. Still, if he was erring, it was in the right direction. He was but showing in an emphatic, not to say exaggerated, way that deep general honesty of his that gave an unmistakable value to his educational results. And this element in his character we do well to preserve in all the work of the institution which bears his name. We may get along without some things; but this we cannot do without, and whatever we have or have not, this is within our reach.

Fortunately for him, Snyder managed to redeem himself before the end of his speech. His final paragraph paid tribute to Lander's influence in developing women who were at the same time scholarly, independent, and good. Most Lander women should be able to accept that accolade in good spirit.

But all the tributes in the world would not answer the question of who would assume the office of president at this most critical point of the college's life. Discussing the transition from the first administration to the second is not a simple matter, and no documentary evidence to explain the choice of John O. Willson as his father-in-law's successor seems to exist. The falling-of-the-mantle-on-his-shoulders idea or other sentimental notions simply will not do; it is necessary to look further, and the Methodist question arises once again at this juncture. Williamston Female College had received conditional acceptance by the South Carolina Conference in 1898. Later editions of the Lander catalog made no mention of the word *conditional* and stated simply, "In 1898 the institution became a part of the educational work of the South Carolina Conference." One clue to the conditions attached to the college's Methodist standing appeared in Faye Tucker Bryant's master's thesis. Citing the *Southern Christian Advocate* for February 8, 1912, Bryant stated that financial support had not been part of the original acceptance in 1898. The actual wording of the report of the Board of Education, which was accepted by the conference, showed that the Methodists got quite a good deal. For example, the conference was allowed to choose five of the nine directors, or trustees, and it required free tuition for "daughters of clerical members of the Conference," as well as "all other benefits now furnished by a Conference institution." All this was to be provided with "no pecuniary liability" to the conference. Conditional acceptance it most certainly was, and the difference in the conference's attitude toward Wofford, Columbia College, and Williamston could not have been more marked, as shown in the conference minutes at the time. The conference appealed "to its friends for their most active support" for Wofford and noted "It is necessary that our people be appealed to very earnestly in behalf of this [Columbia] College." On the other hand, regarding Williamston Female College, the minutes stated merely: "By the action of this Conference the above College is put under our control. This institution has done a noble work for the cause of female education in our State. We cordially recommend it to our people."

The college at Greenwood was again offered to the Methodist Conference in 1903 "on the sole condition that it should be used and maintained as a first-class college." The conference accepted the offer, provided all debt was paid within two years. The Lander College Catalog for 1905-06 supports these statements, except for the date which is given as December 1904. The catalog for the next year settles the question entirely by spelling out the preamble and resolution adopted at the South Carolina Methodist Conference of 1906:

> in December, 1904, the property occupied by Lander College . . . was tendered to this body and was accepted on condition that the debt due on same be paid in two years;
>
> And, whereas, the time for said payments has nearly expired, and the debt, while largely reduced, has not been paid in full,
>
> And, whereas, the value of said property is at market price at least five times the remaining amount due,
>
> *Resolved*, That this Conference hereby accept the property . . . with its unpaid balance of debt. . . .

Thus it was that the college became finally a full-fledged Methodist Conference School. Its acquisition added some $50,000 to the value of college property owned by the conference, according to the minutes. Another source, the *Handbook of South Carolina: Resources, Institutions, and Industries of the State* (1907 edition) placed the value at $60,000.

It is surely reasonable to assume that negotiations between Samuel Lander and the Methodist Conference were in progress at the time of Lander's death. He had been no stranger to the workings of the Methodist hierarchy; his daughter called his conference work "unstinted and multiform." He had served over the years on many important committees and had been re-elected annually "for a great many years" as statistical secretary in tribute to his "painstaking accuracy." He had also served as secretary-treasurer of the benevolent organization known as the Brotherhood from its beginning in 1885 until his death.

Although there is no outright evidence that Samuel Lander was ever at loggerheads with the Methodist leadership over his philosophy of education or his teaching methods, now and then a cryptic comment appears among the accolades. For example, his daughter Kathleen believed there was "slight derision" in his being called an innovator even though he was two generations ahead of his time pedagogically. Further, no one had ever heard of anything like the plan of concentrated study he worked out in an effort to secure more accurate scholarship. It is clear from the record that he discussed this unique method with teacher-friends and others before introducing it at Williamston. Surely those "others" must have included Methodist clergymen-educators who were well versed in the "educational evangelism" that had been part of the denomination since its inception. According to Lander's daughter, "All advised strongly against taking such a radical step and prophesied dismal failure and financial ruin." A fuller discussion of this point appeared in a reminiscence of Samuel Lander written by his son John for the ninth Founder's Day and reprinted in *The Erothesian* for February 1913. Besides describing his father as quite different from the meek and gentle, even saint-like, figure who comes across in other reminiscences, John Lander related the circumstances of one discussion of the concentrated study plan between Lander and a Methodist bishop:

> I well recall a long conversation that he had with Bishop Wightman. The occasion was a district conference (if I am not mistaken) over which the bishop was presiding. They were seated on the front porch, overlooking the quiet shades of the Spring Park. My father presented the matter, developed his arguments, and showed his reasons for the change from the old, time-honored, universal method of carrying on the college course, and for the adoption of his newly-discovered (or newly invented) plan.
>
> The bishop was not in favor of the innovation. He counseled moderation in going counter to long established usages, and well received methods. He thought that the new system proposed by my father might prove a failure and bring financial embarrassment and that it were better to "let well enough alone." Why fly in the face of all past authority and custom? So thought the noble bishop, and so advised the wise authority in the Church.
>
> But the reasons were sufficient to my father's mind, the arguments were convincing to his judgment; he had the "courage of his convictions," and published his new catalogue with the announcement of the "One Study Plan."

The fact that Lander went ahead to introduce the plan, regardless of what others – even the bishop – thought, was the act of a man confident he knew what he was doing and why he was doing it. Lander's own words support this view: while he admitted to "a few real objections" to the plan, he also wrote, "we are perfectly satisfied that we have a plan more consistent with common sense and more promising of good results than the one in general use." In short, Samuel Lander just might have been quite a maverick in his day. The "wise authority in the Church" was evidently not his first consideration where teaching young women was concerned.

An examination of the Methodist question sets the stage for a look at the choice of John O. Willson as the second president of Lander College. All sources appeared to take the position that he was the natural choice, and certainly nothing to his detriment has been found; nevertheless, it is impossible not to wonder why none of Samuel Lander's sons, of whom there were seven to reach adulthood, was chosen to carry on his father's work. The youngest, Ernest, was 27 in 1904, and the oldest, John, was 46. Five others, ranging from 32 to 43 years of age, were in between. Considering the sort of man Samuel Lander was and the sort of family from which he came, surely most, if not all, of these sons were educated and trained in their father's philosophy and methods. As a matter of fact, at least two – William Tertius and John McPherson – had been members of the faculty and helped to manage the school.

Sallie Thompson Hall Lander (1862-1951), who married Lander's oldest son John in 1886, wrote in a letter to her children dated January 16, 1941:

> As he [John Lander] was then [1886] a professor in his father's college I returned to be a teacher in my first Alma Mater [Williamston Female College]. We were very happy there for three and a half years. Then we went to Brazil.
>
> Your father as a young boy always studied in his father's schools, first in Spartanburg and then in Williamston. He graduated as valedictorian at Wofford College in 1879. After that he went to Vanderbilt University. As he planned to be a medical missionary to China, he took the theological and medical courses at the same time. But your grandfather *felt that he needed the help of his own sons;* so your Father and your Uncle Tertius became professors and partners in the Williamston Female College [emphasis added].
>
> In the spring of 1889 your Father was surprised at receiving a letter from Bishop Granbery. He was just back from inspecting the mission to Brazil and full of the idea that there was great need of a school where Brazilian boys might be trained for the ministry. The Bishop asked your Father to go to Juiz de Fora, Minas Geraes, to establish a school. This proposition was favorably received. I'm not sure why, but your grandfather, who had opposed the idea of his son being a medical missionary to China, was enthusiastic over the prospect of founding a school in Brazil. It may have been because your grandfather, while a successful minister and a Doctor of Divinity, was at heart a most devoted teacher. . . .

From this evidence it would appear that Lander was able to work amiably with his sons; indeed, he had sought their help. There is absolutely nothing in any of Mrs. Lander's letters to her children, of which there are four dating from 1941 to 1947, indicating chagrin when Willson was named president. John Lander, in fact, was following in his father's footsteps in a unique way when he founded Granbery College in Brazil and may have had no interest whatever in events at Greenwood. But what of the other son most closely associated with his father's college, William Tertius Lander? Or, for that matter, Angus, Neil, Malcolm, Frank, or Ernest? There are no answers to this question. Dr. Ernest Lander, former Clemson professor, noted historian, and grandson of Samuel Lander, cannot remember that this point ever came up in family gatherings. He stated, however, that his cousin William Hall Lander, youngest son of John and Sallie Hall Lander, always thought his father would have been chosen if he had not been occupied in Brazil at the time.

In this context it is important to look for a moment at Mrs. John O. Willson, nee Kathleen McPherson, seventh child and third daughter of Samuel and Laura Lander (their first child was a daughter, Lily, who died just before her second birthday). Kathleen Lander had four older brothers when she became the second wife of John Owens Willson, who was himself 23 years her senior. Discussing Kathleen Lander Willson is particularly difficult since she became the major chronicler of her father's life and career in the years after his death. She wrote for family circulation a 20-page booklet entitled *A Pioneer/S. Lander/His Educational Ideas and His Life/March 1945,* as well as a 10-page article entitled "Samuel Lander, Educational Pioneer," printed in *The Southern Association Quarterly* for August of the same year. No one knows who actually wrote the text for the little book *The Story of Lander,* a fiftieth birthday sketch of the college dated February 12, 1922, and presented simply as the work of "the collaborators." The description of Kathleen Willson in that book is particularly interesting:

> No one else knew so well nor so heartily sympathized with the ideals and the aims of Dr. and Mrs. Lander; in no child of theirs are blended so perfectly the characteristics of both as in their daughter, Mrs. John O. Willson. She has the graciousness of her mother, the strength of her father, the devotion of both. Through these marvelous years of change, of progress, she has stood like a rock for the finest things but has shown a nice discrimination that welcomes changes in method, which our changing times demand. . . .
>
> Through these seventeen years she has been a tower of strength to her husband, who has planned and accomplished such large things for Lander College.

The most suspicious line, if one were inclined to suspicion, is found earlier in the same book, as well as in the catalog for 1925-26, after Willson's death: ". . . his [Samuel Lander's] mantle fell on his son-in-law,

Dr. John O. Willson, *the one fitted to carry out better than he himself could have done,* his lofty ideals" (emphasis added). This is a strong statement indeed and one that requires some sort of justification. There is really very little from such college records that exist, and it is necessary to turn to other sources even for an adequate biography of this gentleman. Fortunately, many books and records documenting the history of Methodism in South Carolina exist, as well as any number of biographical sketches of early ministers. Information on Willson was drawn primarily from two of these works: *Twentieth Century Sketches of the South Carolina Conference, Methodist Episcopal Church, South,* by Watson B. Duncan (1901) and *Men of Mark in South Carolina, Vol. II,* edited by J. C. Hemphill (1908).

John Owens Willson (1845-1923) was born in St. James Parish, Charleston District (now Goose Creek, Berkeley County). His father was a planter and physician, as well as a member of the General Assembly for many years. Young John grew up on a cotton plantation where he was encouraged to "engage in outdoor exercises, but not to labor on the farm." He was educated in neighborhood schools, King's Mountain Military Academy, the Arsenal, and the South Carolina Military Academy (The Citadel). Willson was a member of the junior class when he left school in 1862 to join the Confederate Army, where he served as a private in cavalry regiments for three years. After the war he read law and was admitted to the bar in 1866, finally locating in Marion. He was "under strong religious conviction" from about 1868, a conviction that persisted until he was converted, licensed to preach, and received by the South Carolina Methodist Conference in 1873. Pastorates in Darlington, Camden, Greenville, Charleston, and Florence followed until 1894 when he became editor of the *Southern Christian Advocate,* a post he held for seven years. Wofford College awarded him the Doctor of Divinity degree in 1896. There is no record that he ever taught school except "for a few months before choosing a new location" in 1868. He was married in 1871 to Mary O. Richardson, who lived less than two years after the marriage. There was one daughter.

In 1896 when he had been a widower for more than twenty years, Willson married Kathleen McPherson Lander. He was 51; she was 28. Their honeymoon was a four-month tour of Europe, Egypt, and the Holy Land. When Samuel Lander died eight years later, Willson was presiding elder of the Cokesbury District. He was called "a man of scholarly attainments, with outstanding executive and financial ability and unusual tact in knowing how to handle people." The "scholarly attainments" were not described. According to his official biography he never aspired to be known as a "modern thinker" or a "critical preacher" but was satisfied "to carry the simple Gospel to the people." He was considered "wise and discreet" in his management of the *Southern Christian*

Advocate and kept that publication "ever . . . true to the institutions of the Church."

This is a portrait of an extremely orthodox man. The differences between Samuel Lander and John O. Willson, except for their common standing as Methodist ministers, could not be more marked. As for Lander's sons, three were mentioned in an entry in the *Cyclopedia of Eminent and Representative Men of the Carolinas of the Nineteenth Century:*

> Dr. Lander . . . [has] nine children living, seven of whom are sons. Three of the sons have graduated from Wofford College: and two of these delivered the valedictory addresses. The eldest, Rev. John McPherson Lander, is principal of the American Granbery College, in Juiz de Fora, Brazil. The second son, William Tertius Lander, is associated with his father, in the Williamston female college. Another son, Malcom [sic] McPherson Lander, is principal of the Kingstree academy, S. C.

The fact that there was no dearth of direct male descendants of Samuel Lander, at least three of whom were qualified scholastically and two of whom had actually worked with their father, is indisputable. The choice of John Willson almost had to be the result of the association of the college with the Methodist Conference, perhaps with a little help from Mrs. Willson who, according to one source, "had been carefully trained as an assistant to her father." But Kathleen Willson gave this credit to her older sister Martha when she wrote that her father "lived before the days of private secretaries and president's assistants, his only helper being his eldest daughter." Martha Lander married in 1878; after that Kathleen noted that Lander himself "conducted all his correspondence, did all the bookkeeping, made out all the reports, and usually taught two or three classes." The preeminence of the Methodist association also accounts for the emphasis in *A Brief History of the Lander Family* (1918) on the first Samuel Lander as "a patriarch of Methodist preachers." This history was written by William Lander Sherrill, yet another member of the ministerial fraternity, who noted that at least nine members of the family, by immediate descent or marriage, were Methodist preachers at that time.

Whether there were negotiations behind the scenes during the scant two weeks between July 14, the day Lander died, and July 26, the day the board named Willson as his successor, we will never know. We do know, however, that "by request of all parties concerned, the Conference of 1904 authorized the change of name from Williamston Female College to Lander College, in honor of Dr. Lander, and the old college under its new name was duly incorporated by the General Assembly of our State in February, 1905." This Act was reproduced in several catalogs and deserves its own place in this narrative:

AN ACT to Amend the Charter of Incorporation of Williamston Female College of Greenwood, South Carolina, so as to Change the Name Thereof to Lander College, and so as to Authorize Said College to Confer Degrees.

SECTION 1. *Be it enacted* by the General Assembly of the State of South Carolina (a Concurrent Resolution granting leave for the introduction of this Bill first having been adopted by the General Assembly by a two-thirds vote of each House), That the charter of incorporation of Williamston Female College, of Greenwood, South Carolina, is hereby amended so as to change the name of said college to Lander College, and the rights, powers and property belonging to Williamston Female College, of Greenwood, South Carolina, are hereby conferred upon Lander College as fully as if the name thereof had not been changed, and all the duties and responsibilities of this college under its former name shall attach to Lander College.

SECTION 2. That Lander College is hereby authorized and empowered, through its Board of Trustees, on recommendation of its Faculty, to confer the usual literary degrees.

SECTION 3. That this Act shall take effect on and immediately after its approval by the Governor, and it shall be deemed a public Act; and all inconsistent Acts and parts of Acts are hereby repealed.

Approved the 21st day of February, A. D. 1905.

A search of the *Minutes* of the 1904 Conference turned up another tiny, but significant, point. It appears the original Greenwood committee had determined, *as early as January 1903,* that the name of the college should be changed at the time of the move to Greenwood. This conclusion is based on the description of two attachments accompanying the written offer of the college property to the conference. One was an extract of the original agreement between Greenwood and the board of trustees of Williamston Female College. The last item of that agreement as printed in the minutes reads: *"By unanimous resolution of the committee on January 14, 1903, we ask the name to be 'Lander College'"* (emphasis added). Typically, Greenwood citizens had anticipated by more than two years the name the college was destined to bear.

The pressure for more dormitory space began almost immediately after Willson took office, even before the debt mentioned in the conference resolution of 1906 was fully liquidated, and the purchase of five acres in front of the college further increased the debt. The conference resolution also contained a line empowering the board of trustees "to take steps necessary to raise money to pay the indebtedness. . . ." The trustees authorized Willson to take on this task "according to his convenience and judgment," but the new president's priorities were centered elsewhere as indicated in a statement from the 1908-09 catalog:

> The pressure of other duties only permitted the President to visit a few places. The liberality of friends called upon, assured the ultimate success of this effort, but the urgent need of an additional dormitory became so manifest that it was decided to concentrate our endeavors on this enterprise. The Trustees asked authority of Conference to prosecute this new building canvass, and that body granted the request in November last. This is our supreme need and effort today.

The proposed new dormitory was designed to "complete the original plan of our building," and a drawing printed in the 1908-09 catalog shows another wing duplicating Laura Lander Hall attached *to the east end of Greenwood Hall* by means of a connector identical to the one already in place. This addition, had it been built as planned, would have resulted in a so-called "five-part Palladian" structure named for the sixteenth century Italian architect Andrea Palladio. The published drawing depicts a building of striking symmetry with the bell tower as the central focus. The inescapable assumption is that the plan was meant to complete R. H. Hunt's original design, only part of which was carried out because of funding constraints in 1903. No one knows why that particular plan did not materialize; it was evidently abandoned at some point between 1908 and early in 1911. Newspaper accounts named five members of the board of trustees, plus President Willson, as the building committee appointed in 1911 "for the express purpose of building the new dormitory which is so greatly needed at Lander College." Willson announced that architect's plans and estimates would be received on March 22 and estimated the building's cost at $30,000. The board, or perhaps Willson, had evidently reconsidered the location and design of the new dormitory during the year between two successive college catalogs: the 39th year edition indicated one design, and the 40th described the construction of an entirely different building in a different location. The newspaper reported the building would be "added to the southern [sic] end of the present building" and would accommodate some eighty boarders. It would be "even handsomer and more comfortable than our first College home."

This time the board looked no further for an architect than "just adjourning [adjoining] the College campus." The newspaper of April 16, 1911, announced the choice of T. W. Cothran of Greenwood as architect. Thomas White Cothran was indeed an architect, probably Greenwood's finest, and also a construction engineer for railroads. He had graduated from Clemson as a member of its first class in 1896; the Lander College commission came during the height of a prolific career in

Greenwood. Cothran's home still stands on Blake Street, and a bridge over the Saluda River perpetuates his name. Cothran's design, while destroying Hunt's elegant symmetry, echoed many features of the original building, including paired windows with granite ledges, fanlight windows in gables, and a veranda matching the one fronting Laura Lander Hall. It also contained living quarters for teachers and the president's family, a feature that recalled earlier times in Williamston when college life was a great deal like family life.

Bids for construction were accepted in the early summer of 1911. Two Greenwood firms, as well as one each from Athens, Raleigh, and Rock Hill, submitted bids. Low bidder was the Rock Hill firm of J. J. Keller & Company at $25,024 (the highest bid, $28,476, came from one of the Greenwood firms, J. Grandy). The heating and plumbing contract went to Greenwood Hardware Company for $4,850. Although the building was three stories high with a full basement, it was substantially completed in less than four months. The newspaper reported that about thirty of its dormitory rooms were ready for occupancy by the time school opened in September.

With the new wing in place the physical plant of the college was considered complete by the opening of the 1911-1912 school year. There would be no more construction for more than ten years, and the campus would not grow beyond its 23-acre size until 1929. The added dormitory space meant that boarding student capacity had nearly doubled; it was important simply to grow in enrollment and trust that the Methodist connection would take care of a rather unfortunate degree of indebtedness. Conference minutes of 1911 showed that the construction of Willson Hall added another $15,000 to that figure. The catalog for 1911-1912 announced for the first time the names of the various sections of the building: "The Administration building, which contains the Auditorium, 'Waller Hall,' has been named GREENWOOD HALL, the first dormitory is called LAURA LANDER HALL, and the new dormitory is WILLSON HALL."

The decision to name Lander's first building by sections, including a section-within-a-section, was probably partly a result of the architect's original design and partly a certain zealousness to honor Greenwood and selected individuals, including a sitting president. Whatever the reasons, Lander's Old Main Building became one structure with four separate names applied to its parts, a situation that was bound to cause confusion at some point. Many people, for example, believe that Old Main will be preserved and restored in the $14 million science building project recently approved for state funding, when in reality only Greenwood Hall will remain. Both Laura Lander Hall and Willson Hall, Greenwood landmarks for 88 and 81 years respectively, will be destroyed.

Even after the building reached its final configuration, much remained to be done to beautify the campus which had been a combination cotton field/briar patch only a few years earlier. Kathleen Lander Willson wrote a little article, "The Plants of the Lander Campus," during the Speake administration (1932-1941) which was published in *The Index-Journal* of September 22, 1937, and used as the basis of Dr. Shelton Stewart's later work. The article suggested that the grounds no less than the original building were stamped from the first with the Lander family imprint. Willson provided her father's rationale for choosing the site over others where trees were already established in a statement he supposedly made to the committee: "Gentlemen, . . . we must find a lot within easy walking distance of the churches and the shopping district. This one is convenient but bare. We can have trees in a few years." As for the suggestion that a landscape architect be employed to plan and plant the campus, Mrs. Lander scorned such indulgence, insisting that the family was perfectly capable of doing the work using native trees and shrubs; the fact that there was really no money for such luxuries was apparently a secondary, albeit practical, concern.

The first plants came from Williamston. Willson wrote that Dr. Lander (presumably her brother Tertius and not Samuel) kept an old trunk which went along every time anyone went to Williamston and came back filled with plants and cuttings for propagation in a special bed until places could be prepared to receive them. She also related that the leftover bricks, which the Greenwood committee hoped to sell, were stacked in an ugly pile near the building for more than a year. After the bricks were moved and neatly stacked near the sidewalk, courtesy of the industrious Landers, they attracted a buyer and sold within two weeks.

There were, of course, mistakes. One turned out to be the mixed hedge of privet and mock orange, which Willson stated "grew phenomenally" and which had to be removed many years later. Others were trees that "refused to live" in the climate, such as eucalyptus and pepper trees sent from California, camphor, palmetto, ginkgo, and redwood burl trees. But there were many more successes; for example, the campus boasted many highly unusual trees such as live oak, cypress, Norway maples, long leaf pine, and mahogany. Local citizens gave trees and shrubs from the first, a tradition that continues to the present time. Willson credited Chris Waller, William Bailey, Belle Yoe, and R. B. Epting for such donations. The Chinaberry trees planted by Waller and Bailey later gave way to Mrs. Bruce Barksdale's dogwoods which still line the driveway. Many friends and alumnae from other parts of the country also contributed. Most Lander people from earlier days remember the Lady Banksia roses and wisteria vines that climbed around the verandas, as well as the huge deodar cedar which still towers over the fountain circle. There were also several varieties of ivy, one of which came from Mount Vernon.

A plot behind Willson Hall, which in Kathleen Willson's day had been one of the barest and least fertile locations on campus, became the "newest beauty spot" after President Speake's wife created a special garden in memory of Laura Lander. Stewart described this spot in 1972 as outlined with two willow oaks, a sweet gum and a red bud, plus a shoe-shaped fish and lily pond, all of which provided an impressive setting for roses, spring-flowering bulbs, and other plants. He credited Dr. L. C. Glenn of Vanderbilt with contributing the irises and described the purple wisteria that twined in the willow oak by the pool. The crowning touch was a sundial placed in the center. The care and maintenance of small plots such as Mrs. Speake's garden was undertaken by local garden clubs during the time Lander was a county institution. When it became part of the state system, that hands-on community connection was unfortunately lost, and "Grounds" became merely another budget category consisting of the staff, supplies, and equipment necessary to maintain the campus acreage. Many small garden club plots were lost entirely, and the Speake garden gradually fell into disuse and disarray. This particular spot, however, managed to regain its identity and secure a new lease on life when it was rescued and redesigned in recent years by the grounds crew.

All students were required to take a course in practical and taxonomic botany during the developmental period of Lander's grounds and gardens, according to Stewart, and "every student was asked to bring a tree which was native to their county and plant it on the campus." Members of the senior classes in the early 1900s observed Arbor Day by planting a new tree on the campus annually. The efforts of Kathleen Willson and the students eventually resulted in a valuable collection of ornamental and forest trees; all of the varieties native to the state of South Carolina were planted on the campus, "many of which lived and formed a massive canopy" overhead. Stewart wrote that 28 state trees were represented on the Lander campus in 1972.

In later years the Lander Alumni Association contributed several times to the beautification of the campus by planting trees in honor of individuals. Stewart mentioned three or four special plantings in honor of Mrs. Fitz Lee, Dr. J. Marvin Rast, and others. One of the latest was a magnolia tree beside the Cultural Center given by her family to honor retired music professor Ann M. Hutto. Nor did Greenwood forget the efforts of its gardeners and the Federation of Garden Clubs on Lander's behalf. Seventeen years after the college passed from county ownership and control, the Greenwood Rotary Club recognized Angelle Penn Adams "for her continuous work on the Lander College campus in landscaping" when it presented her its Community Service Award in June 1990. Other well-known Greenwood women who contributed their skill and expertise to beautify the Lander campus included Mrs. Dewey Johnson and Mrs. J. G. Jenkins, Sr.

The academic work of the college proceeded apace during the Willson administration. Maintaining adequate enrollment was evidently not a problem and, except for ever-increasing immersion in the Methodist girls' school traditions of the day and the nagging question of debt, Lander College appeared to thrive, both inside and out. One ominous prediction of things to come was noted, however, in the 1907 edition of *Handbook of South Carolina*:

> For thirty years this College offered several unique and peculiar features in female education, and under Dr. Lander they were eminently successful. They are summarized briefly as follows: (1) The organization of new classes every session of twenty weeks, instead of once a year. (2) Instead of prizes for excellence, deductions from regular tuition fees were allowed. (3) The "one study plan," so-called, in which the session was subdivided into four sections of five weeks each, and some particular branch was made the major study and some associate branch the minor study. (4) The graduation of the student eight times during the year as soon as she has completed the round of studies. (5) Private graduation with no public exhibition; but the students were subjected to rigid examinations. The Trustees in June, 1907, directed the discontinuance of this system. It remains to be seen whether this action is a wise one or not.

According to an interview with Dr. R. O. Lawton in 1949 cited in Faye T. Bryant's thesis, the predicted changes came about in 1913. Lander College joined other colleges in setting regular standards and guidelines which gradually evolved into a set of objective criteria used for recognition and accreditation. Similarly, the highly individualistic imprint of Samuel Lander gave way inevitably to John Willson's Methodist ideal of education for "womanly women." Perhaps, in view of things to come, this was just as well.

Mrs. Samuel Lander – one is forced to wonder whether she found the appellation of "Little Mother" to her liking – died in 1914. Her will, drawn up seven years earlier, was an amazing document, as much for what it did not say as for what it revealed. There was even a hint or two of family discord, although anything else in a family of seven sons and two daughters would probably be rather odd. Mrs. Lander surely emerges as a person in her own right in two paragraphs from that will:

> 3. I will and bequeath to my son Angus M. Lander the sum of Eight hundred Dollars, and to my son Ernest M. Lander the sum of Four hundred Dollars. In order that my other children may understand this apparent preference I deem it best to here state that these several sums are given my said two sons in lieu of the expenses of a college education which my other sons had at the expense of their father, through whom I received what property I have. This I deem a simple act of justice.

4. I will and bequeath to my sons Wm. T. Lander and John M. Lander each the sum of Five hundred Dollars. This special bequest is made as a token of my appreciation of the sacrifices made by my said two sons, the former for his father and the latter for his church.

Mrs. Lander left an estate valued at about $5,000. Although she inherited the 45.6 acre farm owned by S. Lander & Son, which at the time of her husband's death was heavily mortgaged, she and her son William had sold this property to John O. Willson in 1907 for $4,035 and assumption of the mortgage. Willson in turn left the property in equal shares to his wife and daughter with the admonition that "both of them on receiving same shall at once execute a will in which each shall remember Lander College." Willson's will also contained a provision that seems extremely patronizing, at least at the remove of nearly seventy years: "If I am in charge of Lander College when I depart this life then I direct that each servant working in said college or on its campus shall be paid the sum of five dollars."

John O. Willson's will, as well as the record of property acquisition during his lifetime, gives evidence of his early legal training. For years he had bought and sold, always at a profit, a number of lots near the college, and the will contains a great many individual and special bequests. One bequest provides annual awards, in perpetuity, at both The Citadel and Bailey Military Institute. By the time he wrote his final will in 1918 Willson was able to state, "In former will, I have made bequest to my alma mater, The Citadel Academy, for an annual Honor Ring but I have made permanent provision for it and therefore make no gift – but what she has, my gratitude." Actually the Willson Ring has been given by The Citadel every year since 1911. According to an article in a Citadel publication (c. 1974) the ring "is given to the graduating senior voted by his classmates the manliest, purest, and most courteous member of his class."

President Willson conceived the award as early as 1905 when he wrote perhaps the first of many wills and determined the qualifications *manliest, purest,* and *most courteous* for the recipient. The provision was kept secret until 1910 when The Citadel accepted an invitation to hold its annual summer encampment at Greenwood. Superintendent O. J. Bond wrote that the encampment was held in "a grove of trees behind the Presbyterian Church . . . not far from the business center of the city. . . ." Greenwood provided every convenience, "including water, baths, latrines, electric lights in the tents, and even telephones at headquarters and at the mess hall." The activities were those usually associated with military summer camps; among the special features of the one at Greenwood were morning concerts by the cadet band and target shooting at a rifle range specially constructed to facilitate practice of this "important feature of the work." The encampment lasted two weeks and culminated in commencement exercises featuring a baccalaureate sermon by John O. Willson. Clearly the exhilaration of the moment prompted Willson, in a letter to Bond dated June 14, 1910, to reveal his plans to establish the award immediately. Clearly also he endowed the award soon thereafter with the result that some eighty Citadel alumni share a common bond as recipients of the John O. Willson ring. No doubt most have no idea of their connection with Greenwood and Lander College, and some would probably even misspell Willson's name, but the ring itself is well known among alumni of The Citadel. "An unsurpassed Citadel honor," it is officially described as "gold, with a bloodstone setting, and inscribed with the three words, Manliness, Purity, Courtesy." The ring evidently possesses the power to make strong men cry: *"Few dry-eyed cadets ever accept the fabled John O. Willson Ring,"* according to the article. Winners are described as by turns "awed" . . . "shocked" . . . "stunned" . . . or "breathless" but nearly always unable to articulate their feelings. One inadvertently hilarious letter from a recipient of about twenty years ago reads: "Your letter about the Willson Ring is impossible to answer. My sentiments, on paper at least, are trite. I have really tried to concoct an answer for you and hope you will forgive my inability to do so. I would do almost anything for The Citadel."

The twin issues of debt and money plagued Lander continually during the Willson years, but both enrollment and the value of the college property increased steadily. After Willson Hall was completed, conference minutes placed the college's monetary value at $135,000, yet the conference continued to discriminate against Lander in its educational efforts. For example, a three-year fundraising campaign for the three Methodist colleges authorized in 1912 directed that only one-fourth of the goal of $300,000 would be allocated to Lander. There was no explanation of this inequity. Bryant wrote that Lander actually received only $9,240 from the conference during the six-year period from 1912 to 1918.

Enrollment continued to flourish, and the need for more dormitory space became evident before the end of the decade. Bryant noted that 47 applicants were turned away in 1917 even though no one had canvassed for students that year. Enrollment in 1919 was 271 students, debt amounted to $31,500, and the plant was valued at $239,000. Demand was definitely exceeding supply, and this time the Methodist Conference institution looked to the citizens of Greenwood and a short-term bond issue for help. A building project in 1920 added a third story to the rear wing of the building, as well as a large new kitchen, several additional music rooms, and a greatly enlarged dining room. Most people would probably agree that these renovations added nothing to the beauty of the building, but at least they did not mar the serenity of its front facade, and they did provide space to accommodate more students. The record shows that Lander received $3,365 from the Methodist Conference in 1922; its debt that year stood at $45,000.

The move for an endowment began in 1910 when the Alumnae Association determined to raise $5,000 over the next five years. According to a story in *The Index-Journal* of February 11, 1947, Lander was the only women's college in the state at that time with an endowment of any kind. The alumnae managed to raise about $2,000 in the first year. The emphasis on endowment continued, and slowly but steadily the fund grew; by 1922 the college could boast an endowment totaling about $32,000. The City of Greenwood contributed $6,000 toward an "educational fund" as early as 1917. Lander's first (and presumably only) pipe organ, partially funded by gifts from Sunday School students, was installed in 1920.

The college's golden anniversary celebration was not at all in keeping with Samuel Lander's aversion to showy occasions and students "on parade." A pageant, in eight episodes and three interludes depicting Lander's history, was staged in 1922, and the celebration included a Jubilee Reunion of alumnae with a banquet boasting menu cards printed in gold. Each alumna also received her own copy of the anniversary book *The Story of Lander 1872-1922*, which probably accounts for the number of copies of this 32-page book still extant. By that time the college had been in Greenwood for eighteen years. Its activities contributed in large part to the religious and cultural life of the town, and Lander was making genuine contributions in the field of education that extended well beyond the region. Samuel Lander had initiated a scheme to provide additional training to South Carolina schoolteachers as early as 1887: he divided the state into three regions and offered free tuition and textbooks to twelve selected teachers from one of the regions for three successive years. The only cost to the young women chosen was room and board, and even that was discounted by one-third and could be paid at a later date. Each successful applicant for this training had to be at least eighteen years of age, hold a first or second grade certificate, and bring a recommendation from her county school commissioner. It is not known how long Dr. Lander was able to offer this special program, but Lander College has emphasized the preparation of public school teachers from its earliest beginnings to the present day. A number of statewide short courses, conventions, and special events were held at Lander in the 1920s, among them Dr. Wil Lou Gray's famous Opportunity School program for adult illiterates, the assembly of the Epworth League, short courses in home economics conducted by home demonstration agents for Greenwood County girls, sessions of a convention of the United Daughters of the Confederacy, and Education Week, an annual event at the college for many years.

John O. Willson's administration ended with his death in March 1923 at the age of 78. The college yearbook, *Naiad* (named for a water nymph from ancient mythology, presumably a reference to the spring at Williamston), was first published that year and dedicated to his memory. The yearbook called him "the highest type of Christian gentleman," and the Methodist Conference *Minutes* for 1923 noted that all Lander students were members of the church, including fourteen who were "life service volunteers." Loyal and devoted Methodist minister that he was, Willson would surely have considered this the crowning achievement of his educational career.

But there were other achievements as well. John Willson left an estate valued at just under $20,000, including stocks, bonds, real property, livestock, and a "Ford Sedan – Bought last September" valued at $500. Economist David Dumont placed the value of Willson's estate as the present-day equivalent in purchasing power of $151,500, not bad for a humble preacher. He left real property consisting of the Lander farm with a house and barn, as well as "lots and cottage on Lawson Street," the whole valued at $10,000. Like many others in Greenwood, Willson lost $4,300 from investing in the failed Peoples Bank, and Lander College owed him more than $1,700 at the time of his death. Writers have reminded us since the fourteenth century that comparisons are odious, but they are also sometimes unavoidable and often quite revealing. A case in point might be the comparison between the holographic wills of two nineteenth century Methodist preachers who happened to be related by marriage for about eight years. Samuel Lander's beautifully written last will and testament dated March 30, 1876, consists of fourteen lines, among them, ". . . if I shall die seized and possessed of any property, real, personal, or mixed, over and above the payment of all my debts, my precious wife, Laura Ann, shall be my sole heir and executrix." John Willson's will is equally beautifully written, but there the similarity ends. The document consists of five legal-size pages, fifteen separate items, and two codicils. Whether there is any deeper meaning attached to such a comparison is a moot point.

John O. Willson is buried in Magnolia Cemetery in Greenwood. His wife of twenty-seven years rests by his side.

Kathleen Willson and her step-daughter Mary W. Donaldson held on to the original Lander property for another six years before selling it to the college. That sale was handled over a two-day period in October 1929 when (1) the executors sold a one-half interest in the property to Lander College for $4,000, (2) the executors sold the other one-half interest to Mrs. Willson for $4,000, and (3) Mrs. Willson in turn deeded her interest to Lander in return for a lifetime annuity of $200 per year. By that time the city had opened roads along two boundary lines of the property. One of the roads became Sproles Street which would bisect the campus for many years until the city agreed in the 1970s to close a section to public traffic in order to make the campus whole again.

Dr. R. O. Lawton, who had been Professor of English since 1911 (some sources say 1912), served as acting president until May 11, 1923, when the board elected the well-known Methodist minister Barnwell Rhett Turnipseed as Lander's third president. Lawton was a native of Garnett who had attended Trinity College (now Duke University) and graduated from Wofford in 1904. After teaching at his alma mater, he became a minister and preached for a time in California. He came to Lander in 1911 where he remained until 1926, near the end of the Turnipseed administration. Another teaching stint followed, this time at Columbia College. Lawton retired to Greenwood where he became noted for his "Sermonette" columns in *The Index-Journal.* He received an honorary doctorate from Wofford in 1931.

Turnipseed was at the time of his election as president a member of the Lander board of trustees, presumably one of the conference appointees. He had graduated in the first class at Clemson and prepared, through graduate study at Clemson and the Medical College at Charleston, for a medical career. After three years of study he opted instead to enter the Christian ministry and was licensed to preach in 1900. His appointment as President of Lander for the years 1923-27 appears in the midst of routine ministerial appointments from 1900-1939 in a Methodist publication. It is interesting to note that Turnipseed was awarded not one, but two, Doctor of Divinity degrees after he had been at Lander for a year. Both Wofford and the University of South Carolina obliged in 1924. Turnipseed was cited as a "popular and successful pastor . . . [who] has improved parsonages and church buildings wherever he has gone." With such a record, it is not surprising that Lander's next major building, Chipley Hall, was built during his administration. Nor should it come as a surprise that the 1925-26 catalog indicated the aim of the college's endeavors as "womanly women." The nearest the catalog came to defining these paragons were the words *gentleness, modesty,* and *a charming type of religion.* Dr. Turnipseed resigned in 1927 to return to the active ministry.

Chipley Hall was erected in 1925 at a cost of about $81,000. Trying to trace this building's history in a little more detail was extremely difficult. Although there were fairly regular columns about happenings on the Lander campus, very little information on board meetings seemed to make the newspaper. Finally, *The Index-Journal* reported in a brief story on May 16, 1924, the announcement by President Turnipseed that a new dormitory would be erected on the west side of the college building "in accordance with plans suggested by Landscape Architect George A. Burnap." The president apparently saw nothing strange in a landscape designer determining the placement of buildings; indeed, perhaps the procedure was not strange at all. Turnipseed added that other buildings would be erected "in time"; possibly a quadrangle arrangement was contemplated for the dormitory area.

The rest of the story, until July 15 when a sizable article with the first pictures was run, was laboriously extracted from items in the "Brief City News" columns appearing at intervals through May and June. The names of the architects – R. E. Lee of Clemson and James C. Hemphill of Greenwood – were revealed in an article on May 24, along with the name of the projected building: "This dormitory, which is to be known as Chipley Hall, is to be a three story and basement brick building in the colonial style with a slate roof, with a marble stone foundation front."

Bids were opened in early June. Apparently no Greenwood firm submitted a bid for construction, although Holloway Plumbing and Heating Company tried unsuccessfully to obtain that contract. The low bidder was C. M. Guest of Anderson; his price was $60,850. Bryce Plumbing and Heating of Florence was awarded a contract in the amount of $11,591. Another Greenwood firm, W. J. Snead Lumber Company, became subcontractor for millwork. Groundbreaking and excavation got underway almost immediately after the contracts were awarded.

An article on June 2 noted that subscriptions from Greenwood citizens and businesses amounted to about $23,000. Two lists from about this time, both on letterhead of The American Bank, indicate the progress of the fund-raising campaign. One seems to consist of Greenwood businesses and affluent citizens while the other appears to be a list of donations or pledges from private individuals of much lesser means. John I. Chipley gave $1,000, any number of companies subscribed at the $500 level, and even President Turnipseed promised $150 to the building campaign. There were also a great many gifts of from $1 to $10. More information about the new dormitory was finally revealed in a long newspaper story covering plans for the school year 1924-25. The issue of July 15, 1924, reported: "A benevolent citizen of the community has given $25,000 toward the erection of this new building." That benevolent citizen was Greenwood businessman and Lander board member Marvin S. Chipley, the same man who had offered $5,000 toward a fund to move the Democratic National Convention that summer to some location other than New York City. Chipley actually sent a telegram to South Carolina Governor Thomas Gordon McLeod, addressed to the convention at Madison Square Garden, to make the offer. It seems he deplored New York's "liquor clique" and "foreign tinge and custom." The story of the telegram was front page news, but since there was no follow-up and no one recalls a national political convention moving to a new location in mid-session, apparently nothing came of a Greenwood businessman's offer to the National Democratic Party in 1924.

The newspaper story indicated pledges from the trustees individually amounting to $6,000. It also described the building in detail, noting a foundation of blue granite, walls of "tapestried brick from Kingsport, Tennessee," a slate roof, and white limestone trim. Chipley Hall was occupied in the fall of 1925 and for some reason gained a reputation as the "rich girls' dorm." Possibly Chipley's rooms did cost a little more than those in Willson or Laura Lander Hall. Chipley Hall was designed to house 100 students; it was "of the very latest type, being the first of a new group to be built upon the campus." The planned building boom did not materialize, except for the president's home erected more than fifteen years later, and the physical plant remained substantially the same until after the college came under Greenwood's control in 1948.

The Reverend Richard Heber Bennett, a Virginian whose entire preaching career except for one year had been in Virginia churches, succeeded Turnipseed as President of Lander College. Bennett's educational credentials were impressive. The son of a minister, he earned both the bachelor's and master's degrees at Randolph-Macon and attended the Princeton Theological Seminary. The D. D. was from Hampden-Sydney and was awarded in 1905. Bennett's major extra-ministerial activities centered on his work with the Anti-Saloon League – state, national, and international – and he taught Moral Philosophy at Randolph Macon from 1903 to 1907. Among many other activities, Bennett was credited by the Methodist publication *Builders* with a syndicated weekly column for newspapers entitled "Twitterings of Timothy Twig." Unfortunately, the newspapers which published this column are not known.

Bennett's administration lasted five years; he was transferred to the Virginia Conference in 1932. Methodist support was apparently at its most stable during his tenure. Bryant noted that the conference diligently met a $12,000 per year assessment during the five years of Bennett's presidency. Enrollment was in the 300-400 range, and the debt stood at some $81,000 when he assumed office.

The college first sought regular accreditation from the Southern Association of Colleges and Secondary Schools during this period. Bryant described Lander's "theoretical endowment" in 1930: cash invested – $145,187; unpaid subscriptions – $110,000; wills and legacies – $75,000; assessments from Conference – $200,000; total – $530,187. Evidently these figures had something to do with an application for accreditation; Bryant wrote that the Southern Association agreed to consider the conference appropriation as the equivalent of $200,000 in endowment. But accreditation was not granted, neither then nor later during the entire period of Methodist control. Lander remained on the "approved non-member" list because of the twin deficiencies of debt and lack of real endowment.

Bennett was succeeded by the Reverend John W. Speake, a native of Newberry County. If his biography in *Builders* is correct (it is probably merely incomplete; the publication date is 1932), Speake did not finish high school and had no college at all. Instead, he entered the ministry early and served charges all over the state. By the time he came to Lander as president, he was 58 years old and had been preaching for

35 years. There must have been an honorary degree at some point; a good Methodist minister would hardly have been expected to sit in a college president's chair without one. The important point is that not one of the five Methodist ministers who followed Samuel Lander had any *real* experience as an educator.

Conditions during the nine years of Speake's administration managed to capture the attention of the Methodist Conferences (there were two at this time in South Carolina). The struggle for accreditation must have been something of an embarrassment, so much so that bishops, two conference boards of education, and presiding elders were called together to work out a campaign to increase Lander's endowment. The board of trustees had already been authorized to do something about the college's debt, either refinance or extend the repayment period. So serious were the conferences, in fact, that the year 1937 was to be "assigned" to Lander as the kickoff year of an important endowment campaign. Not only was the campaign a dismal failure, according to Bryant, it actually cost the college nearly $37,000 from its already small endowment fund. Conference appropriations also dropped to less than $4,000 for several years, and the college was forced to give an additional mortgage to build the president's home.

Strangely enough, enrollment actually increased during the late 1930s. At one point Lander enrolled more females than any other college in the state except Winthrop. It also furnished more teachers than any other private school. Scholastically, Lander was a member of both the Association of Colleges for Women and the Association of American Colleges, but Southern Association membership was still denied for financial reasons. Yearbooks for the 1920s and 1930s depict a very active student body, with organizations and groups for every imaginable interest consistent with the wholesome type of young woman who enrolled. Church membership was vitally important, and attendance at Sunday services was mandatory; Bryant noted that the 1938 student body represented eight religious denominations. Lander was featured in a special department, "Do You Know Your South Carolina?" in the Charleston *News and Courier* during this period, a column that was reprinted in *The Index-Journal* of January 21, 1940. The historical sketch noted that the 1938-39 budget of $139,244 came from "students, the church, endowment, and the farm." The farm, mentioned earlier in the context of property, was actually quite a productive enterprise. The article cited its importance in "raising all pork, . . . [conditioning] its own beef cattle, . . . [feeding] the twelve riding horses, [and] . . . [furnishing] fresh vegetables for the table." One line in the article – that Lander lived "strictly within her income" – was not strictly true; nevertheless, day-to-day life for the students was busy and good, even though the atmosphere at board meetings might well have been gloomy. Speake's administration was clearly a mixed bag; he retired for health reasons in 1941 and died the same year.

The charming John Marvin Rast, a native of Georgia, took over the presidency upon Speake's retirement. Rast was a graduate of Emory and held the M. A. from Columbia University. He attended Union Theological Seminary and earned the B. D. from the Candler School of Theology in 1929. The D. D. was awarded by Wofford in 1940, and Rast's career included a two-year teaching stint at Wofford. John M. Rast brought a special brand of urbanity and dignity to his new assignment, as well as three attractive children – Carlisle, Ann, and Sue – who attended Greenwood schools. It was Rast's misfortune to be at the helm of a Methodist school during a time of serious financial retrenchment that affected all three conference institutions. Lander's income from the conference fell to embarrassing lows; in 1944, according to Bryant, it was only $2,000. Normal operating expenses, more or less regular debt service, and free tuition for preachers' daughters continued. The college was able to make only small additions to its resources, although the noted financier and South Carolina native Bernard Baruch gave $10,000 in memory of his wife during this period. The State of South Carolina, which had provided funds for the operation of the Opportunity School every summer at Lander for more than twenty years, withdrew funding when the school was moved permanently to Columbia in 1945. Rast's administration was not notable for great leaps forward, but among its successes was the enrollment of the first male student, O. L. Thomas of Ninety Six, who entered in 1943. It was not necessary to amend the original charter to admit Thomas since the trustees had already provided for such an eventuality in its wording.

The 1940s also saw a rash of commemorations of one type or another, as well as various kinds of contributions to public service during wartime. Bryant noted conventions of the South Carolina Press Association, Women's Society of Christian Service, and Methodist Conference meetings. In addition, some 34 Lander alumnae were cited for various contributions in the field of "war work." The Alumnae Association erected a permanent historical marker in Williamston in 1942, the 70th anniversary of the college. That marker was refurbished in 1972 as part of the college's centennial observance. Its inscription reads:

> Williamston Female College – This college was founded February 12, 1872, by the Reverend Samuel Lander, D. D., Methodist Minister. On this site stood the college building until 1939. The school was moved to Greenwood, S. C., September 27, 1904, becoming Lander College, in honor of the founder who died July 14, 1904. From an humble beginning there arose here a Christian institution of expanding influence, keeping faith with its motto: "Puritas et Scientia."

Although the college was not exactly prone and helpless during Rast's administration – one bright spot was the enrollment of about fifty men, an innovation he actively encouraged — it is true that financial problems continued to plague the college, and enrollment steadily declined. But Lander also continued to hold at least one highly visible asset: its campus was a prime piece of real estate within the city limits, and less than half of its 65 acres had been developed. A city street also effectively bisected the campus, dividing it into "the college" and "the farm." Perhaps no one knows the reasoning of the board of trustees at the time, but the college agreed in February 1941 to lease space in the basement of Willson Hall for offices and studios for a radio broadcasting station, as well as "a sufficient amount of land on the Lander College farm to locate a tower." The lease, to Grenco, Inc., of Greenwood, also contained an option to buy "so much of the Lander College farm property as may be required . . . (but not exceeding five (5) acres) . . ." for $500 per acre. The lease was for fifteen years. Its ten items meant, in all, five dollars to Lander College, while the lessee got "exclusive control," including the right to lay underground wires, to have ingress and egress at its discretion, to erect "such buildings, towers and/or equipment" it considered necessary, and to remove within "a reasonable time" all improvements to the property upon termination of the lease. Lander College did have the right, upon a year's written notice, to terminate the lease if Grenco should be sold. But there was a kicker even in that item: in order to forfeit the lease, it was necessary that the new owners operate the station in a manner "detrimental to the best interest of Lander College," in the opinion of its trustees.

Five months after this extraordinary lease was executed, it was amended, again for the consideration of $5.00, to cover nearly four acres of the college farm for the studios, transmitter building, antenna and other facilities of Grenco "because of mechanical and acoustical difficulties" with the Willson Hall basement. The original option to buy was reconfirmed. In an interesting juxtaposition of dates, that option was exercised nearly seven years later just before the transfer of college assets to Greenwood. On April 19, 1948, Grenco, Inc. bought for $2,500 a five-acre tract of college property. The lease, the amendment, and the deed were all signed by J. B. Gambrell, President of the Board of Trustees. The property was described in the deed as "located on the Northeast side of Willson Street and . . . bounded on the other three sides entirely by other property of Lander College."

Most interesting of all was the property transfer of exactly three days later when the tract was deeded from Grenco, Inc. to Douglas Featherstone, prominent Greenwood attorney and Methodist lay leader. The preamble to that deed reads in part: "the property hereinafter described was deeded by Lander College to Grenco, Inc. *when it should have been deeded to Douglas Featherstone,* who paid the purchase price" (emphasis added). Featherstone kept the property in his own name about seven years; in 1955 it was conveyed back to Grenco at the original purchase price of $2,500. No one has ever suggested that the lease and sale were anything but legal; nevertheless, the college lost acreage it did not regain until 1975 when the State of South Carolina paid Grenco, Inc. $130,000 for it. Evidently the property had appreciated more than 5000% in the 27 years from 1948 to 1975. In the meantime, Featherstone gave the school two lots near the campus totaling less than half an acre. The gift was booked at its appraised value of $3,050 in 1974.

Even as Lander College celebrated its 75th anniversary and Founder's Day on February 12, 1947, with, in Bryant's words, "all the honor and dignity becoming an institution of higher learning," its fate was under serious study by a joint educational commission consisting of six ministers and six laymen which had been created in 1946 "to work out an educational policy for the Methodist colleges in our state." The commission was to make its report at some time in the spring of 1947 at a special session of the conferences.

The special session was held on May 20, 1947, at Washington Street Methodist Church in Columbia. The conference *Minutes* reported the proceedings, but the series of five articles written by Ed Chaffin, editor of *The Index-Journal,* in 1964 was used in preference to the more staid *Minutes* for purposes of this narrative. Chaffin wrote that the commission's report "painted a dark picture of Lander." The failure to obtain accreditation was stressed, along with the committee's opinion that accreditation was not likely to happen. After more than forty years of strictly Methodist control, the Methodist committee called its school "decidedly deficient in meeting the standards concerning training and development of the faculty, the physical plant, library, laboratories and financial support," as though it were someone else's problem. The committee charged that earned doctorates were scarce – only two faculty members held the Ph.D. – and the faculty salary schedule was "not much more than half" the expectation for accredited colleges. Finally the kicker came: in consideration of the "imperative building program" needs of Columbia and Wofford, the Methodists could not supply the estimated $900,000 that Lander would require for new buildings and endowment to place it "on reasonably solid ground as an accredited senior college." The committee's recommendation, therefore, was that the three colleges be merged into one co-educational institution on an entirely new campus.

This so-called solution pleased nobody, except possibly its framers, and Chaffin wrote that "a heated debate" followed, resulting in rejection of the proposal and adoption of a substitute plan presented by W. C. Holroyd of Greenwood. The Holroyd resolution called for further study and recommendations for "the preservation and creditable operation of our three colleges as now located." A committee chosen at a subsequent "mass meeting in Greenwood" charged that the Methodist report had "seen fit to confuse adequate facilities with the cinema version of the ideal campus."

Two months after the May meeting, a story entitled "Plain Facts About Lander College" appeared in *The Index-Journal.* That story was essentially an open letter to Greenwood citizens from C. B. Barksdale and R. F. McCaslan, chairman and vice chairman, respectively, of the steering committee to raise an endowment. Clearly, these men feared Greenwood people were not in possession of the "plain facts," either about the situation with the Methodist Church or the fund-raising drive itself. Barksdale and McCaslan believed the rejection of the consolidation resolution had been "influenced by the representation that Greenwood had started to raise a special endowment fund of $500,000 for Lander College," but they also feared that a great many people believed the money was already in hand. The problem in this regard was a newspaper headline reading "Greenwood Rallies to Support of Lander; Half Million Dollar Endowment to Save College is Pledged." While the body of the article explained that the "endowment" was nothing more than the goal of a 10-year fund-raising campaign just begun, evidently "many members of the Methodist Conference [also] got the definite impression that . . . [funds] had been subscribed in a legal and binding form."

Another troubling result of the Methodist resolution, according to Barksdale and McCaslan, was the public perception that the college "must of necessity remain in its present status." They reminded Greenwood that the resolution had merely charged the committee to undertake further research and bring a recommendation of "Conference policy for the preservation and creditable operation of our three colleges as now located, and, or, different groupings or consolidation of all Methodist institutions." Actually, as matters stood, Greenwood was a long way from assurances of any kind. The next committee report might recommend "common management, standardization of courses, or many different ways of changing the . . . nature of the college. . . ." There was simply no way to tell.

The chairmen evidently thought it necessary to compare the educational efforts of the state's two largest denominations. Although South Carolina represented the smallest unit of Methodism in the country, the denomination was supporting three senior colleges, whereas the much larger Southern Baptist group was concerned with only one senior and one junior college. This seemingly extraneous bit of information was intended to show that there were two sides to the Lander question. No doubt Barksdale and McCaslan understood very well that Greenwood needed to be reminded of the fact "that those who have favored closing Lander as an independent four-year college of the Methodist Church have strong arguments from the standpoint of efficiency and economy. . . ."

Barksdale and McCaslan spelled out in detail their committee's efforts to get the fund-raising campaign off the ground. Recruiting campaign workers had apparently been fairly easy, but only 24 of the 82 who accepted canvassing assignments at the initial meeting had reported at all – 58 had made no response to "repeated requests" – and exactly five had "reached their full quota" of $5,000 in pledges to be paid over a 10-year period. Considering that the entire campaign had raised only $115,000 in bona fide pledges, the chairmen wrote: "If the special endowment fund of $500,000 . . . is not subscribed, we might as well face the fact that it will be difficult to keep Lander at Greenwood in any form." The frustration of the two men was evident: on the one hand it appeared Greenwood was overly confident that the college would remain securely in place, while on the other hand its response to the appeal for endowment funds had been so lackluster as to indicate otherwise. The chairmen felt they were dealing with "a feeling of indifference in many quarters."

Timing was a factor as well. Only a few months remained before the joint conference committee would meet to hear the new report, and the chairmen believed Greenwood needed to be not only ready but also able and willing to meet the challenge Lander College would represent if, indeed, it were offered to the county. The letter stressed the "importance and worth" of the school to the Greenwood area and pointed out that the future of Lander College was not a concern of Methodists alone. Baptists and Presbyterian students combined outnumbered Methodists at the time, according to a table included in the letter, and the regular student body of 330 was only 39% Methodist. In addition Lander served more than 200 Greenwood County students in academic courses and special non-credit instruction in music, art, speech, and riding. Finally, more than half the students came from within a 50-mile radius of Greenwood and 74% from the thirteen counties "in the Northwest corner of South Carolina." Barksdale and McCaslan were sure that, without Lander, many students in the area might never have the advantage of a college education.

The letter ended with a simple statement and a challenge: "It has been our sole purpose to keep the community informed . . . and serve the best interests of Lander College, which we believe is serving the best interests of the community. Is Greenwood willing to serve Lander?"

The new Methodist committee of six ministers and five laymen made its report on November 18, 1947, at Main Street Methodist Church in Greenwood. Three recommendations were proposed for debate: (1) to retain and adequately support Wofford as a fully accredited college for men, to retain and adequately support Columbia as a fully accredited college for women, and to offer all Lander assets "as a gift to the Greenwood community, under certain reservations." If the community should reject the offer, the college property would be sold and its assets divided equally between the other two institutions; (2) to maintain all three colleges at their respective locations; and (3) to retain both Wofford and Columbia as senior accredited colleges and Lander as an accredited junior college under the name Greenwood Junior College. The lead article in the Lander College Centennial Edition of *The Index-Journal* of May 6,

1972, written by Thomas L. Hutto, credited Rast with the idea of giving the college to Greenwood.

Arguments began at 10:30 a.m. and raged until 7 p.m. Chaffin wrote that the result "was told in The Index-Journal lead: 'Methodists yesterday withdrew their support of Lander College, leaving Greenwood with the choice of operating the school itself or of seeing the 75-year old institution abandoned and sold for the benefit of Wofford and Columbia Colleges.'" The first proposal had been adopted! The "certain reservations" stated that Greenwood would own the assets only as long as they were used for educational purposes, and the name Lander could be used only so long as the college remained a senior institution. (This is an extremely interesting condition. Insofar as is known, the name *Lander* had never been copyrighted and was not owned by the Methodist Church, which in any event could not rewrite history.) Further, title would remain with the conference until the college had been granted accreditation; indeed, any Methodist claims against the property would be surrendered only after the first full year of accreditation. The time allowed for attaining accreditation status was ten years. If it were not achieved in that time, the Methodists would sell the property.

Albert Deems Betts wrote in *History of South Carolina Methodism* (1952) that the offer also contained a deadline for acceptance of June 15, 1948. That was plenty of time; Greenwood had already made up its collective mind. Greenwood County Senator Calhoun A. Mays announced on February 20 that the county would accept the offer through a corporation set up for that purpose. In addition, the county pledged $30,000 to operate the school for the 1948-49 year. A corporation named, appropriately, The Lander Foundation was duly chartered "as an agency of the community" on March 17, 1948, and the Methodist offer was formally accepted on May 13. The first trustees under the new charter were: Mary Baker, C. B. Barksdale, Howard L. Burns, J. D. Featherstone, F. E. Grier, J. B. Harris, B. S. Hodges, Mrs. R. O. Lawton, W. D. N. Ouzts, J. B. Sloan, C. Y. Thomason, and W. D. Tinsley. Barksdale was elected chairman; other officers were W. D. Tinsley and Howard L. Burns, vice chairman and secretary-treasurer. All the board members appeared to be keenly aware of the uniqueness of their position, as well as the scope of the challenge they faced. The first priority was obviously that of naming exactly the right man as president. Chaffin wrote that advice had been sought earlier (he did not say by whom) from Limestone College which had faced a similar situation. The advice appeared to boil down to the admonition: "Get a good man to head the college. If you don't, then all the work of the best board of trustees in all the world won't help you any."

The search for that "good man" began at the first board meeting and culminated with the selection of Dr. Boyce McLaughlin Grier, a native of North Carolina who was at that time superintendent of schools in Athens, Georgia. He had held the position of school superintendent for nineteen years, first at Elberton and then at Athens. The board made its choice in early May, and Grier took office on June 16. One of his first public statements on assuming the new position showed a clear understanding of the problems he faced: "Lander has a history rich in the tradition of service," he said, "but it must stand before the bar of public opinion and justify its existence."

As it turned out, the choice of Grier as president was most fortuitous. In addition to possessing the correct credentials, which included degrees from Erskine College, the University of Georgia, and Peabody College, he was not only personable but also a hard-headed and practical businessman who could cut directly through a problem to its source. One example from a newspaper article about a month after he took office illustrates Grier's resourcefulness. The Methodist committee report had come down hard on the inadequacies of the Lander library, both its collection and physical facilities, and estimated that an expenditure of "at least $100,000" would be required to remedy the library situation alone. The ever-practical Grier simply obtained a copy of the *List of Reference Books and Periodicals for School Libraries* put out by the Southern Association and cross-checked to determine actual deficiencies. Next he wrote accredited colleges similar to Lander to see what they had and what their department heads recommended. Then he conferred with Lander's department heads to determine their most urgent needs. By that time he had an actual list of books on which to obtain prices. He discovered that $1,500 would do the job of building a basic collection. He also discovered that a mezzanine, or balcony, which could be built around the entire room for about $500, would solve the space problem, for the moment at least. Thus he managed to overcome a supposed $100,000 problem with an expenditure of $2,000. This attitude carried over throughout the college in those first days. But Grier always knew he was working against time and that band-aid solutions would not suffice on the all-important question of meeting accreditation standards.

Newspaper articles described a number of Grier's early innovations; nothing escaped his notice, not even inadequate light fixtures in dormitory rooms. "The girls can't study with a ceiling bulb," he said. He consolidated, he improvised, he economized, always, it seemed, just a step away from disaster until Chaffin could report after Grier had been on the job about six weeks, "Lander has its feet on the ground and is beginning to crawl a little." That metaphor cannot stand much analysis, but its meaning is perfectly clear. Grier was always deadly serious about the accreditation problem, and he approached it in his characteristically realistic fashion in an address to the Greenwood Rotary Club. "Church schools can struggle along for a time without being accredited because of certain affiliations, loyalties and attachments," he said. "Independent institutions cannot do this. The flow of life's blood depends upon receiving a rank and rating that meets the approval of accrediting agencies. The needs . . . revolve fundamentally around finances, plant, equipment, and faculty personnel." Grier assured his audience that meeting those needs required sound economic principles and good business practices. "We must not only know our problems, but be able to properly evaluate them," he said. "The important and essential ones must come first. We must deal with the realities of life as they are or run the risk of failure." Chaffin used Grier's closing words to the Rotarians to conclude his own article. The thoughts the Lander president expressed more than forty years ago are still applicable today:

> The task is not easy. The paths of worthwhile things never are. The task is challenging, however, and will tax the best there is in us to accomplish. There is a place in the American system of education for small liberal arts colleges. This fact need not be argued. It is generally conceded. We, a people, talk a great deal about the New Order or the New World for which we are to educate the young men and women to actively participate in. Neither you nor I have any definite conception of the tremendous social, economic, and scientific change which lies immediately ahead. Our educational system must produce citizens who understand and who have the intelligence to control this civilization of which they are a part and to adapt themselves to those changes that will enrich it. We do not know what to teach young men and women to think, for they must deal with things we know [nothing] about. The important thing is to teach them how to think. The strength of our civilization lies not in material prosperity . . . but in the character and intelligence of our people, in their ideals and conceptions of life, in their attitudes toward Him who is the Author of Life and Giver of every good and perfect gift.

Grier was a joiner and a team player. He was also gregarious by nature and enjoyed the company of men. These qualities of Lander's new president, as well as those of the carefully chosen board of trustees, were combined in a formidable assault on the problem of shoring up Lander's shaky ship. Everyone knew that a long-term commitment of tax monies would be required if the school were to have any chance of survival. To make fiscal matters worse, the Methodists had been making noises about recovering the endowment fund of some $150,000 which was assumed to have been part of the transfer of assets. Grier loved to talk about the exciting times when he and others covered the entire county appealing for a county-wide tax assessment. His method of working a crowd was to pick out the "leading man" in his audience and speak directly to that person. "Get the support of that man," he would say, "and he will do the job for you with the rest." It worked. Greenwood County taxpayers approved the referendum for a four-mill tax levy for Lander College in the fall of 1951.

The endowment question was not quite so easy, and for a time the matter threatened to wind up in the courts. Many years later Grier took the position that he had wanted absolutely no strings attached to Lander's future, particularly none associated with the years of Methodist control, and for that reason alone favored the college's releasing the endowment. Ernest Lander remembers writing a letter urging that the funds remain with the college, since he believed the original contributors meant to help Lander College in particular and not simply Methodist education. Whatever the position of board members and others at the time, the decision to release the endowment fund was made in a 1951 agreement with the Methodist Conference in return for a deed in fee simple transferring Lander property to the Lander Foundation. Chaffin wrote, "Greenwood again responded to the challenge by raising an endowment of $165,000 for the college."

But the accreditation deadline still loomed, and Lander's future was in real doubt until that goal was accomplished. Grier had made friends everywhere in his long career in public education; having joined everything from the Sons of the American Revolution to high school boosters' clubs, he had built a vast network of cronies and well-wishers. No doubt he had also done a few favors in his time, favors that might well be returned now when he needed all the help he could get. There would be no more selling off of Lander property, but he was not averse to some shared arrangement with the town or the county whereby he could gain some advantage for Lander students. The deal with the City Recreation Commission in 1952 is a case in point. In return for swimming pool and building privileges, Lander allowed the commission to build its facility on college property. In time the city commission became a county commission, and the legal entanglement grew more onerous year by year. College and commission wrangled over everything from clock hours of use to who owned which light bulbs. Finally that too was settled, but only after the college had become a state institution.

The Southern Association agreed to undertake a special study of Lander in 1951. The introduction to that study noted the endowment fund controversy as well as other handicaps of the ten-year stipulation in the Methodist agreement, particularly that the provision had "made it difficult to raise funds, as the title to the property was not clear" for a time. On the positive side the county tax assessment vote was cited, and the third paragraph of the introduction clearly indicated the Southern Association's willingness to do its best to help:

> President Grier has been in touch with the Association ever since he accepted his position. The Executive Secretary, while he was still dean of Queens College, made an informal inspection of the college and offered certain suggestions. President Grier has consulted him and the chairman of the Committee on Admission to Membership frequently. He and the Board have worked diligently to meet the standards.

The eleven-page report concluded with a summary of its findings:

> The committee found that forward strides had been made on those standards which had previously been weak. It is believed that the stage of uncertainty was passed when the ownership of the college was finally settled in 1951.
>
> In those areas in which rapid progress was possible, rapid strides have been made. In areas where progress is necessarily slower, such as the library, improvements were noted even though more remains to be done.

A follow-up report from Lander spelling out the implementation of the Southern Association recommendations was submitted in September 1952. There was nothing left to do but wait for the annual meeting to be held in Memphis in December. Surely everyone in Greenwood County knows the result of that meeting: following Grier's triumphant phone call notifying officials that the 10-year goal had been reached in less than five, classes were dismissed and happy students piled on a firetruck to spread the news throughout the town. Lander was a fully-accredited college for the first time in its 80-year history, and it was at last exclusively the property of Greenwood County.

Grier's administration lasted until his retirement in 1966 at the age of 72. Although he was not noted as an educational innovator, the college made a number of significant advances during the time Grier led the institution. The first separate library building was erected in the late 1950s with local financing; the first black student, Mary Alice Brown, enrolled without a ripple in the early 1960s; Lander accepted its first federal funds for financial aid when it joined the National Defense Student Loan Program in about 1957; and Lander entered the field of nursing education in 1956 with the first two-year associate degree program in South Carolina. The nursing program was a cooperative venture with Self Memorial Hospital and was established with the aid of The Self Foundation. The nursing program had far-reaching ramifications; it led in time to the full-fledged baccalaureate degree program in place today. Building projects during the Grier administration, in addition to the library, included the Lander Apartments, built in cooperation with C. Y. Thomason in 1950 and now part of the college housing complex, and the first separate student center, the second college building to be named in honor of a sitting president. The Barratt Science Hall was also essentially planned and its joint financing arranged during the last months of Grier's administration. College leadership was very much a one-man show in Grier's time, but he depended heavily on three key administrators: Katie H. Hollingsworth, who served as registrar, admissions director, and dean of students; Hugh H. Tucker, who became business manager in 1956; and Thomas L. Hutto, who worked closely with Grier in the fields of public relations and alumni affairs.

From the first to the last of the Grier years the president worked for recognition of the college as fully independent of the Methodist Conference. Always in demand as a speaker, Grier crisscrossed the state – Hutto wrote that in one spring he gave twelve commencement addresses, and he was high on the speakers' lists of civic clubs – appearing always as a spokesman for Lander College. He liked to run newspaper ads and almost invariably used the word *nonsectarian* even before *coeducational* in describing Lander. He was fiercely proud of the college's independence and intensely grateful to Greenwood County and his board of trustees. He was named President Emeritus on his retirement in 1966, and the Greenwood Chamber of Commerce sponsored an appreciation day for him.

Grier was always proud of the quality of Lander's board of trustees. Many of the original members continued to serve throughout his administration, and the names of men such as Bruce Barksdale, Howard Burns, F. E. Grier, J. B. Harris, and W. D. Tinsley became identified with the college almost as strongly as his own. Tinsley and Burns tackled thorny legal questions routinely, heroically, and nearly always successfully, while the prestige and know-how of businessmen Barksdale, Harris, and Grier meant a great deal to the always struggling institution. The college recognized many of its board members with honorary degrees over the years, but Barksdale was also accorded the singular tribute of his name on a college building. That honor came posthumously in 1972 at the dedication of the Barksdale Physical Education Center built during the Herd administration. President Emeritus Boyce Grier gave the memorial tribute on that occasion. He called his friend Barksdale a "distinguished leader in the fields of religion, education, and civic affairs of life, not only on the community level, but on state and national levels." He left out the field of business in which Barksdale also made quite a name as president of Greenwood Telephone Company and director of a bank, an insurance company, two colleges, and a savings and loan association. Barksdale was a Greenwood native, a veteran of both world wars, and an alumnus of Erskine, the University of South Carolina, and the University of Kansas. A lifelong Presbyterian, Barksdale was particularly active in presbytery and synod work. He was also an enthusiastic Rotarian and served as president of both the local and state chambers of commerce. In addition, he was a Mason and an active member of both the American Legion and the Sons of the American Revolution. Barksdale was the first chairman of The Lander Foundation Board of Trustees. Even after an arduous ten-year stint as chairman he remained an active member until his death on July 16, 1966. "Always," said Grier, "he was vitally interested in Lander's welfare and in her development."

Because Grier loomed so large in the life of the college and the community, there was a great deal of interest in who would succeed him as president. The board's choice turned out to be E. Don Herd, Jr., a native of Piedmont who was at that time director of the Lancaster branch of the University of South Carolina. Not exactly an unknown, Herd had already made a reputation as a scholar and South Carolina historian and had published a book on Andrew Jackson in 1963. He was also well known in Methodist circles, having been for some years a lay leader in the church. Like Grier he was a graduate of Erskine, and he held the M. A. in history from the University of South Carolina. He was also very young, only 33 when he took office. Herd joked later that while his Methodist connection might have worked against him, the fact that he too was a member of the SAR probably clinched the decision on Grier's part. Herd took office on February 1, 1966. There was a snowstorm the weekend he moved to Greenwood, and Lander's old furnace chose to conk out, again, to mark his arrival. He said some years afterward that he almost turned around to return to Lancaster, which at that moment seemed a safe haven far removed from the unknowns of Lander College and its future.

But Herd had the advantage of youth, as well as a driving ambition that had led him to set a college presidency as a goal many years before. He realized early that he was destined for a career in education and was a natural, intellectually, for the field; he was not always comfortable, however, with the more homely virtues of small talk, social trivia, and the minutiae of everyday life that accompanied the office of college president. A severe diabetic since childhood, a fact he did not share with many people, Don Herd had already defined and refined his own philosophies of life, religion, education, politics, and human nature, philosophies he shared selectively, if at all, during the years of his presidency.

Everything, simply everything, changed during the Herd administration. He was convinced that Lander was uniquely qualified to become a state school, and he began moving toward that goal from the very first days of his administration. His inaugural address in May 1966 anticipated state tuition grants to private colleges and made an indirect case for Lander's own drive for state support that would bear fruit only six years later. In the meantime he moved swiftly in every direction at once, or so it seemed to those who worked at the college in those days. He restored the title of vice president which had not been used since Turnipseed's day; he launched intercollegiate athletics as an inducement to the enrollment of men; he sought federal funds for any number of academic, administrative, faculty, and student programs, including the new Higher Education Act grants for developing institutions and supplementary training grants for Head Start teachers, as well as the full complement of financial aid programs; and it was Herd who suggested that the new science building be named for Dr. John Perkins Barratt, an early physician and scientist in Greenwood County. He also started the first learning laboratory, a forerunner of the present-day media center, and set up the first print shop. His academic innovations included the first cooperative ventures with the new technical education centers and the "upside down" degree program in vocational education described in another chapter, as well as the "credit-in-escrow" program through which high school students could earn college credits in special high school classes, credits that could be activated upon their enrollment at Lander. Particularly interesting in this regard was his choice of instructor: Herd named Maria Pyles, a Greenwood High School history teacher whose worth he recognized years before she was named South Carolina Teacher of the Year for 1989-90 and became one of four finalists for the national award.

Some of his dreams never materialized, such as a lake which would be ringed with men's dormitories and a fine arts center, but the college managed with strictly local financing to build the physical education center/gymnasium which is part of a physical education complex currently under construction along Willson Street. There was never enough money, but the college budget grew apace and the school operated in the black. Herd was always proud that Lander retired the student center bonds early, thereby earning commendation from a federal lending agency, and that the school entered the state system viable and debt-free. More than $170,000 in operating surplus, in fact, was transferred to The Lander Foundation, Eleemosynary, when the college assumed state status.

Most people would probably agree that two members of the Greenwood County delegation – Representatives James E. Moore and Marion P. Carnell – were largely responsible for Lander's achieving its goal of state support in the spring of 1972. The two men co-authored the legislation and gained the support of six other representatives from the region who acted as co-sponsors of the Lander bill: Julius Baggett, McCormick; Butler Derrick, Edgefield; Rudolph Mitchell, Saluda; and Eugene Stoddard and David Taylor, Laurens. Both the College of Charleston, which had been struggling with debt, and Francis Marion, which began as a two-year branch of the University of South Carolina, had been successful in selling themselves to the state during the preceding three years. Neither the Commission on Higher Education nor the Association of State College Presidents supported Lander's bid, but the General Assembly had acknowledged for several years Lander's contributions in the fields of education and nursing by voting state funds to the school. Those funds had reached $150,000 by 1972.

No brief summary such as this can possibly do justice to the events of the year 1972 at Lander College, particularly those occurring after the Lander bill was signed by Governor John C. West on June 14. Because so many participants in the drama are alive, this narrative will go no further than the bare facts of the case. It is enough to say that the situation became almost unbelievably chaotic. Visions of lucrative sinecures appeared to dance in some people's heads, while others watched with a certain alarm the political maneuverings inherent in the creation of a brand new state agency. Relations reached so strained a point that one board member expressed fear that Herd might refuse to move out of the president's house when it became known he would not continue as president. The State Board of Trustees, which had been created to oversee any new colleges brought into the state system, moved early to consolidate its position but communicated only with the existing board whose lame duck status and divided loyalties created their own problems. One of state board chairman James A. Rogers's most unfortunate utterances was that Lander would be a "new college." Many people, including alumni for scores of years and others who had worked and struggled to keep the college afloat, were not thrilled with any such designation. The first state budget was a problem, the catalog was a problem, everything was a problem because of the lack of communication and the trauma of the transfer. The state board did not choose to retain Don Herd as president, citing "lack of community support" as the reason, and chose instead Larry A. Jackson, a native of Florence who was at that time vice president for financial affairs at the University of Evansville. Boyce Grier must have thought he had come full circle when he read the story of Jackson's appointment in *The Index-Journal* of March 5, 1973. Describing the president-elect as an "ordained layman" of the Methodist Church, Chairman Rogers added: "With Lander's many years of history as a church-affiliated college prior to becoming county-supported, it seemed appropriate that this heritage be considered in the choice of its first president as a state institution." The official transfer date was July 1, 1973.

Lander College has always been important to Greenwood County, as much for its academic and cultural contributions as for its economic impact on the community. As a state institution its importance has merely increased, albeit tremendously and in every conceivable way. Lander's operating budget of some $16 million is spent largely in the area, and the state's capital investment of more than $31 million since 1973 has accrued to the benefit of all South Carolina citizens. If there is ambivalence in some quarters about the college's state agency status and a certain "loss of innocence," Greenwood citizens need only reflect on the school's long history and its struggles to attain some sort of security. Surely Greenwood can be proud that it rallied more than once to guarantee the future of an institution which, if it had not existed, would have had to be invented at some point along the way.

At this point it is probably necessary to bring the Lander-Methodist connection into some sort of perspective. Education in the South, particularly higher education, has always been a mixed bag, and early attempts at higher education for women were almost exclusively the work of the denominations. The Methodists should not be faulted for their zeal in educational evangelism because without it many colleges as we know them would not exist. The South Carolina Methodist Conference simply tried to spread itself too thinly in the early days, probably in response to appeals it felt it could not ignore. Also, the locations of early Methodist institutions must be considered: Methodists did not concentrate their efforts in the more populous lowcountry of South Carolina; indeed, Cokesbury was wilderness when Methodism came, and the Greenwood-Columbia-Spartanburg triangle was not the developed and industrialized area it is today when Methodist colleges began in those towns. Perhaps the reason the conference rejected Samuel Lander's offer three times in the late 1800s was the realization that supporting three colleges would simply be too much. It is important to remember that without the Methodist connection of about fifty years, there probably would have been no college for Greenwood to save. For that reason, Greenwood should salute, with certain reservations, the Methodist Conference years of Lander College, 1898-1948.

The transfer of Lander College to state control brought to an end one of the most interesting chapters of Greenwood County history. For a quarter of a century the county owned and operated a four-year college, the same college its first senator found and convinced to move to Greenwood in its earliest days as a county. Those who have written about Lander have chosen to call this situation unique, but in fact we do not know whether it is true that Lander was the *only* county-owned college in the United States. Whether or not Greenwood was alone in such an endeavor, there can be no question that its intervention saved Lander College from extinction in 1948. Nor were the 25 years that followed merely a period of marking time. The vote of the General Assembly to accept the college as a state institution was interpreted as recognition that Lander's influence was already statewide in scope, particularly in teacher training and nursing programs. While recognizing its history of service to the state, lawmakers also understood that Lander's county status meant serious limitations on its potential for the future. A whole new world opened when the legislature accepted Lander as a state institution. Tuition dropped immediately (it has since risen rather dramatically), enrollment increased, an overall building program/campus plan was drafted, the staff expanded, and Lander entered the most secure phase it had ever known in its hundred years of existence. Lander College today is an established regional state college enrolling approximately 2,500 students, still mostly from South Carolina. It offers the usual range of undergraduate instruction leading to the bachelor of arts or bachelor of science degree, as well as master's programs in selected fields.

In the spring of 1991 Larry A. Jackson announced his retirement as president of Lander College, effective in the summer of 1992. An honorary degree from Clemson at its summer commencement in 1991 cited him for length of service as chief executive of a state college. Jackson's tenure of nineteen years at the time of retirement makes him second only to founder Samuel Lander in terms of longevity. The search for his replacement ended with the announcement on March 3, 1992, that Dr. William C. Moran had been chosen as Lander's eleventh president.

This chapter has concentrated heavily on the college's earlier years, primarily because their history has never been coherently and chronologically documented, but also because Lander was an entirely different type of institution before 1973. The relationship between Greenwood and Lander College is an integral part of county history; even though the college has in a sense left the town and gone on to fulfill its own destiny, its story still says something important about Greenwood people.

The record should reflect that Boyce Grier remained active for some time after retirement in 1966. The President Emeritus maintained an office at the college and took great interest in Lander's progress during both the Herd administration and the first year of Jackson's. The community's regard for Grier is shown in the fact that he was elected to the County Hall of Fame in 1977, only three years after his death at the age of eighty on November 18, 1974. His wife, the former Lois Johnson, lived for another fifteen years. She died on October 30, 1989, only three months before her 89th birthday. Both are buried in Edgewood Cemetery.

Very few people knew that Don Herd was already blind in one eye when he left Lander on June 30, 1973. Despite several laser operations attempting to offset the effects of diabetic retinopathy, a series of hemorrhages that would result in total blindness about a year later was underway. After the inevitable happened, Herd entered a program sponsored by the South Carolina Commission for the Blind to learn Braille, as well as to take advantage of other aids available to blind citizens, such as the long cane, the laser cane, a Braille typewriter, and, most important of all, the talking books program. Although the first priority had to be shoring up his health and adjusting to the new reality of a serious handicap, Herd's fertile mind was able to take stock, regroup, and carry on.

The last five years of Herd's life were full and productive. He undertook a study of Old Cokesbury and published four small volumes documenting three important phases in the life of what he termed the "utopian society" Cokesbury represented. Even as he worked on the Cokesbury project, Herd was also outlining his next venture, a collection of historical and biographical sketches of the South Carolina Upcountry, a book he had been planning for about thirty years. The manuscript was completed less than a month before Herd's death, and the two-volume work, *The South Carolina Upcountry,1540-1980,* was published according to the original schedule he had conceived.

In addition to – or perhaps because of – fighting juvenile-onset diabetes all his life, Herd was always, to use a less than satisfactory modern term, an extremely goal-oriented individual. That trait, coupled with voracious reading in history and philosophy, would bear fruit again and again in his life, not least where Lander College was concerned. When he first took over as president, Herd was given to understand that some people in Greenwood would not be averse to Lander's becoming a two-year satellite of Clemson. Based on his reading of its history and his own assessment of its potential, however, Herd favored an expanded role for the college, not retrenchment, and he was always proud that Lander never regressed from its original baccalaureate-degree standing.

Never a team player nor "one of the boys," Herd kept his own counsel and followed his own vision for Lander's future always, a stance not calculated to endear him to members of boards and commissions in general. His understanding of people, politics, and power was behind the decision to involve Lander alumni and the county delegation in a direct appeal to the General Assembly for state support. He understood exactly what he was doing and whom he was offending with his methods, and no one was less surprised than he when he was not retained as president. But neither did he resign, as many people hoped he would, when that decision was made in the fall of 1972. Instead, he served out his term to the last day as a matter of principle; some people believe the cost of that decision to him personally was great. Herd never earned a doctorate, and no college ever awarded him an honorary degree. Not a single building bears his name, and he is not listed in the Greenwood County Hall of Fame. His memory is perpetuated at Lander College only in a small collection of southern history books in the library. In view of his lifelong love of books, nothing could be more appropriate. Don Herd died suddenly of a heart attack, one of the multiple effects of diabetes, on October 3, 1980. He was 48 years old.

During the early period of Lander's county college status, conventional campus wisdom held that the majority of its faculty members were either on the way up or the way down. Whichever, it was assumed that most of the best ones would not stay long enough to make a career at Lander College. Salaries were low and benefits were negligible; President Grier was notorious for hiring first-time college teachers, as well as some well past retirement age, particularly if they held doctorates. Doubtless the question of salary requirements loomed large in these decisions. He also took a page from Colonel F. N. K. Bailey's book by awarding rank in lieu of salary, and room and board were part of some salary contracts as late as the 1950s. Nevertheless, then as now, student motivation was the most powerful spur to learning, and Lander has always had its share of professors who facilitated that process. No one who sat in Anna Rena Blake's English 101 class could forget that straight back, almost clenched jaw, and deadly eye busily exposing the inadequacy of one's high school background. One simply improved or got out of her class as soon as possible. Even in the early 1950s the fact that Lander was struggling to survive had no discernible effect in the classroom.

Students found a vast difference in the transition from high school seniors to Lander freshmen, and if they were ready for it as many were, there was never a doubt they were in a real college. Learning was the student's responsibility, and even out-of-class hours were somehow different if one were a college student. Many discovered, for example, that even an inadequate college library can be an awesome resource.

Other memorable professors from the more or less modern era include Nell Q. Henry, who taught chemistry; Dr. George Walker, English literature; Samuel McLeod, mathematics; Dr. Joseph Stukes, history; Gladys Wham, education; Marie Chisholm, art; and Elizabeth C. Welborn, librarian. Many readers will remember other Lander personalities such as Elizabeth Alexander, Annie Aunspaugh, Blanche Hanner, Elizabeth K. Ouzts, Mrs. Irving Messick, Estill Blocker, Rennie Hook, and Carrie P. Lander, one of Dr. Samuel's granddaughters, who remained on the staff until well into the Grier administration. Two very important Lander professors might be considered as symbols for all the men and women, no longer living, who ever marched in Lander's academic processions. In another sense, however, Maybelle Coleman and Bill Ricketson represented only themselves. Each left an indelible imprint at Lander College and on those who knew them.

Maybelle Coleman was a native of the New Market section of Greenwood County. She was a granddaughter of Thomas Lipscomb Coleman and made her home for many years in the big house he bought about 1869. Miss Coleman, one of five children of Martin Hackett and Mary Ella Brooks Coleman, was educated in Greenwood and graduated from Lander in 1909. She continued her education, first at Ward Belmont College in Nashville and then Columbia University in New York where she earned the master's degree. Much later she earned the Ph.D. in sociology from Duke University. Coleman was, in fact, one of the two "famous" faculty members with the Ph.D. when the Methodist committee made its study in 1946-47. She was also academic dean at the time, a post she held from 1943 to 1950. In addition, it was Coleman who acted as president from the time Rast resigned in March 1948 until Grier came on board in the middle of June. Maybelle Coleman's Greenwood County credentials were impeccable; Margaret Watson placed the family in Cambridge (Ninety Six) in the early 1900s. It is conceivable that a teen-aged Maybelle Coleman drove in with her family from New Market to see Samuel Lander lay the cornerstone for Greenwood Hall in 1904. The prominence of her position at Lander – she was academic dean and acting president when the county assumed control – must have brought a certain reassurance that a strong county connection already existed through her.

Maybelle Coleman's career spanned 36 years until her retirement in 1962 at the age of 72. In one sense her life paralleled those of other Greenwood County schoolteachers: she never married, and she became something of a fixture in the community and at Mount Lebanon Methodist Church. In another sense, however, Coleman was different, no doubt because of the choice to devote herself to college teaching, and she seemed to know how important her educational attainments were to Lander at a critical time in its history. She and Lander College were practically indistinguishable in people's minds for many years. The college showed its gratitude by awarding her an honorary degree in 1963 and the Medallion of Honor in 1988. A singular honor came when the Edward Arms apartment building, purchased in 1975 for college housing, was rechristened Coleman Hall in tribute.

Although ages and birthdays should not be accorded inordinate importance in describing people's lives, it is somehow significant that Maybelle Coleman died on the first day of January 1990, in her one hundredth year. She was exactly 99 years and three weeks old at the time of her death. Efficient and decisive to the last, it was she who summoned the ambulance, and her final illness was very brief.

On the other hand, William F. Ricketson died on September 15, 1988, at the age of 62, in the full flower of mature intellect and after only 21 years on the Lander faculty. Ricketson was a Georgia native who was educated at Mercer, the University of North Carolina, and the University of Georgia. He was also a graduate of the Southern Baptist Seminary with both bachelor's and master's degrees in theology. An anthropologist and historian, Ricketson was first and foremost a scholar, one whose primary research centered on seventeenth century American history. The scholar was also a teacher: Ricketson's students never doubted that they sat at the feet of a master, and Sunday School lessons on the days he taught at the First Baptist Church were like no others. The scholar/teacher was a stimulating conversationalist as well; a lunch table discussion with Bill Ricketson was an unforgettable experience. Lander alumnus Harris Bailey gave an interesting answer when asked for his assessment of Ricketson: "College faculties fall into three categories," he said. "There are teachers, there are educators, and there are scholars. Dr. Ricketson bridged the gaps; he was all three." When pressed for a one-liner, Bailey added, "He invigorated his students with the love of his craft."

A memorial service was held at the college soon after Ricketson's death. An empty chair draped with his academic regalia was a poignant reminder that a scholar of his particular kind was not likely to be seen again at Lander College.

Colleges assume all sorts of symbolic significance in people's lives. Americans supposedly revere their institutions of learning: reunions, "old school ties," class rings, and fraternity pins evoke nostalgia while all-but-professional sports events, which actually constitute big business in anybody's language, masquerade under the guise of a "schoolboy" network. Lander College, fortunately, is guilty of very few of the excesses that plague American higher education in the late twentieth century, and the sheer variety of its several "lives" marks it as particularly pertinent in the story of Greenwood County. The college is actually 25 years older than the county; its history therefore links Greenwood with more than a century of developments in American higher education as well as with a true pioneer in education for women. A realization something of that sort prompted The Lander Foundation to offer a seminar entitled "Lander College: A Historical Perspective" as a community service in November 1983. Four panelists reviewed Lander in the contexts of South Carolina history, educational history, and local/architectural history, as well as its prospects as a state institution. Among the panelists was a professor of architecture at Clemson University who only a year earlier had led a class of fourth-year students in an adaptive use project focusing on Lander's Old Main Building. Professor Martin A. Davis's presentation was a thought-provoking paper which characterized Old Main not only as representative of the college but also as a "statement of particularity." The building, he said, "represents a very special kind of distinctive personal experience, . . . [one with] different associations to different people."

Old Main's days are numbered. Both Laura Lander Hall and Willson Hall are slated for demolition, and only Greenwood Hall will survive as a small part of a giant new science building planned for the near future. Some people are content that at least one section of Lander's original building will be saved; they believe the planned structure will symbolize the fusion of old and new and thus represent Lander's story in a unique way. Others, who believe there can be no substitute for the genuine article, want the entire building saved and rehabilitated for another round of educational use. Preservationists point to the fact that the building — all of it — was placed on the National Register of Historic Places in 1984. This designation means that a national rather than strictly a local landmark will soon be only a memory. A particularly eloquent section of Professor Davis's paper from 1983 speaks to this issue. He wrote that buildings become truly rich only when they acquire the quality of myth through association with important people and events. Its association with Samuel Lander, R. H. Hunt, and a developing Greenwood was the "unique and endless event" that created for Old Main a special place in the history of Lander College and the county. Davis believes planners should be careful that their perspective in determining the quality of human environment selects from the past as well as the present, since there is more to be gained from a study of actual experience and the factors that molded it than from any amount of conjecture. "We do not start afresh," he wrote. "Our previous cultural . . . inheritance is crucial to our present and future development."

8

TOWNS, SECTIONS, AND PLACE NAMES

Home is the place where, when you
have to go there,
They have to take you in.
Robert Frost

As states and counties go, neither South Carolina nor Greenwood is particularly large. The area of South Carolina, a little more than 30,000 square miles, means the state is about one-tenth the size of Texas and slightly larger than West Virginia. The area of Greenwood County is just under 451 square miles, or something over 288,000 acres. Its 1990 census population of a little more than 59,000, therefore, works out to a ratio of about one person for every five acres. The density of the county's population – or, more correctly, the lack of density – suggests that county residents should be content to view themselves as just that: county residents. Not so. While South Carolina might not actually be unique in this regard, the attachment of its citizens to a sense of specific *place* is so strong that the first place-name journal in the United States, *Names in South Carolina,* was founded at the University of South Carolina in 1954. Its editor, Claude Henry Neuffer, wrote that, aside from the scholarly purpose of the undertaking, the book represented something else to most South Carolinians, both native and adopted: "It does reveal here and there our tastes, our temperament, our quixotic attachment to lost causes and odd ways, our inimitable Southern character sometimes so sadly misjudged by those of a more frigid climate and a colder reason."

Greenwood County is no slouch in the place name game. An early county map from a survey in 1898 is divided into townships as administrative and electoral districts. The first subdivision of the new county resulted in sixteen named townships containing 46 school districts; the changing configuration of the school districts is documented in another chapter. The names of the original townships and other place names contribute to a rich legacy of Greenwood County history. Proceeding roughly north to south, there are Walnut Grove, Hodges, Cokesbury, Coronaca, Greenwood, Ninety-Six, Verdery, Bradley, Troy, Yeldell, Callison, Kirksey, Phoenix, Fellowship, Brooks, and Kinards. Located on the map, which was the work of W. H. Yeldell and W. J. Kirk, are schools, churches, and post offices, as well as rivers and creeks, railroads, stores, and residences. One particular spot in Brooks Township is labeled

"Senator Tilman [sic] Place." The boundary lines changed when McCormick County was created in 1916. This action apparently robbed the county of the Yeldell Section along Hard Labor Creek just below Troy; at any rate, there is no sign of Yeldell on the map included in H. T. Cook's *The Hard Labor Section.* That map, drawn in 1923 by Emmett I. Davis, covers portions of Greenwood, Abbeville, Edgefield, and McCormick Counties and contains even more place names. This chapter sketches the histories of the original townships, as well as a few other place names listed in Neuffer's book.

William R. Walker, the one-man police force of Hodges, wrote the town's history as an assignment for an English class in 1977. That paper, annotated and updated by Betty Emerson Riddle, was the basis of the following sketch. Riddle was also the source for numerous newspaper articles and other memorabilia consulted as background. The "Indian-chief-and-beautiful-white-maiden" story from the early history of the Hodges family is included for its curiosity value and its connection to the Cateechee-Ninety Six legend. The Hodges story appears in several Greenwood sources, including No. 275 of the "Our Old Roads" series in the local newspaper during the 1940s.

Hodges is located about halfway between Greenwood and Ware Shoals just off Highway 25. The origin of the name is perfectly straightforward: the town was named for General George Washington Hodges whose grandfather had settled the area in 1755 with a purchase of property in what is now Greenwood County. The original Hodges's son, Major John Hodges, held a commission in the Revolutionary army, and the two men participated actively in the struggle with both Tories and Indians. The fact that John Hodges also sired twenty children is probably a mixed blessing for present-day genealogists, since southern family names tend to repeat themselves in each generation so that dates assume great importance as the only means of identifying which was which.

George Washington Hodges (1792-1876), the second child of the second marriage of John Hodges, made a name for himself well before a town was named for him. He served in the War of 1812 as a lieutenant; his general's rank was earned in the state militia. He was also appointed a commissioner of Indian affairs, served in the General Assembly, and was elected sheriff of Abbeville County for a four-year term. He was a man of industry and economy who managed to amass a considerable fortune as a very successful cotton farmer. One tangible reminder of the general's fortune remains in the form of the beautiful old house in the heart of town. The Hodges house, built in 1822 and extensively remodeled much later by a grandson, was considered the finest home above Columbia and a landmark that became known as the "White House" by travelers between Greenville and the state capital. Old houses acquire importance in many ways: the fewest owners over the longest time span might be one means of measuring. The Hodges house has had only five owners in its 158-year history, an average tenure of more than thirty years. The house is built in the style known colloquially as the "banker's house" with four Ionic columns in front; it probably reflects more of the Greek Revival style than any other architectural order.

Hodges received its name shortly after the first railroad depot was opened in 1852. At first the stop was called Cokesbury Junction, since nearby Cokesbury had been a thriving community for more than thirty years when the Columbia-Greenville Railroad came. A meeting to discuss proposed routes had been held in Cokesbury on January 2, 1848. Don Herd wrote: "Tradition tells us that the people of Cokesbury were against the route traversing their peaceful village," but one is forced to wonder in retrospect whether that attitude might have been sour grapes after the actual route some two miles west of the village had been determined. Walker, citing Guy Emerson as his source, confirmed the story that Cokesbury really did not want the line, but believed the reason was that landowners were afraid their "little slaves" might be in danger. Whatever the truth about Cokesbury's wishes, the railroad ran through Hodges and the station's name was changed to honor the general about 1855. The first message over the first telegraph line was sent to G. W. Hodges as "Patriarch" of the village; the message was preserved in the family archives. Another family artifact is General Hodges's sword which hangs on the mantel in the Greenwood home of his great-great-niece Louise Hartzog. She believes her uncle carried the sword in his capacity as a state militiaman and not in the War of 1812.

The same family figured in a wildly improbable Indian chief and white maiden love story similar to the Cateechee legend connected to Ninety Six. While the latter has been run to ground conclusively by H. L. Watson, Don Herd, and others, the Hodges tale is reported in several sources as fact. One story from *The Charlotte Observer* of October 7, 1928, repeated it in quotation marks and named as the source the (presumably written) family history of B. S. Hodges. Margaret Watson called it "a family legend," while her father used the term "tradition." Serious historians are opposed to "papering" history with worthless lore, but perhaps the Hodges legend bears repeating one more time, if only for its sheer imaginativeness. It seems that John Hodges's father, while home on furlough during the Revolutionary War, was killed in an Indian attack on his cabin. During the attack four of his daughters were captured, bound, and thrown in the cabin to be burned alive. At this point one of the warriors noticed the beauty of one of the daughters and offered to spare her life if she would become his wife. She promptly accepted the offer and rode off to a new life with her benefactor, presumably leaving her dead father and three living sisters in a burning cabin. Hers must have been a most forgiving nature, for the next thing we know she reappears, along with her half-breed son, for a joyous reunion with whatever was left of the family. Although her devoted husband had extracted a promise that she would return to him, she allowed herself to be persuaded to remain with her family and friends in Hodges. "Being yet of fine personal appearance and possessed of attractive manners," she eventually gained a new husband by the name of Rosemond. The Rosemonds moved west with all their children several years later, and none ever returned to the area. In the meantime the Indian son grew up in the village, but when he began to show the "characteristics of the race," he apparently felt the call of the wild and left to find his father's people, never to be heard from again. It must be admitted that the ending is extremely neat.

One hardly knows where to begin finding problems with this story, even though the newspaper article stressed that General Hodges remembered seeing the Indian boy and hearing the tale from his mother's own lips. John Wayne once starred in a movie with the same theme, but there the similarity ends. His character's entire purpose during the long search was to find and kill the girl who had been kidnapped by her family's murderers in order to remove the taint of association with the villainous redskins. Of course he relented when she was finally found, and of course there was no Indian "marriage" and no Indian child; nevertheless, the story of *The Searchers* is much more plausible than the Hodges family legend in which a white woman exerted "a wonderfully refining influence over the red man" to the point of "sweet communion with each other as to their child."

The first post office in Hodges was established in 1852 but for some unknown reason lasted less than a year. A post office had existed in Cokesbury since 1825; possibly the distance between them was considered too small. The office was, however, re-established about 1855 and managed to outlast the one at Cokesbury, which was discontinued in 1943. Rural service was inaugurated in 1905.

Everyone likes to point out that Hodges was once larger than Greenwood, but so for that matter were both Cokesbury and Ninety Six. The town was a thriving railroad center and farming community in the years just before the Civil War. There was bustling activity, not only at the railroad depots where five passenger trains stopped daily, but also at the two banks, the drug store, the hotel, two doctors' offices, and nearly a dozen stores that made up the town. Riddle commented with a smile that every new newspaper reporter in the area could count on a Hodges article of some kind to combat a slow news day; as a result, any number of stories exist. One from *The Anderson Independent* (c. 1954) documents the 50th anniversary of the Bank of Hodges, famous for the fact that it survived the Great Depression. Only three banks in the third congressional district could claim that distinction. Bob S. Hodges, president of the bank, was inducted into the Half Century Club of the South Carolina Bankers Association in 1954. He is quoted in the accompanying article: "The bank has always protected its depositors and has paid dividends every year except in 1920 and 1921." The Bank of Hodges was acquired by The Palmetto Bank in 1988.

Bob Hodges was noted for wise and progressive farming practices as well as the business acumen to establish a bank in response to the town's needs. His training in banking took the form of visiting a bank in Anderson where he was allowed to stand around and look over people's shoulders for a week or so. Hodges's powers of observation must have been quite keen; he was self-confident enough to say many years later, "Then I went back home and we opened a bank."

A pleasant and peaceful village now, Hodges once had a reputation rivaling that of many wild west towns. When railroad crews were in town, there was plenty of gambling, drinking, and cockfighting, as well as something loosely called "night life" that attracted the attention of traveling salesmen. Ella Hodges Hatcher repeated her father's line that there was a time when a person could get off one train, drink in any of several bars, watch a horse race, and see a cockfight before boarding the next train. Hodges was called a "sin center" and, more frequently, a "hell hole." Nor was violence uncommon. One of the most chilling events took place in 1868 when Benjamin F. Randolph, a black member of the General Assembly, was campaigning for re-election. He had spoken extemporaneously to a group of blacks lounging at the Hodges Depot one day in October, promising them that property would be seized by the federal government and given to them. Randolph was admonished by D. Wyatt Aiken, a prominent citizen of Cokesbury who would later make a name for himself in agricultural reform, about his incendiary speech and warned that his life would be in danger if he persisted in such folly. Randolph spurned Aiken's advice and went on to Abbeville where he spoke in the same vein. The following day he was shot down in broad daylight as he changed trains at the depot in Hodges. Three white assassins managed to escape on horseback before they could be identified. Aiken was arrested as an accessory to murder and incarcerated for two days in Columbia before influential friends managed his release. One of the perpetrators was later caught, and Aiken was never actually tried for the crime.

Walker was able to interview one of the town's most irrepressible citizens, Guy Emerson, for his paper on Hodges. Emerson had followed his father, W. H. Emerson, described as "a well-known horse racer in the early part of the century," in the storekeeping business; Emerson's Store dated from 1883 to its closing upon Guy Emerson's death in 1977 some 94 years later. Guy Emerson was also quoted in nearly every Hodges article; it is easy to regard him as the foremost repository of Hodges lore during his lifetime and his daughter Betty as his successor. A little article by John Bigham in *The Columbia Record* of February 15, 1962, described a conversation between the columnist and the proprietor around "a friendly pot-bellied stove" in Emerson's Store. The writer noted Emerson's warning that poking fun or downgrading the town would not be tolerated. Both the article and Walker's paper indicated that Emerson was well content with the choice to make his home in Hodges where things were "nice and quiet." The store, he said, gave him "a place to loaf and take in a little money occasionally." One of Emerson's specialties was aged hoop cheese, which is fortunately still available at another Hodges landmark, Godfrey's Market.

The slow decline of towns such as Hodges has been attributed to the automobile age and the changing economy. Walker noted that most people now hold jobs in nearby industrial plants and do most of their shopping in larger towns such as Anderson, Greenwood, and Abbeville. There has been, however, a revitalization of sorts in recent years prompted, some say, by a fire which destroyed one of the town's oldest homes a few years ago. The Hodges-Cokesbury Fire Department was established as a result and quickly became the most valued facility in town. A few new businesses appeared also, some housed in the town's historic old buildings. Examples are an antique shop which opened in an old bank building, a gift shop in the old post office, a nightclub in the Southern Railway Depot, and a construction company in the old cotton gin. The news that a Sara Lee textile plant would be built in Greenwood County was announced in early 1990. Ware Shoals was named as its location, and the announcement itself was a media event featuring the governor, county senators and representatives, as well as city and county councils of both Greenwood and Ware Shoals. Hodges, which has both a mayor and a town council, was conspicuously unrepresented, an embarrassing oversight indeed considering that the new plant's mailing address will be Rt. 1, Hodges and its location a mile or two beyond the town limits. Mayor Al Nickles was typically philosophical about the oversight in an interview printed in *The Index-Journal* of February 4, 1990. "Hodges is just not as politically important as Greenwood or Ware Shoals," he said.

An article from *The Greenville News* of October 27, 1978, probably pinpointed the mystique of Hodges best in its title, "Just a Slow, Easy Town." The article consisted primarily of an interview with the then-mayor, William Bagwell, himself a native who came back home after 25 years or so in Greenville. Bagwell named a couple of bank robberies and a tornado as the most exciting events in the town's recent history. The article also provided the best chronology of the evolution of the gazebo as the town's most significant landmark, calling the public well "a reminder of the town's early history." The well itself, according to Bagwell, had gone dry years before and "someone foolishly filled it in." The town council subsequently had to decide whether to tear down the structure surrounding the dry well or renovate it. Apparently there was not much choice since, in Bagwell's words, "there were some people who would have run us out of town if we had torn it down." Accordingly, "the town had the floor cemented, placed an old pump in the center, and built a square gazebo-like, lattice-sided structure over the well. The pump furnishes no water." It does, however, furnish a great deal of symbolic value to the citizens of Hodges.

The population of the town of Hodges, listed in published sources as 350 in 1928, 215 in 1978, and 135 in 1990, attests to its decline as any sort of population center of Greenwood County. Its appeal to the hard core among its inhabitants is, however, of a timeless quality. Most would not consider living anywhere else. One interesting fragment of town lore is an unfinished resolution written by Guy Emerson at some indeterminate time and preserved by his daughter Betty Riddle:

> WHEREAS, Former citizens and our forbears of this Village, in times past, saw the need and advantages of a place whereby the stranger, the passerby, and the wayfaring man could pause, rest in the shade, and quench his thirst, before resuming his or her known and unknown destinations, so had a well digged in center of said Village,
>
> AND WHEREAS, The villagers had a central location where they could come and get a drink, or pail of water, meet with their fellow villagers to discuss crops, weather, politics, religion, or any topic that was current at that time,
>
> AND WHEREAS, It was said that the drugstores of that time availed themselves of copious quantities of this water in concocting the medicines they dispensed in those days,
>
> AND WHEREAS, The well house has been the backdrop of a stage where politicians with choice words have made their appeal to voters of this area, traveling preachers, of many denominations, brought forth the WORD of GOD to both saints and sinners, and also was the setting for tragedies, including shooting and cutting scrapes, and in the early part of this century a murder. On the brighter side we find it a place of gayety with Christmas decorations we placed and young people singing carols and Hosannas to the Lord,
>
> AND WHEREAS, In more modern times our city fathers saw fit to install a modern pump to deliver this crystal water to commercial and industrial places so desiring it at a minimum fee, which we think is right and proper, so long as they have a spigot or fountain so whoever will may quench his thirst at anytime day or night,
>
> AND WHEREAS, The well house and its quaint appearance having been a land mark for so long; in fact it is the exact center of town, as our town limits are measured one half mile in all directions from this well house

At this point the resolution comes to an abrupt halt. Whether or not the writer would agree that his sentiments threatened to get somewhat out of hand, we are not permitted to learn the content of Emerson's final "Now therefore, be it resolved" paragraph, nor do we know to what purpose he proposed to direct his resolution when it was finished. The fragment is, however, notable for the part it plays in that strong sense of place common to most inhabitants of the little town of Hodges.

Quite near Hodges – indeed, the two villages are linked in several ways, not the least of which is the prevalence of the name *Hodges* in local lore – is the Cokesbury community. The result of years of evolution from its beginnings in the late 1700s as Tabernacle and later as Mount Ariel, Cokesbury has an interesting history indeed. It was famous as the site of one of the earliest experiments in Methodist education in the United States and, if one accepts Don Herd's theory, it was at the same time an example of a utopian society similar to those found in Amana, Iowa, and Oneida, New York. Herd emphasized, however, that the utopian aspects of early Cokesbury developed naturally from the processes that created the community; they were not in themselves part of the plan. Cokesbury was in no sense a communal society whose members had taken a vow of personal poverty and shared ownership of resources; rather, it was in Herd's view an independent association of men and women of property who were firm believers in the free enterprise system and for that matter, before the Civil War at least, in slavery. Its settlers came from Maine to Georgia. The attractions seem to have been many: from good schools, good farm land, and thrifty and lucrative agricultural practices to the all-pervasive Methodism that characterized the community.

The earliest settlers, whose names include Connor, Davis, Herndon, Roseman, and Sims, among many others, arrived in various ways. Some had land grants for military service, some came from nearby Cambridge (Ninety Six), and some arrived by way of the "great wagon road" through Virginia. This community of plantations and farms came to be known as Tabernacle, a reference to the meeting house that had sprung up around 1788 to house the Methodist Society and received its official name when regular services were established in 1812. James E. Glenn, a fire-and-brimstone preacher, was the first regular minister.

Methodism had been brought to South Carolina by Bishop Francis Asbury in 1785. A great believer in education, as was the sect's founder John Wesley, Asbury had established a school in the Mount Bethel community of Newberry District. This school lasted less than thirty years; nevertheless, Herd recounted that in its heyday in the early 1800s it furnished the entire graduating class of the South Carolina College (University of South Carolina) for two consecutive years. The difficulty, then as now, lay in attracting and keeping good teachers. Mount Bethel Academy "died" in 1820, only to reappear as Tabernacle Academy in Abbeville District the same year, replacing the Reverend Glenn's field school which had existed for five or six years.

Perhaps the most famous of the early teachers at Tabernacle was Stephen Olin, a native of Vermont whose health problems had forced him to seek a milder climate as well as a somewhat less lofty career than the one he first envisioned. It seems his mind was set on the law and politics. He is supposed to have said that at one time he would have "bartered a seat in Heaven for a seat in Congress." The office of Chief Justice of the United States was another that caught his fancy, and why not? As the valedictorian of Middlebury College, Olin must have thought anything was possible. Instead, at the age of 23 and recovering from a complete breakdown, he found himself bound for Augusta, Georgia, to take a position as schoolmaster. That job fell through, but a place at Tabernacle came to his attention, and he continued his journey into South Carolina. A letter from Olin to a friend in Vermont described the terrain he found on the way:

> The country this side of Savannah River is barren and wretched beyond the power of imagination to conceive. It is a part of the great pine barrens that occupy the middle country of the two Carolinas and Virginia. The soil is formed of yellow sands and small white stones, which have the appearance of burned limestone. The timber is pitch-pine and stunted oaks. This region is but thinly inhabited, and the few human beings who are to be seen exhibit every appearance of want and wretchedness.

Stephen Olin found the Tabernacle community very congenial, however, and wrote: "I board in a rich family; live better than at Savannah or Augusta; have coffee and tea in New England style; good wheat bread and butter, and a plentiful table." He stayed at Tabernacle about three years. During that time, he was converted to Methodism and became a powerful preacher, although recurring health problems prevented full participation in the itinerant ministry. He settled for teaching at the University of Georgia for several years until he was named first president of Randolph Macon College for Men in Virginia. He was later named President of Wesleyan University in Connecticut. Olin died in 1851.

Shortly after Olin left, the entire community decided to relocate to a more suitable site a couple of miles away. Herd believed this was a deliberate move toward a planned community based on the commonly-held beliefs and aspirations of the citizens and not a search for a more "healthful" location as others have suggested. As Olin had pointed out earlier, every man, woman, and child was Methodist. Furthermore, the fledgling school had the patronage of the Methodist Church, and new people were moving to the area to take advantage of the educational and other opportunities offered there. The lifestyle was simple and unpretentious, and vices such as dancing, drinking, smoking, and gambling did not exist. The community was to have a new name as well. The fanciful-sounding, but somehow suitable, name of Mount Ariel was chosen, and the village was laid out quite deliberately. One of the first sites chosen was that for the school, and a post office was established in 1825. A reminiscence by McKendree Glenn in the Connor family papers stated that the area chosen was all woods between the houses of George Connor and G. W. Hodges. The building at the abandoned Tabernacle site continued for another fifty years or so as a church; the adjacent cemetery still exists and is maintained by the Greenwood County Historical Society.

The next big name in Mount Ariel history is that of Joseph Travis, who headed the school for six years. A separate academy for females was erected at some point, and both schools prospered during Travis's tenure in spite of the usual disputes regarding ownership of school property. The question was whether the Methodist Church or the trustees held title to land and buildings. The village was also incorporated during this period and its limits set at three-quarters of a mile in all directions from the male academy building. The school was thus officially the center of village life. Mount Ariel Academy was not fully a conference school, and financial difficulties continually plagued trustees and patrons.

Dr. and Mrs. Thomas Cottrell arrived to take charge of the female school in 1828. Fortunately they were willing to take their chances on making a living; according to the trustees, the Cottrells had agreed to take whatever the school brought in as salary. In spite of a controversy over teaching music, the Cottrells remained at Cokesbury until his death in 1834 and her departure for Alabama two years later.

At this juncture the Methodist Church decided it was time to establish its own school, one that featured the then-prevailing idea of manual labor for its students, to serve as a feeder school for Randolph Macon. Mount Ariel was quick to offer its two schools and their property, with the added inducement of $6,000, if the conference would accept their village as the site. The conference agreed and promptly named a board of trustees which held its first meeting on May 16, 1834. R. E. Stackhouse explained the Church's reasoning:

> Mount Ariel possessed exceptional advantages as a school site in addition to the money consideration. The village was beautiful for situation. Magnificent groves of native oak crowned the crests of several successive eminences, which gradually rolled toward a bold ravine that naturally drained the village. The streets were high and dry and the water was cold and limpid. It is doubtful if there was a healthier village in the State than Mount Ariel. The social and religious environment of the proposed school was superb. The people had every advantage of blood, intelligence and wealth. Many of them had moved there for the purpose of educating their children, and the two flourishing academies were proof that they were thoroughly aroused to the importance of education.

Probably as a consequence of this giant step in Methodism, the citizens of Mount Ariel met just three days after the trustees' meeting and voted to change the name of the village to Cokesbury in honor of Bishops Thomas Coke and Francis Asbury.

Although the manual labor phase of the new Methodist Conference School lasted less than ten years, that period was recalled with particular fondness by a number of distinguished alumni in later years. A brick school building, plus appropriate outbuildings and a house for the rector, or headmaster, came at this period. Advertisements for the school indicated that it owned nearly 1,000 acres of land and facilities to accommodate 100 students. The labor feature had necessitated the school's obtaining more land and farm equipment in order to keep the students in work; these expenditures further taxed its already shaky funding. One 1836 accounting indicated a treasury balance of less than $200. The conference-appointed agents always found excuses for not collecting their quota of contributions from the faithful. In fact, Herd wrote that South Carolina Methodists were never able adequately to fund any program of "educational evangelism" in the state, although they were zealous in founding schools.

While the military school concept was embraced primarily as discipline, proponents of the manual labor provision appeared to view it as useful in what amounts to thought control. One quote from Methodist sources recorded in Herd's book is quite sufficient to illustrate this point: the idea was "to occupy usefully every moment of time either in mental application or manual labor, [which] . . . while it forms and strengthens habits of industry, prevents the dissipation of thought, which invariably follows the ordinary school amusements. . . ." Manual labor was also meant to serve as a deterrent to punishment. "We confidently expect . . . that it will give such sobriety, and manliness to boyish character, as shall prevent much of the mischief and delinquency that call for punishment in common systems of education." It is interesting to note that students were paid for their work by means of credits to their accounts. It was possible to earn from $10 to $20 per year. The going rate was 3¢ per hour.

The emphasis on manual labor began to decline almost as soon as it had begun, and it was always more popular with clerics than with students. Even though the labor requirement was not particularly onerous, many students did not like to work and wanted to leave. Stackhouse wrote that "preconceived prejudices" of the students were defeating the purpose of the school. Leaders had convinced themselves that the manual labor policy was strictly for the students' own good. Herd equated the loss of students to their parents' adoption of James Henry Hammond's "mud-sill" theory that southern culture was built on the necessity of slaves to do the dirty work. People who could afford to send their sons to boarding school liked to believe those sons were becoming young "gentlemen" and not farm laborers. The idea was also dying in other parts of the state. One Cokesbury graduate later called the manual labor period "the delusion of our fathers."

Cokesbury's heyday was the period from 1843 to the mid 1850s. The school was called at that time the Cokesbury Conference Institute, and its rector, a West Pointer named Matthew J. Williams, was apparently a sound and sensible man. Even the financial prospects improved; although a proposed endowment never materialized, the school managed to operate in the black. Williams also introduced the inevitable military training, in the form of a company known as the "Cokesbury Fencibles," along with a military band. The possibilities of this venture were endless, and the groups exploited most of them. No one could resist the combination of snappy uniforms, banners, fife and drum, and real rifles, not to mention opportunities for debates and orations of various kinds. All these extras followed apace, even after Professor Williams left for greener pastures at the South Carolina College.

The conference school declined after it closed its dormitories in 1853. The main building had been declared unsafe after only twenty years and was demolished. The building which replaced it was merely a chapel with recitation rooms on either side. Some of the materials from the old building were sold to the Bascomb Lodge which was preparing to build its own female school at Cokesbury. There was no longer a dining room; students were expected to board with families in the community. The school was now generally regarded as a high school. In addition, Wofford College had opened in 1854, and Methodist interest had quite naturally shifted to the exciting prospect of a bona fide college. The fact that Wofford's first president was William Wightman, who also chaired Cokesbury's board of trustees, was a problem in itself. Divided loyalties were inevitable. To make matters worse, Wofford operated its own preparatory school for a time, a serious blow to Cokesbury's standing as a feeder school. Fortunately, the trustees soon saw the error of their ways, and Wofford's preparatory school was abandoned in favor of Cokesbury.

The population of the Cokesbury community in the 1860 census was 748, of whom 368 were black and, presumably, slaves. The school's enrollment had reached 110 students, and its rector believed it could easily grow to 200. But war was looming, and Cokesbury was drawn into the conflict as fully as every other community in the South. A company of sixty men known as the "Cokesbury Minute Men" was formed, and everything suddenly took second place to the exciting business of waging war.

Female education had been available at Cokesbury since the beginning but had often played second fiddle to the male schools. That changed when members of the Bascomb Masonic Lodge No. 80 decided to establish a female school at Cokesbury. The building still standing is the same one the Masons built in 1854 using materials from the old conference school. The first floor was devoted to classrooms; a chapel, or auditorium, occupied the second floor; and the Bascomb Lodge meeting hall made up the third floor. The first president was Francis A. Connor, a prominent Cokesbury citizen from the earliest days. Seventy students enrolled the first year; there were four teachers. The school was the only one of its kind in the state.

The Masonic Female Collegiate Institute closed for a time in 1865. It reopened the next year and managed to limp along until it finally died in 1874. The building was sold to a group of citizens who wanted to organize a Presbyterian church. The Presbyterians, in turn, swapped buildings with the Methodist Conference school still in operation. Thus the building became a school again.

Cokesbury was never the same after the war. Don Herd believed its ideals were eroded and its disillusionment compounded by the rise of industrial, commercial, and railroad centers across the state. The conference school itself dwindled to almost nothing during the early days of the war and closed entirely in 1864. It managed to reopen in 1866 but never regained anything like its former size. The move to the new building in 1875 was one bright spot, as was the transition to co-ed status in 1882, but it was clear that the school's best days were over. The school was finally absorbed by the public school system of Greenwood County in 1918.

Cokesbury was also the site of an early experiment in education for black children two years before Brewer Institute was founded in Greenwood. The African Methodist Episcopal Church established Payne Institute in 1870 on a 150-acre tract of land less than a mile from the Masonic Female school. Don Herd surmised that Cokesbury was chosen because the conference believed its long history of commitment to educational pursuits would override any community opposition along racial lines. The school was named for Bishop Daniel Alexander Payne, a Charleston native whose outspoken views on black separatism in education and religion had made him unwelcome in the South. Payne Institute evidently lasted some ten years, although little information exists from local sources concerning its enrollment, student makeup, or leadership. The school was moved to Columbia in 1880 and renamed Allen University to honor Bishop Richard Allen, founder of the A. M. E. Church. Allen's centennial celebration in 1970 acknowledged its beginnings in what is now Greenwood County.

H. L. Watson wrote about yet another school and Methodist church located not far from Cokesbury. Evidently Andrew Chapel Church was established about the same time the Tabernacle community was becoming Mt. Ariel (early 1820s), and the one-teacher school was added in the late 1850s. Watson wondered why another Methodist community existed so near Cokesbury and concluded that Andrew Chapel probably pre-dated its more famous neighbor. This surmise lends credence to Don Herd's theory that Mt. Ariel and later Cokesbury were planned communities from the beginning, communities whose members constituted almost the equivalent of a closely-held corporation.

While the story of Cokesbury is primarily the story of its schools, the community was also important for its stability and self-contained lifestyle for many years before it became part of Greenwood County. It was a sort of enclave protected, at least for a time, from outside influences. The rigorous rules enforced at the schools practically guaranteed conformity to village standards of behavior, and the few episodes of expulsion for "gross immorality" probably meant only that a student was caught smoking or playing cards. In addition to the schools and the church, a number of commercial ventures flourished at Cokesbury. While reminiscences by alumni usually described camp meetings and religious conversions first – one says Gabriel Hodges worked boys equally well in a prayer meeting or a cotton patch – they also recalled the placement of particular houses, stores, and other gathering places. Cokesbury had a Jewish merchant and postmaster, Morris Strauss, in the 1840s; Sterling Graydon was a storekeeper; there were a couple of doctors; and so many ministers lived there that a section of the village was known as Preachers' Row. Quite a number of extremely prominent men were educated at Cokesbury, including bishops, college presidents, doctors, lawyers, and at least one Confederate general. A late reminiscence, written by Judge W. C. Benet and printed in *The Index-Journal* of June 14, 1925, described Cokesbury during Reconstruction days. Benet noted that only three public buildings and four stores were left. Thus the village was on the decline well before Greenwood became a county. Only a few of the original houses remain, and hardly any evidence of Cokesbury's glory days can be found. But, thanks to the efforts of Nell S. Graydon, the original building of the Masonic Female Collegiate Institute was saved from demolition in the 1960s. This magnificent structure has been restored and is used for weddings and other gatherings throughout the year. The Cokesbury Historic and Recreational Commission was created by an act of the General Assembly to hold title to the building and adjoining land, and Cokesbury is listed as a historic district in the National Register of Historic Places.

A fuller account of the history of Cokesbury, including many more names and anecdotes than those mentioned here, can be found in *Mount Ariel-Cokesbury, A Biography of an Upcountry Utopian Community*, by E. Don Herd, Jr. (1979). Margaret Watson's *Greenwood County Sketches* also contains accounts of many of Cokesbury's early families.

The town of Ware Shoals in the early township of Walnut Grove evolved, according to *From Hill to Dale to Hollow* (1983), from a "favorite picnic and fishing site" nestled on the banks of the Saluda River where Greenwood, Abbeville, and Laurens counties touch. The authors surmised that it might have been on a fishing trip that Laurens citizen Nat B. Dial was inspired to develop the land as an industrial site and the shoals as a source of energy. Margaret Watson's account is more prosaic and probably also more accurate: she named Dial as only one of seven original incorporators – five from Laurens, one from Hodges, and one from Greenwood – of the Wares Shoals Manufacturing Company, an enterprise that was twelve years getting underway. Although the company purchased about 1,300 acres of land and began the construction of a cotton mill, hydroelectric plant, and mill village, it soon ran into financial difficulties. The officers managed to interest Benjamin Riegel, CEO of the Riegel Sack Company, in the plant's potential as a supplier of cotton cloth for the paper and sack business, and a deal was struck in 1905. At that point Benjamin Riegel moved from New York to Greenwood County to take personal charge of development and construction of the project over the next two years. The company dropped the "s" from "Wares" in 1906 and for the next forty years was known as Ware Shoals Manufacturing Company. Its name changed again in 1946 when the plant became part of Riegel Textile Corporation. As for the name of the town, the strong assumption is that the "Ware" portion comes from a pre-Revolutionary family who lived in the area. A Nicholas and Martha Ware were listed as charter members of Turkey Creek Baptist Church in Abbeville County in 1785. "Shoals" refers to the shallow places in the Saluda River nearby.

The importance of the textile plant to the town cannot be overemphasized; neither, apparently, can the influences of Benjamin Riegel during the two years he lived there. It was Riegel who persuaded the Southern Railway Corporation to build a spur line from the nearest stop at that time, seven miles away in Donalds, into Ware Shoals to facilitate constructing and equipping the mill. It was he also who personally supervised the initial staffing, naming W. C. (Bill) Cobb as first manufacturing superintendent. One source says that "Super" Cobb, as he was affectionately called, left his fingerprints on everything that functioned in Ware Shoals, except the post office, for the next 25 years. The Ware Shoals plant was recognized as one of the best in the South by 1910.

Since Ware Shoals developed strictly as a "company town," it is impossible to escape at least some exploration of the paternalism common to nearly every such town in the early days of the cotton manufacturing industry. Books and articles on the subject abound, nearly all of which for many years vilified mill owners as almost the equivalent of slaveholders. The cotton mill worker became a new force in the South when the agricultural economy began to deteriorate after the Civil War. South Carolina Governor Coleman L. Blease was the first politician to benefit from the vote of mill workers to whom he managed to appeal in language and imagery that stirred their passions. Even folk music has played a part; surely everyone remembers the line "I owe my soul to the company store" from Tennessee Ernie Ford's *Sixteen Tons* written about the coal industry. Author I. A. Newby discussed the question dispassionately and from the clearer vantage point of hindsight in a new book, *Plain Folk in the New South* (1989). Newby noted that approximately 90% of cotton mills in the New South owned residential villages for their operatives, and about the same proportion of mill workers lived in company-owned housing. The reasons were as valid on one side as on the other, he said, and generalizations regarding the practice accomplish nothing since the villages were as diverse on one level as they were alike on another. Ware Shoals appears to have been an example of "good" paternalism. The company store, for example, was described in the town's history as the "Big Friendly," a place providing "everything a person would need to be an efficient and satisfied employee." While one might wonder just what that "everything" might be, the book indicated that charge accounts or advances on next week's wages went a long way toward job satisfaction. The Riegel village's perks included recreational and educational facilities as early as 1913. It would be difficult to brand as evil a building providing a movie theater, library, club rooms, pool room, bowling alley, and showers, such as Katherine Hall in Ware Shoals, even though it was named for the boss's daughter. Newby noted that mill workers accepted the hierarchical structure of the new culture but wanted to have their own place in that structure acknowledged; in other words, they wanted what everybody wants – a little respect. Benjamin Riegel understood that very well indeed. One revealing anecdote noted that management would send Riegel programs from performances held in Katherine Hall annotated with the departments in which performers worked. He would recognize those workers with personal notes of acknowledgement and appreciation.

Ware Shoals Manufacturing Company grew rapidly. The first addition, known as Mill No. 2, opened in 1914 and spurred the growth of the town in terms of even more houses, paved streets, and the organization of schools and churches. A finishing and dyeing plant, the bleachery, opened in 1923 and had to be enlarged only four years later. When the plant added a fabricating department that enabled it to convert goods into finished products, its motto, "From Cotton to Counter," became a reality.

Ware Shoals established a reputation early as a sports town where, once again, the mill took the initiative. Teams in Riegel uniforms competed in baseball, basketball, and bowling games and tournaments. When new athletic facilities were built behind the school in 1933, they were so good that professional baseball teams used them for training grounds.

The downside of being a one-company town, naturally, is that it breeds serious economic dependency. Any decline in that one industry means a loss of jobs and changes in the standard of living of most citizens. Fortunately, by the time Riegel finally closed its doors in the 1980s, progress in both transportation and industrial development in the county was such that nothing catastrophic occurred. Ware Shoals remains a pleasant place to live, and its small business district is still in place.

Other place names in the general vicinity include Stony Point and Coronaca. Both have associations with the famous D. Wyatt Aiken who left his mark on the agrarian movement after the Civil War and who brought national attention to the Grange. This group originated in 1866 as the "Order of the Patrons of Husbandry"; it captured Aiken's attention early as an alternative to what he evidently considered the bureaucratic nonsense perpetrated by the Bureau of Agriculture at its national convention in 1872. The movement was slow to catch on since farmers then, as now, were notorious non-organizers, and only a few local granges had been established in western states when Aiken began his vigorous campaign to organize chapters in South Carolina. Primarily because of his efforts, South Carolina became one of the two leading Grange states in the 1870s (the other was Iowa). Aiken was named a member of the three-man executive committee of the National Grange in 1873. Modern writers, among them Robert West Howard in *The Vanishing Land* (1985), have pointed out that farmers are the only businessmen who buy at retail and sell at wholesale. This upside-down business practice is only one reason for problems in the agricultural sector. Besides the vagaries of the weather, others have been overproduction, extremely costly equipment that might be duplicated at farm after farm, and, particularly in the years after the Civil War, sectional differences that precluded true union of American farmers. Aiken believed the Grange program had the potential of uniting American agrarians in new ways for their own benefit and that of the country.

D. Wyatt Aiken was elected to Congress in 1876 and served five terms. As a congressman he worked continually to elevate the Bureau of Agriculture to cabinet status. That finally happened, but Aiken did not live to see it. He died in 1887, and the bill he supported for so long was signed into law by the president two years later. Aiken's last home was in Cokesbury; his first in the upcountry was Stony Point. Both still stand within a few miles of each other. Aiken's first plan was to build his own manor house when he moved from his native Winnsboro to the upcountry in 1858. The move was the result of Aiken's second marriage, to Virginia Carolina Smith, a granddaughter of original settler William Smith of Stony Point. Smith came to the area from Culpepper, Virginia, in 1793. He built a log cabin by the side of the road from Cambridge, opened a store, and established a post office, the second in the county, in 1808. Only six years before his death in 1824, Smith began construction of a mansion he named Stony Point. His son Joel bought the property from his father's estate and completed the three-story house in 1829. At the time Aiken married into the Smith family, Joel Smith had been dead three years.

Stony Point is an architectural marvel and one of Greenwood County's treasures. The house embodies no specific architectural order; its style is more often found in the Central Atlantic States than the Deep South. The 18-inch thick exterior walls are constructed of handmade brick laid in the Flemish bond pattern, and many of the features are paired: "A double porch, alike upstairs and down, contains four slender Tuscan columns on each level, connected by segmented arches and balustrades," for example. Further, "the house is entered through double doors with transom; an identical door opens onto the balcony above."

Wyatt Aiken never built the manor house he envisioned for his own family, but he did complete a smaller structure of eight rooms which he planned to use as a kitchen and quarters for house servants when the big house was completed. He named his new home "Coronaca" and moved from Stony Point in 1860. Aiken was a successful and enthusiastic planter in the years before the Civil War; he was also skilled as a practical and theoretical writer on agricultural subjects. Aiken considered his profession a science and promoted it as such, first in meticulous plantation records and later in speeches and his own magazine. Aiken is regarded as "the first of the modern soil conservationists in South Carolina." He also took great interest in politics. As the probability of war grew, he embraced secession and joined "Minute Men" companies in both Abbeville and Greenwood. At the time Aiken marched off to war he was among the most substantial citizens in the region; his landholdings totaled more than 2,000 acres in Abbeville and Fairfield Counties.

Aiken saw action in a number of battles and attained the rank of colonel in Confederate service. He was retired from the army under the Invalid Officers Act in 1864. The plantation he came home to was nothing like the one he had left. Even though actual fighting had not touched the South Carolina upcountry, "the crops were in sad shape, fields overgrown or washed, and fences fallen down. The young men had gone off to war, and the hands, without proper direction, had not been wedded to their work." Aiken found conditions much the same at Rock Presbyterian Church: "the Sanctuary was dirty and dilapidated; the congregation composed only of a few old men, women and children." Aiken moved back to the house at Stony Point in 1866 when his family of seven children outgrew the first house at Coronaca.

The rest of Wyatt Aiken's life was spent largely in the public arena even as he continued to farm large acreage. Scorning the sharecropping system, he restored his plantations with the aid of hired farm laborers, a method that demanded both hands-on work and supervision by the landowner. Aiken himself was in the fields every day of the year. The first year's experiment with this system brought "the handsomest profit I have made on my plantation," wrote Aiken. He worked tirelessly as a party canvasser to regain political power for the Democratic Party, speaking all over the state against "the party of villainy" and in favor of resistance "at the ballot box." Aiken also began publication of the *Rural Carolinian*, a monthly illustrated magazine devoted to agricultural reform in a new South, in 1869. The themes he expounded in the pages of his magazine included good advice for the southern farmer, but advice that fell on deaf ears: "The times have changed," he wrote, "and with them must change many of the habits of our people." Aiken was convinced that the southern planter must also change his crops, his culture, and his implements. He advocated growing less cotton and corn and more wheat, oats, barley, and clover. Aiken foresaw the potential disaster of dependence on a one-crop economy in the postwar South and did everything he could to forestall the inevitable. Some of the maxims Aiken stressed in his magazine more than a century ago make a great deal of sense today: "Forget the past; anticipate the future" . . . "Live and farm as if slavery never existed" . . . "Cease your infatuation with cotton" . . . "Raise more stock" . . . "Do not buy what you can raise yourself" . . . "Buy and sell cooperatively."

Aiken moved his family to Cokesbury, primarily for its educational benefits to his eleven children, in 1874, but he continued to operate farms at both Coronaca and Stony Point and write for the *Rural Carolinian*. He lived in the house at Stony Point only eight years, but his name is inextricably linked with three important county place names as well as the Civil War and Reconstruction, politics, agriculture, and religion.

By the time Donald and Marilyn Hawthorne bought Stony Point in 1957, it was "wasting away in the lonesome countryside of Greenwood county." The Hawthornes undertook the task of restoration one step – and one room – at a time, after securing the structure's foundation and shoring up the worst of the problems with the exterior. Stony Point, visible through the pine trees just off Highway 246, stands today as a reminder of an altogether different time, an era of wealth and leisure and landed gentry before the Civil War. Such plantations were rarities in the South Carolina upcountry. The name of the mansion and the community seems to be derived from the terrain, a mixture of abundant loose rocks and stony outcrop, but *Names in South Carolina* suggested it might have been borrowed from a site in New York State where General "Mad Anthony" Wayne won a celebrated victory over the British in the Revolutionary War. The picturesque name, with an "e" added as in "Stoney Point," is perpetuated in a new golf course and residential area currently under development nearby.

The origin of the name Coronaca is obscure. A Coronaca Creek appears on the famous George Hunter map of 1730, and the community's name derived from that, according to *Names in South Carolina*, although two earlier names, Cork and Sim's Cross Roads, were used before the railroad came. Coronaca, or some other spelling thereof, was an Indian word of unknown meaning, or so historian John Henry Logan thought, but Margaret Watson believed the word was probably a slightly scrambled version of Corn Acre, the name Francis Salvador gave to his plantation in 1773. If she is right, what about the notation on Hunter's map? If there were a definitive answer, it probably would have been found before the 1990s. The fact that the name definitely pre-dates the Revolutionary War will have to be enough said about its origins.

The New Market section between Greenwood and Ninety Six derives its name from a town in Virginia near the first home of John Partlow, an early settler in the area. The Virginia town, in turn, was named for Newmarket in England, a town famous for its racetrack. The Partlows were large landowners and prosperous planters. *Greenwood County Sketches* recounts that a son of the original settler was much opposed to the new railroad because of the danger to his livestock; according to one version several of his cows or horses were killed by the train. In retaliation, Partlow built a fence with a gate across the track. He must have meant to stop the train, but the locomotive simply crashed through and arrived in Greenwood with the gate still dangling from the cowcatcher. Undaunted, Partlow next removed a rail and caused the train to wreck. This might have brought him a certain satisfaction, but it enraged the railroad, and he was sued for damages. The record is not clear as to the eventual terms of coexistence between Partlow and the railroad.

New Market is also important as the site of the beginnings of Blyth Funeral Home, one of Greenwood's oldest continuing businesses. Andrew A. Blyth was a master carpenter who came to this country from Scotland. Eventually he turned up in what is now Greenwood County, settling a short distance below the present Epworth. The original Blyth added coffin and buggy-making to his cabinet shop, and one of his sons started his own business in nearby Greenwood in 1884. Blyth was the first undertaker in the state to do embalming, as well as the first to use a motor vehicle instead of a horse-drawn carriage for a hearse.

In a 1991 newspaper article Emmie B. Kinard connected the place name "Epworth" with "the home of the founder of Methodism, John Wesley, in England." While that connection is certainly valid, the name is actually even older and has Church of England connotations as well. Wesley was born in 1703 at "Epworth Rectory" in Lincolnshire; the name therefore pre-dates Methodism. The Methodist Societies Wesley founded were formalized into the Methodist Episcopal Church in 1784, largely for the benefit of Wesley's disciples in America. It is interesting to note that the term "methodist," originally one of derision, had been applied to Wesley in discussions at the Holy Club of Oxford, but the birth date of capital-M Methodism seems to be 1738 when his heart was "strangely warmed" in a religious experience. The Methodist Church is too large a topic for discussion here, but clearly the association with John Wesley forever links the name "Epworth" to Methodism. Epworth is shown as a post office on the 1898 map of Greenwood County, but the same post office was known as Holloway before 1837, according to H. L. Watson, and then as Phoenix.

BAILEY MILITARY INSTITUTE — As it appeared about 1914. Location was at the site of Self Memorial Hospital.

(Right) BAILEY MILITARY INSTITUTE — Another view. Barracks burned in 1936.

LANDER COLLEGE — Established in Williamston in 1872 and opened in Greenwood in 1904. See Chapter Seven.

MARSHAL FOCH DAY — December 9, 1921, was a great day for Greenwood when the Commander-in-Chief of the Allied Forces spoke on the Square.

BOILER EXPLOSION AT GRENDEL MILL — This tragedy in 1920 took only a very few lives.

GRENDEL MILL — After the explosion.

MISS MAUDE PRATT — Longtime teacher at Magnolia School with her 1922 Model T Ford.

WALTER WILLIAM BENSON — "Major." Principal of Greenwood High School, 1924-1953.

GREENWOOD HIGH SCHOOL — (two views above and below) Historic building erected in the 1920s on South Main Street.

BREAKING GROUND FOR CHEMSTRAND — (Now Monsanto). Pictured are locals Jack Lawrence, Howard Burns, Jim Self, Bill Bradford, John Harris, Boykin Curry, and Henderson Barnette.

TRACK RELOCATION COMMITTEE — At lunch with Senator Strom Thurmond and Nancy in the Senate Dining Room. Seated are Bill Charles, Dr. Walter Bishop, Nancy Thurmond, Jim Self, and Carl Seigler. Standing, from left, Travis Higginbotham, Thomas Wingard, Senator Thurmond, Dr. Stanley Baker, Boykin Curry, and unidentified constituent.

MACHINES TAKE OVER — Removing tracks on Hampton Avenue at rear of Citizens Trust Company building.

PULLING UP TRACKS — Dr. Stanley Baker, Boykin Curry, and Charles Moorefield of the South Carolina Highway Department pitch in.

OLD ARMORY — Just before demolition for a downtown office for South Carolina National Bank. Great dancing upstairs in the 1920s and 1930s.

WARE SHOALS HIGH SCHOOL

ht) KATHERINE HALL — Riegel
loyees' Recreation Center, Ware
als.

RIEGEL TEXTILES CORPORATION — A panoramic view.

MILL VILLAGE — at Ware Shoals.

(Right) THE DAM — Saluda River at Ware Shoals.

An early Greenwood County School for black children.

WARE SHOALS INN — as it appears today.

WARE SHOALS — Dirt Road, River, and Smokestacks.

WARE SHOALS RAILROAD, c. 1906

THE DEPOT — at Ninety Six.

SILOAM BAPTIST CHURCH — Old and New.

WEST VIEW OF MAIN STREET — as it appeared in Ninety Six in 1912.

GRAVESTONES – James Mayson and wife at Ninety Six National Historic Site.

OLD NINETY SIX MILL CEMETERY

CHEROKEE TRAIL MARKER – erected by D. A. R. at Ninety Six National Historic Site

LOG CABIN — at Ninety Six National Historic Site.

"POPE'S PALACE" — West Main Street, Ninety Six.

SCHOOL DISTRICT NO. 32 – Bold Spring School, 1940.

COUNTY SCHOOL LUNCHROOM – with sawhorse table and fresh flowers.

BOLD SPRING SCHOOL STUDENT BODY – May 1940 (author shown front row center, with pigtails and bare feet, in dress with dark skirt).

Masonic Female Collegiate Institute Building at Cokesbury. Built in 1854. Restored in the 1960s. Now owned by the Cokesbury Historical and Recreational Commission.

BARRATT HOUSE. Home of former Congressman W. J. Bryan Dorn. Described in Chapter Eight.

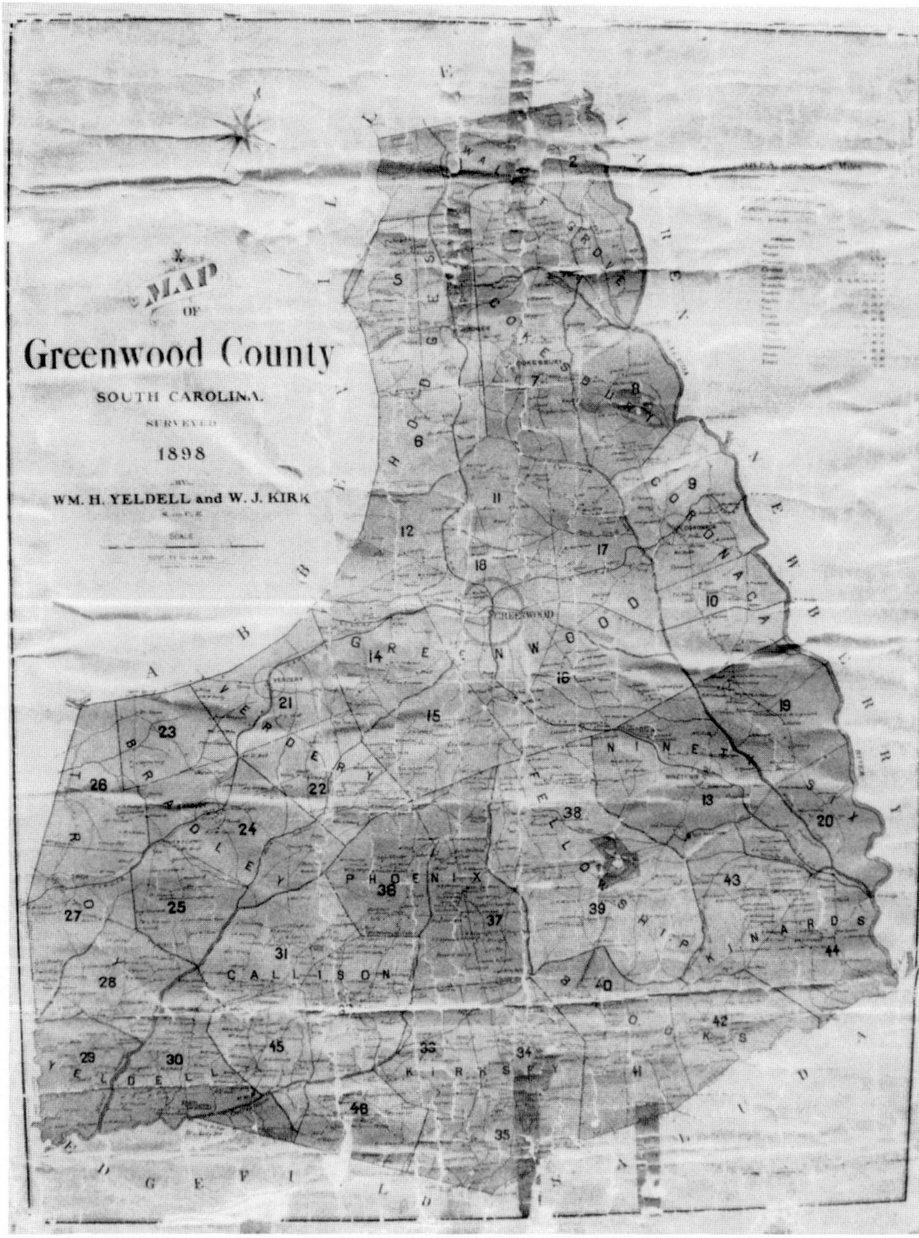

One of three originals of the 1898 county map drawn by Yeldell & Kirk hangs in the president's office at The County Bank.

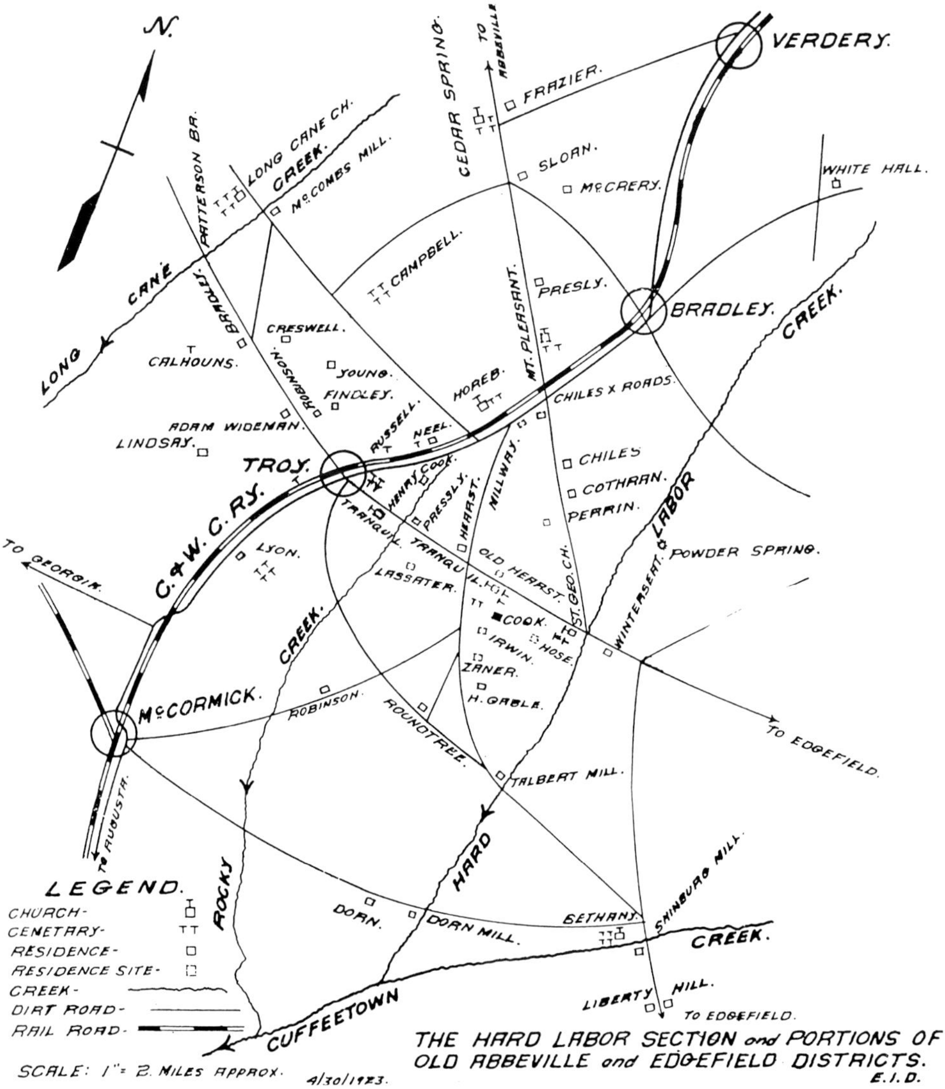

Map drawn in 1923 by Emmett I. Davis for H.T. Cook's book, *The Hard Labor Section*. Cook wrote that Davis's map covered "portions of four counties where our worthy ancestors lived and where many of them now sleep in unbroken silence."

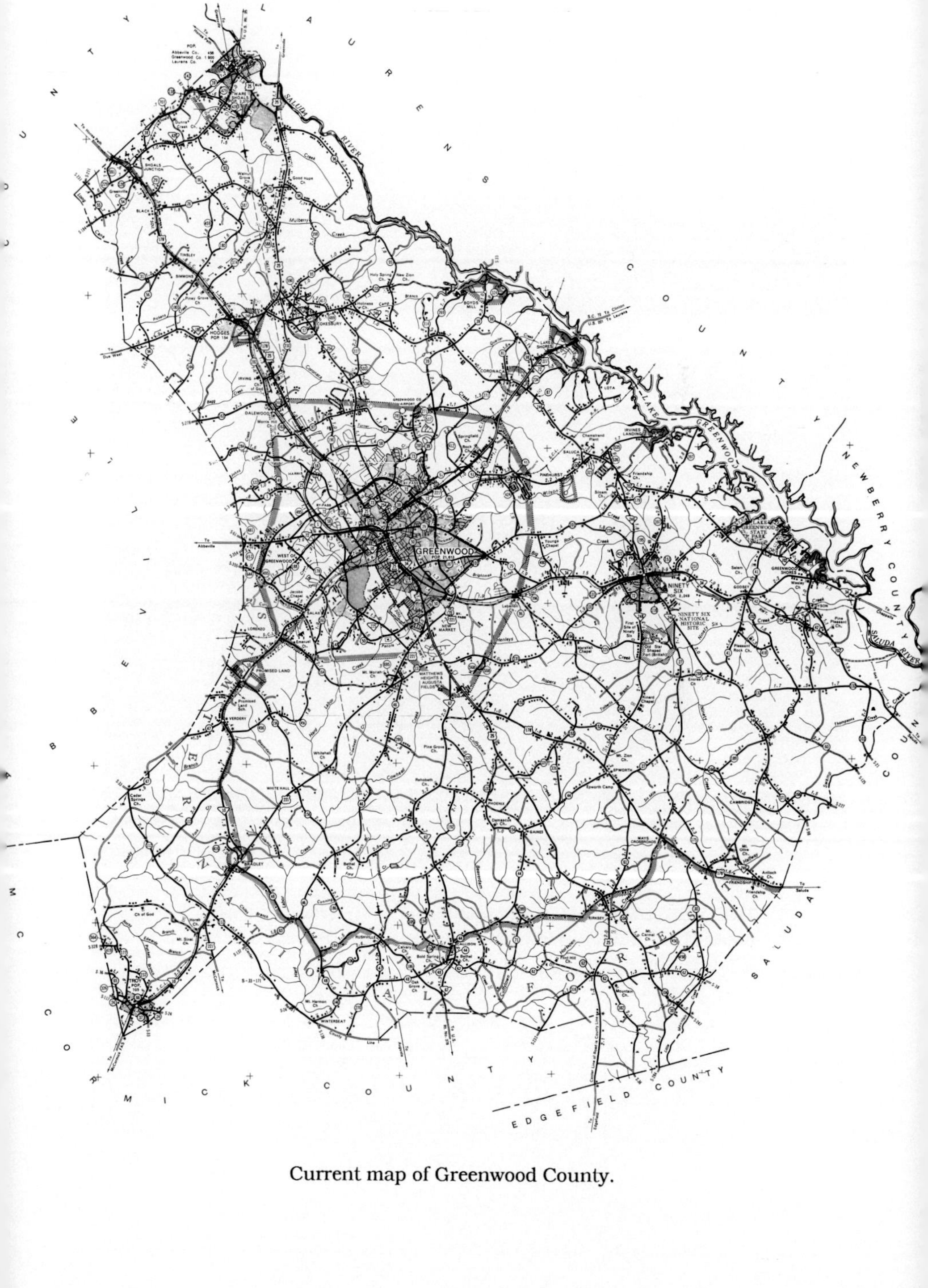

Current map of Greenwood County.

THE MUSEUM. Located on Main Street in Greenwood. Three floors of antiquities, oddities and collectibles. Described in Chapter Three.

The Epworth Camp Meeting site nearby is a modern remnant of the Great Awakening, a religious revival that swept the Southeast about 1800. Camp meetings, or tent revivals, became popular when existing buildings could not accommodate the crowds of people who came. Whole families, along with their household goods, animals, and even servants, would gather for an extended stay of about a week at a general meeting place. These meetings were interdenominational but were made up chiefly of Baptists, Methodists, and Presbyterians. The first such meeting in South Carolina was called by Presbyterians at the Waxhaws (Lancaster County) in 1802, and another was held at Tabernacle (Greenwood County) in 1822, according to Aline Williams Crouch in *Annals of Edgefield District.* Crouch noted that camp meetings were popular as both social and religious gatherings and became annual events at several sites. Still held today, the Epworth Camp Meeting was first conceived by leaders of another camp at St. George in 1905 who dispatched an evangelist and two musicians to assist a Methodist minister, the Reverend W. P. B. Kinard, in founding such a meeting in the upcountry. It was held for two years under a tent at New Market and moved to Epworth when Kinard gave a plot of land as the site for a permanent tabernacle. The original buildings, erected largely at his expense, included a large, open-sided structure for the meetings and small, rustic cabins for the campers. At one time each family prepared its meals over a communal open fire. The facilities have been improved over the years, and meals are now provided for a nominal fee in an air-conditioned dining hall. The property is owned by a self-perpetuating board of trustees, and a ten-day camp meeting is held every July. Methodists have played a dominant role in the Epworth Camp Meeting since its inception, but the gathering itself is non-denominational.

On Highway 178 quite near the Epworth Camp Ground stands the Moore-Kinard house, a fine example of a central-hall farmhouse at least 150 years old. Because of its significance as the only antebellum building remaining in the community, as well as its association with two important families, the house is listed in the National Register of Historic Places. The original owner of the house was Wright Nicholson Moore (1811-1865), and the date of construction is estimated to be somewhere between 1830 and 1840. Moore was a prosperous farmer and landowner; the 1850 Census listed him as the owner of 1,050 acres of land and considerable livestock. The house remained in the Moore family until 1884 when it was sold to the Rev. W. P. B. Kinard and his brother John Michael Calhoun Kinard, who was known as "Big Mike." The distinction was evidently necessary since a cousin, G. M. "Poor Mike" Kinard (interesting nickname for a man who owned 8,000 acres of land), lived just up the road. Both of the Kinard brothers lived in the house for a time, but the Reverend Kinard built his own house just across the road in 1897. That house has recently been restored and is occupied by Tom and Martha Kinard Taylor. The historic Moore-Kinard house has been in the Kinard family since 1884; the present owner is Henry J. Kinard, Jr. The Kinard family actually pre-dates the name of the Epworth community. Possibly the Methodist connection arose when the Rev. William Pierce Bennett Kinard and a couple of brothers moved to the area from Newberry. At this writing, two Kinard cousins, Calvin W., Sr. and H. Bennett, Sr., both in their mid-90s, still live in Greenwood County. These distinguished gentlemen, as well as their forebears and many of their descendants, are practically synonymous with Epworth. The early township of Kinards on the 1898 map is aptly named.

Not far from Epworth just off Highway 25 South at the intersection of state roads 154 and 44 lies a spot loosely known as Gaines. The 1898 map identifies Gaines Post Office and the residence of J. M. Gaines just across the road. The old house on the property was once the home of John Milton Gaines, prominent farmer, merchant, and state senator from both Edgefield and Greenwood Counties. The post office was in Gaines's store at the time Greenwood County was formed. The Gaines house is among the oldest in the county, according to current owners Frank and Cate Townsend, but a number of remodelings over the years have so altered the structure that it no longer meets the criteria of the National Register of Historic Places. Nevertheless, its architectural details have convinced the Townsends that the structure dates from the late 1700s:

> The basic house is a story-and-a-half with an unchinked log structure. The downstairs has the original ceiling boards, flooring, paneling and beams. Until about 1900, the upstairs was an undivided loft with a ladder type staircase. Originally the two rooms downstairs had chairboards (wainscoting) around the walls. Over the years the house has been remodeled and "improved" so that many of the original architectural features are covered or altered. One of the most outstanding features of the house is its double-hipped west chimney with two diamond patterns in black brick.

The Gaines property was known as Langston Acres during the period from 1943 to 1967 when the Henry Langston family owned the house and adjoining 120 acres.

The name of Fellowship for one of the early townships presumably derives from the Baptist church of that name. The church was established as Cambridge Church in 1805 and changed its name to Fellowship a few years later. Margaret Watson wrote that the records were lost in a long-ago fire and the church abandoned in the early 1900s. A large cemetery remains at the site.

Brooks Township links Greenwood County with the family of Whitfield Brooks (1789-1851) who came to the area from Newberry and created the lovely estate "Roselands." One of his sons, Preston Smith Brooks (1819-1857), gained national notoriety in the famous Brooks-

Sumner Affair in the United States Senate in 1856. That "affair" was a sound beating with a gutta percha cane administered by Congressman Brooks to Senator Charles Sumner of Massachusetts in retaliation for a speech that had vilified the South in general and South Carolina and its Senator Andrew P. Butler in particular. Sumner's so-called "Crime Against Kansas" speech, delivered in the United States Senate during a time of national dissension over the extension of slavery to the western territories, shocked many listeners; one senator from Michigan regarded it as "the most un-American and unpatriotic that ever grated on the ears of the members of this high body." As a South Carolinian and nephew of Andrew Butler, Brooks took it upon himself to exact vengeance. The essential facts of the confrontation have never been disputed – several witnesses observed the entire episode – but the public reaction that followed was reported purely along sectional lines. Brooks was denounced in the northern press and burned in effigy during an indignation meeting at Amherst College. Nor were only radical Republicans and abolitionists up in arms; one meeting in New York City was addressed by Columbia College (now University) President Charles King whose denouncement of Preston Brooks inflamed the student body. Southern students managed to rally in time to prevent publication of a "general protest condemnatory of Brooks" that many students wanted. Even Ralph Waldo Emerson got involved by suggesting the nation had now gone too far ever to reconcile the slavery question. Only a few people in the North were brave enough to view the act as one of personal and family outrage. Ironically, the affair brought tremendous attention to Sumner and his speech which otherwise would probably have attracted scant notice, considering the general spirit of the times. Sumner later told Alexis de Tocqueville that a half million copies of the speech were circulated.

Predictably, the South quickly came to Brooks's defense, including at least one additional caning when a South Carolinian attacked Jacob Stanwood of Massachusetts in the lobby of the Metropolitan Hotel in New York City for calling the assault "a cowardly and brutal affair." Southern newspapers came up with some colorful phrases, including "an act in good season," a "classical caning," and "a proper act, done at the proper time and in the proper place." One woman in Brooks's district sent word that the women of the South would supply him with hickory sticks to chastise abolitionists and Republicans whenever he wished. Brooks was flooded with gift canes of all descriptions, and his wife wrote her congratulations and assurances that she would gladly join in accepting any penalty his action might entail. One Baptist minister in Barnwell was run out of town when he dared to criticize Brooks and express "opposition to Southern institutions." The Massachusetts legislature instructed the State Adjutant General to arm its senators and representatives; a Baltimore newspaper suggested it would be better to supply the lawmakers with "broad national views" and "good common sense" umixed with "fanaticism and narrow-minded bigotry."

The actual resolution of the matter was somewhat more prosaic than the battle of words fought in sectional newspapers. Brooks was arrested and brought to trial. Sumner claimed his injuries prevented his presence in the courtroom (a doctor testified that he received only flesh wounds and was in no way incapacitated), and he wished to take no part in the proceedings in any case. Brooks's own statement climaxed with the words, "Can it be expected . . . that I, with a heart to feel and an arm to strike, shall patiently hear and ignobly submit while my political mother is covered with insult, and obloquy, and dishonor? While her character is slandered, and her reputation libeled?" The result of the trial was a $300 fine, paid enthusiastically and twice over, by Brooks's constituents.

Investigative committees were appointed in both houses of Congress. The senate committee called the attack a "breach of its privileges" but saw no way it could punish a member of the other house; it could only register a complaint against "the assault committed by one of its members." The house committee, on the other hand, called for expulsion of Brooks and censure for two of his friends for failing to report the incident before the fact. The resolution failed to pass by the requisite two-thirds majority, but Brooks resigned his seat immediately to appeal to his own people at home for vindication. Brooks announced his candidacy in the special election that followed but conducted no campaign at all. Both Brooks and fellow congressman Laurence M. Keitt, also implicated in the Sumner affair, simply wrote letters to their constituents asking for re-election as a vote of confidence. The response was overwhelming; one barbecue in Ninety Six attracted an estimated 10,000 people, as well as a reporter from *The New York Times* who gave it great play in his newspaper. Brooks was not only returned to office in the special election with a virtually unanimous vote, he also had no opposition in the general election held shortly thereafter. Preston Brooks died a few months into his term.

The Brooks-Sumner affair was so dramatic in every detail, from Sumner's speech to Brooks's triumphant re-entry to Congress, that D. D. Wallace's accounting is a real anticlimax. He chose to castigate both parties who, he believed, knew not what they did in the entire matter. He excused Sumner with the words, "He had no realization of the wounds his words inflicted, and his arrogance made his words doubly intolerable," and said Brooks "did not anticipate the political significance of his act . . . [intervening] in a great public question as though it were a mere personal quarrel." He also wrote that Brooks actually aided his enemy "by adding the sanctity of martyrdom to one of the most dangerous mischief-makers in American history." In spite of Wallace's impartial pox on both houses and in full recognition of its lack of wisdom in the long view, the Brooks-Sumner affair remains one of the most revealing episodes of the period just before the Civil War and, as such, one of the best bits of Greenwood County lore.

The Whitfield Brooks family of Newberry-Edgefield-Greenwood is noted for more than the famous affair of honor in 1856. Military service, politics, and the law have appealed to Brooks men for generations. John Hampden ("Cap'n Ham"), a brother of Preston, was the Brooks most closely identified with Greenwood's bid to become a county. A Confederate soldier who rose to the rank of lieutenant colonel, Brooks also served in the state legislature from both Edgefield and Greenwood. His two marriages, to two daughters of former Governor James H. Adams, not only produced a total of thirteen children but also created a link between Brooks's home "Roselands" and the famous "Rose Hill" plantation in Union County, home of the Gist family. A minor point perhaps, but interesting nevertheless, particularly since Brooks's second wife was the widow of General Gist whose Christian name was States Rights, surely one of the most defiant names ever foisted on an innocent baby. The general was killed in the battle of Franklin, Tennessee, in 1864; Claude and Irene Neuffer wrote in *Correct Mispronunciations of some South Carolina Names* (1983) that States Rights is still a given name in the Gist family. How grand to be able to find a Greenwood connection! One of Ham Brooks's sons, Edward Louden Brooks (1876-1951), who also lived at Roselands, was Greenwood County supervisor for more than twenty years. His children include Carroll Hampden Brooks, immediate past chairman of Greenwood County Council, as well as five other good citizens who call Greenwood home.

The township adjoining Brooks on the 1898 map is Kirksey. What besides a family name could Kirksey possibly be? H. L. Watson named a John Kirksey as a pioneer settler whose tavern existed as early as 1824. There was a post office at Kirksey; the Friendship Masonic Lodge Hall (No. 25 in South Carolina) and an early school building still stand on Highway 25, but neither is an original. In local lore Kirksey is perhaps most closely identified with the Self family. Both James C. Self and his wife, the former Lura Mathews, grew up in the area; and S. P. Mathews, who became Self's father-in-law, was also one of his first employers. The Durst and Mathews store, destroyed by fire in 1953, was a Kirksey landmark for many years. Kirksey and the nearby Pittsburg community where the three counties of Greenwood, Edgefield, and Saluda join are also noted as the home of the Timmerman and Ouzts families. The family name of Kirksey has virtually disappeared in Greenwood County, but the area is perpetuated in the National Register of Historic Places as the site of the Trapp-Chandler pottery factory dating from the middle of the nineteenth century. Recorded during an archaeological survey of Greenwood County in 1978, the spot near Kirksey is the "last known intact site of a production center of Edgefield slip decorated stoneware." The product made at Kirksey is "unique when compared to pieces made in other areas of the country at the same time" because of the distinctive use of alkaline glaze.

The Reverend John Trapp evidently owned the property during the time the pottery was located there. Not only did Trapp preach at nearby Mountain Creek Baptist Church for 42 years, he was also a farmer, landowner, gristmill operator, and sawmill owner. No evidence exists to suggest that Trapp was a potter, but there was definitely an association between himself and Thomas M. Chandler, a rather famous artisan originally from Virginia who came to South Carolina in the 1840s. The partnership between Trapp and Chandler probably involved the lease of the pottery and land and spanned the period from 1844 until Chandler established his own pottery about 1850. The stoneware produced at Kirksey was of "high quality and great diversity," not only in the form of the vessels but in their color as well, color that ranged from pale green to deep olive. Chandler's work is distinguished by swag and tassel designs, flowers, loops, medallions, and various floral themes; much of it is signed "Chandler Maker."

The name of the early township Phoenix seems to have been stolen from Epworth, according to H. L. Watson. Actually, "stolen" may not be quite accurate. Margaret Watson connected the move of the name with the move of her great-great-grandfather Johnson Sale from the original Phoenix in the early 1850s. When a post office was established with Sale as first postmaster, he simply appropriated the name from his former location. No doubt he liked it better than New Boston as the community was then called. Margaret Watson wrote that the name was no longer in use at the time. Her account and that of her father in *Names in South Carolina* do not tally exactly; nevertheless, Greenwood County is fortunate to have retained a community named *Phoenix* even though the name is not at all uncommon. Nothing could be more romantic than the evocation of mythology's fabulous bird which destroys itself after 500 years only to recreate itself out of itself, as it were. The common image of consumption by fire and re-creation from ashes is not supported in Bullfinch's *Mythology*; rather, he wrote that the poet Ovid associated the phoenix with the pleasant odors of frankincense, cinnamon, spikenard, and myrrh with which it builds its nest. At some point the phoenix transfers the nest (its own cradle as well as the grave of its parent) to the temple of the sun in Egypt where it is symbolically consumed "in flames of fragrance." The phoenix was actually thought to be real until its existence was questioned in the seventeenth century by Sir Thomas Browne. He was answered a few years later by one Alexander Ross who must have been an early environmentalist. Ross wrote that appearances of the phoenix were so rare as to be almost nonexistent because "his instinct teaches him to keep out of the way of the tyrant of the creation, *man*, for if he were to be got at some wealthy glutton would surely devour him, though there were no more in the world." Whether the early proponents of the name gave much time to such ruminations is a moot point, but it may be significant that Phoenix native Louis Wright called the area of his birth Arcadia, another name with classical overtones. Wright's rather staggering erudition and fame in later life began, according to him, in a place where someone who could recite Horace's Odes might easily have been found behind a plow. Greenwood County natives should read Wright's *Barefoot in Arcadia* as an exercise in feeling good about themselves. He wrote that the people he knew best were literate and bookish and very much concerned about the education of their children. He also said they had never heard of Freud and therefore could not excuse their own bad behavior by blaming it on someone else.

The Phoenix Wright described was a pleasant and orderly place, even though he admitted it was on the fringe of "the Dark Corner," a section of the state famous for hot-tempered men and a prevailing contempt for so-called "tidewater aristocracy." The early settlers and their descendants were hard-working farmers who managed to live and prosper by the sweat of their own brows. In Wright's day they lived in a virtually moneyless society on farms that had to be self-sustaining. The sale of the money crop, cotton, provided funds for taxes and debts once a year, although a farmer might also sell a few head of livestock from time to time. Wright remembered "a reasonably contented people who enjoyed simple comforts, feasted on the good things of the earth, and were fiercely independent." The Phoenix section today is quite attractive, its houses neat and well-tended, and its rolling landscape a gentle reminder of farms that exist no more. Many landmarks are gone, but Damascus Baptist Church, established in 1831 from an earlier log meeting house and moved to its present site in 1853, remains. It was built by the master carpenter Andrew Blyth, and the eminent Dr. John Perkins Barratt's grave can be found in the cemetery adjoining the church. Elbert Adams's grandfather once practiced medicine in Phoenix; newspaperman Harry L. Watson was a native; and a granddaughter of Phoenix landowner Nathaniel Henderson married Dr. William A. Barnette, a veterinarian who was co-founder and first president of Greenwood Packing Plant, as well as a Greenwood mayor.

Phoenix pioneer Jonathan Sale was a storekeeper and postmaster in Phoenix. His store, which remained in the family for 65 years according to Margaret Watson, was Johnson S. Watson's store at the time of one of the most horrifying episodes of Greenwood County history, the Phoenix Riot of 1898. In our day, the word *riot* somehow connotes an urban disturbance characterized by crowds of people in some sort of "flash fire" conflict. We tend to believe that riots happen quickly, sometimes spontaneously, and are often brought under control just as quickly by law enforcement agencies. The events in Phoenix, however, were anything but an urban conflict, the violence went on for weeks, and the effects on Greenwood County were both far-reaching and long-lasting. Possibly the word *riot* became attached to the incident as a term slightly more palatable than the L-word, but Don Herd's account of the Phoenix incident appears in a chapter entitled "Lynching in the Upcountry, 1784-1980."

A little background is surely required before any accounting of what amounts to mass murder is undertaken. D. D. Wallace wrote that the end of the "discipline of slavery led to a great increase of immorality and crime" among blacks. He pointed out that white citizens were still nervous about the "economic, political, and social dangers" inherent in the race question some twenty or thirty years after the Civil War and suggested wisely, but perhaps tongue-in-cheek, that black citizens probably found the "white problem" rather troubling as well. In other words, nobody had a handle on an answer, and reaction against the intolerable Negro rule under Reconstruction had only intensified racial prejudice. Wallace wrote that while mass violence by blacks was a rare occurrence, rape had become "alarmingly frequent" in the 1880s and 1890s. Considering this jittery state of affairs, as well as the anathema of the Republican party in the South after Reconstruction, perhaps the Phoenix Riot met the criteria of an accident waiting to happen. The power of the ballot box in South Carolina had been jealously guarded since the overthrow of Reconstruction in the election of 1876; the resulting solidarity of whites under the Democrat party was still too new to be taken for granted. Further, the Constitution of 1895 had effectively disfranchised black voters with the poll tax and literacy requirements, and that constitution had not been effectively tested. The situation in Greenwood County paralleled that of the rest of the state as the elections of 1898 approached. Watson's Store was the polling place.

Enter the Tolbert family whose home was nearby. Four Tolbert brothers had served in the Confederate Army even though the family had opposed secession. After the war all four joined the Republican party and worked for party causes, chief among which was registering blacks to vote. Wallace wrote that John R. Tolbert was hated and feared in his county for this activity, and the mere presence of his son Thomas at the polling place that election day was probably enough to anger the election managers and other faithful Democrats waiting to vote. The fact that Tolbert had stationed himself on the porch with his own "ballot box" where he asked blacks to deposit evidence that they had been turned away because they were unregistered or had not paid the poll tax, or both, must have infuriated them. As always on election day groups of men, both white and black, were gathered at the polling place. One white man, J. G. Ethridge, remonstrated with Tolbert and, while accounts differ as to who struck whom first and with what, suddenly shots rang out from the yard and Ethridge fell dead. Neither Tolbert nor Ethridge was armed, but the fact that many others were was not unusual. Several men, including Tolbert, were wounded in the volley of shooting that followed the fatal bullet, but both he and the blacks managed to get away in the wild confusion. D. D. Wallace stated categorically that a black man shot Ethridge; Margaret Watson could not, or would not, say; and James A. Hoyt, who covered the story for *The State* and wrote probably the most exhaustive account more than thirty years later, hinted strongly that one Joe Circuit, a black man who had accompanied Tom Tolbert to the polling place, was the culprit. It is hard not to wonder if Circuit's function that day was to serve as Tolbert's bodyguard. An article by Bruce Lee Kleinschmidt in *The Furman Review* for Spring 1974 stated that the man's name was not Joe Circuit but Joe Syrk and cited Benjamin Mays's book *Born to Rebel* as the source of this information. Mays credited his sister Susie with the name and noted that Syrk was their cousin. Evidently no one ever really knew exactly who fired the shot that killed Ethridge. Tom Tolbert always believed the bullet was fired by a white man and meant for him. Mays questioned whether blacks were even armed and wrote that most people in the black commuity also believed Ethridge's killer was white.

When news of the shooting reached Greenwood and other towns, groups of armed men gathered at Phoenix ready to exact vengeance against both blacks and Tolberts. Cooler heads managed to prevail that afternoon, but the killings began in earnest the next day, at least partly because three young men had been fired on from ambush while traveling from Phoenix to Greenwood on the afternoon of election day. A group of black men who had been recognized, or were suspected of having been at Watson's store, were rounded up and brought to Rehoboth Church to face an "unofficial firing squad." Hoyt stated that the group numbered eleven, four of whom were killed on the spot and two others wounded. Tom Tolbert's father was also fired on as he drove to visit his wounded son. Two more blacks were murdered the next day; perhaps the most gruesome aspect of the whole affair was that the body of one of them was thrown on the pile of bodies still lying in front of the church. The speculation that blacks were assembling preparatory to a general attack was evidently just that; the truth was that they, along with several of the Tolbert men, were shut up in their houses literally in fear for their lives, and with good reason. Hoyt's accounting of the affair listed eight men killed, including Ethridge, before the carnage stopped on November 10. Sporadic violence between blacks and whites continued for weeks.

Aside from an inquest of sorts and a couple of community meetings, nothing happened. No one in authority in the state took any notice of the election day events in Phoenix, in spite of widespread newspaper coverage. A resolution adopted in Phoenix on November 12 deplored the situation and placed the blame squarely on Tolbert shoulders. The resolution actually named John R., R. Red, Joseph W., and Thomas P. Tolbert, as well as a Tolbert cousin, Robert L. Henderson, and while it carried no force of law to banish these men, the attitude of the community was abundantly clear: "We believe their further residence in Greenwood County or its vicinity will tend to imperil the lives and property of both the white and colored people, and we earnestly hope they will choose to remove themselves and their evil influence elsewhere." Further resolutions were adopted the next week when circuit court was held in Greenwood. In addition to approving the one adopted at Phoenix, one Greenwood resolution offered assurances that the Tolbert *property* would be protected. No such protection for their lives was mentioned.

No one ever sought the slightest punishment for the lynchers. They had operated quite openly; many people knew who they were. August Kohn's lines in *The News and Courier* portray the tenor of the times quite well: "There is universal agreement that it is time to stop killing Negroes *through other than legal methods*" (emphasis added). His reasoning included not only points such as brutality and shamelessness, but also the reputation of the state and the loss of farm labor. The last point, while crass, was well taken; an agent from Mississippi arrived seeking laborers, and a so-called "Negro Exodus" ensued soon after the lynchings. Several hundred black families left for Mississippi, Georgia, and other parts of South Carolina. Many farms were left virtually without laborers.

In fairness, it must be reported that many of the state's newspapermen took up the question of the lynchings in the months following the conflict. One editorial in *The State*, presumably written by James Henry Rice, Jr., of Ninety Six, stated that such violence "sets back for years the solution of our race problem and ties the hands of those white men who are most kindly toward the Negro and most anxious for good will between the races. We deplore it greatly."

Robert R. Tolbert, who was at Abbeville on election day, gave his version of the events at Phoenix to a New York newspaper reporter in Washington a week or two later. He said his group had been warned and indirectly threatened by county Democratic Chairman J. M. Gaines and asserted that Tom Tolbert's actions on election day were not only legal but also non-threatening. R. R. Tolbert blamed Ethridge for starting the fight and claimed that Ethridge's friend R. G. Cheatham was the first to fire a pistol. He went on to say that he took his wife and children to Due West for safety the next day and returned to gather his tenants and prepare for a siege at his home. The expected attack did not come, and at 2 a.m. he put his father and brother on a train for Columbia where they registered at Wright's Hotel. Oddly, a military company made up of upcountry South Carolinians happened to be encamped at Columbia when the Tolberts arrived. One of the officers, Wyatt Aiken, Jr., actually swore out a warrant charging three Tolbert men with "inciting to riot" in connection with the Phoenix incident of a few days before. John R. and Joe Tolbert were arrested at the hotel pursuant to the warrant. They engaged an attorney who, fearing for their safety, was wise enough to obtain a court order to hold them in the penitentiary. They were released four days later when no one appeared to prosecute. Meanwhile, R. R. Tolbert himself boarded a train at Donalds bound for Washington on the same morning his father and brother departed. He remained in Washington for several weeks while seeking intervention in the case by the McKinley administration. But sectional differences were in the process of healing after the Spanish American War, and McKinley wanted no trouble with the South. United States attorneys in South Carolina did look into the matter but could find no grounds for federal action.

The Tolberts remained as power brokers in Republican circles for many years, although D. D. Wallace wrote that Joseph Warren ("Tieless Joe") Tolbert "distributed patronage in the manner that sank their party into contempt." Some people still believe that an "a" or an "o" in the family name makes a great deal of difference, while others view the story merely as one relic of a bygone era characterized by violence. Don Herd privately faulted the Watson family for their reticence in chronicling this gruesome episode. Margaret Watson's line, "Objectivity is difficult – Johnson S. Watson is our grandfather," did not satisfy him. He believed the family's repute as local historians demanded more than the bare bones account in *Greenwood County Sketches.* Possibly the Watson family believed that no good purpose would be served by dredging up the dark side of their community's history, and one might argue that they were right. On the other hand, the very horror of the Phoenix Riot might have gone a long way to convince county citizens that the law of the jungle had no place in building a civilized society for themselves and their children. Hoyt related two incidents that tend to support this view. One was that a white man named E. C. Rice succeeded in saving the life of Frank Latimer, one of the eleven blacks captured in the mob's first foray who, Rice knew, was innocent of any wrongdoing. Perhaps there were others; the remarkable thing is that anyone was spared that day. Another revealing episode was that A. C. Stockman gave shelter, not only to the three young men who were ambushed, but also to Elias Tolbert who had taken no part in the affair but whose name alone endangered his life.

Kleinschmidt's article concluded with three theories that attempt to explain the reasons behind the intensity of the Phoenix Riot. All three have some basis in the reality of the times, but none is completely satisfactory. One theory is that the riot was set off simply by the Tolberts' attempt to demonstrate the power of the Republican Party at the polls, and the Democrats, having finally wrested political control of the state after Reconstruction, were having none of that. The second theory holds that the agricultural depression and economic plight of the farmer turned a smoldering discontent into violence. A third suggestion introduces the conspiracy theory – that the riot was actually planned by white farmers to terrorize blacks into leaving and freeing the land for white tenants. The author might have been nearer the mark than he knew when he wrote that the riot was the result of great "personal hatred . . . against the blacks, the Tolberts, or against both groups."

So much for an episode that Margaret Watson called the greatest tragedy in the history of Greenwood County. If an excuse is needed for recording it yet again, the words of D. D. Wallace in the Preface to his *South Carolina, A Short History* might suffice: "May we not hope that the time has arrived when the distance from ancient passionate crises and the maturity of our intellectual life make it possible for South Carolinians to study their past with intellectual frankness?"

While the Phoenix Riot might be considered a study of the evils of Reconstruction in Greenwood County, the community of Promised Land could illustrate just the opposite. The story of Promised Land requires a look at the South Carolina Land Commission, a direct outgrowth of the constitutional convention of 1868, as reconstructionist a gathering as anyone could imagine. Blacks constituted 61% of the voting delegates. Prominent South Carolinians such as James L. Orr, Benjamin Perry, and Wade Hampton had warned that any such convention would mean outright confiscation of land for the benefit of the freedmen. That did not happen, but the convention did work out a land distribution program whereby the state would purchase land and sell it to blacks on a long-term payment plan. The Land Commission was created in 1869 to carry out this project. Two important studies, *The Promised Land, the History of the South Carolina Land Commission, 1869-1890* (1969) by Carol R. Bleser and *Promiseland, A Century of Life in a Negro Community* (1981) by Elizabeth R. Bethel, provided the information for this sketch.

Bleser pointed out that South Carolina was the only southern state to attempt the redistribution of land for the benefit of freedmen after the war. The experiment was undertaken as a means of dealing with the reality of the condition of former slaves who "had emerged from bondage destitute, 'without land, without shelter, without a legal claim even to the clothes on their backs'" Land ownership was the key: "Negroes had acquired from the white man a passion for owning land."

This experiment in land redistribution lasted only about twenty years, and the office of land commissioner was abolished just three years after it was created. The secretary of state was assigned to administer the program in 1872, and the post-Reconstructionists, or Redeemers, managed to remold it after the 1876 elections. There was evidently a great deal of bumbling as well as outright fraud during the life of the program, and toward the end its distortions included harsh conditions of sale and overly strict collection schedules. Fewer and fewer blacks were willing to participate as the program wound down, and some who did soon found themselves evicted and worse off than before. Only a few Land Commission tracts were held together and still remain in the hands of the descendants of their original owners. Promised Land in Greenwood County is one of them.

There was little difficulty in finding people willing to sell land to the commission. Most ex-Confederates were destitute. Even General M. C.

Butler offered to sell 650 acres of his Edgefield plantation for $10 per acre. While his offer was rejected, the Land Commission did buy 2,742 acres of the Samuel Marshall estate in Abbeville at the same price. This purchase, finalized in 1870, was among the earliest to be handled by the first commissioner, Charles P. Leslie, a classic "carpetbagger" who had come to the South for the sole purpose of entering politics. The Marshall tract was renamed by its black settlers at some point during Reconstruction; the reason for the name appears self-evident. The tract consisted of fifty farms, 44 of which were sold by 1873. Bethel noted that few of the new landowners actually paid the full asking price, initially set at about $10 per acre; final purchase prices were greatly reduced, to a low of $3.25 in line with then-prevailing land prices. Bethel also wrote in an end note that the boundary line with Abbeville, re-drawn when Greenwood became a county, bisects this black community rather neatly between two voting precincts, "an obvious instance of nineteenth century gerrymandering." Perhaps that is true, but there is also the possibility that the curve in the boundary line in that area was drawn to satisfy the mileage requirement between county seats and county lines. Bethel noted that residents do not agree among themselves as to the community's boundaries.

Both writers cited Promised Land for its continuity and stability for more than a century. Bleser related a 1963 interview with a resident who recognized the names of nineteen of the original 33 settlers and knew all the families descended from the seven Moragne brothers who settled there. The thrust of Bethel's study was to trace as many of the families as possible, a project that took her as far afield as New York, Chicago, and Washington to interview Promised Landers who had taken part in the "great migration" to those cities. Both writers also described Promised Land as a community of self-reliant and thrifty people whose children largely escaped the "infantilizing effects of the closed society" of whites. Promised Land families were among the few for whom the promises of emancipation were fulfilled. Promised Land is located on Highway 10 between Greenwood and Verdery. It is not shown at all on the 1898 map and is called *Promise Land* on the latest map of Greenwood County.

Three communities beyond Promised Land – Verdery, Bradley, and Troy – grew up along the railroad, and two of the names themselves came directly from that source. Bradley was named for General P. H. Bradley, first president of the line that became the Charleston and Western Carolina (C&WC), and Verdery for a prominent Augusta businessman who was an official of the same railroad. Margaret Watson's account in *Greenwood County Sketches* traced the Bradley family from the arrival of one Patrick Bradley from New York in 1784. Patrick Henry Bradley, a grandson of the original settler, attained his general's rank in the state militia and served in the Civil War as captain of a company raised in the community. One of his privileges as an official of the railroad company was a stop in front of his home. The village that grew up around that stop was named for him in the 1880s. Verdery dates from about the same time. One interesting tidbit of local lore concerns a young classical guitarist from New York, Benjamin Verdery, who spent two weeks as an artist-in-residence at Lander College in 1985. Someone asked him if there were any connection between his name and the community a few miles from Greenwood. He had no idea but was sufficiently intrigued that he followed up with phone calls to his family and a trip to Augusta to look up relatives he didn't know he had. Ben Verdery managed to trace some of his roots between performance dates at several Greenwood locations.

The Ligon house on Highway 10 is a historic landmark in Verdery. Still in good repair, this house has been a stage coach stop and hotel, as well as a post office and a private home. According to a notation in *Greenwood County – The Artist's View* (1976), the front of the house still contains post office furniture and artifacts from 200 years ago. There is no longer a post office at Verdery, but a number of modern houses have been built along the highway, and the A. M. Tuck Construction Company is much in evidence along the road to Cedar Springs in Abbeville County.

Troy lies between Long Cane and Hard Labor Creeks in lower Greenwood County. It is associated with the Long Cane settlement in nearby McCormick County and the Indian massacre of that name during which more than twenty settlers were killed in 1760. Don Herd suggested that the encroachment on Indian lands by white settlers was the major reason for the Long Cane massacre. The Cherokees also feared oppression from the rising strength of the militia and were on their way to attack the fort at Ninety Six when the settlers, attempting to flee to Augusta, got in their way. Regardless of the reasons for the massacre, its historical importance is undeniable, and it serves to place the Troy environs well before the Revolutionary War. It also introduces the Calhoun family to the upcountry. Surely everybody knows that the great John C.'s grandmother was one of the victims of the massacre. Margaret Watson, who noted that there were at one time six different Patricks and six different Williams in the Calhoun family, gave history away too easily when she wrote, "Greenwood has no claim on these pioneer Calhouns. . . ." It would be unthinkable to write about Greenwood County and omit the Long Cane massacre. The site may be, technically, in McCormick County, but its associations with Troy and Greenwood County are indisputable. Fears of Indian attacks did not ease until a treaty with the Cherokees full 25 years after the massacre lessened the threat.

Although local historian and Troy denizen Nora Marshall Davis was credited with pinpointing the exact location of the Long Cane massacre, this was by no means the sole contribution of one of the area's most remarkable citizens; indeed, Davis's painstaking research into a number of historical puzzles led to the directorship of the South Carolina Historical Markers Survey, a position she held from 1936 to 1945. At the time of her death in 1969 at the age of 85, Nora Davis was a noted "historical scholar, English professor and author." A native of Troy, her formal education included degrees from Erskine College and the University of South Carolina as well as graduate study at the University of Chicago and Columbia University. Davis's doctorate was the honorary D. Litt. awarded by Erskine in connection with its Centennial observance in 1939. Although Davis's academic career consisted of teaching English and short story writing at Erskine, LaGrange (Georgia) College, Winthrop, and Lander College, she is best remembered for articles, pamphlets, and monographs on South Carolina history. Among her better known works is "Military and Naval Operations in South Carolina, 1860-1865," published by the South Carolina Archives Department for the Confederate War Centennial Commission in 1959. She also published histories of Fort Charlotte on the Savannah River and Long Cane Associate Reformed Presbyterian Church. Dr. Davis was known as a stickler for accuracy in research; the body of her work was called "a major contribution to the history of South Carolina and especially . . . her own section."

Another important contribution from Dr. Davis was an article entitled "Jefferson Davis's Route from Richmond, Virginia, to Irwinville, Georgia, April 2 - May 10, 1865," which appeared in *Proceedings of the South Carolina Historical Association* for 1941. The Confederate President's flight from Richmond took him through Greenwood County on his way to Abbeville; he spent the night of May 1, 1865, in Cokesbury. Dr. Davis's article refuted some of the information contained in A. J. Hanna's *Flight Into Oblivion* published in 1938. In a recent book on the same subject, *The Long Surrender* (1989), author Burke Davis recalled, and simultaneously downplayed, the controversy between Hanna and Nora Davis:

> *Flight into Oblivion*, the only previous work on the pursuit of Davis and his Cabinet, won a devoted readership over the years after publication by a small Virginia press in 1938. Though the narrative by the late Alfred J. Hanna is rather limited . . . its underlying research was an invaluable guide in the composition of this account. . . .
>
> The chief defect of Hanna's book is a lack of unity, but the accuracy of its chronology was also challenged in considerable (if chiefly minor) detail by Dr. Nora M. Davis of South Carolina. Her article in *Proceedings of the South Carolina Historical Association*, 1941, inspired a challenge to Hanna from the late Monroe F. Cockrell of Chicago, a banker and amateur Civil War historian. A lively correspondence between the two is in the M. F. Cockrell Papers, Manuscript Department, Perkins Library, Duke University, Durham, N. C. Dr. Hanna acknowledged that Dr. Davis had found numerous errors in his text, including some dates. The

little-known controversy was studied, but its outcome had little effect upon the present volume, which does not include such detail. The originality, charm and generally sound background of Hanna's book make it of enduring interest to readers and scholars alike. [Vintage Books paperback ed.]

Nora Davis's work on the state's historical markers alone would be enough to secure her place as an important South Carolina historian; her research in that capacity was called, interestingly enough, "infinite," and it was she who composed many of the inscriptions on historical markers erected during the time she served as director of the survey.

The last years of Davis's life were spent at the family home in Troy where she cared for an invalid sister even as she continued her work in historical research. Some of her papers survive in a collection housed in the Erskine College Library, and nephews Emmett and Robert Davis of Greenwood have preserved other examples of her work.

Another attraction of the Troy area was the covered bridge spanning Long Cane Creek in what is now McCormick County. The bridge, known as Bradley's Covered Bridge, was erected in 1892 to facilitate travel between Troy and Abbeville and was destroyed by fire in 1979. Covered wooden bridges were useful in their day to avoid freeze-overs in severe weather as well as to prevent balking by horses and mules. Simulating a barn door, the entrance was believed less likely to terrify the animals than an open bridge. The distinctive sway in the roof of the bridge over Long Cane was caused by army tanks crossing during maneuvers held there in 1941. The fire, which most people believe was deliberately set, destroyed a national landmark; the bridge had been placed on the National Register of Historic Places only two years before. One of the best extant photographs of the covered bridge is a color study done by Thomas L. Hutto not long before it burned.

The origin of the naming of Troy is obscure. The location was once a post office named "Indian Hill" designated on an 1854 map and used into the twentieth century on voting tally sheets. The nickname of "Trickum" or "Trick-Em" appears to have been just that, but the name did show up on at least one early deed as "Trickemville." There is speculation that the designation referred to some less-than-honest horse trading activity in the area. Evidently there was at one time a racetrack nearby, another place that could conceivably give rise to such a name. H. T. Cook's book *The Hard Labor Section* credited the location of both Bradley and Troy to a single source, Thomas White Chiles, one of whose daughters married General Patrick Bradley and another Captain Robert W. Lites. Chiles supposedly settled a plantation on each daughter when she married, and a village grew up at both locations. Cook called Lites the "founder of Troy" and also instrumental in bringing the railroad, an event that made all the difference. The incorporation of the town with its final name of Troy came in 1882, the year the first train from Augusta reached the village. Whether the idea came from W. K. Bradley or a railroad engineer named McFall is really immaterial. The name is a classic, even if one has heard only of the beauteous Helen who, interestingly enough, was from Sparta and not Troy. She sojourned in Troy only about ten years, just long enough to enjoy the Trojan War, the massive slaughter that followed her abduction by Paris, son of Troy's King Priam. It seems that Paris was already married, to a nymph named Oenone, a circumstance he conveniently forgot when he stole Helen away from her husband. The nymph, however, did not forget, and it was she who caused her unfaithful husband's death when she refused to heal his wounds. Helen's husband Menelaus was more forgiving. After the fall of Troy; he took Helen back home to Sparta where they lived happily ever after. The best part of the whole Helen of Troy story, one of the most famous in Greek mythology, is that nobody ever blamed Helen for the carnage; evidently one look at her famous beauty was enough to set the whole male population at war with each other. Troy folk may find in this story what they will, but the record is plain. Actually, the practice of using names from classical antiquity was well established in the nineteenth century. Consider Rome and Athens in Georgia, and Spartanburg in South Carolina, as well as many other place names in the United States. If nothing else, this practice indicated a certain familiarity with the classics that was evidently more common a century ago than it is today. It also lends further credence to Louis Wright's descriptions.

At one time Troy had prospects of becoming a two-railroad town. The second line was surveyed and actually graded, but the project never materialized. The road through Troy was first called the Augusta and Knoxville (A&K). It merged with the Savannah Valley Railroad and others a few years later to form the Port Royal and Western Carolina Railway and eventually became the Charleston and Western Carolina (C&WC). The C&WC was acquired by the Atlantic Coast Line which eventually merged with the Seaboard to form the Seaboard Coast Line Railway, now operated under the name CSX. But all that was in the future when Troy entered its boom period near the end of the last century. Its prospects must have seemed quite bright when the building boom started. Margaret Watson wrote that Troy was a considerably more bustling place in the first thirty years of its history than it is today. Although no mention of a mineral spring has come to light, Troy somehow gained a reputation as a health resort; excursion trains brought visitors from Augusta to stop at the rambling Park House Hotel and picnic in the park and grove just across the road. The grove contained tennis courts and a bandstand, and thousands came on excursions because no other town on the railroad line had a park as pretty. The old hotel building became a private residence at some point. It remains standing, but only barely, and is known as the Dendy place for the family who were its last occupants. Troy's high point was the period between 1900 and the Great

Depression; Margaret Watson wrote that in 1911 it had fourteen stores, a bank, a telephone exchange, livery stables, three churches, and three resident physicians. There was also a dentist's office at some point. The telephone exchange provided local service to subscribers beginning around 1895 and extending a few years later to adjoining towns. Telephone service was discontinued about 1925 when everybody ran out of money, and no service was available in Troy for the next 25 years or so. There was even a soft drink bottling company in Troy at one time.

Cotton was the mainstay of the economy of towns such as Troy for many years. In addition to two cotton gins, Troy had a cottonseed oil mill at one time. The town is also strongly identified with the lumber industry or, in local parlance and more comprehensively, the wood business. Sawmills were among the first businesses, and a planing operation was established around 1920. That business was bought by Frank Rush whose two sons – Jasper F. and Robert M. – ran Rush Lumber Company until it closed in the mid 1950s. Another business of long standing was White Lumber Company, operated by J. Frank White and his sons Joe and Alfred. Frank White & Sons Lumber Company continues to exist as a chipping mill near McCormick still operated by Alfred White and one of his sons. One of the last remaining businesses in Troy, Cox's Store, closed in 1990.

Two noted nineteenth century houses, Eden Hall and Ivy Gates, are located near Troy, but neither is in Greenwood County. Another fine example of antebellum architecture and Troy family history is the Bowen house just off Highway 10 between Bradley and Troy. Described as an "elegant farm house" in *Greenwood County – The Artist's View*, this structure was built in the 1830s by the Reverend James Chiles and was known as Dr. Neel's place when William R. Bowen bought it in 1925. Currently owned by Bowen's grandson Hamp Warner, the house has been in the family for more than 65 years.

Still another glorious antebellum house nearby is Sylvania, home of Frank and Sally Wideman. Although the county line shift in 1916 placed Sylvania in McCormick County, its location before that time was in the township of Bradley, county of Greenwood. Most important to preservationists is the fact that the house today is almost exactly the same as when it was built in 1825. Sylvania means, literally, a place in the woods; presumably it has always borne that name. This house connects Greenwood with the Hearst family, ancestors of the famous William Randolph and the later and more infamous Patty. John Hearst and his son John, Jr., were among those who received land grants "at or near the Long Canes" about 1766. Margaret Watson wrote that the wording of the Colonial Council minutes indicated the Hearsts had just arrived from Europe. The John Hearst who built Sylvania was a grandson of the first John. His father Joseph owned at one time more than 2,000 acres of land, including the original homesite. Joseph's son was nicknamed "Hard Labor" John, presumably to differentiate him from John "Whitehall" Hearst, a cousin who lived in the White Hall community nearby. "Hard Labor John" built Sylvania; his son Dr. John Wardlaw Hearst built Eden Hall about 25 years later. James H. Wideman bought the property when John Hearst died in 1847 and lived there until his death in 1896. A daughter, Eulalie Wideman, owned the property until 1929. The site is shown on the 1898 map of Greenwood County with the notation "Dr. Wideman." The current owner is Frank J. Wideman, Jr., great-grandson of James H. Wideman. Perrins, Presslys, and Chileses, among other old county families, owned land adjoining the estate in 1825.

Sylvania's location is off the beaten track, but not far from the intersection of Millway Road with Highway 10 below Bradley. Indeed, the house's setting is part of its charm, since the site affords a tantalizing glimpse of serene beauty among the trees to the passerby along the highway. Even one's angle of vision – the house faces its own side road and not the highway – contributes to the pleasantly oblique, if not slightly aloof, ambiance of Sylvania on a summer afternoon. The house is a story-and-a-half frame structure with eight rooms and upper and lower hallways. The upper rooms have dormer windows, and the main rooms on the ground floor are notable for their original hand-carved mantels and woodwork. The wainscoting in the downstairs hallway is decorated with a hand-painted design of grape vines. The color and design are remarkably fresh after more than 160 years. Sylvania was placed on the National Register of Historic Places in 1977.

Troy is located in the extreme southwest corner of Greenwood County, a funny little blip of land that seems logically to belong to McCormick. One persistent legend is that a Troy landowner had no intention of leaving Greenwood County when McCormick was formed in 1916, and the line was drawn to accommodate that gentleman. Stranger things have happened; the story may very well be true.

A great deal of factual information and some interesting old photographs can be found in the little centennial history *An Excursion to Troy* (1982). The booklet is evidence also that Troy citizens cherish their sense of place in much the same way as those of Hodges, Ninety Six, Phoenix, and Cokesbury. Though the founding fathers are long dead, a number of their descendants continue to live in Troy, and even those who have moved away seem to maintain their ties to the community in some way. One interesting reunion is a gathering of Troy School alumni at the old schoolhouse in the grove, now used as a community center. Hundreds come from miles away to greet old classmates and exchange very special memories of the time they spent in Troy.

Between Troy and Phoenix on the 1898 map lies the township of Callison. This community owes neither its existence nor its name to the railroad; instead, it seems to have begun with Captain James Callison, an immigrant from Ireland who came to the new world as a boy. According to Mary Jane Rush Broadwater in *David Rush and His Descendants and Stories of the Community* (1953) or, in the vernacular, "The Rush Book," James Callison came to the upcountry from Charleston to work in the new cotton mill at Graniteville. From there he went to Tennessee for a time but eventually returned to South Carolina and settled in the area between Hard Labor and Cuffeytown Creeks about 1852. Callison organized a company named the "Reedy Branch Boys" and fought in the Civil War. He farmed and operated a store after the war and also served in the General Assembly from Edgefield County. Callison died in 1894 and is buried at Bold Spring Church. The first James Callison had four children; his descendants number a great many more, some of whom still live and work in Greenwood County.

Captain Callison's son James also ran a store and handled mail, evidently on the same site as Rush's Store which still stands at the crossroads. A post office thus evolved, with Callison as its name. Broadwater wrote that the entire area between Hard Labor and Cuffeytown Creeks was once known as "Shatterfield." H. L. Watson agreed and provided, without documentation, 1812 as the earliest date for the name. Watson also believed a post office with that name was established in 1850. Though unconvinced of the existence of a post office, Broadwater wrote that hand-delivered letters bearing the address "Shatterfield, S. C." had been preserved. She stated that the place name eventually became a sort of joke and traced it to the Satterwhite or Satterfield families in Newberry and Edgefield Counties. She wrote that a tavern on the Hamburg (Augusta) road became known as "Shatterfield's Tavern" and surmised that the name evolved from local references to "Old Man Satterwhite's Field and Tavern."

But some people are not satisfied with the notion of Shatterfield as a sort of generic term for a broader area. One native, Angelle Penn Adams, believes it was a more specific spot and speculates that it pre-dated Callison as the community's actual name. That view is supported in an 1877 letter to the *Edgefield Advertiser* reprinted in Broadwater's book. The writer recounted a visit to Shatterfield without a trace of irony; one is forced to wonder why, in Broadwater's words, "no one ever owned that he lived in Shatterfield." The letter described several families – among them Hollingsworths, Rushes, Flinns, and Quattlebaums, names practically synonymous with Callison – as "well-to do farmers, whose farms are generally in repair, with as good small grain crops as any I have seen in the District, and the first cotton I have seen up this spring." The writer stated expressly that he had visited Shatterfield on and off for forty years; this statement establishes a place name much earlier than Captain James Callison's arrival. Although there is no proof, the possibility exists that the community simply changed its name at some point to honor its most distinguished citizen. The letter to the editor closed, in fact, with a tribute to Callison, who was at that time a member of the legislature.

Broadwater gave Rushville and Union as two names for the same place, an area off the Callison-Bradley road near Powder Spring and the old Union School site. Rushville still appears on a general highway map of Greenwood County. The designation was self-evident; nearly a dozen families named Rush lived there, and everybody was kin to everybody else. A short-lived post office was established about 1890 at Aiton's Store nearby. Union was the name chosen when two schools, one in Abbeville and another in Edgefield, were merged into one. Union School became the center of community life in Rushville; early teachers included Mr. and Mrs. T. E. Dorn. The schoolhouse also served for Sunday school and church services. Since the residents lived a good distance from established churches, visiting ministers came from Bradley and other communities to hold services. Union School was the site of square dances and other social gatherings as late as the 1950s.

Shatterfield/Callison/Rushville had its share of natural springs, including one that provided the name for Bold Spring School and Church, as well as a rather famous mineral spring on Hard Labor Creek called Powder Spring. So strong was the sulphur smell that the name was well taken, just as were the waters by people seeking relief from a number of complaints, among them kidney ailments of various kinds. Broadwater wrote that Powder Spring was known and used by the German immigrants who settled on Hard Labor Creek in 1765. She noted that doctors had been known to prescribe the waters for their patients; many others stocked up without benefit of prescription. Powder Spring was a popular site for political gatherings, picnics, and fish fries, as well as a meeting place for people who came on Sunday afternoons to lay in their supply of water for the week. A swimming hole in the creek nearby was also well-known and well-used on long summer afternoons.

The early German settlement at that place was Londonborough, the first known group settlement in Greenwood County. Hard luck cases from the beginning, the settlers were bilked by the promoter of the expedition to the new world, Colonel John Henry Christian de Stumpel, who took their money and disappeared, leaving them stranded in London. A humane clergyman aired their plight in the newspapers and asked for help. It came, from "a great personage" who had to be the King, and London citizens followed his example with food, funds, and medical help for the displaced group. It was King George III who decided they should go to the colony of South Carolina and took care of the transportation in two ships engaged and fitted out for the purpose. Minutes of the 1764 Provisional Council cover arrangements on the South Carolina end: Patrick Calhoun was directed to build a large log house for shelter until the newcomers could be settled on their own farms, build their own houses (the minutes read "Hutts"), and plant their own crops. A grant of about 25,000 acres was allotted and the name Londonborough chosen to honor the settlers' English benefactors. But bad luck continued to plague the settlement, and both food and money ran out within the first few months. Londonborough was never prosperous; it failed to "take hold" as its founders hoped it would. A number of families moved to more established German settlements in nearby counties, but some stayed on and spread out in the area. Names such as Dorn, Durst, Strom, Clem, and Zimmerman are reminders of this early German community. The Ouzts, or Utz, family came to the area from Germany later. The Londonborough settlers had a particularly difficult choice to make when the Revolution came. While some served on the American side, others were loyal to England or tried to remain neutral in gratitude to King George and the people who had come to their aid while they languished in London. A marker commemorating this early German settlement was erected near Powder Spring by the Edgefield and Greenwood Historical Societies in 1964.

Callison in the 1930s and 1940s was much like other farming communities in Greenwood County, except that in some instances its so-called "farmers" were better at idling, talking, hunting, fishing, gambling, and drinking than they were at making a living from the land. In truth, the incidence of shiftlessness was simply part of the charm of the place; except for a long-held grievance or two, no real harm was done. A couple of stories, possibly legend but just as likely true, can justify these statements: one concerns a man who never quite got around to cutting wood into stove lengths for the kitchen, even though his wife admonished him repeatedly about the sorry state of her wood box. Pine slabs, with bark on one side, were often used for kitchen wood, and people simply split and cut these slabs into the right kind of fuel to keep the stove going. This long-suffering housewife, it is said, was often reduced to using the whole slab with one end burning and the other across the back of a chair ready to be shoved farther into the fire box as the slab burned down. If this story is true, it illustrates another aspect of farm life: wood chopping was evidently *not* women's work in the country, at least not in that family. But another story, this one from McCormick, provides a different view. It seems that a man was about to go fishing when his wife tried to stop him because no wood had been chopped. "Dammit!" he said, "I ain't plannin' to take the axe." Yet another story concerns a Callisonian who asked the mail carrier one day if he knew of a buyer for his hogs. The carrier said he would find one and let him know. A few days later, having located a buyer, the mail carrier asked the farmer about the hogs, only to hear that he didn't have them any more. The mailman was concerned and sympathetic until he learned the farmer had lost them in a poker game. One Callison farmer is said to have routinely left his plow and mule in the field whenever someone came by to ask for help with a seining party somewhere.

Community gatherings such as turtle stews and fish fries brought out the best in the storytellers. No one who ever saw T. E. ("Eb") Dorn tell a story could possibly forget it. He never neglected the necessary body language; even when he had grown old and feeble, he would manage by holding on to a chair as he gestured. The moneyless society Louis Wright remembered prevailed in Callison as well. There were no "manor houses" of the sort L. B. Adams associated with years when cotton prices were very high. The nearest fine house was probably the Sproull place a few miles east of Bradley. That house, built about 1825 by Captain James Sproull and named Mount Vernon, eventually became known as Green Pastures; its owner when it burned in 1978 was William Harrison.

The best thing about Callison was probably its people who, just as people everywhere, ran the gamut from worthless to noble. Church and school activities were the primary diversions, but barbecues, fish fries, and an occasional barn dance were also features of the social life. A card game called Set Back was very popular in Callison, although it attained nothing like the prominence of Rook in Troy; the Troy Rook Club lasted more than thirty years. A few people also played Bridge and Pinochle. Every farming community had its "squire" or leading citizen. Just as James Callison filled the role in Callison originally, in modern times that man was G. D. Bell. Although his primary occupation was mail carrier, he was also a lawyer whose name was on a door to a law office in Greenwood but whose "lawyering" was done at mailboxes, across a card table, or in his or someone else's home. His friends said that for every dollar he was paid for legal services he gave away at least ten.

George Dorn Bell was born in 1895 in Callison and lived there all his life. He was educated at the University of South Carolina and taught school as a young man. He married another school teacher, Josie E. Rush, in 1917. Possibly the stature he acquired in the community was a gradual thing, but he seemed a born leader to those who knew him. People gravitated to him naturally, and his interest in them was genuine. He even seemed to suffer fools gladly. No one enjoyed life more than G. D. Bell, and no one person knows the full extent of his influence in the community. He didn't talk about the things he did for people; he just did them. Bell's mail route brought him in contact with simply everybody in Callison and Kirksey, and his activities as a Mason and Shriner took him far afield; the sheer breadth of that exposure was probably necessary to a man like Bell and probably also explains why he never worked out of a narrow office. His was an expansive soul, big enough to embrace both the high and low born. The Bell house reflected the master's personality; the door was never locked, and everyone was welcome.

G. D. Bell almost personified the word *friend* to a remarkable variety of people. He once took a bottle of Scotch to a neighbor who had left the hospital because he wanted to die at home. There was no possibility that the dying man could use the gift, but Bell was making the perfect symbolic gesture without regard to the reality of the situation. At other times he could be almost harsh in his realism. If a young person did not want Bell's opinion or advice, he should by no means ask for it. When G. D. Bell died in 1980, Callison lost a unique personality and many people their best friend. His wife lived another six years; one eulogy at her funeral called her the "mother" of the community.

Callison today has lost much of the cohesiveness of earlier days, even though it is by no means deserted. It was never a town, but there were a couple of stores, and the minute post office at the crossroads gave the place a certain identity. Two notable postmistresses, Mamie Witt and Mary Dorn Burnett, both with long family trees, died in recent years. Callison is now served by post offices in Troy, Bradley, and Greenwood. Bold Spring, once a three-teacher school, was lost to consolidation in the 1950s; the building now serves as a community center of sorts. An active chapter of bowhunters holds regular meets and competitions in Callison, and the volunteer fire department seems to be the primary focus of local interest. Most residents work in Greenwood; no one seems to mind the commute.

Between Callison and Greenwood on Highway 67 lies the community of Breezewood. The name seems to have no particular significance except its own pleasant connotations, but the area itself is of historical importance. For one thing, Dr. John Perkins Barratt's grandson raised his family there, and in more recent years, Breezewood was the home of Mr. and Mrs. Ben Hunter. Mrs. Hunter, the former Mary E. Stockman, was well known in the community for her good works and interest in the well-being of her neighbors. An educated woman herself, she is said to have given the land for Moss Hill School. She also provided help for many young people who wanted to get an education. A Callison neighbor remembers that Mrs. Hunter's house was a favorite boarding place for teachers in nearby county schools. One of those young teachers was Mary Beaudrot Herndon who lived with Mrs. Hunter in 1931. Herndon retains vivid memories of the days when she was a brand new schoolteacher just out of school herself. Unable to accept a fellowship to graduate school, she had sought a teaching job near Greenwood. Offers came from both Calhoun Falls and Bold Spring, but the Calhoun Falls position included such stringent requirements for her personal life that Herndon chose Callison instead. A place in Mrs. Hunter's household turned out to be an unexpected fringe benefit. Among other stories of the friends she made there, Herndon recalled one memorable night when the windmill came loose with a sound that can only be imagined. She and her landlady, nightgowns flapping, had to go outside in the middle of the night to tie it down.

There were books in Mary Hunter's house, and people often gathered there for bridge parties. She was probably the dominant figure in the community, and her example was played out in her daughter Lillian and granddaughter Gladys Estelle who currently lives and works in Breezewood. Mrs. Hunter's husband died when he was only fifty years old, and her only son Carlisle drowned before he was thirty. Her daughter-in-law, Elizabeth Davis Hunter, credited Mrs. Hunter for kindness to everyone, particularly the black families who lived on the farm. She worked to help their children get a decent education; Herndon added that she took particular care to provide eyeglasses for those whose sight was failing. If one wishes to see only the concept of noblesse oblige in people such as Mary Hunter, it is surely there, but the people who knew them observed more than simply a sense of obligation in their day-to-day activities. Theirs were busy and purposeful lives, always, or so it seemed, directed outward. There was no time for introspection; there was too much to be done. Mary Stockman Hunter died in 1946; she is buried in the family plot at Damascus Church.

Continuing toward Greenwood on Highway 67 the modern traveler is dazzled by two magnificent structures, one on either side of the road, that, except for their physical location, could not be more dissimilar. One, Abney Hall, is a modern mansion built in the early 1960s by John S. Abney and now occupied by his widow, and the other is Barratt House, designed and built by Dr. John Perkins Barratt in the 1850s as a residence for his son Jack. Barratt House was long the home of Mr. and Mrs. T. E. Dorn and is now owned by a son, former Congressman W. J. Bryan Dorn. The addition of two major wings was undertaken by the younger Dorns to provide living space for a large family. Because of their concern for the architectural integrity and historic value of this very special house, Bryan and Millie Dorn made sure that the additions were, in the words of the National Register nomination, "in keeping with the exterior design, scale, and materials of the original building."

Don Herd always thought the house had a northern England feel and attributed that quality to Barratt's reminiscences of his birthplace in Wakefield. Officially the structure is described as "a two-story, stuccoed brick residence which displays elements of the Gothic revival style of architecture." At some point (the nomination states simply, "during the Victorian era," which could have been any time from 1837 to 1901, but must have been much nearer the latter date), frame porches and a frame kitchen were built onto the house. These additions were removed when the north wing was built in 1957. "At the same time, stoops and simple wrought iron railings were added to the central bays of the facade and west elevation. A similar wing was built on the south elevation in 1969. Each wing is stuccoed and has a gable roof of standing seam metal. Both wings are set back from the planes of the facade and west elevation. Windows are set in simple surrounds and are smaller than those in the original portion of the house. Care was taken to make the additions compatible with, yet distinctive from, the original building."

The interior of Barratt House is even more remarkable than its gracious exterior. It deserves to be described in the exact words of the National Register nomination:

> The original section of the Barratt House contains a central hall with four large rooms on each story. A small room is also located at the rear of the second story hall. Construction of the 1957 and

> Construction of the 1957 and 1969 wings has enabled the owners to add modern amenities to the house while preserving its interior spaces as originally designed. Interior features include walls of plaster on brick, wooden floors, wide baseboards, plaster ceilings, four-panel doors, and simple door surrounds with plain corner blocks.
>
> Interior ornamentation is concentrated in the parlor, which has an ornate plaster ceiling medallion and elaborately carved window and door surrounds and mantel. In addition, Dr. Barratt painted murals on all four plaster walls; these were obscured by paint in the 1930s, but the owners intend to have this paint removed and the murals restored. Paint removal in selected spots indicates that the murals are intact. [The murals were indeed restored, with professional help, in the late 1980s and add greatly to the beauty and authenticity of the parlor.]
>
> The first story hall has an elaborate plaster cornice and a single-run staircase with rosewood bannister and turned balusters. The stair makes a quarter turn at the top. At the turn the wall forms a rounded corner, in which is located a niche with semicircular arch.
>
> All of the eight major rooms have mantels which were hand-carved and painted with scenes by Dr. Barratt. The mantel paintings have since been obscured by paint. Dr. Barratt, a horticulturist, utilized a variety of leaves and blossoms, as well as geometrical shapes, in his carvings. Several mantels were carved (as well as painted) to give the appearance of marble. Five rooms have original built-in closets.
>
> The north wing of the house . . . is noteworthy for its use of materials salvaged from Dr. Barratt's home, Chinquapin Ridge. . . . Of special interest is a wall in the study, on which is painted a mural and primitively marbelized wainscoating [sic].

Five outbuildings are also part of the estate. They include a gear house, corn crib, granary, and smokehouse, as well as a hewn log structure believed to have been constructed as a schoolhouse. A genuine treasure, one shared generously over the years by Bryan and Millie Dorn, the Barratt House property was placed on the National Register of Historic Places in 1986.

If Barratt's most ambitious plans had materialized, Greenwood County might have developed very differently. Margaret Watson wrote that he planned a village to be called Barrattville not far from his home on the present site of Abney Hall. Part of that vision was a railroad which he anticipated would be built along the ridge followed by Mathews Road; his dream village would be a stop along the railroad. He set out oaks and cedar trees to enhance the site he selected. Don Herd believed he built the schoolhouse that once stood among those trees; Watson made no such declaration but affirmed that a school was built there. The actual route of the railroad when it came, along a ridge similar to the one Barratt anticipated but a few miles to the east, put an end to Barrattville before it began even as it gave new life to Ninety Six and brought the outside world to Greenwood.

Margaret Watson named a spot on the west side of the present Highway 178 as Wallerville, named for the Reverend John Waller who came to this section in 1793. A rather famous figure in Baptist history, John Waller had fought for freedom from the Church of England while preaching in Virginia as well as founded two churches after he came to South Carolina. He was also the great-grandfather of C. A. C. "Chris" Waller. Chris Waller's parents gave most of their children truly remarkable names, among them James Leonidas, Robert Aurelius, Pelius Augustus, Creswell Archimedes Calhoun, Cadmus Garlington, and Codrus. Only two of the eight who lived to maturity had ordinary names: Edward Henry and Rhoda Elizabeth. Three Waller sons were killed in the Civil War, and Chris Waller retained the captain's rank he earned in military service as an honorific throughout his life.

The McKellar family, one of the Greenwood's oldest, also settled on what is now Highway 25 and 178 in Greenwood County near Scotch Cross. Two brothers, John and Donald, evidently arrived in the early 1800s from County Argyle in Scotland. The McKellar family, with its profusion of Donalds, Peters, and Johns, was well traced by Margaret Watson in *Greenwood County Sketches*.

Scotch Cross, almost smack in the middle of Greenwood County, is now associated with the historic house at the crossroads; but the name, according to a sketch by Louise C. Fleming, was originally a reference to the McKellar family settlement and two important roads that happened to cross at that place. Margaret Watson was unwilling to state that the "Scotch" in the name referred to the McKellar family whom she placed about a half mile south and several years later than the name. Instead, she believed a native of Scotland whose name was not recorded ran a store there before 1800. She also wrote that a horse thief was hanged at the store site and buried nearby about 1800, thereby establishing a date earlier than the McKellars' arrival. In any case, the name is another reminder of the homogeneity of Greenwood's early settlers – they were almost exclusively from the British Isles, with a few western Europeans thrown in.

The house at Scotch Cross was built about 1815 by J. Wesley Brooks as one of the most elaborate and elegant of its day. Preparations alone required nearly three years and involved hand-wrought nails, hinges, and other hardware, as well as heavy timbers cut on the property and shaped and fitted by hand. Fleming wrote that mantels, door frames, molding, paneled wainscoting, and other decorative features were hauled by ox-cart from Charleston. None of the eight rooms is smaller than 20 by 12 feet. The cost of the house originally, in money and labor, was estimated at $10,000; its foundation and chimneys are supposed to contain enough brick to build a modern bungalow. The original owner moved to Alabama about 1835, and the house became the property of Zebulon Rudulph, whose wife was Brooks's niece. After him, it passed to a brother-in-law, Dr. Samuel Perryman. After Perryman's death, his widow married Captain Henry H. Creswell, who bought up surrounding land until the plantation contained 2,000 acres. The house passed next to a son-in-law, Robert F. Fleming, in 1896 and remained in the family until 1935. Members of the same family had owned Scotch Cross at that point for more than a century. There have been three owners in the last 55 years: Jane H. Cothran, Dr. S. C. Hodges, and Mr. and Mrs. Olin Turner. At this writing, Turner's widow Virginia maintains, in her words, "the tradition of Scotch Cross."

Louise Fleming's reminiscence of her home detailed both the interior of the house and the extensive gardens that once surrounded it. She compared the grounds at the height of their glory to those at both Roselands and Chinquapin Ridge and named dozens of varieties of trees, shrubs, and flowers once cultivated there. The vegetable garden contained a fine asparagus bed, and tomatoes grown at Scotch Cross were legendary. Fleming wrote that the first tomato plants were grown for ornamental purposes only. Though fairly common since their introduction from Africa in the sixteenth century, tomatoes actually have a checkered history. Whether they are fruits or vegetables is evidently meaningless; the plant is a tropical herb of the nightshade family which probably accounts for the fact that tomatoes were once thought to be poisonous. Fleming found it significant that she made a large part of her living from selling tomatoes grown in the same garden that had provided food for the Scotch Cross table a hundred years earlier.

One final Scotch Cross story concerns Louise Fleming's mother, Zemula Estelle Creswell Fleming, described in Don Herd's book as "the woman who died twice." A bit of oral history from Mary Barratt Park, the story goes that Mrs. Fleming suffered a seizure after several months of declining health and was pronounced dead by the family doctor. Embalming was not the accepted practice in those days, and the body was laid out on the bed for viewing by family and friends during a period of mourning lasting several days. At one point during this period Mr. Fleming happened to notice a faint flickering of his wife's eyelid, an indication that funeral preparations had been a bit premature. Not only was Mrs. Fleming alive, she recovered fully and lived another thirty years or so. Park added that Fleming herself later recounted the experience many times: her spirit, she said, left her body and entered heaven only to be turned away by a "godly creature" who said that her time had not yet come. An amusing sidelight to this story is that the mourners consumed the fruit cakes Mrs. Fleming had baked before she was stricken, and she was much put out that none remained for the Christmas feast that year.

Utopia as a place name in Greenwood County appears to be gone entirely, with the exception of a tiny section called Utopia Acres Road between Scotch Cross and Highway 67. Utopia School was at one time among the larger schools in the county; the record shows it had five teachers in 1948 not long before consolidation. Another classic, the name derives from Sir Thomas More's famous work describing an ideal state. More's *Utopia* was written in Latin in 1515 and translated into English in 1551, but the concept is much older; actually it extends from Aristotle and Plato all the way to treatment by authors of the present day. A whole school of utopian literature exists, as well as a few utopian communities. More coined the name of his ideal place from two Greek words, one signifying "no place" and the other "good place," thus deliberately exploiting a double meaning. The mythical state he described functioned on several interesting premises: one was the scorning of money and finery of all kinds, while another called for a six-hour work day with time for modest relaxation and compulsory education. In addition, everyone in Utopia was taught farming and at least one craft. Laws were few and so clear that lawyers were unnecessary; in any event, the most severe punishment was bondage. Interestingly enough, divorces could be granted in the original Utopia for adultery and intolerable incompatibility (one wonders who defined "intolerable" or, for that matter, "incompatibility" if there were no lawyers), and wars were waged only in self defense or to relieve the oppressed. In short, a community could have many names worse than Utopia. Some writers argue that the word is merely a connotation of unreality; nevertheless, several serious efforts to live out More's and other writers' visions have been made. It is probably safe to assume that Greenwood County's Utopia was not among them.

About six miles below Ninety Six lies the community called Dyson. Little more than a voting precinct along Highway 702 on the road to Saluda today, Dyson was one of the villages that grew up along the railroad. Luther B. Aull, who lives on the Ninety Six highway, is a third generation Dyson native. His grandfather came to the site from Newberry after the Civil War and established a grist mill, flour mill, and planer operation a couple of miles from the depot. Dyson was named for a captain in the Civil War, but the family name seems to have disappeared. Aull recalled that at least one Dyson family member attained local hero status during World War II. John Henry Williamson flew with General Claire Lee Chennault's famous "Flying Tigers," a volunteer group that fought against Japan during the earliest days of the war. The Flying Tigers squadron was almost the equivalent of the French Foreign Legion; Williamson certainly deserves to be remembered for that service.

No place name in Greenwood County holds more sway over the imagination than Ninety Six, and none is more important historically. Its significance as a trading post at the crossing of two important Indian paths in pre-Revolutionary times and as a Tory fort during the War itself is documented elsewhere; this section deals primarily with the evolution of the town through a couple of incarnations and its status as an integral part of Greenwood County's development over the last century.

Ninety Six has the longest memory of any section of the county. Possibly its recollection of a meeting between the royal governor and the Cherokee emperor at that place in May 1746 had something to do with Ninety Six's bid to become a county seat more than a hundred years later. As the farthest outpost inland from Charles Town, Ninety Six was the logical choice as the seat of one of the seven judicial districts established in 1769 "for the more convenient administration of justice." It was, in fact, the seventh such district named, and its jurisdiction included all parts of the colony not specifically named in the other six. The area covered was so large it comprised fourteen of the state's present counties and part of a fifteenth, according to *Greenwood County Sketches*. Once subdivision started in response to the cry of the back-country for some seat of government more convenient than Charles Town, the inexorable march to the modern system of counties began. A steady succession of changes – from districts to counties, back to districts, and, finally, with the constitution of 1868, to counties again – went on for nearly 150 years until Greenwood reached its current configuration in 1916. Ninety Six remained a judicial district for only 31 years; its original size was reduced, first in 1791 and again in 1800 when new districts destined to become counties were formed. In the interim, Ninety Six had officially changed its name to Cambridge in honor of the school which opened in 1785, and the first post office in Greenwood County was established there in 1793.

As the importance of Ninety Six as a judicial center declined in the first years of the nineteenth century, the village grew smaller and smaller until it virtually disappeared. The original settlement that grew up around the fort was never larger than 200-300 inhabitants; even so, Cambridge in its heyday consisted of "four 'hotels' or taverns, more than a dozen stores, a newspaper, blacksmith, shoemaker, tailor, offices of doctors and lawyers and the Cambridge Literary Association which was a gentleman's club with a library." The story of the decline of Cambridge College is documented in another chapter. An episode that plagues researchers to this day was the loss of court records, deeds, and other legal documents originally housed at the courthouse in Ninety Six. When Ninety Six lost out as a judicial seat in 1800, these records were transferred to new courthouses in Abbeville and Edgefield. The records in Abbeville were saved from a courthouse fire in January 1872 and stored in several buildings around the square while repairs were underway. Yet another disastrous fire struck only ten months later; it was the second fire that destroyed the records while they were in protective storage awaiting return to their proper place in the courthouse. Many people know that a hundred years of public records were lost in a fire in Abbeville, but most believe it was a courthouse fire. Margaret Watson set the record straight in *Greenwood County Sketches* and added as a mild afterthought: "That loss poses many unanswerable questions to historians and lawyers."

No doubt in part because of the Abbeville fire, little descriptive information about the physical appearance of the original village of Cambridge exists. Watson stated that both the courthouse and the jail were brick structures, but questioned whether the "two-story brick" courthouse was the original or a later replacement. Evidently both buildings were a short distance southwest of the Star Fort site. The jail was located near a small stream long known as Jailyard Branch. Schoolmaster Edward Hooker wrote in a diary entry dated February 27, 1806:

> The town of Cambridge is nothing more than a snug little village of 15 or 20 houses and stores on the top of a small hill called Cambridge Hill. There is an area in the center of it, where stands an old brick Court House. At a little distance down the hill is the jail – both in a neglected state. . . . The Village has seven stores and three taverns. [Would modern readers agree that proportion is a little strange?] Its appearance is not at all flourishing; and it is said to have been decaying, ever since the new judiciary arrangement, by which the courts were removed to Abbeville. The present town has been built anew since the war; the old town of Ninety Six, as it used to be called, having been destroyed by the British.

Hooker obviously looked on his new situation at Cambridge with a somewhat jaundiced eye. A New Englander, he was critical of nearly every aspect of his brief sojourn in the backcountry of South Carolina, from the infrastructure of roads and bridges to the social amenities. He found a Fourth of July barbecue, for example, poorly handled in the matter of after-dinner toasts: "No notice was given when they were commenced," he sniffed, "and they were drunk by about a dozen at the head of the table, while the rest of the company were, some of them, eating, others talking and laughing and others sauntering about, without knowing of any toasts being drunk, except by the sound of the cannon." He even found fault with Major General Butler of Edgefield who was there to review the militia. While Hooker allowed that the "old Warrior" appeared "pretty well on horseback," he exhibited "far less dignity on foot." All in all Hooker was not impressed: "I did not," he wrote, "perceive in his honor any striking indications of greatness. He seems to be a man of sense and information, but not much polished and improved by education." The military gentleman whom Hooker found so inadequate was Major General William Butler (1759-1821), an important figure in South Carolina history. Not only was his rank earned in the state militia, he was also a member of Congress when Hooker met him in 1806. The general was in his mid-40s; "old Warrior" would not seem the most apt description for a man in the prime of life, though perhaps the military and political life in those days included a great deal of wear and tear. General Butler was also the grandfather of General Matthew Calbraith Butler of Civil War fame and the same Butler for whom Saluda County was almost named. Possibly it was fortunate that the schoolmaster confined his comments to his diary. As Charles Sumner discovered fifty years later when he attacked another statesman with the same surname, South Carolinians do not take kindly to what they call "vilification" of their heroes. What a relief for us that Hooker was much more taken with John C. Calhoun whom he called "a young man of much promise." No doubt their common status as Yale men was a factor in that judgement. Hooker, whose brother was a lawyer in Cambridge, moved on to teach mathematics at South Carolina College after only a year in the village.

While adjusting to the new political reality was probably not easy, Cambridge nevertheless managed to attract some new residents and businesses during the early part of the 1800s. Margaret Watson wrote that the distinction of having the first newspaper in Abbeville District belongs to Cambridge. Thomas M. Davenport's weekly, *The Anti-Monarchist*, began at Edgefield in 1811 and moved the next year to Cambridge. Davenport's printing business lasted until about 1820; the newspaper was published under the name *The Cambridge Republican* for part of that time.

Watson's book contains the names of many early settlers in Ninety Six, but only four families dating from the pre-Revolutionary period have been identified: Robert Goudy, William Moore, John Savage, and William Hagood. Family names of a later period can be found in an account book kept by Dr. Zachariah Meriwether and given to the University of South Carolina library by a descendant of Dr. John Logan, who Watson speculated might have taken over Meriwether's practice. Further recollections, by Dr. Richard C. Griffin and Dr. Ephraim Ramsay Calhoun, appeared in a later newspaper, *The Ninety Six Guardian*, in 1879. Griffin's article named a number of doctors in Cambridge in the 1820s. The practice of medicine was considered primarily an appropriate avocation for the land-owning gentry, in no sense the full-fledged scientific profession we know today. Griffin wrote concerning one practitioner: "We thought him [Dr. Joseph R. Dogan] the finest specimen of the medical gentleman the world ever produced, and we determined in our mind that if we ever lived to be man nothing short of being a doctor, the owner of a fine nicktailed horse and sporting a ruffled shirt would satisfy us." Doctors must have been on the cutting edge of Cambridge society in those days when cock fighting and horse racing were among the most popular diversions for sporting gentlemen. Meriwether was recalled as "a man fond of blooded horses and game chickens."

Calhoun's published recollections were similar to Griffin's. He too wrote in a jocular vein, and both were careful to show their erudition with a liberal sprinkling of multi-syllable words and a Latin phrase or two. Calhoun, a graduate of the medical college in Philadelphia, moved from Cambridge to New Market to Greenwood where he practiced medicine and opened a drug store about 1838. Watson wrote that he also operated a hotel for a time in his home on the east side of the square and was very active in the development of Greenwood. A number of Calhoun's descendants still call Greenwood home. *Greenwood County Sketches* also named a few lawyers who practiced in Cambridge during this period; one was the John C. McGehee whose wife gave Greenwood its name. The lawyers, including McGehee, appear to have moved on after a year or two at Cambridge. Business also dried up; Griffin's account noted that "mountain people" who would come once or twice a year to trade their farm produce for manufactured goods began bypassing Ninety Six in favor of Hamburg and Augusta after the epidemic of 1815-16. Ninety Six was beginning to acquire a dreaded epithet – it was becoming "an unhealthful place."

The courthouse building, which had seen service as a store, post office, library, and men's club, was dismantled about 1855, and the Cambridge post office was dropped in 1860. The village was in process of moving a couple of miles to the site of the new railroad. Evidently there were still a few holdouts for the name Cambridge; Watson wrote that it was revived for about ten years at a new post office established a few miles away along Highway 246. That area is still known as the Cambridge section but is unrelated to the original village except as namesake.

Watson's description of a gala celebration held at Star Fort on June 18, 1878, is particularly interesting in the context of the development of Greenwood County. Ostensibly the celebration was to commemorate the 97th anniversary of the siege of Ninety Six. People wondered, in print, why anyone would choose to celebrate so odd a year. Why had they not celebrated, symbolically, the 96th anniversary? Why not hold out for a centenary which would be appropriate only three years thence? Why celebrate at all, since the siege had ended in defeat for the American side? Notwithstanding, the gala went on as planned. The governor and other state dignitaries came, as well as military units and bands from as far away as Columbia and Anderson. Newspapers estimated the crowd at some four or five thousand people. The actual rationale for the event was to promote the beginnings of a movement for a new county with Ninety Six as the county seat. The two chief promoters, Milledge Lipscomb Bonham and Miles B. McSweeney, had established a new newspaper, *The Ninety Six Guardian*, to boost the proposal. These were prominent men indeed, and both were destined to go on to greater things after their plan to elevate Ninety Six to new prominence came to naught. Bonham, the son of former Confederate General and Governor Milledge Luke Bonham, was born in Edgefield in 1854 and admitted to the bar in 1877. After two years in Ninety Six, he moved first to Newberry and later to Abbeville. He was elected Adjutant and Inspector General of South Carolina in 1886 and became a circuit judge in 1924. *Men of the Times* (1902) stated outright that Bonham settled at Ninety Six "with a view to assist in the establishment of a county seat at that place." McSweeney's career was primarily as a newspaperman, but he was elected to the General Assembly in 1894 and became lieutenant governor two years later. He succeeded to the governor's office upon the death of W. H. Ellerbe in 1899 and was elected in his own right in 1900. McSweeney died in 1909 at the age of 54.

The move for a new county with Ninety Six as county seat was defeated by a narrow margin in the General Assembly. Greenwood had naturally opposed the effort, much as Abbeville would later oppose Greenwood's bid, and it is reasonable to assume that the leading men determined to marshal their forces for another assault on the county-making apparatus of the state, this time in favor of their own town just eight short miles away. Ninety Six historian and raconteur Bruce Ezell put forth the most interesting, and very political, notion that R. F. McCaslan was persuaded to support Greenwood's bid when he was promised the office of first sheriff of the new county. *Greenwood County Sketches* covers the McCaslan family and notes that Robert Foster McCaslan married Rosalie Walker "from the Ninety Six area," but does not state that he lived in Ninety Six in the late 1800s. Perhaps he did, as Ezell suggested, and perhaps he moved to Greenwood in order to throw his support more fully into the county movement. In any event, he did become the first sheriff, and two of his sons, Robert Foster, Jr., and Gustavus Walker, eventually became partners in McCaslan's Book Store, a Greenwood institution.

There is no evidence that Ninety Six renewed its efforts to become a county seat after the 1878 attempt. Instead, it has managed to retain its individuality and cohesiveness even as Greenwood County grew and developed over the last century. The Ninety Six Chamber of Commerce 1988-89 information update, entitled "New Ninety Six," reveals that the town has a population of more than 2,000, a traditional town square housing some forty retail firms, a mayor-council form of government, a 10-man police department, and eighteen volunteer firemen. Ninety Six not only draws on countywide resources for hospital services, cultural opportunities, and higher education, it has its own school district, a branch library housed in a new building constructed with mostly local funds, and a Southern Railway depot preserved and renovated to serve as a community center and focal point on the town square. Ninety Six also has civic and cultural organizations of its own; the book and music clubs are among the oldest in South Carolina.

Ninety Six residents might with justification believe their community embraces the best of all worlds. The Buzzard Roost electricity-generating plant is only six miles away, and many of the county's largest manufacturing plants are located within its school district boundaries. Two plants of the Greenwood Mills chain are located there, as is Southern Brick Company, Ninety Six Manufacturing Company, and Star Fort Cannery. Monsanto, Fuji Photo Film, and Kaiser Aluminum plants are only a few miles away. Two resident doctors and two dentists have offices in Ninety Six, and both NCNB and United Savings Bank operate branches there. As for historic and recreational sites, there are Greenwood State Park, the Star Fort National Golf Club, and the Ninety Six Historical Site, now part of the National Park Service. The elevation of Star Fort to national park status by an act of Congress in 1976 has been a real boon to Greenwood County. Archaeological excavations and other research have identified 24 separate historical sites in three categories from Prehistoric-Historic Aboriginal to English Colonial, American Revolutionary War, and post-American Revolutionary periods, thus adding greatly to current knowledge of the area. Many sites that were previously unknown or purely speculative have been identified and mapped. The historic site is open daily, and a full range of park service amenities, including lectures and tours, is available.

The value of a look at place names, like the definition of beauty, might well lie with the beholder. While the place names of Greenwood County are probably no more numerous or fanciful than those of many other counties in the United States, they do appear to be meaningful to Greenwood people. This chapter was meant to be a sort of leisurely saunter from place to place, with a pause here and there for a little side trip or a bit of refreshment before moving on. Much of the material is probably all too familiar to residents of long standing, but possibly some of Greenwood's newer citizens have found their favorite fantasies about some of the names they have run across either substantiated – or else completely exploded – in these pages.

9

PEOPLE AND EVENTS

There is no contradiction I have not met with in men and women: the rarest combination is to find fundamental humbleness, freedom from self, intrepid courage and the power to love; when you come upon these, you may be quite sure that you are in the presence of greatness.

Margot Asquith

NOBODY knows quite how to define a particular place, generalizations about anything are risky business, and there is no such thing as definitive coverage of anything so nebulous as local history. Nevertheless, no account of Greenwood's past could be considered acceptable if it omitted people and events of significant impact, whether for good or ill, especially those that do not fit neatly into the broad categories that make up the bulk of this book. Indeed, Greenwood would not be Greenwood without its collective memories: of the day in 1921, for example, when Field Marshal Ferdinand Foch came to town . . . of the Sunday morning in April 1944 when county citizens fully realized the extent of the devastation caused by a tornado that roared through in the wee hours before dawn . . . of special people whose personalities and achievements allow Greenwood to bask in the reflection of the glory that still surrounds their names. This chapter sketches a few of the "big days" that stand out in Greenwood's history, as well as a few unforgettable people whose connection with the county forever marks them as Greenwood's own.

Greenwood's entry in the "festival fever" that swept the state in recent years was the Festival of Flowers, an event that began in 1968 primarily as a celebration of the 100th anniversary of Park Seed Company and continued as a major event of every summer since. Greenwood has reason to be grateful that Park deals in a product with universally pleasant connotations. The Aiken County town of Salley is not so fortunate, even though its annual "Chittlin' Strut" is said to bring in enough cash to pay the town's bills every year. The aroma for miles around Salley during preparation of the delicacy for which the festival is named is also said to make additional publicity almost unnecessary. Notwithstanding the southern fondness for gumbo, the name of Irmo's Okra Festival seems just a bit uninspired – what beauty queen would want to be remembered as "Miss Okra"? – but McCormick's "Gold Rush Days" celebration manages to reflect an important historical feature of that county's past. Ware Shoals emphasizes another southern delicacy in its "Catfish Feastival," while Ninety Six occasionally stages re-enactments of the Revolutionary War siege at Star Fort. In short, "big days" in southern towns seem to have become rather structured and certainly well-planned events occurring at regular intervals. Big days of the past, on the other hand, happened in response to big events and managed thereby to hold a special place in people's memories. In a pamphlet called *Rambling Recollections of a Reporter, 1912-1937,* E. P. Wideman described several truly special events that occurred in Greenwood during that period.

Wideman cited Armistice Day on November 11, 1918, as the absolute biggest celebration and one that began with a typical Greenwood touch. It seems that one citizen, N. A. Craig, had stashed several fully-loaded shotguns on top of a building in the Syndicate Block so that he could be the first to blast away when the momentous news of the signing of the armistice came over the telegraph wires. Craig had left the newspaper office about midnight, but not before reminding Wideman to call him first when official word was received. True to his promise, Wideman telephoned Craig about 2 a.m. just after the two words "Armistice signed" came through. Craig showed up a few minutes later to verify the report, then dashed off on his mission. "The next noise I heard," Wideman wrote, "was the booming of the shotguns and the Armistice celebration was on. It lasted during the rest of the night and most of the day, a shifting engine on the C&WC joining in the bedlam with Mr. Craig seated in the fireman's box pulling the string."

Although the celebration of the end of the first world war must have been wonderfully exciting, memories of the day Marshal Ferdinand Foch visited seem dearest to Greenwood for some reason, perhaps because everybody had the armistice, but only Greenwood got Foch, at least in South Carolina. Neither the great day – December 9, 1921 – nor any one of the scant fourteen that preceded the Foch visit, was a slow news day in Greenwood. Committees, formed in a trice, functioned with smooth precision; a war chest of $2,500 was quickly raised to meet expenses; bunting and flags were ordered for decoration; and a wooden replica of the Arc de Triomphe was designed and erected across Maxwell Avenue at the corner of Main Street. When completed, the arch soared four stories above the street. It cost $1,500, the largest single expenditure of the celebration. H. L. Watson later admitted his fear that the arch might be a mistake. Certainly it could have turned out badly, but Watson was delighted with its "wonderfully impressive" effect after bunting and flags and electric lights were added. Louis Wright wrote merely that it was painted white. Other hasty preparations included building a speakers' stand on the square in front of the present Grier Building; procuring souvenirs, presumably for sale, and gifts for visiting dignitaries; teaching Lander girls to sing "The Marseillaise" in French; drilling Bailey cadets in military marches; and preparing invitations to festivities that included not just one, but two, dances. Town leaders wanted to be sure "everything was done to show the rest of South Carolina that Greenwood could handle the important official reception for the state."

Foch's visit to South Carolina was part of an official good will tour in connection with an important speech scheduled for delivery at the annual meeting of the American Legion later in December. Since the meeting was to be held in Kansas City, travel plans included a special train with short stops in at least one city in each state, preferably the capital if routing would permit. Originally Foch was expected to visit Greenville and Spartanburg on the Southern Railway line from Atlanta to Washington, but an extremely odd attitude on the part of Southern's legal department caused the re-routing through Greenwood. Most railroad lines had agreed to move the special train at only nominal cost to the Legion, but Southern held out for the regular charge. Seaboard stepped in and offered its lines at the lesser fee, and Greenwood got the plum.

The whistle that sounded just as Foch's train pulled into the station area at 4:25 p.m. was the prearranged signal for a three-minute blast from every steam whistle in Greenwood. Louise Watson's account gives an idea of the pomp and color of the occasion:

> Attended by French officers, aides, high Legion officials and the local reception committee, Marshal Foch stepped onto the soil of South Carolina, walked through a platoon of B.M.I. cadets to his car, while bands played and the throngs cheered. Mounted police led the parade up Maxwell Avenue to the platform on the Square. Confetti, *upon each piece of which* was printed "Welcome, Foch" was thrown by people on the streets and from office windows. (emphasis added. Imagine!)

As the procession reached the stand and Foch stepped onto the platform, the assembled Lander students broke into the French national anthem. Foch's seat of honor was a chair in which Lafayette had sat at a reception in Columbia in 1825. One wonders whom to credit for this imaginative touch. Watson wrote that the chair's owner had brought it from Columbia for the occasion; perhaps it was the owner's idea. A rug donated by Simmons Furniture Company and used on the platform became the most treasured souvenir of Greenwood's American Legion Post 20. Perhaps it still hangs on the office wall as it did in 1957.

Louis Wright's description of the ceremonies might be a little less detailed than Watson's, but the introduction to his account contains a little extra barb: "Patriotism was still a respected emotion in my youth," he wrote, when "veterans of World War I were honored, and men could still talk about 'my country, right or wrong' without being sneered at." Consequently, Greenwood "boiled with excitement" at the news of Foch's visit, and Ernest Rosenberg, whom Wright credited as "one of the first officer-candidates to be commissioned and to get to France," was the most envied man in town. At the time a reporter for *The Index-Journal*, Wright was assigned to cover the event. "Every elected official and politician who could think of a reason," he wrote, "clamored for a place in the planned parade." Watson did not mention the fact that Rosenberg actually acted as Foch's aide, but Wright called it "a touch that pleased us." He also provided details of the delegation that met the Marshal at the train and escorted him through the crowd of some 15,000 to the reviewing stand on the square: "The governor of South Carolina, military men of sundry sorts, government officials from Washington, the mayor and other local dignitaries, and an assortment of others dressed in their Sunday best got into the sleekest cars Greenwood had ever seen, and the cavalcade rode through the streets to the speakers' platform."

"But the crowd had no eyes for the tail of the comet," ran a typical Wright line; instead,

> their gaze was fixed on the small, compact figure in the sky-blue uniform of the French army. He was a man of quiet dignity — a man, to be sure, who had given the American high command a hard time, but he was now subdued, with a wistful, faraway smile. Intent upon his duty, he greeted his well-wishers graciously and made a modest little speech in French, which he articulated so clearly that even those with a high school knowledge of the language could understand.

Wright added that the speech was translated "for the unlettered" by Colonel Frank Parker, a South Carolina native identified as Foch's "French aide." In his "modest little speech" the Frenchman expressed appreciation for the friendship between the two countries, for the supplies and fighting men America provided during the war, and for the spirit of unity which he said "originated in the United States, swept across the Atlantic to France and carried us victoriously to the Rhine." After Foch's remarks the governor and others spoke briefly, and Greenwood Mayor A. S. Hartzog received a French flag from the Marshal. Greenwood-grown roses were presented by Laura Arrington and Carroll Chipley (Wright recorded that "the little girl got kissed, and the boy received a chuck under the chin"), and the ceremony was over. The procession retraced the route to the station, and the train pulled out at precisely 4:58 p.m. The whole business, two weeks in the planning, was over in just 33 minutes.

The assumption that no one felt cheated is based on the fact that Greenwood threw a 50th anniversary celebration of Foch Day in 1971 with Louis Wright as featured speaker. Wright understood clearly the importance of such a retrospection. "For a few minutes the citizens of Greenwood had touched world history," he wrote; of course he wanted to help celebrate the golden anniversary of that event. And so he did, to his and Greenwood's pleasure, except that one young man had to be enlightened about "who or what Foch was."

Nor was the 1971 occasion the only recollection of Foch Day years after the event itself. The Rotary Club invited H. L. Watson to deliver a reminiscence at its January meeting in 1944. The fact that the United States and France were once again allies in another great world struggle added a particular poignancy to Watson's remarks, and the speech also provided another occasion for assessing the impact of Foch Day on Greenwood. Watson's conclusion that the day was indeed worth the cost in money, time, and work was supported by debriefings from the national American Legion and newspapers around the state, all of which agreed that Greenwood's celebration was among the best organized and most orderly of any on Foch's tour. Watson's Rotary speech differed from his daughter's later account in one rather interesting particular: he wrote that both Foch and his aide Frank Parker "were seated on a dais on which Lafayette had sat," whereas Louise Watson called the seat of honor simply "a chair." The word *dais* is defined as a platform of some sort; we are left to wonder exactly what the artifact was that its Columbia owner, J. R. Allen, brought to Greenwood that day. Some historians might say it matters.

It was not possible to stage much of a "Lindbergh Day" in Greenwood nearly six years after Foch came since the Lone Eagle spent only eight minutes, all of them in the air over the town on his way to Spartanburg, his only stop in South Carolina in October 1927. Wideman reported that Lindbergh reached Spartanburg just twenty minutes after his plane was sighted over Greenwood. And William John Park is sure he saw the airship Hindenburg pass over Greenwood when he was a boy. The Hindenburg, "the ultimate in luxurious air passenger transportation," was a rigid type dirigible built in 1936. After an overseas flight, it burst into flames and crashed while landing at Lakehurst, New Jersey, in 1937.

Although Wideman never actually named the date of another big day, his account of a visit to Greenwood by the "Jefferson Memorial party" is hilarious. The time was somewhere between 1924 and 1928 during D. A. G. Ouzts's term as county senator. It seems that a group of Jeffersonian Democrats was attempting to have Monticello named "a national shrine, or something," in Wideman's words, and considered a visit to southern cities a good way to get started. At first the plan was that Virginia's governor and attorney general would lead a delegation through the South on a special train, whipping up support for the project all along the way; the Greenwood newspaper "emblazoned the fact" that the tour was imminent. The next word was that a whole train-load would not appear, but "a special car filled with simon-pure Jeffersonian Democrats" would surely arrive as scheduled. The date and time, as well as the exact train, were duly publicized; both Governor Thomas G. McLeod and third-district congressman Fred H. Dominick accepted an invitation to be part of the welcoming committee at Greenwood. A dinner at the Oregon Hotel was to be part of the festivities:

> A sufficient number of cars had been readily offered to transport members of "the party" from the Seaboard station to the hotel [,] and Mr. [Kenneth] Baker, Mr. [Marvin S.] Chipley, Dr. [Samuel C.] Hodges and Mr. [Howard B.] Ellis had shined up their Cadillacs and Packards for the "official" members of the party. Soon the train whistle was heard down about Salak and presently it [the train, not the whistle] rounded the curve between the station and the orphanage with all eyes set on the track.

County Senator Daniel Andrew Gaines Ouzts headed the reception committee that hurried alongside the train in order to greet the distinguished guests as they stepped from the special coach. But no special coach was part of the train that day, and the Jefferson Memorial "party" turned out to be a single "gentleman of very small stature" who appeared from a day coach and introduced himself as Theodore Kuper of New York, speaker for the Jefferson Memorial. There was some consternation among members of the welcoming committee, not least about which of the three official cars would be used to transport the single-member delegation; the winner was Chipley's Packard, which Wideman described as "one of those long, lean, roomy vehicles that almost required telephone connection between the driver and the back seat." The local dignitaries, the congressman, and the governor must have been just a tiny bit chagrined as the ceremonial escort formed at the station. "It is a matter of record," Wideman wrote, "that the unoccupied cars looked mighty empty as the procession moved slowly up Maxwell Avenue to the hotel."

But the worst was yet to come. No fewer than four public meetings had been scheduled in anticipation of speeches by various well-known political figures. Instead, Governor McLeod, Congressman Dominick, and Theodore Kuper spoke at all four – the Oregon Hotel dinner as well as gatherings at the courthouse, the First Baptist Church, and Community Hall (the Armory). It is probably to Greenwood's credit that the best face was put on things and nothing was canceled. As the last meeting finally ended, Jefferson Memorial Day seemed an example of "a little more of the same" to Wideman; nevertheless, he valiantly proclaimed that even though the gentlemen spoke often, they spoke well. One interesting variation at the last meeting was a group rendition of "Swing Low, Sweet Chariot" led by Lander President B. Rhett Turnipseed.

No one remembers the net results, if any, of the day the Jefferson Memorial party came to Greenwood. Wideman concluded that the movement made no difference whatever since even Virginia forgot its Jeffersonian Democratic heritage and voted for Herbert Hoover in 1928.

Political campaigns of earlier years provided any number of big days for Greenwood. The most popular method of campaigning – a barbecue featuring mountains of free food and including "stump" speeches by wild-eyed politicians who held what amounted to oratorical contests – practically guaranteed an exciting day. Greenwood had its share of genuine political barbecues and stump meetings and orators (today's efforts are merely pale imitations). A good portion of former Congressman Bryan Dorn's recent book, subtitled "A Political Way of Life," is devoted to the style of campaigning in vogue when he began his career. He wrote that he once asked Senator Olin D. Johnston why he went into politics, and the answer was, "I heard Colie Blease speak." Dorn's description of his own reaction to Blease's oratory is nothing if not graphic. "The first time I heard him, I sat there hypnotized: my mouth hung slap open, my eyes ceased to bat," he told co-author Scott Derks. Dorn considers that South Carolina "belonged" in no uncertain terms to politicians Ben Tillman, Coleman Blease, "Cotton Ed" Smith, and Olin D. Johnston for the "first several decades of this century." Any day when one or more of these men came to town was almost by definition a big day; Greenwood's own orators, notably W. H. Nicholson and Bryan Dorn, could also be counted on to draw an enthusiastic crowd.

The sort of excitement generated by political gatherings was reminiscent of the Preston Brooks "Festival" held in 1856 to return the local hero of the Brooks-Sumner affair to his seat in Congress. That gathering, billed as a "public dinner" at Ninety Six, drew an estimated 10,000 people and was regarded as a national event; at any rate, *The New York Times* sent a special reporter to cover it. Correspondent P. H. Cary spent the preceding day and night in Greenwood since Ninety Six could furnish "no tolerable house of entertainment." His observations of Greenwood about a year before its incorporation were part of the story he filed with his paper:

> The little village . . . is one of the pleasantest I know of; embedded in groves of oaks and persimmon, and surrounded by a beautiful undulating country excellently cultivated, inhabited by planters of respectable means, and quiet as a Sabbath morning. It was to me a very picture of rural peace and happiness. Nor were the people so primitive in their notions as one fresh from the North would be likely to expect.

Cary discovered that on the whole Greenwood people seemed "thoroughly familiar with the politics of the country, and not at all ignorant of public affairs generally," though in some respects they were "lamentably behind the age." An obvious lack of "public enterprise" prevailed in the village even as some few individuals kept "a sharp lookout for the main chance." Greenwood was served by only one railroad in 1856; Cary wrote that travel was "tantalizingly slow," consisting mainly of "stoppages" and locomotion that at best scarcely exceeded the speed of a horse-trot. His trip from Charleston had required 17 1/2 hours of continuous travel. Cary also noted, "as a sort of offset to this tardiness," that accidents on these early railroads were almost unknown.

Not every Greenwood event, political or otherwise, rated a mention in *The New York Times.* Fortunately, the Brooks Festival was covered by a reporter who also gave the village a nice little boost.

Just as South Carolina was forever changed by Hurricane Hugo in September 1989 (indeed, Josephine Humphreys has already written a novel set in post-Hugo Charleston where "nothing is as it used to be"), so was Greenwood brought to its knees and altered ever after by a devastating tornado that roared through the county from Georgia in the early hours of Sunday, April 16, 1944. Louise Watson called the death and destruction it wrought "unparalleled in the history of Greenwood County." Eight Greenwood County residents, as well as five from Abbeville and three from Newberry, lost their lives. There have been other tornadoes – a broad path from Abbeville has been called "tornado alley," and other fierce storms struck in 1973 and 1983 – but the 1944 storm is still The Tornado in the minds of many Greenwood people.

The day preceding the storm was mild and spring-like, with nothing to foreshadow the appearance of "a raging tornado" within a few hours. Apparently no one had any idea that the fierce electrical storm that developed around 1 a.m. presaged a dreaded "funnel cloud" that would dip first at Maxwellton just beyond the orphanage and then in the area of the hospital, South Main Street, Phoenix Street, and Wade Heights before it continued on to Ninety Six where it dipped again. In the "worst case scenario" that was the tornado of 1944, Greenwood County Hospital was among the hardest hit of the buildings, which meant that victims had to be treated at an emergency center hastily put together in the Armory on Phoenix Street. The Servicemen's Center on South Main Street was pressed into service as a delivery room and maternity ward for new mothers and their babies. A temporary operating room was fitted out in the undamaged portion of the hospital and used for several weeks until the regular operating room could be repaired. The hospital board met and voted to begin rebuilding immediately; in a moment of high dramatic impact, James C. Self announced then and there that the two-year-old Self Foundation would build a brand new hospital as soon as building materials became available after the war.

In addition to the dreadful death toll, which included a number of children, Greenwood suffered property damage estimated variously at a quarter to a half million dollars. Watson wrote that 119 buildings were destroyed and 281 damaged. Fifty houses were on the destroyed list, as were ten barns and one church. Although much of the damage was covered by insurance, wartime shortages and restrictions meant that property owners were still seriously hampered in their efforts to rebuild.

Both organized and volunteer workers "sprang to the relief of the stricken city" within minutes after the storm passed through. A distress signal sounding from the fire department siren activated the National Guard which began rescue work and handled patrol duties until other groups joined the action at daybreak. Agencies and volunteers included the Red Cross, the Civilian Defense Corps, city personnel from mayor to street workers, public works personnel, doctors and nurses from Greenwood and surrounding counties, county officers from supervisor to sheriff, soldiers from Coronaca Air Base, state highway patrolmen, the Salvation Army, the Boy Scouts, and many others. The various groups seemed to work well together; Watson wrote that the "thousands of persons visiting Greenwood that Sunday were impressed by the dispatch with which the disaster was . . . handled."

An illustrated booklet entitled "A Tornado and What It Did in Greenwood, S. C." was published only four weeks after the disaster. Its text was prepared by Howard Cooper, then advertising manager of the newspaper, and most of the 87 pictures were made by Dr. Lee Hodges of Hodges Drug Store. In addition to telling one of Greenwood's biggest and most tragic stories, the pamphlet was prepared, in the words of its author, as "a tribute to the heroic fibre of the men and women who are Greenwood." Several copies are on file at the county library.

A special event ten years after the tornado, and one quite far removed from its legacy of destruction and despair, occurred when "Miss Universe" of 1954 was welcomed to her adopted hometown of Greenwood on July 31, 1954, just after winning the international title in Long Beach, California. Miriam Stevenson was a native of Winnsboro, a minor detail almost overlooked in Greenwood's bid for a share of the Lander College senior's triumph. Stevenson had represented the town as Miss Greenwood in preliminary contests and had made the finals of the Miss America Pageant in 1953; the Greenwood Jaycees sponsored her again in another contest that led to the Miss Universe title the following year. Greenwood's excuse for a "mammoth parade" and celebration, complete with speeches and a big banquet at the Oregon Hotel, was Stevenson's homecoming to South Carolina for a few weeks before reporting to Hollywood to fulfill a six-month movie contract, her chief prize as "Miss Universe." A newspaper story in the centennial edition called Greenwood's reaction one of "pride and joy" and estimated the crowd that jammed the square that Saturday at 17,000 people. There were numerous other beauty queens in attendance and photographers galore, as well as representatives of major news networks and dignitaries such as Governor George Bell Timmerman, Congressman Bryan Dorn, Mayor Robert McCaslan, and Greenville Mayor Kenneth Cass standing in for mayors and city officials from across the state. Jaycee President William John Park and Lander President Boyce M. Grier shared the honor of claiming Miriam Stevenson as the particular prize of their respective organizations.

As it turned out, Greenwood had more reason than it knew to rejoice in the honor that came to one of its adopted daughters. Everyone thought those few hours of Stevenson's time in the first flush of a year-long reign were a great gift and the last they would see of a lovely young woman on her way to movie stardom. But Miriam Stevenson was not the stuff of which tinsel dreams are made. A rock-sensible country girl who knew very well what she did not want, Stevenson renounced Hollywood after only a few weeks and came back to complete requirements for a degree in home economics at Lander College and graduate with her class in 1955. Greenwood's wild exhilaration of July 31, 1954, settled into a sort of quiet pride that the most beautiful girl in the entire universe quite obviously preferred Greenwood to any other place in the world. Nor did Miriam Stevenson disappoint her South Carolina public after college. She still lives in Columbia and takes part in alumni activities at her alma mater now and then.

While the big days Greenwood still cherishes were primarily associated with events, special people have also provided a wealth of memories for the town. Many of those special people are profiled under chapter headings covering their particular spheres of influence. Some either defy categorization entirely or fail to fit because their careers were made away from Greenwood. Four people, each with strong Greenwood connections but not one a businessman or politician, are sketched here because of their unique contributions to the Greenwood story. Although the names of Nell Saunders Graydon, Benjamin E. Mays, and Louis Booker Wright are known far beyond the borders of Greenwood County, and Gerald Smart is in a class by himself, none of these individuals has been elevated to the County Hall of Fame established by the Greenwood Area Chamber of Commerce in 1976. Evidently no Greenwood woman has ever qualified for hall of fame honors; at least none appears on the list as it currently stands. For that reason the county is fortunate that one woman who made Greenwood her home for more than fifty years was included in the revised and expanded edition of *South Carolina Women* published in 1991. In fact, without author and preservationist Nell Graydon and the famous educator Wil Lou Gray whose first teaching job was in the county, Idella Bodie's book would have no Greenwood connections at all.

The first half of Nell Saunders Graydon's life was that of a well brought up young woman who did what females of her generation and social class were expected to do. Long before she moved to Greenwood as the wife of Sterling Graydon, the girl from Pineville, North Carolina, had already experienced the death of her mother, a rather solitary youth under the watchful eye of a spinster aunt, and her father's remarriage when she was sixteen years old. Nell Saunders' early life seems to have been serene and well-ordered; the "old maid aunt" in no sense warped the sensibilities of her young charge, and no "wicked stepmother" disturbed the tranquility of the household. Instead, the young woman's world widened with the introduction of a new step-family in Mississippi, and Aunt "Sister" remained part of the household until she died long after her niece's own marriage. Nell Saunders earned a degree in English and drama from Elizabeth College, a Lutheran school in Charlotte, before her marriage to Sterling Graydon when she was 21 years old. The

Graydon family were natives of Laurens County with strong ties to Cokesbury. An earlier Sterling Graydon attended the conference school, married a preacher's daughter, and ran a store there; his grandson and namesake was born in Abbeville where his father Ellis Graydon practiced law. Young Sterling Graydon was working in the textile business in Charlotte when he met and married Nell Saunders in 1914. The Graydons moved to Greenwood in 1930; by that time the family included three children – Virginia, Sterling, and Frank. The Graydon family home was a large red brick and white-columned house on Montague Avenue at about the site of the entrance to Greenwood Plaza.

Graydon's daughter Virginia Davies remembers her mother as a person of a great many interests. She was always a collector with a discriminating eye and rather catholic tastes. Porcelain figurines might capture her fancy for a time, then the emphasis might shift to furniture or china or unusual silver pieces. A display cabinet filled with small and decorative kerosene lamps stands in the parlor of Graydon's last home in Greenwood, and her touch is discernible in any number of interesting objects scattered throughout the house. While she concentrated primarily on collecting antiques, she was fascinated also by old family papers even though genealogy was not a particular interest. Always a great reader, Graydon was gripped by the content of the letters and other documents she collected; accounts of life at an earlier time stimulated a fertile imagination that would hold full sway during the last half of her life. Even as she indulged her interest in collecting historical artifacts, Graydon threw herself wholeheartedly into running a household and raising a family. Her daughter remembers a mother who supervised the children's activities and personally guided their upbringing but who retained the central spot in the household for the adult relationship of husband and wife. Sterling and Nell Graydon always doted on each other. She ran the house to his tastes, and he encouraged her to follow where her interests led. No arrangement could have better suited Graydon's emerging as her own person instead of merely someone's wife. She did not fade as the years passed; she bloomed instead, growing in self confidence every day as she found new avenues to explore.

Everyone who knew Graydon would probably agree that the year 1941 was pivotal to her development as a writer. She was nearly fifty years old when her husband purchased property and built a house on the water at Edisto Beach. Graydon described the island as "a small water bound piece of land forty miles southwest of Charleston" and added, "Along the paved highway that skirts the beach, one finds few of the gaudy commercial enterprises that dot most beach scenes. Primarily it remains a family beach with residents coming back year after year. Many transients come and go without seeing the century old houses that sit far back from the highway facing a tidal creek." Many transients, yes, but not Nell Graydon. She felt such affinity for the place and its people that she adopted them as her own almost from the beginning. Davies remembers that a stay at Edisto always included daily trips to the post office, especially during the war years when sharing news was doubly important. It was there that the summer colony met and mingled with the natives, and it was in the mundane setting of the post office that the tales of Edisto first reached Nell Graydon's ears. She wrote many years later: "The most important part of . . . my first book came before I ever set a word on paper. I never could have written the book before the islanders told me their stories. The stories are not new – they have been told many times. The tales fascinated me, and I often wondered why someone had not compiled them in book form. It did not occur to me to try to do it until a friend, after listening to some of the stories, suggested that I do so." The historical context of Edisto included elements of glamour that would appeal to almost anyone; certainly the nineteenth century sea island cotton plantations with their "elegant homes, avenues of magnolias, orange blossoms, beautiful women, [and] gentleman planters with their mint juleps" were the stuff of which romance is made. Nell Graydon also saw literary possibilities in "the slaves who worked the plantations, sang in the cotton fields, and told ghost stories as they sat around their cabin doors." The underside of this idyllic world would fuel many a writer's imagination in other directions, but Graydon chose the romantic view of her subjects. Her interest was not in the "causes and effects of the broad trends of political and economic development" but simply in people and their stories. She believed that the legends of a region were vital components of its political and social structure even though they might often remain unrecorded by historians. She was also convinced that her adopted state could easily be regarded as "the cradle of culture" in the United States.

Graydon's first book, *Tales of Edisto*, was published in 1955, fourteen years after the author's love affair with her second home began. While this was her first book, it was not the first time Graydon had been published. Davies recalls that her mother was always interested in journalism and contributed articles to the magazine section of *The State* long before she tackled a book. The subject of Graydon's very first piece was not Edisto but the traveling library of the Seaboard Railway, according to her daughter's best recollection. Davies remembers her own fears that the publishing venture might prove disappointing; she worried that a commercial failure would devastate her mother and bring what had been a satisfying hobby to a frustrating end. Nell Graydon harbored no such fears; she had faith that the book would succeed on its own merits. Besides, she never viewed herself as a professional writer, someone with "a definite place and hours to work." She wrote when and where she could, putting the work aside "for the slightest reason" and picking it up again as circumstances allowed "sometimes days later." She also pronounced her writing "fun" and called it an "absorbing and interesting" avocation with "no rhyme or reason" behind it. *Tales of Edisto* caught on very well indeed; the fact that the book is now in its eighth printing is evidence of the enduring popularity of Graydon's work. Its illustrations were the work of engineer-photographer Carl Julien, another Greenwood connection.

Graydon followed the "tales" format in two subsequent books spotlighting Beaufort and Columbia, but a historical novel, *Another Jezebel*, intervened in 1958. This fictional account of a glamorous female spy during the Civil War was based on a real person. Graydon's explanation of her digression from tales to novel was that she learned about the Countess Pourtales while researching material on Columbia and became so intrigued that she could not put the lady out of her mind. Columbia and Beaufort simply had to wait while Graydon created adventures for the countess's real-life mother Amelia Burton Boozer Feaster, the Jezebel of her story.

Five of the ten books credited to Nell Graydon were published in the 1960s; the third came out in 1963, the year of her 70th birthday. And the event that would place Greenwood uniquely in Graydon's debt also occurred in that decade. The South Carolina Methodist Conference regained title to the Cokesbury school building in 1965 under terms of a reverter clause dating from 1918 when the Conference discontinued the school. A committee found the building structurally sound but badly in need of repair and regular maintenance. A proposal to raze the structure and erect a memorial to the 104-year history of Methodist education at the site was not enthusiastically received. Some members of the committee, including Henry McKinney, thought the building should be preserved and restored. Although Nell Graydon was a Presbyterian, she was approached to help raise funds for preservation. Once again Graydon allowed herself to become intrigued; this time there was the added inducement of working on a project with connections to her husband's family. With her usual self-confidence and resolve she immediately set to work: she wrote newspaper articles, sought support from a broad network of friends across the state, and appeared personally at a Methodist meeting in Charleston to lobby for preservation of the building. She was named to the Cokesbury Board of Trustees as a result of that appearance, and her fund-raising efforts on behalf of the project began in earnest. One was the personalized cookbook *From My House to Your House*, the first page of which carried a photograph of the deteriorating building along with the notation that all proceeds from the sale would go to restoration efforts. The first of three printings of the cookbook raised $10,000 for Cokesbury.

Cookbooks as fund raisers are pretty routine stuff, but another of Graydon's efforts on behalf of Cokesbury was something else entirely. She spearheaded a benefit appearance of the world-famous Dali Jewel Collection in Greenwood in 1971. This one sparked a bit of a controversy in the town. The showplace as originally planned was the new Barksdale Physical Education Building on the Lander College campus, but a minor uproar ensued when it appeared the basketball schedule might be disrupted in the process. To no one's surprise, sports managed to win out over a black-tie cultural event, regardless of its rarity, and the showing took place at the county courthouse instead. Many people remember a truly novel evening of the 1971 social season when the Dali Jewels came to town for the benefit of Cokesbury. Nell Graydon contributed greatly to the designation of Cokesbury as a historic district. She helped secure the Thomas Gary House adjacent to the college building as well as a 50-acre tract of land to be used as a youth center. She was also named first chairman of the Cokesbury Historical and Recreational Commission when it was created by the General Assembly.

Securing the future of Cokesbury created hardly a ripple in Graydon's productive literary life. She collaborated as co-author of two books published in 1965 and produced *Eliza of Wappoo,* a biography of indigo planter Eliza Lucas Pinckney, two years later. *South Carolina Ghost Tales* followed in 1971, and Graydon's last book, *South Carolina Gardens,* appeared in 1973. Both *Ghost Tales* and *Tales of Beaufort* are now in their sixth printing.

Other changes came in the 1970s. The Graydons recognized that the house on Montague Avenue had become an anachronism as the business section of town expanded outward, and the appearance of a Pizza Hut next door was enough to convince them it was time to move. The change must have been difficult for a traditionalist such as Nell Graydon. The property had once been a 35-acre farm; Graydon had been fascinated by the emphasis on bountiful food and good cooking from her first visit as a bride in 1914, and she continued the tradition of hospitality when she became mistress of the house that had belonged to her mother-in-law. The Graydons' annual Christmas party became a tradition in Greenwood; family members were not alone in feeling the wrench of the house's demise.

When her husband died in 1974, Graydon lost her biggest fan and a companion of sixty years. Her famous energy and enthusiasm survived the inevitable changes that come with time, and she began to enjoy the compensations of a lifetime of fruitful work. The honors and awards came from all quarters. She received the South Carolina Electric and Gas Company's preservation trophy from the South Carolina Federation of Women's Clubs as well as life membership in the Garden Club of South Carolina in recognition of her work. Lander College awarded her an honorary doctorate, the Greenwood Chapter of the American Association of University Women chose her for its award of honor, and the Greenwood County Historical Society presented its Historical Award of Distinction. Graydon is also listed in *Who's Who of American Women* and the *Dictionary of International Biography.* Not long before her death Nell Graydon received the Community Service Award from the Greenwood Rotary club.

Nell Graydon would have qualified as one of Greenwood's grande dames if she had never written anything more than an invitation to tea or a thank you note. She became a sort of timeless personage as she grew older. Although the word *imperious* comes to mind in describing Graydon, it does not quite fit because she was actually a woman of great personal warmth beneath a somewhat regal facade. Her daughter chuckles at the memory of Graydon's soft spot for almost any charity: the woman who had served as a volunteer nurse's aide for four years during World War II continued quietly to contribute to almost any appeal from a "save a puppy" campaign to famine relief. She genuinely cared. She also grew in understanding and affection as her immediate family expanded. Her children grew up and had children who eventually had children of their own. Graydon's rapport with her great-grandchildren was particularly remarkable. A relaxed understanding seemed to transcend the two generations separating them, and a poem written by a great-grandson was part of her funeral service. Nell Graydon was 93 when she died on July 14, 1986. Idella Bodie's tribute in *South Carolina Women* concludes: "With her enthusiastic love of the past, Mrs. Nell Saunders Graydon contributed to the present and the future by endowing lovers of history and of South Carolina with a rich legacy. Her work of preservation and of capturing the grandeur, romance, and beauty of the past will continue to enrich the lives of people of all ages."

A contemporary of Nell Graydon's, but one whose life could not have been more different, was Benjamin Elijah Mays. His autobiography is especially valuable for its recollection of the lifestyle of a black family in rural Greenwood County at the turn of the century. Even reading the account nearly a hundred years after the time Mays described is painful, yet a large percentage of county citizens can relate directly to a period when the color of their skin not only exacerbated the problems of poverty and illiteracy they shared with the majority of the white population but also constituted the ultimate stigma of the time and place they lived. Mays viewed himself and his people as the "disinherited," which of course they were, and he always felt alienated from the county of his birth.

Benjamin Mays was born on a farm four miles below Epworth on August 1, 1894. He was the youngest of eight children of Hezekiah and Louvenia Mays, both of whom were born in slavery. His family was fairly typical of the times; that is, they were virtually unschooled and very poor. Even so, the fact that Hezekiah Mays owned his mules placed him on a slightly higher level than many blacks who worked for wages or sharecropped; Mays was a renter who paid for the land he farmed at the rate of two bales of cotton for every twenty acres rented. Everyone in the family worked as a day laborer from time to time to supplement the once-a-year cash income from the cotton crop. Mays wrote many years later that he did not leave the farm because it was distasteful to him – he enjoyed the work and considered himself a better than average farmhand – but because he wanted to enter the world of learning in order to find and liberate himself. He felt himself "called" to something else.

The maximum school term for black pupils in that day was four months, November through February, while white children attended for six months. Mays wrote that he was nineteen before he was able to remain in school for a full term. By the time he entered first grade at the age of six he could already count, recite the alphabet, and read a little, thanks to the interest of an older sister. Because he was the only one in the beginners' class who could do all this, he was "praised and highly complimented by the surprised teacher." That "eventful day" seems to have set the tone for Mays's life ever after; his was a veritable thirst for knowledge. He wrote that he "fell in love" with his teacher Ellen Waller and studied as much to please her as to please himself. Waller's educational attainment and qualification to teach consisted of a high school diploma from Benedict College in Columbia. Mays remembered only four county blacks before his time who had earned college degrees, although a "fair number" managed to graduate from high school.

Hezekiah Mays considered that only two honest occupations – preaching and farming – were open to black men, and neither needed more preparation than was available in the local one-room school. He was therefore less than sympathetic with his son's "insatiable desire" to get an education. Mays's practical problems boiled down to just two: how to overcome his father's opposition and how to get the money to go away to school. Even though he knew his father had no money to give, Mays longed for "his sympathetic approval, or at least his consent." The elder Mays finally gave his consent, if not his approval, for the boy to study at a different school so long as it did not interfere with work on the farm. With the help of his pastor, Benjamin Mays enrolled at a small Baptist institution in McCormick at the age of fifteen after he had absorbed all his old school had to offer. Although the new school was little, if any, better than the one he had left, Mays found the train ride from Greenwood to McCormick both a revelation and a liberating experience. For one thing, it seemed symbolic as a way out of his dead end situation on the farm, and for another, a black mail clerk on one of the trains made a tremendous impression on the young man. If more school turned out to be impossible, a railway mail job might be an alternate way out. Mays had his heart set on the high school department of Benedict in Columbia or State College in Orangeburg. He applied to both and chose State only because it was less expensive. He knew he could earn the $6 per month tuition and train fare even without help from his father, so he made his way to Orangeburg "without Father's blessing but with my mother's prayers." The break with his father came after two years at State when Mays disobeyed an order to come home to work on the farm at the end of February. The final act of disobedience came "without regret and with no pangs of conscience." Mays accepted the fact that he had to take control of his life entirely, including his education, if he were to secure any sort of future for himself. Benjamin Mays would never look back.

Mays graduated from the high school department of South Carolina State College as valedictorian in 1916. He was nearly 22 years old and had spent a total of 73 months – the equivalent of only eight years – in school. He regretted the "lost years" of learning the rest of his life, particularly the unread books. A paragraph from *Born to Rebel* is especially poignant:

> Although the high school teachers at State were excellent, I am well aware that there are gaps in my education which I was never able to overcome, despite the fact that the years brought me membership in Phi Beta Kappa, a Ph.D. from a great university, and honorary doctorates from twenty-eight distinguished colleges and universities. There are many things that one must learn and read in elementary and high school; otherwise it is too late, for each passing day makes its own new demands. Even if one had time to catch up on the reading he missed as a child, the end result would be different. I am sure that I would have read many books in my childhood had they been available. They were not. Not in the Brickhouse School, not in my home, not in the community. No library was available.

When the time came to choose a college, Mays would settle for studying only at a non-segregated institution. The reason for the requirement is contained in a simple sentence in the first chapter of his autobiography: "In Greenwood County, for the most part, black was black and white was white, and never the twain did meet except in an *inferior - superior* relationship; this relationship I never sought, cherished, or endured." He longed to test his academic ability in an open arena since it was clear the valedictory from the high school department of State College proved nothing; the great disparity between state support of white and black schools meant that the playing field in South Carolina was anything but level. After one year of preparation at Virginia Union University, a black school in Richmond, Mays enrolled at Bates College in Lewiston, Maine. He found a great difference in the "predominantly white world" at Bates, and for the first time in his life Mays was able to meet and mingle with others "as peers, not as 'superior' and 'inferior' . . . a new experience." During his three years at Bates College Mays learned also that not all whites were his enemies; his own racial attitude underwent a tremendous change when he was able to stop generalizing. And Benjamin Mays proved something to himself once and for all:

> One of my dreams came true at Bates. Through competitive experience, I had finally dismissed from my mind for all time the myth of the inherent inferiority of all Negroes and the inherent superiority of all whites – articles of faith to so many in my previous environment. I had done better in academic performances, in public speaking, and in argumentation and debate than the vast majority of my classmates. I concede academic supe-

> riority to not more than four in my class. I had displayed more initiative as a student leader than the majority of my classmates. Bates College made these things possible. Bates College did not "emancipate" me; it did the far greater service of making it possible for me to emancipate myself, to accept with dignity my own worth as a free man.

Studying at the University of Chicago had been a dream for Benjamin Mays since his high school days in Orangeburg, and he was able to enroll in the graduate school in 1921. Mays left after "three quarters of stimulating and rewarding work" to teach for the first time at Morehouse College in Atlanta, an institution with which he would be identified for the rest of his life. Although his ultimate goal was a doctorate in some phase of religion or theology, Mays succumbed to the offer of a real job, his first since graduating from college, and moved to Atlanta in the fall. His account of race relations in the Georgia capital at that period is graphic; as he put it, "the picture was not pretty." But he was no stranger to perseverance, and a one-year appointment stretched to three. Mays returned to the University of Chicago to complete requirements for the M.A. degree in 1925.

Once again a teaching opportunity interrupted Mays's pursuit of the Ph.D. He accepted a position at South Carolina State College in 1925 and left a year later only because the college would not allow both Mays and his wife to teach there at the same time. An offer from the National Urban League took the Mayses to Tampa for two years, and one from the National Council of the YMCA led them to Atlanta again. After a few years the way was finally clear to resume pursuit of the Ph.D. from the University of Chicago. Mays achieved that goal when the degree was conferred in 1935, the same year he was elected to Phi Beta Kappa and Delta Sigma Rho. Dr. Mays accepted a position as dean of the School of Religion at Howard University in 1934 and stayed for six years. The call to the presidency of Morehouse came in 1940. Mays left Morehouse 27 years later; an account of those years is contained in a chapter of his autobiography entitled "So Much with So Little and So Few."

Benjamin Mays spent a lifetime of rebellion against the "cruel and unjust system" of legalized racial discrimination. He always regarded himself as a "desegregationist," meaning he supported the removal of artificial barriers, rather than an "integrationist," a term he equated with spiritual acceptance that cannot be mandated. Mays confessed he had no answer to the nagging problems of racism in the United States but concluded that "we have no choice but to continue our efforts to make this country a decent place for all Americans." Mays traveled a long way, both literally and figuratively, from his birthplace in Greenwood County. He considered the chasm between black and white so wide that no white person in Greenwood would be interested in him or in anything he did. He was wrong about that; he found a kindred spirit in J. E. Chaffin, editor of the newspaper, when he returned in the late 1960s to gather material for his autobiography, and he received an enthusiastic welcome in 1974 when Lander College awarded him an honorary degree to add to the dozens he had already accumulated.

Benjamin Elijah Mays died on March 28, 1984, at the age of 89. Probably one of the most honored men in the country, Mays held at least 45 honorary degrees and more than 200 honors and awards from organizations all over the world. Throughout a public career that included the presidency of the Atlanta Board of Education as well as Morehouse College, Mays was a "quiet but persistent thorn in the white conscience." He became a legend in higher education, and he never faltered in his fight for racial justice. "I was born a little stubborn on the race issue," he said. Mays was named to the South Carolina Hall of Fame in 1984, and the state officially designated a spot on Highway 178 near his birthplace as "Mays Crossroads." An editorial called this act "indicative of the changes in his state."

If any individual ever seemed to personify Greenwood's conscience, that person would have to be Gerald Smart. Not only did he plead for humanitarian services long before Greenwood had social welfare institutions of any kind, he also helped organize the first Parent-Teacher Association, personally assisted in bringing the Salvation Army to town, and worked to establish both the Humane Society and the first library. Gerald H. Smart was also a fixture in the churches, the schools, the columns of the local newspaper, and the city jail where he presided over Sunday School classes for weekend inmates. Smart's humanist philosophy evidently arose from more or less equal infusions of Baptist fundamentalism, socialism as espoused by Norman Thomas in settlement house work, and a genuinely unselfish and self-sacrificing nature. He was born in Greenwood where his father served as pastor of the First Baptist Church. The Reverend Henry C. Smart established a mission church in Troy, and young Gerald spent several years of his boyhood there. Only eight years old when his father died in 1890, Smart was largely self-educated. He recalled many years later that he was seldom able to attend public school and was taught in bits and pieces by an older sister. He also remembered reading extensively in the library of another minister who lived near his childhood home in Troy.

Smart moved as a teenager to Chicago where he hoped to find employment as well as an opportunity to attend high school. He found work as a street lamplighter and as a turnstile operator at a large hotel, the first job chosen because its working hours did not interfere with school and the other because it included one meal a day at the hotel. He attended a very large high school with a full program of extracurricular activities. Smart later claimed he availed himself of everything the school offered, and it was there he added music to his list of accomplishments. The high school also afforded the young man his first contact with organized social work: its "Sociological Club" provided recreational outlets for children of the Chicago Stockyards, an extensive section of tenements on the south side of the city. The seventeen-year-old Smart participated enthusiastically in trolley car excursions for these inner city children, some of whom had never seen trees or grass or even a pool of clean water, and he never forgot the wonder of their response to an outing at one of Chicago's lakeshore parks. A few years later Smart lived for a time in the slums of New York City while he attended the New York School of Civics and Philanthropy. It was during this stay in about 1914 that he met and became friends with Norman Thomas. Smart never lost his admiration for the man who ran for President of the United States on the Socialist Party ticket no less than six times. He corresponded with the Thomases until the end of his life.

When Gerald Smart came back to Greenwood in the early 1900s, he was able to find work teaching at Connie Maxwell and playing the organ at the First Baptist Church. He also found any number of outlets for his prodigious energies and his overwhelming desire to "do good." Far from lauding Greenwood city and county government as progressive and modern, Smart was always quick to chastise the community for its lack of services for the poor and downtrodden. All sorts of people with a variety of hard-luck stories found their way to his door. Years ahead of his time in race relations and humanitarian causes, Smart became a fixture – some say a gadfly – in the day-to-day life of Greenwood. Nothing escaped his notice, and an issue of the newspaper without a column, an observation, or a letter to the editor signed by Gerald H. Smart was rare indeed.

But perhaps Smart's chief claim to fame lay in his work with young people. He established a summer camp at Lake Jocassee in the late 1920s and later claimed he wore out three buses, a Model A, a Model T, and a Dodge transporting more than 8,000 children to and from a week's stay at Camp Hemlock. The fee was $6 per week, but many children were accepted without regard to fee. This so-called "camp" was totally freestyle – no schedules, no staff, no rules except the single requirement that everybody have a good time. While he might have been lackadaisical about rules, Smart was serious about children learning to swim. He claimed he insisted on swimming lessons at a time when swimsuits were not in vogue; nothing daunted, he bought quantities of black sateen and had a local seamstress make up suits for his swimmers. These diaper-like outfits can be seen in extant camp photographs.

Important as it was, summer camp was not Smart's sole contribution to leisure time activity for Greenwood's youngsters. As both mentor and playmate, often simultaneously, he could organize a day of fun as readily as teach a music lesson. Once he put together a doll buggy parade for a hundred little girls with prizes for the best-dressed doll and best-decorated buggy. He also organized baseball games, May Day festivals, and a successful Community Week held for several years during the 1920s. Smart himself was probably proudest of the live evergreen trees he and a group of boys planted downtown in the dark of night as a Christmas surprise for the town, or "Daffodil Day" at the church when the entire altar was banked with a spectacular display.

In some mystical way Greenwood townfolk seemed to become Gerald Smart's family. His interests were boundless, and he played no favorites; everybody knew him, and he knew everybody. A one-man cheerleading squad for organizations such as the YMCA, the Humane Society, an Octogenarian Club, Boy Scouts, glee club, library, field day, and Chautauqua, not to mention church activities of every description, Smart wanted to draw everybody into an orbit of service to others. A nature lover, Smart planted trees in the tradition of Johnny Appleseed, and a section of the Old Abbeville Highway still boasts a number of oaks, cedars, redbuds, dogwoods, and crepe myrtles from an avenue of trees Smart planted when he owned property in the area that is now Lakewood Heights.

Greenwood made its affection official when it designated his 75th birthday as Gerald H. Smart Day on June 17, 1957. A proclamation signed by Mayor A. R. McAlhaney called him an "esteemed and revered citizen" who had made "inestimable contributions and rendered invaluable service" to the community for many years. As if on cue, other tributes followed. A Sunday School class at the Methodist Church adopted a resolution similar to the city's, letters to the editor appeared, and the newspaper threw its own bouquet when it called him "unsurpassed" and a "natural born leader" in public affairs, religious work, and youth activities. The Kiwanis Club also honored him at its annual banquet, and *Sandlapper* magazine featured Smart in its October 1972 edition.

Gerald Smart lived past his 92nd birthday. Interviewed not long before his death in 1974, Smart told a *Greenville News-Piedmont* reporter: "I've given all my money away. I've spent my life trying to help other people." Everybody who remembers Gerald Smart knows he was telling the simple truth.

When Louis Wright retired as director of the Folger Shakespeare Library in 1968, his colleagues wrote a book to commemorate the occasion and subtitled it "a Bibliography and an Appreciation." The bibliography consists of more than 300 items credited to Wright, and the appreciation is 75 pages of extremely readable prose sprinkled liberally with examples from Wright's own work. Greenwood County rates a mention or two in this memoir. Wright's birthplace is described as "a remarkable region, rich in legend, folklore, and earthy wisdom," elements that "seeped into the consciousness and fiber of the boy who grew up there and who would never forget his background" even after he had become a "very erudite and sophisticated man of the world of scholarship."

Louis Booker Wright was born in 1899 in the Phoenix section of Greenwood County, the son of a schoolteacher who allowed him, among other important freedoms, "free run of the bookshelves." Wright could not remember a time when he did not read, but he always insisted that "equally useful elements of his education came from sources other than books." Rambling in the fields and woods had its place, as did mingling with sawmill hands, black and white, and listening to their conversations. Both literature and history were stressed in Wright's boyhood home, along with "common sense, good humor, and good manners." From an upbringing in the "rural, Protestant South of the early twentieth century, he acquired a keen eye for essential qualities of middle-class culture." Wright's long career as a cultural historian drew heavily on themes and sensibilities familiar to him from the days of his youth in Greenwood County.

Wright graduated from high school in 1917. His college career at Wofford was interrupted by service in World War I and a brief stint as one of the first airmail pilots in the country. "He and a local veteran of the Army Air Corps went in cahoots and purchased an old plane, made a mail contract with the government, and set up in business. The veteran gave him a few hours' instruction in flying, and somehow both of them managed to survive. . . . He had a number of crashes and inspired terror among the mules and cattle of the Dark Corner." After such adventures, accelerating his studies at Wofford must have been easy for Wright. He completed work for a degree in chemistry in less than the usual four years and graduated in 1920. Wright's first job after college was as a reporter for *The Index-Journal.* Work on a newspaper in Spartanburg during his senior year had whetted his appetite for journalism and convinced him that people were far more interesting than precipitate on filter paper. Wright's career in the humanities began with a job that taught him more than he could have learned over many years in a college or university. "Not to have worked on a country newspaper," he claimed, "is to have missed a post graduate instruction in contemporary history."

Although Wright was essentially happy as a small-town reporter, he began to consider the possibilities of producing something more serious and lasting than "the daily rubbish" he ground out at the newspaper office. He was influenced in this regard by Robert O. Lawton, a Lander College professor who wrote a weekly column of "philosophic observations" for *The Index-Journal.* Lawton's example more than his advice convinced Wright that life as a college professor allowed time to study, think, and write; it seemed to be exactly what he wanted, "and the way to become a college professor was to go to graduate school, obtain an advanced degree, and hope for the best." Wright left Greenwood in the summer of 1923 to begin graduate studies in literature at the University of North Carolina.

The three years that followed were among the happiest and most fruitful of Wright's life. The university boasted a "distinguished and dedicated group of scholarly teachers" who inspired the graduate students to work as they had never worked before. Wright found himself drawn more and more to social history rather than literature; he was convinced that knowledge of the accomplishments of men and women of an earlier time was important to an understanding of current life. That conviction led to Wright's first major historical work after obtaining the doctorate in 1926. With the aid of a Guggenheim grant that allowed research in London he produced *Middle-Class Culture in Elizabethan England* in 1935. The book was well received critically; one historian declared it an important work for all students of Anglo-American cultural history. Wright had managed to get at the "mentality and aspirations of the English middle classes as reflected in the printed materials . . . they read." Drawing on an insight gained from histories, poems, and popular books of the day, he was actually "able to draw a literary portrait of Shakespeare's audiences." Wright's horizon had broadened considerably in the few years since his doctoral dissertation on "Vaudeville Elements in Elizabethan Drama." The first Guggenheim Fellowship grant contained an interesting connection: Louis Wright eventually became Chairman of the Guggenheim Foundation's Committee of Selections. As for the first trip to England, a paragraph from the retirement memoir said it best:

> [I]t is certain that he entered into this first experience with a zest and a zeal that goes far to explain his incomparable knowledge of English places and persons, manners and mores, oddities and quiddities, graces and gaucheries, prides and prejudices, glamor and greatness that has kept him in a constant state of oscillation between bewilderment and admiration throughout four decades. It is doubtful, at the same time, whether there are many American scholars who have formed as many fast and enduring friendships with Britons in all walks of life as he has succeeded in achieving.

Although Wright's career path seemed set on college teaching – he was a member of the English faculty at Chapel Hill from 1926 to 1932 – a one-year appointment as visiting scholar at the Huntington Library in San Marino, California, in 1931 changed the course of his life thereafter. The decision to stay at Huntington after the first year meant giving up a professorship at the University of Michigan, a decision he never regretted. Wright continued to teach from time to time on visiting appointments to notable universities, but his career was different from that of most professional social/cultural historians in that he became a scholar-administrator rather than an academician.

The most remarkable single feat Wright accomplished at both the Huntington and the Folger was to open up the "collector's collections" the libraries represented and make them accessible to scholars. The Huntington was particularly deficient as a scholarly resource, having been opened to the public only four years prior to Wright's arrival. It was essentially "a vehicle for the display of an outstanding collection of rare books, manuscripts, and paintings"; its reference section consisted of only 9,000 volumes and other materials not fully catalogued. It was at the time Wright went there "a repository of books waiting to be put to use." He was less interested in rare books for rarity's sake than in making rare books useful, and he always believed a library should be "an active rather than merely a passive research institution." Wright's own work flourished during his tenure at the Huntington. One critic found *The First Gentlemen of Virginia,* published in 1940, "a sane and scholarly reexamination of a way of life that has received too much romanticization." Other works on Anglo-American topics date from the Huntington period, as well as service on the editorial boards of at least three learned journals. One admirer wrote that it would be hard to overestimate the value of Louis Wright's services to scholarship during the time he worked for the Huntington Library.

In 1947 Wright was approached by the trustees of Amherst College to serve as consultant to the search committee seeking a director for the Folger Shakespeare Library in Washington. His name was not among those considered for the position at the time; he was merely invited to meet with the committee, an invitation he readily accepted. During the course of the meeting the "consultant's" contribution to the discussion of library problems in general so impressed the committee that the meeting turned into an interview, and Wright was eventually offered the position. An honorary degree from Princeton University was awarded in 1948 after Wright had accepted, but before he had taken up, the Folger position. The citation accompanying that degree pointed in two directions: "He was the principal force in developing the fabulous collections of Henry Huntington from a repository of literary treasures of the past into one of the most effective research libraries in the world. . . . In the Folger Library he will administer the world's greatest collection of Shakespearean books and manuscripts. The scholars he has served in the past look forward to his greater achievements for learning in his new undertaking."

Thus Greenwood native Louis B. Wright held in a remarkable lifetime two of the most prestigious positions in the academic world. The Folger Shakespeare Library in Washington, described as "one of the proudest honors of the United States," is administered by Amherst College. It is a preeminent resource in the study of Anglo-American relations and influences, second only to the British Museum. Wright's influence at the Folger is best captured in a foreword to the retirement volume written by Amherst President Calvin H. Plimpton in 1968:

> [T]he real reasons for our current pride are the endeavors of a doughty, fearless, sometimes pugnacious scholar and administrator named Louis B. Wright. In his twenty years at the Folger he

> has brought books to life and has brought light, life, and air to books. It will be noted that he installed physical air conditioning to the building, but far more important was his intellectual air conditioning which blew out the mustiness of literary and scholarly disuse. He practiced his philosophy that books are for men and turned the Folger into a working library. He has made the institution popular but has not cheapened scholarship by popularization. The collection was great, but Louis has made it greater by acquisitions both daring and discriminating. Good libraries are the extensions of great people. Louis Wright is such a man and is the real source of our pride in the Folger Shakespeare Library.

Among many other innovations, Wright launched the custom of afternoon tea at the Folger. An eminent Elizabethan historian considered these famous breaks for tea and talk as "inspired and inspiring" and called them a "simple aid to success." The tea break seems to have been typical of Wright's approach to the work of scholarship; no staff work was so urgent that a short break for refreshment and communion with one another could not help, and many a tough job seemed simpler after a civilized mid-afternoon respite.

Like most interesting people, Wright was a sort of paradox: he was a blend of publicist and scholar, good organizer and anti-organization man, political liberal and social conservative. The gruff exterior of the realist concealed the concern for people of the sentimentalist. He was called with good reason "the man of a thousand articles, books, boards, committees, commissions, and commitments," a man who delighted in helping others, even those who could not possibly do anything for him. Perhaps a tribute from Thomas J. Wilson, Director of the Harvard University Press, comes closest to describing the type of man Louis Wright was:

> The breadth and depth of his knowledge of British and European civilization, his understanding of the relationship between the Old World and the New, and his enthusiasm for the unusual book – the esoteric or rare, but important – added enormously to the range of editorial discussion and to the variety and value of the list of publications. . . . Louis Wright's mind never tires; it is always fresh, always imaginative, forever searching for the significant and contemptuous of the trite.

Wright retired from the Folger at the age of 69 before, as he put it, "falling into anecdotage." His scholarly reputation after more than forty years was impeccable; not only had he received dozens of honorary degrees and other awards during that time, he was also a consultant to several publishers and an officer of twenty societies, including the Cosmos Club of which he was president. Among his most significant honors were the O. B. E. (Order of the British Empire) and the Benjamin Franklin

Gold Medal of the Royal Society of Art in London, both awarded in 1969. Wright was also named a Life Trustee of Shakespeare's Birthplace, one of only two non-British life trustees ever named, in 1963. After retirement Wright accepted a position as historical consultant for the National Geographic Society. His output during the 1970s was hardly less prodigious than before retirement. In addition to producing several popular histories, he wrote a tribute to Greenwood entitled *Barefoot in Arcadia* in 1974 and a follow-up personal narrative, *Of Books and Men*, two years later. Louis Booker Wright died on February 29, 1984, the day before his 85th birthday, of cardiovascular disease.

The last two paragraphs of *Barefoot in Arcadia* seem particularly apt as closing comments on Greenwood County history:

> But we are talking about an age that is past and a society that has vanished. The transportation revolution helped to end an era because, with the advent of the automobile, the small town ceased to retain its integrity as a symmetrical social unit. Its citizens could now motor to the nearest city, patronize department stores and supermarkets, and return home in the time it had formerly taken them to drive downtown in their buggies. Paved highways and cheap motorcars sounded the death knell of small towns as we knew them before 1920.
>
> Small towns, of course, would not disappear. If they happened to be within driving distance of a large city, they became dormitories for city workers. Filling stations supplanted livery stables; the horse became a luxury item for sports-loving men and women; the mule virtually disappeared. The prosperous merchant of the small town in premotorcar days sold out and went into real estate or became a stockbroker. Small-town and country churches lost many of their parishioners to fashionable city churches with parking lots. Schools were consolidated, and lo, the school bus became an engine of controversy. Even the cotton field is no more. Instead the Up Country is green with trees, and power dams have made enormous lakes – and have improved the fishing. A social revolution has occurred while we watched, and we live in a changed world. While we may think of the past with a certain nostalgia, few would exchange life today for the "good old days" that never were. Many things today are not to our liking and make a previous era appear more idyllic. But we are in a transition period, and transitions are never comfortable. Our children will probably look back upon this age as one of excitement, stimulation, and progress. In the meantime we can chronicle the problems and pleasures of our generation, lest the memory of them be lost and forgotten. Some of us may also feel an obligation to correct misconceptions before they become crystallized as facts in the histories our children read.

CHAPTER NOTES

1. "Origins and Overview" – Chapter One draws heavily from two main sources and includes collateral information from several others. Louis Wright's bicentennial history of South Carolina, published in 1976 as part of the State and Nation Series of the American Association for State and Local History, was chosen primarily because Wright was a Greenwood County native but also because the book is utterly unpretentious and user-friendly. The general editor, in fact, made clear the purpose of the series: authors were asked not for comprehensive chronicles nor for new data for scholars; instead, the editors wanted "a summing up" of whatever seemed significant to each author about his or her state's history. That sounded a bit like my own agenda in tackling a history of Greenwood County. The second source was a monograph, "Old Ninety Six and the South Carolina Backcountry, 1700-1775," by Dr. Marvin L. Cann, prepared as a tricentennial publication of Lander College in 1970. Cann's work is a no-nonsense look at the area that became Greenwood County at a critical time in its history – from the beginnings to just before the Revolutionary War.

Other details came from Margaret Watson, *Greenwood County Sketches* (Greenwood: Attic Press, 1970); David Duncan Wallace, *South Carolina, A Short History* (Chapel Hill: University of North Carolina Press, 1951); C. M. Calhoun, *Liberty Dethroned* (c. 1901); and the centennial edition of *The Index-Journal* (September 14, 1957).

2. "The County Seat" – Practically the first book to fall into my hands at the beginning of the project was a new volume, *South Carolina in the 1880s: A Gazetteer,* compiled and edited by John Hammond Moore (Orangeburg: Sandlapper Publishing, Inc., 1989). This book consists of material gleaned from files of the Charleston *News and Courier* between 1880 and 1892. Its editor admitted that the picture painted by these articles was only half true, that a rosy "New South" doctrine had set the tone for the overall view of a state emerging from the wreckage of war and reconstruction. Even so, the nearly six pages devoted to Greenwood provided an irresistible view of the bustling little town as it appeared in December 1889.

Most of the material on the Oregon Hotel and the Bailey family came from family scrapbooks maintained by the late May Bailey Smith and provided by nieces Clara Robeson and Margaret Tinsley. Louise Hodges Hartzog shared her collection of Greenwood memorabilia, including documentary material for the sketch of her father, Samuel Connor Hodges, and Henry K. Thayer, Jr., talked to me about his family's business and the building at the corner of Main Street and Maxwell Avenue. Newspaper articles provided the material on Rosenberg's, and a family memoir written by Nicholas E. Sterghos in 1975 and loaned to me by a nephew contained invaluable information on the Star Cafe.

Bonner Harvley's firsthand account of banking in Greenwood occupied an engrossing hour in his office at The County Bank, and Arthur L. Murray graciously shared his scrapbooks and memories of a lifetime in Greenwood. Mary Neel Baker provided information on her father, one-time Greenwood Mayor Kenneth Baker, and current Mayor John Nave talked to me about the way city government operates today. Helen Taylor Barnette and Gee Taylor Poe loaned me clippings about their father Andrew Taylor and talked about the Barr-Taylor house that once stood on South Main Street. A family history with the marvelous title *200 Years of the Beaudrots* was a great help in sorting out the members of a family that has been an integral part of Greenwood for four generations. The fifth generation of Beaudrots, in fact, is well represented in the town today.

For the most part, Chapter Two was pieced together from newspaper accounts appearing from time to time. The centennial edition of *The Index-Journal* contained historical sketches of most of the downtown businesses existing in 1957. Both the building and dismantling of the railroad systems serving Greenwood strongly affected the physical layout of the town center. The limited edition map of downtown Greenwood as it appeared in 1908, prepared in 1973 by Margaret Watson, Kendall Few, and Boykin Curry, is evidence that Greenwood people do not want to lose the record of their town's physical evolution. I attempted to trace in this chapter the development of Greenwood's Uptown, or "Square," from about 1854 to the late 1980s, a period of more than 130 years. While such an experiment cannot possibly have succeeded entirely, perhaps an outline of sorts can be discerned.

3. "The County" – The first part of Chapter Three drew on Watson's book, newspaper articles, and Don Herd, *The South Carolina Upcountry*, Volume I (Greenwood: Attic Press, 1981). The *Greenwood Index* was the sole source for the story of the first courthouse. Information on Greenwood's first senator, C. A. C. Waller, came from several sources, not the least of which was a sketch provided by Jimmy Wade. Calhoun's book contains several Waller anecdotes, as do both Watson's and Wright's. "Captain" Chris Waller was arguably Greenwood's quintessential "character" in the very earliest days.

Greenwood County Sheriff Sam Riley took the time to talk to me about the work of his office and that of his five predecessors. The Buzzard Roost story came together from newspaper accounts, including the Raleigh *News and Observer*, the *Columbia Record*, and *The New York Times*, as well as *The Index-Journal*. W. H. Nicholson, Jr., deserves credit for the research involved. Stories of Greenwood County Hospital, the library, and the first county council came primarily from newspapers, but Director Bruce Heimburger provided a written sketch of the Greenwood Library, and Administrator Despina Panagakos supplied a history of The Museum. Bill Nicholson profiled his father and brother.

4. "Schools and Education" – It seemed to me particularly important to set the scene for Chapter Four by describing in general the deplorable state of education in South Carolina just after the Civil War. The Constitution of 1868, a thoroughly reconstructionist document, nevertheless brought the first state system of education to South Carolina. Sources included Wallace's *Short History*; Ernest M. Lander, *A History of South Carolina, 1865-1960* (Columbia: University of South Carolina Press, 1970); Wilbur J. Cash, *The Mind of the South* (New York: Vintage Books, 1941); newspaper articles; and conversations with former county superintendents Thomas I. Dowling and W. R. Dunn. Much of the Brewer material came from Dowling's collection. The late Miss Ermie Tedards provided a sketch of her mother, and H. L. Watson's description of Woodville Academy came from a pamphlet preserved in the county library. The 1913 Annual Report and the 1948-49 Directory of County Schools are also in the library.

The information on Bailey Military Institute/Academy came mostly from Lillie Fuller Simonson's collection, but William John Park, who lived as a boy just down the street from the academy, added a couple of anecdotes later in a telephone interview. It seems that Bailey boys were notorious for invading the lake and boathouse on the Park property, leaving a telltale trail of initials carved at various places inside the boathouse. Also, Park remembers Bailey publications with pictures of the lake but no mention that it was not part of the school's property. This tactic was a favorite with Lander President Boyce M. Grier as well. It was a rare college publication that failed to include a swimming pool picture with lots of girls in swimsuits, yet the college actually had no pool of its own until after 1973; the on-campus swimming pool was built by the City Recreation Commission on college property as part of a joint venture between the town and the college during the Grier administration.

Ted Wolf provided information on the College of Commerce, the public information office at Piedmont Technical College responded to my request for data, and Thomas Dowling sent me a copy of the vocational school study conducted in 1966. May Smith's scrapbook and the newspaper provided an abundance of material on Nellie Screws, but information on Nannie Major and Maude Pratt was harder to come by. Mary Beaudrot Herndon remembered a few stories, and obituaries and editorials provided the rest. Many people talked to me about Major Benson – including Boykin Curry, Gertrude Brabham, Edgar Davis, Helen Harrison, and Madison Breland – but nobody was able to produce anything he had written. The Citadel Class History of 1907 was a particularly valuable resource for information on Benson. Most of the recollections of Miss Sunbeam Andrews are my own, but Ernest Young and Angelle Adams also shared their memories with me.

5. "Business and Industry" – The very thought of tackling the complicated story of Greenwood's five railroad systems might have been enough to scare me away from the county history project had I not already worked with Jimmy Wade on his detailed manuscript. Wade generously distilled his voluminous railroad information down to a three or four page synopsis for this chapter.

The history commissioned by Greenwood Mills, *The Character of Quality,* is certainly not an unbiased source. For that reason I consulted a number of relatively new works focusing on the mill experience in the South, among them I. A. Newby, *Plain Folk in the New South* (Baton Rouge: Louisiana State University Press, 1989); Jacquelyn Dowd Hall, James Leloudis, Robert Korstad, Mary Murphy, Lu Ann Jones, and Christopher B. Daly, *Like a Family: The Making of a Southern Cotton Mill World* (Chapel Hill: University of North Carolina Press, 1987); and Jack Temple Kirby, *Rural Worlds Lost* (Baton Rouge: Louisiana State University Press, 1987). The subject is vast and the bias rampant, but there seemed to me no way to profile Greenwood's largest industry, not to mention two of its most towering figures, without picking my way as carefully as possible through whatever material presented itself. I gladly leave to professional historians and sociologists the task of exploring the deeper implications of the rise of the textile industry in the South.

Jimmy Wade must be credited once again for the material on Bob Aldrich. Everybody said Aldrich must be sketched, but I did not know where to look for information. Bill Barnette provided a most modest description of Greenwood Packing Plant, and Joe Patrick obligingly wrote out the Southern Brick story. William John Park helped with material on his family's long history in Greenwood, as well as the family business, an import of much more recent vintage.

6. "The Professions" – Material for Chapter Six came primarily from newspaper articles, but Don Herd's South Carolina Upcountry work and Perrin Anderson, *Recollections of my Life* (1989) also provided usable information. Jessie Julien talked to me about growing up in Greenwood – she and the county are about the same age – as well as about her late husband Carl. Gay Scurry Charles wrote a loving memoir of her father, Dr. Carroll Jenkins Scurry, that convinced me I was not the only person who remembered him with respect and affection. The information on Greenwood churches came primarily from Margaret Watson's research.

7. "Lander College" – Most of the material for the first part of Chapter Seven came from newspapers, college publications, and privately printed Lander family papers. One important source was a copy of an unfinished letter written in four installments by Sallie Thompson Hall Lander (1862-1951) to her children. Two of the letter's four parts were dated 1941, another was written in 1944, and Mrs. Lander added the final installment in 1947 when she was 85 years old. For the benefit of her children, Mrs. Lander recalled details of life with their father, John McPherson Lander, oldest son of Samuel Lander, whom she married in 1886. The Landers journeyed to Brazil in 1889 at the suggestion of a Methodist bishop; Granbery College opened a year later as the result of Lander's work. The family remained in Brazil for 35 years, until Lander's death in 1924. Mrs. Lander's descriptions of life in the mission field and the family's travels during furloughs make interesting reading. According to his wife, John Lander was responsible for bringing soccer to Brazil. "It was here," she wrote, "that your Father introduced football in 1894. He had obtained a 'rugby' ball when we were in London. Studying out the rules, he himself taught the boys and played with them daily. The game as they play it now is known as soccer . . . . In after years when there was some dispute about it, your Father proved that he brought the first football to Brazil and that the game was first played at Granbery College. Of course, he had no idea that it would grow to such proportions as now in all Brazil." The family spent the furlough winter of 1911 in Greenwood. Their house on Grace Street was described as "comfortable" and the winter as "busy." John Lander taught a course in psychology that semester at "the new Lander College." According to the Landers' youngest son William, who copied and edited the letter in 1952, Mrs. Lander's narrative ended with the year 1914.

My association with Lander College began in 1950, only two years after the Methodist connection ended and a year before county voters approved a four-mill tax assessment for the college's support. Thus many of the experiences and observations recorded in this chapter are my own. The evolution of the college has always seemed to me extraordinary, particularly the relationship to Greenwood County in the interim period between the Methodist girls' school years and Lander's current status as a regional state college.

8. "Towns, Sections, and Place Names" – A copy of the 1898 map of the county drawn by Yeldell and Kirk, secured by push pins to a piece of heavy cardboard, provided exactly what I needed to launch Chapter Eight. The names of the original townships provided the all-important beginnings; connections came from many sources, not the least of which were works by the Neuffers, Claude Henry and Irene, *Names in South Carolina,* Volume I-XII, 1954-1965 (Columbia: The State Printing Company, 1967) and *Correct Mispronunciations of Some South Carolina Names* (Columbia: University of South Carolina Press, 1983).

Betty Emerson Riddle gave me a morning and stacks of material on Hodges. My own work with Don Herd in the late 1970s when we researched the history of the Mount Ariel-Cokesbury community proved invaluable; I knew exactly where to find what I needed, and the memories that came flooding back were a fringe benefit. The section on D. Wyatt Aiken is based on works by Margaret Watson, Don Herd, and Aiken kinsman Claudius Hornby Pritchard, Jr. Another view entirely was provided in a book by Allen B. Ballard, *One More Day's Journey* (New York: McGraw-Hill Book Company, 1984). Ballard's book, subtitled "The Story of a Family and a People," is an account of a black family, Ballard's own, who left Abbeville County for Philadelphia as part of the "great migration." If Bruce Heimburger had not told me about this book, I would have missed it entirely.

The Brooks-Sumner affair is standard fare in American and South Carolina histories. Similarly, many writers have explored the Phoenix Riot, but the perspectives of black authors such as Allen Ballard and Benjamin Mays should not be overlooked. Thanks to the work of scholars Elizabeth R. Bethel in *Promiseland, A Century of Life in a Negro Community* (Philadelphia: Temple University Press, 1981) and Carol R. Bleser in *The Promised Land, The History of the South Carolina Land Commission, 1869-1890* (Columbia: University of South Carolina Press, 1969), the history of the community called Promised Land is easily available. Troy citizens Rodine Russell and Henry R. Deason, Jr., provided a service to local history when they put together *An Excursion to Troy* in 1982, and the late Mary Jane Rush Broadwater, known to everyone as "Mame," created a stir in Callison when she produced the genealogy/local history book entitled *David Rush and His Descendants and Stories of the Community* in 1953. Family members are currently updating and revising the "Rush Book." Other recollections and observations about Callison are my own.

The sketch of Ninety Six which concludes the chapter drew on a number of sources, most of which are named in the text. Chamber of Commerce President Don L. Going provided information on modern Ninety Six, as well as documents prepared by the National Park Service of the United State Department of the Interior.

9. "People and Events" – For some reason Greenwood seems to cherish the memory of "Foch Day" in 1921 more than any other single event in its history. This 33-minute occasion, two weeks in the planning, made such an impression that the town held a retrospective on at least two occasions in later years. When it became necessary to explain "who or what Foch was," as Louis Wright had to do in 1971, Greenwood evidently decided to rely on written recollections of the original Foch Day and attempt no more re-creations. Reminders cropped up again and again in the research phase of this book. The 50th anniversary Lander College booklet contains a fold-out, wide angle photograph of the

gathering, and a picture of the famous five-story arch over Maxwell Avenue appears in *The Index-Journal* of April 7, 1938.

Reporter E. P. Wideman had a habit of combining bits and pieces from his columns over many years and publishing them as "Rambling Recollections" in the newspaper and in pamphlet form. Louise Hartzog loaned me the pamphlet Wideman inscribed to her father, Dr. Sam Hodges, in 1937. That booklet was the source for information on the ill-fated "Jefferson Memorial Day" celebration in the 1920s.

My friend Virginia Davies not only gave me a morning to talk about her mother, Nell Saunders Graydon, but also loaned me several pages that appeared to be notes, perhaps for a speech Graydon delivered at some point. These notes were an excellent guide to the way she viewed herself and her writing.

Benjamin Mays's autobiography *Born to Rebel* (New York: Scribners, 1971) provided most of the material for the sketch of his life, but personal recollections also played a part. I was in the audience when Lander awarded the honorary degree in 1974, and I attended the reception in Mays's honor that followed the ceremony. It is probably enough to say that he made an unforgettable impression.

The name of Gerald Smart might not evoke the same response as those of the other notables sketched in this chapter, but in one sense he was perhaps the most "Greenwood" of all. Unlike Mays and Wright, whose careers were made away from their home town, or Nell Graydon, the individualist who was not a native, Smart made a name and a life for himself that became almost synonymous with the town. In retrospect it is clear that his was a most adroit use of publicity long before PR was acknowledged as the powerful political tool it is. Smart tooted his own horn constantly and wrote his own history in large letters, even as he pronounced himself the humblest of the humble. This assessment is not meant to be harsh criticism; there is something endearing about a life so open and transparent and touching. In spite of his protestations to the contrary, one senses great looming loneliness and almost overwhelming need. Jean Park is responsible for sorting and preserving Smart's jumble of clippings and memorabilia in a scrapbook she presented to The Museum.

Most of the people and events in this book were of at least passing familiarity to me when I began my research and, as usual, all became more interesting the more I learned about them. But if I had to choose a personal favorite from all of Greenwood's notables, it would have to be Louis Booker Wright. The reason for that choice is simply that Wright seems never to have lost the simplicity of his upbringing in Greenwood County even as he rose to impressive positions in the wide world of scholarship. Not only did he remember, he also celebrated his early life in Greenwood in a charming book, *Barefoot in Arcadia* (Columbia: University of South Carolina Press, 1974). I wish I'd had the chance to discuss that book, or this book, or nearly anything else, with Louis

Wright. It is a shame that whatever part Greenwood played in producing a man as sane, and at the same time as erudite, as Wright cannot be identified, bottled, and distributed as widely as possible. He was an eminently civilized man.

It has always struck me as odd that we Greenwood people seem to exult in the ease with which we can get away from home to someplace more exciting. In just a few hours, we like to say, we can have mountains, or seashore, or the big city lights of Atlanta or Charlotte. On the face of it that is certainly quite true. But, after a couple of years of intense concentration on the Greenwood mystique, I now know what we are really saying is that regardless of where we might find ourselves – whether at Folly Beach, on the crest of Mount Pisgah in the Great Smoky Mountains, in a Charlotte concert hall, or at Braves Stadium in Atlanta – we can be secure in the knowledge that we are really only a few hours away from Greenwood!

Acknowledgments

The late Clyde C. Cole photographed historic houses for a series featured in *Quills* magazine (*Quills*, edited for some years by Edgar Davis, was a publication by and for employees of Abney Mills). The first ten pictures are examples of Cole's work. Other photographs came from The Museum, county libraries, and private collections. Some were issued as post cards.

* * * *

Among the most important elements of a book's impact is its appearance, both inside and out. Appropriately, this volume owes its distinctive look to Greenwood resources: Park Seed Company generously allowed the use of its facilities, and Theresa Ethridge's wizardry at the computer did the rest.

INDEX